THE LAW OF ORGANIZED RELIGIONS

The Law of Organized Religions

Between Establishment and Secularism

JULIAN RIVERS

OXFORD
UNIVERSITY PRESS

OXFORD

UNIVERSITY PRESS

Great Clarendon Street, Oxford OX2 6DP

Oxford University Press is a department of the University of Oxford.
It furthers the University's objective of excellence in research, scholarship,
and education by publishing worldwide in

Oxford   New York

Auckland Cape Town Dar es Salaam Hong Kong Karachi
Kuala Lumpur Madrid Melbourne Mexico City Nairobi
New Delhi Shanghai Taipei Toronto

With offices in

Argentina Austria Brazil Chile Czech Republic France Greece
Guatemala Hungary Italy Japan Poland Portugal Singapore
South Korea Switzerland Thailand Turkey Ukraine Vietnam

Oxford is a registered trade mark of Oxford University Press
in the UK and in certain other countries

Published in the United States
by Oxford University Press Inc., New York

British Library Cataloguing in Publication Data

Data available

Library of Congress Cataloging-in-Publication Data

Data available

Typeset by Newgen Imaging Systems (P) Ltd., Chennai, India
Printed in Great Britain
on acid-free paper by
CPI Group (UK) Ltd, Croydon, CR0 4YY

ISBN 978–0–19–922610–8

3 5 7 9 10 8 6 4 2

…quod Anglicana ecclesia libera sit…

Magna Carta

Preface

This is a systematic study of English law as it applies to organized religions. None of these terms is particularly satisfactory. To start with the latter, it would still have been possible a generation ago to write about the 'law of churches' and even to countenance the development of a new sub-discipline called 'public ecclesiastical law'. In this, one would be doing no more than following the lead of countries such as Germany, Italy, and Spain, whose constitutional arrangements have long since abandoned establishment without committing to a secularizing agenda, such as French *laïcité*. But even then, the rise of non-Christian religions, to say nothing of the long-standing quiet presence of a substantial Jewish minority, were making the terms anachronistic. Yet we have no words akin to 'church' and 'ecclesiastical' which are multicultural enough. Occasional attempts to refer to synagogues, mosques, and temples as churches have not caught on. Yet 'religious organization' is rather too broad—any group of people organized for any purpose can give their organization a religious ethos. 'Religious association' is slightly better, although it makes an assumption about its origins in an agreement to associate for religious purposes. 'Religious body' is useful, if rather vague. So the title refers to organized religions and the text to all these terms as each appears most useful in its context.

If we struggle for words to describe a church/organization/association/body, how much more when it comes to 'religion'. We know what it refers to in a rough, pre-theoretical way. A definition that excluded any of the Bahá'í, Buddhists, Christians, Hindus, Jains, Jews, Muslims, Pagans, Sikhs, and Zoroastrians would be suspect. And there is a substantial literature seeking to give the legal definition of religion more precision. This ranges over approaches that identify necessary and sufficient conditions, paradigms, Wittgensteinian family resemblances, and more. The point of much of it is to find a rational basis on which to control access to legal privilege and to settle the boundaries of legal regulation. If only we knew exactly what religion is, we would know what to do with it. And this, it seems, is to miss the point. One cannot assume that a socio-empirical definition of a cultural phenomenon, the varying expressions of which are deeply implicated in competing value-systems, can straightforwardly control normative (ie legal) consequences. Of course, if the law uses the term, lawyers have to work out what it means. But that is inevitably, in part, an evaluative process in which the law defines 'religion' for the relevant purposes. So no attempt is made anywhere in this book to defend one global definition of religion for all legal purposes. The point is to understand how the law defines—and organizes—religions and what constitutional values are at stake when it does so.

As far as 'English law' is concerned, the arrangements made for the reconstitution of the Church of Ireland on its disestablishment in 1871 have a particular significance: not only does the Irish Church Act 1869 express the common law's general approach to the constitution of non-established religious bodies, it was also reproduced in the reconstitution of the Church in Wales half a century later. Yet this book makes no attempt to trace the distinctive features of the law of Northern Ireland, let alone that of the Republic. On the other hand, 'English law' applies in Wales, except to the extent that devolution has started to produce a body of Welsh law. This has been noted where it differs. Finally, the legal position of the Church of Scotland—whether it is to be considered 'established' or not—is of particular comparative interest. It cannot be ignored, but neither has this study attempted to set out all the distinctive features of Scottish law either. In short, the book is thoroughly Anglocentric, treating other systems as means to the end of shedding light on its subject-matter. This is as much an admission of need and a recognition of practical limits as a cause for apology.

The book falls into four main parts. The first chapter presents some essential background material. It gives an overview of the changing law of Church and State. The old aphorism that the main point of legal history is to understand how quickly the law can change is as true here as elsewhere. Yet echoes of old law live on in sometimes remarkable ways. Since there is no obvious starting-point, one might as well start at the beginning. Apologies are due to constitutional historians for whom the account is familiar and simplistic; in defence it can only be pointed out that experience would suggest that many need the orientation it offers. It also offers a greater focus on the development of legal doctrine than one might normally find in such accounts.

The next two parts are broadly divided into a consideration of what organized religions *are* in law, followed by an account of what they *do*. Chapter 2 shows how international human rights law has come in recent years to treat religious associations as rights-bearers. This has been a particular feature of the case-law of the European Court of Human Rights after 2000. Since the case-law informs domestic understandings of Convention rights under the Human Rights Act 1998, it is also part of any full account of English law. One also notices that all subsequent chapters raise questions of compatibility between English law and the emerging body of international human rights law. Chapters 3 to 5 address, respectively, the legal constitution of religious bodies, the status of ministers of religion, and the ways in which the law creates a category of 'public religion'. Questions of legal constitution raise the problem of the extent to which secular courts will protect legal interests, such as property, and take account of religious perspectives in doing so. There is a considerable, and still unresolved, tension here between justice and justiciability. The same tension emerges in the specific context of the legal relationship between ministers of religion and their organizations. The distinctive treatment of ministers of religion in employment law is part of a broader enjoyment of a special legal status afforded to them by the law.

Here, however, recent equalities legislation is pushing the courts in the direction of secular 'justice'. Chapter 5 gathers together a number of matters of privilege and accountability under the rubric of 'public religion'. The legal term is more commonly 'public worship', but the point is to draw a parallel with European systems that accord a certain higher public status to some religious bodies. In the English context, charitable status is only one dimension of this, albeit clearly the most significant.

As regards the activities of organized religions, Chapters 6 to 10 work outwards from a core of religious activity to various forms of public engagement. Chapter 6 deals with regulated rites: acts of collective worship and religious ceremonies which the law treats as having legal significance. Chapter 7 covers chaplaincies: the access of ministers of religion and similar workers to relatively enclosed public institutions, such as the armed forces, prisons, and hospitals, in order to offer pastoral services. Chapter 8 then sets out the involvement of religious bodies in education. Historically, this involvement has been the most controversial area of overlap between religions and the State, and must have regard to a significant body of relevant human rights law of its own, which is recounted at this point. The degree to which Government has sought an accommodation with religious bodies in the delivery of education contrasts with growing State regulation in other forms of social welfare provision. Here, new tensions are apparent as divergent values produce competing agendas. These are considered in Chapter 9. Chapter 10 then looks at matters furthest from the core of 'private' religious ritual: access to discourse with Government in formal and informal consultation processes, as well as with the general public through the regulated mass media.

The final chapter seeks to pull all this material together in a search for constitutional principle. It argues that the English law of organized religions cannot be understood simply as an expression of individual rights of religious liberty and equality. Instead, it identifies 'establishment' and 'secularism' as two poles within which the law of organized religions must be located. Once questions of definition are clarified, the Church of England is seen to be barely established. But in spite of signs that the law is on a journey from establishment to secularism, this direction of travel is neither descriptively accurate nor prescriptively attractive. The law can be located between the two, but for principle we must look elsewhere. The chapter then takes its cue from the European Court of Human Rights and explores the ideas of religious autonomy and State neutrality as two main constitutional principles. These reflect commitments to a collective guarantee of liberty and equality. Given a rather fuller articulation than they have hitherto received at the hands of the Court, they present a positive alternative which is both in continuity with British constitutional traditions and proof to the deceptive fairness of a new secularism which runs the risk of turning into a Trojan horse for State-sponsored atheism.

It is perhaps worth pointing out what this book does not seek to do. It does not claim to be a complete account of the interaction between law and religion. This can be considered from many different perspectives, embracing matters as diverse as religious laws, canon law, and the ideological foundations of modern law. It does not even claim to explicate a theory, or the content, of religious liberty. As well as a remarkable social achievement, religious liberty is also an individual right, and a complete account of it must also include a discussion of the ways in which English law accommodates individuals. Finally, and this is particularly pertinent to any non-lawyers reading the book, it does not claim that the legal dimension of organized religious activity is its most significant. Most religious believers most of the time are blithely unaware of it, and rightly so. If the law in this area is largely invisible to them it is probably doing its job well. Instead, the focus is primarily on the development of legal doctrine. This means that the book contains rather more doctrinal history than might normally be the case; it also means that there is rather less social and political context than one might ideally like to see. My hope is that there are sufficient indicators of context at least to show where further connections and work may be done. The task, in short, has been to reconstruct, and thus bring into being, an area of law which has for too long been absent from the conceptual maps of English lawyers.

In writing this book I have incurred many debts of gratitude, not least to colleagues and friends whose expertise in particular areas touched on by this work far outstrips my own. I would like to thank Michael Brealey, Jonathan Burnside, Jonathan Chaplin, John Coffey, Malcolm Evans, Emma Hitchings, Mike Kavanagh, Roger Kerridge, Sylvie Langlaude, Morag McDermont, Gerard McMeel, Tonia Novitz, Emile Perreau-Saussine[†], Keith Syrett, and Chris Willmore. They have saved me from many errors. I am also grateful to the Institute for Advanced Studies at the University of Bristol for granting me a research fellowship in 2008–9, during which time the bulk of the book was written. Readers who know the School of Law at the University of Bristol will know what a congenial place it is to pursue work of this nature. To my commissioning editors at OUP, Gwen Booth and Alex Flach, I owe initial enthusiasm and ongoing encouragement. And above all others, my wife, Caroline, and my daughters, Lily and Alice, have been an unstinting support, cheerfully tolerating my preoccupation with 'the book'.

Finally, a word about the caption. It is as easy to plunder Magna Carta for the grand ideas of liberal constitutionalism as it is to sneer at the historical *naïveté* of such an exercise. In the case of 'the liberty of the English church' the irony is completed by the fact that King John secured annulment of the Charter by Pope Innocent III only three days after signing it. Yet as with habeas corpus, trial by one's peers, freedom of commerce, or representative consent to taxation, Magna Carta still stands, in this respect as well, for a constitutional value of enduring significance. If this book revives and rearticulates that value in the very different circumstances obtaining eight centuries later, it will have served its purpose.

Contents

List of Abbreviations

AC	Appeal Cases
ACD	Administrative Court Digest
AJIL	American Journal of International Law
All ER	All England Reports
ASA	Advertising Standards Authority
ASAB	Advertising Standards Authority (Broadcast)
BCAP	Broadcast Committee of Advertising Practice
BCLC	Butterworths Company Law Cases
BHRC	Butterworths Human Rights Cases
CAFOD	Catholic Fund for Overseas Development
Cal L Rev	California Law Review
CCEL	Canadian Cases on Employment Law
CD	Collection of Decisions of the European Commission of Human Rights
Ch	Chancery
CLJ	Cambridge Law Journal
CLWR	Common Law World Review
CMLR	Common Market Law Reports
COD	Crown Office Digest
CRAC	Central Religious Advisory Committee
Cr App R	Criminal Appeal Reports
Crim LR	Criminal Law Review
DCLG	Department of Communities and Local Government
DCMS	Department for Culture, Media and Sport
DCSF	Department for Children, Schools and Families
DEC	Disasters Emergency Committee
DEFRA	Department for Environment, Food and Rural Affairs
DES	Department of Education and Science
DETR	Department of Employment, Training and Rehabilitation
DoH	Department of Health
DoT	Department of Transport
DR	Decisions and Reports of the European Commission of Human Rights
DTI	Department of Trade and Industry
EAT	Employment Appeal Tribunal
Ecc LJ	Ecclesiastical Law Journal
ECHR	European Court of Human Rights
ECR	European Court Reports

EHLR	Environmental Health Law Reports
EHRR	European Human Rights Reports
ER	English Reports
EWCA Civ	Court of Appeal (Civil Division)
EWHC	England and Wales High Court
FCO	Foreign and Commonwealth Office
FCR	Family Court Reports
HO	Home Office
HRA	Human Rights Act
HRC	Human Rights Commission
ICCPR	International Covenant on Civil and Political Rights 1966
ICESCR	International Covenant on Economic, Social and Cultural Rights
ICLQ	International and Comparative Law Quarterly
ICR	Industrial Cases Reports
ICRC	International Committee of the Red Cross
IJCL	International Journal of Constitutional Law
ILJ	Industrial Law Journal
Int ALR	International Arbitration Law Review
IRLR	Industrial Relations Law Reports
ISKCON	International Society for Krishna Consciousness
ITA	Independent Television Authority
ITC	Independent Television Commission
J Env L	Journal of Environmental Law
JPL	Journal of Planning and Environmental Law
KB	King's Bench
LC	Lord Chancellor
LEA	local education authority
LJ	Lord Justice
LQR	Law Quarterly Review
LSG	Law Society's Gazette
LT	Law Times Reports
Med LR	Medical Law Reports
MLR	Modern Law Review
NCVO	National Council for Voluntary Organisations
NDC	New Deal for Communities
NGO	non-governmental organization
NIQB	High Court of Justice Northern Ireland: Queen's Bench Division
NLJ	New Law Journal
NSS	National Secular Society
NSWLR	New South Wales Law Reports

NYUJ Int'l L & Pol	New York University Journal of International Law and Politics
NZLR	New Zealand Law Reports
ODIHR	Office for Democratic Institutions and Human Rights
OFCOM	Office of Communications
OJLS	Oxford Journal of Legal Studies
OSCE	Organization for Security and Co-operation in Europe
P & CR	Property, Planning and Compensation Reports
PAD	Planning Appeal Decisions
PL	Public Law
QB	Queen's Bench
QBD	Queen's Bench Division
R & IT	Rating and Income Tax Reports
SACREs	Standing Advisory Councils on Religious Education
SAGB	Spiritualist Association of Great Britain
SC	Session Cases
SCR	Supreme Court Reports (Canada)
SI	Statutory Instrument
SLT	Scots Law Times
SNU	Spiritualist National Union
TLR	Times Law Reports
UB Col LR	University of British Columbia Law Review
UDHR	Universal Declaration of Human Rights
VATTR	Value Added Tax Tribunal Reports
VC	Vice Chancellor
WLR	Weekly Law Reports

Table of Cases

Table of International Treaties, Conventions and other Legal Instruments

Table of Legislation

Table of Statutory Instruments

Table of European Legislation

Table of Foreign Legislation

1

The Changing Law of Church and State

The relationship between law and religion in any country is a reflection of historical contingencies, controversies, and compromises. Nowhere is this more apparent than in the English law of Church and State. Echoes of legal arrangements centuries-old can still be heard in the practices of today. In order to understand the present law, an overview of the past is indispensable.

I. The First Millennium

We know very little of the Celtic religion the Romans found on their arrival in Britain in AD 43.[1] Classical accounts portray it as centred on sacred groves and springs, led by druids officiating at sacrifices, usually animal, sometimes human. Roman temple-building was an important component of imperial domination, and could give rise to violent resistance, as when the temple to the divine Claudius at Colchester was destroyed by Boudicca's forces in 61. However, for the most part a process of assimilation ensured the reinterpretation of Celtic religion in terms of the Roman pantheon. The association of the sacred spring of Sul with the goddess Minerva at Bath seems typical. With the Romans came also a diversity of other cults: mystery religions, such as the worship of Mithras with its complex sequences of initiation, the drug-assisted ecstatic worship of Bacchus, and at some point before the third century, Christianity.[2]

Once Christianity had been adopted as the official religion of the Empire in 312, it spread increasingly quickly, not least on account of its superior organization into bishoprics, which are known to have existed in Britain even before three bishops were sent to the Council of Arles in 314. By 400 it has been estimated that there were around 20 bishops with churches inside towns exercising a ministry to surrounding areas.[3] Here too, in practice, there is evidence of a degree

---

[1] G Webster, *The British Celts and their Gods* (London: Batsford, 1986); Martin Henig, 'Religion in Roman Britain', in Sheridan Gilley and W J Sheils (eds), *A History of Religion in Britain* (Oxford: Blackwell, 1994).
[2] Charles Thomas, *Christianity in Roman Britain to AD 500* (London: Batsford, 1985), 45–50, tentatively puts the martyrdom of Alban, the first known Christian martyr in the British Isles, during Decius's persecution of AD 250–1.   [3] Thomas, *op cit* n 2, 198.

of syncretism with existing religions. But if Roman Britain could produce the heretic Pelagius (*c*354–418) it could also produce a Patrick (fifth century), who after capture into Irish slavery would convert large numbers and sow the seeds of a vigorous Celtic Christianity capable of surviving in spite of collapsing Roman rule and Germanic invasion.[4]

It used to be thought that Roman-British Christianity was almost totally obliterated by the invasions of Germanic tribes in the fourth and fifth centuries. On this account, Augustine's mission of 597 to convert the English represented a completely fresh start.[5] However, the fact that the wife of his first convert was a Frankish Christian princess, coupled with the speed of his initial success, especially in Northumbria, suggests that Christian belief may well have survived in unorganized form. But the Roman mission had to contend both with a tendency to revert to Anglo-Saxon paganism and with the Celtic missionary movement. Where possible, the church sought to preserve the pagan festivals and names while converting their substance. As a result, the Teutonic gods Tiw, Woden, Thunor, and Frigg live on in the days of our week, while Yul and (most remarkably) Eostre still mark the birth, death, and resurrection of Christ.[6]

After Northumbria had reverted briefly to paganism, King Oswald invited Aidan from Columba's foundation of Iona (563) to establish a new monastery at Lindisfarne (630). As the Celtic and Roman missionary movements met, differences between the traditions came to a head and were resolved in favour of Roman custom at the Synod of Whitby in 664. In fact, apparently trivial disagreements over clerical tonsure and the date of Easter masked more fundamental differences. Celtic Christianity was essentially peripatetic and monastic, in the sense that a 'bishop' might well be a missionary monk under the authority of an abbot, and based in a monastery or minster; Roman Christianity was territorially based and headed by bishops and archbishops seated in cathedrals. Although Augustine's mandate to establish dioceses throughout England was complete by the time of Bede's death in 735, the peripatetic tradition—and the tensions— lived on. Prohibitions on wandering clergy and Irish ordinands first issued by the Council of Hertford in 672 were being repeated as late as 816 by the Council of Chelsea.

As works such as the Lindisfarne gospels and the Venerable Bede's *Ecclesiastical History of the English People* demonstrate, the monasteries of the seventh and eighth centuries were centres of learning unparalleled in Northern Europe. But they were doomed not to survive. Perhaps already weakened through growing

---

[4] For an attempt to disentangle history from legend about Patrick, see Thomas, *op cit* n 2, 307–46.

[5] See, generally, P H Blair, *An Introduction to Anglo-Saxon England*, 2nd edn (Cambridge: Cambridge University Press, 1977); John Blair, *The Church in Anglo-Saxon Society* (Oxford: Oxford University Press, 2005); Gerald Bonner, 'Religion in Anglo-Saxon England', in Sheridan Gilley and W J Sheils (eds), *A History of Religion in Britain* (Oxford: Blackwell, 1994).

[6] Gale R Owen, *Rites and Religions of the Anglo-Saxons* (Newton Abbot: David & Charles, 1981).

corruption and decadence, they were destroyed in the Viking invasions. The sack of Lindisfarne in 793 was only the foretaste of what was to come at the hands of a large Danish force from 865 onwards. By 900 organized monastic life, and with it much of the learning of the early Anglo-Saxon church, had been totally destroyed.

Nevertheless, Christianity itself survived, managing even to affect those areas in which Danelaw was imposed. The monastic revival of the tenth century was due to the efforts of three men in particular: Dunstan, Aethelwold, and Oswald.[7] In time, they came under the influence of the continental monastic revival which had started in 910 at Cluny and then spread to Fleury and Ghent around 930. Within a couple of years of Edgar's accession to the throne of Mercia in 957, Dunstan was Archbishop of Canterbury, Aethelwold bishop of Winchester, and Oswald bishop of Worcester. They were thus in a position to promote the foundation of monasteries throughout the south of England. All monastic life was based on the rule of Benedict (early sixth century), but there was considerable local diversity, and in 970 the Synod of Winchester approved Aethelwold's *Regularis Concordia*, a single harmonized rule for all regular (ie monastic) clergy. This revival of monasticism among the clergy placed increasing pressure on secular (ie married) clergy, who were gradually removed from their positions in cathedrals and minsters.

From the beginning it was assumed that the church in England would be structured as territorially-defined dioceses grouped, as was the old Roman civil Government, into two provinces, with capitals in York and London.[8] The further division of dioceses into parishes only began to occur towards the very end of the first millennium.[9] It was a diocese, headed by a bishop, which constituted the local church. Stone crosses might be erected as places of meeting as the bishop and his clergy moved through their diocese. A church building was more likely to be erected and endowed by a local landowner, perhaps first as a simple oratory—a place for prayer—then later with its own permanent clerk. In this way, lay involvement in clerical appointments first came to play a significant part in the English church. Only gradually were 'ordinary minsters', or mother churches, established within dioceses. These could function like their greater Celtic prototypes as missionary bases for a group of clergy to serve the surrounding area. Even by the time of the Norman Conquest a complete network of parishes was only partially established. Church government was effected through provincial and diocesan synods (assemblies of senior clergy), which could decide disputes and issue canons (rules) for the better ordering of the church. There were no courts and no ecclesiastical lawyers.

---

[7] Blair, *op cit* n 5, 165–70.

[8] The early resistance of the King of Essex to Christianity forced Augustine to base himself in Canterbury instead of London.

[9] R H Helmholz, *The Oxford History of the Laws of England*, Vol 1: *The Canon Law and Ecclesiastical Jurisdiction from 597 to the 1640s* (Oxford: Oxford University Press, 2004), 21–5.

It would seem that under Anglo-Saxon pagan religion, the king took a leading role in securing the goodwill of the gods through sacrifice and divination.[10] There was a unity of government and religion. The seventh-century evangelization of Britain proceeded by way of converting and baptizing kings. But even if the coronation service Dunstan designed for King Edgar in 959 adopted continental Carolingian practice to include anointing in the manner of the godly kings of Old Testament Israel,[11] Christian political theology was fundamentally different from pagan religion in this respect. The Christian King was responsible for the spiritual and temporal good of his people, but he was not the leader of the church. Thus while there was as yet no clear and consistent jurisdictional distinction, some difference of role was undoubtedly recognized.[12] The subject-matter of certain disputes could be allocated to one or the other sphere, as for example the allocation to bishops of certain disputes about marriage in the laws of King Cnut. At least as a general principle, it was accepted that the church should be free from secular obligations, in particular taxation, and that the clergy were in some way exempt from the jurisdiction of temporal courts. They should be subject instead to the authority of their bishops. And clergy should not get entangled in secular affairs, such as the obligation to assume secular judicial office. There was thus to be an area of the church's life free from secular intrusion. At the same time, Cnut's laws also punished witchcraft and pagan religious practices. The reality was that kings maintained control over the appointment of bishops and often required their attendance and participation in secular courts and councils. In the absence of a system of church courts, the immunity of clergy from secular jurisdiction and the allocation of certain matters to the exclusive authority of the church could at this point only be limited.

II. From the Norman Conquest to the Break with Rome

The establishment of Norman rule over England in 1066 coincided with three events which were to have a substantial impact on the organization of the Christian church, in time giving it the character of a complete system of law.[13] The first of these was the radical reform associated with Pope Gregory VII. Although it had long been accepted that the Bishop of Rome had a certain pre-eminence among bishops and was the proper judge of major causes of dispute in the church, in his *Dictatus Papae* (1075) Gregory laid claim to being the necessary single figure who could discipline, order, and reform the entire church. The Roman church was founded by God and inerrant; no synod had authority without his consent.

---

[10] Owen, *op cit* n 6, 51.   [11] Ibid, 180.   [12] Helmholz, *op cit* n 9, 55–8.
[13] See, generally, J C Dickinson, *The Later Middle Ages* (London: A & C Black, 1979); Helmholz, *op cit* n 9, 67–106.

As the person with 'the power to judge all men', the possibility of appeal to him in any cause was created—at first in theory and then increasingly in practice.

The second development of note was the growing number and sophistication of collections of the church's canons. Collections of the rules and decisions of church councils had long been known, but from the eleventh century these started to increase in scale. This process culminated in Gratian's *Decretum* (1140), which not only collected together over 3,500 canons, but attempted to harmonize them into consistent rules. There followed a series of commentaries by the 'Decretists' of which the *glossa ordinaria* of Teutonicus and Brixiensis became the most authoritative. Corresponding to the rise in papal authority was an increase in the number of decretals (decisions) which could re-state and incrementally develop the law. The most significant collections of these were the Gregorian Decretals (1234) and the *Liber Sextus* (1298).

Finally, there was the rediscovery and systematic study of the ancient Roman civil law. Justinian's sixth-century compilation of classical Roman law, the *Corpus Iuris Civilis*, was studied at Bologna from the eleventh century, and its concepts enriched the emerging canon law. Thus was brought into being the *Corpus Iuris Canonici*, a parallel body of ecclesiastical law to match the ancient Roman civil law. Together they constituted a European *ius commune*. By the middle of the thirteenth century they were being studied in distinct faculties at universities across Europe, including those recently founded at Oxford and Cambridge.

William I had already recognized the exclusive jurisdiction of the bishop over spiritual matters, but in general the English monarchs did not take kindly to the limitation of their customary power over the church brought about by the Gregorian reforms. While the conflict over lay investiture to English church offices was compromised and relatively muted in comparison to continental European disputes, Henry II's attempt to refine and limit ecclesiastical jurisdiction, including appeals to the Pope, and to reassert his feudal prerogatives over the bishops and abbots of the church, in the *Constitutions of Clarendon* (1164) brought conflict and eventually martyrdom to Archbishop Thomas Becket. *Magna Carta*'s (1215) opening article guaranteeing the liberty of the church was at the time simply one more round in ongoing attempts to settle the division between spiritual and secular authority.[14] But by about the middle thirteenth century, major conflict with the papacy had settled down to a rather uneasy and pragmatic compromise.

After the Norman Conquest, dioceses had quickly been subdivided into archdeaconries and rural deaneries, offices which carried with them an informal disciplinary power to punish sins. The same period saw the increasing use of papal judges delegate, a use which, however, diminished as consistory courts (the courts of bishops) emerged around the middle of the thirteenth century. These courts not only heard cases within their jurisdiction at first instance, but also appeals

---

[14] J C Holt, *Magna Carta* (Cambridge: Cambridge University Press, 1965).

from the lower courts of archdeacons and rural deans. The royal common law courts also emerged, and had at their disposal the prerogative writ of prohibition to prevent the use of excessive ecclesiastical power. Complaints about the misuse of this writ led to increasingly precise and authoritative statements of the boundaries between the two jurisdictions as in the acts *Circumspecte Agatis* (1286) and *Articuli Cleri* (1316).

The result was that English ecclesiastical law developed a number of distinctive characteristics not provided for by European canon law generally, which were to ensure its survival in significant form right up to the nineteenth century.[15] First, the jurisdiction of its courts—apart from the limited 'benefit of clergy' secured by the martyrdom of Thomas Becket, which ensured the trial of clergy accused of criminal offences before ecclesiastical courts—was based on subject-matter and not the person of the litigant. Secondly, the courts gained jurisdiction over subject-matters not covered by the canon law, in particular an emerging law of defamation and probate. Thirdly, the ecclesiastical courts could by letter of signification request the assistance of the secular power to enforce its sentences, most notably to imprison those they excommunicated.

Thus by around 1300 there was an established system of ecclesiastical courts exercising a tolerably clear jurisdiction over a wide range of disputes (breach of faith, wills and testaments, tithes and other dues, church property, clergy cases, marriage and divorce, defamation and sins/crimes) and enforcing a complex body of law which was subject to systematic study at the Universities. Convocation—a representative body for the clergy parallel to the House of Commons—had come into existence, prompted by clerical objections to being summoned to council by a lay person. Although at first intended as a representative body to approve taxation, it increasingly fulfilled the legislative functions of a provincial synod, and could be used in parallel to Parliament to amend the law of the English church. A systematic valuation of the assets of the church formed the basis of both papal and royal taxation.

The period after 1300 was marked by greater stability in the relations between Church and State, although there were ongoing jurisdictional tensions between royal and ecclesiastical courts, for example in respect of advowsons and debts supported by pledges of faith. The Crown also sought to limit the power of the Roman *curia* (court). The Statutes of Provisors[16] sought to restore to English patrons rights of clerical patronage and election which had been bypassed by papal appointment, while the Statutes of Praemunire[17] subjected those who sued in the Roman *curia* on a matter within the jurisdiction of royal courts to severe penalties. The reaction to this legislation was complex, and enforcement patchy: some clergy approved of the measures, and even the monarch could at times find the use of papal provision convenient.

---

[15] Helmholz, *op cit* n 9, 143–6.   [16] 25 Edw III, St 4 (1351); 13 Ric II, St 2, c 2 (1390).
[17] 27 Edw III, St 1 (1353); 16 Ric II, c 5 (1392).

Although from a modern perspective, medieval England was religiously highly homogeneous, in terms of its institutions there was considerable diversity. Apart from the familiar structure of dioceses, with their well-staffed cathedrals, and parishes, some of the churches of which were also collegiate, one must note the monasteries, which experienced a massive increase in the 150 years following the Norman Conquest.[18] The first Norman monasteries were Benedictine, but there soon followed Cluniacs, Cistercians, and regular canons of St Augustine (Austin canons). Unlike the Benedictines, who formed independent abbeys under the oversight of the local bishop, the Cluniacs and Cistercians had centralized forms of government and oversight within the entire order and were granted papal exemption from episcopal oversight and tithes. Many of the Cluniac monasteries were 'alien priories' dependent on a French mother abbey. Cistercian discipline, coupled with the tendency to establish themselves in isolated places and to stress the value of manual labour, brought about substantial economic success, not least in the wool trade. The Austin canons had been formed out of a variety of previous orders on the basis of Augustine's insistence that the clergy of his cathedral should live a monastic life. They came to serve parishes in small groups with considerable variation in practice, in some cases giving rise to sub-orders such as the Premonstratensians and Gilbertines. Relatively small numbers of preceptories of the two military orders of Templars and Hospitallers (Order of St. John of Jerusalem) were also to be found in England.

Alongside the fixed monasteries were the four orders of friars, which grew rapidly during the thirteenth century: Franciscans (Grey Friars), Dominicans (Black Friars), Carmelites (White Friars), and Augustinians (Austin Friars). The friars were characterized by their theological study—contributing significantly to the early growth of the Universities—their pastoral work of preaching and confession, their radical pursuit of poverty, and their mobility. In terms of their pursuit of poverty they rejected the use of endowments and lived off alms instead. Their higher standards of training compared to the average parish clergy meant that they were generally popular, which in turn led to certain tensions between them and the secular clergy.

The monastic tradition of hospitality ensured that the monasteries provided a certain level of care for the poor and for travellers. The late medieval period also saw the steady rise of semi-monastic hospitals caring for a wide variety of needs, including illness, both physical and mental, as well as for the destitute, orphaned, and aged—sometimes all within the same institution. Typically hospitals had a Warden or Master, assisted by a number of chaplains and brothers and sisters. Less is known about the early history of schools. Informal and basic instruction in reading, singing, and Latin must have existed on a wide scale. Choir schools grew up around the cathedrals, and the rise of the use of chantries—endowments for priests with little else to do save saying a daily mass for the soul

---

[18] Dickinson, *op cit* n 13, ch 4.

of the departed—may well have secured a body of men with sufficient education and time to provide elementary schooling. The substantial foundations of Winchester College (1382) and Eton College (1440) were exceptional. But by the fifteenth century one can detect an increase of interest. When in 1414 Parliament ordered the ejection of foreign monks in a burst of national feeling prompted by the Hundred Years War with France, the endowments were not necessarily to be applied for liturgical purposes but to ecclesiastical or educational corporations.

Alongside institutional diversity within medieval Catholic Christianity one must also note the encounters with Judaism and with Christian dissent in the form of Lollardy. Jews entered England after the Norman Conquest and settled in many major towns, mainly as financiers.[19] Hostility emerged from about the middle of the twelfth century and became violent during the Third Crusade (1189–92), with the Crown imposing irregular and onerous tax demands, as well as occasional sequestrations of property. By the Ordinances of the Jewry (1194), the Crown created an Exchequer of the Jews and the office of Jewish Archpresbyter to regulate their affairs, in particular their financial transactions. Government regulation was not in any sense benign. Throughout the thirteenth century their position worsened: in 1222 the ruling of the Fourth Lateran Council (1215) that Jews should wear distinctive dress was implemented and in 1253 they were forbidden to dwell anywhere other than in existing communities. By the *statutum de judaismo* (1275) usury was prohibited, and an attempt was made to force a change of occupation. Finally, in 1290, frustrated by their unwillingness to convert and needing the consent of the clergy to new taxation, Edward I ordered their expulsion, with property and debts forfeit to the Crown.

Lollardy was an ill-defined movement of protest centred on the proto-reformer John Wyclif (c1330–84).[20] Wyclif was a priest and Oxford don who attacked abuses in the church, in particular aspects of late mediaeval piety such as the veneration of saints and masses for the dead, its wealth, and the exercise by bishops of political power. He also promoted the translation of the Bible into English and a return to a more primitive model of church life. Wycliffite teaching was implicated, almost certainly unfairly, in the Peasants' Revolt (1381) which caused substantial civil unrest. In 1401 Parliament was persuaded by Archbishop Arundel and Convocation to pass the statute *de haeretico comburendo*.[21] This provided that heretics who refused to abjure (ie swear an oath to abandon) their heresy could be handed over to the secular authorities to be burnt. The practice of burning heretics was probably first approved by Pope Innocent III (1198–1216) and it was already practised in continental Europe. But apart from the burning of

---

[19] Cecil Roth, *A History of the Jews in England* (Oxford: Clarendon Press, 1941); Robin R Mundill, *England's Jewish Solution* (Cambridge: Cambridge University Press, 1998).

[20] K B McFarlane, *Wycliffe and English Non-conformity* (Harmondsworth: Penguin, 1972); Anne Hudson, *The Premature Reformation* (Oxford: Clarendon Press, 1988); Richard Rex, *The Lollards* (Basingstoke: Palgrave, 2002).

[21] 2 Hen IV, c 15. The Act also prohibited preaching without a bishop's licence.

some Albigensians in 1210 by royal command,[22] this ultimate sanction had not been used in England until in 1401 William Sawtry became the first of over a hundred Lollards to be burnt for heresy in the fifteenth and early sixteenth centuries. Archbishop Arundel also sought to combat the heresy by strengthening the control of the church over potential dissent. His *Constitutions* (1409) prohibited preaching outside the priest's benefice without a bishop's licence, thus removing a privilege early Wycliffite graduate clergy had exploited to the full. Possession of an English Bible, or any part of it, was also banned, and discussion restricted in the universities.[23]

Lollardy largely lost influence after Oldcastle's unsuccessful rebellion of 1414, but survived as an unpopular lay movement centred on households which repudiated some of the popular orthodox acts of medieval piety and met for the collective reading of the English Bible and Wycliffite tracts. In spite of the similarities between Lollardy and later Protestant views, and with the possible exception of links between Lollardy and early Baptist congregations in Buckinghamshire, there was probably little causal connection between its network of small and poorly educated covert congregations and the sixteenth-century reformation. However, Lollardy is significant in terms of the law of Church and State because it prompted both greater control on the part of the church over unorthodox Christian ideas and cemented a connection between heresy and sedition which ensured the cooperation of the State in suppressing religious dissent for another three centuries.

III. Reformation and Revolution

Although the immediate occasion of Henry VIII's break with Rome was the Pope's refusal to dissolve his marriage to Catherine of Aragon, the broader context was a growing critique by humanists and reformers of many of the practices of the medieval Catholic Church, along with the rise of political absolutism.[24] In fact the transfer of legal business from ecclesiastical to royal courts was already well underway. By the mid-fifteenth century enterprising common lawyers had secured a reading of the Statute of Praemunire to extend its severe penalties to the abuse of jurisdiction by domestic as well as Roman ecclesiastical courts.[25] The old uneasy stand-off in respect of jurisdiction over actions considered both spiritual and temporal, such as breach of faith (contract) and advowsons (clerical appointments), was resolved in favour of the temporal courts. Further statutes

---

[22] Maitland discusses the record of the burning in 1222 of a deacon who converted to Judaism 'The deacon and the Jewess; or, apostasy at common law' (1886) 2 LQR 153.

[23] Hudson, *op cit* n 20, 82f.

[24] General accounts in G R Elton, *England under the Tudors*, 3rd edn (London: Routledge, 1991); John Guy, *Tudor England* (Oxford: Oxford University Press, 1988).

[25] Helmholz, *op cit* n 9, 367–8

were enacted in 1529 reforming mortuary and probate fees and punishing clerical pluralism and non-residence.[26] The novelty here was that while clerical pluralism was undoubtedly a church matter, offenders were to be punished in royal courts. Dispensations from Rome were made ineffective.

As regards political absolutism, the King was much influenced by a collection of authoritative writings (*Collectanea Satis Copiosa*, 1530) designed to show that ever since the Anglo-Saxon monarchs had converted to Christianity, the Kings of England had enjoyed an 'imperial' right to govern the church.[27] Thus although they did not enjoy the sacramental cure of souls, they could call councils, determine the faith, and judge causes. The raft of legislation that followed in the next five years put the imperial theory into practice. In 1532 Thomas Cromwell secured the formal submission of the clergy to the Crown: Convocation was not to assemble without the King's permission, royal assent was needed for new canons, and a Royal Commission was established to review the existing ones. This was secured by statute in 1534.[28] In 1533 the Act in Restraint of Appeals sought to make the Archbishop's court the highest ecclesiastical court,[29] only to be replaced in 1534 with the Court of Delegates, a new royal court which could include laymen. The same year saw the establishment of the Faculty Office to fulfil the papal function of issuing dispensations from the strict provisions of canon law.[30] By the Act of Royal Supremacy (1535), the King was finally declared supreme Head on earth of the Church of England.[31] The Pope's authority over the English church was ended and the church, by unilateral act, had become independent.[32]

For a time it looked as if a thoroughgoing reformation would follow, but the King was Catholic in theology if not in law. Popular resistance to reform found political expression in the Pilgrimage of Grace (1536),[33] and the Act of Six Articles largely restored Catholic orthodoxy.[34] It was thus a paradoxical characteristic of the Henrician reformation that Protestants and Roman Catholics could be executed on the same day—the former for heresy, the latter for treason. But one key component of the reformers' programme succeeded: just one year after William Tyndale's execution for heresy, an English Bible substantially based on his pioneering work from the original languages received royal approval.

There was no obvious connection between the territorial independence of the English Church and the dissolution of the monasteries.[35] Nevertheless, in spite of the reforms carried out during the Hundred Years War, some religious houses still owed their allegiance outside the country. The regular clergy were the most vociferous critics of Henry VIII, and humanists and reformers had combined to criticize enclosed religion, both on account of its corruption in places, and also

---

[26] 21 Hen VIII, cc 5, 6, and 13.   [27] Guy, *op cit* n 24, 129.   [28] 25 Hen VIII, c 19.
[29] 24 Hen VIII, c 12.   [30] 25 Hen VIII, c 21.   [31] 26 Hen VIII, c 1.
[32] 28 Hen VIII, c 10.
[33] On the continuity of popular religion, see Eamon Duffy, *The Stripping of the Altars: traditional religion in England c. 1400–c. 1580*, 2nd edn (London: Yale University Press, 2005).
[34] 31 Hen VIII, c 14.   [35] Guy, *op cit* n 24, 147f.

on account of a belief that religion should confer more obvious public benefits. Alongside the ideological shifts were the desire of the laity for more land, and the plan of Thomas Cromwell to endow the 'imperial' crown with enhanced revenue and patronage. In 1535 a complete valuation of the assets and income of the Church was carried out (*Valor Ecclesiasticus*) and on this basis around 400 religious houses worth under £200 were dissolved. Although there had initially been no plan to dissolve the greater houses, in the period 1538–1540 the remaining 202 monasteries were also dissolved.

To some extent the church benefited. Six new dioceses were founded, and eight other cathedral churches were re-established. Christ Church College, Oxford and Trinity College, Cambridge were refounded, and Regius chairs endowed at both universities. But high-minded original schemes to endow preachers, schools, colleges, hospitals, and other works of charity were abandoned. In the end, not even the Crown was endowed, since most lands were sold. Seven thousand monks were dispossessed, although 2,000 of these subsequently got dispensations to serve as secular clergy, and the church lost about two-thirds of its property, including a large minority of presentations to livings. The impact on charitable giving, and above all on giving to the church, was severe.[36]

The two brief reigns of Edward VI (1547–53) and Mary I (1553–8) saw the extremes of religious dispute. Under Edward, the reformers finally had the chance to implement their programme.[37] By the Act 1 Ed VI, c 14, chantries, fraternities, guilds, and other trusts for the support of local forms of piety were vested in the Crown. Unlike the earlier confiscations of Henry VIII, this statute was subsequently to form the basis for a legal doctrine of superstitious uses until well into the twentieth century. The Act of Six Articles was repealed,[38] and Communion was to be taken in both kinds.[39] A year later, the Act of Uniformity secured a single compulsory form of common prayer,[40] at which attendance was soon required.[41] Books and images associated with Catholic doctrine were banned.[42] Queen Mary sought to reverse these changes, not least by restoring *de haeretico comburendo* and burning 300 Protestants. Another 800 fled to continental Europe, where many experienced first-hand the Presbyterian systems of church government of Leiden, Strasbourg, and Geneva.

The 'Elizabethan Settlement' of 1559 was contained in new Acts of Supremacy[43] and Uniformity,[44] but was largely based on Edward's reformed church. *De haeretico comburendo* was repealed,[45] and the Court of High Commission established instead with powers to fine and imprison, to assist the

---

[36] W K Jordan, *Philanthropy in England 1480–1660* (London: Allen & Unwin, 1959).
[37] Diarmaid MacCulloch, *Tudor Church Militant: Edward VI and the Protestant Reformation* (London: Allen Lane, 1999). [38] 1 Ed VI, c 12.
[39] 1 Ed VI, c 1. [40] 2&3 Ed VI, c 1. [41] 5&6 Ed VI, c 1.
[42] 3&4 Ed VI, c 10. [43] 1 Eliz I, c 1; also 5 Eliz I, c 1. [44] 1 Eliz I, c 2.
[45] 1 Eliz I, c 1, s 6.

ecclesiastical courts in their pursuit of crimes against spiritual laws.[46] The first decade of Elizabeth's reign was reasonably peaceable, with little attempt being made to deal with recusant Catholics. However, in 1570 Pope Pius V excommunicated Elizabeth and declared that Catholics were relieved of any duty of obedience to the English Crown. The legislative response was rapid. It became treasonable to assert that Elizabeth was a heretic, or that the Pope had any authority in England, and a renewed attempt was made to secure uniformity of belief among the clergy.[47] The following years saw increasingly draconian legislation against 'Papists', and in particular against the Jesuits, the counter-reformation missionary movement founded by Ignatius of Loyola in 1534.[48] This legislation was affirmed and strengthened under James I, particularly in the wake of the Gunpowder Plot.[49]

Tensions also grew between those Protestants content with the ecclesiological middle road of the Elizabethan Settlement and Puritans seeking a more radical reformation, particularly an abandonment of episcopal order for presbyterian or congregational forms of church government.[50] Until the 1640s it was an almost universal assumption that there should be one church coordinate with the State. Argument was joined over the correct beliefs, liturgy, and government of that church, but not the basic principle. Early separatists—whether Catholics hearing mass in secret or Presbyterians meeting in an unlawful conventicle—deplored the fact that they had to do so. Catholics had been forced into separation from 1570, but the number of Protestant separatist congregations at that time was tiny. In 1567 a Protestant congregation was discovered at the Plumbers' Hall in London and suppressed, and small numbers of dissenters continued to emerge. In 1593 the Act for Retaining the Queen's Subjects in their Due Obedience decreed immediate imprisonment for those who failed to attend church or who attended an unlawful religious assembly.[51] By 1610 there were several congregations of English refugees in the Netherlands, and in 1612 Helwys returned from exile to establish what became the General Baptists. But even in 1640 it has been estimated that there were still only around 1,000 Protestant separatists in London, gathered into 10 congregations. Members of the Church of England might chafe at the Elizabethan Settlement, but the vast majority sought reform from within.

Charles I's bishops, led by archbishop Laud, sought to adjust the Elizabethan Settlement in a more Catholic direction. By tying the cause of episcopacy to that

---

[46] Background in John Coffey, *Persecution and Toleration in Protestant England* (Harlow: Pearson, 2000).

[47] Treason Act 1571 (13 Eliz I, c 1); Bulls etc. from Rome Act 1571 (13 Eliz I, c 2); Ordination of Ministers Act 1571 (13 Eliz I, c 12).

[48] Religion Act 1580 (23 Eliz I, c 1); Jesuits Act 1584 (27 Eliz I, c 2); Religion Act 1586 (29 Eliz I, c 6); Popish Recusants Act 1593 (35 Eliz I, c 2).

[49] Jesuits etc. Act 1603 (1 Jam I, c 4); Popish Recusants Acts 1605 (3 Jam I, cc 4, 5); Oath of Allegiance Act 1609 (7 Jam I, c 6); see also Popery Act 1627 (3 Cha I, c 3).

[50] Michael Mullett, 'Radical Sects and Dissenting Churches, 1600–1750', in Gilley and Sheils, *op cit* n 1, ch 10.   [51] 35 Eliz I, c 1.

of the King, they achieved its eventual abolition. In a few years after the abolition of the Court of High Commission in 1640,[52] the ecclesiastical courts had collapsed. For a time, it thus seemed as if the 1640s would witness a further reform of the Church of England and the establishment of a united Presbyterian Church embracing the entire British Isles. In 1643 the English Parliament adhered to the Scottish Solemn League and Covenant, and established the Westminster Assembly to reform the doctrine, liturgy, and order of the church. The high-point of the Puritan revolution even saw the abolition of church taxation and the introduction of civil marriage (1653). However, the social and political disturbance of the Civil War, helped in part by the lifting of press censorship, saw an explosion in the numbers and variety of Protestant groups. Although the overall numbers were small in comparison with the population, their impact was substantial. By 1660 the Particular Baptists had 250 congregations, and the Quakers were nearing their peak of 60,000 adherents (1 per cent of the population).[53] Neither Baptists, nor Quakers, nor the multitude of other Independents, wished to see an established Presbyterianism. Their views on the voluntary nature of the church as a gathered congregation of individuals bound by mutual covenant had an increasing impact on assumptions about the legal nature of a church.

The Interregnum also saw the readmission of the Jews.[54] Cromwell organized a public debate on the matter in 1655, but in spite of his hope for a formal statement, conservative opposition was too strong. Instead the conference closed without resolution, and the Jews were given private assurances of security. By 1659 they too had their own synagogue and cemetery. Thus when the republican experiment finally collapsed in 1660, religious diversity was no longer a matter of personal theological difference within a single State church; it was firmly rooted in forms of organized religious belief.

IV. Establishment and Toleration

The Restoration of Charles II (1660–85) opened auspiciously with his Declaration of Breda (1660) offering 'liberty for tender consciences'. A workable plan to produce a national church comprehending both Episcopalians and Presbyterians only narrowly failed to gain Parliamentary approval. However, early in 1661 a Fifth Monarchist uprising produced a massive backlash: 4,000 Baptists and Quakers were arrested and imprisoned, and in May a Cavalier Parliament was elected which was to prove conservative, Anglican, and hard-line. Its legislation determined the shape of the law of religion for the next 170 years. The Act of Uniformity 1662[55] was an explicit reinstatement of the Elizabethan Settlement,

---

[52] 16 Cha I, c 11.   [53] Mullett, *op cit* n 50, 197, 202.
[54] David S Katz, *The Jews in the History of England* (Oxford: Oxford University Press, 1994).
[55] 14 Cha II, c 4.

and the last serious attempt to secure by law 'an universal agreement in the Public Worship of Almighty God'. All clergy had to declare their assent to the revised Book of Common Prayer; other office-holders in universities, colleges and hospitals, teachers and even private tutors had to conform to the liturgy of the Church of England. About 2,000 clergy refused on grounds of conscience and were ejected from their livings to form a new core of educated dissenting leadership.

Associated with the reimposition of religious uniformity were a series of laws designed to suppress the dissent it invigorated, which came to be known as the Clarendon Code. The Corporations Act 1661[56] required local office-holders such as magistrates and councillors to take the oaths of allegiance and supremacy, an oath repudiating armed resistance to the Crown, a declaration that they were not bound by the Solemn League and Covenant, and also to have taken communion within the Church of England within the previous year. The Quakers Act 1662[57] punished the refusal to take oaths as required by law, and also presence at an assembly of five or more adults for religious worship. Penalties were severe: £5 or three months in gaol for the first offence; £10 or six months with hard labour for the second; and deportation for the third. The first Conventicles Act 1664[58] effectively extended this principle to all dissenters, while the Five Mile Act 1665[59] targeted ejected clergy by penalizing them for coming within five miles of any city, town, or parliamentary borough, or parish in which they had ministered, before they had taken an oath of non-resistance and sworn to refrain from seeking an alteration in the government of Church or State. The second— and permanent—Conventicles Act 1670[60] made it an offence to be present at an assembly of five or more adults, and although the penalties for individuals were smaller, preaching or allowing an assembly to meet on one's premises met with substantial fines. Local officials were given the power to break and enter to disperse meetings and were also subject to penalties for failing to enforce the law. The first Test Act 1673[61] required all office-holders under the Crown to take the various oaths of allegiance and supremacy, to take communion once a year, and to make a declaration against transubstantiation. The second Test Act 1678[62] excluded Roman Catholics from Parliament by requiring them to deny transubstantiation and denounce various Roman Catholic practices as superstitious and idolatrous.

In spite of this draconian body of legislation, there was a considerable gap between legality and enforcement. The rigorous ideals of the Cavalier Parliament were not shared by either the Monarch or many local authorities. Until Parliament forced him to withdraw it, Charles II's Second Declaration of Indulgence (1672) suspended all the penal laws and set up a system for the licensing of ministers and houses. In places, quiet protection by the magistracy meant that some dissenting

[56] 13 Cha II, St 2, c 1.   [57] 14 Cha II, c 1.   [58] 16 Cha II, c 4.
[59] 17 Cha II, c 2.   [60] 22 Cha II, c 1.   [61] 25 Cha 11, c 2.
[62] 30 Cha II, St 2, c 1.

congregations could even establish their own places of worship. Thus in respect of the Catholic community, there were no deaths between 1654 and 1678 until the 'Popish Plot' unleashed a final burst of State-sponsored persecution, ending with the death of the last Catholic martyr, Oliver Plunkett, in 1681. In respect of dissenting Protestants, after an initial spate of persecution in 1661, matters quietened down until the final 'Tory Revenge' of 1681–6. Laws were only ever tools for potential persecution—and indeed, it was the older laws, such as Elizabeth's Act of 1593, which kept the Baptist John Bunyan in prison. Generally speaking, rigorous application of the law was the exception, not the rule.

James II's vigorously pro-Catholic policies effectively united Anglicans and Dissenters in their mistrust of his Declaration of Indulgence (1687), unleashing the Revolution and ensuring that the subsequent Act of Toleration had a distinctively Protestant cast. The Toleration Bill was introduced into Parliament alongside a Comprehension Bill designed, as in 1660, to secure a broader settlement of the Church of England, embracing the Presbyterians, who made up a majority of Protestant dissenters. But fears that William III was pursuing a policy too liberal led to its rejection, and the Toleration Act 1689[63] became the principal legislative framework for the regulation of non-conforming religion.

The Toleration Act 1689 relieved Trinitarian Protestant dissenters assenting to all but three of the Church of England's 39 articles of religion from the penalties imposed by the Clarendon Code on meetings for non-established religious worship, their ministers, and schoolmasters, so long as they were registered and licensed as the Act required.[64] As a rough estimate, the Act applied to about 300,000 Protestant dissenters in England, or 5 per cent of the population.[65] Over half of these were Presbyterians. There were about 60,000 Congregationalists, 50,000 General and Particular Baptists, and 40,000 Quakers. There was considerable regional variation and tendency for greater concentrations in urban areas. The Quakers were the most diffuse, being the only Protestant denomination with a presence in every county. They also tended to have much smaller congregations; thus while the Baptists had 328 congregations in the second decade of the eighteenth century, giving an average membership of 150, the Quakers had 672 with an average membership of 59. The Catholic community—to whom the Act did not apply—is also estimated around this time to have numbered about 60,000 or about 1 per cent of the population, with 500 priests, 150 Jesuits, and 30 Catholic peers.

In the early years, the policy of toleration was far from secure. Many dissenters were prepared to practise 'occasional conformity', ie to take communion once a year in the established church to qualify for public office. Those adopting a

---

[63] 1 W&M, c 18.

[64] General accounts in Gordon Rupp, *Religion in England, 1688–1791* (Oxford: Clarendon Press, 1986); Michael Watts, *The Dissenters*, 2 vols (Oxford: Clarendon Press, 1978, 1995).

[65] Figures relate to the early decades of the eighteenth century. K Hylson-Smith, *The Churches in England from Elizabeth I to Elizabeth II*, Vol II (London: SCM Press, 1997), ch 2.

High Church, or Tory, position, some of whom were sympathetic to the claims of the Stuart dynasty, objected to this strategy for undermining the position of the established church. When Dr Sacheverell was narrowly convicted of sedition in 1710 for his intemperate writings, a furious Tory mob attacked dissenting meeting-houses. Although the decision in 1684 finding unlawful a bequest left to the eminent Puritan, Richard Baxter, for the benefit of 60 dissenting ministers was reversed in 1689, the basis was probably not the new legality of its objects, but a judicial reconstruction as individual gifts to persons prompted by the change in political context.[66] In *R v Larwood* (1694), the court held that the Toleration Act was purely personal to dissenters and had not changed the general law.[67] In *AG v Eades* (1713) doubts were still being expressed whether a gift to poor Anabaptists was a good charity.[68] And under Queen Anne, the Tories achieved some success in rooting out compromise with the Occasional Conformity Act 1711[69] and Schism Act 1714.[70] It is hardly surprising that the trusts on which dissenting places of worship were established often made provision in case of future proscription.

The same initial caution can be seen in the case of the Quakers. Their refusal to take oaths was accommodated in the Toleration Act by the provision of alternative affirmations, and this principle was extended by the Quakers Act 1695[71] to all cases in which an oath might be required by law. However the Act was temporary only, and after renewal for a further term in 1701[72] was finally made perpetual only in 1715.[73] The form of the affirmation continued to require amendment and clarification to render it acceptable. However, affirmations did not extend to criminal process or public office, extensions which had to wait for nineteenth-century emancipation. And if the refusal to take oaths was accommodated—at least in theory—unwillingness to pay church rates and tithes most certainly was not. It was the process for seizing goods and selling them in lieu of church taxation set out in the Act of 1695 which was to form the main hardship experienced by Quakers in the following two centuries.

The accession of the Hanoverian George I in 1714 secured the dominance of the Whig interest; the Tory legislation of Queen Anne's reign was repealed in 1719,[74] and occasional conformity restored. The courts established that Protestant dissenting trusts were enforceable and within the policy of the law.[75] Furthermore, as Convocation was no longer summoned after 1717, the Church of England lost its forum for self-government, and Parliament became its supreme legislative

---

[66] *AG v Baxter* (1684) 1 Vern 248, 23 ER 446; *AG v Hughes* (1689) 2 Vern 105, 23 ER 677; *Moggridge v Thackwell* (1803) 7 Ves 36, 30 ER 440, per Lord Eldon LC at 76.

[67] *R v Larwood* (1694) 1 Salk 168, 91 ER 155; 1 Ld Raym 29, 91 ER 916. The point was still worthy of clarification in 1779; see 19 G III, c 44, s 4.

[68] Unreported; see *AG v Cock* (1751) 2 Ves Sen 273, 28 ER 177, at 274.

[69] 10 Anne c 2/6.   [70] 12 Anne c 7.   [71] 7&8 W III, c 34.

[72] 13&14 W III, c 4.   [73] 1 G I, St 2, c 6.   [74] 5 G I, c 4, s 1.

[75] *AG v Hickman* (1732) 2 Eq Cas Abr 193 pl 14, 22 ER 166; *AG v Cock* (1751) 2 Ves Sen 273, 28 ER 177; *Waller v Childs* (1765) Ambl 524, 27 ER 338.

body. From 1726 a series of Indemnity Acts relieved non-communicants from the requirements of the Corporation Act,[76] although this may have been as much about accommodating lax Anglicans as dissenters. Until stopped by the courts in 1767, conscientious dissenters who refused to qualify themselves for those offices still requiring conformity could be exposed to malicious elections and suits for damages.[77] For the most part, they survived by a mixture of occasional conformity and the absence of any party sufficiently interested to bring suit.

Lord Mansfield's remark that the Toleration Act had legally 'established' dissenting Protestants was not wholly without merit when one considers the legal position of Jews.[78] This reflected an underlying ambiguity about their status as subjects or aliens, and an argument that restrictive legislation, such as that requiring weekly attendance at church or chapel, was really only intended to ensure unity among Christians. 'Stranger churches' and ambassadorial chapels outside the establishment had always been tolerated in London extra-legally. Already by 1659 a synagogue and cemetery had been established in reliance on informal assurances of security. On his restoration, Charles II was petitioned by hostile merchants but refused to enforce the expulsion order of 1290. Further prosecutions were blocked by royal command in 1664 and 1685, and William of Orange was so indebted to Jewish merchants for supplying his army that he not only ensured their protection but knighted Solomon de Medina in 1700. It is perhaps not accidental that the Blasphemy Act 1697 only applied to those educated, or having made profession, as Christians.[79] In 1667 the courts ruled that Jews might give evidence by being sworn on the Hebrew Bible and in 1684 confirmed that they could sue to recover debts.[80] This principle was confirmed for both Jews and Muslims in 1744.[81] In 1732 Kitty Villareal, a Jewish heiress, was sued for breach of promise of marriage by her cousin in the Canterbury Court of Arches, an ecclesiastical court. The case was unsuccessful, but there was no question of denying jurisdiction. One brief incident aside, there was no special taxation, and although Jews could not become freemen of the City of London on account of the oath that had to be sworn, restrictions on retail trading were largely ignored. However, the courts did refuse to enforce trusts for Jewish religious purposes,[82] and legislation in 1752 to naturalize Jews born outside the United Kingdom pro-

---

[76] K R M Short, 'The English Indemnity Acts, 1726–1867' (1973) 42 Church History 366.

[77] Finally prevented by the courts in *Evans v Harrison* (1762) Wilm 130, 97 ER 51; (1767) 3 Bro PC 645, 1 ER 1437.

[78] H S Q Henriques, *The Jews and the English Law* (London: J Jacobs, 1908). Relevant cases summarized in Gerald Godfrey, 'The Judges and the Jews' (2003) 7 Ecc LJ 50. For background, see Katz, *op cit* n 54. Lord Mansfield's remark was made in *Evans v Chamberlain of London*, noted in *AG v Pearson* (1817) 3 Mer 353, 36 ER 135, at 420.

[79] 9 Will III, c 32/35. It would appear that no prosecution was ever brought under the Act, which was repealed by the Criminal Law Act 1967.

[80] *Robeley v Langston* (1688) 2 Keb 314, 84 ER 196.

[81] *Omychund v Barker* (1744) Willes 538, 125 ER 1310; 1 Atk 21, 26 ER 15. See also *R v Morgan* (1764) 1 Leach 54, 168 ER 129.   [82] *Da Costa v De Pas* (1753) Amb 228, 27 ER 150.

voked such a public outcry that it was quickly repealed.[83] Thus by a mixture of acceptance and Nelsonian blindness, Jews were largely accommodated in their family, commercial, and religious life. Roman Catholicism, by contrast, grew slowly, but steadily, entirely outside the law.

The restoration of the monarchy in 1660 had also brought about the reinstatement of the ecclesiastical courts with their jurisdiction almost unchanged.[84] Thereafter, a slow process of decline set in as social mores changed and the sanctions of penance and excommunication became increasingly ineffective. At first, there was a considerable number of prosecutions for religious offences such as attending conventicles, neglecting the sacraments, and non-attendance at divine service. Although not formally abolished, these quickly died away after the Toleration Act. Prosecutions for sexual offences, mainly for fornication, adultery, and bastardy rose during the early decades of the eighteenth century, but then also fell away. On the civil side, defamation suits survived somewhat longer. An Act of 1787 introduced limitation periods of six months for defamation, eight months for fornication and brawling, and it abolished the offence of ante-nuptial fornication. By the late eighteenth century the criminal jurisdiction of the ecclesiastical courts was moribund, and by 1830 it had almost completely collapsed.

As far as other civil causes of action were concerned, an act of 1696 had given magistrates parallel jurisdiction over the recovery of small tithes, the limit of which was raised in 1813. The effect of this was to draw most tithe actions into the secular courts. In 1736 the Society of Friends asserted that Quakers had suffered 1,180 prosecutions for non-payment over the previous 40 years, two-thirds of which had been before magistrates.[85] Testamentary and matrimonial causes remained major sources of business, although the former became increasingly dominated by the provincial courts of Canterbury and York, while the latter were dominated by the London Consistory Court and Court of Arches held at Doctors' Commons in London.

One exception to the gradual decline of the role of the church in matters of family law was brought about by Lord Hardwicke's Act of 1753.[86] This was passed to address the problem of clandestine marriages (especially to wealthy heiresses). Marriages could no longer be conducted by simple consent before a renegade clergyman, but had to follow formal publicity in the parishes of the parties involved. Quakers and Jews were allowed to continue their own forms of marriage ceremony, but Protestant dissenters had to use their local Anglican church. This, along with other local instances of establishment such as the continuing need to use Anglican rites for burial in the churchyard formed a constant low-level reminder of subordination.

---

[83] 26 G II, c 26; 27 G II, c 1.

[84] R B Outhwaite, *The Rise and Fall of the English Ecclesiastical Courts, 1500–1860* (Cambridge: Cambridge University Press, 2006).   [85] Outhwaite, *op cit* n 84, 88.

[86] 26 G II, c 33; R B Outhwaite, *Clandestine Marriage in England 1500–1850* (London: The Hambledon Press, 1995).

The Toleration Act was Protestant and Trinitarian, requiring adherence to all but three of the Church of England's 39 articles of religion. These doctrinal constraints were relaxed slightly in the Non-conformist Relief Act 1779,[87] and as the fear of Jacobitism and political Catholicism subsided, the exclusion of Roman Catholics from its terms became increasingly indefensible. The Roman Catholic Relief Act 1791[88] extended much of its protection to them. Similarly, the growth of Unitarianism out of Presbyterianism during the course of the eighteenth century had become so significant that the Doctrine of the Trinity Act 1813[89] removed that restriction as well. In fact, the entire scheme was in need of rationalization. The Places of Religious Worship Act 1812[90] repealed the relevant penal provisions of the Clarendon Code and imposed a new obligation to register on congregations or assemblies for the religious worship of Protestant dissenters at which more than 20 were present beside the occupier and his family. It imposed fines on those permitting unregistered meetings to take place and on those preaching or teaching without a licence. Quakers were exempt and Roman Catholics were not mentioned.

Thus by the early decades of the nineteenth century there was considerable liberty for all religious groups. However, there was still a strong sense of a second-class citizenship, expressed not only in the annual possibility that indemnity from the operation of the Test and Corporation Acts might be removed, but in occasional decisions of the courts as well. The courts were not willing to read relieving statutes any further than strictly necessary. Thus, in spite of the Roman Catholic Relief Act 1791, in *Cary v Abbott* (1802) a bequest for the education of poor Roman Catholic children was held void.[91] This was legally correct: the Act of 1791 expressly preserved the pre-Act legal status of Roman Catholic charities. The same restrictive attitude was shown by Lord Eldon LC in *AG v Pearson* (1817) in which he held that a trust established in 1701 could not have been intended to benefit Unitarians, since Unitarianism was unlawful at the time.[92] This was tantamount to refusing to read the Unitarian Relief Act 1813 retrospectively and was less secure legally. The Toleration Act was generally taken to have had retrospective validating effect on Protestant dissenting trusts settled beforehand.

In fact, with hindsight, it can be seen that the combination of the Clarendon Code and the Toleration Act had a certain ossifying effect on the relations between Protestant Christians who might otherwise have found it easy to blur denominational boundaries. John Wesley was the last person to seek schism from the Church of England, yet the legal insecurity of his Methodist meeting houses meant that he was practically required to settle the trusts and register them as

---

[87] 19 G III, c 44.   [88] 31 G III, c 32.   [89] 53 G III, c 160.   [90] 52 G III, c 155.
[91] *Cary v Abbott* (1802) 7 Ves 490, 32 ER 198.
[92] *AG v Pearson* (1817) 3 Mer 353, 36 ER 135.

belonging to a dissenting religion. Having been forced into a clear position of dissent, Methodism was then socially, and to some extent legally, disadvantaged.

V. Religious Pluralism

The amendment of the Test and Corporation Acts in 1828 marked the start of four decades of rapid change in the law of Church and State.[93] This was driven by a sustained and successful non-conformist campaign to achieve legal equality.[94] For some, such as the Liberation Society founded in 1844, equality required a complete separation of Church and State. In practice—the case of Ireland aside—what was achieved was a combination of the extension of the privileges of the established church to other bodies and the creation of new secular forms of public administration. The Dissenting Deputies had been formed as early as 1732 with Presbyterian, Independent, and Baptist representatives to press for the repeal of the Test and Corporation Acts.[95] Having achieved their principal objective, in 1833 they compiled a list of outstanding practical grievances.[96] These included the need to use the marriage service of the established church, inability to bury their dead with their own minister officiating, the use of church registers for births and deaths, church rates, taxation of dissenting chapels, and exclusion from the old universities. A rather fuller list compiled in 1847 added the ecclesiastical courts, tithes, drawback on building materials for churches, the establishment of colonial bishops, the Maynooth grant and *Regium Donum*, exclusion of dissenters from Doctors' Commons, bias in the appointment of Poor Law chaplains, the declaration on becoming a member of a municipal corporation, burial fees, and State support only for denominational education. By 1870 all these grievances had been addressed.

The Poor Rate Exemption Act 1833[97] exempted those parts of buildings registered and exclusively appropriated to public religious worship from poor rates. The Births, Deaths and Marriages Registration Act 1836[98] created the General Register and compulsory civil registration of all births, deaths, and marriages. This was accompanied by the Marriage Act 1836[99] which not only created the possibility of civil marriage, but allowed the registration of chapels for the solemnization of marriages. This could take place after the issuing of a superintendant registrar's certificate, and in the presence of a registrar. The Roman Catholic Relief

[93] Robert E Rodes, *Law and Modernization in the Church of England* (Notre Dame: University of Notre Dame Press, 1991), ch 2.

[94] Timothy Larsen, *Friends of Religious Equality: Non-conformist Politics in Mid-Victorian England* (Woodbridge: The Boydell Press, 1999).

[95] Bernard, Lord Manning, *The Protestant Dissenting Deputies* (Cambridge: Cambridge University Press, 1952).   [96] Larsen, *op cit* n 94, 43–4.

[97] 3&4 W IV, c 30.   [98] 6&7 W IV, c 86.   [99] 6&7 W IV, c 85.

Act 1829[100] secured the civic participation of Catholics, and the Roman Catholic Charities Act 1832[101] finally required Roman Catholic places of worship to be treated as if they belonged to Protestant dissenters. The Religious Disabilities Act 1846[102] fulfilled both requirements in respect of Jews. A considerable body of old penal legislation was also repealed in the 1846 Act, with the effect that by 1846 none of the penalties from which the Toleration Act relieved dissenters was left on the statute book. The only penalties remaining were those contained in the Places of Religious Worship Act 1812.[103]

The Protestant Dissenters Act 1851[104] made a clumsy attempt to reform the process of registering places of worship by transferring that function to the Registrar-General as well: the new process was compulsory, lists were to be transferred from the former ecclesiastical authorities and magistrates, but it only applied to 'Protestant dissenters'. Strictly speaking, at this point, Roman Catholics and Jews were required to register their churches and synagogues to avoid the penalties of the law, but had no means to do so. In 1855, the situation was remedied. The Liberty of Religious Worship Act 1855[105] confirmed that the obligation to register did not apply to meetings conducted or authorized by an incumbent or curate of the Church of England, to private meetings, or to occasional meetings in buildings not normally appropriated to religious worship. It also confirmed that when the law stated that Roman Catholics and Jews were to be treated as if they were Protestant dissenters, it meant that the law for the time being in respect of Protestant dissenters was to apply to them also. Furthermore, the Places of Worship Registration Act 1855[106] made registration with the Registrar-General an optional alternative to the old modes of registration, and allowed places of worship to be registered in the name of any religious denomination. At this point—from a strict legal perspective—the only penalties left on the statute book applied expressly to Protestant dissenters by virtue of the Act of 1812 and by extension to Roman Catholics and Jews. From a practical perspective, prosecutions for conducting unregistered religious worship were dying out.

The campaign for legal pluralism received a considerable boost from the results of the 1851 national census, which showed both widespread religious non-attendance on the census date (39.2 per cent), and the dominance of non-conformists in a majority of the principal manufacturing districts. On a national average, Anglican attendance barely surpassed that of dissenters, with both a little under 30 per cent.[107] The results gave Anglicans such a shock that a question about

---

[100] 10 G IV, c 7. The Roman Catholic Relief Act 1813 (53 G III, c 128) had already extended the Irish relief of 1793 to those transferring to offices in Great Britain.   [101] 2&3 W IV, c 115.

[102] 9&10 V, c 59.

[103] These penalties were only formally repealed in the Statute Law (Repeals) Act 1977 until which time it was technically an offence to engage in unregistered religious worship.

[104] 15&16 V, c 36.   [105] 18&19 V, c 86.   [106] 18&19 V, c 81.

[107] Detailed tables in Watts, *op cit* n 64, vol 2; average percentages noted in Rodes, *op cit* n 93, 121.

religious affiliation was not repeated until 2001. At the same time, the announcement in 1850 that the Roman Catholic Church intended to re-establish its hierarchy prompted a wave of anti-Catholic feeling. The Ecclesiastical Titles Act 1851[108] made it unlawful for Roman Catholic clergy to adopt territorial designations. In 1871 this restriction was repealed.[109]

In 1830, a Royal Commission of Enquiry into the ecclesiastical courts was established amid increasing public concerns about cost, delay, and abuse.[110] Its recommendations were radical: abolition of the criminal jurisdiction, control over clergy discipline, and reduction of all other cases to the two provincial courts. In the event, political opposition ensured that the only immediate effect was the abolition of the Court of Delegates—the appeal court convened on an *ad hoc* basis—and a transfer of its functions to the Privy Council. After repeated attempts by reformers, defamation jurisdiction was removed in 1855, testamentary and matrimonial causes followed in 1857, and suits for brawling were replaced by a secular criminal offence in 1860. Thereafter the ecclesiastical courts were for practical purposes the domestic tribunals of the Church of England. The advocates of Doctors' Commons who served these courts transferred to the common law bar, and their buildings were sold.[111]

As regards financial support for the Church of England, the Government had made grants totalling £1.5 million in 1818 and 1824 for the building of new churches. These were the last block grants, and from that time the two most contentious forms of financial support for the church were the tithes and rates. Tithes were commuted for a charge on land akin to a rentcharge in 1836.[112] As a form of historic property right they were not so obviously inequitable, although controversy could still emerge in times of economic hardship.[113] Rates proved a more intractable problem, with protracted litigation from 1841 to 1853 over the powers of a vestry to set rates when a majority of the parishioners voting refused to assent. Some dissenters thought they should be applied to benefit all denominations. Parliamentary bills to abolish them were considered in 1834 and 1837, but the church fought off the attacks until 1868, when they became voluntary.[114]

The intertwining of the Church of England with education was much harder to disentangle. Schools and universities were thoroughly Anglican institutions. From 1828 the Government started to make block grants to the National Society (Anglican) and the British Society (Protestant inter-denominational) to support their school building programme. By 1860 it was accepted by even the most die-hard supporters that grant-aided voluntary effort would not meet the needs of

---

[108] 14&15 V, c 160.   [109] 34&35 V, c 53.   [110] Outhwaite, *op cit* n 84, 140ff.

[111] See also J H Baker, *Monuments of Endlesse Labours* (London: The Hambledon Press, 1998).

[112] 6&7 W IV, c 71.

[113] The same debates were reignited in modern times over the obligation of a lay rector to pay for chancel repairs. See *Aston Cantlow and Wilmcote with Billesley PCC v Wallbank* [2002] Ch 51, [2004] 1 AC 546. Chancel repairs were either an inequitable tax (CA) or an unexceptionable proprietory right (HL).   [114] Compulsory Church Rate Abolition Act 1868.

universal basic schooling, and from 1870 the first State elementary education schools were established.[115] When the public schools were reformed in 1868, the governors were empowered to make regulations permitting the attendance of non-Anglicans,[116] and the reform of the other endowed schools contained a comprehensive scheme requiring their accommodation.[117] The process of widening access to the universities of Oxford and Cambridge started in 1854 and 1856 respectively, removing religious tests for matriculation or bachelor's degrees (except in divinity).[118] The Universities Tests Act 1871[119] was much more thoroughgoing, removing tests for any office or teaching position, and for any degree apart from that in divinity. Even this Act did not address the widespread restrictions on college fellowships to clergymen. That had to wait until review of college statutes by commissioners established under the Oxford and Cambridge Act 1877,[120] which swept away almost all restrictions except for college chaplains and professors of divinity. However, new denominational colleges were permitted, and Anglicans made use of this in establishing Keble College, Oxford, and Selwyn College, Cambridge.

The more ambitious desire of radical dissent to disestablish the Church of England was not achieved. But the disestablishment of the Church of Ireland, with which it was united, was. Notwithstanding the fact that the Union with Ireland Act 1800 made unity and establishment an 'essential and fundamental part of the Union', the religious demography of Ireland made it the most obviously inequitable arrangement in the United Kingdom, a fact which was regularly underscored by the felt need to compensate Irish Presbyterian clergymen by the *Regium Donum* and State support for the Roman Catholic training college at Maynooth. The Irish Church Act 1869[121] was passed after a Liberal Government had been returned in the wake of the further widening of the franchise brought about by the Second Reform Act 1868. The church was reconstituted in a legal form familiar both to dissenting denominations and to the Anglican Church in the colonies. Ecclesiastical law and courts ceased to exist as such, but continued as a matter of contract between the members, enforceable in temporal courts only in respect of property rights. The church was free to hold assemblies and synods as it wished. Lay powers of appointment were abolished, and all church property was vested in commissioners to be distributed either as compensation, including to non-conformists for the loss of *Regium Donum*, or to public purposes, or to a newly incorporated representative body of trustees to hold for the purposes of the church.

---

[115] Elementary Education Act 1870.   [116] Public Schools Act 1868, s 12.

[117] Endowed Schools Act 1869, ss 15–19. The scheme was so rigorous that it required emendation to accommodate post-1688 faith-based schools to preserve their ethos: Endowed Schools Act (1869) Amendment Act 1873, s 7.

[118] Oxford University Act 1854 (17&18 V, c 81), ss 44–45; Cambridge University Act 1856 (19&20 V, c 88), ss 45–46.   [119] 34&35 V, c 26.

[120] 40&41 V, c 48.   [121] 32&33 V, c 42.

One simple way of characterizing the changing law of Church and State is as a slow transition from the maintenance of one true religion to the principle that there is, in law, no false religion. At some point in that transition, around the middle decades of the nineteenth century, English law underwent a fundamental reversal of orientation. Rather than assuming that all religion was unlawful except for that of the established church and other 'sects' expressly tolerated by Act of Parliament, the underlying assumption became that all religion was lawful unless it breached some specific prohibition. After 1855, a place of religious worship could be registered under 'any religious denomination', but the reversal of orientation was not brought about by a single statute. Rather, it can be followed most closely in the judgments of the courts concerning superstitious uses, or trusts for unlawful religious purposes.

Lord Eldon's grudging attitude to Unitarians in 1817 has already been noted. In spite of the Roman Catholic Charities Act 1832, which was accepted as having retrospective effect, in *West v Shuttleworth* (1834), the future Lord Chancellor, Lord Cottenham, maintained a doctrine of superstitious uses for specific purposes within Roman Catholicism.[122] Parliament may have made trusts for saying mass lawful, but trusts for saying masses for the repose of a soul were not. His decision was followed as late as 1854,[123] but the tide was beginning to turn. In *Re Michel* (1860) Sir John Romilly MR pointed out the difficulty of holding that a religion was tolerated while some of its central practices were not.[124] Nevertheless he considered himself bound to follow precedent, and the Roman Catholic Charities Act 1860 was passed to ensure that trusts considered superstitious would still at least be applied to lawful Roman Catholic purposes. Romilly's underlying attitude was exposed in the remarkable case of *Thornton v Howe* (1862) in which he upheld a bequest to propagate the writings of Joanna Southcote, a mystic who claimed to be pregnant by the Holy Spirit and to give birth to a second Christ.[125] He robustly insisted that the Court of Chancery would not draw a distinction between one religion and another, and would not object to a trust for religious purposes unless it was adverse to the very foundation of all religion and subversive of all morality. In other words, all religions were permitted unless they were prohibited. Even the doctrine of superstitious uses could be creatively avoided by construing a gift as one to the individual members of an order for the time being.[126]

Odd residual privileges of the established church continued to be addressed. For example, in 1873 a provision of the Church Building Act 1818 which allowed corporations to donate land for building churches was extended to other denominations.[127] It is hard to believe this was a matter of real practical grievance, but it demonstrates a commitment to principle. It was a mark of the new confidence in

---

[122] *West v Shuttleworth* (1835) 2 My & K 684, 39 ER 1106.
[123] *Heath v Chapman* (1854) 2 Drew 417, 61 ER 781.
[124] *Re Michel* (1860) 28 Beav 39, 54 ER 280.
[125] *Thornton v Howe* (1862) 31 Beav 14, 54 ER 1042.
[126] *Cocks v Manners* (1871) LR 12 Eq 574.   [127] Places of Worship Sites Act 1873, s 1.

the State as the neutral organizer of a plurality of religions that the jurisdiction of the Charity Commissioners to settle schemes was extended to cover buildings registered as places of worship in 1869.[128] The first such scheme was a substantial reorganization of Jewish charities settled in the United Synagogues Act 1870.

VI. Towards the Modern State

After 1870 English law begins to take on a shape familiar today. Most dissenters had been content, whether out of pragmatism or principle, to limit their campaigns to the redress of practical grievances, but during the last quarter of the nineteenth century, English law began to move beyond religious pluralism into a more thoroughgoing process of secularization. Four dimensions of this are worth noting by way of general background to the following chapters. First, the law abandoned any attempt to adjudicate expressly between religions and worldviews. Secondly, public and religious services were to be ever more clearly differentiated, with public services open to all regardless of belief. Thirdly, the established churches were to enjoy an increasing measure of independence from State control. Finally, individual conscience took centre-stage in the law's approach to religion. These developments were not unconnected with the widening franchise. Before the Reform Act 1867 the electorate was still drawn from the body of regular attenders at church or chapel. After 1867 that balance had shifted, with substantial numbers of non-attenders becoming enfranchised. This shift became even more marked after 1884.

1. Extending legality to all religions and none

The atheist Charles Bradlaugh's campaign to reform the law of oaths was paradigmatic of a general change.[129] The Toleration Act had made provision for Quakers, who scrupled to take oaths, in respect of licensing meeting-houses. But until the nineteenth century, oath-taking was widespread and posed considerable social difficulties for Quakers. In the course of the eighteenth century, the occasions on which affirmation might be substituted were extended, and other specific denominations, particularly the Moravian Brethren, were added to those who could benefit. An Act of 1854 extended the right of affirmation to all persons willing to declare that the taking of an oath was unlawful according to their religious belief. This requirement was maintained in further statutory extensions through the 1860s. Then in 1869, the law of oaths was completely pluralized to allow for affirmation in any case in which the judge was satisfied that an oath

---

[128] Charitable Trusts Act 1869, s 15.
[129] Constance Braithwaite, *Conscientious Objection to Compulsions under the Law* (York: William Sessions Ltd, 1995), ch 1.

would have 'no binding effect' on the conscience of the individual concerned. Even this was unsatisfactory for those like Bradlaugh who considered themselves bound, but for whom the theistic dimension was irrelevant. In any case, it did not apply to the oath of allegiance required of Bradlaugh as an MP by the Parliamentary Oaths Act 1866. His long campaign to be allowed to take the oath as a known atheist lasted for six years from his first election in 1880, involved two references to the courts,[130] and occasioned considerable public controversy. It finally bore fruit in the Oaths Act 1888, which allowed anybody who objected to being sworn to affirm on any occasion on which an oath was required.

The same development can be seen in the criminal law of blasphemy. From the case of *Taylor* (1676) onwards, judges would regularly insist that Christianity was part of the law of England, and that to reproach Christianity was to speak in subversion of the law.[131] While in practice only egregious abuses would be prosecuted, in theory any public disagreement with established belief could be considered criminal. The underlying judicial attitude can be seen in *Waddington* (1822) in which it was held that the Doctrine of the Trinity Act 1813 extended the benefits of the Toleration Act and provided relief from the operation of the Blasphemy Act to Unitarians, but had not affected the common law of blasphemous libel.[132] Best J refused to say whether he thought it was libellous to argue from Scripture against the divinity of Jesus Christ, rather implying that he thought it was. The first hints of a formal narrowing of the offence by reference to the manner and tone of the publication appeared in the judgment of Lord Denman CJ in *Hetherington* (1841),[133] then right in the middle of the Bradlaugh controversy, Lord Coleridge CJ told the jury in the case of *Ramsey and Foote* (1883) that 'if the decencies of controversy are observed, even the fundamentals of religion may be attacked without the writer being guilty of blasphemy'.[134] The eminent criminal lawyer, Sir James Stephen, publicly disagreed, but it was Lord Coleridge's view that survived.

As far as the civil law was concerned, the question was whether irreligious purposes were unlawful. Early in the nineteenth century, Lord Eldon LC had denied injunctions to prevent the circulation of pirated copies of works he considered antithetical to Christianity.[135] When in 1861, Sir John Romilly MR allowed the Rational Society to recover a contract debt it was on the basis that it was not to be considered as propagating 'irreligious and immoral doctrines'.[136] As late as 1867 the courts could hold that a contract to let a room on behalf of a secular society for a lecture impugning the character and teaching of Christ was unen-

---

[130] *Clarke v Bradlaugh* (1881) 7 QBD 38; *AG v Bradlaugh* (1885) 14 QBD 667.
[131] *R v Taylor* (1676) 1 Vent 293.   [132] *R v Waddington* (1822) 1 St Tr NS 1339.
[133] *R v Hetherington* (1841) 4 St Tr NS 563.
[134] *R v Ramsey and Foote* (1883) 15 Cox CC 231 at 238.
[135] *Murray v Benbow* (1822) 4 St Tr NS 1409; *Lawrence v Smith* (1822) Jac 471.
[136] *Pare v Clegg* (1861) 29 Beav 589, 54 ER 756.

forceable.[137] This line of cases was not overruled until *Bowman v Secular Society* (1917).[138] The judge and Court of Appeal had upheld a gift to the society since it was not subversive of morality. Significantly, they did not refer to the promotion of irreligion. In the House of Lords, Lord Finlay LC was a lone dissenting voice in his mid-Victorian attempt to argue that since toleration had never been extended to atheists or humanists, the purposes of the secular society must be unlawful. The attitude of the majority could be summed up in the words of Lord Sumner, 'it is not necessary to consider whether or why any given body was relieved by the law at one time or frowned on at another'.[139]

It took until *Bourne v Keen* (1919), for the House of Lords to overrule the *West v Shuttleworth* line of cases on superstitious uses,[140] at times expressing incomprehension as to how the decision could ever have been reached in the first place. Although Lord Birkenhead LC expressly left open the possibility that there might still be unlawful superstitious uses, given the decision in *Bowman*, for practical purposes attention shifted to the question of public benefit, where it remains today. The final, genuine, statutory restriction on trusts for Jesuits and other male Catholic monastic orders was removed by statute in 1926.[141]

2. Distinguishing public and religious services

The removal of public registration functions from churches in 1836 has already been noted. The significance of the parish vestry with its churchwardens as an organ of local Government had also declined from the 1830s as new boards and functions were created. New urban parishes created by statute from the Church Building Act 1818 onwards tended to be for solely ecclesiastical purposes, leaving the original parish out of which they were carved with the secular functions. However, in London, the Metropolitan Management Act 1855 had reorganized and renewed the parish vestries with mixed functions. It was the Local Government Act 1894 which created secular rural parishes, and the London Government Act 1899 which abolished secular vestries in favour of new London Borough Councils. The last remaining dual-function vestries were finally reformed under the Local Government Act 1933.

The Local Government Act 1894 also 'disestablished' local charities by distinguishing clearly between parochial charities with secular purposes (ie the relief of the poor) and 'ecclesiastical charities' which were for spiritual purposes or the benefit of a particular church or denomination.[142] The former were vested in or accountable to the new parish councils. In the case of mixed charities, the Charity Commissioners could apportion the property.

---

[137] *Cowan v Milbourn* (1867) LR 2 Ex 230.
[138] *Bowman v Secular Society* [1917] AC 406. [139] Ibid, 466.
[140] *Bourne v Keen* [1919] AC 815. [141] Roman Catholic Relief Act 1926.
[142] Local Government Act 1894, s 75(2).

The period from 1870 to 1902 saw the steady rise of the better resourced State elementary schools as opposed to their denominational counterparts. Fears that the latter would be completely supplanted were allayed by Morant's Education Act 1902, which brought the denominational schools within the State funding mechanism. Thus churches became junior partners in a State-guaranteed universal system of education.[143] The same narrative can be told in respect of other social welfare services, with a delay of about four decades. Public services could thus be conceived as essentially non-religious, with an option for a religious dimension for those who wished to deliver and receive it.[144]

The same change can be seen in the law of burial. Before 1880, dissenters never gained a really satisfactory solution to the problem that they could not be buried in the churchyard without the rites of the Church of England.[145] Strictly speaking, unbaptized persons could not be buried in the churchyard at all, so the problem was most acute for Quakers, who did not baptize, and Baptists, who only baptized adults. There was some dispute as to whether this really was a practical grievance: private burial grounds could always be established, and, at their best, the clergy were sensitive to other religious requirements. The Burial Acts of the mid-nineteenth century attempted a solution by requiring Burial Boards to mark off portions of unconsecrated ground and build chapels for non-members of the Church of England. However, this failed to satisfy dissenters, and when the solution finally came in the Burial Laws Amendment Act 1880 it gave individuals the right to be buried in their local churchyard without any religious service or with such Christian and orderly religious service that any church, denomination, or person might choose.[146] The solution was both individual and secular.

3. Enhancing the independence of established churches

The Irish Church Act 1869 reconstituted the Church of Ireland according to the principles of trust and contract applied by the courts to dissenting churches and colonial Anglican Churches. If the causes of discontent with establishment in Ireland had been present from the beginning of the union of 1800, in Wales they grew during the nineteenth century. Unlike Scotland, Wales had no institutional bearers of cultural identity, and the Anglican Church had a historic presence there.[147] During the nineteenth century, Calvinistic Methodism grew rapidly, becoming separate from the Church of England in 1818. In its unified form, the Presbyterian Church of Wales increasingly represented a Welsh-speaking, chapel-going, national identity. In 1862 the Liberation Society marked the bicentenary of the Great Ejection by holding a conference in Swansea, which was

---

[143] See further Ch 8 below.   [144] See further Ch 9 below.
[145] Larsen, *op cit* n 94, 53–7.   [146] Burial Laws Amendment Act 1880, s 6.
[147] Keith Robbins, 'Religion and Community in Scotland and Wales since 1800', in Gilley and Sheils, *op cit* n 1; Roger L Brown, 'The Disestablishment of the Church in Wales' (1999) 5 Ecc LJ 252.

instrumental in persuading both the Presbyterians and the Methodists to join the political cause of disestablishment. In 1870, the first Parliamentary motion was presented, and between 1894 and 1914 four bills to disestablish the church were introduced. It took Lloyd George and the Parliament Act 1911 to overcome English opposition, and even then the operation of the Welsh Church Act 1914 was delayed until 1920 on account of the Great War. The non-conformist campaign was, in one sense, too successful. Church endowments were applied to new national institutions such as the University of Wales and the National Library of Wales, and the continuing rise of Welsh national consciousness began to lose its distinctively religious cast.

This is not the place even to sketch the complex ecclesiastical history of Scotland, but the reunification of the Church of Scotland which came to be anchored in the Church of Scotland Act 1921 has a wider constitutional significance.[148] The established position of the Presbyterian Church was secured in the Union Treaties and Acts of Union 1706, but the church was riven by schism in the eighteenth and nineteenth centuries over the question of the degree of secular involvement in church affairs. The outcome was the recognition of dual sovereignty in the Act of 1921, so pure in its form, that the Act recognizes—it does not confer—an exclusive jurisdiction on the church in spiritual matters. The Act confirms in law the complete jurisdictional autonomy of the church in matters of doctrine, worship, government, and discipline. It stands as a reminder that establishment and autonomy are not mutually exclusive. The Act also holds out the possibility of a similar legal position to other religious bodies.[149] It expresses a widespread twentieth-century constitutional assumption about the place of organized religions.

At the same time as being divested of the responsibilities of public administration, the Church of England also gained substantial autonomy from the State.[150] Convocation started meeting again in the two provinces from the early 1850s as merely consultative bodies rather unsure of the relevance of their historical role. From the 1880s, houses of lay representatives were added. Around this time, clergy were also increasingly promoting the election of voluntary parish councils to provide advice in place of moribund vestries. Consolidation and rationalization produced the Representative Church Council in 1903 with a combined House of Bishops, a House of Clergy, and a House of Laymen. A plan to give this body an official status and role was delayed by the war, but in 1919 the Enabling Act constituted this body the Church Assembly with power to legislate on matters concerning the Church of England (including the amendment of primary legislation) subject to review of the draft Measure by a joint Parliamentary Committee and a vote in favour. Parliament could thus still veto proposed legislation, as it did most

---

[148] See Lord Rodger of Earlsferry, *The Courts, the Church and the Constitution: Aspects of the Disruption of 1843* (Edinburgh: Edinburgh University Press, 2008).
[149] Church of Scotland Act 1921, s 2.   [150] Rodes, *op cit* n 93, ch 5.

notably in the attempts to revise the Book of Common Prayer in 1927 and 1928. In 1969, the Synodical Government Measure transferred the remaining powers of Convocation to the Church Assembly, now renamed the General Synod. Under the Worship and Doctrine Measure 1974, the church gained almost complete control over these central aspects of its identity. Apart from residual rights associated with local residence, the basis of lay involvement in the Church of England has been, from 1919, the voluntary parish electoral roll.

4. Focusing on individual conscience

The rooting of religion in individual conscience has a long history in Western thought. After all, the Toleration Act was designed to offer relief to 'tender consciences'. But its solution was essentially collective, and from a legal perspective the protection of the individual conscience has been until recent times a relatively minor theme. The law only gradually made a transition from exemptions for specified religious groups to more general provisions in favour of the individual religious (or even non-religious) conscience. It has already been pointed out that it was not until the Oaths Act 1888 that general provision was made for affirmation in any circumstance requiring an oath. Apart from the vexed issue of oath-taking, Quakers and Moravians had also objected to military service, and here accommodation was slower. A few concessions were made in the Militia Act 1757, but full exemption from personal military service was only finally guaranteed in the Militia Act of 1803. A general conscience clause in matters of religion was accepted on the introduction of compulsory schooling in 1870.[151] Similarly, a conscience clause was finally included in the scheme for compulsory vaccination in 1898, after considerable public pressure.[152] By the time of the re-introduction of conscription in the Military Service Act 1916, it was accepted—not without some debate in Parliament—that conscientious objection should not be limited to members of religious groups known to object, but should be available to all as individuals.[153]

Thus it was that the protection of individual conscience came to be the dominant twentieth-century paradigm in the law's relationship to religion. It could explain both the formation of voluntary religious associations and the existence of legal exceptions from general obligations. It is reflected pre-eminently in the international human rights documents of the second half of the century, which protect 'freedom of thought, conscience and religion' and then refer to the subsidiary right to manifest religion or belief either individually or in community with others.[154] Many current practical legal problems turn on whether some

---

[151] Elementary Education Act 1870, s 7.
[152] Vaccination ceased to be compulsory in 1948 when the National Health Service Act 1946 came into force.   [153] Military Service Act 1916, s 2(1)(d).
[154] Universal Declaration of Human Rights 1948, art 18; International Covenant on Civil and Political Rights 1966, art 18; European Convention on Human Rights and Fundamental Freedoms 1950, art 9.

onerous legal obligation can be justified as a permitted limitation on freedom of religion, or whether an exception should be granted. This is the case whether one considers the matter as a limit on freedom or, in very recent times, as a potentially justified act of indirect discrimination.

Modern statutory examples still waver between adopting specifically religious and more general exceptions. The Abortion Act 1967 protected the right of conscientious objectors not to participate in a lawful abortion;[155] likewise the Industrial Relations Act 1971 allowed those who objected on grounds of conscience to trade union membership to donate their dues to charity instead.[156] However, industrial tribunals struggled to accept claims of conscience in the absence of a religious grounding,[157] and under the Trades Unions and Labour Relations Act 1974, the wording was changed to protect only those who 'genuinely object[ed] on grounds of religious belief'.[158] The Employment Appeal Tribunal found it necessary to insist both that this was a genuine limitation against some dicta suggesting that conscientious objection could only ever be religiously motivated, and also that the body of beliefs commonly held by the group of which the individual concerned was a member was merely a strong indicator of the genuine beliefs of the individual, not conclusive.[159] In the case of Sikhs, the law relating to exemptions from wearing turbans on motorcycles[160] and on building sites[161] goes to the other extreme and specifically refers to Sikhs, whereas the legal exemption from the prohibition on carrying knives in public places refers more generally to 'religious reasons'.[162] Recent litigation has often concerned the accommodation of religious individuals in non-religious contexts.[163]

VII. Conclusion

From the perspective of English legal history, it is relatively novel to locate the relationship between organized religions and the law in individual conscience. Much of the law can only be understood as an attempt to regulate belief and

---

[155] Abortion Act 1967, s 4(1). See *Janaway v Salford Area Health Authority* [1989] AC 537.

[156] Industrial Relations Act 1971, s 9(1)(b).

[157] *Drury v The Bakers' Union* [1973] IRLR 171.

[158] Trades Union and Labour Relations Act 1974, sched 1, para 6(5).

[159] *Saggers v British Railways Board* [1977] 1 WLR 1090. Saggers, a Jehovah's Witness, only won his case after a second appeal; see [1978] ICR 1111. A highly restrictive approach by the British Railways Board had already been challenged in *Cave v British Railways Board* [1976] IRLR 400.

[160] Road Traffic Act 1988, s 16(2).   [161] Employment Act 1989, s 11.

[162] Criminal Justice Act 1988, s 139(5)(b). On exceptions for Sikhs generally, see Sebastian Poulter, *Ethnicity, Law and Human Rights: the English Experience* (Oxford: Clarendon Press, 1998), ch 8.

[163] Among the more prominent cases, see *Ahmad v Inner London Education Authority* [1978] QB 36; *Mandla v Dowell Lee* [1983] 2 AC 548; *Copsey v WWB Devon Clays Ltd* [2005] ICR 1789; *R(Begum) v Denbigh High School Governors* [2007] 1 AC 100; *Eweida v British Airways plc* [2009] ICR 303; *Ladele v Islington LBC* [2009] ICR 387, [2009] EWCA Civ 1357; *Azmi v Kirklees MBC* [2007] ICR 1154.

action which is inescapably—if imprecisely—religious and collective in orientation. With hindsight we can see that around 1920, the law entered a period of relative stability in the relationship between 'Church' and 'State', which was in some sense connected with respect for conscience, but which was still substantially marked by the outcome of earlier struggles over the place of organized religion in public life. A gap emerged between the assumed theoretical basis for the legal place of religion and its actual expression in the law. It is the main object of this book to trace the contours of what we can now see to have been a constitutional settlement of the legal position of organized religions. This was much more than the expression of respect for conscience.

Furthermore, we shall also see that in many areas of the relevant law, changes are now taking place which cannot be fitted into the twentieth-century trajectory. The settlement is being challenged, so it is important not only to state the law, but to understand the principles at stake. If individual conscience is descriptively incomplete, it is also unlikely that it will provide the necessary normative grounding for the law. It is striking that in the last decade or so international human rights law has begun to take tentative steps towards a more comprehensive account of the rights of religious associations, which moves beyond its original individualistic cast in a direction which reconnects religious liberty and equality to the substance of the law of organized religions. The purpose of subsequent chapters is thus also to state how English law gives concrete expression to—and even limits—those human rights.

2

The Human Rights of Religious Associations

International law has recently started to protect the human rights of religious associations. This is only one of a variety of ways in which international law engages with religious belief and practice. If its historical aim has been to prevent religious diversity from becoming a cause of conflict, modern developments have added the protection of religious liberty and combating internal persecution and discrimination. Protecting the human rights of religious associations must be seen against the background of these wider agendas.

I. The Place of Religion in International Law

The Westphalian Treaties of Münster and Osnabrück (1648) ended the Thirty Years War and marked the final demise of two-sword mediaeval imperialism, which juxtaposed spiritual and temporal empires in a 'united' Christendom. Henceforth, sovereign States could determine whether they were to be Catholic, Lutheran, or Reformed, as their ruler decided: *cuius regio eius religio*. Citizens of a different religious persuasion were to be tolerated in public and private worship, and free to send their children to foreign schools or have private tutors. They could emigrate immediately, and indeed, after five years could be required to do so.[1]

Echoes of Westphalia live on. From a formal, constitutional, perspective, a large number of States, both with and without strong 'human rights records' have a religious foundation. Apart from the United Kingdom, to pick just a few examples, one thinks of Norway (Protestant), the Republic of Ireland (Catholic), Greece (Orthodox), Israel (Jewish), Iran (Muslim), Nepal (Hindu), and Sri Lanka (Buddhist). Furthermore, one should not ignore the position of the Roman Catholic Church itself.[2] The Holy See is unique among religious associations in

---

[1] Malcolm D Evans, *Religious Liberty and International Law in Europe* (Cambridge: Cambridge University Press, 1997), ch 2.

[2] Josef L Kunz, 'The status of the Holy See in International Law' 46 AJIL 308. James Crawford, *The Creation of States in International Law*, 2nd edn (Oxford: Clarendon Press, 2006), 221–33.

having sustained its international legal personality through a time when international law was dominated by concepts of the sovereign nation-state. The Holy See is also the Government of Vatican City, which recovered statehood after the Lateran Treaties of 1929. However while Vatican City maintains diplomatic relations with the vast majority of States in the world, and has entered into concordats (treaties) with a number of them, it cannot be a member of the United Nations and other international organizations. Instead, the Holy See typically has the status of 'permanent observer'.[3]

The Covenant of the League of Nations (1919) failed to include a provision concerning religious liberty.[4] Instead a Polish Minorities Treaty specifically designed to protect the position of the Jews in Poland was signed alongside the Treaty of Versailles. This treaty was subsequently to become the model for treaties with Czechoslovakia, the Serb-Croat-Slovene State, Romania, and Greece. Their purpose was to preserve the legal status of threatened religious minorities by ensuring both individual and collective aspects of their distinctive forms of life. New members were admitted to the League on making declarations of conformity to similar principles. In some cases there were additional requirements. Thus Albania was required to present the League Council with detailed information concerning 'the legal status of the religious communities, churches, convents, schools, voluntary establishments, and associations of racial, religious and linguistic minorities'.[5]

The minorities system collapsed in the 1930s, but its legacy lives on in article 27 International Covenant on Civil and Political Rights (1966). This includes the right of minorities to profess and practise their own religion in community with the other members of their group. The idea of a religious minority for these purposes contains a certain tension: a 'minority' must display an element of stability over time, but membership of religious minorities must be established by a personal voluntary act.[6] In this it differs from membership of a linguistic or ethnic minority. Many religious groupings in the modern State will satisfy Capotorti's fourfold minorities test of being numerically inferior, in a non-dominant position, with distinctive religious characteristics, and displaying a sense of solidarity,[7] yet they will not be treated as minorities for the purposes of article 27. The relatively small number of cases heard by the Human Rights Committee under this article involves ethnic minorities. Ethnicity often contains a traditional religious element,[8] but it is suggested that it would now be rare to find a minority defined solely by reference to religion protected by article 27.

[3] The relation between Vatican City and the Holy See is, as Crawford points out (ibid, 226) 'a matter of some perpelexity'.   [4] Evans, *op cit* n 1, chs 4–6.

[5] Evans, *op cit* n 1, 140.

[6] Manfred Nowak, *CCPR Commentary* (Kehl am Rhein: Engel, 1993), 490–1.

[7] Ibid, 487.

[8] *Ilmari Länsman et al v Finland*, Comm No 511/1992; *Francis Hopu and Tepoaitu Bessert v France*, Comm No 549/1993.

It is probably more accurate to think of article 27 as protecting the religious rights of minorities which are defined by more than religion alone, rather than the rights of religious minorities as such. In respect of purely religious rights, the protection afforded by article 27 probably does not extend beyond that of article 18 (freedom of religion).

In the second half of the twentieth century, international law has sought to manage religious diversity by protecting religious liberty as a human right. This is understood essentially as an aspect of freedom of conscience: the right of each individual to decide for him or herself what to believe and to live (within limits) accordingly. It is reflected above all in the formulations of the post-Second World War human rights instruments which combine 'thought, conscience and religion' into a single article.[9] Religious liberty as freedom of conscience has a limiting individualistic tendency. For example, it is hard to see how one would construct a claim of an Eastern European church to restitution of its cathedral confiscated by a Soviet Government 70 years ago as a right of individual conscience. Individual religious liberty also struggles to find a workable distinction between forms of behaviour which are and are not protected.[10] Inevitably the case-law finds itself forced back on familiar notions of religious manifestation, which are themselves often the expression of the practices of a long-standing community of belief.

Non-discrimination approaches in international human rights law were dominant from the 1960s to the 1980s and became apparent in a series of declarations and conventions,[11] culminating in the Declaration on the Elimination of All Forms of Intolerance and of Discrimination based on Religion or Belief (1981).[12] It is far from clear what the practical consequences of a non-discrimination approach to religion really are. The problem is often one of substance: should the claim of a religious minority to distinctive beneficial legal treatment be granted? Comparison with the position of the majority (whether religious or not) is not always very illuminating. In practice, instruments based on non-discrimination contain substantive commitments as well. Furthermore, while liberty rights admit of horizontal effect without much modification, equality rights often do not. The statement in article 2(1) of the 1981 Declaration that, 'no-one

[9] Universal Declaration of Human Rights (1948), art 18; European Convention on Human Rights (1950), art 9; International Covenant on Civil and Political Rights (1966), art 18; American Convention on Human Rights (1969), art 12; African Charter on Human and Peoples' Rights (1981), art 8.

[10] As far as the ECHR is concerned, see, classically, *Arrowsmith v United Kingdom* No 7050/75, 19 DR 5 (1980); on the ICCPR see Nowak, *op cit* n 6, 322.

[11] See, eg, the Declaration and Convention on the Elimination of All Forms of Racial Discrimination (1963, 1966 respectively) and the Declaration and Convention on the Elimination of All Forms of Discrimination against Women (1967, 1979 respectively).

[12] For general analysis, see Donna J Sullivan, 'Advancing the Freedom of Religion or Belief through the UN Declaration on the Elimination of Religious Intolerance and Discrimination' (1988) 82 AJIL 487. See Evans, *op cit* n 1, ch 9, on the drafting history.

shall be subject to discrimination by any State, institution, group of persons or person on the grounds of religion or other belief' cannot be accepted without the substantial gloss that 'discrimination' can only mean unjustified differentiation, and that the reasons for permitting differentiation on grounds of religion are much greater in the private sphere than they are on the part of the State. One only needs to consider cases in which the 'institution' or 'group of persons' involved are themselves religious.

Nevertheless, in an expansive application of the equalities approach, international human rights discourse has recently started to apply the standards once only expected of States to religions and religious associations themselves. Attention is drawn to the potential of religious belief to become a cause of violence and discrimination, and the focus of human rights activity is said to be the fostering of 'tolerance' and 'mutual respect'. General doctrines such as the positive obligations of States and the horizontal effect of rights are prayed in aid of an agenda of State intervention to promote inter-religious dialogue and equalities obligations on the part of religions. Dangers to public order supposed to arise from sects and new religious movements are taken to justify State regulation and restriction.

At present, this approach is seen more in the work of international bodies than in formal instruments. The agenda of the UN Special Rapporteur on Freedom of Religion from 1993 to 2004 was particularly characterized by a mutual respect agenda, and the events of 11 September 2001 only served to strengthen efforts to combat both religiously-sponsored violence and Islamophobia. The 2005 Cordoba Declaration of the OSCE[13] focuses on inter-faith and intercultural dialogues and partnerships, racism, xenophobia, anti-Semitism, and other forms of intolerance and discrimination. It recognizes the primary responsibility of States to address this by information gathering, legislation, and law-enforcement, and by using education and the media to promote integration and highlight the positive contributions of diversity. For a number of years the United Nations Human Rights Council and General Assembly have passed resolutions condemning 'defamation of religions', the limits of which are quite uncertain.[14]

The mutual respect approach often fails to observe that transforming religious individuals and associations from the subjects to the objects of human rights standards carries with it an enormous risk to existing standards of liberty and non-discrimination. Human rights were primarily designed as an ethic for Governments, to protect (among others) religious individuals and groups from their excesses. The reinvention of government as the benign promoter of a new syncretistic public orthodoxy is only one step from oppression.

---

[13] CIO.GAL/76/05/Rev.2.

[14] Brief critical account in Julian Rivers, 'The Question of Freedom of Religion or Belief and Defamation' (2007) 2 Religion and Human Rights 113.

II. From Individual to Collective International Religious Rights

During the 1980s and 1990s, international law also witnessed a shift from individual to collective approaches to questions of religious rights. The celebrated Krishnaswami Report was an early harbinger of this development, and since 2000 the European Court of Human Rights has also begun to make a substantial contribution.

1. The Krishnaswami Report

In 1956, the Sub-Commission on Prevention of Discrimination and Protection of Minorities appointed a Special Rapporteur, Arcot Krishnaswami, to produce a study of discrimination in the matter of religious rights and practices.[15] After taking evidence from Governments, specialized agencies of the United Nations, non-Governmental organizations, and independent experts, Krishnaswami produced a report that is still considered a classic in its field.[16]

At an early stage in his report, Krishnaswami established the 'particular importance' of collective aspects of the right to manifest religion or belief to his study, since State intervention was more frequent when manifestations occurred in community with others.[17] He noted that in general terms, freedom of association and the right to organize are often denied or severely curtailed in the specific field of religion, on the grounds that new and permanent organizations may be considered dangerous. He also noted that questions of structure and management of religious affairs were often distinctively determined by religious doctrine.

This sensitivity to collective aspects of religious liberty and non-discrimination was clearly expressed in the concrete examples Krishnaswami discussed. Chapter III of the report considers the licensing of places of public worship, public processions, pilgrimages, religious holidays, acquisition of equipment, display of symbols, arrangements for disposal of dead, dietary practices, regulation of marriage and divorce, taxation, dissemination of religion, particularly in the context of social welfare institutions such as schools, hospitals and orphanages, training of personnel, and the secrecy of the confessional. In chapter IV he argued against any assumption that the separation of Church and State was a model preferable to an established church or to the recognition of a fixed plurality of religions, pointing out that the actual level of discrimination in practice seemed independent of

---

[15] Arcot Krishnaswami, 'Study of Discrimination in the matter of Religious Rights and Practices' UN Doc. E/CN.4/Sub.2/200/Rev.1 (1960), reproduced at (1978–9) 11 NYUJ Int'l L & Pol 227.

[16] Brice Dickson, 'The United Nations and freedom of religion' (1995) 44 ICLQ 327, 334.

[17] *Op cit* n 15, 236–7.

this largely historical matter. Instead he insisted on the greatest possible freedom in the management of internal religious affairs.[18]

In spite of this emphasis, the right to religious association as such did not figure in the catalogue of 16 'basic rules' or 'principles'[19] elucidated by way of conclusion to his report. Comparison of the rules with the body of the report reveals an individualizing tendency. For example, Rule 1 states:

Everyone should be free to adhere, or not to adhere, to a religion or belief, in accordance with the dictates of his conscience.

By itself, this could be construed as a matter of private mental assent. However, the relevant paragraph from the report is strikingly collective in tone:

...it must be recollected that the followers of most religions and beliefs are members of some form of organization, such as a church or community. If it is to be considered that freedom to maintain or to change religion or belief does not admit of any restraint—and it seems to be rightly considered by the consensus of world opinion—any instance of compelling an individual to join or to prevent him from leaving the organization of a religion or belief in which he has no faith must be considered to be an infringement of the right to freedom of thought, conscience and religion.[20]

To take another example, Rule 9, which refers to a right to religious marriage, needs to be read in the light of the body of the report, which makes plain that systems in which no religious ceremony has civil effect, and systems of recognized religious forms with the alternative of civil marriage are both acceptable modes of regulation.[21] The closest the Rules get to acknowledging a genuine collective right is in Rule 11:

No group professing a religion or belief shall be prevented from training the personnel required for the performance of practices or observances prescribed by that religion or belief.

Nevertheless, in spite of their final formulation, many of the Krishnaswami principles can only be exercised in a context of collective religious activity, and in a modern State can hardly fail to be subject to legal regulation.

2. The International Covenant on Civil and Political Rights

Krishnaswami closed his report with a call for the further codification of religious rights. But in the light of the failure to agree any specific convention on religious liberty or non-discrimination, it is still the International Covenant on Civil and Political Rights 1966 (ICCPR) which provides the primary legal basis for international human rights obligations in respect of religious associations.

---

[18] *Op cit* n 15, 263–6.
[19] The 'rules' reappear with slight verbal changes as 'principles' in Annex 1 to the Report.
[20] Ibid, 231.   [21] Ibid, 251–2.

Article 18 ICCPR guarantees the right to freedom of thought, conscience, and religion.[22] It includes freedom to have or to adopt a religion or belief of choice and freedom, 'either individually or in community with others and in public or private' to manifest religion or belief in 'worship, observance, practice and teaching'. The only significant textual difference from the Universal Declaration of Human Rights (1950) is the omission of an express right to change religion. Historically, it is probably the case that this omission was deliberate in order to achieve consensus.[23] However, it is often assumed now that the compromise alternative, 'have or adopt' includes a right to change religion.[24]

Article 18 is phrased individualistically: it is the individual person who may manifest his or her religion in community with others. But the fact that individuals normally require like-minded communities to be able to exercise their religious rights effectively is sufficient justification for accepting that religious associations as juridical persons are also beneficiaries of subjective rights under article 18.[25] The basic relationship between the individual and their association is indicated by the phrase 'have or adopt', which implies that the individual must be free to leave one association and join another.[26] Article 18(4) extends to the freedom to found private religious schools,[27] and by analogy with article 18(1) such schools also have subjective rights as legal persons once founded.

Any doubts about the enjoyment of article 18 rights by collective persons can be laid to rest by reference to article 22 ICCPR. Article 22 guarantees the 'right to freedom of association with others'. This embraces several related rights: the right of an individual to found an association with like-minded people, the right of a group of people to a legal framework making possible the creation of juridical persons, the collective right of an existing association to represent the common interests of its members, the individual negative freedom to leave freely, or not to join an association, and the collective negative freedom of an association to expel a member who has breached the terms of association.[28] These rights extend as much to associations for religious purposes as they do to associations for any other lawful purpose. Article 22 does not by itself give a right to a certain status of association, such as a public law corporation. However, should a State make available a range of types of association for religious purposes, the obligation in article 2 to 'respect and to ensure to all individuals within its territory and subject to its jurisdiction the rights recognized in the present Convention, without distinction of any kind, such as ... religion ...' ought to ensure that the types of association represented are accessible on a non-discriminatory basis. Furthermore, the general independent equality right contained in article 26 will apply to ensure

---

[22] For background, see Evans, *op cit* n 1, ch 8. General accounts can be found in Nowak, *op cit* n 6, and Sarah Harris, Jenny Schultz, and Melissa Castan, *The International Covenant on Civil and Political Rights*, 2nd edn (Oxford: Oxford University Press, 2004).
[23] Evans, *op cit* n 1, 201–7.   [24] See eg General Comment no 22 (1993), para 5.
[25] Nowak, *op cit* n 6, 313.   [26] Ibid, 316.   [27] Ibid, 332.   [28] Ibid, 386–9.

that the exclusion of religious bodies from legal forms and their associated powers and privileges must be justifiable on reasonable and objective criteria.

3. Human Rights Committee

Given that associations have substantive rights under the ICCPR, and that States have duties under article 2(3) to make domestic legal remedies available to associations, it is surprising that the First Optional Protocol to the ICCPR restricts the right to submit communications to the Human Rights Committee to 'individuals'.[29] Any concern to prevent popular actions by pressure groups would be met by the accompanying victim test, and the restriction is better explained by an unwillingness to give 'peoples' a cause of action to vindicate their right to self-determination.[30] The word 'individual' could thus, if desired, be given an expansive interpretation to cover corporate persons. Nevertheless, the Human Rights Committee has stuck rigidly to an insistence that only natural persons may submit communications. Groups may only be represented by way of a specific mandate from each affected individual.[31]

The necessarily individualistic cast of human rights cases which results from this procedural constraint is reflected in a number of ways. In terms of the type of religious case resolved under the Optional Protocol, the Committee has had to consider religiously-motivated drug consumption,[32] prisoners' religious rights,[33] dismissal for religiously offensive speech,[34] safety helmets in the construction industry,[35] the right to change one's name,[36] and conscientious objection.[37] Although the litigants may in some cases have been representative of a class of believers, there is nothing intrinsically associational about these disputes. In the case of prisoners' rights, the matter was considered solely from the perspective of the individual prisoner. It has been suggested that the *Coeriel* case on Hindu name changes was characterized by a failure to consider sufficiently the international nature of some religious organizations.[38] In *Sister Immaculate Joseph v Sri Lanka*, violations were found in a case concerning obstacles to educational and charitable work arising from the refusal to incorporate a Roman Catholic order, but the Committee focused on the question of improper proselytism rather

---

[29] First Optional Protocol, arts 1 and 2. See, generally, Martin Scheinin, 'The Human Rights Committee and Freedom of Religion or Belief', in Tore Lindholm *et al* (eds), *Facilitating Freedom of Religion or Belief: A Deskbook* (Leiden: Martinus Nijhoff, 2004).   [30] See art 1.

[31] *JT v Canada*, Comm No 104/1981; Nowak, *op cit* n 6, 657–9.

[32] *MAB et al. v Canada*, Comm No 570/1993.

[33] *Clement Boodoo v Trinidad and Tobago*, Comm No 721/1996.

[34] *Malcolm Ross v Canada*, Comm No 736/1997.

[35] *K. Singh Bhinder v Canada*, Comm No 208/1986.

[36] *Coeriel v Netherlands*, Comm No 453/1991.

[37] *LTK v Finland*, Comm No 185/1984; *Brinkhof v Netherlands*, Comm No 402/1990; *Westerman v Netherlands*, Comm No 682/1996.

[38] Harris, Schultz, and Castan, *op cit* n 22, 510.

than access to corporate legal status.[39] When the Committee had to consider the problem of access to a certain status for religious associations, it disaggregated this into the component rights of individuals to engage in specific protected religious activities.[40]

One exception to this downplaying of collective rights has been in the area of religious education. In *Delgado Paez* the Committee accepted the involvement of the Roman Catholic Church in the State's decision to assign to other duties a religious education teacher who propounded a liberation theology disapproved by the church.[41] In *Hartikainen*, the Committee held that compulsory classes in religion and ethics, as an alternative to religious instruction, are compatible with the Convention, so long as instruction is given in a neutral and objective manner.[42] In *Waldman v Canada*, the Committee found a violation of article 26 in the provision made by the Ontario Constitution for the public funding of Roman Catholic schools.[43] Accordingly, the Committee held that public funding should either be withdrawn or made available to other minority religious communities as well.

Some members of the Committee have taken the straightforward view that article 18 does not deal with the freedom of churches or religious organizations.[44] General Comment 22 (1993) on Article 18 also shows individualistic tendencies.[45] Paragraph 4 downplays collective aspects of religious liberty by comparison with article 6 of the 1981 Declaration, on which it is based.[46] General Comment no 22 also considers the question of State religion,[47] considering it acceptable as long as it does not impair the enjoyment of Covenant rights or have a discriminatory effect on adherents of other religions or non-believers. The brief discussion that follows moves through examples of discrimination against individuals to minority rights more generally. Substantive questions of religious liberty disappear, and there is no consideration of the structural discrimination between religious bodies consequent upon the existence of a State church or religion.[48]

However, in spite of this relative absence of associational disputes, comments relating to the law of religious associations can be found reasonably frequently in the Concluding Observations to State Reports issued by the Human Rights Committee since 1992. For example, in 1997, the Committee commented on Slovakia's restrictive laws requiring the registration of churches and religious

---

[39] *Sister Immaculate Joseph and 80 Teaching Sisters of the Holy Cross of the Third Order of St Francis in Menzingen of Sri Lanka v Sri Lanka*, Comm No 1249/2004.

[40] *Malakhovsky and Pikul v Belarus*, Comm No 1207/2003.

[41] *Delgado Paez v Colombia*, Comm No 195/1985. This may be incompatible with statements made by the Committee elsewhere. See Harris, Schultz, and Castan, *op cit* n 22, 515.

[42] *Hartikainen et al. v Finland*, Comm No 40/1978.   [43] Comm No 694/1996.

[44] See the views recorded in Evans, *op cit* n 1, 213.

[45] CCPR/C/21/Rev.1/Add.4, General Comment No 22.

[46] Dickson, *op cit* n 16, 345–6.   [47] Para 9.

[48] Evans comments on the way in which the HRC often views article 18 in terms of non-discrimination: *op cit* n 1, 207–12.

associations, recommending that 'all necessary measures be adopted in order to amend the relevant legislation so as to bring it into conformity with articles 18 and 22 of the Covenant'.[49] More recently, in the case of Georgia it has expressed concern about discrimination as a result of differential access to legal status of religious groups.[50] This is a clear recognition of the relevance of substantive human rights to religious associations, notwithstanding the individualistic cast of their textual formulation and processes for enforcement, and the general tendency to ignore or suppress collective dimensions of religious liberty in the context of individual communications. Clearly the divergent processes for raising matters before the Human Rights Committee is having an impact on the substance of its concerns.

4. 1981 Declaration

The Declaration on the Elimination of all Forms of Intolerance and of Discrimination Based on Religion or Belief (1981) takes as its starting point the first three paragraphs on freedom of religion in the ICCPR.[51] This it supplements with three potentially far-reaching non-discrimination provisions, a specific reference to the child's religious rights, and, in article 6, a detailed enumeration of specific religious rights. The enumerated rights must be available in domestic law, and rights already contained in the UDHR, the ICCPR, and the ICESCR are preserved from restriction or derogation.

Article 6 enumerates nine specific religious rights. While some of these may be exercised by individuals as such (eg writing religious material and observing a day of rest) the majority require collective, coordinated activity, and some, notably the maintenance of places of worship and the establishment of appropriate institutions, practically demand the recognition of religious associations as legal entities and right-holders themselves. In Lerner's view this means that the Declaration 'contemplates the needs of religious communities or congregations—needs that are not satisfied by the instruments that follow the orientation of the early years of the UN, based exclusively on individual rights'.[52] Sullivan observes that the Declaration presupposes a 'Western model of religion, in which religious institutions and authority are structurally separable from political and other social institutions',[53] but also points out that a majority of the specific article 6 rights apply equally well to non-religious beliefs.[54]

---

[49] Cited in Scheinin, *op cit* n 29, 201.
[50] Concluding Observations: Georgia (2007) UN Doc CCPR/C/GEO/CO/3, para 15.
[51] See, generally, Nazila Ghanea, 'The 1981 UN Declaration...Some Observations', in Nazila Ghanea (ed), *The Challenge of Religious Discrimination at the Dawn of the New Millennium* (Leiden: Martinus Nijhoff, 2003).
[52] Natan Lerner, 'Religious Human Rights under the United Nations', in Johann D van der Vyver and John Witte, Jr (eds), *Religious Human Rights in Global Perspective: legal perspectives* (The Hague: Kluwer Law International, 1996), 120.   [53] *Op cit* n 12, 490.
[54] Ibid, 500–1.

The status of the 1981 Declaration is not entirely clear. Formally speaking, it is a non-binding declaration of the UN General Assembly. Nevertheless, the formal position must be qualified by three factors. First, the text itself treats much of its content as declaratory. This is clearest in the context of article 6 rights which are said to be 'included' in article 1. This in turn is based on the (binding) ICCPR. Secondly, the Declaration has been used to inform the Human Rights Committee's understanding of article 18 ICCPR. Finally, the Special Rapporteur on Freedom of Religion and Belief has effectively acted as if the 1981 Declaration were derived from other binding human rights norms. For practical purposes article 6, which is of the greatest interest for present purposes, can therefore be treated as declaratory of existing law.[55]

5. UN Special Rapporteurs

The 1981 Declaration has formed the foundation for the work of a series of United Nations Special Rapporteurs.[56] In 1983, a Special Rapporteur was requested to report on the 'various manifestations of intolerance and discrimination on the grounds of religion or belief in the contemporary world and on specific rights violated, using the Declaration as a standard'. Mrs Elizabeth Odio Benito was appointed and reported in 1986. Then in 1987 Mr Angelo d'Almeida Ribeiro was appointed Special Rapporteur on Religious Intolerance and Discrimination to examine incidents and Government measures incompatible with the 1981 Declaration and to make recommendations. Ever since, the mandate has been regularly renewed. Ribeiro was replaced in 1993 by Mr Abdelfattah Amor, who was in turn replaced in 2004 by Mrs Asma Jahangir.[57] In 2001, the title was formally changed to Special Rapporteur on Freedom of Religion or Belief. The Special Rapporteur receives and investigates allegations of human rights violations, makes communications to Governments concerning prima facie breaches of human rights, receives responses, and submits annual general reports to the Human Rights Council. Since 1994, interim reports to the General Assembly on communications and *in situ* visits to specific countries have also been submitted.

The Special Rapporteur has considerable control over her own role, and is able to stamp it with her own agenda. The first Report of the third Special Rapporteur (Amor) made clear a new concern for preventing human rights violations through education and the need to address 'the increasing number of problems posed by religious extremism, religious minorities, and sects and other similar

---

[55] Dickson, *op cit* n 16, 345. Evans, *op cit* n 1, 257–8, is slightly more cautious.

[56] Dickson, *op cit*, n 16; Evans, *op cit* n 1, 245–57; Carolyn Evans, 'The Special Rapporteur on Freedom of religion or Belief', in Ghanea, *op cit* n 51; Theo van Boven, 'The United Nations Commission on Human Rights and Freedom of religion or Belief' in Lindholm *et al*, *op cit* n 29.

[57] Since the mandate can now only be held for up to two three-year terms, Mrs Jahangir will be replaced at the end of 2010.

or comparable communities'.[58] The three top priorities identified in the Annual Reports for 1998 and 1999 were the need to tackle religious extremism, the need to tackle discrimination and intolerance against women, prescribed by religion or tradition, and the need to examine closely the issue of sects or new religious movements.[59] It is striking that all three represent religious communities as a threat to human rights, not as the beneficiaries. The concern with inter-religious dialogue eventually led him to propose formal visits to major religious communities and institutions. The first such visit, to the Vatican, took place in 1999 and is substantially reported in the Annual Report following.[60] The visit has not been followed by others, although the Special Rapporteur meets with representatives of religions during country visits.

The review of communications made to specific countries contained in the interim and annual reports of the Special Rapporteur are in no sense a statistically balanced sample of human rights violations. For present purposes, the interesting question concerns the extent to which prima facie violations appearing in the communications can be traced back to problems in the relevant domestic laws of religious associations. The largest category of violations, namely those which amount to discrimination, harassment, or violence by State actors on account of individual religious beliefs or individual activities such as proselytism or possession of religious literature, can be excluded. Of course, those beliefs may be shared by a community, but they are not necessarily connected with the community's status as a legal entity. Violations in connection with conscientious objection can also be excluded, as can cases of intercommunal and non-State-sanctioned violence and situations of complete civil disorder. That leaves a range of violations including refusals to register religious associations, harassment for failures to register, administrative difficulties in building, accessing or recovering places of worship, refusals to recognize priests and other religious officials, restrictions on seminaries, schools and other places of religious education, bans on religious processions and festivals, refusals to recognize marriages, and lack of access to broadcasting media. All caveats notwithstanding, roughly a third of the human rights violations picked up by the Special Rapporteurs seem to involve the status and regulation of religious associations, and problems in this field have affected about half of the States referred to in the reports, or about a third of the Member States of the UN.

At the end of his 2004 report,[61] the Special Rapporteur drew a number of conclusions, and made recommendations expressly based on a retrospect of his 11 years' experience. One cannot help noticing a certain imbalance between the typical cases of violation recorded in the communications to States and the final analysis presented by the Rapporteur.[62] Some cases of inter-communal violence

---

[58] E/CN.4/1994/79, 139.   [59] E/CN.4/1998/6; E/CN.4/1999/58.
[60] E/CN.4/2000/65, 30–45.   [61] E/CN.4/2004/63.
[62] Cf the Interim Report A/58/296 (2003), para 135, which clearly highlights 'the new upsurge in administrative regulations'.

aside, the communications portray religious communities as victims of State oppression or indifference. And yet the principal remedy is supposed to be State intervention in the life of religious communities to teach them universal human rights values.[63] The three specific examples of preventive action proposed are the control of media stereotyping, the need for States to involve themselves more formally in the process of inter-religious dialogue, and the need for greater concern on the part of States about the role of education in promoting respect for freedom of religion or belief. One cannot help concluding that Amor thought of religious associations as very much akin to States, sometimes responsible for human rights violations, containing intolerant elements, but potentially persuadable to take human rights seriously.

The first Annual Reports submitted by Asma Jahangir display a shift back to a more traditional State-focused conception of religious liberty, albeit one that includes positive obligations on States to protect religious groups from third party attack.[64] It includes several matters relating to religious associations. As well as the depressingly predictable litany of violence against religious believers, she notes a significant number of cases involving attacks or restrictions on places of worship and other religious buildings. Emerging general issues of compatibility with human rights law include questions of registration and the categorization of religions, as well as the appointment of clergy, teaching and disseminating materials, international communications, and the maintenance of charitable and humanitarian institutions.[65] It is noticeable that although clearly guided by article 6 1981 Declaration, there are few explicit references. This has largely been supplanted by article 18 ICCPR and the Human Rights Committee's General Comment no 22 as the main substantive source of relevant obligations.

6. OSCE and ODIHR

The Conference on Security and Cooperation in Europe was a cold-war political process initiated in the 1970s.[66] 'Security' was from the start broadly conceived to include a human as well as an economic and environmental dimension. The human dimension referred to norms and activities related to human rights and democracy. After the collapse of Eastern European communism, the Charter of Paris (1990) transformed the CSCE from a forum for dialogue into an organization with a range of institutions, although the name change to OSCE did not take

---

[63] Evans makes a similar point: '... the chief difficulty is seen to lie in the intolerant attitude of believers themselves. This is seen as a handicap which can be overcome with copious doses of education concerning human rights.' *Op cit* n 1, 259.

[64] E/CN.4/2005/61 and subsequent reports.

[65] See especially A/HRC/6/5 (2007), paras 10–22.

[66] For a general account of the OSCE's work in relation to religion, see Urban Gibson and Karen S Lord, 'Advancements in Standard Setting: Religious Liberty and OSCE Commitments', in Lindholm *et al*, *op cit* n 29.

place until 1995. One of the 1990 institutions was the Office for Free Elections, which in 1992 was broadened to become the Office for Democratic Institutions and Human Rights (ODIHR), based in Warsaw. This office has responsibility for the promotion of free and fair elections, democracy-building, and monitoring and implementation of human dimension commitments. The ODIHR now deals with questions relating to associational religious liberty as part of its programme on tolerance and non-discrimination, which was established in 2004. This programme has three main strands: combating hate-motivated crimes and violent manifestations of intolerance; freedom of religion and belief; and combating tolerance through the promotion of intercultural and inter-religious respect and mutual understanding.

It has been suggested that the success of the OSCE has been due to the combination of soft approaches to the enforcement of international norms with a high degree of precision in the specification of those norms.[67] The right to religious liberty provides a good example of this. The Declaration of Principles contained in the Helsinki Final Act (1975) gave a noted emphasis on religious liberty to its commitment to protecting human rights, and the 'Human Contacts' part of Cooperation in Humanitarian and Other Fields contained a specific right of free communication for religious associations. To this right of free movement, the Madrid Concluding Document (1983) added rights of public consultation and legal status. It is noteworthy that the phrase, 'take the action necessary' implies that these commitments are to be seen as outworkings of an existing right.[68] Substantial codification followed in Principle 16 of the Vienna Concluding Document (1989). Once again, Principle 16 is cast as a gloss on an existing right and contains a remarkably full codification of rights benefiting religious associations. Likewise, at Vienna, the 'human contacts' provision concerning travel for religious purposes received further elaboration.

The Vienna Concluding Document goes beyond the 1981 UN Declaration in two general respects. First, it makes clear that the beneficiaries of the various rights are collective entities. Thus Principle 16.1 adds into article 4(1) of the 1981 Declaration the phrase 'against individuals or communities'; Principle 16.3 grants a right to legal entity status to communities of believers, which is then elaborated in Principle 16.4 in terms of specific rights: to maintain places of worship, to autonomy in internal structure and personnel, to voluntary financial and other support. Principles 16.10 and 16.11, which are essentially aspects of freedom of religious expression, are tied to 'faiths', 'institutions', 'organizations', and 'communities'.

The second general respect in which the Vienna Concluding Document is distinctive is in the high degree of specificity it gives to the rights it enumerates.

---

[67] Janne Haaland Matlary, 'Implementing Freedom of Religion or Belief: Experiences from the Norwegian Chairmanship', in Lindholm *et al*, *op cit* n 29, 259–61.

[68] Gibson and Lord, *op cit* n 66, 247.

A comparison with the 1981 Declaration shows a noticeable tightening up in almost every case. Places of worship or assembly are to be 'freely accessible', internal organization may be 'hierarchical' if wished, there are rights both to give and receive religious education, and public dialogue includes access to mass media. The one obvious omission is the right to observe days of rest, holidays, and ceremonies. The Copenhagen Concluding Document (1990) is also significant for its restatement of a number of rights relating to religion, but in respect of religious associations adds nothing to the Vienna Concluding Document.

From the mid-1990s, a number of NGOs started to press the ODIHR to take a more active role in respect of these norms. In April 1996 a seminar was held in Warsaw on constitutional, legal, and administrative aspects of freedom of religion. As a result of this seminar, the ODIHR established an Advisory Panel of Experts on Freedom of Religion or Belief. Under Norway's chairmanship, the first Supplementary Meeting to the human dimension implementation process was held in Vienna on 22 March 1999 on the topic of freedom of religion and belief. This considered religious dialogue and conflict prevention, religious pluralism and limitations of freedom of religion, and possible future activities of the Advisory Panel. Calls for dialogue necessarily imply processes of collective representation, and many of the limitations discussed in the Meeting concerned the legal status and rights of religious communities. The Supplementary Meeting resulted in a strengthening and relaunching of the ODIHR Advisory Panel of Experts on Freedom of Religion or Belief with a more focused remit.[69]

A further seminar was held in The Hague on 26 June 2001 with a particular focus on religious communities.[70] Its two working sessions addressed the recognition and registration of religious and belief communities, and restrictions on the activities of religious and belief communities respectively. Apart from the reiteration of existing standards and the need for better compliance, transparency, and dialogue, the work of the Advisory Panel was welcomed and promoted. This validation of the Advisory Panel's work received formal support in the Ministerial Council Decision on Tolerance and Non-Discrimination, which encouraged States to seek its assistance.[71]

The Advisory Panel engages in a number of activities, including the legislative review of laws relating to religion at the request of Governments to help them comply with international standards,[72] the development of new legislation to foster improved relations among religious groups, and the promotion of

---

[69] Matlary, *op cit* n 67, 270

[70] Seminar on Freedom of Religion or Belief in the OSCE Region: Challenges to Law and Practice, Ministry of Foreign Affairs, The Hague, Netherlands, 2001.

[71] Maastricht Ministerial Council Decision 4/03 on Tolerance and Non-Discrimination.

[72] See, for example, the analysis of the February 2002 Draft Law of the Kyrgyz Republic 'On Freedom of Religion and Belief and on Religious Organizations (Congregations)' prepared by the Advisory Panel of Experts on Freedom of Religion and Belief of the OSCE/ODIHR, 7 March 2002.

dialogue between Governments and religious groups. In the course of 2004 it was reformed to consist of two experts nominated by each State with a separate Advisory Council of 15 appointed by ODIHR to give focus and direction to its work.[73]

The Advisory Panel has prepared a set of Guidelines for Review of Legislation Pertaining to Religion or Belief, which were adopted by the Council of Europe Venice Commission at its 59th Plenary Session and welcomed by the OSCE Parliamentary Assembly at its 2004 Annual Session.[74] These Guidelines draw on the texts already considered as well as the case-law of the European Court of Human Rights discussed below. Although relatively brief and cautious to avoid articulating specific normative constraints on States which cannot be clearly justified from existing international and regional law, the Guidelines give a clear sense of the areas which can prove problematic in religious association law. Initial questions which are identified include the question whether legislation is necessary at all, how religion and belief are to be defined, whether the legislation is an overreaction to problems of extremism, the interrelationship with other human rights norms, and the relevance of a (limited) margin of appreciation.

The Guidelines identify nine basic values underlying the relevant human rights standards: internal freedom, external freedom, equality and non-discrimination, neutrality and impartiality, non-coercion, parental rights, tolerance and respect, the right to association, and the right to effective remedies. These values are then considered in the context of questions of education, organizational autonomy, clergy and religious leaders, registration, immigration, proselytizing activity, financing, and access to State institutions. In some cases—in particular in education and financing—there is clearly a range of acceptable models. In general, the imposition of obligations must be justified and non-discrimination between majority, generally traditional, faiths and minority ones assured. Finally, the potential need for exemptions from laws of general applicability in areas such as military service, food, religious holidays, medical treatment, and oaths is also noted.

The Guidelines also identify a number of areas of legal regulation in which a religious dimension touching on associations may arise. These include general criminal and administrative law penalties, national security, planning law, property law, electoral law, family law, broadcasting law, employment law, and the law relating to burial and cemeteries. The Guidelines set out standardized procedures for the review of draft legislation and for the production of reports on such legislation.[75]

[73] ODIHR Annual Report 2004, p 66.

[74] OSCE/ODIHR 2004. The Rapporteur was T Jeremy Gunn, and the work drew on the earlier report by Cole Durham, *Freedom of Religion or Belief: Laws affecting the Structuring of Religious Communities* (Warsaw: OSCE/ODIHR, 1999).

[75] The Guidelines are currently subject to a review.

Thus, over the course of the last decade, the OSCE has proved to be an influential actor at international level not only in the articulation of human rights norms as they apply to religious associations, but also in the practical process of encouraging States party towards better compliance.

7. The Council of Europe

Considerable activity in relation to the law of religious associations takes place under the umbrella of the Council of Europe. The most significant part of that activity consists of the development of the case-law on article 9 ECHR by the European Court of Human Rights, which will be considered in detail below. Apart from that, one should note the recommendations and resolutions of the Parliamentary Assembly in the field of religious liberty and non-discrimination, the replies and work of the Committee of Ministers, and the opinions of the European Commission for Democracy through Law (Venice Commission). This was established in 1990 to provide independent expert advice on matters of constitutional law. It adopted the OSCE Guidelines referred to above in 2004. It has provided opinions on draft laws relating to religious associations, recent examples of which include those of Georgia and Serbia.

In Recommendation 1086 on the situation of the church and freedom of religion in Eastern Europe,[76] the Parliamentary Assembly called on the Committee of Ministers to invite Governments of Council of Europe Member States then participating in the OSCE Review Conference in Vienna to ensure that the concluding document contained a set of 17 rights relating to religious associations. By Resolution 908 of the same date it also called directly on Eastern European Governments to address specific related issues. Most of the components of this remarkably comprehensive checklist found their way into the Vienna Concluding Document, although often in slightly attenuated form. The two clear omissions were the right to engage in pastoral work in public institutions and the right to run religious courses and congresses without official permission. In keeping with this approach, Recommendation 1178 on sects and new religious movements advised against specific legislation on sects, while at the same time calling for their registration, corporate status, and the inclusion of their workers under social welfare regimes.[77] Recommendation 1202 repeated the call to guarantee freedom of religion with particular reference to the Recommendation 1086 set of rights.[78]

By the end of the 1990s, there was a noticeable change of emphasis toward the tolerance and mutual respect agenda.[79] This is as much concerned with regulating

---

[76] 6 October 1988. The Committee of Ministers replied (no 424) on 1 February 1989.

[77] 5 February 1992.   [78] 2 February 1993.

[79] See Recommendation 1396 (27 January 1999); Recommendation 1412 (22 June 1999); Resolution 1278 (23 April 2002); Recommendation 1556 (24 April 2002). For the Committee of Ministers' reply to the latter, see CM/AS(2003)Rec1556 final 10 June 2003.

the behaviour of 'dangerous sects' and preserving national cultural heritage as it is about freedom of religion. Intriguingly, in Standing Committee Resolution 1309 on freedom of religion and religious minorities in France,[80] the Assembly stated baldly:

After examination of this French law, the Assembly cannot but conclude that ultimately, should the case arise, it will be for the European Court of Human Rights, and it alone, to say whether or not this law is compatible with the ECHR.

Standing Committee Resolution 1390 on the new Bulgarian Law on Religion also makes no reference to any of the older Recommendations, but draws instead on the ECHR case-law to make a series of specific criticisms.[81] At present, there is therefore no sign that the Parliamentary Assembly will play much further positive role in developing the law relating to religious associations.

III. Collective Religious Rights under the European Convention

The European Convention for the Protection of Human Rights and Fundamental Freedoms (1950) is arguably the most significant regional human rights instrument, not least on account of the early development of the right of individual petition. Article 9 provides:

1. Everyone has the right to freedom of thought, conscience and religion; this right includes freedom to change his religion or belief, and freedom, either alone or in community with others and in public or private, to manifest his religion or belief, in worship, teaching, practice and observance.
2. Freedom to manifest one's religion or belief shall be subject only to such limitations as are prescribed by law and are necessary in a democratic society in the interests of public safety, for the protection of public order, health or morals, or for the protection of the rights and freedoms of others.

Article 11 guarantees the right to freedom of association, article 14 prohibits discrimination on grounds of religion in the enjoyment of Convention rights, and article 2 of the First Protocol (1952) states that,

In the exercise of any functions which it assumes in relation to education and to teaching, the State shall respect the right of parents to ensure such education and teaching in conformity with their own religious and philosophical convictions.

The wording of article 9(1) is almost identical to that of the UDHR and the ICCPR. Article 2 First Protocol is closely followed by article 18(4) ICCPR, although the ECHR is arguably broader when it refers to education and teaching in

---

[80] 18 November 2002.   [81] 7 September 2004.

conformity with . . . religious and philosophical convictions, whereas the ICCPR refers to 'religious and moral education'. Unlike the general equality norm contained in article 26 ICCPR, the non-discrimination provision of the ECHR is limited to areas connected with other substantive rights provisions.[82] There is no specific minorities protection in the ECHR similar to article 27 ICCPR, a matter finally addressed in the 1995 European Framework Convention for the Protection of National Minorities. Article 8 of this Convention is as follows:

The Parties undertake to recognise that every person belonging to a national minority has the right to manifest his or her religion or belief and to establish religious institutions, organisations and associations.

1. Substantive development

The general case-law on freedom of religion under the Convention is well covered elsewhere.[83] The purpose of this section is to trace the recent developments which extend Convention rights to religious associations.[84] Religious associations are now clearly protected as such. Their existence is rooted in the individual's right to manifest a religion or belief in community with others and in his or her freedom of association with others. Having accepted that religious associations have a separate corporate personality for the purposes of European human rights law, they have then become the beneficiaries of a set of relevant rights derived both from article 9 and from other provisions such as the right to a fair trial, freedom of expression, non-discrimination, and property. This development can be seen clearly in the determination and subsequent reworking of three cases: *Manoussakis v Greece*, *Serif v Greece*, and *Canea Catholic Church v Greece*.

The Court in *Manoussakis* held that the conviction of the Jehovah's Witness applicants for operating a place of religious worship without Government

---

[82] This is different for those States party to Protocol no 12. The UK has not signed that protocol.

[83] Apart from relevant chapters in general accounts, see Evans, *op cit* n 1, chs 10–13; Carolyn Evans, *Freedom of Religion under the European Convention on Human Rights* (Oxford: Oxford University Press, 2001); Paul M Taylor, *Freedom of Religion* (Cambridge: Cambridge University Press, 2005). For a recent analysis of the current state of development, see Malcolm D Evans, 'Freedom of religion and the European Convention on Human Rights: approaches, trends and tensions', in Peter Cane, Carolyn Evans, and Zoë Robinson, *Law and Religion in Theoretical and Historical Context* (Cambridge: Cambridge University Press, 2008).

[84] An early attempt to capture this development can be found in Julian Rivers, 'Religious Liberty as a Collective Right', in Richard O'Dair and Andrew Lewis (eds), *Law and Religion* (Oxford: Oxford University Press, 2001). It is striking how little one had to go on then. See also Malcolm D Evans, 'Believing in Communities, European Style', in Ghanea, *op cit* n 51. For a parallel—and critical—exercise from the perspective of individual conscience, see T Jeremy Gunn, 'Adjudicating Rights of Conscience under the European Convention on Human Rights', in Johan D van der Vyver and John Witte, Jr (eds), *Religious Human Rights in Global Perspective: legal perspectives* (The Hague: Kluwer Law International, 1996).

consent was unjustified in the circumstances.[85] In a concurring opinion, Judge Martens pointed out that the issue was not so much that of injustice to these particular applicants, but the injustice caused to Jehovah's Witnesses and other religious minorities by the entire system for registering places of religious worship. However, the approach of the majority was still based on a paradigm of individual rights.

The applicant in *Serif v Greece* was convicted of various criminal offences including usurping the functions of a minister of a known religion.[86] Serif claimed to be the elected and true Chief Mufti of Rodopi in Thrace, in opposition to the Government-appointed Chief Mufti. The Court accepted that Serif's religious liberty was infringed and approached the problem by asking whether his conviction was necessary in a democratic society. They held that since allegations of his performing administrative functions (such as conducting weddings) were unsubstantiated, the only ground for his conviction was his wearing the clothes traditionally associated with the office, and issuing messages of spiritual guidance and encouragement. Even if he were not Chief Mufti, to convict somebody in those circumstances would be an unjustifiable breach of their liberty. This surely misses the point. The issue at the heart of this dispute was whether the Muslim community had the right under the European Convention collectively to elect their spiritual leader if they so wished. The Court ducked that central issue.

The case of *Canea Catholic Church v Greece* concerned a property dispute between the church and a neighbour, which the church lost for want of legal personality.[87] The church had been founded before 1830, and had acted since time immemorial as if it had personality. The Commission took the view that the (collective) right to bring a legal action was an aspect of article 9, but the Court deliberately rejected this position and simply considered the Catholic Church's right as an aspect of article 6. Thus the Court saw no need to distinguish the church from a secular company.

The shift occurred in 2000, in *Hasan & Chaush v Bulgaria*.[88] The case arose from the interference of the Bulgarian Directorate of Religious Denominations in the internal life of the Muslim community, in particular by removing the first applicant as Chief Mufti. In expounding article 9, the Court said this:

The Court recalls that religious communities traditionally and universally exist in the form of organised structures. They abide by rules which are often seen by followers as being of a divine origin. Religious ceremonies have their meaning and sacred value for the believers if they have been conducted by ministers empowered for that purpose in compliance with these rules. The personality of the religious ministers is undoubtedly of

---

[85] *Manoussakis v Greece*, no 18748/91 RJD 1996-IV 1346 (1996) See also *Pentidis v Greece*, no 23238/94 (1997); *Tsavachidis v Greece*, no 28802/95 (1997).

[86] *Serif v Greece*, no 38178/97 (1999).

[87] *Canea Catholic Church v Greece*, no 25528/94 (1997), Reports 1997-VIII 2857.

[88] *Hasan & Chaush v Bulgaria*, no 30985/96 (2000).

importance to every member of the community. Participation in the life of the community is thus a manifestation of one's religion, protected by Article 9 of the Convention.

Where the organization of the religious community is at issue, Article 9 of the Convention must be interpreted in the light of article 11, which safeguards associative life against unjustified State interference. Seen in this perspective, the believers' right to freedom of religion encompasses the expectation that the community will be allowed to function peacefully, free from arbitrary State intervention. Indeed, the autonomous existence of religious communities is indispensable for pluralism in a democratic society and is thus an issue at the very heart of the protection which article 9 affords. It directly concerns not only the organization of the community as such but also the effective enjoyment of the right to freedom of religion by all its active members. Were the organizational life of the community not protected by article 9 of the Convention, all other aspects of the individual's freedom of religion would become vulnerable.[89]

The Court went on to find that the actions of the Government had had an adverse effect on the internal life of the religious community and that the legal basis for such interference was unacceptably vague.

This decision was reinforced in *Metropolitan Church of Bessarabia v Moldova*.[90] Moldova had refused to recognize and register the applicant church because it was attached to the Romanian Orthodox Church, which was attached to the patriarchate of Bucharest, rather than the Russian Orthodox Church, attached to the patriarchate of Moscow. In finding a violation of article 9 the Court quoted from the judgment in *Hasan and Chaush*, and continued:

In addition one of the means of exercising the right to manifest one's religion, especially for a religious community, in its collective dimension, is the possibility of ensuring judicial protection of the community, its members and its assets, so that article 9 must be seen not only in the light of article 11, but also in the light of article 6.[91]

At this point, the court referred back to *Canea*, showing that it now considered the right of the church to have legal personality and own property to be an aspect of its religious freedom. This line of cases has since then been extended in several others, in some of which *Serif* has also been recast as a collective liberty case. The Court has repeatedly emphasized the importance of the autonomous existence of religious communities, the existence of associations to enable collective action, and the need for the State to remain neutral and impartial in exercising its regulatory power over them.[92]

---

[89] Ibid, para 62.
[90] *Metropolitan Church of Bessarabia v Moldova*, no 43701/99 (2001), 35 EHRR 13.
[91] Ibid, para 118.
[92] The principal cases are now: *Supreme Holy Council of the Muslim Community v Bulgaria*, no 39023/97 (2004); *Moscow Branch of the Salvation Army v Russia*, no 72881/01 (2006); *Biserica Adeverat Ortodoxa din Moldova v Moldova*, no 952/03 (2007); *Church of Scientology Moscow v Russia*, no 18147/02 (2007); *Svyato-Mykhaylivska Parafiya v Ukraine*, no 77703/01 (2007);

2. Procedural development

One of the key incidents of legal personality is the right to bring legal actions. The law on admissibility has also followed the transition from religious liberty as a purely individual to a collective right. The Commission had initially taken the view that applications from religious organizations were inadmissible, since article 9 only protected individual interests.[93] This untenable position was soon changed. It is clear that religious associations can be 'non-governmental organisations' for the purposes of article 34 ECHR and thus as 'victims' have the right to bring individual applications alleging breaches of their human rights.[94] This applies even if they are part of an established church, since these are treated as exercising non-Governmental functions.[95] It is also irrelevant whether the association has legal personality in domestic law or not.[96] Parts of larger organizations which are socially, but not legally, distinct can bring applications.[97]

However, the reasoning for allowing applications by religious associations has long been ambiguous: 'a church body is capable of possessing and exercising the rights contained in article 9(1) in its own capacity as a representative of its members'. This formula reappears at regular intervals, but it is not clear whether religious liberty is a right of the association itself, or whether the association simply represents the common individual interests of its members. In cases involving religious property, the collective right is unavoidable, since in most cases such property is held by a religious organization as a legal person, or on trust for religious purposes. Thus in the *Holy Monasteries* case[98] there was no question that the applicants were the monasteries as corporate bodies. In *Serbo-Greek Orthodox Church in Vienna v Austria*,[99] which concerned the occupation of church premises in the aftermath of a church schism, the Commission accepted that the victim was the church itself, and not the particular priests who would be the beneficiaries of the tenancy agreement in issue. In *ISKCON v United Kingdom*,[100] the reasoning of the Commission shows that it considered the primary victim of planning constraints on Bhaktivedanta Manor to be the International Society for Krishna Consciousness, and not the individual priests who also applied.

Religionsgemeinschaft der Zeugen Jehovahs v Austria, no 40825/98 (2008); *Leela Förderkreis eV v Germany*, no 58911/01 (2008); *Holy Synod of the Bulgarian Orthodox Church (Metropolitan Inokentiy) v Bulgaria*, nos 412/03 and 35677/04 (2009).

[93] *Church of X v UK*, no 3798/68 (1968), 29 CD 70, 75. The Commission maintained its view that freedom of conscience could not be enjoyed by a collective body: *Verein Kontakt-Information-Therapie v Austria*, no 11921/86 (1988), 57 DR 81, 88.

[94] *X & Church of Scientology v Sweden*, no 7805/77 (1979), 16 DR 68, and subsequent cases.

[95] *Holy Monasteries v Greece* 310-A (1994), para 49.

[96] *Christian Association of Jehovah's Witnesses v Bulgaria*, no 28626/95 (1997), 90 DR 77.

[97] See, for example, *Spetz v Sweden*, no 20402/92 (1994).

[98] *Holy Monasteries v Greece*, no 13092/87, 13984/88, A301-A.

[99] *Serbo-Greek Orthodox Church in Vienna v Austria*, no 13712/88 (1990).

[100] *ISKCON v United Kingdom*, no 20490/92 (1994), 76 DR 90.

At times, the Commission would give preference to the individual right by denying standing to an organization because of the existence of an individual breach. The last occurrence would seem to be the *Scientology* decision of 1997,[101] in which the Commission reaffirmed a strand in the case-law stating that 'a corporate applicant cannot claim to be itself a victim of measures alleged to have interfered with the Convention rights of its individual members'. Where an association claimed to represent its members, it had to identify them and show it had received specific instructions from each of them, as their agent.[102] But practice was erratic. In *Hautaniemi v Sweden*,[103] which concerned the right of a Finnish-speaking congregation in the Church of Sweden to use a liturgy of the Finnish Lutheran Church, the Commission accepted that both the congregation (parish) and the minister were victims. In *Christian Association of Jehovah's Witnesses v Bulgaria*,[104] the Bulgarian Government had refused to register the Jehovah's Witnesses as a recognized religion in Bulgaria, and various Jehovah's Witnesses suffered serious injustices as a result.[105] The Association made an application in its own name, and the Bulgarian Government tried to argue that standing should be denied, because the individuals claiming injustice were the real victims. However, the Commission was quite happy to accept the argument that the individual injustices were examples of the consequences of the failure to register the association, which could plead a breach of religious liberty in its own right.

In the light of the developments in the case-law since 2000, it should be clear that individuals and communities have independent rights, and that the existence of a breach of one does not foreclose the possibility of a breach of the other. The 'new' Court[106] appears to be adopting this approach. Thus, in a recent registration case, the Court even denied the standing of the individuals affected, effectively accepting that the only proper plaintiff was the association.[107]

IV. The Human Rights of Religious Associations

International human rights law thus shows a growing recognition that religious associations enjoy human rights. The principal detailed expressions of these rights can be found in article 6 of the 1981 Declaration, Paragraph 4 of General Comment no 22, Principle 16 Vienna Concluding Document, Recommendation 1086 Parliamentary Assembly of the Council of Europe, and the case-law arising

---

[101] *Scientology Kirche Deutschland eV v Germany*, no 36283/97 (1997).
[102] As has already been seen, this is the approach of the Human Rights Committee under the First Optional Protocol to the ICCPR.
[103] *Hautaniemi v Sweden*, no 24019/94 (1996), 85 DR 94.
[104] *Christian Association of Jehovah's Witnesses v Bulgaria*, no 28626/95 (1997), 90 DR 77.
[105] See also *Lotter and Lotter v Bulgaria*, no 39015/97 (2003).
[106] The reorganization under Protocol no 11 has now operated for over a decade.
[107] *Church of Scientology Moscow v Russia*, no 18147/02 (2004).

from the European Convention on Human Rights. On this basis, the specific human rights of religious associations may now be enumerated. It should be noted that the law is still unfolding rapidly, but that as a matter of general principle these rights derive from a general right of autonomy of religious communities under a system of law maintained by a State that is neutral, or impartial, subject to limitations in accordance with the doctrine of proportionality, if these are necessary to protect some legitimate public interest.

1. Right to legal and religious entity status

Religious associations have the right to acquire basic legal entity status with the associated rights to own real and moveable property, enter into contracts, employ persons, sue, and be sued.[108] The right to acquire legal entity status is a civil right for the purposes of article 6. While groups of believers must be free to assemble without registration, there is no support for the proposition that legal systems must make corporate personality available to religious associations without any State involvement at all. Not every legal system can recognize corporate personality as a matter of purely private legal act. The Court has not so far seen any significance in the distinction between systems that treat religious entities differently from non-religious association and systems that combine them. However, States are presumably not permitted to insist that religious associations register under a distinctive system of registration more restrictive than that available to commercial, artistic, sporting, or other associations. The combination of article 11 and article 9 would seem to indicate that any registration system should be *less* onerous and restrictive in the case of religious associations. One can also argue that the criteria for registration should be purely formal and based on the least number of individuals necessary to make the grant of corporate status reasonable.

There is no right to any distinctive religious entity status beyond that necessarily implied by corporate legal personality, although where such a status is made available, associations must be able to access it on a non-discriminatory basis. In *Religionsgemeinschaft der Zeugen Jehovahs v Austria*,[109] the Court held that substantial delay in granting an association of Jehovah's Witnesses basic private-law entity status as a 'religious community' amounted to a violation of article 9. The Court did not consider whether the mere existence of a separate regime for religious groups, which was only created in 1998, itself represented a violation. However, the 10-year waiting period imposed by Austria on 'religious

---

[108] *Christian Association of Jehovah's Witnesses v Bulgaria*, no 28626/95 (1997); Refusals to register have been found to result in violations in *Moscow Branch of the Salvation Army v Russia*, no 72881/01 (2006); *Biserica Adeverat Ortodoxa din Moldova v Moldova*, no 952/03 (2007); *Church of Scientology Moscow v Russia*, no 18147/02 (2007).

[109] *Religionsgemeinschaft der Zeugen Jehovahs v Austria*, no 40825/98 (2008). See also *Verein der Freunde der Christengemeinschaft v Austria*, no 76581/01 (2009).

communities' wishing to access the privileges associated with being a 'religious society' (the older public-law entity status dating from 1874) was disproportionate and discriminatory in the case of an established and familiar religious body such as this. Higher status included tax advantages, military exemptions, rights to operate schools, and rights of representation on various public bodies. Each religion must have a fair chance of accessing those privileges. Judge Steiner, dissenting, was not convinced that basic level status was not available by registration as an ordinary society,[110] and in addition argued that the further privileges associated with being a 'religious society' should not be treated as a single status, but on an issue-by-issue basis.

The difficulties of the majority's approach can be seen in the subsequent cases involving military exemption for Jehovah's Witnesses.[111] The Court has found discrimination simply by reason of the refusal to grant exemption on account of the lack of public law status. The Court did not address the fact that Witnesses do not straightforwardly have ministerial or clerical offices, and so in many cases may not qualify anyway. However, the root of the problem lies with the use by Austrian law of a monolithic category for access to privilege, and the approach of the majority is perhaps designed to challenge that. Furthermore, the approach of the majority raises questions about any form of religious establishment, however residual, if that is construed as a unique 'status' to which only one church has access. Convention organs have generally insisted that the existence of a State church is not instrinsically incompatible with the Convention.[112] However, as recent cases have construed liberty and non-discrimination requirements more broadly, their position is not as secure as it once was.[113]

Profit-making corporations in general cannot benefit from article 9 rights, at least in respect of matters associated with the profit, such as the payment of taxes.[114] The case-law leaves open the possibility that a profit-making company might in some other respects be a bearer of rights under article 9.

2. Right of internal structural autonomy

Religious associations have the right to structure themselves in accordance with their precepts. This may be hierarchical, or more 'democratic', and positions and offices may be more or less formally conceived. States have no interest in bringing religious bodies under a common leadership, or in preferring one form of structure

---

[110] The point would have needed argument and required changing an earlier decision of the Constitutional Court.

[111] *Lang v Austria*, no 28648/03 (2009), *Gütl v Austria*, no 49686/99 (2009), *Löffelmann v Austria*, no 42967/98 (2009).   [112] *Darby v Sweden*, no 11581/85 (1990).

[113] The vigorous dissent of the (large) minority of the Grand Chamber in *Folgerø v Norway*, no 15472/02 (2007) is grounded in part in a defence of the position of the State church. See also the Italian crucifix decision, *Lautsi v Italy*, no 30814/06 (2009).

[114] *Kustannus v Finland*, no 20471/92 (1996).

over another.[115] It follows from the freedom of association that religious associations are not obliged to grant complete freedom to their members or component associations while remaining within the main body.[116] The ultimate guarantee of liberty is the freedom to leave the association individually or collectively as a schismatic group. Of course, that may result in the forfeiting of civil rights.[117]

The solution to internal conflicts over the life of the association must be to respect decisions taken in accordance with its internal order. The closest the Commission came to considering this problem was in the case of *Williamson*,[118] in which they were prepared to accept that the General Synod's approval of the ordination of women might have amounted to an infringement of the applicant's rights. However, they noted that the decision was in the direction of gender equality and that it was in line with a view as to the proper interpretation of Scripture, which could be treated as within the meaning of 'protection of morals'. All three of these arguments are unsound: the first implies a substantive judgment about the relative value of different lawful religions, which the Court is not competent to make. In an internal dispute, judges are clearly not to prefer that faction with whom they happen to agree. The Court has recently stressed the importance of State neutrality and non-competence over questions of canon law.[119] The second point ignores the real problem, which is about how conflicts over proper interpretations of Scripture are resolved. Both sides could claim sincerity in their interpretations. The third (implicit) argument is that this was a justified restriction of the applicant's individual liberty under article 9(2). This implies that the Church of England was bound in its decision-taking by article 9(1), when it is not—at least not without considerable modification.

The only relevant question is one of procedural propriety. Members of associations—particularly large associations such as national churches—have to accept that they join dynamic bodies capable of formal decision-taking, internal development, and change. The only interest of a secular court is in ensuring that such change happens in an orderly and fair way, in accordance with the constitution of the association. This requires the Court first to locate authority within the organization, which on the facts can admittedly be difficult. It is possible that the connection between articles 9 and 11 at times leads the Court inappropriately

[115] *Hasan & Chaush v Bulgaria*, no 30985/96 (2000); *Svyato-Mykhaylviska Parafiya v Ukraine*, no 77703/01 (2007).

[116] *X v Denmark*, no 7374/76, 5 DR 157; *E & GR v Austria*, no 9781/82, 37 DR 42; *Gottesmann v Sweden*, no 10616/83 (1984), 40 DR 284; *Knudsen v Norway*, no 11045/84 (1985), 42 DR 247; *Karlsson v Sweden*, no 12356/86 (1988), 57 DR 172; *Spetz v Sweden*, no 20402/92 (1994); *Hautaniemi v Finland*, no 24019/94 (1996); *Williamson v United Kingdom*, no 27008/95 (1995); *Sijakova v Former Yugoslav Republic of Macedonia*, no 67914/01 (2003). See also *Skordas v Greece*, no 48895/99 (2000), although inadmissible here for failure to exhaust domestic remedies.

[117] *Griechische Kirchengemeinde München v Germany*, no 52336/99 (2007).

[118] *Williamson v United Kingdom*, no 27008/95.

[119] *Holy Synod of the Bulgarian Orthodox Church (Metropolitan Inokentiy) v Bulgaria*, no 412/03 and 35677/04 (2009).

to prefer the lowest level unit within a hierarchical organization.[120] Having located authority for the disputed decision, the Court should respect it, following through any civil consequences.[121] This is not incompatible with the insistence on a basic minimum of procedural justice derivable from article 6. But it does prevent the Court from adjudicating on the substantive merits of the changes. Cases of schism, as distinct from secession, are problematic, because they represent the breakdown of the internal structure. The State is not obliged to refrain entirely from intervention, but may (cautiously) attempt to broker an agreement. However, it must not prefer one side or the other, nor should it seek to force unity.[122] The need to restore legality can only justify neutral measures to ensure legal certainty and foreseeable procedures for settling disputes.

Article 6(i) of the 1981 Declaration refers to the right to establish and maintain communications with individuals and communities at the national and international levels. Recommendation 1086 refers to the right to 'contact' with other bodies. Clearly this embraces meetings such as congresses and assemblies. Although it does not on its terms refer to permanent national or transnational arrangements, when taken together with the right of internal structuring, it must include these as well. There are potential tensions here between international organization and the requirements of national jurisdictions. A State could insist that religious associations active within its jurisdiction comply with its law (eg on legal personality or property ownership), but not that they maintain complete autonomy in relation to other associations in other jurisdictions.

3. Right to select, train, appoint, and dismiss leaders

The right of internal structural autonomy is closely related to the right to select, train, appoint, and dismiss leaders such as ministers, priests, and other office-holders. Freedom of choice over the mode of appointment is emphasized by article 6(g) 1981 Declaration with the words, 'appoint, elect or designate by succession...'. This right includes the right to establish suitable training institutions. It also extends to the removal of leaders: Principle 16.4 Vienna Concluding Document refers to 'replacing their personnel in accordance with their respective requirements and standards.'

The State has no general interest in the qualifications and appointment of ministers of religion, although such an interest arises under systems which permit ministers to carry out acts with civil effect such as marriages.[123] Any intervention here must be the least necessary to ensure the competent and orderly carrying out

---

[120] It is not clear that the Court was right to locate authority in the individual parish in *Svyato-Mykhaylviska Parafiya v Ukraine*, no 77703/01 (2007); see also *Mirolubovs v Latvia*, no 798/05 (2009).   [121] *Kohn v Germany*, no 47021/99 (2000).

[122] *Supreme Holy Council of the Muslim Community v Bulgaria*, no 39023/97 (2004).

[123] *Serif v Greece*, no 38178/97 (1999); *Agga v Greece (No 2)*, nos 50776/99 and 52912/99 (2002).

of such administrative duties. Apart from that, joint arrangements between the State and religious associations must be freely accepted on both sides.

Although there is no right to immigration under the Convention, the Court has held that the State may not ban the entry of a religious worker if the ban is designed to repress the exercise of the right to freedom of religion and stifle the spreading of the teaching of a religious body.[124] This is a narrow right against targeted exclusions; a general refusal of entry on national security grounds applied without regard to the religious activity to be engaged in could survive scrutiny. It is not yet clear, but it is at least arguable, that a religious association unable to recruit a suitable minister locally has its own right to secure the services of an immigrant.[125] As the judges pointed out, it is not even obvious why the association should have to show that a local appointee is unavailable if it prefers the services of an immigrant.

4. Right to establish places of worship and meeting

Religious associations have the right to erect, purchase, or hire churches, prayer centres, and other places of worship and meeting. The claim of Recommendation 1086 that this must be without the need for official approval is too strong, and correctly appears in the Vienna Concluding Document as a requirement instead that such places be freely accessible.

Under the European Convention, religious associations as legal persons may own property and enjoy property rights under article 1 First Protocol.[126] However, some property also benefits from article 9 protection. Since this grants a higher level of protection, requiring correspondingly stronger reasons for State interference, a distinction must be drawn between the two classes of 'secular' and 'religious' property. Clear cases on either side include agricultural land held as an investment to produce income (secular)[127] and places of worship (religious).[128] However, the test for distinguishing the two classes is unclear. In *Holy Monasteries v Greece*, the Court asked whether the object was intended for the celebration of divine worship.[129] This is probably too narrow. In *Johannische Kirche and Peters v Germany* the Court accepted that the layout and regulation of a cemetery was included in the scope of article 9 as an 'essential aspect of the religious practice' of the association.[130] This suggests that the test is akin to the manifestation/motivation test developed in the context of individual manifestations.[131]

---

[124] *Perry v Latvia*, no 30273/03 (2007); *Nolan v Russia*, no 2512/04 (2009).
[125] Thus the minority in *El Majjaoui and Stichting Touba Moskee v Netherlands*, no 25525/03 (2007).   [126] *Fener Rum Erkek Lisesi Vakfı v Turkey*, no 34478/97 (2007).
[127] *Holy Monasteries v Greece*, nos 13092/87, 13984/88 (1994).
[128] *Canea Catholic Church v Greece*, no 25528/94 (1997), as interpreted in *Metropolitan Church of Bessarabia v Moldova*, no 43701/99 (2001).   [129] *Op cit*, para 87.
[130] *Johannische Kirche and Peters v Germany*, no 41754/98 (2001).
[131] See discussion in Carolyn Evans, *op cit* n 83, 111–27.

It is questionable whether the distinction between religious and secular property carries with it any real consequences. The cases are not always clear about the extent to which interferences with religious property (however defined) require greater justification. In *ISKCON v United Kingdom*,[132] the Commission stated:

In particular, the Commission does not consider that Article 9 of the Convention can be used to circumvent existing planning legislation, provided that in the proceedings under that legislation, adequate weight is given to freedom of religion. In contending that inadequate weight was given to ISKCON's freedom of religion, the applicants rely on statements in letters sent by Ministers and an official of the Department of the Environment to the effect that the decision on ISKCON's appeal against the enforcement notice was based on the relevant land-use planning grounds and that 'the religious aspects of the Society's activities at Bhaktivedanta Manor were not relevant'. The Commission does not interpret these statements as suggesting that the religious importance of the Manor to the members of ISKCON was not fully taken into account and weighed against the general planning considerations, but rather as making clear that the refusal of planning permission was based on proper planning grounds and not on any objections to the religious aspects of the activities of ISKCON. It is in any event clear from the terms of the Inspector's Report and the decision letter of the Secretary of State that considerable weight was attached to the religious needs and interests of the members of ISKCON and to the importance of the Manor in relation to the religious activities of the members.

However, elsewhere the Court has been more concerned to establish that there is no discrimination on account of the religious dimension, rather than that appropriate consideration was given to this factor.[133] In a case arising from an investigation by German authorities into a large payment made to an Islamic association in the closing months of the German Democratic Republic, the Court doubted whether article 9 was implicated, since the investigation

concerned neither the internal organisation of the applicant association nor its official recognition by the State...Furthermore, there was nothing in their decision to suggest that they had deliberately sought to interfere with the applicant association's religious activities.[134]

5. Right to raise funds

Religious associations have the right to solicit and receive voluntary contributions, whether financial or otherwise. A number of cases concerning church tax regimes have been considered under the European Convention. A church tax regime is not incompatible with the individual's freedom of religion so long as he or she is free to leave the church in question.[135] The State has a discretion in

---

[132] *ISKCON v United Kingdom*, no 20490/92 (1994).
[133] *Johannische Kirche and Peters v Germany,* no 41754/98 (2001).
[134] *Islamische Religionsgemeinschaft eV v Germany*, no 53871/00 (2002).
[135] *E & GR v Austria*, no 9781/82 (1984) 37 DR 42.

setting the formalities for departure.[136] Where the tax is imposed autonomously by the church it is in the nature of a civil obligation of membership.[137] In general, individuals may not insist on a hypothecated tax regime to reflect their religious or ideological convictions,[138] but a tax system which distributes revenue to religious associations against the will of a non-member breaches his or her article 9 rights.[139] Religious associations cannot therefore insist that the State establishes a system for the collection and distribution of tax from members to religious associations. If it chooses to do so, such a system must be non-discriminatory.[140] This is not incompatible with differential distributions, so long as such differences reflect 'neutral' criteria such as the civil functions of a State church. Such civil functions might be the conduct of marriages and burials, the maintenance of buildings of historic value, or the keeping of ancient public records.[141] The extent of general contributions to the association for these functions must be proportionate to their actual cost.

6. Right to uphold religious community life

The rights of religious associations grow out of the rights of religious communities. A number of matters thus lie at the transition point between individual and collective aspects of rights, since the relevant rights are exercised by individuals in community, and can be considered from either perspective.[142] Generally speaking, religious associations have the right to uphold the community life of which they are the organizational expression. A number of aspects of this are worth noting.

The right to uphold community life includes the right to worship or assemble in connection with a religion or belief. Assemblies for religious purposes can be considered either from the perspective of the article 9 right to manifest belief in community with others, or from the perspective of the article 11 right of assembly.[143] Groups of religious believers must be free to meet without official permission,[144]

---

[136] *Gottesmann v Switzerland*, no 10616/83 (1984), 40 DR 284.

[137] *E & GR v Austria*, no 9781 (1984), 37 DR 42.

[138] *H, B v United Kingdom*, no 11991/86 (1986).

[139] *Darby v Sweden*, no 11581/85 (1990). Although this case was not decided under article 9, subsequent cases have treated the problem as one of impermissible forced 'involvement' in religion: *Bruno v Sweden*, no 32196/96 (2001); *Lundberg v Sweden*, no 36846/97 (2001).

[140] *Iglesia Bautista El Salvador v Spain*, no 17522/90 (1992), 72 DR 256.

[141] *Bruno v Sweden*, no 32196/96 (2001); *Lundberg v Sweden*, no 36846/97 (2001).

[142] For example, the Commission accepted that both the individual and the Secular Order of Druids were proper applicants in *Chappell v United Kingdom*, no 12587/86 (1987), 53 DR 241.

[143] Compare *Chappell v United Kingdom*, no 12587/86 (1987), in which article 9 predominates, with *Pendragon v United Kingdom*, no 31416/96 (1998), in which article 11 is considered. *Moscow Branch of the Salvation Army v Russia*, no 72881/01 (2006) involved a violation of article 11 in the light of article 9, while *Biserica Adeverat Ortodoxa din Moldova v Moldova*, no 952/03 (2007) concerned a violation of article 9. It is not clear if there is any significance to this variation.

[144] *Kuznetsov v Russia*, no 184/02 (2004).

and public assemblies must not be refused except for sufficient reason.[145] The Commission has held that not every religious assembly is a protected manifestation of religious belief, holding that a group who broke into an abortion clinic to engage in a communal praying session were properly convicted on the grounds that their action was merely motivated by their belief.[146] It would presumably be hard to deny that the procession of a religious image, or a 'prayer walk', is a manifestation of religion. Quite why it stops being religious once it trespasses is unclear. The outcome is better justified by reference to the legitimate proprietory and privacy rights of the clinic staff and its clients, which cannot be overridden in these circumstances. The decision of the Commission in *Logan* is similarly problematic.[147] A man attempted to argue that an obligation to pay child maintenance was a breach of his article 9 right to attend a Buddhist priory, since he could no longer afford the travel costs. Instead of holding either that legitimate financial constraints do not constitute a breach of rights, or that the parental obligation to support a child was justified, the Commission held that attendance at the priory was not a manifestation of belief, since it was not an indispensable element of the applicant's religious worship. This unnecessarily opens up tricky questions about the strength and nature of religious duties.

The right to uphold community life may involve a religious association in seeking to protect many different aspects of the religious practice of its members.[148] These include the right to manifest religion in ritual or ceremonial acts, and the observance of customs such as distinctive dress, dietary regulations, the observance of holidays and days of rest, or the use of a distinctive language. Naming a child need not represent a belief as such,[149] but practices of religious initiation are presumably protected. Modes of burial can also amount to a manifestation of religious belief.[150] Religious freedom includes the right to bear witness to one's faith and to seek converts.[151] Religious associations thus have the right to make, acquire, and use the necessary articles and materials related to the rites or customs of a religion or belief. This includes sacred books and other publications in the language of their choice.[152]

In general terms, limitations of the right to uphold religious community life must be prescribed by law and necessary in pursuit of one of the legitimate aims set out in article 9 paragraph 2.[153] The Court has recently emphasized that this list

---

[145] *Barankevich v Russia*, no 10519/03 (2007).
[146] *Van Schijndel v Netherlands*, no 30936/96 (1997).
[147] *Logan v United Kingdom*, no 24875/94 (1996).
[148] See General Comment no 22 (1993), para 4.
[149] *Salonen v Finland*, no 27868/95 (1997).
[150] *Johannische Kirche and Peters v Germany*, no 41754/98 (2001).
[151] *Kokkinakis v Greece*, no 14307/88 (1993); *Larissis v Greece*, no 23372/94 (1998).
[152] Art 6(c), 1981 Declaration; Principle 16.9 Vienna Concluding Document.
[153] *Stankov and the United Macedonian Organisation Ilinden v Bulgaria*, nos 29221/95 and 29225/95 (2001).

is narrowly tailored and does not include national security.[154] The Commission drew no distinction between religious and other assemblies and meetings. Thus where religious assemblies and processions have been prevented by a more general police prohibition, so long as the general prohibition is considered necessary and proportionate, the particular impact on specific assemblies and processions has been discounted.[155] This is clearest in the case of *Pendragon v United Kingdom*, in which Druids complained about their inability to celebrate the summer solstice at Stonehenge. The Commission denied that the ban on trespassory assemblies was any more onerous on Druids than on people having other beliefs, effectively equating them with anyone else who might just want to be there. One can question whether this can survive the Court's recent emphasis on religious pluralism.

In *Cha'are Shalom ve Tsedek v France*,[156] the applicant association represented ultra-orthodox Jews unsatisfied with the quality of kosher meat certified by the Jewish Consistorial Association of Paris, which had the exclusive privilege of carrying out ritual slaughter under French law. Applications to the authorities for approval were turned down. The Government defended this before the European Court on the grounds, first, that the applicants were not a religious body, but a commercial body, being set up simply to produce pure ('glatt') kosher meat, and secondly that its support among the Jewish community was small (about 5 per cent).

The Court accepted that the association had an article 9 right to manifest religion by engaging in ritual slaughter. However, it denied by a majority that there was any interference in that right, or that there was discrimination in the ambit of the right. The reasoning is highly problematic. The test proposed by the majority for establishing the existence of an interference is whether the refusal made it 'impossible' for ultra-orthodox Jews to eat 'glatt' meat. It was not impossible, because such meat could be imported from Belgium, and because the Beth Din did certify some meat as 'glatt'. The second reason is the easiest to dispense with: it is no function of the State to bring a religious community under a unified leadership.[157] If a viable part of a community does not trust the majority's Beth Din, the State may not prefer one part or the other. As regards the first reason, the majority clearly forgot that it was dealing with the rights of the association, not individuals. It is arguable that there is no interference with religious liberty if an individual can satisfy their religious needs from freely available, although imported, materials. But if an association wishes to engage in one form of slaughter it is no answer to direct them to the lawful activities of a different association.

While there can be little doubt that regulation serves important public interests, the question of infringement is first of all a question of fact. If a religious

---

[154] *Nolan v Russia*, no 2512/04 (2009).
[155] *Christians against Racism and Fascism v United Kingdom*, no 8440/78 (1980), 21 DR 138; *Chappell v United Kingdom*, no 12587/86 (1987); *Pendragon v United Kingdom*, no 31416/96 (1998).
[156] *Cha'are Shalom ve Tsedek v France*, no 27417/95 (2000).
[157] *Supreme Holy Council of the Muslim Community v Bulgaria*, no 39023/97 (2004).

body is unable to carry out ritual slaughter as it would otherwise do, there is surely a limitation. If one religious body is permitted to carry out ritual slaughter and another prevented without any objective justification, there is discrimination in the limitation. It is suggested that the seven judges who dissented were quite correct. In particular, they pointed out that authorizations had been given to much smaller, less organized, Muslim communities, such that there was no plausible State interest in dealing with just one Jewish body. The case was decided a few months before *Hasan and Chaush*, and it is suggested that it is both intrinsically indefensible and incompatible with that and later decisions.

Apart from cases of clear religious bias,[158] the organs of the European Convention have been very willing to recognize general limitations on the enjoyment of these rights arising from participation in public institutions[159] or in the context of employment.[160] Clearly, the domain within which religious belief and practice are protected is fairly narrowly conceived as operating in the private lives of adherents and unstructured public spaces.

7. Right of pastoral access to restricted institutions

Religious associations often have access to a variety of public institutions, most notably, schools, prisons, hospitals, and the armed forces in order to provide pastoral services to their inmates.[161] Recommendation 1086 calls for the right to operate pastoral work without restriction anywhere in the territory, particularly in hospitals, old people's homes, and prisons. While there are a variety of models for such interactions, Convention rights establish certain principles and limits. It is clear that the Court has rejected any notion of 'special regimes' for public institutions which in themselves imply a limitation of rights.[162] At the same time, it is apparent that States are permitted a wide discretion in structuring religious practice in public institutions.

In *VRU v Netherlands*,[163] the Commission found no breach of an article 9 right when the leave to enter a prison granted to an organization providing free legal advice to prisoners was withdrawn. However, individual prisoners have the right to manifest their religion within necessary institutional constraints.[164] This includes a right to an appropriate diet,[165] to visits from a minister of religion, and to participation in services.[166] Rights to proselytize other inmates or to attend religious activities outside their prison may be curtailed for the

---

[158] *Thlimmenos v Greece*, no 34369/97 (2000); *Ivanova v Bulgaria*, no 52435/99 (2007).

[159] *Leyla Sahin v Turkey*, no 44774/98 (2005).

[160] *Stedman v United Kingdom*, no 29107/95 (1997); *Konttinen v Finland*, no 24949/94 (1996); *Kosteski v Macedonia*, no 55170/00 (2006).   [161] See Ch 7 below.

[162] *Larissis v Greece*, no 23372/94 (1998).

[163] *VRU v Netherlands*, no 11308/84 (1986), 46 DR 200.

[164] *JL v Finland*, no 32526/96 (2000).   [165] *S v United Kingdom*, no 13669/88 (1990).

[166] *Poltoratskiy v Ukraine*, no 38812/97 (2003); *Kuznetsov v Ukraine*, no 39042/97 (2003).

purposes of good order. Thus although religious associations have no right as such to enter a prison, their imprisoned members do have rights to access their services.

Armed forces personnel enjoy the same rights as everyone else, including rights to manifest religious belief in community with others. However, the enjoyment of these rights may be limited by the requirements of military discipline.[167] In particular, the State may prevent those in positions of authority from using that authority to lend weight to proselytizing activity.[168]

8. Right to provide educational, charitable, and humanitarian institutions

Religious associations have the right to establish schools and other educational institutions to provide education according to their precepts. The Convention case-law on the interaction of religion with education under article 9 and article 2 First Protocol is sufficiently complex to warrant separate consideration.[169] For now it is sufficient to note that the Commission originally held that associations could not claim to be victims of breaches of article 2 First Protocol which give rights specifically to children and parents.[170] However, once it had been accepted that the article included an individual right to start and run a private school (albeit subject to State regulation),[171] it would have been odd to resist applications by such schools. In *Verein Gemeinsam Lernen v Austria*,[172] the Commission accepted that differential State subsidies for church and non-religious private schools raised a question of a possible breach of article 14 in connection with article 2 First Protocol. Indeed, in the parallel individual application it was doubted whether the parents could claim to be victims in such circumstances.[173] One would expect the case-law to settle into the position already obtaining with religious associations more generally: the proper applicant is the primary victim, which in the case of the legal framework for religious schools is likely to be the schools themselves.

Article 6(b) of the 1981 Declaration refers to the right to establish and maintain appropriate charitable or humanitarian institutions, and Recommendation 1086 called for the right to operate charitable aid schemes. There would appear to be as yet no case under the European Convention addressing the extent of a religious organization's freedom to provide health and social welfare services. As noted above, hostility to charitable work by a Roman Catholic order in Sri Lanka has come before the Human Rights Committee.

---

[167] *Kalac v Turkey*, no 20704/92 (1997); *Akbulut v Turkey*, no 45624/99 (2003).

[168] *Larissis v Greece*, no 23372/94 (1998).   [169] See Ch 8 below.

[170] *Ingrid Jordebo Foundation of Christian Schools v Sweden*, no 11533/85 (1987). But withdrawal of State approval did raise a question of potential breach of article 6 rights.   [171] Ibid.

[172] *Verein Gemeinsam Lernen v Austria*, no 23419/94 (1995).

[173] *Bachmann, Hofreiter and Gulyn v Austria*, no 19315/92 (1995).

9. Right to public presence

There can be no question about the right of religious associations to produce, import, and disseminate religious publications and materials. This includes the right to print religious works in sufficient quantity and without official approval. It is protected by article 10 in connection with article 9 ECHR. More problematic is the question of access to mass media. Recommendation 1086 called for a right of access including a right to broadcast religious services on Fridays, Saturdays, or Sundays as well as major religious festivals. The Vienna Concluding Document reduced this to an obligation on States to 'favourably consider the interests of religious communities to participate... through the mass media'. However, religious associations have so far had no success in seeking specifically religious rights of access to broadcasting media under the European Convention.

In principle, access to broadcasting media is protected by article 10.[174] In *United Christian Broadcasters v United Kingdom*,[175] the Commission held the blanket prohibition on religious bodies seeking national radio broadcasting licences was justifiable in the light of the small number of bands available (three analogue and one digital) and the extreme unlikelihood that a balanced provision of services would be possible if one were allocated to a religious group. *Murphy v Ireland*,[176] which concerned a ban on religious advertising in commercial broadcasting, raised rather more complex issues. The advertisement in question was a short radio announcement of a showing of a religious film open to the public. The broadcaster was willing to air it, but was prevented by laws preventing religious advertisements. The Court accepted the blanket ban as a proportionate restriction of free expression rights, but for reasons that were at times incompatible. Thus the Court accepted that members of the 'particular church'[177] to which religious Irish tend to belong might find the advertisement an instance of offensive proselytism, that the State had an interest in ensuring that religious broadcasts were impartial, neutral, and balanced (with every citizen having the same right to participate),[178] and that freedom to advertise would be likely to benefit a dominant religion.[179] The first and third arguments cancel each other out, while a case for equal rights of access can be made for regimes that both permit and do not permit advertisements. It is hard to resist the conclusion that the Court is unwilling seriously to question State control of the major influence on public ideology.

A recent case has found a violation in the refusal of a broadcasting licence to a Christian broadcaster on straightforward grounds.[180] The refusal was discretionary, unexplained, and unreviewable. It was therefore not 'prescribed by law'.

---

[174] *Informationsverein Lentia v Austria*, no 13914/88 (1993).
[175] *United Christian Broadcasters v United Kingdom*, no 44802/98 (2000).
[176] *Murphy v Ireland*, no 44179/98 (2003).   [177] Ibid, para 73.   [178] Ibid, para 74.
[179] Ibid, para 78.   [180] *Eood and Elenkov v Bulgaria*, no 14134/02 (2007).

Reading between the lines, there is some evidence that it was motivated by anti-Christian prejudice, but this did not figure in the judgment.

The right of religious associations to political participation is similarly under-developed, but is recognized to some extent in the Vienna Concluding Document. States are under an obligation to 'engage in consultations with religious faiths, institutions and organizations in order to achieve a better understanding of the requirements of religious freedom'. They must also 'favourably consider the interest of religious communities to participate in public dialogue'.

10. Right to protection

Article 9 embraces a positive right to be protected by State officials from the hostile acts of third parties seeking to disrupt religious meetings.[181] Religious associations also enjoy a right to adequate protection from hostile speech and behaviour, whether on the part of the State or private individuals. Originally, the Commission dealt with restrictions on religious hate speech as a permissible limitation to freedom of expression under article 10(2). An application brought in the wake of the failed prosecution in respect of Salman Rushdie's *Satanic Verses* failed on the grounds that there was no actionable violation of a Convention right.[182] However, in *Otto-Preminger Institut v Austria*, the Court held that the right to be protected from offence was a component of article 9.[183] Failure to protect believers from the provocative portrayal of objects of veneration may amount to a violation of article 9. This was confirmed in *Wingrove v United Kingdom*.[184]

In *Keller v Germany*,[185] the applicants complained of State information about Scientology which they claimed was a prejudiced and offensive attack on their religion in breach of article 9. The Commission rejected the complaint on the grounds that the applicants were insufficiently directly affected by it to count as victims. In *Scientology Kirche eV v Germany*,[186] the association made a similar claim, alleging violation of a series of Convention rights. The Commission rejected the claim in respect of rights which it considered could only be exercised by individuals (privacy, parental rights, and the right to free elections), noted that the complaints arose substantially in respect of the activities of non-State actors, accepted that the failure by the State to protect the association from hostility could amount to a breach of positive State obligations, but held that the association had failed to exhaust domestic remedies. The problem of 'anti-sect' information has now come before the Court in *Leela Förderkreis eV v Germany*.[187]

---

[181] *97 Members of the Gldani Congregation of Jehovah's Witnesses v Georgia*, no 71156/01 (2007).
[182] *Choudhury v United Kingdom*, no 17439/90 (1991).
[183] *Otto-Preminger Institut v Austria* (1994), 295-A, (1995) 19 EHRR 34.
[184] *Wingrove v United Kingdom*, no 17419/90, (1997) 24 EHRR 1; see also *Dubowska and Skup v Poland*, nos 33490/96 and 34055/96 (1997).   [185] *Keller v Germany*, no 36283/97 (1998).
[186] *Scientology Kirche eV v Germany*, no 34614/97 (1997).
[187] *Leela Förderkreis eV v Germany*, no 58911/00 (2008).

The Court accepted that the Shree Bhagwan association's reputation was a protected civil right for the purposes of article 6(1), and that the State's negative information campaign had amounted to an interference with this right. But by a 5:2 majority they found no violation on account of the restrained language with which the Government had expressed its warning, along with the public interest in information about 'youth sects'. The minority found a violation simply on account of the Government's breach of neutrality in matters of religious belief. Judge Kalaydjieva drew an unfavourable comparison with the activities of communist regimes. An obligation to avoid religious stereotyping by public bodies can be found in a series of decisions concerning child custody for religious believers.[188]

Cases may therefore arise in which a specific association or organization may be the proper victim in the case of false and hostile portrayals of religion reaching a sufficiently high degree of severity and focused on the activities of the association or organization concerned. However, there is a considerable difference between this and a general right to act as defender of the religion.[189]

11. Convention rights not enjoyed by associations

It has been accepted that religious associations enjoy rights not only directly derived from article 9, but also in respect of articles 6 (fair trial), 10 (expression), 11 (assembly and association), 13 (effective remedy), 14 (equality), and articles 1 (property) and 2 (education) of the First Protocol. It is hard to see how corporate bodies could enjoy rights derived from articles 2 (life), 3 (torture etc.), 4 (slavery), 5 (personal liberty), 7 (no retrospective punishment), or article 3 First Protocol (free elections). This leaves an intermediate category in which religious association may or may not have rights.

Associations have been denied freedom of conscience.[190] This would only be plausible if 'religion' were implicit in the structure and activity of an association in the way that 'conscience' is not. The Commission clearly thought that the two were distinguishable, but it is far from clear why a freethinking individual should be able to object to a church tax on the grounds of freedom of thought, conscience, and religion,[191] but a freethinking association is unable to object.[192] It may be that this early approach has now been surpassed, not least on account of implicit discrimination between religious and non-religious viewpoints.

---

[188] *Hoffmann v Austria*, no 12875/87 (1990), A-255 C; *Palau-Martinez v France*, no 64927/01 (2003).

[189] This is tendency of UN resolutions on the 'defamation of religions'. See Rivers, *op cit* n 14.

[190] *Verein 'Kontakt-Information-Therapie' and Hagen v Austria*, no 11921/86 (1988); *Kustannus v Finland*, no 20471/92 (1996).

[191] *Bruno v Sweden*, no 32196/96 (2001); *Lundberg v Sweden*, no 36846/97 (2001).

[192] *Kustannus v Finland*, no 20471/92 (1996).

Associations have also been denied rights of privacy.[193] Although the Commission's view that article 8 had more of an individual cast than article 9 is plausible, and although in many cases the proper applicants may well be the individuals concerned, cases could arise in which confidential information is held primarily about the activities of an organization, and in which the association might be the proper victim. As far as article 12 is concerned, an association clearly cannot marry and found a family. However, there is no reason why an association should not enjoy the right to conduct marriages with civil effect on a non-discriminatory basis, and failure to secure this could properly be cast as a breach of article 14 in the context of article 12.[194] A case might be more likely to succeed if framed as an individual right to enjoy a religious ceremony with civil effect on a non-discriminatory basis, ie presuming in principle the availability of such ceremonies.

V. Conclusion

The purpose of this chapter has been to gain a sense of the emerging international legal environment within which the English law of organized religions must be located. Although the formal binding commitments of international law have not changed, their implications for collective manifestations of religious belief have been increasingly recognized. In spite of variations in the relevant instruments and their associated case-law, and notwithstanding important formal legal differences in the nature of obligation and processes for enforcement, a reasonably constant core of human rights standards in respect of religious communities and associations is becoming apparent. These are based on a recognition of associations as right-bearers on behalf of autonomous religious communities under a law characterized by State neutrality or impartiality. As more cases involving religious associations are heard by the European Court of Human Rights, the details of these rights are being clarified.

The Court is clearly willing to protect associational activity within the 'private' sphere of religious worship. However, the rights of religious associations also include a certain public presence, as well as an area of overlap with State activity. Restrictions on activities in these areas are much easier for States to justify. The relatively lax application of the doctrine of proportionality coupled with the margin of appreciation give States a wide discretion. Here, some of the commitments emerging elsewhere in the international community are, arguably, more extensive. While non-discrimination requirements are also beginning to have some effect in opening up the privileged positions of established churches more

---

[193] *Church of Scientology of Paris v France*, no 19509/92 (1995).
[194] The nearest case is *Spetz v Sweden*, no 20402/92 (1994), which was treated individualistically, as the right of a pastor.

widely, article 14 can lead as easily in the longer term to 'levelling down' as to 'levelling up'.

A number of fundamental questions are thus beginning to emerge about the relationship between organized religions and the State. In spite of an early acceptance of a range of forms of establishment among the European States party to the Convention, this is looking increasingly insecure. What forms of privilege can survive scrutiny, and why? At the same time there is an ongoing uncertainty about the extent to which the law of organized religions needs to be different from the law applying to non-religious bodies. Does the religious dimension need accounting for, or are purely secular models of regulation adequate? And in what domain—over what range of subject-matter—do religious communities enjoy their right to autonomy? English law provides a set of answers to these questions, but it also has its own trajectory of development which in some ways is misaligned to that of international and European human rights law.

3

The Constitution of Religious Bodies

At the centre of the law of organized religions lies the question of the legal constitution of religious bodies. It is possible for a religion to have an organizational structure to which the law is completely blind. The structure still exists as a matter of social reality dependent for its continued viability on the beliefs and practices of individuals and groups, but without any validation or support from the law. As we have seen in Chapter 1, the clearest historical examples in English law are the Roman Catholic Church prior to 1791 and Judaism prior to 1846. Arrangements and bodies for Roman Catholic or Jewish purposes could still exist and even operate reasonably effectively,[1] but they were vulnerable to disruption in the event of litigation.

In some ways, modern law also has tendencies to be blind to the social form of religious bodies, albeit without the active hostility of earlier centuries. In the light of this dynamic it is easy to suppose that the fundamental tension in the constitution of religious bodies is between organized religions seeking legal expression and secular courts and legislatures unwilling to grant it. But this is too simplistic. Rather, religious and secular institutions both struggle with the same tension between a desire to give legal expression to religious form and a desire to preserve distance between the questions of religion and questions of law. The problematic relationship between religious form and legal expression is key to the constitution of religious bodies.

I. Religious Form and Legal Expression

It is entirely understandable that religious bodies should seek the protection of the law from those who would disrupt the basis on which they are formed. If an individual holds property for the purposes of a church, it is not unreasonable for the church to seek redress should he or she divert it to personal ends. At the same time, religious adherents may well be unwilling to see disputes resolved by 'outsiders', who lack sympathy and legitimacy. The same tension is replicated on

---

[1] This point is made by H S Q Henriques, *The Jews and the English Law* (London: J Jacobs, 1908).

the part of secular legal institutions, which struggle with the desire to uphold the rule of law and protect legally recognized interests on one hand, and an understandable caution about being drawn into the resolution of theological disputes on the other. The law becomes problematic not simply because of the existence of this tension, but when there is a mismatch of expectation and approach as to its proper resolution.

Judges increasingly appeal to doctrines of non-justiciability in relation to religious disputes.[2] When nineteenth-century British judges disclaimed any authority to determine disputes about religious doctrine or government, they were offering assurances of neutrality to the parties. They were pointing out that it was no role of a court of law to act as a religious insider delivering 'correct' answers to the underlying substantive theological or ecclesiological dispute between the parties. However, they would regularly proceed to point out that questions of doctrine and discipline might well be relevant as questions of fact to determine the outcome of the case. Evidence could be heard and conclusions reached in a detached, and supposedly neutral, way.

The modern doctrine of non-justiciability holds that courts should not even resolve disputed questions of religious doctrine and government as matters of fact. If the two factions to a schism both claim to be legitimate successors to the historic body—if the minority faction alleges that the majority have departed from historic fundamental doctrine and the majority faction alleges that the minority are refusing to accept the legitimate decisions of correctly constituted bodies— courts *cannot tell* which doctrines are fundamental or what the decision-taking remit of the relevant bodies is.

The modern doctrine of non-justiciability is thus a form of blindness to social reality and the expectations of the parties. It leads to a curious instability in the law. On one hand, it can lead to the denial of any legal remedy. The religious dimension infuses the entire dispute and takes it out of court. An example of this would be the refusal of a court to interfere with procedural irregularity on the part of a religious decision-taking body.[3] On the other hand, remembering their duty to uphold the rule of law, non-justiciability can lead the courts to filter out the religious dimensions of a dispute, leaving a residue of legally-cognizable fact, which then forms the basis of a legal decision. An example of this would be treating the refusal of a religious body to ordain women as priests as straightforward employer discrimination on grounds of sex. After all, the court cannot decide between the theological protagonists in such a debate.

Non-justiciability is not a helpful guide to resolving the tension between judicial abstention and judicial oversight, precisely on account of this instability. Nor does it reflect the weight of legal authority. Rather, the law has developed by reference to two principles: a respect for internal autonomy, and a commitment

---

[2] eg *R v Chief Rabbi, ex parte Wachmann* [1992] 1 WLR 1036; *Blake v Associated Newspapers* [2003] EWHC 1960.   [3] *Scandrett v Dowling* (1992) 27 NSWLR 483.

to protecting legal interests. This leads to a limited secular judicial oversight of churches and religious bodies. The trigger for such oversight is the infringement of a legal interest; but the standard of judgment is the body of internal rules or 'law' adopted by the organization.

The basic legal structure of organized religions in English law developed by way of a private law analogy to the position of the established Church of England, almost entirely through the extension of trust principles. The first part of this chapter summarizes that development up to 1869. The date is significant. In that year, part of the United Church of England and Ireland was disestablished and reconstituted in Ireland as the Church of Ireland on the basis of the existing private law analogy. When the Church in Wales was formed in 1920 out of another part of the Church of England, the disestablishing legislation adopted the same basic model. In 1869 the Charity Commissioners also gained the jurisdiction to certify schemes for the administration of trusts of registered places of worship for confirmation by local Act of Parliament. After this date private legislation has regularly been used to constitute, or partially constitute, churches and other religious bodies. Finally, a number of cases from the 1860s tend to form the starting-point of modern discussions of the law, and it is important to set these in the context of the law at the time.

The chapter then proceeds to consider the modern law by reference to four questions. The first concerns the choice of legal form open to churches and religious associations, in particular the use of statutory constitutions and the availability of different modes of incorporation. The second question concerns the occasions on which courts will construe members' interests as legal, and resolve disputes concerning those interests. One area in which there is little doubt that the courts will get involved is where property interests are at stake. Thus the third question concerns the approach of the courts in resolving disputes about religious property, particularly where the dispute is internal to a church or religious association in a context of schism. The final question to be considered in this chapter is the extent and basis of the secular courts' oversight of religious courts. There is a fifth question—about the legal position of ministers of religion—but this is complex enough to warrant a chapter of its own.

II. The Law up to 1869

Lord Mansfield once commented that the effect of the Toleration Act was not merely to remove the penalties attaching to religious dissent, but to bring about the legal establishment of non-conforming Protestantism.[4] Accordingly, he held that it would be 'putting Protestant Dissenters and their religious worship out of the protection of the law' to deny the writ of mandamus to members of a

---

[4] In *Evans v Chamberlain of London*, noted in *AG v Pearson* (1817) 3 Mer 353, 420, 36 ER 135.

congregation requiring trustees to hold an election for an endowed pastor and to admit the person duly elected.[5] Mandamus was also available to restore a pastor to the office to which he had a *prima facie* title.[6] Alternatively, an action for money had and received for the profits of the office might be brought.[7] The point was that in some way, doubts about the validity of an appointment or dismissal of a minister could be litigated.

As regards the occupation of premises, the minister was at law the mere tenant at will of the trustees.[8] Litigation was almost always in equity and depended on the correct application of trust property for the use of a congregation for the time being.[9] The minister was not *cestui que trust* (beneficiary) in a personal capacity, but only for the duration of his office.[10] Once a minister was properly dismissed, the trustees could bring an action for possession of the chapel and dwelling-house.[11] The existence of partial parallel remedies at law in respect of the office of minister did not prevent the exercise of the broader equitable jurisdiction.[12]

The trust did not need to be declared in a deed or in writing, but could be proved by usage.[13] If necessary, the court would give effect to the trust by filling up the number of trustees,[14] who must be of the same religion as the congregation.[15] The court would look to any trust deed to determine how the property was to be applied, including the conditions for the appointment and dismissal of a minister to his office, and could also inquire into past usage to clarify any uncertainties.[16] However, the courts were unwilling to imply an expectation that a ministerial appointment was for life, whether by analogy with the parson's freehold, or even on the basis of practice within the relevant denomination.[17] The precise nature of the inquiry into usage was not always clear. Considered as a matter of private right, the beneficiaries could bind themselves to exercise their rights in any mode they chose.[18] Thus the rules of the society for the time being were relevant either as extrinsic evidence to assist in the construction of the trust deeds, or as the disposal by the congregation of their beneficial interests. For Lord Eldon,

---

[5] *R v Barker* (1762) 3 Burr 1265, 97 ER 823. Parke J later commented that the use of the pulpit as a pastor, minister, or preacher was an easement like a right of common or way. See *Doe d Jones v Jones* (1830) 10 B & C 718, 109 ER 616.   [6] *R v Jotham* (1790) 3 TR 574, 100 ER 741.

[7] Ibid, per Buller J at 578.   [8] *Doe d Nicholl v M'Kaeg* (1830) 10 B & C 721, 109 ER 618.

[9] *Davis v Jenkins* (1814) 3 V & B 151, 35 ER 436; *Foley v Wontner* (1820) 2 Jac & W 245, 37 ER 621; *Leslie v Birnie* (1826) 2 Russ 114, 38 ER 279; *Newsome v Flowers* (1861) 30 Beav 461, 54 ER 968.   [10] *Cooper v Gordon* (1869) LR 8 Eq 249.

[11] *AG v Aked* (1835) 7 Sim 321, 58 ER 861.

[12] *Daugars v Rivaz* (1860) 28 Beav 233, 54 ER 355.

[13] *AG v Murdoch* (1849) 7 Hare 445, 68 ER 183.

[14] *Davis v Jenkins* (1814) 3 V & B 151, 35 ER 436; *Foley v Wontner* (1820) 2 Jac & W 245, 37 ER 621.

[15] *Shore v Wilson* (1839) 9 Cl & F 355, 8 ER 450; *AG v Shore* (1843) 11 Sim 591, 59 ER 1002; *Newsome v Flowers* (1861) 30 Beav 461, 54 ER 968.

[16] *Davis v Jenkins* (1814) 3 V & B 151, 35 ER 436; *AG v Pearson* (1817) 3 Mer 353, 36 ER 135.

[17] *Porter v Clarke* (1829) 2 Sim 520, 57 ER 882; *Cooper v Gordon* (1869) LR 8 Eq 249.

[18] *AG v Newcombe* (1807) 14 Ves 1, 33 ER 422.

it did not seem to matter very much.[19] Where the trustees, or the congregation, had a power of appointment, they could act by a majority.[20] If the trust was clear that the congregation were part of a wider denomination or church, they could not withdraw themselves from that association, even by a majority vote.[21] The rules of the wider denomination would be followed where applicable,[22] and decisions of its domestic tribunals within the scope of their authority upheld.[23] Each member of the congregation had the right to secure the due execution of the trusts, and hence (indirectly) to secure the enforcement of any relevant rules of the association.[24]

The distinction between private and public (ie charitable) trusts was procedurally significant, but not entirely clear. Sometimes parties proceeded by private bill, sometimes by information at the relation of the Attorney-General; usually by both combined. After some initial uncertainty, it became clear in the course of the eighteenth century that lawful dissenting trusts were charitable,[25] and that Protestant dissenters could proceed by information, but Lord Eldon held they were not obliged to do so unless the case concerned an income-generating endowment.[26] By the 1860s the charitable nature of dissenting religious trusts was settled, and the distinction between proceeding by information or by bill turned on whether the Attorney-General could be persuaded to intervene.[27] Generally speaking, however, whether the trust were private or public made little difference to the power of the congregation collectively to determine the disposal of their interests. They were the beneficiaries either way.

Lord Eldon considered that one of the most difficult questions facing him in his time as Lord Chancellor was what to do when some of the congregation had changed their religious opinions.[28] Generally, the trust deed—if there was one

---

[19] *Leslie v Birnie* (1826) 2 Russ 114, 38 ER 279, in which a seat-holder failed to show that he had a right to participate in the election of a minister according to the rules of the Scottish Presbyterian Church, is nicely ambiguous on this point.
[20] *Fearon v Webb* (1802) 14 Ves 14, 33 ER 427; *Wilkinson v Malin* (1832) 2 C & J 636, 149 ER 268; *Perry v Shipway* (1859) 1 Giff 1, 65 ER 799, 4 De G & J 353, 45 ER 136; *Cooper v Gordon* (1869) LR 8 Eq 249. [21] *Broom v Summers* (1840) 11 Sim 353, 59 ER 909.
[22] *Leslie v Birnie* (1826) 2 Russ 114, 38 ER 279; *AG v Welsh* (1844) 4 Hare 572, 67 ER 775.
[23] *Dr. Warren's Case* (1833) Grindrod's Compendium; *AG v Clapham* (1853) 10 Hare 540, 68 ER 1042. [24] *Perry v Shipway* (1859) 1 Giff 1, 65 ER 799, 4 De G & J 353, 45 ER 136.
[25] The earlier cases reject the argument that dissenting uses are superstitious, but lean against the recognition of a permanent endowment for lawful dissenters: *AG v Baxter* (1684) 1 Vern 248, 23 ER 446; *AG v Hughes* (1689) 2 Vern 105, 23 ER 677; *AG v Eades* (1711) cited in *AG v Cock* (1751) 2 Ves Sen 273, 275, 28 ER 177; *AG v Hickman* (1732) 2 Eq Cas Abr 193 pl 14, 22 ER 166. Charitable nature was accepted in *AG v Cock* and *AG v Wansay* (1808) 15 Ves Jun 231, 33 ER 742, although the point that they were purely private could still be argued in *AG v Fowler* (1808) 15 Ves 85, 33 ER 687.
[26] *Davis v Jenkins* (1814) 3 V & B 151, 35 ER 436, referring to Lord Hardwicke's decision in *AG v Parker* (1747) 1 Ves Sen 43, 27 ER 879.
[27] *Lang v Purves* (1862) 15 Moo PC 389, 15 ER 541.
[28] See *Foley v Wontner* (1820) 2 Jac & W 245, 37 ER 621; see also his frustration in *Davis v Jenkins* (1814) 3 V & B 151, 35 ER 436: 'it is very difficult to know, what to do with these dissenting societies'.

at all—made no provision for this. Presumably the matter was difficult precisely because it was arguable that considered as a matter of private trust the congregation could agree to wind the trust up and distribute the proceeds, and hence also change the doctrine, if not by majority, at least unanimously. Alternatively, it could be argued that the trust had failed and the property should be divided among the original contributors. However, Lord Eldon decided that the leaning of the Court must be to support those adhering to the original system.[29] Moreover, where the trust deed was broadly phrased, evidence could be heard to determine what that original system was.[30] Thus it came about that a trust for 'Protestant dissenters' could only be applied to the use of that particular denomination of Protestant dissenters which was originally intended.[31]

In the light of subsequent developments, it is important to note the way in which Lord Eldon applied his own principles. When *Craigdallie v Aikman* returned to the House of Lords in 1820, he held that Craigdallie and his party had failed to show that the controverted resolution of the synod amounted to a departure from the original terms of the trust. The seceding 'Burgher' church of which he was a part was to have the same form of government as the Church of Scotland, so its synod was to have the normal powers of a synod, which included the resolution of the disputed point about the power of the civil magistrate. Craigdallie was therefore to be considered a person voluntarily separating himself from the congregation without any cause. The question was not whether Craigdallie and his party were the more faithful adherents to the original settlement, but whether the governing institutions of the church had crossed the doctrinal limits which determined its essential identity.

A number of consequences flowed from this decision. One of the privileges of membership (as *cestui que trust*) was to ensure that the religious body maintained its original principles,[32] thus creating a justiciable distinction between matters in the disposition of the congregation and matters which were entrenched. Any power on the part of the congregation to make rules for their society was subject to the trust deeds and the fundamental religious principles.[33] This focused attention on the freedom left to a congregation by the original trusts, and forced a clearer distinction between the relevance of usage to construe the deeds and the power of the congregation to make rules from time to time.[34] Although conceptually clearer, the distinction in practice could be hard to draw. It also effectively leaned in the direction of public trust, for who—logically—would otherwise

---

[29] *Craigdallie v Aikman* (1813) 1 Dow 1, 3 ER 601; *AG v Pearson* (1817) 3 Mer 353, 36 ER 135; see also *Shore v Wilson* (1839) 9 Cl & F 355, 8 ER 450.

[30] *AG v Pearson* (1817) 3 Mer 353, 36 ER 135.

[31] Ibid. See also *AG v Murdoch* (1849) 7 Hare 445, 68 ER 183, distinguishing the establishment of a specific chapel from the general bequest in *Shore v Wilson* (1839) 9 Cl & F 355, 8 ER 450.

[32] *Milligan v Mitchell* (1837) 3 My & Cr 72, 40 ER 852; *AG v Gould* (1860) 28 Beav 485, 54 ER 452.   [33] *Milligan v Mitchell* (1837) 3 My & Cr 72, 40 ER 852.

[34] Clearly explained in *AG v Gould* (1860) 28 Beav 485, 54 ER 452. See also *AG v Murdoch* (1852) 1 De GM & G 86, 68 ER 183, per Knight Bruce LJ.

represent the interest in doctrinal continuity against the unanimous wishes of the congregation? It followed that actions alleging breach of fundamental doctrine had to be brought by information at the relation of the Attorney-General, and not by bill.[35] It also followed that where a congregation was associated with a larger denomination, it became important to show that that denomination had not changed its fundamental doctrines if its rules were to be considered still applicable to the individual congregation.[36]

The law thus created a tension between the fundamental identity of a religious society as established by its founders and its dynamic character as a community over time. The ruling on fundamental changes of doctrine caused severe practical difficulties in the case of denominations such as the Presbyterians, who had undergone major doctrinal change in the course of the eighteenth century. In *Shore v Wilson*, the House of Lords followed the earlier lead of Lord Eldon and ruled that the illegality of Unitarianism at the time of creation was a relevant consideration in construing Lady Hewley's substantial bequests to exclude Unitarians.[37] Litigation rumbled on and was eventually settled when a mixture of Baptists, Congregationalists, and Presbyterians were appointed trustees.

Lord Lyndhurst, who was Lord Chancellor in *Shore v Wilson*, was sufficiently perturbed by the effect of his judgment in that case to secure the passage of the Nonconformists' (or Dissenters') Chapels Act 1844, section 1 of which required courts in construing trust deeds to assume that any religion currently within the policy of the law was so at the time of creation. Section 2 granted a prescriptive right to the benefit of any trusts on the basis of 25 years' continuous practice by a congregation, so long as the use was not actually contrary to the trusts. Section 2 is still in force in relation to any charities taking effect before 1844.[38] The effect of this was fairly limited: in line with the growing emphasis on founder's intent,[39] it was not effective if extrinsic evidence showed that the founders would not have counted those who denied the doctrine of the Trinity as 'Protestant dissenters' at all.[40] However, its use was demonstrated in *AG v Bunce* in which property given to 'Presbyterians' at Devizes between 1716 and 1803 was held to be for the benefit of a congregation that had been overwhelmingly Baptist for the previous 60 years.[41]

The idea that a congregation might do things unanimously that could not be done by majority never quite died out. As the nineteenth century proceeded, a threefold distinction began to emerge between entrenched matters, matters

---

[35] This was recognized in *AG v Gould* (1860) 28 Beav 485, 54 ER 452; *Newsome v Flowers* (1861) 30 Beav 461, 54 ER 968.

[36] *AG v Welsh* (1844) 4 Hare 572, 67 ER 775; *AG v Munro* (1848) 2 De G & S 191, 64 ER 55; *AG v Murdoch* (1849) 7 Hare 445, 68 ER 183.

[37] *Shore v Wilson* (1839) 9 Cl & F 355, 8 ER 450; only Maule J disagreed. The bequests were to benefit 'poor and godly preachers of Christ's holy gospel'.

[38] Charities Act 1960, s 39 and sched 5.

[39] See *AG v Calvert* (1857) 23 Beav 248, 53 ER 97.

[40] *Drummond v AG* (1849) II HLC 837.   [41] *AG v Bunce* (1868) LR 6 Eq 563.

determinable only by a unanimous resolution, and matters determinable by a majority in accordance with established procedures. In *AG v Murdoch*, as well as disagreeing on the facts, the judges adopted different formulations in respect of the power of a congregation of dissenters to adopt new regulations.[42] Knight-Bruce VC required unanimity whereas Lord Cranworth LJ referred to a majority. The distinction continued to cause some puzzlement.[43]

The question whether (if at all) the rules of a religious association constituted a contract hardly arose in the context of an individual congregation. In *Israel v Simmons* a contract for pew-rents in a synagogue was upheld, and a claim for fees in respect of other rites and ceremonies could have been, but for problems of privity.[44] The relationship between a minister and the appointing trustees might also constitute a special contract,[45] but in *Porter v Clarke* the court refused jurisdiction in a case concerning the dismissal of a minister supported by voluntary contributions alone.[46] Given that the 'use of the pulpit' was as much a benefit as the occupation of any dwelling attached to the chapel,[47] it is not clear why the court refused jurisdiction.[48] The better explanation is perhaps not the absence of any statement of the mode of election or duration of office in the trust deed, as the court claimed, but the subsidiary point that it was also reasonable that a minister depending on voluntary contributions by the congregation should be dismissible at will.[49] Even if there were a contract for services in a context within the jurisdiction of courts of common law, it would not have aided the minister much, and the breadth of the beneficial interests of parties was such that there was generally little point in proceeding at law instead of in equity.

The relevance of contract became apparent once litigation involved churches and denominations larger than individual congregations.[50] The courts showed some hesitation in accepting that the use of property—which was assumed to be for the benefit of a specific congregation—could be directed by an 'extraneous' body, such as a synod, in the absence of a specific contract or express statement in the trust deeds.[51] As we have seen, the law was essentially congregationalist

---

[42] *AG v Murdoch* (1849) 7 Hare 445, 68 ER 183.

[43] See *AG v Clapham* (1853) 10 Hare 540, 68 ER 1042; *AG v Gould* (1860) 28 Beav 485, 54 ER 452; for a later expression of the confusion, see *AG v Anderson* (1888) 57 LJ Ch 547.

[44] *Israel v Simmons* (1818) 2 Stark 356, 171 ER 671.

[45] *Daugars v Rivaz* (1860) 28 Beav 233, 54 ER 355.

[46] *Porter v Clarke* (1829) 2 Sim 520, 57 ER 882.

[47] In *Doe d Jones v Jones* (1830) 10 B & C 718, 109 ER 616, Parke J stated that the use of the pulpit to which mandamus was granted in *R v Barker* (1762) 3 Burr 1265, 97 ER 823, was 'an easement like a right of common or of way'.

[48] Perhaps it was influenced by the fact that he was not paid from pew-rents, which would have been impressed with the same trust as the chapel; see *AG v Fowler* (1808) 15 Ves 85, 33 ER 687.

[49] Ibid, at 523.

[50] *AG v Welsh* (1844) 4 Hare 572, 67 ER 775, per Sir James Wigram VC, contains an unusual early use of 'contract' to describe the relationship between the members of the congregation.

[51] *AG v Pearson* (1817), 36 ER 135, per Lord Eldon LC. See also *Lang v Purves* (1862) 15 Moo PC 389, 15 ER 541.

in orientation: trusts were assumed to be for the use of a congregation, not any wider church. It was one thing to imply a trust for the benefit of a congregation as defined by the settlor's doctrine, quite another to read the trust deed as requiring integration into a wider body. It was for this reason that the outcome in Dr Warren's case involving the power of the Methodist Conference was not entirely guaranteed,[52] although in the event the courts did accept the linkage. Contract analysis seems to have developed first in Scotland. *Craigie v Marshall* concerned the power of a synod to effect a union against the wishes of the majority of a congregation.[53] The three judgments of the court vary in whether they construe the authority of the synod as a matter of contract of submission by the congregation subsequent to the formation of the trust, or as a condition on the enjoyment of the beneficial interest. *McMillan v General Assembly of the Free Church of Scotland* seems to be the first case to be argued solely on the basis of the terms of the contract of association.[54]

In 1863 the Privy Council decided that the Crown had no power to establish ecclesiastical offices and courts exercising coercive jurisdiction in colonies having an independent legislature.[55] Discipline within the colonial Church of England therefore had to be based on a consensual jurisdiction arising from the voluntary submission of members to a contract based on the rules and regulations of the entire body.[56] This placed the church in exactly the same legal position as any other religious society.[57] From then on it was clear that the rules and regulations of the religious body were not only conditions on the exercise of trust powers, but also formed a contract enforceable to the extent that civil or temporal interests were affected.[58] Of course, it was still an open question whether the trust deeds of any church property, properly construed, did in fact associate the property with a denomination, or according to some independently defined set of doctrines and procedures, which might prevent it from joining, or remaining part of, that denomination.[59]

---

[52] See the discussion in *AG v Clapham* (1853) 10 Hare 540, 68 ER 1042, which still does not use the idea of contract.   [53] *Craigie v Marshall* (1850) 12 D 523.

[54] *McMillan v General Assembly of the Free Church of Scotland* (1859) 22 D 290, (1861) 23 D 1314. The case later collapsed on the basis of the General Assembly's lack of legal personality: (1862) 24 D 1282, (1864) 2 M 1444.

[55] *Long v Bishop of Capetown* (1863) 1 Moo PC (NS) 411, 15 ER 756.

[56] In *Re Lord Bishop of Natal* (1864) 3 Moo PC (NS) 115, 16 ER 43, there was no doubt on the part of counsel for the Bishop of Natal that there was a contractual relationship between him and the Metropolitan Bishop of Cape Town. The point was simply that the law of the Church of England (albeit treated as a contract) did not grant Metropolitan bishops the power to depose diocesan bishops. Hence the brief dismissal of the contract point at 155; there was no *additional* agreement modifying existing Anglican ecclesiastical law.

[57] *Long v Bishop of Capetown* (1863) 1 Moo PC (NS) 411, 461, 15 ER 756.

[58] *Bishop of Natal v Gladstone* (1866) LR 3 Eq 1; *Murray v Burgess* (1867) LR 1 PC 362; *Forbes v Eden* (1867) 1 Sc & Div AC 568.

[59] The alternative is clearly set out by Lord Romilly MR in *Bishop of Natal v Gladstone* (1866) LR 3 Eq 1 at 3. *Merriman v Williams* (1882) 7 AC 484 is a good example of the problems that might arise.

The limitation on enforceability caused—and still causes—doubt about whether one should characterize the agreement as a contract.[60] In *Bishop of Natal v Gladstone*, Lord Romilly MR stated:

If any number of persons, either in England or any of its dependencies, associate themselves together, professing to follow a particular religion, not being the religion of the state, the Court must, when applied to, inquire into what the doctrine and discipline of that religion are, and must then enforce obedience to them accordingly ... It is needless to cite authorities to establish this proposition.[61]

Lord Romilly can be read as asserting that the secular courts will determine every internal dispute, or at least every dispute which, had it occurred within the Church of England, would be determinable by ecclesiastical courts, including the Privy Council. This was at the height of litigation arising from the nineteenth-century doctrinal and liturgical controversies and caused some public consternation.[62] But such a broad reading is unfair. The question was whether the fact that the bishop lacked coercive jurisdiction made any substantial difference for the purposes of a trust to endow his bishopric. Lord Romilly's point was that it did not, because to the extent that he needed to act coercively, eg by defrocking a clergyman and excluding him from his benefice, the secular courts would hold that so long as he acted in accordance with internal law, his acts were effective and enforceable. The civil law provided an analogy to public ecclesiastical law. In the light of the existing case-law, which Lord Romilly was very familiar with, situations in which it might be necessary to exercise a coercive ecclesiastical jurisdiction would always raise questions of enforceable civil legal interest.

Thus when Lord Chelmsford LC stated in *Forbes v Eden* that the canons of the Scottish Episcopal Church did not form the contract between the members, it is clear that he did not mean they were legally irrelevant or unenforceable when the enjoyment of a legally recognized interest was concerned. In citing *McMillan* he showed that he accepted the existence of a legal interest (the status of ordained clergyman) which was a creature of contract. Forbes's problem was that the revision of the canons he objected to was procedurally proper, and thus within the terms of the contract. Rather, Lord Chelmsford was referring to the fact that the alleged change of the canons by that church's synod was not actionable *per se*, since the change concerned 'nothing with regard to the fundamental doctrines or articles of faith upon which the constitution of a religious community depends'. In other words he was suggesting a contractual equivalent to the rule that individual beneficiaries under a religious trust had a right to ensure that the fundamental doctrines of the church were not denied. Attempting to raise Forbes's

---

[60] *Scandrett v Dowling* (1992) 27 NSWLR 483 denies that there is a contract, and thus misses the key question about whether the plaintiff's interest is an enforceable one.

[61] *Bishop of Natal v Gladstone* (1866) LR 3 Eq 1, 36.

[62] Noted in *Scandrett v Dowling* (1992) 27 NSWLR 483.

objections to the status of fundamental doctrine was the most plausible way of arguing his case. Unfortunately for him it was not plausible enough.

In summary, by 1869 the courts had secured the legal right of each member of a congregation of religious dissenters to obtain the ministry of a pastor in accordance with the fundamental doctrines of the denomination in question, and subject to its internal rules. The internal rules applied either as conditions on the exercise of trust powers, or as a matter of contract between the members of the congregation and other denominational bodies extraneous to the specific congregation. The contract was only enforceable in respect of interests variously described as beneficial, proprietory, patrimonial, temporal, or legal. The formulation of section 20 Irish Church Act 1869 is thus about as neat a summary of the general law as one could wish for:

The present ecclesiastical law of Ireland, and the present articles, doctrines, rites, rules, discipline, and ordinances of the said Church, with and subject to such (if any) modification or alteration as may be duly made therein according to the constitution of the said Church for the time being, shall be deemed to be binding on the members for the time being thereof in the same manner as if such members had mutually contracted and agreed to abide by and observe the same, and shall be capable of being enforced in the temporal courts in relation to any property which under and by virtue of this Act is reserved or given to or taken and enjoyed by the said Church or any members thereof, in the same manner and to the same extent as if such property had been expressly given, granted, or conveyed upon trust to be held, occupied, and enjoyed by persons who should observe and keep and be in all respects bound by the said ecclesiastical law, and the said articles, doctrines, rites, rules, discipline, and ordinances of the said Church, subject as aforesaid; but nothing herein contained shall be construed to confer on any archbishop, bishop, or other ecclesiastical person any coercive jurisdiction whatsoever...[63]

At the same time, this formulation is nicely ambiguous as to the precise extent of enforcement 'in relation to any property'. It is an ambiguity that lives on.

III. Modern Statutory and Corporate Structures

The basic legal principles established by 1869 suffer from a certain rigidity. They assume that the identity of the religious body rests in the religious doctrine it maintains, and they assume that questions of discipline and government are to be determined by the individual congregation, subject to any wider form of church government to which the congregation might expressly be bound. In the case of societies such as the Methodists, for whom John Wesley had had the foresight to draft model trust deeds which ensured that church property was held subject to his form of association and the powers of the Annual Conference, this was not such a problem. In the case of other religious denominations wishing to combine

---

[63] The Primitive Wesleyan Methodist Society of Ireland Act 1871, s 6, is in the same terms.

and form regional or national churches, legal restrictions on the variation of trusts represented a considerable obstacle. In addition, the general law did not enable religious bodies outside the established church to incorporate.

1. Statutory constitution

From 1870, the typical solution to these problems was to secure partial constitution by Act of Parliament. The significance of this should not be overstated. Acts of Parliament have regularly been used to constitute commercial and civil society organizations from banks, building societies, and insurance companies to colleges and universities. The Irish Church Act 1869, which disestablished the Church of Ireland, was precedent-setting in respect of two other denominations in Ireland: the Presbyterian Church and the Methodist Church. These were also partially constituted at around the same time by public Act of Parliament.[64] Apart from that, legislative constitution came with the assistance of the Charity Commissioners, who gained the jurisdiction in 1869 to certify schemes for the administration of charities in respect of places of religious worship.[65] Until 1960 such schemes required Parliamentary confirmation by private act to take effect.[66] Today, apart from the Church in Wales, which was disestablished and reconstituted by public Act of Parliament on the model of the Church of Ireland, the United Synagogues, the Methodist Church, the United Reformed Church, the Salvation Army, the Baptist Union, and the Presbyterian Church of Wales are substantially constituted on the basis of private Acts of Parliament. Strictly speaking, legislation is only to be used if the objects cannot be achieved by other means. Given subsequent changes in the general law, the only object which cannot now be achieved without Act of Parliament is the creation of a corporation sole. However, the historic practice has been to use Acts of Parliament for purposes beyond those strictly necessary, and this practice has continued in the case of major Christian denominations. The three main modern examples of this are the Methodist Church Act 1976, the Salvation Army Act 1980, and the United Reformed Church Act 2000.

The majority of the legislation confirms charitable schemes in respect of individual Baptist or Congregational chapels. These schemes, which were very common in the period 1907–23, usually transfer ownership to regional or national incorporated trustees and contain provisions concerning the direction of the use of the property, meetings, resolutions, and a basic doctrinal statement; a smaller

---

[64] Irish Presbyterian Church Act 1871; Primitive Wesleyan Methodist Society of Ireland Act 1871. These were subsequently amended by private Act of Parliament in the normal way. See the Irish Presbyterian Church Act 1901, c liii, and the Methodist Church in Ireland Act 1915, c xlvi.

[65] Charitable Trusts Act 1869, s 15.

[66] Charities Act 1960, s 18, set out the new powers. Section 19 provided for the amendment of schemes previously confirmed by Act of Parliament by ministerial order. See now Charities Act 1993, s 17.

number are concerned to grant powers of sale and reinvestment.[67] In the case of fully independent chapels, the constitution tends to be more complete. This process culminated in the Baptist and Congregational Trusts Act 1951,[68] which allows for the transfer of any appropriate trust of a chapel, hall, or manse to national incorporated trustees. The national trustees can then adopt and adapt existing model trust deeds in respect of the property. There is no power to vary doctrinal standards, the qualifications of ministers, elders, deacons or members, or the identity of the ultimate beneficiaries. Similar purposes were fulfilled by the Calvinistic Methodist or Presbyterian Church of Wales Act 1933.[69] This body of legislation can be contrasted with the arrangements within Methodism, in which centralization has been apparent from the start. As a result, very few chapels have needed to be transferred by legislation to the Wesleyan model trust deed.[70]

Another significant purpose of legislation has been to facilitate schemes of union by reconstituting a new united organization. The Jewish United Synagogues Act 1870 brought together a number of Jewish charities, annulled existing internal laws and regulations, and set out the new objects and powers, committees, and office-holders.[71] The United Methodist Church Act 1907 joined together three of the smaller Methodist off-shoots by granting the power to adopt a deed poll of foundation and a new model trust deed, transferring property, construing gifts etc.[72] The Methodist Church Union Act 1929 was closely modelled on this legislation and joined together the Wesleyan Methodist Church, the Primitive Methodist Church, and the United Methodist Church.[73] The same process can be seen in the formation of the Presbyterian Church of England by Act of 1960, which harmonizes slight doctrinal differences in the various model trust deeds adopted in the bodies out of which it was formed.[74] The same process of expanding union and harmonization underlies each of the United Reformed Church Acts 1972, 1981, and 2000.[75]

The Salvation Army Acts have been required not by processes of incremental union, but by a desire for internal reconstitution, the outstanding feature of which has been the gradual diminution in the powers of the General. As established by William Booth, the General was to have considerable powers of direction, including the power to appoint his own successor, who was to hold office for

---

[67] In total, schemes were confirmed involving about 100 chapels. This is, of course, a very small proportion of the total number of non-Anglican places of worship.

[68] Baptist and Congregational Trusts Act 1951, c xvii.

[69] Calvinistic Methodist or Presbyterian Church of Wales Act 1933, c xxxvii.

[70] Exceptions can be found for chapels in Birstall (1890, c clxxxiv), Bosden (1913, c clxxiii), Eatington (1919, c lxxxvii) and Hawkeshead (1923, c lv).

[71] Jewish United Synagogues Act 1870, c cxvi.

[72] United Methodist Church Act 1907, c lxxv.

[73] Methodist Church Union Act 1929, c lix.

[74] Presbyterian Church of England Act 1960, c xxxii.

[75] United Reformed Church Act 1972, c xviii; United Reformed Church Act 1981, c xxiv; United Reformed Church Act 2000, c ii.

life. This was reduced in the Salvation Army Act 1931 to appointment by election, with the possibility of resignation, and further reduced in the Salvation Army Act 1980.[76] Thus by section 12 of that Act, the Salvation Army Trustee Company is made an ordinary trustee of the property, rather than a custodian trustee with the General as managing trustee, which had been the arrangement hitherto.

The tendency of recent legislation has been to give churches increasing control over their own doctrinal standards. Not surprisingly, in the light of the general law, the inclusion of a doctrinal statement is very common, and these can be more or less detailed. The development towards doctrinal autonomy can be seen in the Presbyterian Church of England Act 1960, which incorporated into every trust deed a declaration as to the doctrine of the church, subject to interpretation, modification, or alteration by the General Assembly.[77] When the Presbyterians joined with the Congregationalists in the United Reformed Church, the Act of 1972 simply set out the principal object of chapel trusts to be 'the public worship of God according to the principles and usages for the time being of the United Reformed Church'.[78] Whereas the Methodist Church Union Act 1929 gave that church no power to alter or affect its doctrinal standards, the Methodist Church Act 1976 gives the Conference the power to amend doctrinal standards by deferred special resolution.[79] Under the Salvation Army Act 1980, its object is the advancement of the Christian religion, as set out in Schedule 1, which may be altered by the General with the prior written approval of two-thirds of the Commissioners.[80]

2. Corporate personality

At a very early stage the common law recognized the existence of ecclesiastical corporations sole, separating out the office of parson from the human being occupying that office.[81] In this way courts were able to solve problems of rights to glebe land for church uses by means of a perpetual succession of the office. Later on, ecclesiastical corporations aggregate, such as the dean and chapter of a cathedral, were also recognized. The ability of the common law creatively to recognize new legal corporations died out long before the rise of religious diversity raised the possibility that there might need to be ecclesiastical corporations other than those of the established church. Unlike their Anglican counterparts, Roman Catholic bishops and non-conforming ministers are not corporations sole.[82] Common law ecclesiastical corporations are a unique feature of establishment, dissolved

---

[76] Salvation Army Act 1931, c xciv; Salvation Army Act 1980, c xxx.
[77] Presbyterian Church of England Act 1960, c xxxii, s 3.
[78] United Reformed Church Act 1972, c xviii, sched 2, pt 1.
[79] Methodist Church Act 1976, c xxx, s 5(2).   [80] Salvation Army Act 1980, c xxx, s 14.
[81] F W Maitland, 'The Corporation Sole' (1900) 16 LQR 335.
[82] *AG v Power* (1809) 1 Ball & B 145, 149; *Kehoe v Marquess of Lansdowne* [1893] AC 451, 457 per Lord Herschell LC.

in their respective countries by the legislation providing for disestablishment in Ireland and Wales.[83]

Corporate personality thus became a privilege only to be granted by the Crown, by royal charter, or letters patent; or by Parliament, by statute, or under a statute. Apart from educational and other charitable bodies, religious associations in the narrow sense have rarely been incorporated by the Crown for fairly obvious reasons of establishment. In the case of the Church of England, one can note a small number of Royal Peculiars and colonial Anglican trusts. The only early example of a non-established church incorporated by Royal Charter appears to be that of the French Protestant Church in London, the superintendent and four pastors of which were incorporated by Edward VI in 1550.[84] Effectively this created them an ecclesiastical corporation aggregate similar to the dean and chapter of a cathedral. It is unique. Royal charters were then used to incorporate the representative bodies of the Church of Ireland and the Church in Wales following their statutory disestablishment.[85] Exceptionally, one was also used under the Irish Presbyterian Church Act 1871, which is perhaps best understood as a vestige of Crown patronage consequent on the abolition of *Regium Donum*.[86] These representative bodies are quite different from the corporations aggregate of ecclesiastical common law, being property-holding companies for their respective churches acting under the direction of synods or assemblies.[87]

The principal advantage of incorporating the trustees of property is that one thereby secures perpetual succession and a common seal by which the company can sue and be sued. The Charitable Trusts Incorporation Act 1872 created a straightforward means of incorporation of charity trustees by registration with the Charity Commissioners.[88] It was not widely used, although some religious charities did use it.[89] The Companies Act 1862 had already enabled the formation by registration of companies limited by guarantee, which had the added advantage of limited liability. This would appear to be the preferred mode of incorporation for church property-holding bodies. Notwithstanding these potential routes, it is not uncommon for the church-related acts of Parliament to incorporate trustees directly.

More hierarchical religions might prefer to incorporate their most senior office-holders as corporations sole. There is no provision of the general law to facilitate this. In fact, as Maitland pointed out, the old ecclesiastical corporation sole is a

---

[83] Religious corporations other than those in the Church of England are to be classified as 'lay' and not 'spiritual', or 'ecclesiastical'. The Local Government Act 1894 contains a rare legal use of 'ecclesiastical' to refer to non-established religious denominations.

[84] *Daugars v Rivaz* (1860) 28 Beav 233, 54 ER 355.

[85] Irish Church Act 1869, s 2; Welsh Church Act 1914, s 3(2).

[86] Irish Presbyterian Church Act 1871, s 13. See also the lengthy preamble to the Act.

[87] Irish Church Act 1869, s 9; Welsh Church Act 1914, s 13(1); Irish Presbyterian Church Act 1871, ss 18, 21, 29, and 30.   [88] See now Charities Act 1993, ss 50–62.

[89] Hubert Picarda, *The Law and Practice relating to Charities*, 3rd edn (London: Butterworths, 1999), 432.

'juristic abortion' since it is not clear that the fictitious personality is truly separate from the real personality of the office-holder.[90] Rather, it is an unsatisfactory device to explain the distinctive nature of church property ownership, conceived as freehold without the power to deal as freeholder, but held for the benefit of successors in office. Thus when the office-holder dies, the freehold goes into abeyance; it does not subsist in the corporation. An ecclesiastical corporation sole also cannot hold chattels and is severely circumscribed in its capacity to contract.[91] It would seem, then, that it is not vicariously liable for the acts of its incumbent, nor could one sue a successor for the acts of a predecessor.

Nevertheless, corporations sole have been widely created by statute in the United States, and used for the purposes of, among others, the Roman Catholic Church.[92] These modern corporations sole are born in full health, with the capacity to sue and be sued, deal with property, enter into contracts, and otherwise perform any other acts incidental to the office they incorporate. There is no reason why these corporations could not employ others, and it is even arguable that they could contract with their incumbent and be liable for their acts, either as principal or vicariously.

In only two cases have English religious denominations sought the form of the corporation sole. The General of the Salvation Army and the Dai al-Mutlak, who is worldwide spiritual leader of the Dawoodi Bohra Muslims, are statutory corporations sole.[93] Statute also partially resolves questions of legal standing that might otherwise affect the capacity of an unincorporated association to sue or be sued: the President of the Methodist Conference for the time being has capacity to represent the Methodist Church in any legal proceedings.[94]

There would appear to be no example in which the entire church is incorporated in a manner akin to a commercial company. Rather, it is simply the property-holding components which are incorporated and as often as not rendered subject to the directions of other church decision-taking bodies. It is worth considering briefly why this is so. In a commercial, or even educational or other charitable context, it is possible to conceive of a basic division between 'the company' and the section of the public it seeks to serve. Of course, the bigger the company, the less likely it will be that all working in it will be partners, directors/trustees, or shareholders/members. But even where there are substantial numbers of employees, the basic division between insiders and the public will be clear. Few religious associations will conceive of themselves in this way. Membership of a religious association is often too fluid to admit of being assimilated to membership of (say)

---

[90] *Op cit* n 81, 354.

[91] *Fulwood's* case, 4 Co Rep 65, 76 ER 1031; *Arundel's* case, Hob 64, 80 ER 212; *Howley v Knight* 14 QB 240.

[92] Paul G Kauper and Stephen C Ellis, 'Religious Corporations and the Law' (1972–3) 71 Mich L Rev 1499; James B O'Hara, 'The Modern Corporation Sole' (1988–9) 93 Dick L Rev 23.

[93] See Salvation Army Act 1980, c xxx, s 4(2) and Dawat-e-Hadiyah Act 1993, c x, ss 2–3.

[94] Methodist Church Act 1976, c xxx, s 21.

a company limited by guarantee, or even the relatively clear and certain status of being a member of a university. On the other hand, it would generally be misleading to incorporate the ministers of religion and some senior lay office-holders, and conceive of them as providing a service to a section of the public. The complexity of incorporation within the Church of England—which is a network of benefices, parochial church councils, bishops, diocesan boards of finance, and much more, bound together by law—provides an obvious example. Although it offers a simplified regulatory regime, one therefore suspects that the new Charitable Incorporated Organization is unlikely to appeal to religious bodies.[95]

In law, a church or religious association is thus a more-or-less complex network of persons, both natural and artificial, fulfilling different and interlocking functions in accordance with the internal rules. The unwillingness to conceive of a networked denomination as enjoying a single legal personality creates difficulties in conceiving of the relationship between ministers and their association as one of bilateral contract.[96] It also makes the attribution of vicarious liability for tortious acts difficult.[97] Whether one sees this as an unjustifiable immunity depends on whether one thinks that the religious body is 'really' a single entity.[98] Tendencies in this direction should be treated with caution: it is at least as legitimate to see the internal arrangements as sufficiently loose to allow one component to disclaim responsibility for the defaults of another, even as we disclaim legal responsibility for each other in civil society more generally. In that respect it is often better to think of larger churches and religious associations as self-governing polities rather than homogeneous organizations.[99]

IV. Members' Rights

Courts are not always clear as to the basis on which members of churches or religious associations have legally enforceable rights. As we have seen, their origins lie in the beneficial interests of a specific congregation. However, where the trustees incorporate, the property is often not held on trust any more, but is owned absolutely by the corporate body for application to its purposes in accordance with the charter or memorandum and articles of association.[100] There will be 'members' of such a company, but they are unlikely to include the vast majority of members

---

[95] Overview and discussion in Stuart R Cross, 'New Legal Forms for Charities in the United Kingdom' [2008] JBL 662.   [96] See discussion in Ch 4 below.

[97] Nafees Meah and Philip Petchey, 'Liability of Churches and Religious Organizations for Sexual Abuse of Children by Ministers of Religion' (2005) 34 CLWR 39.

[98] *Percy v Board of National Mission of the Church of Scotland* [2006] 2 AC 28, contrasting Lord Nicholls at paras 27–8 with Lord Hope at paras 116–18.

[99] See, already, *Free Church of Scotland v Overtoun* [1904] AC 515 per Lord Macnaghten at 634–6 and Lord Lindley at 701–2.

[100] Alternatively, the incorporated body may be custodian trustee acting under the direction of local managing trustees.

of the church or association, in the ordinary sense of the word. The central legal identity of a religious association is therefore likely to be in the contract of association, as it is for any other unincorporated association.

However, as has already been suggested, contract analysis is not universally accepted. First, there is a line of authority which continues to prefer a proprietary, or quasi-proprietary analysis of unincorporated associations. In *Rigby v Connol*, Sir George Jessel MR held that the courts had no jurisdiction to resolve disputes about the rules of voluntary associations in the absence of any property interest.[101] This was later qualified, doubted, and finally abandoned under the influence of Lord Denning.[102] Courts may resolve disputes internal to trade and professional associations on the basis of an implied contract where the dispute affects the ability of an individual to practise his or her trade or profession. Interestingly, the principal authorities Denning relied upon to develop the law were the church cases of *McMillan* and *Forbes v Eden*. But later, even he abandoned implied contract as unnecessarily fictitious and returned to a quasi-proprietary analysis.[103] The conceptual debate rumbles on. In this country, implied contract analysis still tends to be preferred, whereas in Australia, for example, the courts are much more cautious about characterizing the rules of an unincorporated association as contractual.[104]

There are arguments to be made on both sides. The principal difficulty with implied contract analysis is that one must immediately limit its scope: courts will not enforce every rule of an association at the suit of each and every member. There must be some legally cognizable interest at stake. On the other hand, the suggestion that this must be some sort of property interest, let alone a legal or beneficial interest in real property, is too narrow. Indeed, taken to its logical conclusion, it is hard to see why the courts should take any account of the larger associational context in which an incorporated property-holding company is located. Yet there are plenty of cases in which the courts will take account of the context, and will find that legally enforceable rights have been created by the rule-structure of the organization. The agreement between the parties is central to the question of the extent and enjoyment of relevant interests. Cases in which the existence of a contract is denied are better read as cases in which the courts concluded that the alleged right of the member was not legally enforceable.

Even if one is prepared to place the agreement to associate centrally, the second doubt which sometimes leads courts to deny a remedy is whether the parties intended to create legal relations.[105] In practice this usually has to operate by way

---

[101] *Rigby v Connol* (1880) LR 14 ChD 482.
[102] *Abbott v Sullivan* [1952] 1 KB 189; *Lee v Showman's Guild* [1952] 2 QB 329.
[103] *Nagle v Fielden* [1966] QB 633.
[104] Compare *Modahl v British Athletic Federation Ltd (No 2)* [2002] 1 WLR 1192 with *Cameron v Hogan* (1934) 51 CLR 358, the legacy of which lives on in church cases such as *Scandrett v Dowling* (1992) 27 NSWLR 483.
[105] In truth, there are 'too many doctrines chasing a limited number of problems' here: A W B Simpson, 'Innovation in 19th century contract law' (1975) 91 LQR 247, 263.

of presumption, and sometimes courts have presumed that the religious nature of the association means that the rules are not intended to create legal relations. It is certainly the case that a religious association could prevent legal relations from arising by clear and express words. The clearest example of this from the case-law is the Salvation Army in *Rogers v Booth*.[106] But it is far less obvious that courts should presume an absence of intention where legal interests are at stake. There is something ironic about the development of the law here. The need to find a proprietory interest was, in part at least, founded upon a presumption that when people enter into voluntary associations they only intend to create legal rights if property interests are at stake. Having recognized that this test is too narrow, it would be odd to presume an absence of contractual intention to defeat the necessary expansion.[107] The doctrine of intention to create legal relations should only come into play if the parties evince a clear intention that in those cases in which their agreement might be supposed to have a legal effect, it actually has none.[108]

As has already been noted, courts have also on occasions refused to uphold agreements to associate on the grounds that to do so would require them to determine questions that are non-justiciable. The fundamental weakness of justiciability as an explanation of the occasions on which courts will intervene, is that it focuses attention on the wrong question. The real question is not about the categorization of substantive views of individuals and associations, but on the nature of the interest that the individual is seeking to defend. Where that interest is legal ('patrimonial', 'temporal', 'secular', 'material', or 'civil') the courts will protect it and take cognizance of the terms of the agreement to associate in order to protect it. Where it is non-legal ('merely moral', 'religious', 'theological', etc) they will not. The question in each case is whether the interest a claimant is seeking to defend is one the courts will uphold as a legal one.

1. Right to membership

In principle, individuals are free to associate and dissociate with any other persons on the basis of any religion or belief. No-one has the right to join an existing religious association, and, unless there is a rule stating automatic eligibility on fulfilment of certain conditions, a person can be refused membership arbitrarily.[109]

---

[106] *Rogers v Booth* [1937] 2 All ER 751; see also *New Testament Church of God v Stewart* [2008] ICR 282.

[107] Simpson (*op cit* n 105, 265) notes that in the 1882 edition of *Anson on Contract*, the author states that intention may be tested by asking whether it relates to something of value in the eyes of the law. The late nineteenth-century innovation of 'intention to create legal relations' can thus be seen as a transmutation of the cognizable legal interest approach defended here into terms more compatible with a will-theory of contract.

[108] See also Stephen Hedley, 'Keeping Contract in its Place' (1985) 5 OJLS 391, 401. This point is not compatible with his subsequent critique of *Rogers v Booth* at 414.

[109] *Nagle v Fielden* [1966] 2 QB 633; *McInnes v Onslow-Fane* [1978] 1 WLR 1520; *Woodford v Smith* [1970] 1 WLR 806.

A member can resign at any time, even if there is no provision for resignation.[110] Resignation must normally be in compliance with any relevant procedures, but in the case of a religious association courts should not uphold restrictions on resignation other than pure formalities. To do so would be to deny the right to change one's religion or belief. Membership will not lapse unless there is provision for this in the rules,[111] and it cannot be terminated arbitrarily. Courts will review whether an individual has been expelled from a religious community in good faith, according to the rules, and in accordance with the principles of natural justice.[112] It has been held in Canada that even if the expulsion has the effect of completely depriving the individual of all personal property, the courts will uphold the decision of the community.[113] In principle it must be correct that the incidents of membership are determined by the association. However, one wonders whether really drastic material effects would not fall foul of the principle of freedom of religious choice, since this might have the same practical effect as an attempted ban on leaving.

It is not unlawful for an organization relating to religion or belief to restrict membership of the organization with reference to the religion or belief of the applicant so long as this is done by reason of or on the grounds of the purposes of the organization, or with a view to avoiding offence.[114] This exception to general non-discrimination provisions must be read in the light of the fundamental right of each individual to associate and dissociate on religious grounds.[115] It is unlawful for any association with more than 25 members to discriminate on racial grounds in the terms of admission to membership.[116] Since being Jewish or Sikh can be a matter of ethnicity within the scope of the Race Relations Act 1976,[117] such organizations presumably discriminate on such grounds, but may fall within the express exception of section 26 (benefits restricted to members of a particular racial group). In theory, other religious groups might discriminate indirectly on grounds of race. The boundaries between race, ethnicity, and religion are complex in this context. Where the criterion for membership is expressly religious, cases can be found in which the courts may find the discrimination justified,[118] unjustified,[119] or not even within the scope of the Act.[120] The recent decision of the Supreme Court in the *JFS* case lends support to the view that religious tests are only justifiable if they refer to the belief and practice of the individuals concerned.

---

[110] *Finch v Oake* (1896) 1 Ch 409; *Re Sick and Funeral Society of St John's Sunday School, Golcar* [1973] 1 Ch 51.   [111] *Conejera v Webb* [2002] EWHC 1644.

[112] *Dawkins v Antrobus* (1881) 17 ChD 615.

[113] See *Hofer v Hofer* [1970] SCR 958 (Supreme Court of Canada).

[114] Equality Act 2006, s 57.

[115] See, by analogy, *RSPCA v Attorney-General* [2002] 1 WLR 448.

[116] Race Relations Act 1976, s 25.   [117] *Mandla v Dowell Lee* [1983] 2 AC 548.

[118] *Board of Governors of St Matthias CE School v Crizzle* [1993] ICR 401.

[119] *R (E) v JFS Governing Body* [2009] 1 WLR 2353, [2010] 2 WLR 153.

[120] *Seide v Gillette Industries Ltd* [1980] IRLR 427.

In the context of membership, potential pitfalls resulting from the interplay between different protected characteristics should in future be avoidable. The Equality Act 2010 contains harmonized provisions making it unlawful for an association of at least 25 members, admission to which is regulated by the association's rules and includes a process of selection, to discriminate on the grounds of any protected characteristic.[121] It is irrelevant whether the association is incorporated or non-profit-making.[122] However, there is an exception for 'single characteristic associations'.[123] It is not unlawful for an association to restrict membership, along with related access to benefits, facilities, and services, to persons who share a protected characteristic. In spite of the sub-heading, this exception must apply equally to associations which restrict membership on grounds of multiple characteristics.

There would appear to be no basis in law for requiring an amendment of baptismal registers on leaving a Christian church. The register records a matter of historical fact; it does not constitute a current register of members. Whether the church sees continuing significance in the rite is—from a legal perspective—neither here nor there.

2. Right to occupy an office or enjoy a status

In *Forbes v Eden*, Lord Cranworth LC was prepared to accept that the status of ordained clergyman, as opposed to the interest in a salary or occupation of property, was a protectable interest. The principle extends to those taking monastic vows.[124] It is possible that this reflects a slightly broader concept of a patrimonial interest applicable in Scottish law, although in general there is no reason to suppose that Scottish and English law differ in this area as a matter of substance.[125] In *R v Provincial Court of the Church in Wales, ex parte Williams*, the court did not distinguish between the removal of a clergyman from his parish, expulsion from the office of cleric, and deposition from holy orders.[126] Having said that, it is hard to find any authority for the proposition that a religious office-holder other than a minister of religion can sue for wrongful deprivation.[127] It may be that there must be some indirect material advantage connected with the office for the court to interfere. Of course, in the case of specific jobs such as organist, librarian, or secretary there may well be a bilateral contract for services or of service.

---

[121] Equality Act 2010, ss 101–103, 107(2).   [122] Ibid, s 107(4).
[123] Ibid, s 107(9) and sched 16, para 1.   [124] *McDonald v Burns* 1940 SC 376.
[125] But see *Parker's* Case (1610) 2 Brownl & Golds 37, in which a parson deprived of his living by the High Commissioners for drunkenness sought prohibition. This was refused and he was directed to have an action for the tithe 'and upon that the validity of the sentence shall be drawn in question'.
[126] *R v Provincial Court of the Church in Wales, ex parte Williams*, unreported, 23 October 1998.   [127] But *Hothi v Khella*, unreported, 10 May 1999, could be construed as such a case.

It has been held that the question whether a person is a bishop of a non-established church is non-justiciable in the context of a defamation action turning on this question.[128] This cannot apply as a general rule. A Roman Catholic bishop deprived of his office in breach of canon law could surely seek a legal remedy, and the court would easily be able to tell whether he was, or was not, a bishop.

3. Right to secure proper application of property

Even in cases where there is no beneficial interest, members of unincorporated associations have the right to ensure that property is not applied *ultra vires*.[129] Members of churches and religious associations also have the right to secure the proper application of property held for the benefit of their church.[130] This applies regardless of whether the property is held on trust or immediately by an incorporated body within the organization.

4. Right to prevent departure from fundamental doctrine

Most of the cases concerning departure from fundamental doctrine concern property disputes on schism, but in *Re Methodist Church Union Act 1929*,[131] Megarry J was asked to rule on whether it was within the powers of the Methodist Conference, as set out in the Methodist Church Union Act 1929 and the Deed of Union 1932, to agree to inaugurate the first stage of a proposed union between that church and the Church of England. A minister of the church and others objected that this would involve a change in the doctrinal standards of the church, which was beyond the powers of the Conference. Megarry J held that the union was within the powers of the Conference, since it involved only the interpretation of doctrine, over which the Conference had a final power of decision. If it had been *ultra vires*, the union would have required a new Act of Parliament. At no point was it argued or even considered that the plaintiffs had no legally enforceable interest to ensure compliance with the constitution. The old law giving members the right to prevent a departure from fundamental doctrine would therefore seem to be still good.

5. Right to rites

Members may have an enforceable right to the rites of their religion. This derives from the intriguing case of *Brown v Curé de Montreal*.[132] Brown belonged to an

---

[128] *Blake v Associated Newspapers Ltd* [2003] EWHC 1960.

[129] *Baker v Jones* [1954] 1 WLR 1005.

[130] *The Bahamas District of the Methodist Church in the Caribbean and the Americas v The Hon Vernon J Symonette*, Privy Council (unreported), 26 July 2000 (Lord Nicholls).

[131] *Re Methodist Church Union Act 1929, Barker v O'Gorman* [1971] Ch 215.

[132] *Dame Hanriette Brown v Les Curés et Marguilliers de l'Oeuvre et Fabrique de Notre Dame de Montreal* (1874–5) LR 6 PC 157.

organization called the Canadian Institute which had incurred the displeasure of the Roman Catholic Church since its library contained books on the Index. He was refused communion, but never formally excommunicated by name. On his death, burial was refused in the main part of the burial ground; instead his widow was only offered a place without rites in the smaller separate part reserved for unbaptized infants, suicides, and murderers. Sir Robert Phillimore, in giving the advice of the Privy Council, held that

> even if this Church were to be regarded merely as a private and voluntary religious society resting only upon a consensual basis, Courts of Justice are still bound, when due complaint is made that a member of the society has been injured as to his rights, in any matter of a mixed spiritual and temporal matter, to inquire into the laws or rules of the tribunal or authority which has inflicted the alleged injury.[133]

After citing with approval the statement of the legal status of the Anglican Church in the colonies contained in *Long v Bishop of Capetown*, he continued:

> Their Lordships are disposed to concur…in the opinion expressed by Mr. Justice Berthelot as to the mixed character of these questions: '…Le baptême, le mariage et la sépulture sont de matière mixte, et les ecclésiastiques ne peuvent se refuser de les administrer à ceux de leur paroissiens qui y ont droit…'[134]

The case was made easier by the fact that there was no formal act of excommunication, the validity of which the judicial committee might have to inquire into; nor had the plaintiff's representatives requested that he be buried with certain rites; instead the committee simply expressed its hope that the parties would come to an agreement as to the ceremonies necessary for burial in the larger part of the cemetery. However, Sir Robert Phillimore was effectively prepared to equate the rights of members of religious associations to those of parishioners of the established church, who are generally taken to have legal rights (subject to certain constraints) to be baptized, married, and buried in their parish church.[135] Of course, the key word here is 'right'. The mere fact that a minister of religion is empowered to conduct marriages with civil effect does not itself mean that members of his church have the right to demand that he perform that service. However, in an appropriate case, where the rules of the association or established practice indicate an expectation that such services will be provided, the case is at least persuasive authority for the view that they are legally enforceable.

6. Right to procedural propriety

Inevitably, the question of whether a person has properly been deprived of a substantive interest will raise questions of internal procedure. As we have

---

[133] Ibid, 207–8   [134] Ibid, 209.
[135] Norman Doe, *The Legal Framework of the Church of England* (Oxford: Clarendon Press, 1996), 226–7.

seen, the early cases saw courts defending the rights of members to vote on the appointment of a minister. In general, however, procedural propriety on the part of other members, officers, and committees is not a legally protected interest as such.[136]

In *Motlib v Latif*, the plaintiff sought orders that an association (the Masjid-E-Noor Mosque Association) should be administered according to its constitution.[137] The defendants had registered a constitution with the Charity Commissioners, and the association had been granted charitable status. Nevertheless, they then tried to argue that the association did not actually exist and was merely a sham. The case was further complicated by the fact that the plaintiff sought to bring his action in the name of a non-existent organization, the Masjid-E-Noor Defence Committee. Nevertheless, the judge at first instance held that the plaintiff had sufficient standing in his personal capacity as someone eligible for membership under the registered constitution. The Court of Appeal upheld the orders granted by the judge.[138]

In *Hothi v Khella*, the parties were all members of the Guru Nanak Durbar Association, which managed a Sikh temple in Kent.[139] The plaintiffs sought a declaration that Hothi had been validly elected president and that the constitution of the association had been validly amended. They also sought an injunction preventing the defendant trustees from acting otherwise than on their instructions. The action was dismissed on trial, first on the grounds of lack of jurisdiction (which the Court of Appeal doubted) and secondly on the grounds that the constitution had not been validly amended, since not all members of the association had agreed, and that there was no power to amend the old constitution otherwise than by unanimous consent of the members. The case is not clear authority for the proposition that a pure procedural interest will suffice, since the ultimate reason for the action could be taken to be a power to direct trustees of property. However, that power would only have been exercisable by the executive committee as a whole, of which the two plaintiffs formed only a small part. Again, one could surmise that the interest was that in being a certain office-holder (president and executive committee member respectively). Or one could take the view that the court was upholding a qua-member interest in the enforcement of the proper processes for the amendment of the constitution.

The better view is thus that members have a legally enforceable right to enjoy whatever mode of participation is held out to them by the association of which they are a member. This will extend to constitutional changes, in the absence of a process for amendment which excludes them, in which case they have no legally recognized interest.

---

[136] See also the final section below.   [137] CA, unreported, 3 November 1992.
[138] See also *R v Imam of Bury Park Jame Masjid, ex parte Ali* [1992] COD 132.
[139] CA, unreported, 10 May 1999.

V. Religious Property and the Problem of Schism

Property disputes provide the paradigmatic case for the involvement of secular courts in the internal affairs of religious bodies to prevent injustice. The basis on which secular courts resolve such disputes has been a matter of considerable debate in the United States, in the course of which three basic positions have emerged.[140] The historic position is the 'departure-from-doctrine' principle, which awards property to those who have maintained the original doctrines of the church. This was disapproved by the Supreme Court in *Watson v Jones* (1872) in favour of a 'deference-to-polity' approach.[141] Under this approach, the court identifies the location of decision-taking authority within the church—in the case the court distinguished congregational and hierarchical polities—and defers to the wishes of the appropriate authority. Then in two further cases, the Supreme Court ruled departure-from-doctrine completely unconstitutional, since it requires secular Governmental bodies (courts) to determine religious doctrinal disputes in breach of the First Amendment, and made a call for such disputes to be resolved by 'neutral principles', ie those that would be applied to non-religious organizations as well.[142] State practice varies between deference-to-polity and more or less strict adherence to 'neutral principles'.

It is important to note the real target of the 'neutral principles' approach. It is the application of implied trust doctrine to regulate the use to which church property is put. The argument is that implied trust doctrine arose at a time when corporate structures were not readily available to ensure that property was preserved indefinitely for the purposes of the religion. It does not fit into standard trust analysis of express, resulting, or constructive trusts, making it unique to religious property disputes. It thus represents an inappropriate entanglement of the State with religion, and a favouring of one party against another.[143]

English law has seen the same debate about the proper approach of courts to property disputes. However, as regards English law, there is an important distinction within the departure-from-doctrine approach. The strong version always prefers the party which maintains the historic position of the church or religious association. The weak version allows the organization to act as a polity, but only within the doctrinal limits which are fundamental or constitutive of its identity. This weak version accepts that there are doctrinal matters which are secondary from a constitutional perspective, and about which the church may move between positions of disapproval, comprehension, or positive approbation.

---

[140] H Reese Hansen, 'Religious Organizations and the Law of Trusts'; Patty Gerstenblith, 'Civil Court Resolution of Property Disputes among Religious Organizations', both in James A Serritella *et al* (eds), *Religious Organizations in the United States* (Durham: Carolina Academic Press, 2006).

[141] *Watson v Jones* (1872) 80 US 679.

[142] *United States v Mary Elizabeth Blue Hull Memorial Presbyterian Church* (1969) 393 US 440; *Jones v Wolf* (1979) 443 US 595.   [143] Gerstenblith, *op cit* n 140, 333.

As we have seen, there is clear support for the weak version in the case-law prior to 1869. The question is whether subsequent cases, and in particular the leading case of *Free Church of Scotland v Overtoun*,[144] change anything. In that case a small minority of the Free Church of Scotland opposed the union in 1900 with the United Presbyterian Church to form the United Free Church of Scotland. The minority claimed that the money raised for the Free Church on the schism within the Church of Scotland in 1843 was held on trust for them, as the true successors to the Free Church, rather than for the new United Free Church. And the House of Lords, by a majority, agreed. The problem was that the money was held on very simple terms—essentially 'for the Free Church of Scotland'—so it became necessary to determine what that church was. A majority of the House held that 'the identity of a religious community described as a Church must consist in the unity of its doctrines'.[145] Since the majority of the church had departed slightly from its original doctrines to effect the union of 1900, but the minority maintained the doctrines of 1843 in their unsullied purity, the money had to be held on trust for the minority.

The central difficulty is to establish what divided the majority from the minority of the House of Lords. Not surprisingly, the judgments contain a range of formulations. However, on one point all their lordships were agreed: there is a distinction between fundamental matters and matters susceptible of change by the General Assembly. As regards the majority, the Earl of Halsbury's judgment is most unsatisfactory in that he simply rebutted the argument that a General Assembly has full power to change any of the church's doctrines with a reassertion of the principle of trusts law that property must not be diverted from its proper purpose. This assumes, rather than argues, that the purpose of the trust is defined by all the doctrines maintained by the founder. By contrast, Lord Davey argued expressly that there was no test to determine which tenets were fundamental and which not, so in the absence of any express declaration or power to change, one should assume that every tenet held by the founder is fundamental. Lords James, Robertson, and Alverstone argued that, as a matter of fact, the founders of the Free Church in 1843 did regard the relevant point of doctrine as foundational.[146] As regards the minority, Lords MacNaghten and Lindley were highly critical of an approach that effectively forced the church to subordinate Scripture to the Westminster confession of faith. Lord MacNaghten argued that the polity the Free Church adopted on its formation in 1843 included the right of the General Assembly to reformulate the formal expression of its doctrine. Indeed, in what was at times a passionate judgment, he was critical of an approach which treated Dr Chalmers' address preached before the First Free Church Assembly as 'a sort

---

[144] *Free Church of Scotland v Overtoun* [1904] AC 515. See the discussion by Frank Cranmer, 'Christian Doctrine and Judicial Review: the Free Church Case revisited' in (2002) 6 Ecc LJ 318.

[145] Lord Halsbury LC at 612.

[146] The relevant point of doctrine was an arguably quixotic commitment to the ideal of an established church.

of prospectus on the faith of which the fund of the Free Church was collected, as if the Free Church were a joint stock concern, and that sermon an invitation to the public to put their money in it'.[147] 'A sect could make any point or punctilio however absurd an article of faith',[148] but this church had not. Lord Lindley recognized the difficulty of drawing a line between fundamental and non-essential matters. The church had to remain Christian, Protestant, Reformed, and probably Presbyterian, but apart from that

[a] trust for the Free Church is in my opinion a trust for such persons as shall hold the doctrine and submit in ecclesiastical matters to the government and discipline adopted by the Founders of the Free Church, with such modifications as may be made from time to time by the General Assembly of that church … [149]

Thus it is not an adequate analysis of *Overtoun* to suggest that the majority adopted a departure-from-doctrine test while the minority adopted deference-to-polity. Only Lord Davey, and possibly the Earl of Halsbury, supported a strong departure-from-doctrine test which always prefers the doctrinally more conservative party. None of their lordships accepted a full deference-to-polity test, which would allow a church a right to total change. Rather the case stands for the proposition that deference-to-polity is limited by the need to uphold fundamental and essential principles, as determined by the intentions of the founders. What made the case so difficult—and what their lordships divided on—is that it is not at all clear how the founders put together their motivation for secession in 1843 with their commitment to a form of church polity which would have given that motivation only a subordinate position in the doctrines of their church.

Scottish cases subsequent to *Overtoun* have stressed that what is at stake is whether the doctrine in question amounts to one of the 'essential and distinguishing tenets' of the church.[150] In 2005 the Outer House of the Court of Session found that an alleged 'continuing right of protest' by a minority against the decision of the General Assembly of the Free Church of Scotland to close the file on allegations of sexual abuse against a professor at its training college was not such a fundamental constitutional principle.[151] The seceders thus had no interest in the property of the church.

The immediate practical effect of *Overtoun* was highly problematic. It vested substantial amounts of property in a very small group of persons who had no practical use for endowments of that size, let alone the capacity to administer them. The decision was therefore reversed by the Churches (Scotland) Act 1905 which empowered commissioners to distribute the property among the parties.

---

[147] Ibid, 634.   [148] Ibid, 636.   [149] Ibid, 701.

[150] *Mackay v Macleod*, unreported, 10 January 1952; See also *Brentnall v Free Presbyterian Church of Scotland* 1986 SLT 471.

[151] *General Assembly of the Free Church of Scotland (Continuing) v General Assembly of the Free Church of Scotland* 2005 SLT 348; Gordon Junor, 'Church heritage—law and religion' [2008] SLT 167.

The distribution was required to be 'fair and equitable having regard to all the circumstances' subject to the principles that congregational property was to go to any congregation in which at least one third adhered to the minority Free Church, and adequate provision was to be made for the education, stipends and pensions, administration, and management of that church.[152]

Modern schisms within the jurisdiction of English courts are likely now to give rise to the application of the expanded *cy-près* jurisdiction which has been available since 1960.[153] This gives the court considerable discretion in redistributing charitable assets. Until *cy-près* was liberalized the circumstances of its use were rare.[154] The case of *Varsani v Jesani* concerned a schism among a group of Hindus involving a Hindu temple; the Court of Appeal thought that the problems raised by *Overtoun* had thereby been resolved.[155] The court is no longer obliged to institute an inquiry into the precise limits of the purpose of a charity before redistributing the assets. However, the idea that a free-wheeling jurisdiction to redistribute trust funds on schism avoids theological disputes is mistaken. In order to redistribute *cy-près*, the court must (on one alternative) be satisfied that there is 'no longer a suitable and effective method of using the property available by virtue of the gift, regard being had to the spirit of the gift'.[156] This implies (at least) that neither of the schismatic groups is clearly the successor to the original body of worshippers; but this, too, is a doctrinal judgment, albeit perhaps an easier one than the judgment as to which of the groups is the successor. The danger of proportionate redistribution while apparently avoiding any doctrinal judgment at all is that of unfairness in favour of a faction which may genuinely have split away and wants to take with it whatever property it can get its hands on.

The Privy Council has recently had to consider the constitutionality of a statutory scheme consequent on a schism within the Methodist Church in the Bahamas.[157] A majority wished what was hitherto the Bahamas District of the Caribbean Church to become autonomous. The statute allowed for individual congregations to be non-participating, but with the title still vesting in the new body, and rather unclear compensation provisions. The Privy Council held that the constitutional protection of property applied to the 'real and legitimate interest' that members have in seeing church property correctly applied. The legislature had to make a 'genuine attempt' to divide the property in a 'fair and reasonable manner'. The absence of sufficiently certain factual background meant that the court could only indicate the relevant factors. A simple division whereby each congregation got its own church building was not bound to achieve overall fairness.

---

[152] Churches (Scotland) Act 1905, s 1(1)–(3).   [153] See, now, Charities Act 1993, s 13.

[154] For the old approach, see *AG v Bunce* (1868) LR 6 Eq 563 (trust for 'presbyterians' applicable to long-standing Baptist congregation, not newly formed 'strict presbyterian' splinter group.)

[155] *Varsani v Jesani* [1999] Ch 219.   [156] s 13(1)(e)(iii).

[157] *The Bahamas District of the Methodist Church in the Caribbean and the Americas v The Hon Vernon J Symonette*, Privy Council, unreported, 26 July 2000.

Factors such as geographical distribution, the comparative wealth and size and financial needs of individual churches, and their relative importance in the historic traditions of Methodism might call from departures from this simple basis or, at the least, provision for compensation.[158]

Whether one solves problems of schism by reference to a reworking of implied trust doctrines,[159] statutory apportionment, or an expanded *cy-près* jurisdiction, one is still left with the basic problem of how to deal justly between the parties. Recent cases show a tendency towards proportionate distribution in the name of a deliberate agnosticism by the court as to the respective religious credentials of the competing parties.[160] But proportionate distribution is only fair if the parties are indistinguishable. It is unfair on the majority if they were acting in accordance with the decision-taking powers of a properly constituted organization. And it is a fraud on the minority if the majority are seeking to turn that organization into something fundamentally different. Since people join churches and religious associations in exercise of their rights to manifest their religious convictions in worship, teaching, practice, and observance, an inquiry into what they could plausibly have supposed the association was basically committed to in that respect seems unavoidable. Neutrality cannot mean total blindness to religious and organizational standards which the participants consider fundamental.

VI. Religious Courts, Natural Justice, and Judicial Review

Many religions have courts for the formal determination of disputes. In the case of Christian denominations these are typically internal to a specific church and rather narrowly focused on questions of doctrine, liturgy, and discipline. In the case of Islam and Judaism they can function more broadly as community courts resolving a range of disputes from questions of status and diet, through matters of family and inheritance law, to commercial litigation.[161] The distinction should not be overstated; it was only comparatively recently that ecclesiastical courts finally lost their jurisdiction in marriage and divorce, testamentary, and defamation cases. Other religious minorities tend to manifest themselves in less legalistic forms, at least in this country, if not abroad.

The hostile public reaction to the Archbishop of Canterbury's suggestion that Islamic courts might have a larger role to play in the English legal system exposed

---

[158] *Op cit.*

[159] It is possible that the judgment in the recent case of *Dean v Burne* [2009] EWHC 1250 (Ch) displays a new preference for 'neutral principles' over an inquiry into decision-taking authority within the Russian Orthodox Church.   [160] See *Varsani v Jesani* [2002] 1 P & CR DG11.

[161] While Jewish courts are well established, Islamic Sharia councils are still embryonic from a legal point of view. See Samia Bano, 'In pursuit of Religious and Legal Diversity: A Response to the Archbishop of Canterbury and the "Sharia Debate" in Britain' (2008) 10 Ecc LJ 283; Polly Botsford, 'Sharia Unveiled' (2008) 105 LSG 16.

considerable levels of ignorance about the current law.[162] The decisions of religious courts already acquire legal significance in a variety of ways. Obviously, where the court is internal to a church or religious association its decision may be binding on members according to the contract of association and may be relevant to the determination and protection of legal interests. The other main situation arises where the parties have entered into a contract of arbitration under the Arbitration Act 1996. It is by this means that the London *Beth Din* and other Jewish and Islamic courts have the power to give legally enforceable judgments in commercial and inheritance matters. Some subsidiary routes by which the judgments of religious courts gain legal significance are also worth noting. At common law, parties resident in this country, but domiciled in a foreign State which recognized the judgments of religious courts, could secure legally effective divorces through religious courts located in this country.[163] That power was removed by statute in 1973,[164] but the misalignment of civil and religious divorce continued to create difficulties, principally for wives who were divorced as a matter of civil law, but not according to their religion. It is now clear that civil courts have the power to delay the grant of a decree absolute until the husband has secured a *talaq* or *get* in religious proceedings.[165] Determinations of personal status or compliance with religious law can also have an indirect effect on legal rights, as for example where the admissions arrangements of maintained faith schools depend on an exercise of religious certification or judgment.[166] Finally, in rare cases religious courts exercise public regulatory functions and do so under the oversight of the High Court by way of judicial review.[167]

Agreements to arbitrate must be expressed in writing by the parties.[168] A religious court may have a standard form of arbitration agreement which sets out the law to be applied. While the agreement itself must be governed by some system of national law, assumed in this country to be English law unless otherwise expressed,[169] the substantive and procedural law to be applied by the arbitrator can be a body of religious law.[170] In the past it was arguable that arbitrators were restricted to applying a fixed and settled system of law, and thus it was possible that Jewish or Islamic law might not be applicable since they are better seen

---

[162] Rowan Williams, 'Civil and Religious Law in England: a Religious Perspective' (2008) 10 Ecc LJ 262. For responses, see Bano, *op cit* n 161; Adam Tucker, 'The Archbishop's unsatisfactory legal pluralism' [2008] PL 463.   [163] *Qureshi v Qureshi* [1972] Fam 173.
[164] Domicile and Matrimonial Proceedings Act 1973, s 16; *Chaudhary v Chaudhary* [1985] Fam 19.
[165] *O v O* [2000] 2 FLR 147; Family Law Act 1996, s 9(3) and (4); Matrimonial Causes Act 1973, s 10A inserted by the Divorce (Religious Marriages) Act 2002. See, further, Ch 6 below.
[166] *R (E) v JFS Governing Body* [2009] 1 WLR 2353.
[167] See *R v Rabbinical Commission, ex parte Cohen* (unreported, 12 December 1987) concerning the licensing of *shochetim*.
[168] Arbitration Act 1996, s 5. A mere reference to a power on executors to refer a question to the Islamic Sharia Council is not adequate to bind potential beneficiaries: *Al-Midani v Al-Midani* [1999] 1 Lloyd's Rep 923.   [169] Arbitration Act 1996, s 2(1).
[170] *Halpern v Halpern* [2008] QB 195.

as legal traditions rather than systems.[171] The Arbitration Act 1996 now makes clear that parties can agree to have their dispute settled by reference to considerations other than the rules of a national legal system.[172] This clearly includes a body of religious law.

There is a general duty on arbitrators to act fairly and impartially and to avoid unnecessary delay or expense.[173] It is the principles of natural justice that apply, not their instantiation in the rules of typical common law adversarial proceedings.[174] Civil courts will not enforce arbitral awards contrary to public policy,[175] and this has created difficulties where Jewish law has differed from English law as regards the vexed problem of the enforcement of contracts for an unlawful purpose.[176] But in general terms the requirements of procedural fairness and the public policy filter do not seem to have created difficulties in practice.

However, two limitations on the use of arbitration are relevant. One is the extent of arbitrability. English courts have not had much occasion to consider the precise limits of arbitrability.[177] Individual rights of contract and property are clearly within the private disposition of parties. If the potential beneficiaries under a disputed will wish to arbitrate, they are free to do so. At the other extreme, criminal cases are clearly not arbitrable. Nor can one arbitrate cases involving the public interest (eg welfare of children) or personal status (paternity, legitimacy, marriage, divorce, etc). For practical purposes this means that most family disputes cannot be arbitrated.

However, as a general principle, family law is highly dependent on the cooperation of the parties, and domestic living arrangements are largely designed by the individuals concerned responding to the various social and economic pressures upon them. This is patently the case in arrangements made after separation and divorce, in which the court in practice encourages the parties to settle their dispute and then approves their agreement. There is nothing to stop the parties seeking informal mediation and bringing the mediator's solution to the court as their own. So long as it is not patently unreasonable, the court is likely to 'rubber stamp' it. Thus, even if not acting under a formal arbitration agreement, religious courts may still function as mediators producing court-approved settlements.[178] In the light of this reality, there would seem to be scope for clarifying the precise

---

[171] See discussion in Hong-lin Yu, 'Section 46(1)(b) of the English Arbitration Act 1996: its past and future' [1999] Int ALR 43.   [172] s 46(1)(b).

[173] s 33.

[174] John Tackaberry and Arthur Marriott *et al*, *Bernstein on Arbitration*, 4th edn (London: Sweet & Maxwell, 2003), para 2–415.   [175] s 68(2)(g).

[176] *Soleimany v Soleimany* [1999] QB 785. This—and another decision on illegality (*Westacre Investments Inc v Jugoimport SPDR Holding Co Ltd* [2000] QB 288) tending the opposite way—has spawned a considerable literature.

[177] David St John Sutton *et al*, *Russell on Arbitration*, 23rd edn (London: Sweet & Maxwell, 2007), para 1–033.

[178] The Islamic Sharia Council was founded in 1982 and has considered over 7,000 cases to date, most of them involving marriage breakdown. Its work thus falls into the category of mediation, not binding arbitration.

extent of arbitrability for religious minorities particularly in matters of family law and family property.

The other limitation is the requirement of party consent.[179] Conceived of as community courts, this is indeed odd, and some within religious minorities might wish to dispense with the requirement. But to do so would not only contravene the fundamental principle of English law that religious adherence is voluntary, and the requirement of the rule of law that there be one court system for all people; it would also create new problems of defining the personal scope of the coercive jurisdiction of such courts. Needless to say, there is considerable opposition to any suggestion that religious courts should enjoy a criminal jurisdiction.[180]

Apart from emerging debates about the extent of arbitration, there is ongoing uncertainty about the most appropriate procedural route for the civil courts to exercise oversight over religious courts. Within the Church of England, ecclesiastical courts are inferior courts of law, subject historically to the availability of the prerogative writs,[181] and still ultimately subject to the control of the High Court by way of judicial review.[182] It is generally assumed that this is a unique feature of establishment, but common law jurisdictions are not uniform in their approach to this problem. In *The State (Colquhoun) v D'Arcy*,[183] Hanna J held that prohibition did not lie against the Court of the General Synod of the Church of Ireland, since its jurisdiction was consensual and not statutory. On the other hand, one could envisage a broader notion of public interest which embraces certain non-Governmental purposes. In Canada, judicial review has been accepted as a legitimate way of regulating church courts. This was justified in the case of *Lindenburger v United Church of Canada* by reference to the fact that the church in question was 'a creature of statute' and that 'it minister[ed] to the spiritual needs of a large segment of the Canadian public'.[184] As to the first argument, while it is true that many non-established churches in England also have a statutory basis to their constitution, the statute does not create mutual rights and obligations in public law but on the basis of an assumed contract between members. The rights might be created by statute, but they are not 'statutory rights'.[185] As to the second, it depends on whether one sees the purpose of judicial review procedure to be more narrowly Governmental or more broadly public.

---

[179] This does not mean that arbitral awards are completely incapable of producing rights *in rem*: *Kastner v Jason* [2005] 1 Lloyd's Rep 397, per Rix LJ.

[180] Lord Phillips of Worth Matravers, 'Equality before the Law' [2008] Law & Justice 75; Adam Tucker, 'The Archbishop's unsatisfactory legal pluralism' [2008] PL 463.

[181] *R v Tristram* [1902] 1 KB 816; see the summary in Doe, *op cit* n 135, 149–50.

[182] *R v Archbishop of Canterbury, ex parte Williamson*, unreported, 10 March 1994; *R v Bishop of Stafford, ex parte Owen* [2001] ACD 14; *R (Gibbs) v Bishop of Manchester* [2007] EWHC 480 (Admin).   [183] *The State (Colquhoun) v D'Arcy* [1936] IR 641.

[184] *Lindenburger v United Church of Canada* (1985) 17 CCEL 143, 153.

[185] See, by analogy, *Roy v Kensington and Chelsea and Westminster Family Practitioner Committee* [1992] 1 AC 624.

English courts have resisted the extension of judicial review as a way of controlling domestic religious tribunals. In *R v Chief Rabbi, ex parte Wachmann*,[186] Simon Brown J (as he then was) had to consider whether to grant judicial review of the Chief Rabbi's decision that Wachmann was no longer morally and religiously fit to hold rabbinical office. He was invited to reject the application on three grounds, two of which he followed. He did not follow the argument that submission was consensual in any relevant sense. It was no more consensual than the submission of 'members of the Bar or members of a university'. But, first, there had to be 'not merely a public but potentially a Governmental interest'[187] and secondly, 'the court is hardly in a position to regulate what is essentially a religious function'.[188]

The first argument was disposed of too quickly. Submission to the jurisdiction of a domestic tribunal is only conditionally coercive. If one wishes to become or remain a member of the association, one must be prepared to abide by its rules and the decision-taking power of any of its tribunals. This is, of course, true of the Bar or a university as well. The difference is that there is a public interest in ensuring that access to these institutions is freely available to all suitably qualified members of the public. There is no equivalent public interest in the case of religious bodies. Thus submission to the jurisdiction of a religious court is indeed consensual in the sense that one is free to join and leave the religious body, and the State has no interest in ensuring that the conditions of joining are reasonable for all people.

The second argument depends on whether judicial review has a broader public role. Writing extra-judicially in 1992, Lord Woolf suggested that judicial review should develop to provide a remedy of last resort for anyone caused material prejudice by the unlawful exercise of authority: 'Why should a policeman be in a better position than a sportsman or a minister of religion?'[189] This argument presupposes that there are particular advantages from the perspective of procedural justice for making judicial review more widely available.

Judicial review is obviously less attractive to a potential litigant in respect of the time available to bring the action and the need for permission. Available remedies may also be less suitable, in that courts might prefer to grant damages rather than interfere with the internal workings of an organized religion by insisting on reconsideration or reinstatement.[190] On the other hand, judicial review procedure is generally quicker and cheaper than proceeding by claim. The two key substantive questions are, first, whether the range of interests deemed legally protectable by way of judicial review is broader than those enforceable under the agreement to associate, and, secondly, whether the ability of the court to imply

---

[186] *R v Chief Rabbi, ex parte Wachmann* [1992] 1 WLR 1036.   [187] Ibid, 1041.
[188] Ibid, 1042.
[189] Lord Woolf, 'Judicial Review: A Possible Programme for Reform' [1992] PL 211, 235.
[190] See *Lindenburger v United Church of Canada*, n 184 above.

standards of fairness into the relationship is more extensive than it would be were it construing the contract of association.

In the light of the relatively broad view of members' legal interests set out in the earlier part of this chapter it is suggested that the restrictive view of the availability of judicial review poses no significant practical obstacle to the redress of grievance. For example, it has been suggested that judicial review might also be available for breach of charter or constitution.[191] However, in *R v Imam of Bury Park Jame Masjid, ex parte Ali* a judge of the Chancery Division issued injunctions restraining unconstitutional practice by the executive committee of the mosque in question.[192] The Court of Appeal recognized that there was an effective remedy for alleged bias on the part of the Imam in drawing up a new list of voters, namely an appeal from the decision of the judge. Judicial review is not necessary in this context either.

It is suggested that this contractual route would have been the proper approach in *R v London Beth Din, ex parte Bloom*.[193] Bloom had had his *kashrut* licence withdrawn on account of the presence in his restaurant of non-kosher meat. The President of the court withdrawing his licence had known of the admission by an employee that the matter was entirely the fault of that employee, but he had not apprised Bloom of the fact, on account of an obligation of confidentiality. When Bloom later became aware of this key piece of evidence, he sought judicial review of the court's refusal to reconstitute itself without the judge in question. On the facts, Lightman J did not consider there to have been a breach of natural justice warranting his intervention, but if there had been it is suggested that the proper way to frame the action would have been to argue that the possession of a *kashrut* licence is a legally cognizable interest, in that it entitles one to sell food to a sector of the public who would not otherwise buy it. This has a commercial value. The licence may therefore only be withdrawn in accordance with the rules of the association providing it and subject to the principles of natural justice. A remedy could have been sought by private claim against the religious court.

All the recent judicial review cases involving religious courts and officers have effectively sought to argue that the procedures adopted were in some way unfair to the claimant. Even if commenced by claim, this raises the question of the relationship between religious law and the internal rules of religious associations on one hand and common law standards of natural justice and reasonableness on the other. Tensions arise particularly in the case of inquisitorial modes of procedure, whereby a senior office-holder has both a duty to inquire and a duty to decide. Other problems can involve the admissibility of evidence or rights of appeal. The third ground offered by Simon Brown J for rejecting Wachmann's application for judicial review was that courts of law are not competent to regulate religious

---

[191] *R v London Beth Din, ex parte Bloom* [1998] COD 131, per Lightman J.
[192] *R v Imam of Bury Park Jame Masjid, ex parte Ali* [1992] COD 132.
[193] *R v London Beth Din, ex parte Bloom* [1998] COD 131.

functions. If correct, this argument applies as much to the implication of standards of procedural propriety into the rules of religious associations, as it does to the enforcement of such standards by way of judicial review. But complete judicial abstention on these grounds is unpersuasive.

It is true that the older cases betray a certain ambiguity as to the extent to which a secular court can impose its own procedural standards on the behaviour of a religious domestic tribunal. The rules of natural justice could be seen as a supplement to the procedural rules of the association, or as an essential requirement.[194] In *Lee v Showman's Guild of Great Britain*, the Court of Appeal clearly preferred the latter position, with Denning LJ (as he then was) expressing the position with particular force.[195] Domestic tribunals must observe the requirements of natural justice, and members of associations cannot by consent oust the jurisdiction of the courts to determine questions of law. The case arose in the context of a trade association, and can only be applied to religious associations if the robust views of the court are glossed in two respects. First, some religious bodies take exception to the determination of disputes by secular courts. It must therefore be open to the parties to make clear their intention not to create any legally binding relationship,[196] or to subject their invocation of the civil courts' powers to a formal religious consent.[197] Secondly, all domestic bodies have some discretion as to how they frame their internal procedures. This is particularly so in the case of religious bodies which may be acting in the light of a long and complex tradition of religious law. Just as the general principles of arbitration law allow flexibility in the expression of fairness and impartiality, the question is not whether the procedures adopted were the most fair or in accord with those rules that would apply in the context of a secular common law court, but whether the procedure adopted was fundamentally objectionable. The requirements of article 6 ECHR may provide some guidance here, although they do not apply directly.[198] Secular courts should recognize a reasonable pluralism of fair internal procedures.

Ultimately, the procedural route by which secular courts oversee the determinations of religious courts should not make any difference to the extent of their oversight.[199] This oversight depends on the interplay of substantive principles of the protection of legal interests and the requirements of natural justice along with a respect for collective religious autonomy and non-competence in questions of

---

[194] Both positions are stated by Lord Kingsdown in *Long v Bishop of Cape Town* (1863) 1 Moo PC NS 411.   [195] [1952] 2 QB 329.

[196] *Rogers v Booth* [1937] 2 All ER 751.

[197] As is the case with *Beth Din* arbitration agreements.

[198] Domestic religious tribunals are not courts or tribunals for the purposes of Human Rights Act 1998, s 6(3)(a).

[199] In *R v Provincial Court of the Church in Wales, ex parte Williams*, unreported, 23 October 1998, Latham J was therefore correct in permitting Williams to abandon his claim by way of judicial review and continue it as if commenced by writ, and correct to apply the same standards of natural justice by way of implied term in the contract of association.

religious law. The distinction between private claim and judicial review should be one of convenience only.

VII. Conclusion

It will have become apparent from this chapter that it is not easy to state the legal constitution of non-established churches and other religious bodies with full accuracy and confidence. In deciding what legal significance to accord to various aspects of the collective life of an organized religion, courts have struggled with the tensions inherent in upholding the rule of law, preserving the autonomy of religious groups and maintaining neutrality while doing so. Authority after 1869 is relatively sparse, and it is not entirely clear to what extent principles laid down during the nineteenth century still hold good.

However, it is suggested that the weight of authority in English law lies with an approach which sees the constitution of a religious body as fundamentally contractual in nature, even where there is some statutory underpinning. The contract of association binds together natural and any corporate persons, as well as trustees holding property for the organization. Religious law can thus become private law. However, the contract is only enforceable on the part of members when legally-cognizable interests are at stake. These interests are wider than the purely proprietary or financial, extending also to the status of membership itself, participation rights associated with membership, as well as adherence to the fundamental constitution of the association. It may also secure aspects to certain guaranteed religious rites. Where religious courts are a feature of the organized life of the religion, they too gain their authority either as domestic tribunals or as arbitrators.

This approach must be glossed in two ways. First of all, the rules of natural justice apply to internal decision-takers as a matter of law, regardless of the content of the religious law in question, albeit not insensitively. Secondly, courts in recent years have become more overtly conscious of the need to avoid taking sides on matters of religious dispute. Such matters are supposedly non-justiciable. Although motivated by a commitment to neutrality and fairness, this studied agnosticism can lead to a refusal to make inquiry into the religious context of the dispute. This in turn risks widening the gap between religious form and legal expression, and may result in unfairness, for example, when dealing with the aftermath of schism. At the same time one detects the recent occasional hint of impatience with the structural complexity of some organized religions. If courts are to do justice between the parties, they should not avoid taking evidence on the internal structures of religious bodies, taking the procedurally valid decisions of properly constituted decision-takers into account.

4

Ministers of Religion

Ministers of religion have long enjoyed a distinctive position in English law. However, it is remarkably hard to state accurately what that position is. Employment law attaches a range of different consequences to different categories of worker. The principal categories are those of 'employee' under a contract of service and 'self-employed' with a contract for services, reflecting a major distinction between dependent and independent labour.[1] However, a distinctive category of 'worker', which is inclusive of, and broader than, that of employee, has also increasingly been adopted, and this brings with it another set of rights. Some legislation stated to apply to 'employees' actually covers this broader category instead.[2] Furthermore, the old category of 'office-holder' has recently acquired new significance as a result of the extension of employment equality legislation. And in some respects, legal protection has moved well beyond employment categorization altogether, of which the protection offered by health and safety legislation is a prime example. Health, safety, and welfare duties are owed not only to employees but also to anyone affected by the conduct of an undertaking and to those who use non-domestic premises as a place of work or as a place where they may use plant or substances provided for their use.[3]

Complexity is increased by the fact that categorization for the purposes of employment rights correlates only imperfectly with taxation and social security status. For example, individuals may be treated for tax purposes as employed under a contract of service without prejudice to their status for the purposes of protected employment rights. Or again, the fact that a minister is taxed as if self-employed does not necessarily mean that there is a binding contract for services. Courts and tribunals are cautious before relying on tax and social security arrangements to determine questions of employment status.

Complexity risks collapsing into confusion when one seeks correctly to classify particular ministers of religion and others who work for organized religions. Courts have doubted whether there is even a contract, let alone a contract of

---

[1] Simon Deakin and Gillian Morris, *Labour Law*, 4th edn (Oxford: Hart Publishing, 2005), 136–80.
[2] See eg Sex Discrimination Act 1975, s 82; Transfer of Undertakings (Protection of Employment) Regulations 2006, SI 2006/246, reg 2(1).
[3] Health and Safety at Work etc Act 1974, ss 3 and 4.

service. They have disagreed over the relationship between contract and office-holding, even hypothesizing a new employment relationship for ministers *sui generis*. It is not clear whether considerations leading one to deny a contract of service also take ministers out of the category of 'worker'. Perhaps the spiritual or religious nature of a minister's work makes it legally distinctive? What if the religion has no relevant legal personality? And overarching all these technical matters is the question of the relevance, if any, of Convention rights.

Moreover, this confusion tends to overshadow the important substantive question, which is the extent to which the law ought to be regulating the relationship between a minister and his or her religious body by reference to norms which have been developed primarily for secular and generally commercial contexts. To some extent, formal debates have acted as proxies for that underlying substantive problem. Since the mid-1980s, it has generally been presumed that ministers of religion do not have contracts of employment (or possibly even contracts at all) on account of the nature of their work. That view has been subject to criticism in the secondary literature, and the law in this area has recently been re-directed by the judgments of the House of Lords in *Percy v National Board of Mission of the Church of Scotland*.[4] However, while that case resolves some of the formal confusion, it also raises more starkly the underlying substantive problem.

This chapter seeks to clarify the factors leading to the allocation of one or another employment status, it considers the tensions arising from recent employment equality legislation, and it sets out the ways in which the law in areas other than employment treats minister of religion as having a distinctive legal position.

I. Office-holders, Contractors, Employees, or Workers?

1. Office-holding as baseline

An office has been defined as:

a subsisting, permanent, substantive position, which has an existence independent from the person who fills it, which goes on and is filled in succession by successive holders.[5]

At common law it was advantageous to hold an office as opposed to being employed under a mere contract of service. Servants could be dismissed at will, courts would not enforce a contract for personal service, and the only possible remedy was damages for breach of contract, which were fairly minimal. By contrast, an office-holder—unless they held office 'at pleasure', as did some office-holders under the Crown—was protected in law and could not be removed

---

[4] *Percy v National Board of Mission of the Church of Scotland* [2006] 2 AC 28.
[5] Rowlatt J in *Great Western Railway Co v Bater* [1920] 3 KB 266, 274.

except in compliance with the terms of the office and the requirements of natural justice.[6]

Clergy in the Churches of England and Scotland are office-holders.[7] The relationship is determined by the rights and duties attached in ecclesiastical law to the office in question. The nature of lesser positions in the Church of England is not so clear. Secretaries and organists are likely to be employed;[8] assistant curates are probably not.[9] A sexton is not presumed to hold an office for these purposes,[10] while the position of stipendiary lay reader (lay minister) is unclear.[11] They are likely to be office-holders by analogy with other clergy. The question of office-holding in the Church of England was considered at some length by Mummery LJ in *Diocese of Southwark v Coker*.[12] The Court of Appeal had to consider whether Coker had a contract of service as an assistant curate such that he could bring a claim of unfair dismissal when the church failed to find him a position. The court held that it had to be positively established that there was an intention to create contractual relations, because he was ordained to an ecclesiastical office established by law. This meant that a contract was not necessary, that his functions made the special jurisdiction of ecclesiastical courts more appropriate and that his spiritual duties were defined by public law rather than private contract. Office-holding in the Church of England is also public in the sense that judicial review is ultimately available to remedy unlawful decision-taking, whereas it is not available in the case of other religious bodies.[13]

The criterion of permanency in the definition of office-holding has on occasion caused doubts to be expressed about the nature of curacies, readerships, and other ministerial appointments on a personal or *ad hoc* basis. It seems entirely possible to appoint an assistant minister, simply because a well-qualified person is available and there are sufficient funds to do so, without there necessarily being a permanent position to be filled on their departure. But the criterion of permanency should not be overstated. In *Edwards v Clinch*, Lord Lowry pointed out that even a relatively short-term appointment which is not purely personal and which could be filled by a succession of people (even if in fact it was not) could be an office.[14]

---

[6] H W R Wade and C Forsyth, *Administrative Law*, 8th edn (Oxford: Oxford University Press, 2000), 531–4.
[7] See Norman Doe, *The Legal Framework of the Church of England* (Oxford: Clarendon Press, 1996), 198–201; see also *Scottish Insurance Commissioners v Paul* [1914] SC 16. For a helpful recent account, see Philip Petchey, 'Ministers of Religion and Employment Rights: an examination of the issues' (2003) 7 Ecc LJ 157.   [8] See eg *Neary v Dean of Westminster* [1999] IRLR 288.
[9] *In re Employment of Church of England Curates* [1912] 2 Ch 563.
[10] *R v Vicar and Churchwardens of Dymock, ex parte Brooke* [1915] 1 KB 147.
[11] *Barthorpe v Exeter Diocesan Board of Finance* [1979] ICR 900.
[12] *Diocese of Southwark v Coker* [1998] ICR 140.
[13] Mark Hill, 'Judicial Review of Ecclesiastical Courts', in Norman Doe, Mark Hill, and Robert Ombres, *English Canon Law* (Cardiff: University of Wales Press, 1998). *R v Bishop of Stafford, ex parte Owen* [2001] ACD 14. See, by analogy, police constables, who are public office-holders only dismissible for cause: Wade and Forsyth, *op cit* n 6, 153–5.
[14] *Edwards v Clinch* [1982] AC 845, 876.

The right question would therefore seem to be, not 'is there always an assistant minister in this church?' but 'has there been or could there be another assistant with broadly the same duties?'

It is sometimes thought that a position must have some public element before amounting to an office.[15] A public element to office-holding was originally significant for income tax purposes. The Income Tax Act 1842 distinguished between profits or gains arising from any profession, trade, employment, or vocation, which were taxed under Schedule D, and emoluments arising from any 'public office or employment of profit', which were taxed under Schedule E. This was further defined as:

> any office or employment of profit held under any ecclesiastical body, whether aggregate or sole, or under any public corporation, or under any company or society, whether corporate or not corporate, any office or employment of profit under any public institution, or any public foundation, of whatever nature, or for whatever purpose the same may be established.

Company directors (even of private companies) were expressly included, it was suggested, because their office had some statutory underpinning.[16] The test was held to include the office of college bursar in a university.[17] By contrast, in *Poynting v Faulkner* (1905), the minister of a Unitarian chapel had been taxed under Schedule D.[18] But office-holders and employees not already under Schedule E were transferred in 1922, and from that date, if not before, the stipends of ministers of religion were taxed under Schedule E.[19]

The old tax distinction is a red herring. Nineteenth-century courts were generally unwilling to hear extrinsic evidence to find that non-conformist ministers of religion held their positions for life, and certainly unwilling to assume any automatic analogy with the freehold interest of a rector or vicar.[20] Furthermore, where a minister depended solely on the voluntary contributions of the congregation he was dismissible at will.[21] However, in most cases, a minister enjoyed the benefit of some trust property: if not endowment income, then occupation of a residence or income from pew rents. At the very least he had the 'right to occupy the pulpit'.[22] The courts would protect his position according to the terms of any trust deed and the rules of his church. There was thus a proprietary analogy to public office-holding. When contract-analysis of the legal basis of religious societies began to emerge in the 1860s, a clergyman's stipend, and even his ordained status, gave him sufficient legal interest to warrant judicial intervention to enforce the terms of the association at his suit.[23] The most straightforward reading is that

[15] eg Petchey, *op cit*, n 7, 166; see discussion in *Edwards v Clinch* [1981] Ch 1, CA, [1982] AC 845.
[16] *McMillan v Guest* [1942] AC 561.   [17] *Langston v Glasson* [1891] 1 QB 567.
[18] *Poynting v Faulkner* (1905) 93 LT 367.   [19] See eg *Reed v Cattermole* [1937] 1 KB 613.
[20] *Porter v Clarke* (1829) 2 Sim 520, 57 ER 882; *Cooper v Gordon* (1869) LR 8 Eq 249.
[21] *Porter v Clarke* (1829) 2 Sim 520, 57 ER 882.
[22] *R v Barker* (1762) 3 Burr 1265, 97 ER 823.
[23] *Forbes v Eden* (1867) 1 Sc & Div AC 568.

the courts recognized and protected ministers of religion as private law office-holders. A public element is thus, at most, only one factor in finding the existence of an office.[24]

In broad terms, the development of labour law has seen the protection offered to employees overtake that formerly given to office-holders. Recent developments affecting ministers of religion are part of a wider process of enhancing the rights of individual workers against their employers. However, there are several good reasons for still taking office-holding as a baseline for analysis in the case of ministers of religion. First, the terms and conditions of the office can be set by the organization in question. This may make the individual office-holder more or less secure than an employee, but this is a matter for the organization. Secondly, office-holding still has a proprietary dimension, in the sense that an individual can occupy an office without there being any need to identify any other legal persons party to a bilateral contract. The terms and conditions can be set by the internal 'law' of the organization. Thirdly, enjoyment of the office can be protected by the courts according to its terms and subject only to the requirements of natural justice.[25] The whole point about natural justice is that it represents a universal floor of procedural fairness. In short, office-holding offers the most flexible concept for translating the self-understanding of religious bodies into legal terms, it optimizes the autonomy of the religious body, and it preserves the neutrality of the State in any dispute.

2. The no-contract presumption

Discussions of the legal status of ministers of religion in the twentieth century have typically lost sight of the earlier law, and started from scratch with two cases under the National Insurance Act 1911. In *Re Employment of Ministers of the United Methodist Church*, Joyce J held that it was impossible to argue in the light of the cases and the agreed facts that Methodist ministers had a contract of service for the purposes of the National Insurance Act 1911.[26] There was almost no discussion in the judgment of why this might be so, apart from the brief point that it might be difficult to identify the employer. In *Re National Insurance Act 1911*, Parker J held that curates and assistant curates of the established church were not covered either.[27] The three reasons given in the judgment, of which the second predominated, were that (1) their duties were owed to different people to different degrees; (2) their duties were owed by virtue of ecclesiastical jurisdiction, not

---

[24] In *McMenamin v Diggles* [1991] STC 419 the absence of a public factor counted against a barristers' clerk being treated as an office-holder.

[25] *R v Provincial Court of the Church in Wales, ex parte Williams* (1998), unreported, 23 October 1998, noted at (1999) 5 Ecc LJ 217.

[26] *Re Employment of Ministers of the United Methodist Church* (1912) 107 LT 143.

[27] *Re National Insurance Act 1911* [1912] 2 Ch 563.

contract at all; (3) by holding curates to be employees there was a risk of imposing serious liabilities on a vicar from which he ought to be exempt.

In *Rogers v Booth*, the Court of Appeal had to consider whether an officer of the Salvation Army was a workman for the purposes of the Workman's Compensation Act 1925.[28] This turned on whether she had a contract of service. The constitutional documents of the Salvation Army and the forms used in appointing officers went to great lengths to stress the purely voluntary nature of the arrangement. After citing these clauses, Sir Wilfred Greene MR found the necessary contractual element to be entirely absent. The officer therefore did not qualify for compensation. It should be noted that this was not based on any presumption, but on a careful review of the evidence concerning the nature of the Salvation Army and the status of its officers.

As such cases showed, the legal environment was beginning to change in favour of 'servants'. The most significant change came with the Industrial Relations Act 1971, which gave 'servants' protection from unfair dismissal and rights to reinstatement. Increasingly, it became advantageous to be an employee under a contract of service rather than an office-holder. The process of enhancing protection for dependent labour has continued, and employees in this narrow sense now benefit from a substantial range of rights, including protection from unfair dismissal, redundancy compensation, notice upon termination, guaranteed pay, the right to maternity and paternity leave and the right to return thereafter.[29] There is nothing to stop an ecclesiastical office-holder also having a contractual relationship.[30] After all, company directors might well have a service contract to perform their office, in addition to the office itself. But cases from the 1980s saw the emergence of two paradoxical lines of reasoning. On one hand, there were increasing attempts by ministers to invite courts to analyse their relationship in terms of a contract of service; on the other hand, the courts often resisted this by denying the existence of any contractual intention at all in the relationship between the parties.

In *President of the Methodist Conference v Parfitt*, Dillon LJ asserted that the spiritual nature of the functions of the minister '…make it impossible to conclude that any contract, let alone a contract of service, came into being between the newly ordained minister and the Methodist Church when the minister was received into full connection…'[31] although he was prepared to concede that there probably were some binding contracts in relation to ancillary matters, and that it was possible to conceive of a contract of service to fulfil ministerial functions.[32] May LJ was more cautious, being willing to countenance the possibility that he was wrong on the contractual point, while nevertheless clear that it was no contract of service. He cited with approval the view of Waterman J at first instance that a consideration

---

[28] *Rogers v Booth* [1937] 2 All ER 751.   [29] Deakin and Morris, *op cit* n 1, 138.
[30] *Barthorpe v Exeter Diocesan Board of Finance* [1979] ICR 900, 906.
[31] *President of the Methodist Conference v Parfitt* [1984] QB 368, 375.   [32] Ibid, 376.

of the faith and doctrines of the Methodist Church led to the conclusion that a minister was called by God and a servant of God, not of any other human being.[33] *Parfitt* was implicitly approved by the House of Lords in *Davies v Presbyterian Church of Wales*.[34] Lord Templeman held that 'by no stretch of the imagination' could the appointment of a minister to that church be considered as based on a contract of service. When put together with the *National Insurance Act* cases and *Rogers v Booth*, it could easily seem as if the courts were holding that there was a legal presumption that ministers of religion had no contractual relationship with their religious bodies.

It is worth emphasizing that in denying the existence of a contract, neither the Court of Appeal nor the House of Lords were denying the enforceability of the rules of the association. Although at one point Dillon LJ stated that the relationship is 'not founded on contract' it is clear that he meant there was no bilateral contract between Parfitt and his church. Lord Templeman twice stated that the reciprocal duties owed by a pastor and his church are not contractual at all,[35] let alone being in the nature of a contract of service. But at the same time he insisted that the law would ensure that a salaried pastor would not be deprived of his position save in accordance with the provisions of the book of rules. The obligation was not to pay a stipend, but to pay it out of the fund set up for that purpose.[36] Confusingly, his Lordship then stated:

There is indeed an agreement between all members of the church to perform and observe the provisions of the book of rules, but that agreement will only be enforceable at law in respect of any property rights to which a member is entitled under the terms of the agreement.[37]

As we have seen, the language of 'property rights' is too narrow.[38] Ironically, Lord Templeman cited *Forbes v Eden* at this point, which, as Lord Denning recognized,[39] marks the transition from older trust-based notions of jurisdiction over unincorporated associations to implied contract analysis. But we should not let the question of the basis of the court's jurisdiction stand in the way of the main point: in both *Parfitt* and *Davies* the courts held that the ministers were legally protected office-holders, but with no additional bilateral contract of service.

In a series of subsequent cases, the Employment Appeal Tribunal held that ministers of religion were presumed not to be employed. Over time, the rationale for this presumption shifted and the presumption itself strengthened.[40] Thus although in *Santokh Singh v Guru Nanak Gurdwara*, the exercise of spiritual

[33] Ibid, 379.   [34] *Davies v Presbyterian Church of Wales* [1986] 1 WLR 323.
[35] Ibid, 329B and D.   [36] Ibid, 329.   [37] Ibid, 330.   [38] 88–95 above
[39] *Abbott v Sullivan* [1952] 1 KB 189; *Lee v Showman's Guild* [1952] 2 QB 329.
[40] *Guru Nanak Sikh Temple v Sharry*, unreported, 21 December 1990; *Sharma v Hindu Temple*, unreported, 28 November 1991; *Birmingham Mosque Trust Ltd v Alavi* [1992] ICR 435; *Subhan v Enfield Mosque Society*, unreported, 7 February 1995; *Khan v Oxford City Mosque Society*, unreported, 23 July 1998.

functions was understood by the Court of Appeal to give rise to a factual presumption that the relationship was governed by a contract for services;[41] by the time the Tribunal heard *Khan v Oxford City Mosque* the spiritual nature of Khan's duties as an imam was the determining factor which excluded contractual intention by necessary implication, even though the documentation was couched in terms strongly suggestive of a contract of employment.

The decisions of the Employment Appeal Tribunal give very little guidance as to why the exercise of spiritual or religious functions leads to a no-contract presumption. If one accepts the possibility that one can be employed as a chaplain or religious teacher, the presumption seems simply obscure.[42] But if we look more closely at *Parfitt* and *Davies*, we can see that there are important points lurking underneath the decisions. Both judgments are quite clear that one could conceive of a contract to perform spiritual functions: this would involve 'enforceable clauses as to the stipend and the manse and its contents, and an enforceable obligation on the part of the minister to hold a particular number of services on particular days...'.[43] In other words, a bilateral contract of service is entirely conceivable, but it presupposes that the relationship can be appropriately characterized as a set of tasks to be completed for the benefit of the other party: *do ut des*. As both Dillon LJ and Lord Templeman emphasized, such a construction radically distorts the church's own understanding of the relationship.

At the centre of that understanding lies an idea of vocation: the complete and lifelong call of God to exercise ministry in his Church. The task of the specific organizational church is to recognize and affirm that call. Dillon LJ draws the parallel with a professional regulatory body recognizing a person's fitness to practise and exercising disciplinary oversight.[44] The purpose of the material emoluments (house and stipend) is to free the individual to exercise their calling without having to work to support themselves or their family. It is not so much pay for services rendered, but a material gift to release the minister's spiritual gifts. The discipline of the church is merely subsidiary to the conscientious fulfilment of his calling by the minister. To translate such an understanding into a bilateral contract is fundamentally to distort the religious perception.

This explains why it is perfectly possible to be employed as a chaplain. In such a case one might well conceive of the relationship from the perspective of the employer as a set of functions needing fulfilment. The employer is simply willing to pay what it takes to get someone qualified to perform the relevant religious tasks. In such a case, the legal construction mirrors the social construction reasonably well. It also explains why it is wrong to read *Parfitt* and *Davies* as containing anything other than a factual presumption in the case of the Christian churches

---

[41] [1990] ICR 309.
[42] Emma Brodin, 'The employment status of ministers of religion' (1996) 25 ILJ 211.
[43] *President of the Methodist Conference v Parfitt* [1984] QB 368, 376.   [44] Ibid, 375.

involved.[45] For example, the arrangement entered into between Dr Alavi and the Birmingham Central Mosque looks much more like a negotiated agreement to perform certain tasks for an indefinite period of time eminently capable of being construed as a contract of service.[46]

3. The impact of *Percy* and *Stewart*

In *Percy v Board of National Mission of the Church of Scotland*, the House of Lords decided by a 4:1 majority that an associate minister in the Church of Scotland was appointed under a contract 'personally to execute any work or labour' thus bringing her claim of discrimination within the scope of the Sex Discrimination Act 1975 and the jurisdiction of the Employment Tribunal.[47] The claimant had accepted that she did not have a contract of service and had withdrawn a claim for unfair dismissal; however, the definition of 'employment' for the purposes of sex discrimination law is broader. Furthermore, the court rejected the church's other argument that the claim was within the exclusive spiritual jurisdiction of the church under the Church of Scotland Act 1921.

Although none of the earlier cases was expressly overruled, a number of more general propositions emerge from the judgments with varying degrees of support. The court helpfully clarified the fact that there is a distinction between holding an office and having a contract, but that the two are not mutually exclusive. There would also appear to be agreement that the mere fact that someone is engaged to fulfil religious or spiritual duties does not in itself stand in the way of finding a contract. Finally, all the judges in some way disapproved of the idea that employment by a religious organization gives rise to a presumption that there is no intention to create legal relations.

In his dissent, Lord Hoffmann argued strongly (and it is suggested, correctly) for a distinction between the intention to create legal relations and the type of legal relations that were intended to be created. He argued that Percy's legal rights and duties were defined solely by the office she was appointed to, and that there was no additional contract.[48] Lord Scott completely elided these two points.[49] Lord Nicholls, rather confusingly, defended the decisions in *Parfitt* and *Davies* on the basis of a lack of intention to create legal relations, but then went on to state that 'it is time to recognise that employment arrangements between a church

---

[45] *Davies* arguably represents a high point in the willingness of appeal courts to treat questions of employment status as questions of law. This has been restricted by the House of Lords to cases in which the relationship is entirely reduced to writing (*Carmichael v National Power plc* [1999] 1 WLR 2042 per Lord Hoffmann).

[46] *Birmingham Mosque Trust Ltd v Alavi* [1992] ICR 435.

[47] *Percy v Board of National Mission of the Church of Scotland* [2006] 2 AC 28. Divergent evaluations in Frank Cranmer and Scot Peterson, 'Employment: sex discrimination and the churches: the Percy case' (2006) 8 Ecc LJ 392.   [48] *Percy*, n 47 above, 49.

[49] Ibid, 69.

and its ministers should not lightly be taken as intended to have no legal effect'.[50] Lord Hope thought that the effect of the presumption was to require positive contracting-in, which was against the policy of employment law.[51] Baroness Hale considered that office-holders were covered already by the Sex Discrimination Act 1975, so she could deal with the matter simply by expressing doubts about the presumption that the exercise of spiritual or religious functions is incompatible with legal relations.[52]

On one final point, two of their Lordships expressed directly divergent views. In considering the problem of multiple legal personality within the Church of Scotland, Lord Nicholls suggested that

the fragmentation of functions within an 'umbrella' organisation may make it difficult to pin the role of employer on any particular board or committee. But this internal fragmentation ought not to stand in the way of otherwise well-founded claims.[53]

Lord Hope, by contrast, expressly distanced himself from such a view. He stressed the complex nature of the church and the fact that there was a contract with the Board of National Mission as a distinct person within the church.[54]

The impact of the judgments in Percy can be seen in the decision of the Court of Appeal in *New Testament Church of God v Stewart*.[55] In that case the court upheld a ruling of the Employment Tribunal, previously upheld by the Employment Appeal Tribunal, that the claimant was employed by his church under a contract of service. All three judges recognized that article 9 European Convention applied in the court's construction of the relationship.[56] The court accepted that the effect of Percy was to remove the presumption that there is no intention to create legal relations, but at the same time recognized the relevance of religious doctrinal considerations to the factual question whether there was such an intention. However, their treatment of this point varied slightly. Pill and Lawrence Collins LJJ seemed to limit its relevance to the rather extreme situation in which the religious body considers that as a matter of religious doctrine no legal relationship cognizable by a secular court arises at all.[57] Arden LJ was more nuanced, recognizing that religious beliefs may be incompatible with finding a contract or a contract of employment.[58] She called for careful and conscientious fact-finding.

The recognition of the relevance of article 9 is welcome, but it leaves the law in a considerable muddle.[59] Article 9 was not argued in Percy's case. The failure of the majority in both *Percy* and *Stewart* to leave open a clear possibility that ministers may occupy a legally cognizable office, without becoming employees by virtue

---

[50] Ibid, 41. [51] Ibid, 60. [52] Ibid, 73. [53] Ibid, 41. [54] Ibid, 63.
[55] *New Testament Church of God v Stewart* [2008] ICR 282.
[56] Ibid, 296 (Pill LJ), 299 (Arden LJ) and 301 (Lawrence Collins LJ).
[57] Ibid, 296–7 and 301. [58] Ibid, 300.
[59] John Duddington, 'God, Caesar and the Employment Rights of Ministers of Religion' [2007] Law and Justice 129.

of an intention to create legal (or contractual) relations, is unhelpful. It removes from organized religions the possibility of ensuring legal protection for ministers, but on terms over which they are fully in control. All we can be sure of is that religious considerations are still relevant in some way, but that the law is now neutral on whether ministers are only office-holders and/or are workers for the purposes of some employment rights (*Percy*) or have bilateral contracts of service (*Stewart*).

4. When is there a contract of service?

The general question of when an employment relationship amounts to a contract of service can best be seen as a multi-factor test, in which various subordinate tests are balanced against each other. The older 'control' test considers whether the employer has the power of deciding the thing to be done, the means to do it, and the time and place at which it is to be done.[60] This could be used to exclude various professionals who exercise considerable discretion in their work with minimal personal oversight. But there is now no question that professionals can be employed, and that the 'control' test is less dominant, at least as regards the detail to which it formerly referred.[61] Other tests consider whether the individual is an integral part of the business,[62] whether they are in a position of economic dependency on the organization and not in business on their own account,[63] and whether there is a mutual commitment to each other.[64] With the necessary adjustments, all these tests would normally be satisfied in the case of ministers of religion. They certainly indicate that a contract of service is typically more plausible than a contract for services.

However, a religious association has the right under article 9 ECHR by express words to render its internal affairs immune from secular judicial consideration, in short to take the steps taken by the Salvation Army in *Rogers v Booth* to keep internal disputes out of the secular courts.[65] This applies both to office-holding and to any possible contract of service. This is not an attempt to exclude the proper obligations of employment law, which would be unlawful;[66] it simply prevents the legal relationship on which those obligations depend from arising in the first place. So long as the intention to exclude secular legal and contractual relations is clearly expressed and rooted in religious doctrine, it is not a sham but a genuine expression of autonomy, which the courts should respect. When the law wishes to impose inescapable obligations in such circumstances, it has done so, and can do so again.

---

[60] *Yewens v Noakes* (1880) 6 QBD 530; *Ready-Mixed Concrete (South East) Ltd v Minister for Pensions and National Insurance* [1968] 2 QB 497.
[61] It is still significant in the case of, eg, agency workers: *Montgomery v Johnson Underwood* [2001] ICR 819.
[62] *Stevenson, Jordan and Harrison v Macdonald and Evans* [1952] 1 TLR 101.
[63] *Lee Ting Sang v Chung Chi-Keung* [1990] ICR 409.
[64] See discussion in Deakin and Morris, *op cit* n 1, 153–9.
[65] *New Testament Church of God v Stewart* [2008] ICR 282; *Koeller v Coleg Elidyr (Camphill Communities Wales) Ltd* [2005] 2 BCLC 379.   [66] Employment Rights Act 1996, s 203.

Furthermore, once it is accepted that 'doctrine' affects internal government and discipline—as it surely does—article 9 is not only significant in cases in which the religious body seeks to oust entirely the jurisdiction of secular courts. It also affects the translation of the religiously-conceived relationship into the most analogous legal terms. It must therefore be open to a religious body to argue that although they are willing to subject themselves to the jurisdiction of the secular courts in respect of adherence to the established terms of an office, they do not accept the expectations and norms of a bilateral contract of service. It is part of the association's right of religious liberty to design the relationship with its ministers as it sees fit, and it is the obligation of the court to translate that relationship into the best legal analogy. This is what the courts were trying to do in *Parfitt* and *Davies*, and what they arguably failed to do in *Percy* and *Stewart*. It is a nice question how far this approach can be extended to other workers whose work seems much closer to that of secular employment, but there is no reason in principle why the factual investigation should not be made. It may be less plausible that a secretary or cleaner is actually required to be an adherent of the religion subject only to the internal ethos or 'law' of the relevant body, to the exclusion of other forms of secular legal relationship, but it is not impossible.

The mere fact that spiritual or religious functions are being exercised is not incompatible with a contract of service. A chaplain can be employed by a secular employer to fulfil spiritual or religious functions. Rather, as well as the usual tests, it is suggested that the following questions should be considered:

(i) Does the religious body conceive of itself more as a polity or more as an artificial person? The absence of a clear 'employer' is an important indication that the religious body is not to be treated as a single company, but as a community under its own internal law. It should not be assumed that there is a 'central government', perhaps of its trustees or directors. The fact that there is a fund that pays a salary does not make the controllers of the fund into an employer, any more than the trustees of a place of worship or accommodation are thereby employers. The distributed personality of many religious bodies is what makes office-holding—on the analogy with public office-holding—particularly apt.

(ii) Assuming, however, that a plausible employer can be found, how does the religious body view their role? Is it true to characterize their responsibility as securing and ensuring ministry in a particular place or role—are they more like a hospital trust or prison governor making sure that there is a chaplain—or is their function rather merely administrative, like the personnel and payroll departments of a company?

(iii) How does the relationship look from the perspective of the putative 'employees'? Do they think they are working for *this* employer? From a religious perspective, they might find that a very odd way of viewing the relationship, either because the ministers in question do not consider that they are really working for anyone except God, or because if they are working for anyone it is for a group of people who benefit from their ministry, not the formal body that happened to appoint or happens to pay them.

(iv) It is also relevant to consider the place of remuneration and other benefits in the thinking of the organization. Is ministry a way of making a living, or is a living what frees up the individual to engage in the ministry to which they have been called? Of course, it is hard to disentangle motives, but there is a distinction between being paid for the work one does and being provided with resources so that one can do it. In a domestic context, a partner who stays at home is not employed by the one who 'works', even if they are 'paid' a regular allowance. There is no reason to prefer an analogy with commercial organizations over one with domestic arrangements.

(v) Finally, what are the legal implications of selecting a particular categorization? Is the bundle of rights associated with the categorization compatible with the ethos of the body, or is it more-or-less at odds with it?

None of these factors is conclusive in itself; however they should lead to more sensitive fact-finding by the court. Certainly the court should not evade such fact-finding by reference to the non-justiciable nature of the religious doctrinal questions which will inevitably be implicated in the inquiry.

5. 'Workers' rights

Employment law also attaches a number of rights to the status of 'worker'. As we have seen, the Sex Discrimination Act 1975 applies to a broad category including those appointed under a contract personally to execute any work or labour. Other workers' rights include rights in respect of the national minimum wage,[67] protection from excessive working time,[68] protection from arbitrary deductions from pay,[69] and protection in respect of disclosures of wrongdoing, or 'whistleblowing'.[70] Workers are also protected from detriments on grounds related to trade union membership or activities, although not from dismissal if they take industrial action.[71] The precise definitions vary somewhat. In the context of equal pay a worker has been defined as 'a person who, for a certain period of time, performs services for, and under the direction of, another person in return for which he receives remuneration'.[72] It extends beyond employees with a contract of service to include an individual who works under

any other contract, whether express or implied and (if it is express) whether oral or in writing, whereby the individual undertakes to do or perform personally any work or services

---

[67] National Minimum Wage Act 1998.
[68] Working Time Regulations 1998, SI 1998/1833.
[69] Employment Rights Act 1996, pt II.   [70] Employment Rights Act 1996, pt IVA.
[71] Trade Union and Labour Relations (Consolidation) Act 1992, ss 146 and 238A. The definition of 'worker' for these purposes is slightly, but not materially, different: s 296(1)(b).
[72] *Allonby v Accrington & Rossendale College* [2004] CMLR, para 67.

for another party to the contract whose status is not by virtue of the contract that of a client or customer of any profession or business undertaking carried on by the individual.[73]

If the argument above is correct, it not obvious that fulfilling a religious office amounts to doing work or services 'for another party to the contract'. The problem is once again that this is likely significantly to mischaracterize the internal relationships. When a minister carries out some spiritual function, it is unlikely that there is any other specific person or persons for whom it is done. Rather, it is done because it is right to do it—the duty is imperfect—or possibly it is done for 'us', ie the religious community as a whole, in accordance with the law and/or practice of the community. There is also a question whether 'any other contract' includes a multilateral contract of association, and it must be at least arguable that the context indicates a bilateral contract. However, the majority decision in *Percy* suggests that many ministers of religion will be considered 'workers', even if they do not have contracts of service.

Workers employed by charities and other voluntary organizations are excluded from the minimum wage provisions, so long as they are not paid anything other than expenses, and do not receive any benefits in kind other than subsistence and accommodation that is reasonable in the circumstances.[74] Of course, being a volunteer may mean there is no contract at all, although this conclusion does not follow automatically. Residential members of charitable communities who are living together, where the purpose of the community is to 'practise or advance a belief of a religious or similar nature', are also excluded from the minimum wage provisions, so long as the community is not an independent school or providing a course of further or higher education.[75] Finally, the main operative parts of the Working Time Regulations such as the 48-hour week, the eight-hour working night, eleven consecutive hours' rest, and one day off in seven, do not apply where the duration of working time is not measured or predetermined or can be determined by the worker on account of the specific characteristics of the activity.[76] Workers officiating at religious ceremonies in churches and religious communities are expressly cited by way of example.

6. Conclusion

In 2004, the Government established a Clergy Working Group to consider working conditions as part of its review of employment status issues. This resulted in a Model Statement of Good Practice,[77] which encourages the provision of statements of terms and conditions, clear procedures for grievance, disciplinary cases and complaints, support during the application process and for personal development, and information and consultation on significant and relevant changes.

---

[73] Employment Rights Act 1996, s 230(3).
[74] National Minimum Wage Act 1998, s 44.   [75] Ibid, s 44A.
[76] Working Time Regulations 1998, reg 20(1).   [77] DTI, March 2007.

Review of implementation and further consultation is still ongoing, and legislative action has not been ruled out.

The question of the nature of the employment status of ministers of religion is ultimately one of fact, to be determined on a case-by-case basis. However, there is a danger that as religious diversity increases and religious literacy drops, secular courts and tribunals will lose their sensitivity to the ways in which organized religions conceive of themselves. Instead, they will treat religious bodies as if they were secular organizations operating on some religious equivalent to economic rationality, paying what it takes to get the job done. Perhaps, with more subtlety, assumptions about relative bargaining power and individual vulnerability will be carried over unthinkingly into the religious context. On such accounts, ministers are just another sort of employee. But this may distort considerably how the religious body views itself. Courts and tribunals need to take considerable care to translate correctly religious understandings into secular categories. The rather crude device of preserving a right to prevent legal relations coming into being at all hardly shows sufficient respect for the self-government of religious bodies.

Perhaps most importantly, where a religious organization has formed a considered view as to the legal status of its ministers and other workers, which is grounded in its religious doctrine and an awareness of secular labour law standards, secular courts and legislatures should be slow to overturn such judgments.

II. Employment Equality and Religious Ethos

The second area to be considered is the growing tension between general standards of non-discrimination in contexts of employment and occupation and the views of religious bodies as to the proper persons to be appointed to offices and positions.[78] It is hardly surprising if a religious organization takes the view that one needs to be an adherent of the religion in question in order to hold an office. Religions may also take the view that certain positions may only be filled by men, or occasionally, women. Moreover, their conception of gender may be incompatible with medically reassigned gender (ie a female-to-male transsexual person may not be treated as a man for certain purposes). Some religions, such as Judaism and Sikhism, are closely aligned to race. Many have views on appropriate forms of sexual behaviour, perhaps requiring celibacy, or limiting legitimate sexual behaviour to lifelong marriage between a man and a woman. Examples can even be found, albeit rare in this country, of religions that set standards of

---

[78] The topic is now substantial. General introduction in Sandra Fredman, *Discrimination Law* (Oxford: Oxford University Press, 2002). Comprehensive and up-to-date account in Nicholas Bamforth, Maleiha Malik, and Colm O'Cinneide, *Discrimination Law: Theory and Context* (London: Sweet & Maxwell, 2008). As regards specifically religious dimensions, see ibid, ch 13 and Lucy Vickers, *Religious Freedom, Religious Discrimination and the Workplace* (Oxford: Hart Publishing, 2008).

physical excellence incompatible with certain disabilities, or impose unusual age requirements, whether young or old.

Until fairly recently, religious organizations have been the beneficiary of the general absence of any legal protection for the individual against discrimination except in respect of sex, marital status, and race. Just as a secular employer could discriminate against a faith, so a religious employer could discriminate in favour of it. But even the familiar grounds of sex, marital status, and race could give rise to difficulty. Section 19 of the Sex Discrimination Act 1975 created an exception in the case of employment

for purposes of an organised religion where the employment is limited to one sex so as to comply with the doctrines of the religion or avoid offending the religious susceptibilities of a significant number of its followers.

Given the prevailing view that ministers of religion did not generally work under a contract of service or contract personally to execute any work or labour,[79] the section was redundant. It was also quite limited. In *O'Neill v Governors of St Thomas More School*, a religious education teacher was dismissed for becoming pregnant by a priest, hence rendering her unsuitable in the view of the school governors to teach Roman Catholic ethics.[80] Section 19 was not even considered and her claim for sex discrimination was upheld. Any attempt to rely on the section would have met with the insuperable objection that it was not a requirement of her job that she be female. The reach of the exception, even when it was relevant, was smaller than the *prima facie* unlawfulness from which it was supposed to except. In short, section 19 did not cover all forms of 'sex discrimination' to satisfy a religious ethos, but only one specific type which in practice hardly ever arose.[81] There would appear to be no case which directly considered the old section 19.

The partially religious definition of ethnicity adopted by the House of Lords in *Mandla v Dowell Lee* also created potential difficulties for organizations applying religious tests.[82] In *Board of Governors of St Matthias Church of England School v Crizzle* an unsuccessful Asian applicant argued that the requirement for a 'committed communicant Christian' as a headteacher for a Church of England school was unlawful.[83] The court treated the requirement as only indirectly discriminatory on grounds of race rather than directly discriminatory on grounds of ethnicity, as it could have been had the applicant been Sikh or Jewish. Being only indirectly discriminatory, it could be justified by appeal to objective criteria, which included the need to maintain the school's religious ethos. As regards

---

[79] This was the relevant test in s 82(1).
[80] *O'Neill v Governors of St Thomas More School* [1997] ICR 33. Vickers questions whether the finding of discrimination was correct: *op cit* n 78, 166.
[81] Strictly speaking, there was no religious exception for a marital status requirement either.
[82] *Mandla v Dowell Lee* [1983] 2 AC 548.
[83] *Board of Governors of St Matthias Church of England School v Crizzle* [1993] ICR 401.

schools, the matter is now comprehensively regulated by statute,[84] but it is not easy to see how the court could have defended the requirement under the then current law in the face of a Sikh or Jewish applicant.

Over the last 10 years, anti-discrimination law has expanded significantly to protect a much wider range of personal characteristics. This has been a Europe-wide development, which can be dated from the inclusion of a general empowering clause in the Treaty of Amsterdam (1997) to combat discrimination on grounds beyond those of race and sex.[85] This resulted most notably in the Directive establishing a general framework for equal treatment in employment and occupation.[86] Anti-discrimination law now exists in relation to protected characteristics of sex and pregnancy, gender reassignment, marital and civil part-nership status,[87] sexual orientation, colour, race, ethnicity, nationality, national origins, religion, belief, disability, and age. One of the advantages of this devel-opment has been a clarification of the boundaries between different grounds of discrimination, in particular between sex and sexuality,[88] and to some extent between race and religion also.[89] At the same time, the new law has substantially increased the regulatory reach of the State and raised a new set of problems for religious organizations. Fitting the grounds together into a coherent body of law has proved a considerable challenge, and the arguments of religious organizations for accommodation have not always been well received.

It is facile to conceive of this as a problem with religions that 'discriminate'. Anti-discrimination law is itself based on judgments of the significance or insig-nificance of difference in different contexts. The primary context has been secular employment. It is not obvious that these judgments are more 'equal' than alter-native judgments of significance adopted by religious minorities for specific and different religious contexts. 'Discrimination', or for the sake of clarity 'unlaw-ful discrimination', is constituted by the drawing of distinctions or the failure to accommodate difference in contexts and in ways which the law considers inappropriate. Those judgments of inappropriateness are always open to revision, and it is entirely possible for the law itself to 'discriminate' by treating certain criteria of appointment as 'discriminatory'.

---

[84] School Standards and Framework Act 1998, s 60; see ch 8 below.

[85] According to EC Treaty, art 13, the Community 'may take appropriate action to combat discrimination based on sex, racial or ethnic origin, religion or belief, disability, age or sexual orientation'.

[86] Directive 2000/78/EC. For background in relation to exceptions for religious organizations, see Julian Rivers, 'In Pursuit of Pluralism: the Ecclesiastical Policy of the European Union' (2004) 7 Ecc LJ 267.

[87] Or, strictly, 'being married' etc. Discrimination against someone for being single is, perhaps surprisingly, still lawful.

[88] The courts tended to resist a conflation of sex and sexual orientation, even though a restriction of benefits to opposite-sex partners could be construed as sex discrimination. See Case C-249/96 *Grant v South-West Trains Ltd* [1998] ECR I-621.

[89] See *R(E) v JFS Governing Body* [2008] ELR 445; [2009] 1 WLR 2353, CA and Supreme Court [2010] 2 WLR 153.

There are various legal techniques for managing the tensions. The law could simply insist on applying general non-discrimination standards to churches and religious associations; this would be more or less oppressive depending on the degree to which the religious body diverges from the new legal norm. At the other extreme, the law could exempt religious bodies from its operation. In between are positions in which the law is applicable, but some freedom is carved out for the religious body. This can be done in various ways: by building the religious perspective into the structure of judgments of appropriateness, such that requiring a priest to be a man, for example, does not even count as discrimination in the first place; by allowing the organization to demonstrate a 'genuine occupational requirement' in respect of the position; or by creating an exception for religious bodies which would otherwise be covered.

1. The legal framework

The legal framework is complex and spread over several statutes. The Equality Act 2010 codifies, harmonizes, and also extends the existing legislation, particularly in relation to public sector duties. The law as it currently stands can be outlined as follows.

Originally, the law only covered employment, defined as employment under a contract of service or a contract personally to do work. From 2003, the provisions of anti-discrimination law in the employment field have also been extended to office-holders.[90] The definition of office-holding is uniform in respect of all the protected characteristics. Non-discrimination requirements are applied to any office or post to which persons are appointed to discharge functions personally under the direction of another person and for which they are entitled to remuneration.[91] There is a sufficient degree of 'direction' if the other person is entitled to direct the office-holder as to when and where the functions are discharged.[92] However, 'remuneration' does not include expenses or compensation for loss of income or benefits the person might otherwise have received;[93] and 'appointment' does not include election.[94] Categorization as an employee takes precedence: the fact that one is also an office-holder then becomes irrelevant for these purposes. In general then, the definitions of 'employee' and 'office-holder' are such that volunteers are not included.

The definition of discrimination has a broadly similar, albeit not identical, structure in respect of each protected characteristic. In particular, disability

---

[90] Race Relations Act 1976 (Amendment) Regulations 2003, SI 2003/1626; Employment Equality (Religion or Belief) Regulations 2003, SI 2003/1660; Employment Equality (Sexual Orientation) Regulations 2003, SI 2003/1661; Disability Discrimination Act 1995 (Amendment) Regulations 2003, SI 2003/1673; Employment Equality (Sex Discrimination) Regulations 2005, SI 2005/2467; Employment Equality (Age) Regulations 2006, SI 2006/1031.
[91] eg Employment Equality (Religion or Belief) Regulations 2003, SI 2003/1660, reg 10(8)(a).
[92] Ibid, reg 10(9)(a).   [93] Ibid, reg 10(9)(b).   [94] Ibid, reg 10(10)(a).

discrimination is differently structured. *Direct discrimination* arises when one person treats another less favourably on grounds of their protected characteristic. This requires a comparison with others whose circumstances are not materially different except for the characteristic in question. The logic of direct discrimination is that protected characteristics are in principle irrelevant to the just treatment of individuals. Cases in which those characteristics are relevant are thus exceptional. This basic structure is then glossed in various ways: in the case of discrimination on grounds of religion or belief, direct discrimination may also arise if the less favourable treatment arises on account of someone else's religion or belief (eg that of a partner).[95] In the case of sexual orientation discrimination, the difference between being married or being a civil partner is not to be treated as material.[96] In the case of sex discrimination, special treatment afforded to women in connection with pregnancy or childbirth does not amount to discrimination against men.[97] In the case of gender reassignment, whether treatment in relation to absence from work is less favourable is to be determined by reference to treatment for absence for sickness, injury, or any other cause.[98] In the case of disability, direct discrimination is narrowed down in that the comparator is someone who has the same abilities as the disabled person.[99] Less favourable treatment is justifiable if based on 'substantial and material circumstances'.[100]

The legislation also renders *indirect discrimination* unlawful. The tendency has been to harmonize the definition of this and to supplant earlier definitions contained in the race and sex discrimination legislation. It is now generally defined as the equal application of a provision, criterion, or practice which puts the individual concerned and others like him or her at a particular disadvantage and which cannot be shown to be a proportionate means of achieving a legitimate aim.[101] The logic of indirect discrimination is that implicit barriers to entry are undesirable, but may be reasonable. The potential for justification is built into the structure of the definition. Disability discrimination is once again different in that there is an express obligation to make reasonable adjustments to accommodate a person with a disability.[102] One should not overemphasize the significance of this; indirect discrimination can also arise where an employer has refused to make a reasonable adjustment, since it is disproportionate uniformly to apply a provision, criterion, or practice if a reasonable adjustment is possible. The legislation typically outlaws *harassment* and *victimization* in the context of employment and occupation as well.

The legislation shows some variety as regards exceptions for employment in religious contexts. In the case of disability discrimination, there are no relevant

---

[95] Ibid, reg 3(1)(a).
[96] Employment Equality (Sexual Orientation) Regulations 2003, SI 2003/1661, reg 3(3).
[97] Sex Discrimination Act 1975, s 2.   [98] Ibid, s 2A(3).
[99] Disability Discrimination Act 1995, s 3A(5).   [100] Ibid, s 3A(3).
[101] eg Employment Equality (Religion or Belief) Regulations 2003, SI 2003/1660, reg 3(b).
[102] Disability Discrimination Act 1995, s 3A(2).

exceptions, since the very definition of discrimination involves the question of whether the treatment is justified, or necessary adjustments are reasonable. The only form of treatment which cannot be justified is that based on pure stigma or prejudice (ie less favourable treatment compared with someone else with similar abilities). This is unlikely to pose difficulties for the vast majority of religious organizations, although beliefs about physical 'purity' are not unknown. In the case of age and race discrimination, there is a general provision for genuine and determining occupational requirements, so long as it is proportionate to apply them in the particular case.[103] In the case of race legislation, this approach represents a change from the original scheme of the Race Relations Act 1976. The Act used to contain a set of very specific genuine occupational qualifications, which did not include requirements for religious purposes, hence the potential difficulty noted above.

As regards religious discrimination, there is provision for proportionate application of genuine and determining occupational requirements and in addition a broader provision for the proportionate application of a genuine occupational requirement where the employer has an ethos based on religion or belief.[104] Regard must be had to the ethos and the nature of the employment or the context in which it is carried out. The key difference is that the requirement does not need to be 'determining'.

As regards sexual orientation, there is provision for proportionate application of a genuine and determining occupational requirement and in addition a broader provision for employment for the purposes of an organized religion.[105] Here, discrimination is not unlawful if the requirement is applied so as to comply with the doctrines of the religion or because of the nature of the employment and the context in which it is carried out, so as to avoid conflicting with the strongly held religious convictions of a significant number of the religion's followers. These have subsequently become known as the 'compliance' and 'non-conflict' principles.

In the case of sex, marital/civil partnership status, and gender reassignment discrimination there is no general genuine occupational requirement, but a set of complex provisions relating to specific occupational qualifications, which do not include requirements or qualifications for religious purposes. Section 19 of the Sex Discrimination Act 1975, which has been substantially recast from its original version, is thus the only basis for special exceptions for religious bodies. As with the sexual orientation regulations, the basic test is that the employment must be for purposes of an organized religion, with requirements so as to comply

---

[103] Employment Equality (Age) Regulations 2006, SI 2006/1031, reg 8(2); Race Relations Act 1976, s 4A(2).

[104] Employment Equality (Religion or Belief) Regulations 2003, SI 2003/1660, reg 7(2) and (3) respectively. *Glasgow City Council v McNab* [2007] IRLR 476 illustrates the need for complete clarity over which posts carry with them a religion or belief requirement.

[105] Employment Equality (Sexual Orientation) Regulations 2003, SI 2003/1661, reg 7(2) and (3) respectively.

with the doctrines of the religion or to avoid conflicting with the strongly-held convictions of a significant number of its followers. However, it only applies to requirements to be of a particular sex, not to undergo or have undergone gender reassignment, not being married or not being a civil partner, or a requirement in relation to a previous spouse or civil partner.

Access to educational establishments in respect of training which helps fit a person for a job or office from which they may lawfully be excluded may also be restricted.[106] Courses at theological colleges are an obvious example.

A group of unions sought judicial review of aspects of the sexual orientation regulations, including the exception for organized religions.[107] The main ground was that the exception was so broad that it failed correctly to implement the European Equal Treatment Directive; the applicants also claimed that it unlawfully infringed the Convention rights of homosexual people under the Human Rights Act 1998. However, the Government successfully defended the exception. The court accepted that it was designed to balance the rights of non-discrimination and religious liberty.[108] Although it was clear that a requirement based on sexual behaviour would be *prima facie* discriminatory,[109] it was not clear that the general occupational qualification exception in terms of 'being of a particular orientation' was broad enough to cover behaviour. The wording of the organized religion exception (a 'requirement related to sexual orientation') was therefore prudent.[110] It was legitimate not to impose a proportionality test on employment for the purposes of an organized religion: this was designed to reduce the risk of inappropriate litigation.[111] However, the requirement not to derogate from the principle of equal treatment meant that the exception should be narrowly construed: an organized religion was not a religious organization, such as a faith-based school or welfare organization.[112] The tests were objective and not easy to satisfy.[113] The exception was also not apt to cover ancillary posts such as sales assistants, teachers, librarians, and cleaners.[114]

In the light of the minor variations between the various non-discrimination regimes, it is entirely understandable that the Equality Act 2010 seeks to codify and harmonize them. In respect of employment and office-holding, the exceptions are reduced to a single scheme and set out in Schedule 9. From the perspective of religious organizations, there are three levels of exception: a general exception for occupational requirements, a slightly broader—or perhaps only clarificatory—exception for employers with an ethos based on religion or belief,

[106] Employment Equality (Religion or Belief) Regulations 2003/1660, reg 20(3); Employment Equality (Sexual Orientation) Regulations 2003, SI 2003/1661, reg 20(3); Sex Discrimination Act 1975, s 19(2).

[107] *R (Amicus) v Secretary of State for Trade and Industry* [2004] EWHC 860 (Admin) 26 April 2004.   [108] Ibid, paras 27–44, 123.

[109] Ibid, paras 29, 119.   [110] Ibid, para 119.   [111] Ibid, para 123.

[112] Ibid, para 116.   [113] Ibid, para 117.   [114] By implication: ibid, paras 121 and 95.

and a special exception for employment or office-holding for the purposes of an organized religion.

The general exception follows the now-familiar test. A requirement to have a particular protected characteristic is lawful if, having regard to the nature or the context of the work, it is an occupational requirement, the application of which is a proportionate means of achieving a legitimate aim, and which the person to whom it is applied does not meet (or there are reasonable grounds for not being satisfied that the person meets it).[115] As for employers with an ethos based on religion or belief, the test is identical to that for general occupational requirement except to clarify that the ethos, nature, or context of the work is relevant to the question of legitimacy and proportionality.[116]

It is the category of exception for the purposes of an organized religion which has proved most contentious. This exception allows organized religions to impose requirements to be of a particular sex, or not to be a transsexual person, or not to be married or a civil partner, or not to be married to, or the civil partner of, a person with a living former spouse or civil partner, or relating to the circumstances in which a marriage or civil partnership came to an end, or related to sexual orientation. It applies to the arrangements for job offers, the offers themselves, opportunities for training and promotion, dismissal, and qualifications. It is not permissible to offer the job on different terms.

As introduced, the Equality Bill contained two new glosses. The test, 'for the purposes of an organised religion' was glossed in the Bill to exclude those not in positions of leadership or involved in promoting the religion. Employment was only to count for the purposes of an organized religion if it

wholly or mainly involves leading or assisting in the observation of liturgical or ritualistic practices of the religion or promoting or explaining the doctrines of the religion, whether to followers of the religion or others.[117]

The compliance and non-conflict principles were glossed by the addition of a proportionality test.[118] The compliance principle was satisfied if the application of the requirement were a proportionate means of complying with the doctrines of the religion.[119] The non-conflict principle was satisfied if, because of the nature or context of the work, the application of the requirement would be a proportionate means of avoiding conflict with the strongly-held religious convictions of a significant number of the religion's followers.[120]

The former gloss was in line with the judgment of Richards J in *Amicus*; the latter was not, since the judge held that the non-interposition of a proportionality test was reasonable to protect organized religions from litigation. The version as introduced in the Equality Bill thus raised the possibility that a court might

---

[115] Equality Act 2010, sched 9, para 1.
[116] Ibid, sched 9, para 3.
[117] Equality Bill, sched 9, para 2(8) as introduced.
[118] Ibid, paras 2(1)–(4).
[119] Ibid, para 2(5).
[120] Ibid, para 2(6).

find that imposing a requirement is a disproportionate way of addressing the tension with doctrine or convictions. The explanatory memorandum accompanying the Bill stated that the requirement must be 'crucial', not merely one of several important factors, and it only applied in a 'very narrow range of circumstances'. The memorandum also suggested that it did apply to the requirement that a Catholic priest be a man, but not to the requirement that a church youth worker or accountant be heterosexual.

The Government's two glosses were removed by narrow margins after vigorous debate at Committee stage in the House of Lords to restore the law to its current form.[121]

2. Puzzles and problems

When applied to the context of religious bodies the anti-discrimination legislation gives rise to numerous puzzles and problems, not all of which are resolved by the Equality Act 2010.

(a) Positions and organizations affected

In practice, it is not at all clear which ministers of religion or other workers are employees or office-holders in the sense required by the legislation. The explanatory memorandum simply says that the category is 'very broad' and 'may include...members of the clergy and other ministers of religion'.[122] But it should not be automatically assumed that ministers of religion are office-holders for these purposes. Office-holding is given a special statutory definition for these purposes. The individual concerned may be sufficiently independent of direction by another person; there may be no entitlement to remuneration, or it may be minimal enough to amount only to expenses and compensation; and the appointment may be subject to an election. Apart from being appointed to a particular parish, and subject to the requirements of ecclesiastical law, a rector or vicar in the Church of England is remarkably free from oversight. Roman Catholic priests typically live off the offerings of their congregations, so may not be 'entitled to remuneration'. Quite apart from being volunteers, churchwardens, elders, and deacons may be elected, although whether this is what the legislation intends in referring to 'elections' may be questioned.

If the boundaries between those holding positions covered by the legislation are unclear, so also are those between organized religions and religious organizations (ie those with 'an ethos based on religion or belief').[123] In relation to the provision of goods and services, the Equality Act 2006 uses a third term, 'organization relating to religion or belief'. All that can be said with certainty is that 'religious

---

[121] HL Deb 25 Jan 2010, cols 1211–1248.   [122] Para 116.
[123] Russell Sandberg and Norman Doe, 'Religious Exemptions in Discrimination Law' (2007) 66 CLJ 302.

organization' is the broadest category, 'organization relating to religion or belief' lies in the middle, and 'organized religion' is the narrowest. Clearly there are some paradigm cases: a church, synagogue, mosque, or temple is an organized religion, while an independent faith-based school, a faith-based children's home, or a *haj* travel agency are, presumably, only religious organizations, although if they are non-commercial and sufficiently distinctive they might count as middle-ranking organizations relating to religion or belief.[124] But there are plenty of hybrids as well: a convent school, a missionary society, a religious publisher, and a kosher slaughterhouse subject to regular rabbinnical inspection all spring to mind. An additional complication may arise in the case of faith-based organizations which are linked to a public authority. If the latter is the employer, it will not have an ethos based on religion or belief, so only the narrower genuine occupational requirement will apply.[125]

(b) The distinction between direct and indirect discrimination

The significance of the distinction between direct and indirect discrimination lies in the test of justification. Direct discrimination is *prima facie* unlawful unless there is an exception based on or akin to a genuine occupational requirement. Indirect discrimination only arises if a uniform provision, criterion, or practice is either disproportionate or fails to pursue a legitimate aim.

A religious test for a position is unlikely to be cast as excluding one specific religion. Rather, it is more likely to exclude all religions and beliefs except one. This could still be treated as direct discrimination on grounds that the applicant is 'not-X'.[126] However, the point is far from secure. A clear line between direct and indirect discrimination can only be drawn if there is a clear line between who a person is and what they believe or do. Since those lines are particularly obscure in the cases of religion or belief and sexual orientation, the distinctions between direct and indirect discrimination are likewise rather fuzzy.

As an example of indirect discrimination the Explanatory Notes to the Employment Equality Regulations cite the case of a requirement that a play group leader be familiar with the teachings of the Koran.[127] Presumably, this is indirect discrimination, because it is possible (although unlikely) to be a non-Muslim and sufficiently familiar with the Koran. The difficulty is that from a legal point of view, a Muslim simply is someone who believes, knows, and does certain things. Would it still be indirect discrimination if one had to be prepared to attend Friday prayers once a week and teach basic precepts as well? Or to take the example of *Crizzle* above, a requirement that someone be a 'committed communicant Christian' could simply be recast as a 'committed communicant member of a Christian church', which is entirely behaviour-based. It is, of course,

---

124 See the definition in Equality Act 2006, s 57.
125 *Glasgow City Council v McNab* [2007] IRLR 476.
126 DTI Explanatory Notes, para 14.   127 Ibid, para 36.

harder to be a committed communicant member of a Christian church if one is not also a committed communicant Christian, but where exactly does one draw the line?

Later on in the Explanatory Notes, a contrast is drawn in the case of sexual orientation between a requirement that someone be heterosexual (direct discrimination) and a requirement that someone have certain beliefs about the inappropriateness of homosexual intercourse (indirect discrimination).[128] The Explanatory Notes are also clear that sexual orientation does not include sexual practices or sexual conduct.[129] These examples imply a clear distinction between identity on one hand and belief and behaviour on the other. But some courts and commentators resist the suggestion that there is a clear line between sexual orientation and sexual behaviour. In the same vein, there is an ongoing debate about whether general rules which in practice only affect an ethnic minority (eg a ban on headscarves) amount to direct or indirect discrimination.

The Equality Act 2010 follows a current tendency to weaken the distinction between direct and indirect discrimination. The imposition of an occupational requirement in relation to a protected characteristic, and the imposition of a provision, criterion, or practice that puts a person at a particular disadvantage in relation to a protected characteristic are both unlawful unless justified as a proportionate means of pursuing a legitimate aim. Proportionality is becoming the answer to everything, and it is not clear how much difference the initial characterization as direct or indirect discrimination will make in the future.

(c) The need for the 'organized religion' and 'religious ethos' exceptions

When the organized religion exception was introduced in the Sex Discrimination Act 1975 it served a specific purpose, which was to allow organized religions to impose a sex-specific requirement for a position of employment. It is still rendered necessary in the case of sex, marital/civil partnership status, and gender reassignment by the fact that the only permissible occupational requirements relating to these protected characteristics are narrowly defined. If section 19 did not exist, it would probably be unlawful to require a priest to be a man, or celibate.[130]

In the case of the Sexual Orientation Regulations, the organized religion exception fulfils a different function. Here it is a wider and additional alternative to the general 'genuine and determining occupational requirement' test. A requirement relating to sexual orientation is also lawful if the employment is for the purposes of the organized religion and it satisfies the compliance or the non-conflict principle. As was highlighted in *Amicus*, and unlike the general occupational

---

[128] Ibid, para 87.   [129] Ibid, para 9.

[130] Assuming the priest is employed or an office-holder for these purposes. The doubt arises because one might be able to argue for a genuine occupational qualification based on the provision to individuals of 'personal services promoting their welfare or education, or similar personal services', Sex Discrimination Act 1975, s 7(e). See Aileen McColgan, 'Class wars? Religion and (in) equality in the workplace' [2009] ILJ 1, 3–4.

requirement, there is no proportionality test. This is significant, because it means that the courts to some extent are kept out of tricky questions around the moral evaluation of religions.

The Religion or Belief Regulations set out two types of exception: a general exception where 'being of a particular religion or belief is a genuine and determining occupational requirement' and 'it is proportionate to apply that requirement in the particular case'; and a specific exception where an employer has 'an ethos based on religion or belief, and, having regard to that ethos and to the nature of the employment or the context in which it is carried out' 'being of a particular religion or belief is a genuine occupational requirement for the job' and 'it is proportionate to apply that requirement in the particular case'. The specific exception is supposedly 'slightly broader' in that it does not require being of a particular religion or belief to be a 'determining' characteristic of the job. It simply has to be a 'genuine requirement'. But if a 'requirement' must be more than one of many relevant factors, it is completely obscure as to what the term 'determining' adds. The distinction is impossible to grasp.

The Equality Bill as introduced into Parliament was thus doubly curious. Having understandably abandoned the additional 'determining' requirement, it left the religious ethos exception in place in a form which almost exactly replicated the test for occupational requirements in general. As has just been pointed out, it also subjected the organized religion exception to a proportionality test. Thus all the 'organized religion' exception did was to clarify that complying with the doctrines of the religion or avoiding conflict with religious convictions is a legitimate aim for a religious body. Since it is obvious by reference to the Convention rights of religious associations that it is a legitimate aim for an organized religion or an organization with an ethos based on religion to seek to preserve their identity by appointing to offices and positions those who are able to do that, the religious exceptions as they appeared in the Equality Bill added nothing.[131] Of course, the restoration of the original wording of the law in the House of Lords has preserved the distinctive function of the organized religion exception, although the religious ethos exception has survived without any obvious purpose.

(d) Discretion and the claims of religious community

It is ultimately up to the court or tribunal to consider whether a religious or other requirement relating to a protected characteristic is necessary for a particular job. It is tolerably clear that the courts are unlikely to accept arguments from religious community, ie arguments of the form that although the tasks of a particular employee may only be mundane such as cleaning, portering, or secretarial work, the organization nevertheless wants to create a community spirit by ensuring that all jobs are limited to co-religionists. The law is thus forcing an 'instrumental'

---

[131] With one caveat: the organized religions exception allows a requirement 'in relation to' sexual orientation, while the general exception only allows a requirement 'to have' an orientation.

or 'functional' view of work on religious bodies, which is opposed to a view that work is 'organic' (ie part of a religious community's whole activity) or 'vocational' (ie part of a person's whole identity).[132]

Quite apart from the distorting affect this may have on a religious body's self-perception, there is an impact on the degree of integration and separation between the religious community and society. One suspects that in practice, preference was often given to co-religionists in cases of lower level employment, but was not always rigidly insisted on: a factor, not a requirement. It seems that this is now unlawful. The freedom to decide on how open or closed the community should be has been taken away from religious bodies and handed to the secular courts.

It follows that discretion in the individual case is hard to preserve. As the Bishop of Hereford found to his cost, it might be lawful to write a requirement concerning beliefs about sexual ethics and behaviour into the job description for diocesan youth officer, but what he could not do is decide as a matter of discretion that a person not currently in a homosexual relationship was not a suitable candidate, even given that a previous relationship had only just come to an end.[133] The obvious solution from the point of view of the diocese is to become stricter in its criteria.[134]

The rational response to anti-discrimination legislation is thus at least as likely to be ghettoization as 'liberalization'.[135] Paradoxically, this may lead to a greater degree of separation between religious and secular employment, since participation in religious activity may be written into job descriptions and insisted on, where previously there was a measure of flexibility.

(e) Non-discrimination and the minister as exemplar

The underlying problem is the fundamental mismatch between secular non-discrimination norms and the typical expectation on the part of organized religions that their ministers and workers should be exemplary people. Of course, one of the features of religious difference is fundamental disagreement about the ways in which religious personnel should be exemplary. Having increasingly abandoned marital-status and sex-based qualifications, modern Protestant Christianity may now only want to insist on lifestyle qualifications—if that—but many religions restrict their priesthood, or equivalent, to identity-related criteria. They tend to be less strict in respect of mere members and volunteers. From a

---

[132] Rex Ahdar and Ian Leigh, *Religious Freedom in the Liberal State* (Oxford: Oxford University Press, 2005), 323–4.

[133] *Reaney v Hereford Diocesan Board of Finance*, noted in [2007] Law & Justice 153; Case Comment, [2008] Ecc LJ 131.

[134] See the response of the diocesan spokesperson, *Daily Telegraph*, 8 February 2008.

[135] See the 'advice to religious organizations' given by Patrick J Schiltz and Douglas Laycock, 'Employment in Religious Organizations', in James A Serritella (ed.), *Religious Organizations in the United States* (Durham: Carolina Academic Press, 2006), 527, 559. Why not create an 'assistant cleaning minister' with regular prayer written into the job description?

legal point of view it might be entirely sensible to distinguish between those who make their living from a certain profession and those who are mere volunteers or adherents. But from a religious perspective the 'professionals' are precisely the people from whom one expects exemplary standards of identity, belief, and practice. Since the logic of non-discrimination law is to remove the significance of some of these distinctive attributes in normal contexts of employment, one wonders if its extension to religious organizations was appropriate in the first place.

Rex Ahdar and Ian Leigh suggest that exemptions are to be preferred to exceptions.[136] Exemptions have the advantage of clearly specifying the limits of freedom in advance, rather than subjecting instances to case-by-case proportionality analysis by the courts. It is right for the State to recognize 'islands of exclusivity'[137] at any rate in the core dimension of collective religious activity. The current organized religion exception is properly to be regarded as an exemption, since it does not subject the relevant requirement to a proportionality test. The argument in *Amicus* that the non-interposition of a proportionality test simply served the purpose of protecting organized religions from unnecessary litigation is only half the story. It also expresses a preference for the judgment of the organized religion as to the relevance of protected characteristics over the judgment of the secular court.

(f) The values at stake

It is usually accepted that the values underlying this area of law are those of non-discrimination and religious liberty. However, the way in which they are related to each other is often confused. Should we conceive of a principle of non-discrimination which only admits of narrow exceptions to protect religious belief and practice, or a principle of religious liberty which only admits of narrow exceptions to protect non-discrimination, or should we simply accept that these two values are in tension and need to be balanced?

A full answer would need to consider carefully the sense in which there is a right to equal treatment of equivalent status to the Convention rights protected in the Human Rights Act 1998. This raises complex questions of constitutional hierarchies as well as structural differences between equality and liberty rights. A shorter answer will have to suffice here. Disputes between individual ministers or other workers and their religious organizations which present as problems of discrimination in employment almost always reflect deeper underlying internal debates about religious doctrine and practice. The European Court of Human Rights is clear (a) that the State should be neutral on such debates;[138] and (b) that

---

[136] Ahdar and Leigh, *op cit* n 132, 309–11.

[137] The phrase comes from A Esau, '"Islands of Exclusivity": Religious Organizations and Employment Discrimination' (1993) 33 UB Col LR 719.

[138] *Hasan & Chaush v Bulgaria*, no 30985/96 (2000); *Svyato-Mykhaylviska Parafiya v Ukraine* no 77703/01 (2007); see, most recently, *Holy Synod of the Bulgarian Orthodox Church (Metropolitan Inokentiy) v Bulgaria*, nos 412/03 and 35677/04 (2009).

the law should in principle side with the collective body, not the individual.[139] To give the most obvious example, the State is not to have a view on whether the Roman Catholic priesthood should be restricted to celibate men, and should side with the church if an individual tries to exploit secular law to impose a dissident theological agenda. If the law sides with the individual, there is no way of protecting collective freedom to unite around a given conception of priesthood, but if the law sides with the collective body, there is always the option of exit and founding a new organization. Indeed, liberty and equality are not really in tension here. Rather, liberty is the solution to disagreements about the conceptions and limits of equality within a defined domain of the religious. While the State may legitimately adopt a particular, more-or-less controversial, conception of equality, it should not impose such a conception uniformly on the whole of civil society.[140] Protection from uniform State ideologies is one of the main points of collective religious liberty.[141]

In line with this basic orientation, the values at stake in this area of law should thus be constructed not as a limited exception to a higher principle of non-discrimination, nor even as a balance, but as exceptions to the Convention right of collective religious liberty. This requires the court to explain why forcing an organized religion to accept a person they consider unqualified, or penalizing them for rejecting such a person, is the least intrusive means of pursuing an 'equalities' agenda. Given the minority position of all people practising a religion in the United Kingdom today, it is hard to see how such an intrusion can ever be justified.

3. Conclusion

The trend of anti-discrimination legislation in the last decade has been to become both more extensive and less precise. Proportionality tests abound, which inevitably bring with them a chilling effect as well as the risks and costs of litigation. One cannot be sure that the court or tribunal will agree that a requirement in respect of a protected characteristic was proportionate. Moreover, the attempt to provide exceptions for religious organizations has been characterized by considerable restrictions on the discretion of such organizations to consider for themselves

---

[139] *X v Denmark*, no 7374/76, 5 DR 157; *E & GR v Austria*, no 9781/82, 37 DR 42; *Gottesmann v Sweden*, no 10616/83 (1984), 40 DR 284; *Knudsen v Norway*, no 11045/84 (1985), 42 DR 247; *Karlsson v Sweden*, no 12356/86 (1988), 57 DR 172; *Spetz v Sweden*, no 20402/92; *Hautaniemi v Finland* no 24019/94; *Williamson v United Kingdom*, no 27008/95; *Sijakova v Former Yugoslav Republic of Macedonia*, no 67914/01.

[140] For an example of such an attempt under the guise of a supposedly universal commitment to dignity and humanity, see Mark Coen, 'Religious ethos and employment equality: a comparative Irish perspective' (2008) 28 Legal Studies 452.

[141] See Julian Rivers, 'Law, Religion and Gender Equality' (2007) 9 Ecc LJ 24, for a fuller account of this argument, and see Ch 11 below.

who is appropriate to fill positions. Whilst legal interference with their autonomy has not been completely restrictive, it has been vaguely so.

These defects need remedying. The law should be read to ensure that occupational requirements can 'relate to' all protected characteristics; they are not limited to 'having' a characteristic. Secondly, it should by now be clear that the preservation of a religious identity or ethos is one of many legitimate aims that any organization may pursue in its appointment policy and practices. Proportionality review can then operate in the normal way, with reasonable deference to the views of the organization as to how it should seek to preserve its ethos. These two clarifications would remove the need for any special exception for religious organizations in the broader sense.

Thirdly, the logic of the narrow organized religion exception should be seen as a genuine exemption in respect of certain core posts and extended to all protected characteristics. There is a real risk of an irrational bifurcation of approach, even under the harmonizing Equality Act 2010, in which religion-related characteristics are relevant to a wide range of posts, but always subject to proportionality-analysis, while sex-related characteristics are only relevant to a narrow range of posts, albeit immune from proportionality-analysis.[142]

If the narrow organized religion exception is to exist at all—and it should—there is no reason why it should not cover the easier cases of requirements related to religion or belief as well as the harder cases of sex and sexuality. The Government's attempt to gloss the type of posts covered was not wholly misconceived, although the terms were excessively narrow. In relation to core liturgical, ritual, and doctrinal teaching posts, organized religions should be completely exempt from the requirements of secular non-discrimination law. Secular bodies, including legislatures and courts, have no competence to assess any supposed 'balance' between religious factors and requirements of non-discrimination operating outside the religious sphere.

III. The Legal Status of Ministers of Religion

In terms of the source of their power, and legal remedies, there is clearly a sense in which ministers of the established churches are public office-holders and ministers of other religious associations are merely private office-holders, possibly workers, or even employees. The former derive their position from statute and the common law; the latter by voluntary submission to the rules of their association. As employment law has expanded to create new obligations of non-discrimination, exceptions have been included to accommodate—to some extent—the distinctive requirements of religious organizations. The final section of this chapter

---

[142] See Lucy Vickers, *Religious Freedom, Religious Discrimination and the Workplace* (Oxford: Hart Publishing, 2008), 141–2.

considers the ways in which, apart from questions of employment and occupation, the law treats ministers of religion as enjoying a special status, subject to distinctive disabilities and privileges.

1. Disqualification from public office

The House of Commons (Clergy Disqualification) Act 1801 prevented any person having been ordained to the office of priest or deacon, or being a minister of the Church of Scotland, from sitting in the House of Commons. This was later extended to persons in holy orders in the Church of Rome[143] and expressly removed in the case of ordained persons in the Church in Wales.[144] In *Re Macmanaway*, the Privy Council advised that all episcopally ordained clergymen were included in the disqualification, rejecting the argument that the Act of 1801 could be limited to clergymen within the established churches.[145] This decision was not unproblematic, in that the statute clearly did not extend to ministers of lawful non-Episcopalian churches. While the view that political office is incompatible with one's position as a minister of religion might be adopted by a religion, it is not clear why the law should have distinguished between different non-established churches on the basis of the established church's view as to the legitimacy of ordination.

Regardless of the precise extent of the 1801 Act, disabilities have now been removed by the House of Commons (Removal of Clergy Disqualification) Act 2001, which removes the disqualification of any person 'merely because he has been ordained or is a minister of any religious denomination'.[146] This wording is broader than is strictly necessary, but reflects sound constitutional principle that any restriction must come from the side of the religion, not the general law.

The Municipal Corporations Act 1835 contained a broader disqualification for any person 'in holy orders or the regular minister of a dissenting congregation'.[147] In *R v Oldham*, a town councillor was held not to be disqualified by the fact that he was a deacon of a Baptist church and had preached on a temporary basis at an Independent chapel.[148] He had refused permanent appointment in his church, and in any case would have been prevented by the doctrinal statement of the trust deed from accepting office. There was nothing in the way of a contract between him and the chapel, and no salary was paid. The disability was repealed by the Ministers of Religion (Repeal of Disqualifications) Act 1925.[149]

A person is still disqualified from any registration office if he holds any office as authorized person, secretary (for marriages) of a synagogue, or registering officer

---

[143] Roman Catholic Relief Act 1829, s 9.   [144] Welsh Church Act 1914, s 2(4).
[145] *Re Macmanaway* [1951] AC 161.
[146] s 1. The restriction is maintained for lords spiritual.
[147] 5&6 Will 4, c 76, s 28; Municipal Corporations Act 1882, 45&46 V, c 50, s12(1)(b).
[148] *R v Oldham* (1868–9) LR 4 QB 290.
[149] s 1 now itself repealed by Local Government Act 1933, ss 307, 308 and sched 11.

of the Society of Friends, or if he is a minister of religion, or a person engaged in any other calling which would conflict with or prevent the proper performance in person of the duties of the office for which he is a candidate.[150] Again, it is not entirely clear why merely being a minister of religion should disqualify one, unless one is also licensed for the registration of marriages. The point is hardly problematic in practice, although strictly speaking the law seems over-inclusive.

2. Notarial and registration functions

Ministers of religion are expressly granted notarial powers in a wide range of miscellaneous circumstances. They may endorse the photograph of an applicant for a personal licence,[151] confirm personal data for certain student loan purposes,[152] verify an application for a shotgun licence,[153] provide certificates of identity and good character for dental auxiliaries,[154] certify cases of posthumous eligibility to public lending rights,[155] take declarations from certain claimants under the will of a seaman or marine,[156] certify for national insurance purposes that a person is unable to manage his affairs by reason of mental disability,[157] and issue certificates of existence under the Government Annuities Act.[158]

These notarial functions are increasingly shared with other 'responsible persons' or 'persons of standing in the community', and the tendency seems to be to draft this class increasingly widely. Most recently, other faiths have also been expressly included. The Health Professions Council (Registration and Fees) Rules Order of Council 2003[159] defines a person of standing in the community as including a registered professional, doctor, solicitor, accountant, bank manager, Justice of the Peace, principal of the institution which granted the applicant an approved qualification, or a person authorized to provide character references by the principal of that institution, minister of the church, rabbi, imam, or other religious official acceptable to the Council.[160]

The fulfilment of notarial functions by a minister of religion is not associated with his or her office as such, but fulfils a legal need in a system which

---

[150] Registration of Births, Deaths and Marriages Regulations 1968, SI 1968/2049, reg 5 (a) (iv) and (v) as amended by SI 1974/571, reg 3(2).
[151] Licensing Act 2003 (Personal Licences) Regulations 2005, SI 2005/41, s 2.
[152] Education (Student Loans) Regulations 1998, SI 1998/211, s 8.
[153] Firearms Rules 1998, SI 1998/1941, s 6.
[154] Dental Auxiliaries Regulations 1986, SI 1986/887, s 5.
[155] Public Lending Right Scheme 1982 (Commencement) Order 1982, SI 1982/719, Appendix, art 2.
[156] Navy and Marines (Property of Deceased) Order 1956, SI 1956/1217, ss 12, 14, 16.
[157] National Insurance (Compensation) Regulations 1948, SI 1948/2729, s 6.
[158] Government Annuities Act 1929, s 10(2) (certificates of existence) Treasury Warrant, 1930/754, sched.   [159] SI 2003/1572.
[160] See also General Osteopathic Council (Application for Registration and Fees) Rules Order of Council 2000/1038; General Chiropractic Council (Registration) Rules Order Of Council 1999/1856.

fails to provide a distinct and easily accessible service in that respect. It simply reflects traditional cultural assumptions about typical levels of professional qualification.

3. Military exemptions

During periods of conscription in the twentieth century, exemptions were granted to 'a man in holy orders or a regular minister of any religious denomination'.[161] The courts have tended to interpret the test restrictively, excluding lay readers of the Church of England,[162] people working as pastors but without formal appointment,[163] and people working for non-denominational societies.[164] The last example is questionable, since any religious association has a certain doctrinal basis, more or less broad, and should not be denied classification as a 'denomination' merely because it is relatively broad in its views. In *Walsh v Lord Advocate*,[165] the House of Lords held that the test did not apply to a 'congregation servant' and 'pioneer publisher' of the Jehovah's Witnesses, since all members of that religion were regarded as ministers of the gospel. There was thus an insufficiently distinct status of minister of religion.

The House of Lords in *Walsh* drew a clear distinction between clergy and laity, limiting the term 'minister of religion' to those having a 'superior and distinct standing' in spiritual matters.[166] This is understandable in the context of exemptions from conscription, but should not be applied to other areas of law without caution. It is plain, for example, that the definition of 'minister of religion' for immigration purposes is much wider.

Ministers of religion also have a protected status under the Geneva Conventions. When prisoners of war they are to be treated as military chaplains with the right to minister to their co-religionists and in situations of occupation and internment they have rights of access and correspondence to enable them to provide spiritual assistance.[167]

4. Immigration status

Full-time ministers of religion, missionaries, and members of religious orders not otherwise entitled to enter the United Kingdom have always enjoyed relatively

---

[161] Military Service Act 1916, s 1(1) and sched 1, para 4; National Service (Armed Forces) Act 1939; National Service Act 1948, sched 1, para 2. The wording appears to have derived substantially from the Municipal Corporations Act 1835, s 28.
[162] *Simmonds v Elliott* [1917] 2 KB 894.   [163] *Stone v Wood* [1917] 2 KB 885.
[164] *Flint v Attorney General* [1918] 2 Ch 50 note.
[165] *Walsh v Lord Advocate* [1956] 1 WLR 1002.
[166] Ibid, 1010–11 per Lord Macdermott.
[167] See, further, H McCoubrey, 'The Protection of Creed and Opinion in the Laws of Armed Conflict' [2000] Journal of Conflict and Security Law 135, and 213–15 below.

unrestricted entry.[168] Prior to the Immigration Rules 1994, the definition of these terms was a matter of administrative practice and tribunal decision-taking. The term, 'member of a religious order' was given a fairly narrow meaning, effectively covering only Christian and Buddhist monastic communities.[169] By contrast, the term 'minister of religion' was broadly applied and sensitive to the context of the relevant religion. It did not require formal qualifications, but did imply some officiating role and a role involving religious leadership.[170] There was considerable discretion in practice. For example, Mormon missionaries were usually granted a two-year clearance in place of the usual 12 months, in line with the practice of that church. Scientologists and ministers of the Unification Church (Moonies) were not treated as ministers of religion, but as ordinary visitors.[171]

The 1994 Rules form the basis of the current immigration regime and contain much fuller statements of definition largely reflecting existing practice. A minister of religion is 'a religious functionary whose main regular duties comprise the leading of a congregation in performing the rites and rituals of the faith and in preaching the essentials of the creed'; a missionary is 'a person who is directly engaged in spreading a religious doctrine and whose work is not in essence administrative or clerical'; and a member of a religious order is 'a person who is coming to live in a community run by that order'.[172] Guidance gives further definition to each of these categories.[173] Police registration has never normally been imposed on ministers of religion.[174] Substantive change occurred in 2004, when the Government introduced new targeted English-language requirements, on account of their perceived leadership role in community affairs and the need to ensure adequate integration of religious and ethnic minorities.[175] This more restrictive approach was balanced to some extent in 2006, when a new category of short-term non-work-permit employment was introduced embracing visiting religious workers and religious workers in non-pastoral roles.[176]

Under the new points-based system, ministers of religion have been transferred to Tier 2 (skilled migrants), while short-term religious workers have been transferred to Tier 5 (temporary workers).[177] In brief, in order to gain entry clearance or leave to remain, ministers of religion must have a certificate of sponsorship from a licensed UK sponsor, a good grasp of English, and sufficient funds to establish themselves or a guarantee of accommodation and mainte-

---

[168] Immigration Rules 1973 (HC 79–82) para 29(c). *R v Secretary of State for the Home Department, ex parte Ademosu*, unreported, 1988, CA refers to a 'special status'. See, generally, Ian A Macdonald and Frances Webber (eds), *Immigration Law and Practice in the United Kingdom*, 6th edn (London: LexisNexis Butterworths, 2005), paras 10.22–10.29.
[169] *Abdul Hamid* [1986] Imm AR 469.
[170] *Begum* [1988] Imm AR 325. Doubts had been expressed about a Sikh *granthi* in *Singh* [1977] Imm AR 1.　　　[171] Immigration Directorates' Instructions (August 2004), ch 5 s 6, para 1.
[172] Immigration Rules 1994 (HC 395) as amended, rl 169.
[173] Immigration Directorates' Instructions (August 2004), ch 5 s 6, and Annexes Q–V.
[174] Rl 326(2)(iii).　　　　　[175] Cm 6297 (August 2004).
[176] HC 769 (19 December 2005).　　　[177] HC 1113 (27 November 2008).

nance from their sponsor.[178] Leave is granted for up to three years in the first instance and is then extendable to five years, after which they may apply for indefinite leave to remain. As well as showing a continued need for employment, this requires the applicant to demonstrate sufficient knowledge of the English language and sufficient knowledge about life in the UK.[179] However, applicants who only lack this qualification are automatically considered for an extension of stay.[180] In the case of temporary religious workers there is no English-language requirement. Leave to enter is granted for three months and is extendable up to two years.[181]

The new system no longer singles out ministers of religion in respect of the English-language requirement, although the level of English required is higher than for Tier 2 migrants generally.[182] In-country switching from other Tier 1 (highly skilled) and Tier 2 occupations, as well as student status, has also been made easier. However, the rules are more restrictive in other ways. Whereas previously, missionaries had to be trained or sent as a missionary by an overseas organization, they—along with members of religious orders—have now been subsumed into the single category of minister of religion and thus require a domestic sponsor. Furthermore, sponsoring organizations must satisfy the resident labour market test 'in respect of the job'.[183] This is arguably plausible in respect of ministers of religion in the older narrow sense, but hardly makes sense for missionaries and members of religious orders. Seeking to assimilate all religious workers to the general pattern of skilled employees is clearly awkward.

5. Personal taxation and national insurance

Ministers of religion are in some respects treated distinctively by the law of taxation and national insurance, but this only reflects the typical features of their financial position: relatively low-paid, perhaps depending on donations, often occupying a residence owned by their church or religious association, and in a distinctive employment relationship.[184]

While some ministers of religion are treated as self-employed,[185] the majority are taxed on 'employment income' under the Income Tax (Employment and Pensions) Act 2003. This does not differentiate between salary under a contract of service and the emoluments of an office.[186] A series of cases culminating in *Blakiston v Cooper* had to consider whether voluntary donations to ministers were

---

[178] Rls 245ZD(c), (e) and (f); 245ZF(f).   [179] Rl 245ZH(e) and rls 33B–33F.
[180] Rl 33E.   [181] Rl 245ZM.
[182] The level is defined as at or above B2 of the Council of Europe Common European Framework for Language Learning, ie 'independent user' on the 4th point of the six-point CEFR scale: Appendix B para 6.   [183] Appendix A, para 92.
[184] See, generally, Keith Gordon, *Tolley's Guide to the Tax Treatment of Specialist Occupations* (Haywards Heath: Tottel Publishing Ltd, 2008), ch 12.
[185] eg ministers of the Elim Pentecostal Church.   [186] ITEPA 2003, s 5.

assessable for tax.[187] The courts draw a distinction between payments in augmentation of stipend, and hence taxable emoluments of the office, and purely voluntary gifts to the individual as such. A pure gift might be a gift of an exceptional amount, or for a specific purpose such as a holiday, or on account of personal qualities. Many of the cases in which gifts were held taxable concerned Easter offerings to the vicar, which, as Lord Phillimore later explained in *Seymour v Reed*, represent and supersede in some respects legal dues. His Lordship pointed out that those cases in which the payments were held taxable involved gifts that were 'voluntary but not spontaneous' and included 'some element of periodicity or recurrence'.[188] However, periodicity should not be overemphasized: a single collection for an individual can still be an emolument of the office.[189]

As regards the occupation of premises owned by a religious organization, the law draws a distinction between occupation for the better performance of ministerial duties, which is the normal case, and occupation in part-payment of salary.[190] Only the value of the latter is taxable. Statute now provides that any statutory amount payable on premises (such as council tax and water rates) is not assessable to income tax where a charity or ecclesiastical corporation has an interest in the property and it is occupied by a minister employed by it for the performance of the duties of the employment.[191] Furthermore, the taxable value of benefits-in-kind such as heating, lighting, cleaning, repairs, maintenance, decoration, furniture, and domestic equipment is limited to 10 per cent of the stipend.[192]

Until recently, the law on allowable expenses for ministers of religion used to be anomalous in that income from all sources, both employed and self-employed, could be combined, but the test was the stricter one of 'wholly, exclusively and necessarily' normally applied to Schedule E earnings, rather than the more generous 'wholly and exclusively' for Schedule D.[193] The two have now been disaggregated, and the normal tests apply.[194] However, ministers of religion may still combine income from different employments, and their deductible expenses in respect of one employment are not limited by the earnings from that employment.[195] Ministers of religion may also get relief for up to a quarter of rent and maintenance costs for a dwelling used mainly and substantially for the duties of the employment.[196] Cases on clergy expenses tend to be restrictive,[197] but

---

[187] *Re Strong* (1878) 1 Tax Cas 207; *Turner v Cuxson* (1888) 22 QBD 150; *Poynting v Faulkner* (1905) 5 Tax Cas 145; *Herbert v McQuade* [1902] 2 KB 631; *Blakiston v Cooper* [1909] AC 104.
[188] *Seymour v Reed* [1927] AC 554.   [189] *Slaney v Starkey* [1931] 2 KB 148.
[190] *Reed v Cattermole* [1937] 1 KB 613, ITEPA 2003, s 99(2)(b).
[191] ITEPA 2003, s 290; ITTOI 2005, s 159.   [192] ITEPA 2003, s 315.
[193] ICTA 1988, s 332.   [194] ITEPA 2003, s 351(1) and ITTOI 2005, s 34(1).
[195] ITEPA 2003, ss 328(2) and 329(4).   [196] Ibid, s 351(2)–(5)
[197] *Mitchell v Mayhew* (1954) 47 R & IT 435: clergyman had to show that it was 'necessary' to have a visiting clergy minister in his church to claim entertainment expenses. *White v Higginbotham* [1983] 1 WLR 416, Ch D. Purchase of a slide projector by a vicar not a 'necessary' expenditure, notwithstanding the fact that one should not challenge the judgement by a clergyman of the precise extent of his duties.

in practice the Inland Revenue allows reasonable work-related costs including books, computers, robes, communion elements, travel expenses, etc.

For National Insurance purposes, ministers of religion may have no employment, be self-employed, or may be 'employed earners'. The latter two categories are not mutually exclusive. Ministers with a contract of service, office-holders, and those whose remuneration consists 'wholly or mainly' of salary or stipend are all treated as 'employed earners' and pay class 1 contributions.[198] Their employer, or the persons responsible for the administration of the fund that pays them, are liable for secondary class 1 contributions.[199] Where the employer's contribution is paid by the minister for reasons of convenience it is, of course, an allowable deduction for income tax purposes.[200] However, those depending substantially on voluntary contributions are likely to be treated as self-employed on the grounds that they have no right to remuneration.[201] This would appear to be the case even though, strictly speaking, it is arguable that they are office-holders and the gifts on which they depend emoluments of their office.

Members of religious communities the principal occupation of which consists of prayer, contemplation, education, or the relief of suffering, who have no income or capital of their own and who are dependent on the community to provide for their material needs, enjoy partial relief from council tax liability.[202]

6. Regulation of titles and styles

Unlike the award of academic degrees, 'reverend' and other associated titles and styles are applied to ministers of religion by social convention and not by law. Anyone can call themselves a minister of religion—indeed the European Court of Human Rights has taken the view that this is an aspect of the Convention right to freedom of religion.[203] However, the criminal courts may well order a person to desist from impersonating an ordained minister of religion if they have done so to assist in the commission of an offence,[204] and immigration authorities are under no obligation to accept that a claim to the status is genuine. There is one historic example of the law seeking to regulate religious titles: the Ecclesiastical Titles Act 1851 made it an offence to style oneself bishop of any 'city, town or place, or

---

[198] Social Security Contributions and Benefits Act 1992, s 2(1)(a); Social Security (Categorisation of Earners) Regulations 1978, SI 1978/1689, sched 1 para 5.   [199] Ibid, sched 3.
[200] ITEPA 2003, s 360A(2)(c).
[201] John Newth instances Elim Pentecostal ministers and Roman Catholic clergy: 'NIC and Special Occupations—Part I' *Tolley's Practical NIC Newsletter*, 15 PNN 6, 46 (1 June 2006).
[202] Local Government Finance Act 1992, s 11(5), sched 1, para 11 and Council Tax (Additional Provisions for Discount Disregards) Regulations 1992, SI 1992/552, para 3.
[203] *Serif v Greece* (2001) 31 EHRR 20; conviction for 'usurping the functions of a religious minister and for publicly wearing the uniform of such a minister' a violation of article 9.
[204] *R v Norkett* [2003] EWCA Crim 2083.

of any territory or district (under any designation or description whatsoever) in the United Kingdom'.[205] The Act had been passed in an outburst of Protestant indignation at Pope Pius IX's decision to restore the Roman Catholic diocesan hierarchy, and was repealed 20 years later.[206]

In *Blake v Associated Newspapers Ltd*,[207] Gray J stayed a libel action by the claimant on the grounds that the issues raised were non-justiciable, and that there was no way of adapting the pleadings to avoid those issues. The claimant had appeared on a television programme as a bishop officiating in a ceremony described as a marriage of two homosexual men. Subsequent reports in the *Daily Mail* described him as a 'self-styled' and 'imitation' bishop. He claimed that he was a real bishop, consecrated by Bishop Richard Palmer into the Province for Open Episcopal Ministry and Jurisdiction, within The Open Episcopal Church, and part of the Society for Independent Christian Ministry.[208] The judge thought that the case could not fairly be tried without determining complex questions of theology which a secular court was not capable of answering. So the action was stayed.

Although the outcome is understandable, the view that questions of status and title are completely non-justiciable must be incorrect. One can easily distinguish between claims which are simply true or false (eg that a person does or does not hold a certain position in a certain religious organization) and claims which depend on a theological judgment (eg that bishops of a certain church are not 'real' bishops) and are in the nature of fair comment. The statement that a certain man is not a real bishop must imply an underlying theological judgment as to legitimacy. As can be seen in the context of the regulation of religious property, the problem with non-justiciability is that it risks putting people entirely outside the protection of the secular courts in respect of their legitimate legal interests. And the interest of a minster of religion in his reputation is surely as worthy of legal protection as that of anyone else.

7. Criminal law protection

The Offences against the Person Act 1961 contains a specific offence of obstructing or preventing a minister from performing his duties.[209] It derives from ancient legislation protecting clergy from arrest while going to or from divine service.[210]

---

[205] 14&15 V, c 60, s 2.
[206] Ecclesiastical Titles Act 1871, 34&35 V, c 53.
[207] *Blake v Associated Newspapers Ltd* [2003] EWHC 1960, 31 July 2003. The case is noted at 7 Ecc LJ 369. See also Christopher Hill, 'Episcopal lineage: a theological reflection on Blake v Associated Newspapers Ltd' (2004) 7 Ecc LJ 334.
[208] The relationship between these two churches is not clear from the judgment.
[209] Offences against the Person Act 1861, s 36.
[210] Paul Barber, 'Outrageous behaviour' (1996) 4 Ecc LJ 584.

IV. Conclusion

There is an intriguing contrast between the way employment law treats ministers of religion and the way it treats other disputes involving religious bodies. In the latter case, as we saw in the previous chapter, the law has tended to draw back, to resist finding cognizable legal interests and to avoid getting entangled in internal disputes. Courts are very aware of their limited jurisdiction to resolve what are at root religious doctrinal disputes. By contrast, in the case of ministers of religion, employment law has increasingly concerned itself with managing the relationship. Furthermore, it has recently started to do this by reference to norms that sometimes fit awkwardly with the internal values of the religion in question. In this specific area there is therefore a growing loss of autonomy on the part of religious bodies and—effectively—religious partiality on the part of the State in favour of those religions which share the predominant secular values and against those which are more traditional, or just different.

Convention rights have been recognized to be relevant both in the legal construction of the relationship between a minister of religion and his or her religious body, and in shaping the exceptions to employment equality legislation. Once again, a contrast is apparent: in terms of the basic relationship, the courts seem to be moving to a position in which an organized religion has to choose between accepting that its ministers are employees and completely excluding legal oversight. In respect of the equalities exceptions, it is the State which is deciding which roles and positions are allowed to remain bearers of religious identity. In the light of this instability, the older approach, whereby ministers had a legally protected interest in their office subject to the internal law of the religious body and the requirements of natural justice expresses a preferable default position.

5

Public Religion

The idea of public religion is an unfamiliar one to English lawyers. However, it is of considerable value from a European comparative perspective. Several European States distinguish between a basic level of organizational structure, typically shared with other non-religious organizations, and a higher level which gives access to a set of privileges and responsibilities related to a certain public presence and role. Moreover, the term is fully justified from the perspective of English law. One might think that it is only the established church which enjoys the status of public religion, with all other religions being in some sense 'private' or 'personal'. But such a view is 200 years out of date. The argument that the Toleration Act 1689 was purely for the personal relief of individual dissenters, and that trusts for non-conformist places of worship were private and not charitable, was (at the latest) moribund by the end of the eighteenth century and killed off by the courts at the start of the nineteenth. The two principal candidates for a regime of public religion—the registration of places of worship and charitable status—are both rooted in the idea that certain religious practices are both publicly accessible and publicly beneficial.

The conditions of access to such a higher status naturally give rise to questions of exclusion and discrimination. Austrian law has recently been held to violate the European Convention on such grounds.[1] The current law must therefore be read in the light of the Human Rights Act 1998 with its requirements of non-discrimination in the ambit of the free manifestation of religion or belief.

I. The Registration of Places of Worship

The phrase 'place of public religious worship' is occasionally defined in legislation as

a place of public religious worship which belongs to the Church of England or to the Church in Wales (within the meaning of the Welsh Church Act 1914), or which is for the time being certified as required by law as a place of religious worship.[2]

---

[1] *Religionsgemeinschaft der Zeugen Jehovahs v Austria*, no 40825/98 (2008) and see 56–7 above.
[2] eg Highways Act 1980, s 203(3); Local Government (Miscellaneous Provisions) Act 1982, sched 1, para 22.

The definition implies that there is an obligation to register places of religious worship. It also assumes that certifiable religious worship is public.

The principal legislation is still the Places of Worship Registration Act 1855,[3] which provides for registration and certification by the Registrar-General. It raises a number of tricky points of construction. It is not clear that there is an obligation to register under the Act, and if there is, to which bodies that obligation extends. Furthermore, while the Act itself grants few privileges to registered places of worship, registration is a precondition for the grant of a number of other privileges in other legislation. There is therefore an incentive to register on the part of religious organizations. The difficulty here is not simply what is to count as 'religious worship' for these purposes, but whether that worship has to be 'public', what that means, and what happens if the premises are used in part for purposes other than religious worship. The difficulties flow from the change of the function of registration from the 1830s onwards. Prior to that date, registration was a way of avoiding criminal penalties and a means of State regulation; subsequently it determined access to privilege.

1. No obligation to register

At first sight, the Act seems to emphasize the optional nature of registration. However, the words, '...may, if the congregation so wish, but not otherwise, register...'[4] must be read both in the context of a long legislative history, and in the light of the immediate background of a short-lived Act of 1852, which first provided for registration by the Registrar-General. Although it is correct that there is no obligation to register, this is not on account of these words.

The preamble to the Act implies that an obligation to register arises from the Toleration Act 1689. The words appear to be taken verbatim from the Toleration Act: 'whereas...no Congregation or Assembly for Religious Worship shall be permitted or allowed until the Place of Meeting shall be certified and registered'. But in fact this quotation omits the crucial words, '*by this Act*' after the word 'allowed'. The purpose of the Toleration Act was not to create obligations on Protestant dissenters to register, but to provide a limited scheme of relief from existing penalties for persons taking certain oaths and subscribing certain declarations. Congregations and their ministers would be free from the penalties of the Clarendon Code if they were certified and registered as provided for. There was originally no obligation as such to register. Rather, registration was a legal means of avoiding other existing criminal penalties, inevitably committed by those conducting religious meetings outside the established church.

The Places of Religious Worship Act 1812 repealed the key elements of the Clarendon Code and created a new, indeed the only, obligation to register. The obligation was imposed on congregations or assemblies for religious worship at

---

[3] Places of Worship Registration Act 1855, 18&19 V, c 81.   [4] Ibid, s 2.

which more than 20 persons were present besides the occupier and his immediate family and servants,[5] and repeated the requirement inherited from the Toleration Act that doors should not be locked, bolted, or barred so as to prevent any persons from entering during the time of the meeting.[6] This Act created new criminal offences relating to meetings for religious worship above a certain size which either were not registered at all or, even if registered, were held in private. The Act's reference to 'Protestant dissenters' was curious, since the Roman Catholic Relief Act 1791 had already created a regime parallel to the Toleration Act for Roman Catholics.[7] But the application of the 1812 Act to Roman Catholics was confirmed in 1832,[8] and extended to Jews by the Religious Disabilities Act 1846.[9] Intriguingly, however, it expressly did not apply to Quakers.[10]

The Liberty of Religious Worship Act 1855 further limited the obligation to register.[11] Again, this misleadingly referred in its preamble to an obligation to register arising from the Toleration Act, but then correctly recited the penalties created by the Places of Worship Act 1812. It exempted three classes of religious meeting from the operation of the 1812 Act: those conducted by or with the consent of an incumbent in his parish, those in a private dwelling-house (ie whatever the size) and those held in a place not generally used for religious worship. By implication, all other meetings were required to register as before. Thus the law in 1855 required all regular religious meetings other than the merely domestic, or those associated with the established church, to be registered and open to the public if they were to be lawful.

The explanation for the permissive language used in the Places of Worship Registration Act 1855 lies in the attempt three years earlier to transfer the entire registration process from ecclesiastical officers and Justices of the Peace to the Registrar-General. The 1852 Registration Act, which was repealed and replaced by the 1855 Act, made it impossible to register by the old means created under the Toleration Act.[12] It required lists of registered places of worship to be transferred to the Registrar-General, and required congregations henceforth to register in the new way. This had obviously proved too onerous, so the 1855 Act adopted a 'softer' approach whereby congregations already registered and those wishing to register for the first time could choose whether to register with the Registrar-General or not. Permission related to the mode of registration, not the obligation.

The obligation to register was not formally repealed until 1977.[13] Strictly speaking, until that date, there was an obligation to register places of regular religious worship on the part of 20 or more persons, and an obligation not to prevent members of the public from attending such worship. In practice, prosecutions

---

[5] 52 G III c 155, s 2.   [6] Toleration Act 1689, s 11.   [7] 31 G III, c 32.
[8] 2&3 W IV, c 115.   [9] 9&10 V, c 59, s 2.   [10] 52 G III, c 155, s 14.
[11] 18&19 V, c 86.   [12] 15&16 V, c 36.
[13] Statute Law (Repeals) Act 1977 s 1 and sched 1, pt 5.

died out in the mid-nineteenth century, so that now the incentive to register arises solely from its associated privileges.

2. The right to register

It is now clear that the Registrar-General does not have a purely ministerial function in respect of registration, but must be prepared to look behind the certificate to ensure that a place of religious worship truly is a place qualifying for registration. The argument that the function is active, in particular because registration brings with it privileges, failed before the courts in 1766 on account of the dominance of the penal dimension,[14] but was successful before the Court of Appeal two centuries later.[15]

The question therefore arises as to who is entitled to register. The simple solution is to suggest that only those required to register in 1855 are entitled to register now. But the example of the Quakers, noted above, shows that this is inadequate. There is, in general terms, no reason why the test for accessing privileges should be as restrictive as the old obligation to register. It would, however, be odd if those religious associations able to avoid criminal penalties by registering in 1855 were to be prevented from registering now. Problems arise in respect of the religion of the body seeking registration, the size of the congregation, other usage of the premises, and the assumption that religious worship must be public.

The 1855 Act allows bodies to register in the name of any religion, or even no specific religion.[16] Clearly this can, and should, be read to apply to every religion present now or in the future. The question is what is to count as a religion for these purposes. In *R v Registrar-General, ex parte Segerdal* it was held that a chapel for Scientology was correctly not registered on the grounds that Scientologists do not engage in worship.[17] Lord Denning MR found the key in reverence to, or veneration of, a deity, and while recognizing exceptions such as Buddhist Temples, found that Scientology was more in the nature of a philosophy. Winn LJ, while prepared to hold that Scientology shared certain affinities with ancient Greek religious thought, was certain that they did not meet for worship. Buckley LJ looked for 'submission to the object worshipped, veneration of that object, praise, thanksgiving, prayer or intercession' and held that the mere presence of a sermon or a creed of themselves did not amount to worship. It is questionable whether this narrow definition can survive the broadening effect of the Human Rights Act 1998.

---

[14] *R v Justices of Derbyshire* 1 Black W 605, 607.
[15] *R v Registrar General, ex parte Segerdal* [1970] 1 QB 430 per Ashworth J (DC) and [1970] 2 QB 697 per Lord Denning MR.
[16] Places of Worship Registration Act 1855, s 2. '...any other body or denomination of persons' in context refers to those not Protestant, Roman Catholic, or Jewish. Form 76 Direction (d) is unhelpfully restrictive in suggesting 'Christians not otherwise designated' as a general default description.   [17] [1970] 1 QB 430, [1970] 2 QB 697.

As regards the size of the congregation, there would seem to be no reason to restrict groups to those greater than 20. Originally, groups of five or more persons were required to register; the increase was a liberalizing measure. The administrative hurdle of registration is arguably sufficient disincentive for tiny and transitory groups to register, and if the argument below about public access is correct, openness imposes an additional disincentive. However, a further requirement relating to size is expressly imposed in respect of marriage licensing.

The Registrar-General assumes that for a building to be registered, its *principal* use must be for religious worship. This would appear to derive from Lord Denning MR's passing words in *Segerdal* defining 'place of meeting for religious worship'. Under the Places of Religious Worship Act 1812 a congregation would have committed an offence if they met regularly in (eg) a school room which was not registered. Occasional meetings were exempted by the Liberty of Religious Worship Act 1855, but not regular meetings on premises also used for other purposes. While one may not wish to extend certain privileges, such as exemption from local taxation, to a place which is mainly used for an activity which would, of itself, attract such taxation, this is no reason to refuse registration for other purposes. And in practice it would seem that rooms used once a week for religious worship and at other times for other purposes can be registered. Indeed, there is something rather odd about registering a building which is empty for most of the week, leaving that registration unchanged as it gets used more frequently for weekday non-worship purposes, but refusing to register a building that is initially not used for worship, but then starts being used for worship in addition at weekends. As is so often the case, the law assumes that religious and non-religious uses are easy to disentangle.

It is less clear that the religious worship being carried on must be 'public' for the place to be registered, and if so, what that might mean. In *Henning*, the House of Lords assumed that one could register whether the religious worship was public or not, but that the privilege of exemption from taxation was further limited by the requirement that the worship be public.[18] Since this further criterion exists in the case of all relevant privileges, the point is not of great practical significance. However, the better view is that the religious worship should be public even to register at all.

Until 1977, strictly speaking, the occupiers of (eg) a Mormon Temple were committing an offence by conducting regular religious worship for more than 20 people from which the public were excluded. The possibility of registering a religion which intended throughout not to admit the public would have been as inconceivable as registering a place of Roman Catholic worship before Roman Catholic toleration. The Poor Rate Exemption Act 1833,[19] the Marriage Act

---

[18] *Church of Jesus Christ of Latter-Day Saints v Henning* [1964] AC 420.
[19] 3&4 G IV, c 30, s 1.

1836,[20] and indeed all subsequent legislation granting privileges clearly imply that a place registered for religious worship is *ipso facto* registered for public religious worship. The 1855 Act for the most part implicitly assumes that the religious worship in question is to be public, and at one point, easily overlooked, it expressly states this. That point arises at the end of Schedule B which creates a standard form certificate to be sent to the registrar if a place ceases to be a place of 'public religious worship' in which case he is to remove it from the register.

The meaning of 'public' in this context is not entirely clear. In *Henning*, Lord Evershed argued that 'public' simply referred to the size of the congregation, consisting of 20 or more people, not its openness.[21] However, the majority of the House of Lords held that the Mormon Temple, which is only accessible to practising Mormons on a 'recommend' from their bishop, was not public, since it was not 'open to all properly disposed persons who wish to be present'.[22] In *Broxtowe v Birch*,[23] the Court of Appeal held further that there must be some evidence of invitation—for example in the architectural design of the building, or in a notice-board. Exclusive brethren who had taken steps to remove public information about their meetings no longer engaged in public religious worship, even if they would not actually have prevented a member of the public who managed to join them.[24]

The majority view in *Henning* certainly does more justice to the history of the legislation; one should note in particular the way in which the Places of Religious Worship Act 1812 connects the obligation not to prevent public access with the specific criminal offence of disturbing an act of worship.[25] Originally, the reason for requiring public access was almost certainly the analogy with worship in the established church, which was compulsory. Worshipping in a dissenting congregation was a permitted alternative, but the condition for the licence was that all dissenters of that persuasion could fulfil their obligations of attendance.[26] Coupled to this was the fear of sedition. Public access allowed potential officials and informers to check that the group was not planning political overthrow.

In the recent case of *Gallagher v Church of Jesus Christ of Latter-Day Saints*,[27] the Mormon Church failed to overturn the judgment in *Henning*. A majority of the House of Lords considered that the relationship between taxation relief and the exercise of religion was too remote for a question of non-discrimination in the ambit of article 9 European Convention even to arise. In the light of the recent case-law of the European Court this is almost certainly incorrect. A law

---

[20] 6&7 G IV, c 85, s 18.   [21] *Op cit* n 18 at 432.

[22] Per Lord Morris at 435. Lord Pearce (with whom the majority agreed) used 'open to the public' (at 439).   [23] *Broxtowe BC v Birch* [1983] 1 WLR 314.

[24] None ever had.

[25] Section 11, which makes it an offence to exclude the public, is followed by section 12, which makes it an offence to disquiet or disturb a lawful religious assembly.

[26] See, still, Roman Catholic Relief Act 1791, s 9.

[27] *Gallagher v Church of Jesus Christ of Latter-Day Saints* [2008] 1 WLR 1852.

that grants a financial privilege to 'religion' but defines 'religion' restrictively *prima facie* raises a question of discrimination. Lord Scott's caution on this point was justified. However, Lord Scott went on to suggest that the policy of conferring privileges on religious worship that was open to the public was well within a State's discretion both to encourage its presence in the community and discourage its potential for divisiveness and danger to the public.[28]

Finally, questions might arise about the requirement that the public attending an act of public religious worship be 'properly disposed'. Quite apart from the obvious forms of disorderly behaviour, the usual examples given are that members of the public must be prepared to perform acts of respect such as removing shoes or covering one's head as required. It is suggested that the proper question should be whether the condition requires one, whether by participation or otherwise, to affirm the truth or validity of the religion in question as opposed to avoiding offence. If an act of religious worship is to be open to the public it must be possible to be a sympathetic onlooker rather than an unwilling adherent.

3. Consequences of registration

Registration as a place of public religious worship brings with it several privileges. In terms of their historical development one should note (a) specific protection under public order law; (b) exemption from Local Government taxation; (c) the capacity to conduct marriages with civil effect; (d) exemption from registration with the Charity Commissioners.

(a) Public order law

The oldest privilege associated with registration is special protection by the criminal law from disturbance. Although the older statutory offences have been repealed, a similar offence to those originally created by the Toleration Act 1689 and the Places of Worship Act 1812 was enacted in the Ecclesiastical Courts Jurisdiction Act 1860, section 2, and this remains in force.[29]

The section makes it an offence to engage in

riotous, violent, or indecent behaviour in England or Ireland in any cathedral church, parish or district church or chapel of the Church of England, or in any chapel of any religious denomination, or in England in any places of religious worship duly certified under the provisions of the Places of Worship Registration Act 1855, whether during the celebration of divine service or at any other time, or in any churchyard or burial ground, or [to] molest, let, disturb, vex, or trouble, or by any other unlawful means disquiet or misuse any preacher duly authorized to preach therein, or any clergyman in holy orders ministering or celebrating any sacrament, or any divine service, rite, or office, in any cathedral, church, or chapel, or in any churchyard or burial ground.

---

[28] Ibid, para 51.   [29] See Paul Barber, 'Outrageous behaviour' (1996) 4 Ecc LJ 584.

The reference to 'any chapel of any religious denomination' presumably refers only to Ireland, so that in England, places of worship must be registered to gain protection. Otherwise the words would be unnecessary. The object of protection is the sacredness of the place or event itself.[30] 'Indecent' behaviour need not be riotous, violent, or actually cause offence to anyone.[31] It can include sexual activity in a churchyard[32] or a night-time occult ceremony attempting to raise the dead.[33] An offence is committed if a service is disrupted by shouting a political protest,[34] or even by the loud singing of hymns to disrupt a service arguably unlawful according to the internal law of the church.[35] It can also be committed by the unwarranted insistence on raising an impediment to ordination.[36] The point is that personal, political, or theological disputes are not to be continued by disrupting religious ceremonies. Having said that, the offence is highly context-sensitive: behaviour which is out of place during a religious ceremony might be entirely unobjectionable on other occasions.

In its *Working Paper on Offences against Religion and Public Worship*, the Law Commission took the view that the offence was the only one of a small group of common law and statutory offences relating to public worship which, in spite of archaic language, still fulfilled a useful function.[37] They proposed in its place a new offence which would have penalized anyone who, with intent to wound or outrage the feelings of those using the premises concerned, used threatening, abusive, and insulting words or behaviour at any time in any place of worship of the Church of England, in any other certified place of religious worship, or in any burial ground. However, after consultation, the Commissioners were persuaded that this was too narrow in its references to the type of behaviour prohibited, the mental element, and the restriction to certified places of worship.[38] Instead, the final Report proposed two offences, one of disrupting services of religious worship, the other of offensive behaviour in places of worship.[39] Although not applicable to behaviour in purely private places, the offences would cover public religious gatherings not taking place in recognized places of worship. The Commissioners took the view that acts of worship should be protected from disruption which may not meet the normal public order threshold of 'threatening, abusive or insulting'[40] and that acts of desecration, such as placing a pig's head in a mosque, should likewise be prohibited, even in the absence of criminal damage.

The House of Lords Select Committee on Religious Offences in England and Wales was primarily established to consider reform to the law of blasphemy in the

---

[30] *Abrahams v Cavey* [1968] 1 QB 479. [31] *R v Farrant* [1973] Crim LR 240.
[32] As in *Blake v DPP* (1993) 97 Cr App R 169. [33] *R v Farrant* [1973] Crim LR 240.
[34] *Abrahams v Cavey* [1968] 1 QB 479; background in T Hughie Jones, 'Outrageous behaviour—a postscript' (1997) 4 Ecc LJ 664. [35] *Matthews v King* [1934] 1 KB 505.
[36] *Kensit v Dean and Chapter of St Paul's Cathedral* [1905] 2 KB 249.
[37] Law Commission, *Working Paper on Offences against Religion and Public Worship*, no 79 (1981).
[38] Law Commission, *Report on Offences against Religion and Public Worship*, no 145 (1985).
[39] Ibid, paras 3.19–3.22. [40] Public Order Act 1986, s 5.

wake of the Government's failed attempt to introduce an offence of incitement to religious hatred in the Anti-terrorism, Crime and Security Act 2001.[41] The Select Committee likewise concluded that although prosecutions under the Act formed a tiny minority of crimes in relation to churches and places of worship, the offence was not obsolete, but covered a small area of behaviour not otherwise covered by public order law. Intriguingly, the Committee also made the long-standing connection between public access and special protection for places and acts of worship. The Committee drew attention as a possible model to the Fijian Penal Code which creates four offences: damaging, destroying, or defiling a place of worship; disturbing a religious assembly; trespass to burial places; and writing or uttering words with intent to wound religious feelings. The Committee also pointed out that the boundaries of protection might not match precisely the criteria for registration of the definition of charitable religion.

In the course of passage of the Racial and Religious Hatred Bill, Lord Avebury sought to repeal the various offences relating to public worship.[42] However, while the common law offences of blasphemy and blasphemous libel have now been abolished,[43] the Government was not prepared for such wider-scale reform. The offence created by the Ecclesiastical Courts Jurisdiction Act 1860, for all its archaic language, remains on the statute book.

(b) Exemption from local taxation

The most significant privilege associated with registration, and the one which has given rise to the most litigation, is exemption from local taxation. The Poor Rate Exemption Act 1833 created a fairly narrow exemption from the obligation to pay local rates in respect of buildings 'exclusively appropriated to public religious worship' and for buildings used for Sunday and Infant Schools. The test survived changes in local taxation until the mid-1950s, but gave rise to difficulties on account of its narrowness. For example, the Lands Tribunal ruled—contrary to the view of the rating officer—that the regular showing of a religious film in a mission hall did not jeopardize the requirement of 'exclusive appropriation', since it was in the nature of a 'visual sermon'.[44] And in *Rogers v Lewisham Borough Council*, the Court of Appeal managed by dint of a certain degree of creativity to exempt a Brethren Hall which was used during the week as a youth club on the grounds that it was a Sunday School.[45] The Local Government Finance Act 1955 abandoned the exclusive appropriation test in favour of an exemption for places of public religious worship and associated premises. The boundaries of these associated premises were then widened in 1988 and again in 1992.

---

[41] House of Lords Select Committee on Religious Offences in England and Wales, HL Paper 95-I (2003), paras 25–27 and 54–68.   [42] Hansard HL 675 cols 544–547 (8 Nov 2005).

[43] Criminal Justice and Immigration Act 2008, s 79.

[44] *British Advent Missions Ltd v Cane* (1954) 48 R & IT 60.

[45] *Rogers v Lewisham Borough Council* [1951] 2 KB 768.

The Local Government Finance Act 1988, as amended, now exempts hereditaments consisting of places of public religious worship belonging to the Church of England, the Church in Wales, or for the time being certified as a place of religious worship, a church hall, chapel hall, or similar building used in connection with such a place of worship for the purposes of the same organization, and hereditaments occupied by an organization responsible for the conduct of public religious worship and used for related administrative or office purposes, including administration, clerical work, and handling money.[46]

A place of worship must be certified to be exempt, so a private chapel is not exempt, nor is a room set aside as a chapel in a private hospital, business premises, or social club.[47] Where a plot of land is used for several purposes, only those parts used for public religious worship, connected buildings and associated purposes will be covered.[48] Even if public access is not a requirement for registration, some indication that the building is open to the public is required for rating exemption.[49] As the Act makes clear, exemption is no longer limited to places of public religious worship but also extends to halls etc used in connection with worship and for the purposes of the same organization. This covers social centres attached to places of worship and even an independent school in the grounds of a mosque.[50]

The incumbent or minister, or trustee, of a place of public religious worship is also exempt as the owner of that place or of a churchyard or burial ground attached to it from liability under the private street works code.[51] This exemption originated in the Local Government Act 1858[52] which amended the new duty to repair or be chargeable for the expense of repair, of a private street, imposed by the Public Health Act 1848.[53] The reason appears to have been that since places of worship were exempt from 'poor rates' which could be used to repair public highways, they should also be exempt for other charges for similar purposes. The meaning of 'attached' has been subject to litigation in which it was held that a burial ground five miles away from the two synagogues it served was not 'attached' and therefore not exempt.[54]

In addition, it is worth noting that premises occupied by charities or charity trustees and used wholly or mainly for charitable purposes are taxed at 20 per cent of the normal rate.[55] Local authorities have a discretion to extend

---

[46] Local Government Finance Act 1988, s 51 and sched 5, para 11 as amended. This effectively changes the outcome in cases such as *Church House Trustees v Dimmick* (1959) 5 RRC 185.

[47] See eg *Morley v SPCK* (1960) 6 RRC 391 (business premises); *Sacred Heart v Veness* [1971] RA 394 (hospital); *Thomas v Mission to Seamen* [1988] RA 97 (social club).

[48] *Gallagher v Church of Jesus Christ of Latter-Day Saints* [2008] 1 WLR 1852 is an example.

[49] *Broxtowe BC v Birch* [1983] 1 WLR 314.

[50] *Liverpool Roman Catholic Archdiocesan Trustees Inc v Mackay* [1988] RA 90; *Ludkin v Trustees of Anjuman E Isthahul Muslimeen of UK* [1988] RA 209.   [51] Highways Act 1980, s 215.

[52] Ibid, s 38.   [53] Ibid, s 69.

[54] *Holy Law South Broughton Burial Board v Failsworth UDC* [1928] 1 KB 231.

[55] Local Government Finance Act 1988, s 43(5) and (6).

full exemption.[56] Local authorities also have the power to make grants towards adaptions to fireplaces in certified places of religious worship.[57] The Local Government Act 2003 removes the requirement of registration and certification for the purposes of exemption from non-domestic rates. Instead, it is proposed that the exemption should attach simply to 'place[s] of public religious worship'. To date, this change has not been brought into force.

(c) Registration for the solemnization of marriages

Apart from the existing exception for marriages between Quakers and between Jews, the Marriage Act 1836 for the first time allowed marriages to be solemnized in registered places of public religious worship. At the time, the general registration of places of worship had not been brought within the competence of the newly established Registrar-General, and so a further application was necessary by 20 householders to certify that they had used a 'separate building' as their usual place of public religious worship for at least a year. This was then overtaken by, but not wholly subsumed within, the 1855 Act procedure. The Marriage Act 1949 substantially re-enacted the 1836 scheme, with the one-year period later being reduced to one month. Failure to certify the place of worship under the 1855 Act does not affect the validity of a marriage carried out on premises registered with the Registrar-General.[58]

Buildings are not required to be registered for the solemnization of marriages between Quakers or Jews. Given that there is no longer any obligation to register under the 1855 Act (and, in fact, Quakers were relieved from that obligation in 1812), it is possible for such marriages to take place on wholly unregistered premises. Since there is still a need for civil preliminaries and the presence of a registrar or the authorization of a minister or other suitable person to conduct and register the marriage, there would now seem to be little added by the requirement of registration for the solemnization of marriage. In 2002 the Government proposed adopting a celebrant-based system, in which the time and place of the ceremony would be by negotiation with the religious celebrant.[59] If implemented, this would render any registration of places for the celebration of marriages redundant.

(d) Exception from registration with the Charity Commission

The only privilege directly associated with registration in the 1855 Act was that no charity was required to be registered with the Charity Commissioners in respect of any registered place of worship.[60] This exception had existed from the

---

[56] Local Government Finance Act 1988, s 47.   [57] Clean Air Act 1993, s 26.
[58] Marriage Act 1949, s 48(1)(c) and 48(2).
[59] ONS, *Civil Registration: vital change*, Cm 5355 (Jan 2002), paras 3.16–3.21.
[60] s 9; Charities Act 1993, s 3(5) now repealed.

creation of the Charity Commissioners a couple of years previously.[61] It extends to any forecourt, yard, garden, burial ground, vestry, or caretaker's house connected with the place of worship and held on the same trusts, as well as any Sunday-school house or other land or building which is certified by an order of the Charity Commissioners and connected with the building that it cannot conveniently be separated from it.

Under the Charities Act 2006, this exemption has now been modified, so that such charities are now to be treated as if they were excepted by ministerial regulation.[62] This is subject to an income limit of £100,000, and in any case charities excepted from registration are subject to new forms of oversight. The matter is therefore better considered as part of the new regulation of churches and religious bodies by the Charity Commission.

II. Charitable Religion

The second candidate for a category of public religion can be found in the law of charities. The advancement of religion is a charitable purpose, so long as the means adopted for its advancement confer a public benefit, and the objects are sufficiently certain to allow the court to oversee its due execution. These simple propositions mask a host of difficulties.

The most familiar difficulty is that of definition. What is to count as charitable religion?[63] The Charities Act 2006 was intended to address this by clarifying the point that religion need not involve belief in one god, but could involve belief in many gods or none.[64] The extent to which this was already reflected in the case-law is open to debate; it had certainly come to be reflected in the registration practice of the Charity Commissioners.[65] The Act also seeks to remove the potential for preferential treatment by removing the presumption of public benefit.[66] Charities for the advancement of religion are no longer presumed to confer a public benefit in the absence of evidence to the contrary; rather, public benefit must be demonstrated in every case. There is a certain logic in this. The financial

---

[61] Charitable Trusts Act 1853, s 62.

[62] Places of Worship Registration Act 1855 as amended, referring to Charities Act 1993, s 3A(4)(b).

[63] General Accounts in Jean Warburton (ed), *Tudor on Charities*, 9th edn (London: Sweet & Maxwell, 2003), paras 2–048–2–070; Hubert Picarda, *The Law and Practice relating to Charities*, 3rd edn (London: Butterworths, 1999), ch 4; Peter Luxton, *The Law of Charities* (Oxford: Oxford University Press, 2001), paras 4.31–4.62. Overviews in Miguel Rodriguez Blanco, 'Religion and the law of charities' (2005) 8 Ecc LJ 246; G E Dal Pont, 'Charity Law and Religion', in Peter Radan, Denise Meyerson, and Rosalind F Croucher, *Law and Religion: God, the State and the Common Law* (London: Routledge, 2005).   [64] Charities Act 2006, s 2(3)(a).

[65] Andrew Iwobi, 'Out with the old, in with the new: religion, charitable status and the Charities Act 2006' (2009) 29 Legal Studies 619.   [66] Charities Act 2006, s 3(2).

advantages attendant on charitable status are ultimately justified by the fact that some activities are publicly beneficial, and not just a matter of private interest. The State gives financial encouragement to organizations which confer a public benefit, but is indifferent to private interest associations.

However, at the heart of the problem of a definition of charitable religion lies the uncomfortable fact that it is not possible completely to transcend religious difference. The gradual expansion of 'religion' for these purposes was based on a model of toleration which took as its central case the established church, and accepted those other religions which Parliament tolerated. Once the courts had decided that they were not to take sides on the relative merits of any religion, they were left searching for supposedly neutral or secular principles by which to determine which religious objects do and do not merit public recognition and privilege. But wherever one draws the lines, it is relatively easy to show that the criteria of distinction are themselves bound up in controverted value-judgements. It has been suggested that with all its profession of neutrality, the law still shows a 'Protestant bias'.[67] Analogical expansion from historically dominant forms seems inevitable, yet in recent times is rendered still more problematic by enhanced expectations of neutrality under the Human Rights Act 1998.

The second difficulty flows from the fact that some lawful religious practices have never been charitable. Indeed, religious bodies have sometimes even preferred the private trust device. When John Wesley settled his Methodist meeting-houses, it was he and the ministers he nominated who were the beneficiaries. Wesley's power of nomination was then later transferred to the Annual Conference, keeping control clearly within the emerging organization. At the time the distinction between private and public trust was far from clear. Counsel in 1808 could still make a fair shot at arguing that in principle a trust for a dissenting congregation was not a public institution under the oversight of the Attorney-General, but a purely private society, like a club or a subscription library.[68] In *Cooper v Gordon* (1869) the congregation of Independent Protestants was deliberately established on the basis of a private trust for the congregation, and treated as such by the court.[69] Against this background, the decision of *Cocks v Manners* (1871) that gifts to closed monastic orders are not charitable is entirely understandable.[70] On the facts, it actually suited the Dominican convent, because it prevented the gift from falling foul of the Statute of Mortmain. And in *Re Price*, it was confirmed that a gift to the Anthroposophical Society was neither charitable nor to each current member absolutely but for the membership as bound by the rules of their society for their common purposes.[71] The invalidity of non-charitable purpose

---

[67] Michael Blakeney, 'Sequestered Piety and Charity—a comparative analysis' (1981) 2 J Leg Hist 207. [68] *AG v Fowler* (1808) 15 Ves 85, 33 ER 687.
[69] *Cooper v Gordon* (1869) LR 8 Eq 249. [70] *Cocks v Manners* (1871) LR 12 Eq 574.
[71] *Re Price* [1943] Ch 422.

trusts is, in practice, not normally problematic for religious organizations.[72] A religious society need not be charitable.

The problem is that large religious organizations can encompass a range of activities only some of which the law will consider charitable. A charity must have exclusively charitable objects. Thus gifts to churches are construed as gifts on trust to be applied for those of the church's purposes that are charitable.[73] This solves the problem of the individual gift for inheritance tax purposes, but then raises problems about the tax position and regulation of the organization more generally.

The problem of the public/private religious purpose distinction in the context of organized religions is exacerbated by the trust/person distinction. The charitable trust was a substitute for the lack of availability of forms of corporate personality for public institutions. Charitable trusts are only peripheral in the legal structure of the Church of England, since ecclesiastical corporations hold their property absolutely. Of course, a trust for the repair of a church, or maintenance of a clergyman, is charitable, but it is also incidental. This complexity was not fully understood by those who drafted the Charities Act 1960. They ensured that companies with charitable objects came within the definition of charity, but then defined ecclesiastical corporations in such a way as to ensure that what might loosely be called the 'property of the Church of England' was mostly—but not entirely—outside the jurisdiction of the Commissioners.[74] Once a religious organization incorporates under the Companies Act it is potentially subject to different regulatory regimes, with different rationales. It might hold some of its property absolutely for objects only mainly charitable, and some of its property as a trust corporation for exclusively charitable purposes.

Lurking behind these difficulties is the question of regulation. Charitable status gives access to fiscal privilege, but it also brings regulation in its wake. Historically, it allowed one to evade the rule against perpetual trusts. It made possible the concept of a protected endowment: an income-producing resource applied in perpetuity to certain purposes. A charitable object was a public one, which the courts would uphold even in the absence of ascertainable beneficiaries. At the same time, the Attorney-General asserted an interest in ensuring that the property was properly applied, and royal commissioners might be appointed from time to time to investigate and redress abuse. Moreover, if the religion were unlawful, a general charitable intent might be held to override the failure of the trust, and warrant the diversion of the property to quite different purposes.[75]

---

[72] *Leahy v Attorney-General for New South Wales* [1959] AC 457 is, of course, an example of the problem of combining charitable and non-charitable religious objects. But properly advised, the testator's intention to benefit both active (charitable) and contemplative (non-charitable) nuns could have been achieved.   [73] *Re White* [1893] 2 Ch 41.

[74] See Lord Nathan, *The Charities Act 1960* (London: Butterworths, 1962), 26–8.

[75] See *West v Shuttleworth* (1835) 2 Myl & K 684, 39 ER 1106, and cases cited therein.

From the perspective of a religious organization this represented a potentially unwelcome degree of constraint and Governmental oversight.

To some extent, the law has always relieved charitable religious organizations from regulation by Government. It is well-known that, with one minor exception, the preamble to the Statute of Elizabeth makes no mention of religious trusts. Its widespread adoption as a working definition of charity was thus potentially problematic—although not actually so, because the courts had no hesitation in holding trusts for purposes connected with the established church charitable, and soon enough accepted that tolerated dissent was also charitable. The reason for its silence is not entirely clear, but was presumably connected with its purpose, which was to authorize royal commissioners to investigate and redress the misappropriation of property given to charitable uses. Sir Francis Moore thought that religious trusts were excluded because the question of whether a religious purpose was lawful or superstitious turned on the pleasure of the sovereign.[76] But this explanation is only partially plausible. The doctrine of superstitious uses derived from a common law development of the statutory appropriation of chantries by Edward VI. The appointment of royal commissioners might have made it practically easier for the sovereign to appropriate and redirect the use of charitable property by way of prerogative *cy-près*, but exclusion from the preamble of the Statute of Elizabeth made no difference to the state of the law. The more obvious explanation is that the Act was simply not intended to interfere with relatively well-governed charitable institutions, and indeed relied on the church to produce the commissioners.[77] It did not apply to colleges in Oxford and Cambridge; Eton, Winchester, and Westminster; cathedrals and collegiate churches; colleges, hospitals, or free schools with visitors, governors, or overseers appointed by the founder; nor was it to affect the jurisdiction or power of the ordinary.[78] There was only one national church, which had a system of government, and which could redress abuses of its property, and was in any case intimately involved in the enforcement of the Act.

When the modern Charity Commissioners were established in 1853, their jurisdiction over religious charities was again limited, this time out of a concern for autonomy from Government interference. This autonomy continues in attenuated form even today, although it is in the process of being dismantled, and self-regulation is giving way to compulsory Government regulation. Depending on the practical tax implications of being non-charitable and non-profit-making, a religious organization might well now prefer to avoid the 'privilege' of charitable status. The three areas of law which require further exploration are therefore the definition of charitable religion, the degree of public regulation now involved

---

[76] Gareth Jones, *History of the Law of Charity, 1532–1827* (Cambridge: Cambridge University Press, 1969), 26–39.

[77] Kathryn Bromley and E Blake Bromley, 'John Pemsel goes to the Supreme Court of Canada in 2001' (1999) CL & PR 115.   [78] Statute of Elizabeth 1601, 43 Eliz, c 4, s 4.

in being a charity, and the comparative financial advantages associated with charitable status.

1. The definition of charitable religion

The advancement of religion was one of four categories of purpose identified by Lord Macnaghten as charitable.[79] This has recently been reaffirmed in the Charities Act 2006, albeit as one of a much longer list of purposes.[80] Until that Act, the courts would presume that the advancement of religion conferred a public benefit unless the religion in question was 'subversive of all morality',[81] or it was clear that the mode of advancing the religion conferred no cognizable public benefit at all. There was thus a certain elision of the question of 'advancement' into the question of 'public benefit'. One impact of the removal of the presumption of public benefit has been to make clearer the three-stage nature of the enquiry: is there a religion, is it being advanced, and does it confer a public benefit?

As regards the first question, the courts have long professed neutrality and adopted a broad definition. Even when it was formulated, the requirement of Lord Denning MR in *ex parte Segerdal* that religion required faith in some sort of supreme being or entity and worship, reverence or veneration of that being was recognized to be too narrow.[82] Buddhism is a religion regardless of that test. The concern to be as broad as possible has been continued in the Charities Act 2006, which states that religion includes those which involve belief in more than one god or none.[83]

Nevertheless, there must be limits, and the Charity Commission has found that Scientology is on the far side of those limits.[84] There is ongoing debate as to the best formulation of what counts as a religion. It is still not clear to what extent the religion must engage in 'worship'. One attractive suggestion draws on the judgments in a leading Australian case[85] and requires belief in some transcendental reality or supernatural being, thing, or principle together with a system of conduct or practice giving effect to that belief.[86] On this account, Scientology would be over the first hurdle. It has also been suggested that the effect of the 2006 Act has been to change the Commission's view that paganism is not a religion for these purposes.[87]

An important consequence of this breadth, which is only paradoxical at first sight, is that it can be a charitable purpose to seek to convert a person from

---

[79] *Income Tax Commissioners v Pemsel* [1891] AC 531.   [80] Charities Act 2006, s 2(2).

[81] *Thornton v Howe* (1862) 31 Beav 14, 54 ER 1042.

[82] *R v Registrar General, ex parte Segerdal* [1970] 2 QB 697, 707.

[83] Charities Act 2006, s 2(3).   [84] Decision of 17 November 1999.

[85] *Church of the New Faith v Commissioner for Payroll Tax* (1982) 154 CLR 120 per Mason ACJ and Brennan J.

[86] Thomas Spring and Francesca Quint, 'Religion, Charity Law and Human Rights' (1999) 5 CL & PR 153.   [87] Iwobi, *op cit* n 65, 628.

religion X to religion Y and it can be a charitable purpose to seek to convert them back again.[88] That is simply the effect of liberty and equality on the State's law. The law does not prefer non-proselytizing religions over proselytizing ones; indeed there is probably even a stronger positive policy in favour of public questioning, debate, and change, with limits on proper modes of proselytism.

The case-law on what counts as advancement is likewise broad. The fullest definition is that of Donovan J in which he defined it as taking 'positive steps to sustain and increase religious belief and these things are done in a variety of ways which may be comprehensively described as pastoral and missionary'.[89] Since this must include the maintenance of religious practice even among those already committed, practices which can only be described at best as 'maintaining' the religion count as advancement for these purposes.

Thus if there is any bias in the law it arises from the apparently neutral test of 'public benefit'. The courts have long insisted that there is religion which is private and personal only, and there is religion which confers a public benefit. This has been most apparent in two groups of decisions: those involving enclosed monastic orders and those involving private rituals. In the case of monastic orders which have withdrawn from society and whose impact is only through the bare knowledge of their existence by other believers and by divine agency in response to their prayers, the House of Lords has ruled that neither of these is judicially cognizable.[90] Monastic orders which engage with society in the provision of pastoral or social welfare services are clearly charitable.[91] The second group of decisions concern private rituals such as masses for the repose of individual souls which are offered in private, or other forms of private devotion.[92]

In truth, it is difficult to reconcile all the cases. However, these two examples seem to express a policy that affects all religions. The endowment of a private chapel—even Anglican—is not charitable; a trust to endow a public chapel is.[93] A trust to endow individual prayer is not charitable; generally accessible corporate prayer is.[94] A trust to erect and maintain a tomb or gravestone to an individual is not charitable, unless it also adorns a public place of worship.[95] A trust to maintain an entire churchyard is charitable.[96] Gifts for 'religious' purposes or to specific religious organizations are presumed to be applied to charitable purposes, but gifts for the purposes of a religious denomination, such as 'Roman Catholic

---

[88] See *AG v Becher* [1910] Ir R 251.
[89] *United Grand Lodge v Holborn BC* [1957] 1 WLR 1080.
[90] *Gilmour v Coates* [1949] AC 426; see also *Re Warre's Will Trusts* [1953] 1 WLR 725.
[91] *Cocks v Manners* (1871) LR 12 Eq 574; *Re Banfield* [1968] 1 WLR 546.
[92] *Yeap Cheah Neo v Ong Cheng Neo* (1875) LR 6 PC 381; *Re Hetherington* [1990] Ch 1.
[93] Compare *Hoare v Hoare* (1886) 56 LT 147 with *Re Robinson* [1897] 1 Ch 85.
[94] *Re Joy* (1889) 60 LT 175.
[95] *Re Vaughan* (1886) LR 33 Ch D 187; *Re Barker* (1909) 25 TLR 753.
[96] *Re Pardoe* [1906] 2 Ch 184.

purposes' or 'parish (ie Anglican) purposes' are not.[97] Gifts to religious office-holders are divided into those to be applied to charitable purposes in accordance with the duties of the office and those where the purpose is vague and thus the gift is void for uncertainty.[98]

The case-law suggests that public benefit can generally be determined by applying a primary test and a subsidiary test. The primary test is one of public access. If the general public, or a sufficiently broad section of the public, can access the rituals and ceremonies, the pastoral services, the teaching or the literature of a religion, a public benefit is conferred regardless of the religion in question.[99] One could adopt the words of article 9 ECHR, that where there is public access to 'worship, teaching, practice or observance' there is charity. The class of beneficiaries can be very small.[100] Certainly, adherents of a given religion constitute a section of the public.[101] In cases where the direct benefit is restricted to members of a particular organization, a subsidiary test of public impact may come into play. If the religion is such that by participating in it the members are in some way supported and encouraged in their spiritual life, which has a wider social effect outside the organized religion, that too amounts to a sufficient public benefit.[102] Of course, if there is a definite social action programme, that will clearly show a public benefit. Thus in one way or another, the activity must tend, either directly or indirectly, to the instruction or edification of the public.[103]

Against this background, the recent statutory guidance of the Charity Commission displays a subtle but strong secularizing tendency.[104] This tendency was clearer in the draft guidance, but is still present in muted form in the final version. First, there is a tendency to see religions in monolithic terms. This is perhaps best captured in a careless limitation of charitable status to 'recognised' religions,[105] but is expressed in a variety of ways: hostility to distinctive individual positions within religions,[106] suspicion of purposes based around only a few tenets of a religion,[107] a limitation of relevant social welfare activities to those required by 'specific obligations' of the religion,[108] and worry about the 'abuse or misuse of religious teachings'.[109]

Secondly, there is a thinly-disguised sense that religions are often morally suspect. The Commission disclaims any desire to 'modernise' religions (as if a

---

[97] Compare *Re Schoales* [1930] 2 Ch 75 with *MacLaughlin v Campbell* [1906] 1 IR 588 and *Re Stratton* [1931] 1 Ch 197.

[98] *Re Garrard* [1907] 1 Ch 382 and *Dunne v Byrne* [1912] AC 407; see also *Re Rumball* [1956] Ch 105.

[99] See, above all, *Re Hetherington* [1990] Ch 1; *Holmes v Attorney-General*, The Times, 12 Feb., 1981.   [100] *IRC v Baddeley* [1955] AC 572, per Lord Somervell at 615.

[101] eg a trust for the benefit of Methodists: P S Atiyah, 'Public Benefit and Charities' (1958) 21 MLR 138, 153.   [102] *Neville Estates v Madden* [1962] Ch 832.

[103] *Cocks v Manners* (1871) LR 12 Eq 574.

[104] See Charity Commission *Draft Supplementary Guidance*, 'Public Benefit and the Advancement of Religion' (February 2008); *Supplementary Guidance*, 'The Advancement of Religion for the Public Benefit' (December 2008).   [105] *Draft Guidance*, 17.

[106] Ibid, 16–17.   [107] Ibid, 24–5.   [108] Ibid, 19.   [109] Ibid, 26.

modern orthodox Jew were not as modern as a modern atheist!).[110] Thus religions are allowed to be 'discriminatory', whatever that means in an undifferentiated sense, but must be open and clear to others about the ways in which they are discriminatory.[111] Proselytism is rather regrettable.[112]

Thirdly, and most problematic of all, there is a deep-rooted instrumentalization of religion to Governmental ends. This has been achieved by recasting the cases on public access as cases on 'advancement' and then requiring an additional demonstration of 'public benefit' in terms of a beneficial moral impact on society, that is, according to modern mores.[113] If one takes this seriously, it would no longer be sufficient to show merely that a place of worship is open to the public.[114] Rather one would need to satisfy the public impact test that the religious worship taking place makes a worthwhile moral contribution to society as a whole. There are even suggestions that religious organizations need to provide evidence of this contribution, although these are muted elsewhere.[115] This re-interpretation of the law is strengthened by the view that the adherents of one religion do not count as a section of the public, which assimilates all religious belief to private club membership.[116] The muddle is compounded when it is suggested that any 'interested' member of the public must be able to join an organized religion as a formal member, or perhaps that tests should not 'deny legitimate access to those who truly wish to join'.[117]

The secularizing tendency has been assisted by confusion as to the meaning of the public benefit presumption, and therefore what it means to remove it.[118] The presumption seems to be understood by the Commission in an evaluative sense. On this account, 'religion' used to be seen as a good thing—it was better for a person to have some religion rather than none—unless the religion was subversive of all morality.[119] Since religion was a good thing (a few uncommon exceptions aside), the presumption meant that advancing a religion typically conferred a public benefit. Removing the presumption then means that the law no longer assumes that some religion is better than none. The positive ethical value of each religion must now be shown. However, the presumption should actually be understood in an evidential sense. Most methods of advancing a religion just happened to satisfy the relevant legal tests for public benefit in practice, so the presumption was just a practical short-cut. Removing the presumption removes the short-cut, but leaves the tests intact.

It remains to be seen whether the secularizing reading of religious charity law by the Commission will take root. The numbers of charities with purposes

---

[110] Ibid, 22. [111] Ibid, 31; *Guidance*, E3.

[112] *Draft Guidance*, 26–9. The negative tone was picked up in the consultation responses, 'Summary of Consultation Responses', 5. [113] *Draft Guidance*, 23; *Guidance*, E2.

[114] This was cited as a paradigm example in the Government's Review and subsequent Report.

[115] eg 'research studies' (*Draft Guidance*, 7); 'factual evidence' (*Draft Guidance*, 23).

[116] *Draft Guidance*, 30; *Guidance*, E3. [117] *Draft Guidance*, 31, 33.

[118] Summary of debate in Iwobi, *op cit* n 65, 639–43.

[119] *Re Watson* [1973] 1 WLR 1472.

including the advancement of religion continues to rise,[120] and in the light of the fact that the Charities Act 2006 was not intended to change the substance of the law, it would be hard to strike off a charity which was properly registered in the past. However, the potential is clearly present for restricting religious charitable purposes to large familiar religions, and only to the extent that they 'provide a moral and ethical framework for people to live by and play an important part in building social capital and community cohesion'.[121] As public morality departs from traditional accounts, largely influenced by Christianity, the charitable nature of religion will be increasingly vulnerable.

2. Regulation by the Charity Commission

The Charity Commissioners were established by the Charitable Trusts Act 1853 for the due administration of charitable trusts and for the more beneficial application of charitable funds in certain cases. Initially, their powers were relatively limited, with the pressing need to reform certain major ancient charitable institutions balanced by a concern about excessive Government intervention. Over time, their powers have been expanded, and the considerable body of subsequent legislation was eventually reformed and consolidated by the Charities Act 1960. This in turn was replaced by the Charities Act 1993, which has now been substantially amended by the Charities Act 2006.

Prior to 1960, charities associated with organized religions were substantially outside the jurisdiction of the Commissioners.[122] At common law, ecclesiastical corporations were not charitable trusts, since they held their corporate property directly.[123] Under the Act of 1853, registered places of worship bona fide used as such were excluded, as were institutions wholly maintained by voluntary contributions. The extra-territorial property of missionary organizations was also excluded. All Roman Catholic charities were excluded until 1861, when they were assimilated to the position of other non-established religious bodies.[124] The purpose of the exception was to take certain institutions out of the operation of the Act, and it meant, for example, that the trustees of a church did not need the consent of the Commissioners before taking legal action to eject a minister who had departed from the doctrinal standards of the church.[125] The policy of the law was reaffirmed in the Charitable Trusts Amendment Act 1869, which, as we have seen, gave religious charity trustees access to the powers of the Commissioners to request the appointment of new trustees, the vesting of property and the approval of schemes, but expressly protected them from any regulation.[126]

---

[120] The Guidelines give a figure of 29,000 registered charities which advance religion (*Guidance*, section A). [121] *Draft Guidance*, 3.

[122] *Halsbury's Laws of England*, 3rd edn (London: Butterworths, 1953), vol 4, paras 902–12.

[123] *AG v St John's Hospital, Bedford* (1865) 2 De GJ & S 621, 635, 46 ER 516.

[124] Roman Catholic Charities Act 1860.

[125] *Glen v Gregg* (1882) 21 Ch D 513, per Lord Jessel MR at 518.

[126] Charitable Trusts Amendment Act 1869, s 15.

The exceptions contained in the Act of 1853 did not provide a blanket exclusion for religious bodies. If capital could be expended, there was no endowment, and thus no jurisdiction.[127] However, in *Re St John's Street Wesleyan Methodist Chapel*, the court rejected an argument of counsel that the entire 'estate' associated with a registered place of worship was exempt.[128] The court held that the Commissioners could require the trustees to account for income derived from any land other than the registered building itself. However, this decision was controversial, and quickly confined by both the legislature and the Court of Appeal. The Charitable Trusts (Places of Religious Worship) Act 1894 extended the exemption for registered buildings to any 'forecourt, yard, garden, burial ground, vestry or caretaker's house' connected with the building and held on the same trusts. A Sunday school house or other land or buildings used in connection with the building and held on the same trusts could be added by order of the Commissioners at the request of the trustees. In *Re Clergy Orphan Corporation*, the Court of Appeal decided that although any investment income might normally constitute 'endowment', in the case of mixed charities whose income derived from both investments and voluntary contributions for the general purposes of the charity, the decision of trustees to lay out some of the funds in investments did not constitute endowments under the jurisdiction of the Commissioners.[129] As subsequent cases showed, even where the land was no longer used as a place of religious worship, but as an income-generating asset, consent from the Commissioners for its disposal was not needed.[130] Since most of the funds of non-established religious bodies were derived from donations, the effect was to exclude the jurisdiction of the Commissioners over organized religions for most practical purposes.

The law was substantially reformed and consolidated in the Charities Act 1960 as part of the rationalization of charities in the wake of the establishment of the Welfare State. The principal effect of this Act was to create new general obligations on all charities to register, to account to the Commissioners, and to seek their consent for major dispositions of property. The independence of religious bodies was a matter of some debate in Parliament,[131] and was dealt with in a variety of ways. The law effectively created a fourfold classification of charities: charities not included within the definition of charity at all for the purposes of the Act, exempt charities, excepted charities, and all other charities subject to the oversight of the Charity Commissioners. The basic policy was that where adequate oversight was provided by a religious denominational structure, that of the Charity Commissioners was not necessary.[132]

---

[127] Charitable Trusts Act 1853, s 62.
[128] *Re St John's Street Wesleyan Methodist Chapel* [1893] 2 Ch 618.
[129] *Re Clergy Orphan Corporation* [1894] 3 Ch 145; *AG v Mathieson* [1907] 2 Ch 383.
[130] *Re Wesleyan Methodist Chapel* [1909] 1 Ch 454; See also *Re Church Army* (1906) 94 LT 559.
[131] Lord Nathan, *The Charities Act, 1960* (London: Butterworths, 1962), 46.
[132] Ibid, 29–30, 46.

Ecclesiastical corporations were wholly outside the Act. The representative Body of the Church in Wales was an exempt body, as were the Church of England's Clergy Pensions Board and funds coming within the Church Funds Investment Measure 1958.[133] So too was the Central Finance Board of the Methodist Church.[134] No charity was required to be registered in respect of a registered place of worship, as under the old law.[135] Several other religious charities were excepted by regulation of the Secretary of State. After initial temporary blanket exception, permanent regulations were created which relieved religious charities from the principal duties to the Charity Commissioners.[136] Trusts connected with the Methodist Conference, various Baptist and Congregational Trust Corporations, the Friends Trusts Ltd, the British and Foreign Unitarian Association, the Federation of Independent Evangelical Churches, the Presbyterian Church of England, and the Properties Board of the Presbyterian Church of Wales were excepted from the requirement to register or account to the Commissioners. So too were diocesan and archdiocesan boards of finance in the Church of England. Another series of regulations also excepted trustees of all religious premises from the requirement to seek consent for dispositions of property under certain conditions.[137] General religious funds of bodies other than those already listed were excepted in respect of any property other than land unless the income was more than £100.[138]

The Charities Act 1993 changed this regime slightly, but not in its essentials. The obligation to gain consent for dealings in land was replaced for all charities with obligations to secure a fair valuation, so the need for an exception fell away. The consequences of designation as an excepted charity were harmonized within the Act, in line with the existing regulations, rather than being dependent on each specific regulation.

The Strategy Review Unit report of 2002 suggested that 'in the context of today's more extensive reporting and monitoring regime for registered charities, designed to improve accountability for charitable funds, these exceptions no longer make sense'.[139] The report went on to suggest that the fact that the privilege of exception was limited to Christian religious denominations was unlikely to be compatible with the Human Rights Act 1998, and recommended its staged

---

[133] Ibid, 31. See currently, Charities Act 1993, s 96(1) and sched 2, paras (x) and (a) respectively. The Places of Worship Registration Act 1855, s 9 is excluded from the scope of para (a); Welsh Church (Temporalities) Act 1919, s 7(1).

[134] Methodist Church Funds Act 1960, c xxxiii, s 8(1).   [135] Charities Act 1960, s 4(4).

[136] Charities (Exception from Registration and Accounts) Regulations 1963/2074 and 1964/1825.

[137] Charities (Religious Premises) Regulations 1962/1421; Charities (Society of Friends, Federation of Independent Evangelical Churches and Presbyterian Church of Wales) Regulations 1962/1815; Charities (Church of England) Regulations) 1963/1062.

[138] SI 1963/2074, reg 1.

[139] Cabinet Office Strategy Unit, Private Action Public Benefit—A Review of Charities and the Wider Not-For-Profit Sector (Sept 2002), para 7.90.

abolition.[140] The Government noted three responses of excepted bodies—that there was no practical need for change, that the constitution of some component churches might be incompatible with Charity Commission requirements, and that the bureaucratic burden would be increased—but nonetheless agreed with the report.[141] The register was a national database of all charities and an important element of accountability. Regulatory oversight through annual monitoring was justified. In consequence, the Charities Act 2006 has now substantially amended the 1993 Act and strengthened the regulatory oversight of the Commission over organized religions.

(a) Religious charities outside the Act

Parts of the Church of England are outside the jurisdiction of the Charity Commission, since the term 'charity' does not apply for the purposes of the Charities Act 1993:

(a) to any ecclesiastical corporation (that is to say, any corporation in the Church of England, whether sole or aggregate, which is established for spiritual purposes) in respect of the corporate property of the corporation, except to a corporation aggregate having some purposes which are not ecclesiastical in respect of its corporate property held for those purposes; or

(b) to any Diocesan Board of Finance (or any subsidiary thereof) within the meaning of the Endowments and Glebe Measure 1976 for any diocese in respect of the diocesan glebe land of that diocese within the meaning of that Measure; or

(c) to any trust of property for purposes for which the property has been consecrated.[142]

'Consecrated' for these purposes means consecrated for spiritual use according to the rites of the Church of England, not according to any other religious denomination, since consecration is a spiritual office exercised by a bishop changing the legal nature of the land in question.[143] These provisions remain unaffected by recent changes.

(b) Exempt religious charities

The list of exempt charities contained in the Act consists substantially of public institutions such as universities, museums, art galleries, and registered industrial, provident and friendly societies. In many cases these are self-regulated, under their own statutory regimes. Exempt charities are not required to register and

---

[140] Ibid, para 7.91.

[141] Home Office, 'Charities and Not-for-Profits: a modern legal framework' (July 2003), paras 6.44–6.50.   [142] Charities Act 1993, s 96(2), as amended.

[143] *Sedgwick v Bourne* [1920] 2 KB 267.

are largely free from the oversight of the Commissioners.[144] In particular, the Commissioners have no power to institute inquiries,[145] to impose a scheme where the trustees unreasonably refuse or neglect to apply for one,[146] or to act for the protection of the charity in question.[147] Furthermore the Charities Act 1993 relieves them from the duty to keep and audit annual accounts in the prescribed form or make annual reports to the Commissioners, except that where no other statute (such as that constituting the charity in question) imposes an obligation to prepare periodical statements of account, there is a subsidiary obligation to prepare consecutive statements of account.[148]

The Charities Act 2006 removes the Church Commissioners from the schedule of exempt charities and excludes investment and deposit funds of the Church of England and the Methodist Church from the older statutory exemptions.[149] The Representative Body of the Church in Wales also loses its exemption.

(c) Excepted religious charities

The Regulations of 1963 and 1964 were replaced by the Charities (Exception from Registration) Regulations 1996, which, as amended, remain in force.[150] They have only ever been temporary, but have recently been extended to 1 October 2012. However, their significance has become attenuated. Charities wholly or mainly concerned with the advancement of religion and connected with one of the major Christian denominations listed in the Regulation are excepted if they fulfil one of three conditions. The charity must either have as its trustee, or one of its trustees, a trust corporation connected with the body or one of the bodies with which the charity is connected, or it must be established wholly or mainly to make provision for public religious worship, or it must be one in respect of which accounts are sent annually to the Methodist Conference, a Methodist Synod, or any connexional or other committee or department appointed or established by the Methodist Conference.[151] For the purpose of the Regulations, the advancement of religion includes the relief of ministers and former ministers of religion and their families.[152] The relevant Christian denominations are: a church within the meaning of section 2 of the Baptist and Congregational Trusts Act 1951; a church which is affiliated to the Fellowship of Independent Evangelical Churches; a church which is a member of the General Assembly of Unitarian and Free Christian Churches; the Calvinistic Methodist or Presbyterian Church of Wales; the Church of England; the Church in Wales; the Methodist Church; the Religious Society of Friends; and the United Reformed Church.[153]

---

[144] Charities Act 1993, s 3A(2)(a). A request by an exempt charity to register need not be accepted: s 3A(6).   [145] Ibid, s 8(1).
[146] Ibid, s 16(6).   [147] Ibid, s 18(16).   [148] Ibid, s 46(1).
[149] Charities Act 2006, s 11.
[150] Charities (Exception from Registration) Regulations 1996, SI 1996/180, as extended by SI 2007/2655.   [151] Ibid, reg 4(1) and (2).
[152] Ibid, reg 2.   [153] Ibid, reg 4(3).

Trusts of less than £1,000 income per year conditional on the upkeep of graves are permanently excepted.[154] There is also exemption by individual order of the Charity Commissioners for charities vested in the diocesan trustees of the Church in Wales and the Roman Catholic Church.[155] Until 2009, charities in respect of a registered place of worship were not required to register and were largely excluded from the jurisdiction of the Charity Commissioners.[156] This has been removed, and instead, they are now excepted by regulation for the purposes of the Charities Act 1993.[157] The term, 'registered place of worship' carries with it the expansive meaning adopted in the Act of 1894 noted above. The list of excepted charities cannot be further increased, but is limited to those institutions excepted before the 2006 Act came into force.[158]

A charity can now only be excepted if its annual gross income is less than £100,000.[159] This value may only be changed to reduce the scope of the exception.[160] Excepted charities are not required to register and are thus also not subject to those obligations imposed on 'registered charities' such as the duty to carry the name and details of the charity on official publications[161] and the duty to make an annual return to the Commission in the prescribed form.[162] Excepted charities are subject to the normal accounting and auditing requirements, but are not required to transmit annual reports to the Commissioners.[163] However, the Commissioners may request the trustees to prepare and transmit to them a report in respect of any given financial year.[164]

3. Financial advantages

Given that problems around the invalidity of non-charitable purpose trusts can be circumvented relatively easy, not least through incorporation, the principal advantage associated with charitable status today is financial. Charities have benefited from exemptions from direct taxation ever since the introduction of income tax in 1799.[165] The meaning of 'charitable' for the purposes of these exemptions became controversial towards the end of the nineteenth century. In *Pemsel's Case*, the Income Tax Commissioners had argued for a more popular meaning restricted to the relief of poverty, but the House of Lords asserted that it should be read in

---

[154] Ibid, reg 5.

[155] Picarda, *The Law and Practice relating to Charities*, 3rd edn (London: Butterworths 1999), 605.

[156] Places of Worship Registration Act 1855, s 9 and Charities Act 1993, s 3(5) as originally passed.

[157] Charities Act 1993 (Exception from Registration) Regulations 2008, SI 2008/3268, reg 2.

[158] Charities Act 1993, s 3A(4)(c).   [159] Ibid, s 3A(2).   [160] Ibid, s 3A(8)(a).

[161] Ibid, s 5.   [162] Ibid, s 48.   [163] Ibid, ss 46(4) and 45(3).

[164] Ibid, s 46(5) to (7).

[165] Some historians blame Addington in 1803. The tax was repealed at the end of the Napoleonic War. The modern income tax, annual but renewed without fail, derives from the Income Tax Act 1842.

its wider and technical meaning.[166] It was in this context that Lord Macnaghten formulated his well-known four categories of charitable purpose, and on the facts it meant that the missionary objectives of the Protestant Episcopal, or Moravian, Church, benefited from the relevant exemption. On the other hand, there has never been a blanket exemption from tax liability. It all depends on the arrangements and activities of the religious body in question as assessed in the light of the statutes. Thus, in principle, where a religious organization carries on a trade, it cannot set the losses of associated charitable activity off against the profits of the trade.[167] Subject now to some exceptions, the courts treat the trading component as a separate enterprise which is donating its profits to the religious or charitable object.

The question for current purposes is the extent to which organized religions benefit from the tax advantages associated with charitable status. The tax reliefs available to charities fall into two distinct groups. First, there are those associated with the taxation of the charity as an entity. Secondly, there are those accruing to other persons in respect of donations to charity. Tax law is highly complex and currently undergoing a process of major restatement, so only the most general of principles can be stated here.[168]

If applied to charitable purposes only,[169] the following main types of income are exempt from taxation:

(i) The profits of charitable trades, that is trades exercised in the course of carrying out a primary purpose of the charity or mainly carried out by its beneficiaries.[170] There is also an allowance for non-exempt trades up to 25 per cent incoming resources, up to a limit of £50,000.[171]

(ii) Income deriving from VAT-exempt fundraising events and lotteries exempt from regulation under the Gambling Act 2005.[172]

(iii) Income derived from land, investments and securities.[173]

(iv) Public revenue dividends are not taken into account so far as the dividends are applicable and applied to the repair of a cathedral, college, church, chapel, or a building used only for the purposes of divine worship.[174]

(v) Charities are also exempt from capital gains tax if the gain is applied to charitable purposes.[175]

(vi) Stamp duty is not chargeable on conveyances, transfers, or leases made to bodies established for charitable purposes only.[176]

---

[166] *Special Income Tax Commissioners v Pemsel* [1891] AC 531.

[167] *Trustees of Psalms and Hymns v Whitwell* (1890) 3 TC 7; *Religious Tract and Book Society of Scotland v Forbes* (1896) 3 TC 415; *Grove v YMCA* (1903) 4 TC 613.

[168] See, further, general treatments such as John Tiley, *Revenue Law*, 6th edn (Oxford: Hart Publishing, 2008) esp ch 53; Natalie Lee (ed), *Revenue Law—Principles and Practice*, 26th edn (Haywards Heath: Tottel Publishing, 2008) esp ch 53.

[169] *IRC v Helen Slater Charitable Trust Ltd* [1982] Ch 49.

[170] Income Tax Act 2007, ss 524–5.   [171] Ibid, ss 526, 528.

[172] Ibid, ss 529 and 530.   [173] Ibid, ss 531–2.   [174] Ibid, s 533.

[175] Taxation of Chargeable Gains Act 1992, s 256.   [176] Finance Act 1982, s 129.

If an organized religion were not charitable it would typically be an unincorporated or partially incorporated private association, potentially liable to corporation tax.[177] Larger denominations might be looser associations not even amounting to unincorporated associations for tax purposes.[178] The closest analogies would seem to be private sports clubs and political parties. Gifts *inter vivos* or by will are not profits or gains and would not be taxable anyway.[179] Nor would members' subscriptions be taxable, since one cannot make a profit from oneself.[180] Fees charged to non-members (eg for services such as rites of passage) could potentially be treated as being by way of trade,[181] profession, or vocation, although the nature of the service and the relatively peripheral contribution to the overall enterprise must make the matter subject to considerable doubt. Of course, expenses incurred in offering the service could be offset against the takings, but tax could not be avoided by applying profits to the non-trading element. Given the current constitution and activities of most organized religions, one suspects that the main difference would be a liability for tax on various forms of endowment income.[182]

So far as Value Added Tax is concerned, many of the activities of religious organizations are not taxable anyway, regardless of charitable status. Yet there are additional benefits in respect of charities. VAT is only charged on taxable supplies.[183] Taxable business activity requires the existence of a continuing activity predominantly concerned with supplying of goods and services to others for consideration. The provision of a place of worship as such is not a business activity for these purposes, but charging for admittance is.[184] A person must be registered if his or her annual turnover exceeds £68,000.[185] Non-business activities and exempt activities are not taxable. Zero-rated supplies are technically 'taxable', even though no tax is paid while zero-rating applies.[186] Educational services, including the provision of a fee-paying members' youth club, are exempt, as are spiritual welfare services provided by a charity or in the context of a religious community or retreat, along with burial and cremation services.[187] Subscriptions to non-profit making bodies with religious objects in the public domain are exempt.[188] Charitable fund-raising is also exempt.[189] The sale of books and other publications is zero-rated, as is the sale of goods donated to charity and

---

[177] Corporation Tax Act 2009, s 2(1); Income and Corporation Taxes Act 1988, s 832(1).

[178] *Conservative and Unionist Central Office v Burrell* [1982] 1 WLR 522.

[179] *Ryall v Hoare* [1923] 2 KB 447.

[180] *New York Life Insurance Company v Styles* (1889) LR 14 App Cas 381.

[181] *Carlisle and Silloth Golf Club v Smith* [1913] 3 KB 75.

[182] See eg *Blackpool Marton Rotary Club v Martin* [1990] STC 1.

[183] Value Added Tax Act 1994, s 4(1).

[184] *Dean and Chapter of Hereford Cathedral v Customs and Excise Commissioners* [1995] VATTR 159. The finding of a partial business activity allowed the cathedral to recover input tax on repairs to the vergers' accommodation.   [185] Value Added Tax Act 1994, s 3 and sched 1, para 1.

[186] Ibid, s 4(2).   [187] Ibid, sched 9, groups 6–8.   [188] Ibid, sched 9, group 9.

[189] Ibid, sched 9, group 12.

advertisements supplied to charities.[190] The construction of buildings for residential or charitable purposes is zero-rated, and the relevant residential purposes include those of a religious community.[191] The biggest practical concern of religious and charitable organizations is the inability to recover input tax on goods and services supplied in the upkeep of historic buildings. This can represent a substantial additional cost.

It is also the policy of taxation law to encourage donations to charity by offering relief from a range of taxes. The Finance Acts 1990 and 2000 extended this policy substantially by making even one-off gifts to charity of any amount eligible for relief from personal income tax and corporation tax. Relief up to the amount of income and capital gains tax paid in any year by a donor is now available through Gift Aid on donations to charities.[192] The value of any benefit the individual may receive in return is limited on a sliding scale, starting at 25 per cent for small gifts, and currently capped at £500.[193] Gifts of shares, securities, and real property are likewise eligible for relief if the individual makes a claim.[194] Regular donations can be assisted through payroll deduction schemes, whereby the employer deducts a designated amount before tax and pays it to an approved agent for distribution to the charities of the employee's choice.[195] Gifts to charities are also exempt from capital gains tax and inheritance tax.[196] Similar reliefs on donations to charities are available to companies,[197] gifts in kind are not accountable as trading receipts,[198] and in some circumstances some donations can be treated as business expenses.

The Inland Revenue provisionally calculate that the total value of tax reliefs granted to charities in 2008–9 was £3.12 billion.[199] The single largest component of this figure is £1,010 million in relief from non-domestic rates. It will be recalled that places of public worship pay no rates at all and other charities pay at 20 per cent. Presumably the figure here does not include a sum representing rates foregone in respect of the former, which is unquantifiable in the absence of any regime for this type of activity. The rest of the value is made up as follows: return of basic rate income tax to charities through Gift Aid etc. £967 million; relief from VAT £200 million; relief from stamp duty land tax £190 million; inheritance tax foregone £380 million; payroll giving relief £30 million; capital gains tax foregone on individual gifts of shares and property £70 million; and higher rate tax relief to individuals on Gift Aid etc £270 million. The figures do not include income such as rent from land and interest on investments which is paid gross to charities, and for which no return is made.

---

[190] Ibid, sched 8, groups 3 and 15.   [191] Ibid, sched 8, group 5.
[192] Income Tax Act 2007, ss 413–430.   [193] Ibid, s 418.   [194] Ibid, ss 431–446.
[195] Income Tax (Earnings and Pensions) Act 2003, ss 713–715.
[196] Taxation of Chargeable Gains Act 1992, s 257; Inheritance Tax Act 1984, s 23.
[197] Income and Corporation Taxes Act 1988, s 339.   [198] Ibid, s 83A.
[199] HM Revenue and Customs, Statistics, Table 10.2.

There is an understandable tendency on the part of some tax lawyers to confuse tax reliefs with subscriptions and to fail to distinguish reliefs by way of exceptions to rules and the limits of those rules.[200] The unspoken presupposition is that all property belongs to the State and is given back to the extent that it is not taxed. If one combines this with an assumption that the State should not be promoting religion, it is easy to conclude that organized religions should be taxed like anyone else. The logic is at least intelligible in the case of individual tax reliefs designed to encourage donations to religious organizations. It is much less so in the case of taxing religious organizations as entities. The view that 'religion' is none of the State's business could equally well lead one to conclude that it should not be taxed at all.

III. The Ecclesiastical Exemption

More briefly, one should note the existence of the 'ecclesiastical exemption' as a final example of public religion. Certain ecclesiastical buildings in use for ecclesiastical purposes are exempt from listed building and conservation area consent in respect of developments.[201] However, they are still subject to planning permission in the same way as every other building. Planning permission only covers external developments, and since it can refer to more or less the same criteria over the matters to which it extends as listed building and conservation area consent, the practical significance of the exemption is to remove Government control of changes to the internal fabric of listed ecclesiastical buildings.[202] Of course, the religious dimension of any planning proposal is a relevant factor in support of the religious needs of the applicant and should be taken into account by the planning authority in every case.[203] However, the exemption goes beyond this to make certain changes subject only to the determination of the religious organization itself. It is of considerable significance to the Church of England, a substantial majority of whose churches are listed.[204] However, a large number of buildings of other Christian denominations are also listed, as are a small but steadily growing number of those of other religions.[205]

---

[200] In *Pemsel's Case*, Lord Bramwell objected to a decision which made the State a subscriber of £17 a year to the missionary establishment of the Protestant Episcopal Chuch. See also Peter Edge, 'Charitable Status for the advancement of religion: an abolitionist's view' (1995/6) 3 CL & PR 29.

[201] Planning (Listed Buildings and Conservation Areas) Act 1990, ss 60 and 75(1)b).

[202] Charles Mynors, *Listed Buildings, Conservation Areas and Monuments*, 4th edn (London: Sweet & Maxwell, 2006), para 16.2.1.

[203] *ISKCON v United Kingdom* (1994) 18 EHRR CD 133; *R (Alconbury) v Secretary of State for the Environment, Transport and the Regions* [2003] 2 AC 295.

[204] Around three quarters of all churches (roughly 16,000) in the Church of England are listed, and 45 per cent of Grade 1 listed buildings are owned by the Church of England.

[205] Mynors notes around 3,000 owned by the Roman Catholic Church, Methodist Church, United Reformed Church, and Baptist Church. There are smaller numbers of highly significant Unitarian chapels and Quaker meeting houses. A few historic synagogues and mosques are also listed, including the first purpose-built mosque in Woking in 1889.

The exemption derives ultimately from the Ancient Monument Consolidation and Amendment Act 1913,[206] in which the Church of England successfully argued that the preservation of ancient churches could be better achieved though its own internal faculty jurisdiction.[207] The price of autonomy was the agreement that the church would not seek financial assistance for repairs and maintenance. The exemption was extended when local authorities gained the power to make orders preventing buildings of historic or architectural interest from being demolished,[208] when the grade listing system was introduced,[209] and when conservation area controls were imposed.[210] Although not technically part of the ecclesiastical exemption, the same logic was applied to the demolition of redundant churches.[211]

The exemption was not lost when an agreement on (limited) State aid for the support of ancient churches was reached in 1976. However, after re-listing in 1982 brought a significant number of non-established places of worship into the lists, agreement was reached that it should only extend to those denominations which could show an adequate system of internal regulation. Powers included for the first time in the Housing and Planning Act 1986 resulted eventually in the Ecclesiastical Exemption (Listed Buildings and Conservation Areas) Order 1994,[212] which is the current law.

The 1994 Order exempts buildings administered by the Church of England, the Church in Wales, the Roman Catholic Church, the Methodist Church, the Baptist Union, and the United Reformed Church.[213] The organizations were selected as a result of the application of criteria such as independent expertise and decision-taking, notification to relevant stakeholders such as English Heritage/ Cadw, taking account of relevant historical and architectural factors, appeal and enforcement mechanisms, record-keeping, and regular inspection.[214] The exemption also extends on a temporary basis to Church of England peculiars and religious communities, some Roman Catholic institutions, various Scottish churches in England, and shared church buildings and places of worship in any university, college, school, hospital, Inn of Court, or other public or charitable institution used by any of the six exempt denominations.[215] The idea is that eventually every building will be subject either to internal or secular control. A review conducted in 1997 essentially approved the operation of the new internal sys-

---

[206] s 22.
[207] Historical development in Kathryn Last, 'The privileged position of the Church of England in the control of works to historic buildings: the provenance of the ecclesiastical exemption from listed building control' [2002] CLWR 205.
[208] Town and Country Planning Act 1932, s 17(5)(1)(a).
[209] Town and Country Planning Act 1947.   [210] Civic Amenities Act 1967.
[211] Redundant Churches and other Religious Buildings Act 1969, s 2.
[212] Ecclesiastical Exemption (Listed Buildings and Conservation Areas) Order 1994, SI 1994/1771.   [213] Ibid, art 4.
[214] DCMS Planning Policy Guidance Note 15, para 8.4.
[215] Ecclesiastical Exemption (Listed Buildings and Conservation Areas) Order 1994/1771, art 6.

tems, while making several recommendations for improvements.[216] These have largely been acted on.[217]

The terms, 'ecclesiastical building' and 'ecclesiastical purposes' are not entirely clear.[218] Although it would be straining language to apply them to other faiths, the legislation now implies that other faith organizations could potentially benefit.[219] In practice none of them has. 'Buildings' do not include residences for ministers of religion.[220] Once an ecclesiastical building is redundant it is out of use and no longer covered by the exemption. However, the Church of England enjoys an additional exemption to determine for itself questions of redundancy and demolition.[221]

The faculty jurisdiction of the Church of England represents the most developed and accessible system of internal control. Indeed, like those in respect of cathedrals[222] and the other five exempt denominations, it has developed in response to Governmental pressure and the desire to preserve autonomy.[223] Nevertheless, the way in which pastoral and heritage considerations are balanced causes some difficulty. The Court of Ecclesiastical Causes Reserved, which deals with rare appeals on questions of doctrine and ceremony and has a more theological than legal composition, took the view that the test for change should not be as strict as 'necessity'.[224] However, several chancellors and the Canterbury Court of Arches have developed a series of questions which make clear that there is a strong presumption against change in the case of listed buildings.[225] Commentators observe that the dissatisfaction of both heritage bodies (change is too easy) and local congregations (change is too hard) might indicate that chancellors are, on the whole, achieving an appropriate balance.[226] It is hard to believe that the same balance would be achieved by a local planning authority.

Major plans to reform the system of heritage protection involve the creation of national heritage registers of heritage assets and a unified system of consent

---

[216] John Newman, *A Review of the Ecclesiastical Exemption from Listed Buildings Controls*, DCMS (September 1997).

[217] DCMS and Welsh Office, *Follow Up to the Review of the Ecclesiastical Exemption (The Newman Report)* (January 1999).

[218] See discussion in *AG ex rel Bedfordshire CC v Howard United Reformed Church Trustees, Bedford* [1976] AC 363.

[219] Planning (Listed Buildings and Conservation Areas) Act 1990, s 60(6)(b).

[220] Ibid, s 60(3).

[221] Ibid, s 60(7) and the Pastoral Measure 1983 as amended by the Pastoral (Amendment) Measure 1993.

[222] Cathedrals are not subject to the faculty jurisdiction but are regulated under the Care of Cathedrals Measure 1990 as amended.   [223] See Last, *op cit* n 207.

[224] *Re St Stephen's, Walbrook* [1987] Fam 146.

[225] The principal cases setting out and elaborating the 'Bishopsgate Questions' are: *Re St Luke the Evangelist, Maidstone* [1995] Fam 1; *Re St Mary the Virgin, Sherborne* [1996] Fam 63; *Re Holy Cross, Pershore* [2002] Fam 1.

[226] Alexandra Fairclough, 'Whose voice prevails? Faculties, hearings and heritage' [2002] JPL 1444, echoing the views of Chancellor Mark Hill.

for development.[227] The Government recognizes the value of the exemption in relieving itself from an administrative burden and in addressing the particular needs of historic assets in use as places of worship.[228] It is therefore content to let the current ecclesiastical exemption continue to operate on the understanding that it continues to provide a similar level of consultation and engagement as the general secular system.[229] It also proposes the introduction of Heritage Partnership Agreements to allow for the strategic management of historic sites, including agreed categories of change. These will be voluntary and also open to non-exempt denominations responsible for heritage assets. There will be a slight loss of autonomy if conservation area control is assimilated to the normal planning process as envisaged.[230]

IV. Conclusion

Two main observations emerge from a consideration of public religion in English law. The first is that the category is not nearly as significant as it is in some other European jurisdictions. It is not connected to privileges such as military exemption, chaplaincies in public institutions, the operation of schools and social welfare institutions, and access to formal and semi-formal processes of consultation. Rather, its main significance is financial. Other matters are dealt with by reference to their own criteria, which allows (at least potentially) for a more nuanced approach.

The second observation is that English law in practice works with two categories of public religion, one extremely broad, the other fairly narrow. At one level, all religious purposes which are not a matter of purely personal devotion or organized as a private club (of which the best example is the enclosed monastic order) are treated as public and privileged accordingly. On the other hand, there is a secondary level which only includes the major Christian denominations. These have been granted a certain freedom from Government regulation, being trusted to be self-regulatory. If the former category is tolerably secure, notwithstanding some calls for the denial of charitable status to organized religions, the latter category is vulnerable to levelling down and increased Government regulation. The Charities Act 2006 has ended it in one area, while the ecclesiastical exemption has survived.

---

[227] DCMS/Welsh Assembly Government White Paper, *Heritage Protection for the 21st Century*, Cm 7057 (March 2007); Draft Heritage Protection Bill (April 2008).

[228] DCMS, *The Ecclesiastical Exemption: the Way Forward* (July 2005); White Paper, section 1.3 paras 21–4.

[229] The temporary exemptions in art 6 of the current order have largely been resolved one way or the other in the draft Ecclesiastical Exemption (Registered Heritage Structures) Order 200X.

[230] Noted by Frank Cranmer, 'Parliamentary Report' (2008) 10 Ecc LJ 352–3.

It is arguable that registration under the Places of Worship Act 1855 is no longer necessary. In the case of public order offences, they would be better drafted to be independent of registration. One might just argue that if there is to be an offence of desecration of a sacred place, some formal act of recognizing a place as sacred is useful, although the idea that potential desecrators might check the register is fanciful. Of the two major consequences (local taxation and marriage registration) there is an amendment pending which removes the requirement of registration as a precondition for non-domestic rating exemption, and a proposal to remove the legal significance of place from religious marriages with civil effect. The exception from Charity Commission registration now seems anomalous in the light of their growing regulatory function, or at any rate should be coordinated with exemptions for charitable religious organizations more generally.

Other forms of regulation, and exceptions thereto, do not depend on registration. Premises appropriated to, and used solely or mainly for, public religious worship were once exempt from fire certification requirements.[231] They are so no longer. The provision of any entertainment for the purposes of a religious meeting or service, or at a place of public religious worship, is not regulated under the Licensing Act 2003.[232] Religious relics for public display at a place of public religious worship are exempt from human tissue regulation.[233] None of these exemptions relied, or rely, on registration.

In an important article published in 1946, F H Newark argued that there is no requirement of public benefit in the case of charities for the advancement of religion.[234] Apart from cases of purely individual benefit, the worship of God was, without more ado, charitable. That position is not sustainable against the background of the current case-law, and yet the article succeeded in showing the elusive quality of public benefit in a political context that professes religious neutrality.[235] It is not difficult to mount an argument for levelling down religious belief and practice to other forms of hobby towards which the State is indifferent.[236] As this chapter has shown, law and Government policy in recent years has drifted towards the subordination of religion to Governmental ends and the combining of public financial privilege with Governmental regulation.

However, if one accepts that religion is in an important sense public and non-Governmental, two linked arguments in favour of some form of registration might carry some weight. The first is that registration as a place of public

---

[231] Fire Precautions Act 1971, s 2(d), repealed by the Fire Safety and Safety of Places of Sport Act 1987, s 13.　　　　　[232] Licensing Act 2003, s 1(4) and sched 1, para 9.

[233] Human Tissue Act 2004, s 40.

[234] F H Newark, 'Public Benefit and Religious Trusts' (1946) 62 LQR 234.

[235] Matthew Harding, 'Trusts for Religious Purposes and the Question of Public Benefit (2008) 71 MLR 159 discusses the evidential problems and notes that the Irish Charities Bill 2007 retains the presumption of public benefit for religious charities.

[236] Peter W Edge, 'Charitable Status for the Advancement of Religion: an abolitionist's view' (1995/6) 3 CL & PR 29; Peter W Edge and Joan Loughrey, 'Religious charities and the juridification of the Charity Commission' (2001) 21 Legal Studies 36.

religious worship has been associated with a bundle of privileges which might be jeopardized if they were divided out among their respective regulatory regimes. It has functioned as a general religious analogy to the position of the established church. If both were to change, it would not be obvious where in the law the distinctive position and needs of organized religions would be anchored. By the same token, as religions diversify, registration provides a simple and controllable point of entry to those privileges. This has the potential for reducing variation in access to privilege across different religions. It may be that what is needed is not assimilation to the legal position of charities more generally, but a specific regime more protective of the autonomy of organized religions in relation to Government. The Convention rights of organized religions would be better protected by a regime that 'levels up' rather than 'down', as is the current tendency. This would also permit the reconstruction of the remainder of charity law around a more homogeneous conception of the public interest.[237]

---

[237] Christine R Barker, 'Religion and Charity Law' [1999] Jur Rev 303, reaches a similar conclusion.

6

Regulated Rites

Worship and ritual acts represent the most distinctive manifestations of religious belief. The law engages with them in a variety of ways. On one hand, a particular ritual act may be legally indifferent: reading from scriptures, reciting a prayer, or singing a hymn are matters of which the law takes no notice.[1] On the other hand, the ritual nature of some acts is legally irrelevant. If a child is abused, a criminal offence is committed regardless of any religious dimension. It makes no difference that speech inciting to religious hatred is contained in a sermon. This chapter considers a number of aspects of religious life which fall between these two limits. Some matters of worship and ritual are specifically accommodated, or are accorded legal significance, or are even subject to their own distinctive legal regime.

Two historic examples, which linger on in popular memory, are the legal privileges formerly accorded to sanctuary and confession. The English common law of sanctuary provided a safe haven for 40 days after the commission of certain serious criminal offences.[2] Thereafter one had to abjure the realm, ie take oneself into exile. Having been broadly interpreted during medieval times, it was restricted in line with canon law after the Reformation and finally abolished completely in 1624.[3] Its modern use to shelter asylum seekers facing deportation with a view to encouraging the Home Office to review their cases rests on no legal basis.[4]

As far as confession is concerned, whatever the historic position may have been, it would seem that clergy enjoy no privilege in law, and thus may not refuse to answer any question properly put to them by appealing to the secret of the confessional.[5] This, at any rate, is the general view of judges and commentators, although the matter has never been fully argued, and there is a legal difficulty in the case of clergy of the Church of England. Under ecclesiastical law, Anglican clergy are bound to respect secrets imparted during confession. Since ecclesiastical law is part of the law of England, an argument can be made that this

---

[1] In rare cases of course, such acts *may* give rise to a criminal offence, as, for example, the singing of a hymn to disrupt a service in *Abrahams v Cavey* [1968] 1 QB 479.

[2] J H Baker, 'The English Law of Sanctuary' (1990) 2 Ecc LJ 8; R H Helmholz, *The ius commune in England: Four Studies* (Oxford: Oxford University Press, 2001), ch 1.

[3] 21 Jam I, c 28, s 7.   [4] Teresa Sutton, 'Modern Sanctuary' (1996) 4 Ecc LJ 487.

[5] D W Elliott, 'An evidential privilege for priest-penitent communications' (1995) 3 Ecc LJ 272.

obligation should be recognized by civil courts as well.[6] In Ireland, by contrast, a broad privilege covering priest–penitent relationships has been recognized.[7] The reasoning is broad enough to embrace all religious denominations engaging in a practice such as confession.[8]

In cases both of sanctuary and confession, representatives of the law may attempt to mitigate the tensions. The police may be unwilling to break into a place of worship, and a judge may seek to dissuade one party from putting a minister of religion into a moral or legal dilemma. However, such attempts aside, the law can be and has been enforced, even in places of worship, and awkward questions can be put.[9] Both sanctuary and confession are examples of aspects of worship and ritual which the law once accommodated, but does so no longer.

The chapter falls into three main parts. The first part considers rites of passage centred on birth, marriage, and death. The second part addresses questions of diet. In the final part, various other aspects of the legal regulation of unconventional collective worship are covered.

I. Rites of Passage

At common law, parishioners have the right to present their children for baptism, to be married, and to be buried by the Church of England.[10] It has been suggested that members of religious associations have an equivalent enforceable civil right to receive these rites of passage according to the rules of their association.[11] These rights are not unconditional. In the case of the Church of England, the conditions are part of the general law, whereas in the case of other religious bodies they are part of their domestic rules. Thus where the civil law of marriage has departed from the formal position of the Church of England, an exception has had to be created in the general law in order to secure to the established church the freedom which would automatically be enjoyed by any other religion. A priest may refuse to marry a divorcé(e), or parties related in certain ways, on grounds of conscience.[12] The extent to which he or she is free to exercise this civil privilege is a matter of canon law, which could have adopted a collective position on the point.[13]

---

[6] Rupert D H Bursell, 'The seal of the confessional' (1990) 2 Ecc LJ 84.

[7] *Cook v Carroll* [1945] Ir R 515. For a wider comparative acount, see Simon Fisher, 'Clergy confidentiality and privileges: themes and prospects', in Peter Radan, Denise Meyerson and Rosalind F Croucher, *Law and Religion: God, the State and the Common Law* (London: Routledge, 2005).

[8] Ibid, 521.

[9] See, for example, the case of Viraj Mendis summarized in Sutton, *op cit* n 4, 488.

[10] See the discussion in Norman Doe, *The Legal Framework of the Church of England* (Oxford: Oxford University Press, 1996), 358–62.

[11] *Brown v Curé de Montreal* (1874–5) LR 6 PC 157.

[12] Matrimonial Causes Act 1965, s 8; Marriage (Prohibited Degrees of Relationship) Act 1986, s 3.

[13] See, for example, Canon B31, which commences, 'Subject to the provisions of the Marriage (Prohibited Degrees of Relationship) Act 1986 no person shall marry …'.

1. Baptism and naming ceremonies; circumcision

The obligation to register births and christenings in the parish registers of the Church of England represented one of the five principal grievances listed by the Dissenting Deputies in 1833.[14] The Registration Act 1836 met this concern by providing for a general system of non-religious registration of births. The Act also made provision for the subsequent addition of a name certified as given in baptism. The current legislation, which is the Births and Deaths Registration Act 1953, still makes provision for the addition or change of a name up to 12 months after the registration of the birth.[15] The new name may be certified in the pre-scribed form by one performing the rite of baptism or by the one having custody of the baptismal register, if any, or if not given in baptism may be notified by a parent, guardian, or other person procuring the name of the child to be altered or given. No more than £1.00 may be charged for such a certificate.[16]

Baptism still carries with it a curious residual civil significance. In *Re Parrott*, Vaisey J held that it is not possible to change a Christian name, that is, a name given in baptism, except by Act of Parliament or on confirmation.[17] A testamen-tary gift conditional on changing one's Christian name is therefore void. Baptism occurs whenever there is the use of water and invocation of the Holy Trinity,[18] so this rule would apply to all (Trinitarian) Christian denominations. Registrations of changes of name by deed poll are nevertheless accepted notwithstanding this decision,[19] and it is possible that this formality would now be treated as sufficient fulfilment of the condition were the facts of *Re Parrott* to arise again. There is no right to have one's name removed from a baptismal register, which unlike a mem-bership roll is a record of an historical event rather than a guarantee of current affiliation.

Male circumcision is an important marker of identity within Judaism and Islam. In the case of the former it occurs soon after birth, in the case of the lat-ter it may take place later in the boy's childhood.[20] It is generally assumed that it is lawful,[21] whether or not carried out by a medically qualified practitioner,[22] although of course a remedy exists for negligently performed operations,[23] which may also give rise to fitness to practise proceedings.[24] If both parents do not agree

---

[14] Timothy Larsen, *Friends of Religious Equality: Non-conformist politics in mid-Victorian England* (Woodbridge: The Boydell Press, 1990), 43.

[15] Births and Deaths Registration Act 1953, s 13(1).   [16] Ibid, s 13(2).

[17] *Re Parrott* [1943] 1 Ch 183.   [18] *Kemp v Wickes* (1809) 3 Phillim 264, 276.

[19] *Halsbury's Laws of England*, 4th edn (London: Butterworths, 1994), vol 35 'Personal Property', para 1273 n 8.

[20] This is entirely different from female 'circumcision', which is a form of genital mutilation and unlawful under the Female Genital Mutilation Act 2003.

[21] *R v Brown* [1994] 1 AC 212, 231 per Lord Templeman.

[22] Law Commission, *Consent in the Criminal Law*, Consultation Paper no 139 (1995), para 9.2.

[23] See eg *Ibrahim (a minor) v Muhammad*, unreported, 21 May 1984.

[24] See eg *General Medical Council v Dirir* [2009] EWHC (Admin); *Nicholas-Pillai v General Medical Council* [2009] EWHC 1048 (Admin).

to the circumcision of their child, it may not be done without court order.[25] The court will consider the best interests of the child, in which the religious character of his home environment and upbringing will be a key factor.[26] However, once a boy of mixed religious heritage reaches a certain age, the court may require the parent to wait until the boy himself is Gillick-competent.[27] The court is not bound to decide the matter according to the internal law of the faith in question. It has been argued that the approach of English law to circumcision is incompatible with the State's duty to prevent harm to children.[28] There may be a case for ensuring better regulation, but in the absence of any indication that significant numbers of Jewish or Muslim men later object to the fact that they were subject to the operation, arguments based on the lack of the child's consent are implausible.

Recent years have seen a renewed desire to provide secular alternatives to traditional religious practices. Many registration offices now offer civil naming ceremonies as an alternative to religious ceremonies. Such ceremonies are of no legal effect, and thus strictly speaking could have any religious component the parties and the registrar consent to.[29] In 2004 Frank Field MP introduced into Parliament a Rite of Passage (Welcoming and Coming of Age) Bill, which would have made it compulsory for parents to participate in a non-religious welcoming ceremony before the registrar. It also contained provision for a coming-of-age ceremony. The Bill was anomalous in failing to permit the obligations to be satisfied by religious alternatives, such as baptism/circumcision and confirmation/Bar Mitzvah/Bar Mitzvoth, on which it was presumably loosely modelled.

Rites of initiation for children are controversial among those who think that it is possible for a child to be brought up in an environment of religious neutrality. Circumcision, and even baptism, seems to foreclose later choice. But quite apart from the fact that prohibition would require considerable State interference in family and religious life, the assumption that a non-religious upbringing is really neutral between faiths is questionable.

2. Marriage and divorce

The requirement imposed by Lord Hardwicke's Act of 1753 that one had to marry in the established church after the publication of banns was another practical grievance of dissenters in the early part of the nineteenth century. Apart from

---

[25] *Re J* (child's religious upbringing and circumcision) [2000] 1 FCR 307, CA.

[26] Circumcision not ordered: *Re U* (child), unreported, 25 November 1999, CA; *Re J* (child's religious upbringing and circumcision) [1999] 2 FLR 345; *Re J* (child's religious upbringing and circumcision) [2000] 1 FCR 307. Circumcision ordered: *Re S* (change of names: cultural factors) [2001] 3 FCR 648.

[27] *Re S* [2005] 1 FLR 236, upheld [2004] EWCA 1257 Fam, CA. The boy was 10 years old.

[28] Howard Gilbert, 'Time to reconsider the lawfulness of ritual male circumcision' [2007] EHRLR 279.   [29] Cf Marriage Act 1949, s 45(2).

the existing exception for marriages among Quakers and Jews, the Marriage Act 1836 for the first time allowed marriages to be solemnized in registered places of public religious worship. At the time, the general registration of places of worship had not yet been brought within the competence of the newly established Registrar-General, so a further application was necessary by 20 householders to certify that they had used a 'separate building' as their usual place of public religious worship for at least a year. The Registrar-General was obliged to publish annually a list of places of public worship registered under the Act. Ministers of religion could be authorized to solemnize marriages in the place of the registrar.

The Marriage Act 1949 substantially re-enacts the 1836 scheme.[30] One year after registration of the building, a person may be authorized to conduct marriages and certified to the Registrar-General by the trustees or governing body of the building.[31] The requirement that the building be 'separate' was recognized to be problematic, in that special provision was made for Roman Catholic chapels under the same roof as another building or forming part only of a building. This condition was eventually removed in its entirety by the Marriage (Registration of Buildings) Act 1990. The provision for religious denominations other than the established church is becoming less distinctive, in that provision has recently been made for civil marriage ceremonies to be carried out in a wide range of approved premises. However, premises may not be licensed if they are used solely or mainly for religious purposes.[32] The same restriction applies to civil partnerships.[33] This rigorous divide between the religious and the secular is also reflected in the exclusion of the use of a 'religious service' from civil ceremonies,[34] which is often interpreted to mean any reading or music which the registrar considers has a religious dimension. This is an exclusion which one suspects might struggle to survive a Human Rights Act challenge. For now, however, the two regimes of civil and religious celebration operate in parallel.

The consequences of solemnizing a marriage on unregistered premises are not entirely clear. Such a 'marriage' may be a purely religious ceremony and thus without any legal effect.[35] Purely religious ceremonies are not unlawful, and it is not a criminal offence to conduct a marriage which does not purport to be valid under English law.[36] However, if the parties knowingly and wilfully intermarry without satisfying the formal requirements, the marriage will be void and the parties entitled to a decree of nullity and appropriate relief.[37] In *Chief Adjudication Officer v Bath*, the Court of Appeal had to consider the case of a Sikh couple who

---

[30] Marriage Act 1949, s 41, as amended by the Marriage Acts Amendment Act 1958, s 1(1)(a).

[31] Ibid, s 43(1).   [32] Marriage Act 1994.

[33] Civil Partnerships Act 2004, ss 2(5), 6(1)(b) and (2); Marriages and Civil Partnerships (Approved Premises) Regulations 2005/3168, sched 1, para 4.

[34] Marriage Act 1949, ss 45(2) and 46B(4); Marriages and Civil Partnerships (Approved Premises) Regulations 2005/3168, sched 2, para 11.

[35] The Marriage Act 1949, s 46, makes provision for post-marriage religious ceremonies which are not themselves valid marriages.   [36] *R v Bham* [1966] 1 QB 159.

[37] Marriage Act 1949, s 49.

had married in an unregistered *gurdwara* assuming that they were contracting a valid marriage.[38] While the majority of the Court merely considered that the presumption of marriage from long cohabitation had not been rebutted, Evans LJ was prepared to hold that the solemnization of a marriage in premises which could have been registered, by a person who could have been authorized, was valid unless the conditions for nullity (ie knowing and wilful intermarriage in breach of formal requirements) were satisfied. But the boundary between a purely religious ceremony and a formally defective marriage is not entirely clear.[39] Given the potential criminal liability,[40] religious bodies would be well advised to make explicit whether the ceremony is, or is not, intended to have civil effect, and ensure that the necessary formalities are satisfied accordingly.

Marriages between two persons professing the Jewish religion or between two persons authorized by the Society of Friends (Quakers) to be married according to their usages are still subject to distinctive rules.[41] In both cases, superintendant registrar's certificates are necessary, with the usual preliminaries.[42] But buildings or places of celebration do not need to be registered,[43] and the need to certify an authorized person is expressly disapplied.[44] The normal time constraints for celebration do not apply.[45] The marriage is to be registered by the district registering officer (Quakers) or the secretary of the husband's synagogue (Jews).[46]

Commentators have observed a gap between registrations as places of worship and further registration for the solemnization of marriage.[47] This may have been caused by the former requirement for a separate building, and it has also been suggested that the requirement that worship must be 'public' may act as a constraint.[48] The Marriage Act contains additional formalities: doors must be open, the marriage must be conducted in the presence of a register or authorized person, and certain words must be used.[49] However, the figures may simply be a result of the fact that very small religious groups will not consider it worth their while to register for these purposes. It is noticeable that while the proportion of buildings of larger Christian denominations registered for marriage is just

---

[38] *Chief Adjudication Officer v Bath* [2000] 1 FLR 8.

[39] *Gereis v Yagoub* [1997] 1 FLR 854 concerned a marriage in an unregistered Coptic Orthodox church (held effective). See the discussion in J M Masson, R Bailey-Harris, and R J Probert (eds), *Cretney's Principles of Family Law*, 8th edn (London: Sweet & Maxwell, 2008), 38.

[40] Marriage Act 1949, s 75.

[41] Ibid, s 47; Frank Cranmer, 'Regulation with the Religious Society of Friends' (2003) 7 Ecc LJ 176, 190–1.   [42] Marriage Act 1949, s 26(1)(c) and (d).

[43] Ibid, s 35(4) implies this by referring to a 'building or place' rather than a 'registered building'.   [44] Ibid, s 43(3).

[45] Ibid, s 75(1)(a).

[46] Ibid, s 53(b) and (c). See also s 67 for the identification of such officers and secretaries.

[47] See Office for National Statistics, *Marriage, divorce and adoption statistics, 2005* (Series FM2, no 32).

[48] Anthony Bradney, 'How not to marry people: formalities of the marriage ceremony' [1989] Fam Law 408; see discussion in Carolyn Hamilton, *Family, Law and Religion* (London: Sweet & Maxwell, 1995), 47–51.   [49] Marriage Act 1949, s 44.

under 90 per cent, the proportion for small Christian groups is about 70 per cent. The figure for Sikh buildings is about 80 per cent, similar to that for Christian Brethren and the Salvation Army. The figure for Muslims is still substantially lower—about 20 per cent of registered places of worship are registered for the solemnization of marriage—but this may be a result of more general tensions between current legal and Islamic conceptions of marriage than the formalities of registration.

Given the universal requirement for civil preliminaries and the need for the presence of a registrar or the authorization of a minister or other suitable person to conduct and register the marriage, there would seem now to be little added by the requirement of separate registration for the solemnization of marriage. It is an historical accident. In any case, in 2002 the Government proposed adopting a celebrant-based system, in which the time and place of the ceremony would be by negotiation with the religious celebrant.[50] This is close to the way the current arrangements work in respect of Jews and Quakers, and would render any registration for the celebration of marriages redundant.

As far as the substantive law of marriage is concerned, English law is still rooted in a conception of marriage as the life-long voluntary union of one man and one woman to the exclusion of all others.[51] It makes few concessions to other cultural conceptions, other than the relatively easy availability of divorce and, more recently, a broadly equivalent same-sex civil partnership. Parties must be at least 16 years of age,[52] and require parental consent if they are under 18.[53] Lack of consent between the parties makes the marriage voidable.[54] Both parties must be physically present at the ceremony.[55] In spite of a series of relaxations, restrictions on marriages between certain close relatives are still in place.[56] While marriages between cousins are permitted, those between uncles and nieces (for example) are not. Polygamous marriages are ineffective and potentially criminal.[57] This position is made much more complex when the parties are domiciled abroad.[58] The common law initially refused to recognize even marriages that were only potentially polygamous according to the law of the place of celebration.[59] The effect was to refuse matrimonial relief to parties who for all practical purposes complied with the English conception of marriage simply on account of the law of their

---

[50] White Paper, *Civil Registration: vital change*, Cm 5355 (Jan 2002), paras 3.16–3.21.
[51] *Hyde v Hyde* (1866) LR 1 P&D 130.
[52] Marriage Act 1949, s 2; Matrimonial Causes Act 1973, s 11(a)(2).
[53] Marriage Act 1949, s 3(1).   [54] Matrimonial Causes Act 1973, s 12(c).
[55] Marriage Act 1949, s 44(3).
[56] Marriage Act 1949, s 1 and sched 1. Most recently, in *B v UK* [2006] 42 EHRR 11, the European Court found the prohibition on fathers-in-law and daughters-in-law to constitute a violation of article 12 ECHR. See Marriage Act 1949 (Remedial) Order, SI 2007/438.
[57] Matrimonial Causes Act 1973, s 11(b); Offences against the Person Act 1861, s 57.
[58] See, generally, Lawrence Collins (ed), *Dicey, Morris and Collins on the Conflict of Laws*, 14th edn (London: Sweet & Maxwell, 2006), vol II, 835–57.
[59] *Hyde v Hyde* (1866) LR 1 P&D 130.

country of origin. This was eventually modified by the Matrimonial Proceedings (Polygamous Marriages) Act 1972, and for most practical purposes polygamous marriages are now recognized if permitted by both parties' law of domicile and according to the law of the place of celebration.

With one limited exception, a religious divorce is legally irrelevant. At common law, parties resident in this country, but domiciled in a foreign State which recognized the judgments of religious courts, could secure legally effective divorces through religious courts located in this country.[60] That power was removed by statute in 1973,[61] but the misalignment of civil and religious divorce continued to create difficulties, principally for wives who were divorced as a matter of civil law, but not according to their religion. It is now clear that civil courts have the power to delay the grant of a decree absolute until the husband has secured a *get* in religious proceedings.[62] The statute only covers Jewish usages and other religious usages as prescribed by order, of which there has been none to date. However, the courts still have a general discretion to refuse the decree absolute in such cases.[63]

3. Burial and cremation

As regards rites related to death, two general questions arise for our purposes.[64] What constraints does the law impose as to the mode of disposal of human remains, and how are places set aside for the disposal of human remains regulated? In practice the two questions are related, since a legal right to dispose of a body in an unconventional manner may be little use in the absence of a public facility to do so.

At common law, the requirements as to the disposal of human remains were minimal: those in possession of the body were required to dispose of it decently and in such a way as to avoid a public nuisance.[65] As a result of Christian influence, burial was universally assumed to be the only appropriate mode of disposal. How the burial took place was a matter of ecclesiastical cognizance alone.[66] Largely for practical reasons, cremation was increasingly debated as an alternative

---

[60] *Qureshi v Qureshi* [1972] Fam 173.
[61] Domicile and Matrimonial Proceedings Act 1973, s 16; *Chaudhary v Chaudhary* [1985] Fam 19.
[62] Matrimonial Causes Act 1973, s 10A inserted by the Divorce (Religious Marriages) Act 2002.   [63] *O v O* [2000] 2 FLR 147.
[64] Full accounts of relevant law in *Halsbury's Laws of England*, 4th edn, vol 10 'Cremation and Burial' (London: Butterworths, 2002); David A Smale (ed), *Davies' Law of Burial, Cremation and Exhumation*, 7th edn (London: Shaw & Sons, 2002). For a discussion of family disputes over modes of burial, see Heather Conway, 'Dead but not buried: bodies, burial and family conflicts' (2003) 23 Legal Studies 423. Conway argues that art 9 ECHR requires greater respect to be shown to the religious and cultural values of the deceased in such disputes; ibid, 429–32.
[65] *R v Stewart* (1840) 12 Ad & E 773.
[66] *R v Coleridge* (1819) 2 B & Ald 806; *Gilbert v Buzzard* (1821) 2 Hag Con 333 (the 'iron coffin case').

as the nineteenth century drew to a close.[67] When the question finally came to be considered as a matter of law, Stephen J held that disposal by burning was not criminal, so long as it was not done in such a place and such a manner as to annoy persons passing along public roads or other places where they have a right to go.[68] In reaching this conclusion he referred not only to the range of different cultural practices, but also the civil power to require the exposure of the bodies of criminals, disposal at sea, and the practice of anatomy. However, disposal of human remains by burning other than in accordance with the provision for public crematoria was made a criminal offence by the Cremation Act 1902.[69] Apart from that, and perhaps surprisingly, it is not obvious that an offence is committed by a person who decides to dispose of a body discreetly on private land by way of exposure followed by burial of the remains.[70]

There was nothing at common law to prevent the maintenance of a private burial ground, and non-conformists often did this. However, in practice before the mid-nineteenth century, the parish churchyard was often the only place for burial. Strictly speaking, suicides, the excommunicate, and the unbaptized could not be buried there, the clergyman had to officiate and use the Book of Common Prayer, and fees had to be paid. In the hands of an intolerant incumbent, this could be distressing, not least because some non-conformists either only baptized adults, or did not baptize at all.[71] General private burial grounds were made possible after 1847,[72] as were municipal burial grounds after 1852,[73] albeit on terms that privileged the established church.[74] The land was to be divided into consecrated and unconsecrated land. In some cases an Anglican chapel had to be built,[75] and in only some cases did a non-denominational chapel also need to be provided.[76] More problematically, customary fees were still collected and paid to the incumbent and churchwardens of the parish church, thus treating the new burial grounds in some respects as extensions of the churchyard.[77] The Burial Act 1900 eventually removed the more egregious privileges of the established church. A non-denominational chapel could be built by the burial authority, or one exclusively reserved to a denomination (including Anglicans) at the expense of that denomination. It also removed the preferential fee structure, by harmonizing them for all religions. Thus the contours of the modern law were settled.

[67] Peter C Jupp, *From Dust to Ashes: Cremation and the British way of life* (Basingstoke: Palgrave Macmillan, 2005).
[68] *R v Price* (1884) 12 QBD 247. See also *R v Clark* (1883) 15 Cox CC 171.
[69] s 8(1). It is still in force.
[70] See John R Hinnells, *Zoroastrians in Britain* (Oxford: Clarendon Press, 1996), 13–16 and 134–7 for traditional practices and British accommodations.   [71] Larsen, *op cit* n 14, 53–7.
[72] The Cemeteries Clauses Act 1847 set out general terms to be applied to specific grounds by private Act of Parliament.   [73] Burial Acts 1852 (metropolis) and 1853 (elsewhere).
[74] Robert E Rodes Jr, *Law and Modernisation in the Church of England* (Notre Dame: The University of Notre Dame Press, 1991), 140–7.   [75] Cemeteries Clauses Act 1847, s 25.
[76] Burial Act 1853, s 7, in this respect differing from the 1852 Act.
[77] Burial Act 1852, s 36.

It is still the case that anyone may maintain a burial ground.[78] In practice most cemeteries are maintained by local authorities. In the case of the Church in Wales, a special statutory scheme applies effectively treating graveyards as public burial grounds.[79] Just as local authorities may authorize the consecration of part of the burial ground, so too they may set apart portions of the ground for any other religious denomination.[80] In some respects the position for other religious denominations parallels that of the established church: for both, chapels may be established at the expense of the religious denomination.[81] In other respects the established church still has a greater degree of control: consecration brings the land under the jurisdiction of the ordinary, and the bishop may object to a proposed monument on consecrated land, whereas the only express element of control granted to other religious associations is the right to object to the scattering of ashes.[82] Although the purpose of setting aside is to create land for the exclusive use of the denomination in question, no individual has the right to object to the burial of another in the area set aside.[83]

The current subordinate legislation is problematic in that it allows a burial authority to authorize a burial in consecrated or 'set apart' portions. Such burials may be conducted 'without any religious service or with . . . [a] Christian and orderly service'. It is not clear why the lines should be drawn at just this point. In practice, some local authorities make extensive provision for Muslim and Jewish burial customs.[84] This raises questions about control over the use of the land set aside. Judge Rupert Bursell QC, sitting in the St Alban's Consistory Court, recently hinted at this problem in granting a faculty for the exhumation of the remains of a humanist from consecrated grounds.[85] In *Preston Corporation v Pyke*,[86] Clauson J had ruled that action to prevent misuse of set apart portions of the burial ground may only be instituted by the Attorney-General. This ruling may need to be revisited in the light of collective religious liberty. The implications of the Human Rights Act 1998 may be that religious associations are to be accorded a greater degree of control over 'their' parts of public burial grounds, if a burial were proposed using rites fundamentally at odds with the doctrine of the association in question.[87] It may imply what could loosely be described as a type of 'co-ownership' of public burial grounds. Yet this would require a certain degree of coordinated organizational structure on the part of the religions concerned, which may not always be present.

---

[78] *Halsbury's Laws, op cit* n 64, para 1002.

[79] See Norman Doe, *The Law of the Church in Wales* (Cardiff: University of Wales Press, 2002), 23 n 139.   [80] Local Authorities' Cemeteries Order 1977, SI 1977/204, art 5(1)(b).

[81] Ibid, art 6.   [82] Ibid, art 5(6).   [83] *Halsbury's Laws, op cit* n 64, para 1023.

[84] Urfan Khaliq, 'The Accommodation and Regulation of Islam and Muslim Practices in English Law' (2002) 6 Ecc LJ 332, 341.

[85] *Re Crawley Green Road Cemetery, Luton* [2001] Fam 308, 311. See also *In re Durrington Cemetery* [2000] 3 WLR 1322.   [86] [1929] 2 Ch 338.

[87] See *Johannische Kirche and Peters v Germany*, no 41754/98 (2001), as well as discussion at 62–5 above.

Cremation is still regulated by the Cremation Act 1902 and Regulations thereunder.[88] There are also environmental regulations bearing on the disposal of human remains by burning.[89] The current arrangements for cremation were recently challenged in the High Court in *Ghai v Newcastle City Council*.[90] The Hindu applicant sought declarations that disposal of his body on an open-air funeral pyre would be lawful, or that restrictions were contrary to his Convention rights. A Sikh organization also intervened. Cranston J held that the law prohibiting disposal outside a regulated crematorium was clear, and that it amounted to an interference with the manifestation of Ghai's religious beliefs under article 9, but not with Sikh views, which only amounted to a cultural preference. However the law was justified primarily on the grounds of preventing offence to the public. This was a sensitive area in which he should defer to the judgment of the legislature. The proper route for the applicant to challenge the law was through political campaigning.[91] In reaching this conclusion, he was influenced by the facts that English law contained no blanket prohibition of Hindu practices surrounding death, that the majority of Hindus did not consider open air cremation necessary, that the law had been recently reconsidered by Government, and that there was no European consensus that open air facilities should be provided.[92]

Notwithstanding a very careful review of the evidential background, the judge's analysis of the relevant Convention rights is not entirely satisfactory. It was effectively conceded during the proceedings that the public health and safety risks of open air cremation could be satisfactorily managed by regulation. This only left public offence as a plausible ground for complete prohibition. But the avoidance of offence is the weakest possible justification for interfering with an individual's rights, and it is not clear that it justifies the limitation of article 9 rights.[93] Different religions are quite likely to be mutually offended by each other's practices. The judge carried out no proper proportionality analysis, in particular failing to consider whether the prohibition was necessary (ie the least intrusive means of achieving the desired end). If bare knowledge and dislike can justify the limitation of rights, rights have lost almost all significance. Furthermore, he dismissed too quickly an argument based on non-discrimination. At the centre of the case was not the criminalization of a private ceremony.[94] It was the provision of local authority facilities and their inability to accommodate the religious practices of a minority. While the argument that there simply was no suitable land

---

[88] The most recent regulations under the Act are the Cremation (England and Wales) Regulations 2008, SI 2008/2841.
[89] Environmental Permitting (England and Wales) Regulations 2007, SI 2007/3258.
[90] *Ghai v Newcastle City Council* [2009] EWHC 978 (Admin).   [91] Ibid, paras 121–123.
[92] Ibid, paras 116–119.
[93] *Otto-Preminger Institut v Austria* (1995) 19 EHRR 34 concerned the limitation of article 10 rights and is the strongest authority for the proposition that offence justifies a limitation of rights.
[94] It was admitted in proceedings that one had recently taken place, with police knowledge and non-intervention.

available is a good one,[95] the legal restrictions imposed on the local authority by the legislation were too quickly dismissed.[96] However, on appeal the Master of the Rolls found that accommodation could be reached on the grounds that the claimant would be satisfied with a form of structure which could be termed a 'building' for the relevant purposes.[97] It was appropriate to give the legislation a generous construction.[98]

II. Dietary Requirements

Modern considerations of animal welfare require the stunning of animals before slaughter, which is incompatible with traditional Jewish and Muslim practices. In *Jewish Liturgical Association Cha'are Shalom ve Tsedek v France*, the applicant was a minority Jewish association which employed slaughtermen and inspectors for the purposes of producing kosher meat in accordance with its own *glatt* (pure) precepts.[99] The European Court of Human Rights held that there was no question but that the association's activities came within the scope of article 9 ECHR as an essential aspect of the practice of the Jewish religion. However, the refusal of France to approve the association did not amount to a breach, since alternative supplies of the meat could be readily imported. Quite how this complies with requirements of non-discrimination between the Jewish majority and minority remains obscure.

Ritual slaughter for the production of *kosher* and *halal* meat is governed by the Welfare of Animals (Slaughter or Killing) Regulations 1995,[100] which is in turn based on European Union legislation.[101] Regulation 22 removes the requirement to stun an animal before slaughter in the case of slaughter by a religious method in accordance with Schedule 12. Schedule 12 covers slaughter 'without the infliction of unnecessary suffering' by Jews or Muslims licensed in the normal way as slaughtermen. In addition, Jewish slaughtermen in England and Wales must be licensed by the Rabbinnical Commission; there is no further formal religious licensing for Muslims.[102] Part II of the Schedule sets out in some detail the implications of the requirement to avoid unnecessary suffering: slaughtering may only take place in a licensed slaughterhouse;[103] cattle must be restrained in an approved pen designed to prevent avoidable pain or injury;[104] the animal must immediately be killed by rapid uninterrupted movements of a knife of sufficient

---

[95] Para 148.   [96] Para 149.
[97] *R (Ghai) v Newcastle City Council* [2010] EWCA Civ 59.   [98] Ibid, para 38.
[99] *Jewish Liturgical Association Cha'are Shalom ve Tsedek v France* [2000] EHRR 351.
[100] SI 1995/731, as amended.
[101] Directive 93/119/EEC; European Convention for the Protection of Animals for Slaughter 1979. See Julian Rivers, 'In pursuit of pluralism: the ecclesiastical policy of the European Union,' (2004) 7 Ecc LJ 267, 281–2.   [102] Sched 12, para 2.
[103] Para 8, as substituted by SI 1999/400.   [104] Ibid, para 3.

size and sharpness;[105] a captive bolt instrument must be kept close at hand for immediate use should the animal suffer any avoidable pain or injury;[106] and the animal must not be moved until it is unconscious.[107] Part III contains similar, albeit less extensive, requirements in respect of birds.

Part IV of the Schedule sets out the composition of the Rabbinnical Commission for the licensing of *shochetim* (slaughtermen).[108] The Chief Rabbi of the United Hebrew Congregations of Great Britain and the Commonwealth is the permanent chairman *ex officio*. Of the nine other members one is to be appointed by the Spanish and Portuguese Synagogue, London, and is the vice-chairman. Three are to appointed by the Beth Din appointed by the United Synagogue; two are to be appointed by the Federation of Synagogues; one is to be appointed by the Union of Orthodox Hebrew Congregations; and two are to be appointed by the president for the time being of the London committee of Deputies of British Jews to represent provincial congregations.[109] The Rabbinnical Commission is subject to judicial review of the exercise of its licensing function.[110] However, it has been held that the statutory background does not have the effect of rendering licences issued by the Beth Din for the sale of meat certified *kashrut* (being *kosher*) subject to judicial review.[111] This is a purely religious and consensual matter.

Where a local authority operates a public slaughterhouse, it is expressly prevented from using its powers to deny to religious communities reasonable facilities for obtaining food slaughtered by the method required by their religion.[112]

If a shop which engages in retail trade selling, among other things, poultry, starts to keep and slaughter live chickens according to a religious ritual, that may amount to a material change of use in breach of planning law, even if it is normal among the religious community concerned for a shop also to fulfil that function. The question is whether the activity is ordinarily incidental to retail trade generally, without regard to the requirements of particular localities or customers.[113]

The permission granted to Jews and Muslim to produce meat in accordance with traditional modes of slaughter is at times criticized for allowing religious precepts to override considerations of animal welfare. But the approach of the law has been to require *kosher* and *halal* methods to be applied in as strict and careful a fashion as possible, thus reducing the suffering experienced by the animal to a minimum. The difference between these methods, if carried out in accordance with the law, and pre-slaughter stunning is a matter of seconds. The argument that the exception for religious slaughter makes other attempts to outlaw certain

---

[105] Ibid, para 6(b).   [106] Ibid, para 5(d).   [107] Ibid, para 7.   [108] Ibid, para 12.
[109] Ibid, para 13.
[110] *R v Rabbinical Commissioner for the Licensing of Shochetim, ex parte Cohen*, The Times, 22 December 1987, CA.
[111] *R v London Beth Din (Court of the Chief Rabbi), ex parte Bloom* [1998] COD 131, QBD.
[112] Slaughterhouses Act 1974, s 16(2).
[113] *Hussain v Secretary of State for the Environment* (1971) 23 P & CR 330.

forms of suffering to animals discriminatory has been rejected by the Court of Session.[114]

Although the production of meat in accordance with traditional Jewish and Muslim practice is treated as a religious observance, it is not closely or strictly connected with worship and ritual. Occasionally, the law can give rise to potential conflict even here. During the era of prohibition in the United States, an exception was made for the supply of communion wine. More problematic today is the Rastafarian use of *ganja* (cannabis).[115] In *R v Taylor*, the Court of Appeal upheld the conviction of a Rastafarian for the possession and supply of cannabis.[116] The prosecution had conceded that Rastafarianism was a religion for the purposes of article 9 ECHR, and that the significant quantity of cannabis found on the accused was all for religious purposes. Nevertheless, the absolute ban contained in the Misuse of Drugs Act 1973 was based on an international consensus, on which it was proper to rely. A religious exception would not be read into the legislation. However, the court was prepared to note, extremely cautiously, the possibility that simple possession of the drug by a Rastafarian for religious purposes in a private place might raise different considerations.[117] Furthermore, the religious dimension was a mitigating factor in sentencing, and the sentence was reduced from 12 months to five months thus securing an immediate release. The approach of the court was later affirmed in respect of importation,[118] with the court being rather more sceptical of the distinction between possession and supply.[119] The court also pointed out that the religion did not strictly *require* the consumption of cannabis.[120]

The Rastafarian use of cannabis has received substantial consideration by the Constitutional Court of South Africa, which concluded (by a majority) that the failure of legislation to provide an exception for religious purposes was justified.[121] Any exception broad enough to satisfy the requirements of the religion would substantially impair the ability of the State to protect the public generally and honour its international obligations. However, the possibility of sufficiently narrowly tailored exceptions for ritual drug use continues to be controversial, with US courts and commentators taking different sides on the question.[122]

III. Unconventional Worship

English law is unmistakeably constructed around a conventional conception of religious worship. This centres on an old building set apart for public services involving prayer, teaching, liturgical music, and the celebration of rites

---

[114] *Whaley and Friend v Lord Advocate* [2004] SC 78.
[115] See discussion in Sebastian Poulter, *Ethnicity, Law and Human Rights: the English Experience* (Oxford: Clarendon Press, 1998), 355–63.   [116] [2002] 1 Cr App R 37.
[117] Ibid, para 17.   [118] *R v Andrews* [2004] EWCA Crim 947, CA.
[119] Ibid, para 19.   [120] Ibid, para 21.
[121] *Prince v President of the Law Society of the Cape of Good Hope* (2001) 12 BHRC 1. See Anashri Pillay, 'South Africa: freedom of religion—religiously motivated use of cannabis' (2003) 1 IJCL 152.   [122] See Derek O'Brien, 'Rastafarianism and the Law' (2001) 151 NLJ 509.

such as baptism and communion. To the extent that other religions comply with this Protestant Christian model, there are few legal difficulties. However, as other religions move beyond the boundaries of conventional worship, a range of legal obstacles arises. This in turn gives rise to questions of legal accommodation.

1. Planning control of new places of worship

Religious minorities have not always found it easy to establish new places of worship. Until 1987, use of a building for public worship or religious instruction and associated social and recreational activities constituted a separate use for planning purposes.[123] Change to or from any other use, such as residential or commercial use, required planning permission. Thus regardless of any change to the exterior building itself, using a house as a mosque, for example, required local authority consent. Nielsen notes a change of attitude from the late 1970s on the part of Local Government authorities led by Birmingham. This local authority then issued new Guidelines in 1981 making it easier to convert houses into mosques, and it even permitted the Central Mosque to play the call to noon prayer on Fridays over an external loudspeaker.[124] However, a review of enforcement notices across the country for the period 1980–3 found a small, but significant, number of appeals relating to unauthorized places of worship, mostly residential in origin.[125] There is evidence that local authorities are often slow to accept applications for planning consent.[126]

Under the Town and Country Planning (Use Classes) Order 1987, certain uses are grouped together.[127] Changes within the same class do not amount to development and so do not require permission.[128] Class D1 now includes non-residential institutions for the provision of medical or health services; as a crèche, day nursery, or day centre; for the provision of education or the display of works of art; as a museum, public library, or public reading room; as a public hall or exhibition hall; for or in connection with public worship or religious instruction; or as a law court. Thus permission is not required to use a former school as a place of worship, but it is required to use a former cinema or concert hall.[129] Ancillary uses are permitted so long as they are ordinarily incidental to the principal use, even if they feature as a separate class of use.[130] It has been held that a certain frequency and size of public worship is a use ancillary to the provision of residential

---

[123] Town and Country Planning (Use Classes) Order 1972.

[124] Jørgen Nielsen, *Muslims in Western Europe* (Edinburgh: Edinburgh University Press, 1992), 51.

[125] R K Home, 'Planning decision statistics and the Use Classes debate' [1987] JPL 167, identi-fied about 50 cases. See eg *Cherwell DC v Vardivale* (1991) 6 PAD 433.

[126] Urfan Khaliq, 'The Accommodation and Regulation of Islam and Muslim Practices in English Law' (2002) 6 Ecc LJ 332, 337–41.   [127] SI 1987/764.

[128] Town and Country Planning Act 1990, s 55(2)(f).   [129] Class D2.

[130] Town and Country Planning (Use Classes) Order 1987, reg 3(3).

theological education, but public entertainment is not.[131] Permanent activities within part of a building may make that part a separate planning unit, and if outside the use class will require consent. For example, a restaurant or bookshop open to the public and linked to a place of worship will generally require consent.[132] There are additional restrictions on developments in specially protected areas such as conservation areas and designated green belts, although even in the case of the latter, very special circumstances can justify what would otherwise be an inappropriate development.

The question for present purposes is the extent to which the law protects the religious interest in the planning process. Does the fact that the sought-after development enables a religious community to establish a place of worship have any particular weight? In general terms, planning authorities have a wide discretion in granting, refusing, or setting conditions on planning permission. The law simply requires them to take account of the relevant local development plan and any other material considerations.[133] While the question of materiality is one of law, the weight to be given to a material consideration is a matter for the authority.[134] In principle this means that so long as a planning authority acknowledges the existence of the relevant religious dimension, the decision is proof against judicial review.

The advent of the Human Rights Act 1998 raised several questions about the entire planning regime. In *Lough v First Secretary of State*, Pill LJ stated that the provisions of the Convention should be considered as an integral part of the decision-taker's approach to material considerations, and that the concept of proportionality, or balance between relevant private and public interests, was inherent to the whole process, both before and after the Human Rights Act came into force.[135] Given that the conduct of a place of worship lies at the heart of the manifestation of religion protected by article 9, this suggests that decision-takers should not only take account of the religious interest, but may also be acting unlawfully if that factor is given insufficient weight.

This point is confirmed by the decisions reached in the course of the most protracted planning dispute involving a religious organization: the use by the International Society for Krishna Consciousness (the Hare Krishna movement) of Bhaktivedanta Manor in Hertfordshire.[136] The Manor fell into a use class which allowed it to be used as a residential theological college, but not as a place of public worship. Being in a green belt area, any development also needed to be justified by 'very special circumstances'.[137] From the mid-1970s the number

---

[131] *International Society for Krishna Consciousness v Secretary of State for the Environment* (1992) 64 P & CR 85.
[132] Discussed in Charles George, 'Shared use of church buildings, or is nothing sacred?' (2002) 6 Ecc LJ 306.   [133] Town and Country Planning Act 1990, s 70(2).
[134] *Tesco Stores v Secretary of State for the Environment* [1995] 1 WLR 759.
[135] *Lough v First Secretary of State* [2004] 1 WLR 2557.
[136] See the full account in Poulter, *op cit* n 115, ch 7.
[137] See now PPG 2: *Green Belts* (2006), para 3.1.

of visitors rose to over 1,000 each Sunday and to several thousands at festivals. Since access lay through the local village, this caused regular and severe disruption. The local authority sought to limit the number of visitors by agreement in 1983, but when that failed to have the desired effect, they issued an enforcement notice in 1987. This was upheld at a subsequent public inquiry (1988), by the Secretary of State (1990), and in the High Court (1991).[138] A challenge under the European Convention on Human Rights was rejected by the Commission (1994).[139] Eventually, after an abortive attempt to find an alternative site nearby, and another public inquiry, permission was granted subject to the construction of a new access driveway (1996).

The inspector at the first public inquiry considered in some depth the place of the Manor in the life of Hindus in Britain, its special association with the founder of the group, the growing number of adherents, and the lack of facilities for Hindus elsewhere, especially in North London and surrounding counties. However, in the light of the experience that limiting conditions had not been observed and were hard to enforce, he considered that the interests of the local inhabitants should prevail. The location was simply not suited for mass gatherings of worshippers. Permission for a change of use should not be given. The Human Rights Commission found that the limitation of ISKCON's freedom of religion was justified as being necessary in a democratic society. Article 9 could not be used to evade the planning system in general, so long as adequate weight was given to freedom of religion in the course of the decision. On the facts, in this case, the inspector had given careful attention to the religious interest at stake, and was entitled to conclude that it was overridden.

While the place of the religious interest in planning disputes is thus broadly clear, there are three outstanding problems.

The first is the question of how one constructs the 'balance of interests'. Convention rights such as article 9 are constructed by way of principle and limitation. Freedom of religion should take precedence unless a limitation is justified. On the other hand, planning applications which are incompatible with a local development plan or in a green belt area are in principle to be refused unless special considerations apply. It is not clear what the base-line is for considering the application. The difference is exposed in the second public inquiry concerning Bhaktivedanta Manor. While remaining within the structure of planning-based reasoning, the inspector sought to give greater weight to the religious interest by characterizing it as a public interest. In this he was modified by the Secretary of State.[140] While agreeing that the planned driveway was acceptable, the Secretary of State pointed out that, 'the religious needs of one section of the community are not in themselves of such paramount importance that they can automatically

---

[138] *International Society for Krishna Consciousness v Secretary of State for the Environment* (1992) 64 P & CR 85.　　　　　　　　　　　　　　　[139] *ISKCON v UK* (1994) 76 DR 90.

[140] See Poulter, *op cit* n 115, 273.

override national or local planning policies'.[141] Given the status of freedom of religion as an important human right, one would have thought that the former approach was preferable. The difference of approach had no impact on the outcome at this stage, but may affect other decisions. A further inquiry was recently held in respect of an application to build a large agricultural and visitor centre at the Manor.[142] The centre was intended to house an expanded dairy herd and an estimated 30,000 to 40,000 visitors and devotees a year. The inspector found that the venerated position of the cow in the Hindu religion and the need to improve the care of the herd did not amount to very special circumstances justifying the overriding the general prohibition of development in a green belt area.

The second problem concerns a tension between the procedural approach of the European Commission and recent attempts by the House of Lords to resist this proceduralization of human rights. In a number of cases, the House of Lords has refused applications for judicial review which were argued on the basis that the decision-taker failed to consider a relevant Convention interest.[143] Instead, the House has insisted that the role of courts is to focus purely on the output-related question: did the concrete decision actually breach the claimant's rights? The difficulty is that planning disputes are highly fact-sensitive, and a court will find it hard to say that a decision is substantively wrong. If it does not also insist that thorough consideration be given to the religious interest in the course of the initial decision-taking process, there is a risk that the pre-Human Rights Act 1998 position whereby the weight to be given to a material consideration lay purely in the discretion of the decision-taker could be *de facto* re-created.

The final problem is the absence of neutral criteria to assist the decision-taker in a correct solution to clashes of interest. The recent case of *R (Bello) v London Borough of Lewisham* illustrates this problem well.[144] In 1988 the applicant had been served with a demolition notice in respect of a rear extension to premises erected without planning permission and in breach of several building regulations. In 2000, after an inexplicable delay, the Council sought to enforce the notice after receiving complaints from local residents. The building's use had changed from that of an educational college to 'The Church of the Cherubim' holding all-night services, and, in the words of one complainant:

there is loud drumming, bell-ringing and chanting, singing and screaming and what appear to be exorcisms of cars have been held on the open road in front our building on Sunday afternoons and in the early hours of Saturday morning.[145]

The challenge to the enforcement notice was rejected by the High Court and the Court of Appeal. The Court of Appeal stressed that it was legitimate for the

---

[141] Cited *loc cit.*   [142] [2006] JPL 1410.

[143] *R (SB) v Governors of Denbigh High School* [2007] 1 AC 100; *Belfast City Council v Miss Behavin' Ltd* [2007] 1 WLR 1420.

[144] *R (Bello) v London Borough of Lewisham* [2002] EHLR 19.   [145] Ibid, para 20.

Council to take public reaction into account in relation to the timing of the enforcement proceedings. Schiemann LJ stated:

Of course Mr Bello feels that hymns and songs emanating from a building should be a cause of joy, not a cause of irritation from his neighbours. It sometimes happens in villages that church bells are rung and some people like the bells and other people do not. But I am persuaded that the Council is in principle entitled to take public reaction into account when it comes to the timing of enforcement proceedings.[146]

Planning control is ultimately sensitive to aesthetic values, which are themselves culturally and religiously contingent. The further religious practices depart from conventional norms, the harder it is to achieve accommodation.

2. Bell-ringing and calls to prayer

The use of bells to announce the start of a service at Christian churches, or calls to prayer within Islam, is of considerable antiquity and predates the invention of clocks and watches. But it would be simplistic to reduce its function to a pre-modern mode of time-keeping. It can also be an audible sign of the public presence of a religious building, a reminder even to those with watches, the concomitant of a ritual act (as in the ringing of a sanctus bell), an act of commemoration, or of celebration. However, simply as a form of noise, it has the potential to amount to an actionable nuisance, and can give rise to disputes even today.[147]

Bell-ringing probably cannot amount to a public nuisance, since the activity is not intrinsically harmful.[148] Indeed, it gives positive pleasure to some people. But it can amount to a private nuisance, and thus also a statutory nuisance, under certain circumstances. The question is whether the ringing materially interferes with the ordinary physical comfort of human existence according to plain, sober, and simple notions of living. On the facts of the leading case of *Soltau v de Held*, the plaintiff lived in a building half of which had been recently converted to a place of Roman Catholic worship, which rang its peal of six substantial bells incessantly from morning to night. The plaintiff got an injunction, although the judge refused to apply a total ban. It did not follow that there was no way of ringing the bells which did not amount to a private nuisance. However, in *Hardman v Halberton*, the plaintiff failed to establish that the chiming of a clock on the quarter-hours through the night amounted to a nuisance.[149]

Bell-ringing is more likely today to be treated as a statutory nuisance under the Environmental Protection Act 1990. Noise constitutes a statutory nuisance if it could amount to a common law nuisance or is prejudicial to health.[150] Local

---

[146] *R (Bello) v London Borough of Lewisham* [2004] 2 PLR 1, para 12.

[147] Recent cases include *Houston v PCC of St Mary's, Belton* (noted by R H Bloor, 'Clocks, Bells and Cockerels' (1995) 3 Ecc LJ 393) and *Calvert v Gardiner* (noted by Will Adam at (2003) 7 Ecc LJ 99). [148] *Soltau v de Held* (1851) 2 Sim (NS) 133.

[149] [1866] WN 379. [150] Environmental Protection Act 1990, s 79(1)(g).

authorities have powers to issue abatement notices in respect of such noise, prohibiting or restricting its occurrence, or requiring works to be done. They may
take any other steps necessary to persuade those responsible to desist.[151] It is an
offence to refuse to comply with an abatement notice.

The incumbents of parishes in the Church of England are under a statutory
duty to ensure that a bell is rung before daily morning and evening prayer, 'that
the people may come to hear God's Word, and to pray with him'.[152] It is this long-
standing duty that probably lay behind the dictum of Kindersley VC that the
bells of churches in the Church of England were privileged in comparison with
those of other faiths.[153] In theory, bell-ringing which would amount to a nuisance at common law if performed by a non-Anglican church, is privileged under
ecclesiastical law.[154] Since this is effectively a statutory defence based on the Act
of Uniformity 1662, there is no reason why it should not apply in the context of
statutory nuisance as well. However, the ecclesiastical obligation to ring a bell
does not cover every mode of its performance, and it has rightly been suggested
that 'much would depend on time, the level of noise involved and the question of
whether any nuisance caused was reasonably avoidable'.[155] It is unlikely that this
argument could be extended to the Church in Wales merely on account of the
fact that its contract of association has a statutory basis.[156]

However, the requirement of non-discrimination in the enjoyment of
Convention rights suggests that such an exclusive privilege can no longer be
sustained. In the Australian case of *Haddon v Lynch*, the judge effectively 'levelled down' by holding that there was no general immunity for church bells
from the law of nuisance.[157] However, it is arguable that the judge took inadequate account of the practice as itself a form of religious expression. There is
a difference between industrial noise, which is a regrettable by-product of no
intrinsic merit, and bell-ringing, which is a deliberate act closely related to religious worship and desired by some. One can therefore expect a greater degree of
tolerance for the latter, or a form of 'levelling up'. The same arguments apply to
Islamic calls for prayer, with at least the modification that traditional practice
is to call five times each day. However, just as noise can reasonably be required
to be reduced through the installation of louvres to belfries, it does not follow
that mosques have the right to use the latest sound technology to amplify the

---

[151] s 80(2A).
[152] *Book of Common Prayer* (1662), 'Concerning the Service of the Church'. The Book of
Common Prayer is given statutory force by the Act of Uniformity 1662. See also Canon B11 passed
under the Church of England (Worship and Doctrine) Measure 1974.
[153] *Soltau v de Held* (1851) 2 Sim (NS) 133 at 160–1.
[154] Thomas Glyn Watkin and Sarah Thomas, 'Oh, Noisy Bells, be Dumb: Church Bells,
Statutory Nuisance and Ecclesiastical Duties' [1995] JPL 1097; Thomas Glyn Watkin, 'A Happy
Noise to Hear?' (1996) 4 Ecc LJ 545.
[155] Watkin, 'A Happy Noise to Hear?' *op cit* n 154, 552.
[156] Watkin (ibid, 554–5) is slightly more open to this possibility.
[157] *Haddon v Lynch* [1911] WLR 5.

call on every occasion. The practical point is that noise from such activities is not to be treated merely as noise, but as worthy of a degree of protection and accommodation.[158]

3. Access to ancient monuments

The need to reconcile competing religious and public interests has found its most enduring expression in events surrounding Stonehenge.[159] Here, too, the law has been required to accommodate the interests of religious believers, in this case various orders of Druids and other pagans. Druidism is the most structured and public form of paganism in the UK. It sees itself as a revival of pre-Christian Celtic religion stemming from the foundation of the Ancient Druid Order in 1717. It is quite diverse, with some Druids combining beliefs with forms of Christianity and Buddhism, some with close associations to Wicca and Shamanism. The Council of British Druid Orders was established in 1989 to represent the interests of Druids in Stonehenge and currently has 19 member orders, although one of the largest founder-members, the Order of Bards, Ovates and Druids, has now left.[160]

What makes Stonehenge so complex is the variety and strength of other interests in the site. Stonehenge is a world heritage site, in the ownership of English Heritage, with much of the surrounding land owned by the National Trust. To the interest in conserving a fascinating, if obscure, ancient monument must be added the large numbers of the public who wish to visit it, many of them tourists from overseas. From the mid-1970s, Stonehenge also became a location for the convergence of travellers, 'hippies', and others seeking to express their rejection of conventional social and political norms. The Stonehenge Free Festival grew from 1974 until it was attracting 30,000 people at its peak. The era of toleration ended in 1985 with a substantial police presence and violent clashes. The attempt to close off Stonehenge also resulted in Druids being prevented from celebrating the summer solstice there from 1986.

Access to Stonehenge has been contested legally for over a century. In *Attorney-General v Antrobus* (1905), members of the public failed to persuade the court that they had established a general right of access against the owner of the site.[161] It was given to the nation in 1918, and is now managed by English Heritage. In principle, it must be open to the public, although conditions may be set and the public may be entirely excluded if necessary in the interests of safety or the

---

[158] See *R (Hackney LBC) v Rottenburg* [2007] Env LR 24 per David Clarke J at para 23.
[159] Background in Penny English, 'Disputing Stonehenge: Law and Access to a National Symbol' (2002) 1 Entertainment Law 1; legal dimensions in Peter W Edge, *Legal Responses to Religious Difference* (The Hague: Kluwer Law International, 2002), 370–7; also in id, 'The construction of sacred places in English law' [2002] J Env L 161.
[160] <http://www.cobdo.org.uk/html/members.html>, accessed 7 July 2009.
[161] [1905] 2 Ch 188.

maintenance or preservation of the monument.[162] Regulations made under the Ancient Monuments and Archaeological Areas Act 1979 create criminal offences in respect of Stonehenge, such as climbing on it and being there when access is restricted.[163] They also state that prior consent must be obtained for 'organising or taking part in any assembly, display, performance, representation, review, theatrical event, festival, ceremony or ritual within the site of the monument'.[164] The use of public order law to control access to the surrounding area has met with mixed success. Convictions for offences have not always been easy to secure.[165] Under the Criminal Justice and Public Order Act 1994, a new police power was created enabling an application to be made to the local authority for an order banning 'trespassory assemblies' within a defined area.[166] This was, at least in part, motivated by events at Stonehenge.

The exclusion of Druids has twice led to applications under the European Convention on Human Rights. In *Chappell v UK*, the applicant unsuccessfully challenged the decision by English Heritage to exclude all people from the site for the 1986 summer solstice.[167] The Commission were willing to accept that his freedom to manfest his religious beliefs was limited, but held that the application was manifestly ill-founded as it was a necessary public safety measure. The second case to be brought under the Convention sought to challenge the impact of the 1995 police exclusion order.[168] King Arthur Pendragon argued that the fact that the order prevented him from celebrating the solstice at the Hele stone, which was outside the perimeter fence, but within the exclusion zone, was in breach of his rights to religious assembly and discriminatory against Druids. Once again, the Commission found the application manifestly ill-founded on the grounds that the limitation of his rights was proportionate. They pointed to the fact that although he had been arrested for breaching the order, he was subsequently acquitted, that he was permitted to assemble in groups of under 20, and that the threat of public disorder was real. The Commission also held that there was no discrimination since the law drew no distinction between those who wished to attend for religious or secular reasons.[169] However, in a case brought in the domestic courts in respect of the same exclusion order, the House of Lords held that a gathering on the highway was not necessarily trespassory, so long as the use was reasonable and did not cause an obstruction or a public nuisance.[170]

---

[162] Ancient Monuments and Archaeological Areas Act 1979, s 19(1) and (2). The argument (see Edge, *op cit* n 159 at 373 and n 181) that Stonehenge is excluded as the remains of an 'ecclesiastical building' is highly implausible given the near uniform use of 'ecclesiastical' in English law to refer to the Church of England.   [163] Stonehenge Regulations 1997, SI 1997/2038, reg 3.

[164] Ibid, reg 4(c).

[165] See eg *Smith v Reynolds, Smith v Hancock, Smith v Lowe* [1986] Crim LR 559.

[166] Public Order Act 1986, ss 14A–14C.   [167] No 12587/86, 53 DR 241.

[168] *Pendragon v UK*, no 31416/96 (1998).

[169] The failure to take seriously a claim for accommodation is in line with the undeveloped nature of the concept of indirect discrimination under art 14 ECHR.

[170] *DPP v Jones* [1999] 2 AC 240.

In 1999, after this judgment, the Chief Constable did not apply for an exclusion order.

From that time on, a concerted effort has been made to find ways to allow more open access to Stonehenge, even during the Summer solstice. This has been granted from 2000, and Druids have been able to celebrate, albeit amongst growing numbers of secular party-goers. King Arthur Pendragon continues his campaign to secure full open access, protesting at the withdrawal of Government plans to build an underpass for the A344 and remove the fences.[171]

4. Spiritualist services

In the 2001 National Census, approximately 32,000 respondents indicated their religion as 'spiritualist'.[172] Spiritualists share a conviction that it is possible to communicate in various ways with the spirits of the departed, thus offering consolation to the bereaved and emotional healing.[173] Interest in clairvoyance and mediumship became socially acceptable during the latter part of the nineteenth century. A number of societies emerged with an interest in the subject, which in 1890 formed a Federation and started annual conferences. This incorporated in 1901 as the Spiritualist National Union (SNU), which remains the largest body with almost 340 churches containing around 17,500 members.[174] The SNU estimates a weekly attendance at its services of around 40,000. The relationship with Christianity has always been variable, with some seeing spiritualism as a legitimate adjunct to their faith, others agnostic. The SNU itself simply affirms the fatherhood of God and the brotherhood of man. After Arthur Conan Doyle lost his motion to give the SNU a more explicitly Christian basis in 1927, a split occurred leading to the formation of the Greater World Christian Spiritualist League in 1931, which is closer to Christianity of a unitarian expression. Other federations of spiritualist groups also exist, such as the Spiritualist Association of Great Britain (SAGB, founded 1872) and the White Eagle Lodge (from 1931). The SAGB's express purpose has a scientific and apologetic orientation, being 'to offer evidence through Mediumship of the continuation of the personality after physical death, and to relieve suffering through spiritual healing'.[175] It is much less Christian and more individualist, offering mediumship and healing services to any interested persons.

The potential for prosecution under old statutes prohibiting witchcraft and vagrancy was confirmed in 1876.[176] In upholding a conviction under section 4 of the Vagrancy Act 1824, Cleasby B insisted that it would be inappropriate to pass

---

[171] 'Stonehenge protestor King Arthur Pendragon defies eviction order', *The Guardian*, 3 May 2009. [172] Office for National Statistics, *Focus on Religion* (Oct 2004), 2.
[173] Nigel Scotland, *Sectarian Religion in Contemporary Britain* (Carlisle: Paternoster Press, 2000), ch 8. [174] <http://www.snu.org.uk/> accessed 16 December 2009.
[175] <http://www.sagb.org.uk/> accessed 16 December 2009.
[176] *Monck v Hilton* (1876–77) LR 2 Ex D 268.

judgment on the merits or efficacy of spiritualism in general. On the facts, there was clear evidence that the accused was an imposter. But not every prosecution involved imposters: even one genuinely believing in their clairvoyant powers was at risk of being convicted as 'a rogue and a vagabond'.[177] Nor was it necessary to have sought payment for the services rendered. For some time, there was considerable doubt as to whether the prosecution needed to show an intent to deceive. In England, after some hesitation, the court held not, Laurence CJ robustly asserting that he could not imagine anyone who did not know perfectly well that he was deceiving in such circumstances.[178] In Scotland, where the use of the law to prosecute spiritualists was generally disliked by the judiciary, the courts held (under the same statute) that proof of *mens rea* was necessary.[179] In spite of a Government commitment not to use the law except against those who were fraudulent and subject to public complaint,[180] in 1944 a well-known medium, Helen Duncan, was convicted under the Witchcraft Act 1735 instead.[181] The outcry was sufficient to secure the passage of a private member's bill, which became the Fraudulent Mediums Act 1951.

The Act repealed the Witchcraft Act 1735 and stated that section 4 of the Vagrancy Act 1824 did not apply

so far as it extends to persons purporting to act as spiritualistic mediums or to exercise any powers of telepathy, clairvoyance or other similar powers, or to persons who in purporting so to act or to exercise such powers, use fraudulent devices.[182]

In its place a new offence was created which was committed by any person who with intent to deceive purported to act as a spiritualistic medium or to exercise any powers of telepathy, clairvoyance, or other similar powers or who used any fraudulent device in that connection.[183] The person had to have acted for reward.[184] By limiting, rather than repealing, section 4 of the Vagrancy Act, the Fraudulent Mediums Act 1951 was itself not entirely clear. In 1955, a conviction for 'psychometry' at a spiritualist church was upheld on the grounds that fortune-telling remained an offence whether practised by a genuine medium, a fraudulent one, or by anyone.[185] A different view was adopted in 1981.[186] This time, the court considered that the phrase 'other similar powers' was broad and designed to cover all activities professing the ability to see beyond the normal powers of a human being. In short, the Act was intended to draw a distinction between (a) sincere spiritualist activities and (b) mere entertainment, both of which were lawful since there was no intent to deceive, and (c) unlawful spiritualist activities

---

[177] *Penny v Hanson* (1887) LR 18 QBD 478; *R v Entwistle, ex parte Jones* [1899] 1 QB 846.

[178] *Davis v Curry* [1918] 1 KB 109; *Stonehouse v Masson* [1921] 2 KB 818.

[179] *Lee or Smith v Nielson* (1895) 3 SLT 318; *Farmer v Mill* [1948] JC 4.

[180] Rachel Morris and Luke Clements, 'Fraudulent and incompetent mediums' (1996) 146 NLJ 1574, 1575.   [181] *R v Duncan* [1944] 1 KB 713.

[182] Fraudulent Mediums Act 1951, s 2(b).   [183] Ibid, s 1(1).   [184] Ibid, s 1(2).

[185] *Doheny v England* [1955] Crim. LR 255.   [186] *R v Martin* [1981] Crim LR 109.

which were presented as genuine but were actually insincere and performed with a desire for financial gain.

It has been suggested that the Act was absurd as it amounted to the professional recognition of mediums and presupposed an afterlife.[187] The difficulty with this view can be illustrated by the problems caused by its recent repeal and replacement by the Consumer Protection from Unfair Trading Regulations 2008.[188] This makes unlawful a wide range of misleading commercial practices such as those containing 'false information … in relation to … the existence or nature of the product'[189] or 'falsely claiming that a product is able to cure illnesses, dysfunction or malformations'.[190] Assuming that a court wishes to maintain its studied agnosticism on the efficacy of spiritualist practices,[191] what is it to do in the face of a claim that a person can contact the dead or predict the future? If a person fails to provide evidence as to the accuracy of a factual claim, or the court considers the evidence provided inadequate, the court may consider that the factual claim is inaccurate.[192] Since the matter cannot be proved to the satisfaction of a court, it seems that an offence is committed whenever such claims are made. On the other hand, if one wishes to tolerate 'legitimate' spiritualist practices, it is not clear how one is to distinguish these from the actions of mere money-making charlatans without some distinction between the genuine (ie sincere) and the fraudulent.

IV. Conclusion

It is hard to draw clear conclusions from this rather miscellaneous collection of tensions between the law and collective religious practices. Although the cultural dominance of Anglicanism obviously has had an impact on the law, in the sense that the general law tends to be cast in terms which make special accommodation for it largely unnecessary, it is by no means the case that the 'fit' is perfect. Religions whose presence in the United Kingdom is more recent have in some respects been accommodated without too much difficulty, in other respects not. There is no clear Anglican versus non-Anglican or Christian versus non-Christian divide. Rather, the overwhelming impression is of a moderately tolerant pragmatism.

What one can observe is the relatively small part played by the courts in securing accommodation. Where compromises have been found, these have typically been as a result of local administrative discretion, or by way of express legislative

---

[187] Morris and Clements, *op cit* n 180, 1575–6.   [188] SI 2008/1277.
[189] Ibid, regs 5 and 9.   [190] Ibid, reg 12 and sched 1, para 17.
[191] In *R v Duncan* [1944] 1 KB 713, the accused offered to provide evidence of her abilities in open court, but this was rejected.
[192] Enterprise Act 2002, s 218A, as inserted by Consumer Protection from Unfair Trading Regulations 2008, reg 27.

regime. Courts are willing enough to find that the relevant general law is not as restrictive as might be thought, and thus that there is no tension to be resolved. They seem generally unwilling to carve collective exceptions out of the general law, even now that they are mandated by the Human Rights Act 1998 to find general laws unnecessarily or discriminatorily restrictive of religious practice. The reason for this may lie in the basic point that the accommodation of religious groups, rather than individuals, tends to require specially-formulated regulatory regimes. It is not simply a matter of relieving an individual from an obligation. To accommodate a group is potentially to legislate in a much more obvious way than to accommodate an individual.

This point indicates that religious organizations seeking to preserve some aspect of their collective life from legal regulation or restriction should be looking rather to the democratic process than to their human rights for a solution, even if that aspect lies at the heart of their religion. It suggests that a degree of negotiation and political compromise needs to take place. The problem then becomes the minority status of unconventional religious groups, and their lack of political influence. This might indicate that one needs to consider more secure forms of representation and consultation.[193] It also suggests that the courts should be willing to stimulate legislative action, even without a clear view of the correct solution, by finding breaches of Convention rights by way of declaration.

---

[193] See Ch 10 below.

7

Chaplaincies

A chaplaincy may be defined as a position held by a minister of religion within an organization or institution in order to provide spiritual services to its members or inmates. The reasons for the existence of chaplaincies are, first, that the organization is to some extent a restricted community, whose members would otherwise be unable to access the services normally offered by a religious body to the general public. Secondly, the organization may embrace a distinctive cross-section of the public who warrant a specific type of spiritual ministry. Finally, chaplaincies offer the possibility of an independent presence in what are often hierarchical contexts, acting both as bridge-builders and whistle-blowers. Chaplaincies are to be found in the armed forces, prisons, hospitals, universities, schools, and in certain professions and industries. From a purely financial perspective, it has recently been noted that chaplaincies in the first three categories make up 10 per cent of all employed clergy—and these are employed, of course, by the State and not by their respective religious bodies.[1]

Chaplaincies can be considered both from an individual and a collective perspective. As a matter of individual religious right they are required by the need of the individual to access spiritual advice and assistance even when confined or constrained in some way; as a matter of collective right they are required by the need for religious communities to sustain their collective identity between members unable to meet and participate in their collective life under normal circumstances.

This chapter reviews the legal provision for chaplaincies in the contexts just outlined. From a strictly legal point of view, this provision is more extensive within the armed forces and prisons. A key question to be addressed is the extent of the human rights obligations resting on the organization to make chaplaincies available. At a minimum there must be a bare permission for ministers to access the institution concerned which would not normally be accorded to members of the public, but the obligation may extend to the provision of facilities, the payment of expenses or a salary and the integration of religious acts into the regular programme of activities. Indeed, there is a spectrum of potential involvement between organizations that do not themselves fulfil religious purposes in any

---

[1] Christopher Swift, *Hospital Chaplaincy in the Twenty-first Century: the crisis of spiritual care on the NHS* (Farnham: Ashgate, 2009), 154.

central sense and those which do. At its most extensive this can give the entire organization a religious character. The question of extent also touches on the religions embraced. Here there is abundant evidence of an expanding establishment, with Anglican chaplains being supplemented by those of other Christian denominations and more recently by non-Christian ministers of religion. This gives rise to tricky questions of equal treatment and accreditation in the context of faith groups of different sizes, different internal structures, and with different needs.

I. Armed Forces Chaplaincies

1. Chaplaincies in British armed forces

The maintenance and administration of the armed forces takes place largely under prerogative powers with the consent of Parliament, and with a certain degree of statutory intervention.[2] This complex relationship of prerogative and statutory authority is no less true of the armed forces chaplaincy. Furthermore, as G R Rubin has recently noted, the largely hidden world of autonomous military regulation has been subject since the early 1960s to a process of civilianization and juridification.[3] Civilianization is the convergence between military and civilian law where there is no detriment to military effectiveness, whereas juridification in Rubin's use refers to the imposition of external legal norms on the military law system, typically under pressure from international and European human rights law and equality requirements.[4] Quite apart from the general judicial assertion of a right to review justiciable exercises of prerogative power,[5] the Crown is bound by the Human Rights Act 1998 in the exercise of its prerogative powers in respect of the armed forces.[6] It is also bound by the Employment Equality (Religion or Belief) Regulations[7] and, with some exceptions, the Equality Act 2006.[8] An important recent example of juridification has been the extension of the jurisdiction of Employment Tribunals to hear cases arising from the armed forces.[9] To the extent that they apply at all, considerations of non-justiciability are unlikely to be relevant in matters concerning the access of religious bodies to members serving in the armed forces, or in meeting the spiritual needs of servicemen and women. Thus the existence of enforceable legal rights in respect of chaplains in

---

[2] Overview in Peter Rowe, *Defence: the Legal Implications* (London: Brassey's, 1987), ch 1.

[3] G R Rubin, 'United Kingdom Military Law: autonomy, civilianisation, juridification' (2002) 65 MLR 36.

[4] Peter Rowe, *The Impact of Human Rights Law on Armed Forces* (Cambridge: Cambridge University Press, 2006). For a comparative study, see Georg Nolte (ed), *European Military Law Systems* (Berlin: W de Gruyter, 2003).

[5] *Council of Civil Service Unions v Minister for the Civil Service* [1985] AC 374.

[6] Human Rights Act 1998, s 22(5).

[7] Employment Equality (Religion or Belief) Regulations 2003, reg 36(2)(c).

[8] Equality Act, s 52.   [9] Armed Forces Act 1996, ss 21–27.

the armed forces falls to be considered as a matter of prerogative power, statutory obligation, and general principle on the basis of human rights and equality law.

In words regularly re-enacted almost verbatim for 350 years, the Naval Discipline Act 1957 commenced as follows:

All officers in command of Her Majesty's ships shall cause public worship of Almighty God to be solemnly, orderly and reverently performed in their respective ships, and shall take care that prayers and preaching, by the chaplains of those ships, be performed diligently and that the Lord's Day be observed.[10]

However, in general terms, chaplains in the armed forces are appointed and carry out their duties not under statute, but under the royal prerogative, with the basic provisions set out in Queen's Regulations. Military chaplains have always been present within the armed forces. The Royal Army Chaplain's Department was formed in 1796 to assist in recruiting clergy as chaplains to the army. Roman Catholic chaplains have been appointed since the Crimean War, and the first Jewish chaplain was appointed in 1892. Uniformed rabbis were present to minister to Jewish soldiers during the Second World War, although generally Jewish chaplains have been non-commissioned. Buddhist, Muslim, Hindu, and Sikh chaplains have now also been appointed as fully integrated members of the armed services chaplaincy, albeit as civil servants.[11] It has been suggested that the failure to make an appropriate spiritual adviser available to give advice to a Muslim reservist who objected to being called up to serve in the Gulf War might ground a human rights complaint on account of inequality of treatment in the ambit of freedom of religion.[12] The new policy has been summed up in these words:

The Armed Forces make every effort to accommodate religious or cultural requirements, and encourage people from all faiths to practise their religious observances. Whenever practicable personnel are allowed to observe religious festivals or holidays and to say prayers at a certain time. Halal, Kosher and vegetarian meals and operational ration packs are provided.[13]

The three armed forces are subject to slightly different regimes in respect of chaplaincies, although in some matters identical wording is used and certain aspects are subject to joint regulation. The Regulations for the Army and the Royal Air Force are particularly close. The Royal Naval Chaplaincy Service is led by a Director General with the historic title of Chaplain of the Fleet.[14] The Royal Army Chaplain's Department is led by a Chaplain-General with the rank of

---

[10] Naval Discipline Act 1957, s 1. The original source is Charles II's Act for the establishing Articles and Orders for the regulating and better Government of His Majesty's Navies, Ships of War and Forces by Sea, 13 Car II, St 1 c 9 (1661). The section was repealed by the Armed Forces Act 2006, s 378.   [11] Hansard, HL, 18 October 2005.

[12] *Khan v Royal Air Force Summary Court of Appeal* [2004] HRLR 40 per Rix LJ at para 20.

[13] <http://www.mod.uk/DefenceInternet/AboutDefence/WhatWeDo/Personnel/EqualityAndDiversity/EqualOpportunitiesInTheArmedForces.htm>, accessed 4 September 2006.   [14] J.1602(3) (Navy).

Major-General,[15] and the Royal Air Force Chaplaincy Service is led by a Chaplain-in-Chief with the rank of Air Vice-Marshal.[16] In general terms, the armed forces chaplaincies are responsible for the provision of religious ministration to armed forces personnel of the Army in peace and war, as well as to their families. They are expected to promote the spiritual and moral welfare of the entire military community.[17] Chaplains are commissioned to provide for the spiritual and pastoral well-being of Service personnel and their families.[18] Where commissioned chaplains are not available, civilian clergymen of the appropriate denomination may be appointed officiating chaplains.[19] Chaplains are not to perform executive or operational duties save those proper to their profession, and should be treated with the respect due to their sacred office.[20] They are thus unarmed.

The Queen's Regulations for the Royal Navy state the principal duties of chaplains to be:

(a) to conduct worship;
(b) to administer the sacraments;
(c) to preach and instruct in the faith;
(d) to visit the sick and all in their care;
(e) to further the life of the Christian Church;
(f) to work together ecumenically, whilst retaining denominational integrity;
(g) to co-operate with others in the caring professions and agencies;
(h) to facilitate the religious and spiritual needs of all regardless of faith group.[21]

The Queen's Regulations for the Army provide a somewhat different list, stating that chaplains are responsible for:

(a) conducting divine service in accordance with the official usage of their Church;

(b) ensuring that provision is made for the administration of the sacraments and other services in accordance with the practice of the Church;

(c) giving religious instruction to the personnel of armed forces and to their families and children;

(d) visiting the sick and personnel in detention or under sentence and caring for their spiritual needs;

(e) ensuring that all the necessary legal requirements have been complied with before they solemnise a marriage.[22]

The reverent observance of religion in the armed forces is said to be of the highest importance.[23] Attendance at divine service is voluntary, but commanding officers

---

[15] 2.034 (Army).   [16] RAF, *Air Rank Appointments List* (April 2009).
[17] 4.020 and Annexe B (Army).   [18] J.1601 (Navy).
[19] J.1601 (Navy) and J5.261 (Army).   [20] Ibid.   [21] J.1603.
[22] 5.276 (Army).   [23] J.7501(1) (Navy) and J5.262 (Army).

are to encourage attendance and set a good example themselves.[24] Sundays, Good Friday, and Christmas Day are to be, so far as possible, observed as days of rest,[25] and provision is to be made for the care of Jewish personnel as the occasion arises.[26] Corporate duties and organized sports are not to be arranged so as to interfere with acts of worship.[27] Courses of religious and spiritual instruction are to be arranged, and commanding officers are expected to encourage attendance.[28] Appropriate rooms and facilities are to be provided.[29] It should, however, be noted that as a matter of human rights law, higher ranking officers must be careful not to abuse their position to bring improper pressure to bear on junior personnel in matters of faith or religion.[30]

Provision is made for the registration and subsequent change of religious denomination of every member of the armed forces on entry to the Service.[31] This includes registration as atheist, agnostic, or no denomination. Change of registered denomination is a formal process requiring the individual concerned to consult with the chaplains and his or her commanding officer.[32] The consent of parents or guardians must be given for personnel under the age of 17½. In general terms, religious observance is voluntary and 'sympathetic consideration' is to be given to the needs of officially recognized non-Christian religious minorities.[33] Parades are not to be ordered in connection with divine service except by a sufficiently senior officer on special occasions of national or local importance.[34] No-one can be compelled to attend divine service or any joint or ecumenical service against his wishes, with the exception of those under the age of 17, and in the case of parades involving divine service of his own denomination.[35]

Chaplains in the Royal Navy assume the rank of the person they are counselling, but for purposes of discipline are treated as officers.[36] Army Chaplains are commissioned officers with rank.[37] For certain pension purposes, military chaplains have the rank as laid down in the Pay Warrant, and chaplains in the naval and air forces are treated as having a rank indicated as appropriate by their

---

[24] J.7501(2) (Navy) and J5.263 (Army).   [25] 7506 (Navy) and 5.266.

[26] 5.267 (Army).   [27] 7506 (Navy).   [28] 7510 (Navy) and 5.277 (Army).

[29] 7.511 (Navy) and 5.268(b), 5.275 (Army)

[30] *Larissis v Greece* (1999) 27 EHRR 329. Brief discussion in Rowe, *op cit* n 4, 50–3.

[31] J.7501 (Navy) and J5.271 (Army).   [32] 7502 (Navy) and J5.272 (Army).

[33] J.7501(3) (Navy) and J5.264 (Army). It is questionable whether permission need be given to practise a religion such as Satanism, which would also fail to gain recognition as a 'public' religion for other legal purposes (BBC News Report, 24 October 2004).

[34] 7509 (Navy) and 5.268(e) (Army)

[35] 5.268(e) (Army). Compulsion at joint services and parades would appear more general in the case of the Navy: see J.7501(3), 7508 and 7509, but may be unsustainable in an individual case of conscience on human rights grounds.

[36] Armed Forces Act 2006, s 371; Armed Forces (Naval Chaplains) Regulations 2009, SI 2009/826.

[37] Officers' Commissions (Army) Order 1967 SI 1967/9200 art 3 and sched, pt II.

length of service.[38] Chaplains are exempt from serving as jury members in courts martial or the new summary appeals court.[39]

By statute, chaplains serving with the armed forces abroad are, with the consent of the commanding officer, able to celebrate marriages of a wide range of service and related personnel.[40] This includes overseas civilians subject to military law as well as their resident children.[41] Such marriages are as valid as if they had been solemnized in the United Kingdom. Armed services chaplains also have responsibilities in respect of baptism (and their registration), funerals, and the consecration of standards, guidons, and colours.

One area in which the royal prerogative is inadequate to regulate the appointment and functions of Church of England chaplains is in respect of the adjustments to ecclesiastical law necessary to secure their ministrations in barracks and other military stations on land. The Army Chaplains Act 1868 grants the power to the Secretary of State to declare army precincts within existing dioceses and parishes an extra-parochial district.[42] An army chaplain may be appointed to the district,[43] and any chapel erected and consecrated in the precinct is an extra-parochial chapel.[44] An army chaplain can be authorized to perform his functions in an unconsecrated building on certification to the bishop.[45] Such extra-parochial districts can by Order in Council be brought under the exclusive jurisdiction of one bishop or archbishop.[46] The Act confirms that this has no effect on the ministrations of Church of Scotland chaplains.[47] It also applies to air force stations.[48]

As noted above, regimes of military discipline are also—for good constitutional reasons—regulated by statute. Military chaplains are accorded a special role in these processes. The Naval Detention Quarters Rules 1973 still have a distinctively Christian tone.[49] On admission, a man under sentence is to have his religious denomination recorded and the chaplain of his denomination informed. If he gives no religious affiliation, or if there is no chaplain of his denomination, notification is to be given to the Church of England, or some other chaplain.[50] Sentenced men are to have access to a Bible and other appropriate books of religious observance or instruction.[51] Chaplains are required to abide by the rules, consult, and cooperate with the commanding officer.[52] They are to see every sentenced man as far as is practicable and be afforded facilities for doing so.[53] They are to celebrate divine service in detention quarters every Sunday, on other

---

[38] Naval, Military and Air Forces etc. (Disablement and Death) Service Pensions Order 2006, SI 2006/206, s 3(9).   [39] Armed Forces Act 2006, ss 156(4)(d) and 143(4)(d) respectively.
[40] Foreign Marriage Act 1892, s 22(1) as amended.
[41] s 22(1A) and Foreign Marriage (Armed Forces) Order 1964, SI 1964/1000 as substituted by Foreign Marriage (Armed Forces) (Amendment No 2) Order 1990, SI 1990/2592.
[42] Army Chaplains Act 1868, s 4.   [43] Ibid, s 6.   [44] Ibid, s 7.   [45] Ibid, s 8.
[46] Ibid, s 9.   [47] Ibid, s 10.
[48] Air Force (Constitution) Act 1917, s 13 and Air Force (Application of Enactments) (No 2) Order 1918, SI 1918/548, art 1 and sched.
[49] Naval Detention Quarters Rules 1973, SI 1973/270.   [50] Ibid, rl 23(7).
[51] Ibid, rl 67.   [52] Ibid, rl 68.   [53] Ibid, rls 68 and 69.

customary days, and at other convenient times,[54] at which sentenced men are entitled to attend unless excluded by disorderly conduct, illness, or other reasonable cause.[55]

The legal framework in respect of chaplaincy duties in the context of army and air force discipline is slightly more comprehensive and slightly less rooted in established Christianity. Under the Imprisonment and Detention (Army) Rules, soldiers who are sentenced to punishment are to have their religious denomination recorded and a chaplain of that denomination is to be informed as soon as possible.[56] They are to have access to books of religious instruction or observation recognized by their denomination and approved by the Secretary of State.[57] Chaplains shall have access to them for visiting and religious instruction.[58] The basic duties of the chaplain as set out in rule 103 are very similar to those in respect of civil prisons. They are to visit the soldier on admission, at reasonable times, and shortly before release.[59] Chaplains are to be given lists of sentenced soldiers who are sick or undergoing punishment, and visits must be facilitated if either the soldier or the chaplain wishes it.[60] Where there is no chaplain of the same denomination, the commandant must arrange for a visit by a minister of the same denomination, if this is practicable and the soldier wishes it.[61] Chaplains are also expected to officiate at burials of soldiers under sentence who die in a military establishment.[62] Chaplains are expected to celebrate divine service on Sundays, other customary days, and on such convenient occasions as they may decide with the consent of the commandant. Sentenced soldiers are entitled to attend, unless they are in close confinement or if they have forfeited the right by reason of their disorderly conduct.[63] The Imprisonment and Detention (Air Force) Rules 1980 make the same substantive provision with respect to airmen.[64]

2. Chaplaincies under the Geneva Conventions

International law contains quite detailed regulations for the provision of chaplaincies under the Geneva Conventions 1949 and their Protocols. These have the force of law within the United Kingdom by virtue of the Geneva Conventions Act 1957 as amended.[65] The context, which is the treatment of prisoners of war, provides a useful bridge between armed forces chaplaincies and prison chaplaincies, which will be considered in the next section.

---

[54] Ibid, rl 70.   [55] Ibid, rl 71.

[56] Imprisonment and Detention (Army) Rules 1979, SI 1979/1456, rl.55(f).

[57] Ibid, rl 101.   [58] Ibid, rl 102(2).   [59] Ibid, rl 103(1).   [60] Ibid, rl 103(3).

[61] Ibid, rl 103(2).   [62] Ibid, rl 103(4).   [63] Ibid, rl 104.

[64] Imprisonment and Detention (Air Force) Rules 1980, SI 1980/2005, rls 55, 101–4.

[65] The First and Second Additional Protocols (1977) were transposed into English Law by the Geneva Conventions (Amendment) Act 1995; the Third Additional Protocol 2005 was transposed by the Geneva Conventions and United Nations Personnel Act 2009.

The Geneva Conventions originally made provision for 'chaplains', but the Additional Protocol use a potentially broader category of 'religious personnel', defined as military or civilian persons, such as chaplains, who are exclusively engaged in the work of their ministry and attached on a permanent or temporary basis to the armed forces of a Party to the conflict, to medical units or medical transports of a Party to the conflict, to various other medical units or medical transports, or to civil defence organizations of a Party to the conflict.[66] The adoption of the broader terminology of 'religious personnel' would seem to have derived from the (arguably mistaken) assumption that 'chaplains' are specific to Christianity.[67] The legal position of religious personnel largely mirrors that of medical personnel. Under the first two Geneva Conventions,[68] they are expressly listed as the object of protection along with the wounded, sick, and medical personnel. In ministering to the sick and wounded, they have specific rights to respect and protection.[69] They are to be treated as non-combatant and thus not as prisoners of war.[70] They may not be captured, but only retained if necessary to minister to prisoners of war.[71] They may not be required to do work other than their spiritual ministry, and have direct access to camp authorities.[72] The Geneva Convention relative to the treatment of prisoners of war contains a fuller codification. Prisoners of war are to be granted complete latitude in the exercise of their religious duties subject to compliance with the disciplinary routine.[73] Chaplains must be granted all facilities necessary to perform their religious ministrations,[74] including adequate premises for religious services.[75] They have the right to visit all prisoners periodically and to deal with the competent authorities.[76]

Article 35 provides a substantial set of rights:

Chaplains who fall into the hands of the enemy Power and who remain or are retained with a view to assisting prisoners of war, shall be allowed to minister to them and to exercise freely their ministry amongst prisoners of war of the same religion, in accordance with their religious conscience. They shall be allocated among the various camps and labour detachments containing prisoners of war belonging to the same forces, speaking the same language or practising the same religion. They shall enjoy the necessary facilities, including the means of transport provided for in Article 33, for visiting the prisoners of war outside their camp. They shall be free to correspond, subject to censorship, on matters concerning their religious duties with the ecclesiastical authorities in the country of detention and with international religious organisations. Letters and cards which they may send for this purpose shall be in addition to the quota provided for in Article 71.

---

[66] First Additional Protocol, art 8.

[67] Hilaire McCoubrey, 'The Protection of Creed and Opinion in the Laws of Armed Conflict' (2000) 5 Journal of Conflict and Security Law 135.

[68] ie for the amelioration of the condition of the wounded and sick in armed forces in the field.

[69] Geneva Conventions, art 24.   [70] Ibid, art 28.   [71] *Loc cit.*   [72] *Loc cit.*

[73] Ibid, art 34.   [74] Ibid, art 33.   [75] Ibid, art 34.   [76] Ibid, art 33.

Prisoners of war who are not chaplains but who are ministers of religion are also to be allowed to minister freely as if they were chaplains,[77] and in the absence of any chaplain or such minister an alternative local minister must be provided.[78]

The Additional Protocols seek to enhance the protection of chaplains and other religious personnel by ensuring that they carry suitable identification and use the distinctive emblems of red cross, crescent, crystal etc.[79] The Second Additional Protocol emphasizes that they are to be granted all available help and that they are not to be compelled to carry out tasks incompatible with their humanitarian mission.[80]

Although the Geneva Conventions and their Protocols only apply to the arrangement of chaplaincies in the relatively unusual contexts of armed conflict and its immediate aftermath, they nonetheless represent a minimum standard potentially applicable on the basis of the right to religious freedom within domestic law. It would be surprising if the standard set by international human rights law in respect of domestic provision for the armed forces and civilian prisons fell below the level required by international humanitarian law should such forces be captured.[81]

II. Prison Chaplaincies

Legislation in the late eighteenth century authorized justices to appoint and pay chaplains in all their penal establishments, and religion was a core feature of the design and life of Victorian prisons.[82] The scope of chaplaincy was widened beyond the established church by the Prison Ministers Act 1863.[83] This authorized those responsible for county and borough prisons to appoint and pay ministers of churches and religious persuasions other than the Church of England if the number of prisoners warranted it.[84] Furthermore, where no minister was appointed, one was permitted to visit without any special request being made by the prisoner, but not against his will. The religious affiliation of each prisoner was to be entered in a book on admission, and a list of relevant prisoners was to be given to each minister.[85] There was to be no compulsion on prisoners to attend any service held by a minister of a persuasion they did not share.[86]

---

[77] Ibid, art 36.   [78] Ibid, art 37.

[79] First Additional Protocol, art 18; Second Additional Protocol, art 12; Third Additional Protocol, arts 2 and 5.   [80] Ibid, art 9.

[81] In this connection, Hilaire McCoubrey (*op cit* n 67) comments adversely on the constraints imposed by the British Army on Christian celebrations in Saudi Arabia during the Gulf War.

[82] James A Beckford and Sophie Gilliat, *Religion in Prisons: equal rites in a multi-faith society* (Cambridge: Cambridge University Press, 1998), 26–7.

[83] Objections to the immediate appointment of a Roman Catholic chaplain to Liverpool Borough Gaol gave rise to a libel action: see *Kelly v Sherlock* (1866) LR 1 QB 686.

[84] Prison Ministers Act 1863, s 3.   [85] Ibid, s 4.   [86] Ibid, s 5.

The current basic statutory framework for prison chaplaincies is contained in the Prison Act 1952. In essence this continues the pattern established by the Prison Ministers Act. Every prison is required to have a chaplain and may have an assistant chaplain if the Secretary of State considers it large enough to require it.[87] The chaplain and any assistant chaplain shall be clergy of the Church of England,[88] licensed for such purpose by the bishop of the diocese in which the prison is situated, who must be given notice of the nomination within one month.[89] A person may not be chaplain of two prisons unless they are within a convenient distance of each other and together are designed to receive not more than 100 prisoners.[90] If there are sufficient prisoners of another religious denomination to require the appointment of a prison minister, the Secretary of State may do so,[91] and may pay him or her reasonable remuneration.[92] Where no prison minister has been appointed, the Secretary of State may allow a minister to visit prisoners of his denomination,[93] but such a visiting minister is not allowed to visit prisoners against their will.[94] The governor of a prison is obliged to record the religious denomination of each prisoner on reception and give a list of the relevant prisoners to any appointed or permitted minister.[95] These are only allowed to visit their co-religionists.[96] Subject to whatever arrangements are in force, every prisoner is allowed to attend chapel or be visited by the chaplain, whatever their denomination.[97]

The Prison Rules amplify these provisions. Chaplains and prison ministers are obliged to interview prisoners of their denomination after reception and before release.[98] They are also obliged to read the burial service for any prisoner of their denomination who dies in prison, if other arrangements have not been made.[99] The chaplain must visit daily all prisoners of the Church of England who are sick, under restraint, or confined to their cells,[100] and any prisoner of any other denomination in similar circumstances who is not visited by a minister of his own denomination, so long as the prisoner is not unwilling.[101] Prison ministers are obliged to visit such prisoners of their own denomination so far as they reasonably can.[102] More generally, the chaplain shall visit the prisoners belonging to the Church of England;[103] prison ministers shall visit the prisoners of their denomination as regularly as is reasonable,[104] and where there is no prison minister of the relevant denomination, if the prisoner so requests, the governor must do what he reasonably can to ensure regular visits by one who is.[105] The chaplain is obliged to conduct services for prisoners belonging to the Church of England at least once every Sunday, Christmas Day, and Good Friday, and to celebrate

---

[87] Prison Act 1952, s 7(1) and (3).　　[88] Ibid, s 7(4).　　[89] Ibid, s 9(2).
[90] Ibid, s 9(1).　　[91] Ibid, s 10(1).　　[92] Ibid, s 10(2).　　[93] Ibid, s 10(3).
[94] Ibid, s 10(4).　　[95] Ibid, s 10(5).　　[96] Ibid, s 10(5).　　[97] Ibid, s 10(4).
[98] Prison Rules 1999, SI 1999/ 728, rl 14(1)(a).　　[99] Ibid, rl 14(1)(b).
[100] Ibid, rl 14(2).　　[101] Ibid, rl 14(3).　　[102] Ibid, rl 14(2).　　[103] Ibid, rl 15(1).
[104] Ibid, rl 15(2).　　[105] Ibid, rl 15(3).

Holy Communion and conduct other weekday services by arrangement.[106] Prison ministers are to conduct services for their prisoners at such times as may be arranged.[107] Arrangements shall be made so as not to require prisoners of the Christian religion to do any unnecessary work on Sunday, Christmas Day, or Good Friday, or prisoners of other religions to do any such work on their recognized days of religious observance.[108] Religious books recognized by the relevant denomination and approved by the Secretary of State are to be available for the personal use of prisoners.[109] In practice, an important additional function includes writing parole reports on prisoners, including discretionary life prisoners, for Parole Boards.[110]

Provision is made for substitute chaplains and ministers with the permission of the Secretary of State.[111] By the terms of Prison Act 1952, section 7, chaplains and assistant chaplains are unlike prison ministers of other denominations in that they are officers of the prison.[112] As such, they have an overall responsibility for religious matters within prisons. It should also be noted that the statutory duties of chaplains and prison ministers do not extend to visiting ministers, and only rarely are the latter involved in such duties in practice.[113] Strictly speaking, the use of 'chaplain' should be restricted to the officer who is a member of the clergy of the Church of England occupying the distinctive legal position just outlined, but the tendency for some time has been to use the term 'chaplain' for any prison minister,[114] and occasionally even for a visiting minister.[115] In the case of many Christian chaplains, this development reflects the terms of a concordat entered into between the Church of England, Roman Catholic, and Methodist Churches in 1971, which although it retains the Church of England clergyman as team leader recognizes that 'all chaplains are colleagues with no relationship of superiority or inferiority'.[116] In practice, popular use goes even further and seems to distinguish between chaplains, defined as full- or part-time employed ministers who are part of a chaplaincy team, and visiting ministers, generally of non-Christian faiths, who are brought in on an *ad hoc* basis to minister to their co-religionists, and who at best are paid an hourly rate and expenses. The Prison Service Chaplaincy now refers to chaplains of all faiths whether permanently employed or appointed on a fee basis.

---

[106] Ibid, rl 16(1).　　[107] Ibid, rl 16(2).　　[108] Ibid, rl 18.　　[109] Ibid, rl 19.

[110] Julian Gibbons, 'Discretionary Life Panels' (1994) 144 NLJ 524.

[111] Prison Rules 1999, rl 17(1) and (2).

[112] Although along with the medical officer, they are excluded from the definition of 'prison service' for the purposes of the Secretary of State's power to provide by regulation for procedures relating to pay and conditions: Criminal Justice and Public Order Act 1994, s 128(5).

[113] The finding of Beckford and Gilliat about the general non-involvement of visiting ministers in fulfilling the basic statutory duties (*op cit* n 82, 64–5) is therefore unsurprising.

[114] See *Chilton v HM Prison Service*, EAT, unreported 23 July 1999.

[115] For a recent example of the use of 'Buddhist chaplain' for a visiting minister, see the Parole Board report cited in *Re Cadman* [2006] 3 All ER 1255.

[116] Beckford and Gilliat, *op cit* n 82, 42–3.

There is some uncertainty as to the employment status of chaplains and prison ministers. Prison chaplains are often cited as examples of clergy who are employed as distinct from merely holding an office.[117] By contrast, in *Miller v Secretary of State for Home Affairs*, the Employment Appeal Tribunal held that a visiting Quaker prison minister was not an employee but subject to a contract to provide services and thus unable to bring a complaint of unfair dismissal.[118] She had been sent a letter of appointment together with *Notes for the Guidance of Visiting Ministers*. She was paid an hourly rate for attendance as well as expenses. By arrangement with the chaplaincy she became very involved in the life of the prison, facilitating programmes and sitting on committees. Towards the end of her time she had acted as assistant chaplain fulfilling some of the duties which by the terms of the Prison Act 1952 fall on the Anglican chaplain. However, she did not receive holiday or sick pay, and was not subject to targets, appraisal, or the disciplinary and grievance procedures which applied to the chaplain. Accordingly, the Tribunal held that the requisite degree of control was lacking, and the EAT found no flaw in its approach. Nevertheless, it should not be assumed that visiting ministers are not 'employed' for all purposes. Remedies in respect of anti-discrimination law are available to a wider range of persons.[119] One can assume, however, that volunteers have no contractual relationship at all with the Prison Service.

The space provided for religious worship in prisons varies considerably. In some cases the original substantial Church of England chapel has been converted, more or less effectively. Some prisons have purpose-built synagogues, and now mosques. Some have rooms which are supposed to be multi-faith, and even multi-purpose, doubling up as concert or meeting rooms, and some of the newest prisons have multi-faith chaplaincy centres with a chapel, offices, multi-faith rooms, and ritual washing facilities.[120]

The statutory and administrative framework for the regulation of religion in prisons presupposes the centrality of the Church of England in the prison chaplaincy, with toleration for those of other denominations and faiths. In a substantial piece of research published in 1998, James A Beckford and Sophie Gilliat found that practice diverged from this model to some extent, although not to the extent of creating *de facto* a situation of equality of treatment in a multi-faith context. They found that although chaplains act as gatekeepers to the provision of religious services, they are generally ill-prepared for interaction with those of other faiths. They found that lack of resources and the perceived inequity of the system acted against a large supply of goodwill on the part of chaplains to produce rather mixed relationships between the chaplaincy and visiting ministers.

---

[117] *Diocese of Southward v Coker* [1998] ICR 140 per Mummery LJ. See Ch 4 above for the general position of ministers of religion.   [118] Unreported, 4 May 2004.

[119] See *Chilton v HM Prison Service*, EAT, unreported 23 July 1999.

[120] Beckford and Gilliat, *op cit* n 82, 51–4.

While chaplains were ready to facilitate and broker the resources necessary for non-Christian prisoners to worship and practise their faiths, there was a general unwillingness to include non-Christian ministers in the chaplaincy teams as equal partners. The model of chaplaincy was essentially Christian, albeit tolerant, and Anglican chaplains were resistant to changes which might undermine that model.[121] One of the authors subsequently wrote of the dilemma facing those who would seek a more neutral provision of religious services, in that by comparison with the United States, the British (Christian) Prison Service Chaplaincy has been able to secure a more advantageous position for minority faiths.[122] In spite of the practical advantages of toleration, there have been problems in the past securing recognition of certain religious groups such as Rastafarians.[123]

Within the last decade, the monopoly position of the Christian chaplaincy has weakened significantly. Responsibility for the provision of religious chaplaincy services lies with the Prison Service Chaplaincy, which is part of the Directorate for operational policy and commissioning at the National Offenders Management Services Headquarters. The Chaplain-General is a Church of England clergyman, but the chaplaincy itself is developing into a multi-faith body. Its fundamental purpose statement is non-faith-specific, and in its recruitment practice it draws no formal distinction between faiths. In addition, the Prison Service has recently entered into formal relationships with representatives of seven faiths: Buddhism, Hinduism, Islam, Judaism, Mormonism, Sikhism, and—from 2005—Paganism, constituting them as Religious Consultative Services. Together they make up an Advisory Group on Religion in Prisons. The significance of this is that the Prison Service Order on religion makes clear that the responsibility for operational matters, including religious worship and practice, rests with governors. There has thus been a formal shift away from the monopoly of the Prison Service Chaplaincy in all matters religious, with new direct relationships between non-Christian faiths and the governor. In line with this development, the Chaplaincy Council contains not only representatives of the Roman Catholic and Free Churches, but also of the Religious Consultative Services. Its remit is to advise both the Prison Service Chaplaincy and the National Offenders Management Service more generally on matters to do with the faith needs of prisoners. Furthermore, the coordinating chaplain role may now be exercised by any employed chaplain.

The main advisory document on religion in prisons is the now the Religion Manual,[124] which has largely superseded the Directory and Guide on Religious Practice in HM Prison Service.[125] The Manual was drafted to reflect 'a more

---

[121] Ibid, 68–70, 124–30.

[122] James A Beckford, 'Rational Choice Theory and prison chaplaincy: the chaplain's dilemma' (1999) 50 British Journal of Sociology 671.

[123] Sebastian Poulter, *Ethnicity, Law and Human Rights: the English experience* (Oxford: Clarendon Press, 1998), 347–50.   [124] Prison Service Order 4550 (2000) as updated.

[125] HM Prison Service, *Directory and Guide on Religious Practice in HM Prison Service* (1988).

inclusive approach'[126] to prison ministry and much of it is taken up with a wealth of detailed information about private and corporate worship and practice, rites, diet, and dress in respect of the eight recognized religions. It sets out general principles along with guidelines on changes of religious registration, the provision of multi-faith rooms, veganism, and permitted religious artefacts. It deals at length with security issues to ensure that personal searches, searches of books, artefacts and food, and the oversight of corporate worship are carried out in a way that is sensitive and effective. It establishes the Religious Consultative Services for the seven non-Christian recognized religions, although in the case of other religions, the Directory and Guide remains the principal resource.[127] The final chapter introduces the 'religion card' containing symbols for 10 major world religions to assist non-English speaking prisoners in identifying their religion.[128] The Religion Manual is supported by a distinct Performance Standard.[129]

Alongside the multicultural shift within prison chaplaincy over the last decade, there has also been a series of experiments with (Christian) faith-based units within prisons, inspired by pioneering volunteers in Brazil and the United States from the 1970s.[130] The Prison Service (England and Wales) was the first prison service in the world to introduce a residential faith-based unit in a prison, a lead that was quickly followed by other countries, notably the US.[131] The development was challenged by secular pressure groups and representatives of some non-Christian faith groups.[132] A subsequent academic evaluation, while highlighting areas of concern nevertheless concluded that the presence of such units 'may act as a sign-post to the Prison Service in terms of promoting standards of decency, humanity and order in prisons'.[133] One difficulty was the risk of tensions with the prison chaplaincy, not least because such units provide a completely different model for the role of religion in prisons.

III. Hospital Chaplaincies

The earliest hospitals were religious foundations, and the hospitals established in the course of the eighteenth and nineteenth centuries uniformly took care to provide for the spiritual and emotional needs of their patients.[134] This was done

---

[126] Prison Service Order 4550, Introduction, para 1.   [127] Ibid, para 3.9.

[128] There is no distinctive symbol for Mormonism or Paganism; the four others are Baha'i, Chinese religion, Jainism, and Zoroastrianism.

[129] Performance Standard no 51 on Religion (presently suspended). Both the Religion Manual and Standard 51 are due for re-drafting.

[130] Jonathan Burnside *et al*, *My Brother's Keeper: Faith-based units in prisons* (Cullompton: Willan Publishing, 2005), 1–67.   [131] Ibid, 196–266.

[132] In the US, a similar initiative gave rise to litigation, a reflective account of which can be found in Winnifred Fallers Sullivan, *Prison Religion: Faith-based Reform and the Constitution* (Princeton; Princeton University Press, 2009).   [133] Quoted at *op cit* n 130, 353.

[134] Christopher Swift, *Hospital Chaplaincy in the Twenty-first Century: the crisis of spiritual care on the NHS* (Farnham: Ashgate, 2009), chs 1 and 2.

at least by appointing a local clergyman as honorary chaplain, and sometimes by employing one full-time. The reform to the Poor Law had the effect of strengthening the position of Anglican chaplains in workhouses and their associated infirmaries.[135] Strictly speaking, attendance at religious services and religious instruction for children were not to be compulsory for those of other denominations; instead it was lawful for a licensed minister to visit at any time to afford religious assistance and offer instruction.[136] In practice there was considerable institutional preference for the established church. Likewise, the Lunacy Act 1890 required the visiting committee of every local asylum to appoint a chaplain in priest's orders and licensed for such purposes by the bishop.[137] He was obliged to perform divine service every Sunday in the chapel or other convenient place.[138] The Act also provided that patients or their friends had the right to request the assistance of a minister of a religious persuasion differing from that of the established church.[139]

The creation of the National Health Service in 1948 caused considerable anxiety about the position of chaplains on the part of church authorities.[140] However the Government gave firm assurances that chaplains and chapels would be funded in each hospital.[141] In fact, nationalization marked a period of significant growth and gradual 'professionalization'. From an initial complement in 1948 of 28 full-time chaplains, by 1999 there were about 400 full-time paid chaplains and about 3,500 other clergy or spiritual care-givers. Whereas it had been normal before nationalization for a chaplain to have a relatively short-term appointment before returning to parish ministry, and for close links between local church and local hospital to be maintained, hospital chaplaincy became a parallel career, with chaplains employed by the NHS and increasingly connected to the churches only through high-level bodies such as the Church of England's Hospital Chaplaincies Council (from 1951). In 1992 the College of Healthcare Chaplains was formed as a non-denominational professional body.

Under New Labour the process of professionalization accelerated; at the same time there was a new emphasis on the public presence of religion (in the less threatening guise of 'spirituality') as well as a commitment to multicultural inclusivity. The question of multi-faith chaplaincy was raised already in 1998, and bore fruit in the formation in 2002 of the Multi-faith Group for Healthcare Chaplaincy.[142] Then in November 2003, after a wide-ranging consultation process, the Department of Health issued its own best practice guidance: *Meeting the religious and spiritual needs of patients and staff*. This insists that 'meeting the spiritual needs of patients, staff and visitors is fundamental to the care the NHS

---

[135] Swift, *op cit* n 134, 36.   [136] Poor Law Amendment Act 1834, s 19.
[137] Lunacy Act 1890, s 276(1)(a). The licence was revocable: s 277(1).   [138] Ibid, s 277(2).
[139] Ibid, s 277(3).   [140] Swift, *op cit* n 134, 40–51.
[141] National Health Service, *Appointment of Chaplains*, HMC (48) 62 (1948).
[142] Swift, *op cit* n 134, 70.

provides'.[143] Intriguingly, it assumes that the introduction of the Human Rights Act 1998 'underlines the need for NHS Trusts to provide appropriate world faith representatives and worship spaces for faith communities within the healthcare population'.[144] The guidance contains a framework for chaplaincy/spiritual care along with methods for calculating the appropriate amount of resource to be allocated. The work of the chaplaincy team should be monitored by the Trust Board and led by one of its Directors; the chaplaincy service should be headed by a designated member of the team; provision must be available out of normal hours; each member of the team should retain responsibility for their own faith community; adequate arrangements should be made for the 'spiritual, religious, sacramental, ritual and cultural requirements' of all patients and staff; suitable appointments are to be made to posts in partnership with appropriate faith communities and their representatives; standard human resource procedures are to be followed and clear lines of management and accountability established; and appropriate and timely access to services from smaller faith communities is to be provided.

More specific guidance follows in a number of areas. As regards confidentiality and data protection, the need to obtain patient consent for details to be passed to the chaplaincy is stressed, while also remaining open to changes of mind on the part of patients. The need to integrate and train volunteers as well as the need to ensure more general training and development is highlighted. Some quite detailed suggestions are made, for example as to the 'units' of chaplaincy time to be made available per bed and number of staff in different contexts of healthcare provision. The guidance also recommends a space for prayer, reflection, and religious services that can hold at least 20, with flexibility as to furnishing and religious symbolism, secure storage for different artefacts, a code of conduct on use, and involvement of the chaplaincy team in planning and development. Throughout, the guidance gives examples of good practice from hospitals across the country.

The growing identity of hospital chaplaincy as an independent profession is more apparent in the accompanying NHS publication, *Caring for the Spirit*. This sets out a 10-year plan for development for spiritual services based on a healthcare model of assessment, planning, delivery, and review. Soon afterwards, the various bodies that had grown out of the College of Healthcare Chaplains came together in 2005 to agree a UK-wide Code of Conduct. In 2007, the Chaplaincy Academic and Accreditation Board was formed to provide training and professional development services. In his recent study of NHS chaplaincy, Swift notes the discomfort felt by many chaplains about the impact of modern healthcare models of service provision on their own understanding of their spiritual and pastoral role.[145] He also notes the resource pressures on budgets which in practice inhibit the appointment of other-faith chaplains. In practice existing hospital chaplains are stretched to provide religious services of last resort to many whose

---

[143] NHS, *Meeting the religious and spiritual needs of patients and staff* (Nov 2003), 'Introduction'.
[144] *Loc cit.*   [145] Swift, *op cit* n 134, 69.

residual faith has severed any substantial connection with a local church, but who still understand themselves to be in some sense Christian.[146]

The most fundamental legal question to arise in respect of hospital chaplains of any faith is the extent of the obligation on NHS Trusts to secure their provision. This question came to a head in 2006, when the Worcestershire Acute Hospitals Trust announced that it intended to cut six of its seven chaplaincy posts.[147] The decision provoked a national media campaign and substantial political debate which caused the Trust to negotiate a compromise with local church leaders and charities, and then finally to reinstate chaplaincy services within its main budget, but which left the fundamental question unresolved. Since there is no longer any specific legal obligation on NHS bodies to appoint chaplains, any duty must be derived ultimately from the general duty of the Secretary of State to provide 'such other services or facilities for the prevention of illness, the care of persons suffering from illness and the after-care of persons who have suffered from illness as he considers are appropriate as part of the health service'[148] together with the duty on NHS Acute Trusts to use their resources 'effectively, efficiently and economically'.[149] It would be hard to argue on general judicial review principles that a decision to cease providing chaplaincy services is unlawful, although to prevent ministers of religion from visiting members of their own congregation would probably cross the boundaries of reasonableness. At this point, general human rights provide a more helpful guide to the legal limits which need to be observed.

IV. University, Professional, and Industrial Chaplaincies

The rapid growth in higher education after the Second World War, and particularly after the Robbins Report of 1963,[150] led to a corresponding growth in university chaplaincies.[151] In the early 1950s the Church of England decided to set aside money for the appointment of Anglican university chaplains and coordinate their work nationally. This lead was followed by other Christian denominations in the mid-1960s and by the creation of the National Jewish Chaplaincy Board in the mid-1970s.[152]

---

[146] Ibid, 73.

[147] See the announcement of the. BBC News 5 September 2006. Full account in Swift, *op cit* n 134, ch 4.

[148] National Health Service Act 2006, s 3(1)(e). Note that regard must be had in the general administration of a former voluntary hospital to any character or association it had by virtue of any link with a particular religious denomination: National Health Service Act 2006, s 221.

[149] Ibid, s 26.

[150] *Report of the Committee on Higher Education* (The 'Robbins Report'), Cmnd 2154 (1963).

[151] See, generally, Sophie Gilliat-Ray, *Religion in Higher Education: the politics of the multi-faith campus* (Aldershot: Ashgate, 2000).   [152] Ibid, 26–9 and 181–2.

Here, as elsewhere, there were ancient precedents. The universities of Oxford and Cambridge were essentially ecclesiastical institutions restricting membership and office to members of the established church. The University of Durham was established on a similar basis. Indeed this restriction formed one of the principal non-conformist grievances of the nineteenth century, and failure to address the matter quickly enough led to the formation of University College, London, on expressly non-religious terms. The process of widening access started in the 1850s, culminating in the Universities Tests Act 1871. This prohibits the imposition of any religious test or requirement in respect of taking a degree or holding any office and exempts students from any obligation to attend a lecture to which they have a religious objection in the Universities of Oxford, Cambridge, and Durham. At the same time the Act preserves specific offices which are lawfully restricted to persons in holy orders or members of the Church of England. It also expressly preserves the lawfully established system of religious instruction, worship, and discipline, and imposes obligations to provide sufficient religious instruction to members of the Church of England *in statu pupillari*, and daily public worship according to the Book of Common Prayer. Section 58 of the Universities of Oxford and Cambridge Act 1877 includes a power on the part of the Commissioners for those universities to establish new denominationally-specific theological offices.

In respect of colleges, as distinct from the Universities generally, the Act only applies to those colleges subsisting on 16 June 1871. Colleges founded since that date may be established with a specific denominational character, may have a multi-faith chaplaincy service, or may make no such provision at all. Thus it is that the older colleges replicate the general political and legal situation with established Anglican chapels and chaplains, toleration for other denominations and faiths, and equal rights for students and staff as individuals. Chaplains are college appointments, supported financially on relatively generous terms.[153]

As regards other older universities, the matter is subject to the charter and statutes of the institution in question. They are autonomous institutions. Many used to reflect the legacy of Victorian disestablishment debates by incorporating a clause preventing the adoption of any religious test,[154] and still think of themselves as 'secular'. In these contexts, the typical position would seem to be that universities tolerate the existence of a chaplaincy centre, which is staffed by full-time minsters of religion paid by their church or association, and assisted on an honorary basis by local representatives of other faiths.[155] The degree of recognition and integration into the formal structures of the university, as well as the provision of premises and financial support for administration, varies. The perceived secular nature of the institution can lead to an unwillingness to make clear

---

[153] Ibid, 71–2.
[154] Such a test would now be unlawful: Employment Equality (Religion or Belief) Regulations 2003, SI 2003/1660, reg 20.   [155] Gilliat-Ray, *op cit* n 151, 65–8.

budgeted provision—although money may well be provided in practice—or to establish formal accreditation processes.[156] There is no general legal requirement for newer universities established under the Higher Education Act to make provision for chaplaincies. In these contexts there is typically a higher degree of institutional support, and a clearer multi-faith orientation. Funding is more likely to be collaborative between the HE institution and one or more religious bodies, and the chaplaincy may exist as an independent charitable trust.[157]

Given that university staff and students are as free to engage in active membership of organized religions as other members of the working public, it is hard to see that the same imperative for the provision of their spiritual needs exists as it does in the other contexts considered so far. It should, of course, not be forgotten that university staff and students themselves enjoy rights to religious liberty and may organize themselves into religious clubs and societies, with or without affiliation to other external religious bodies. In that sense, the context is much freer, and closer to civil society more generally, than in the armed forces, prisons, or hospitals. Gilliat-Ray notes that the role of university chaplains has shifted over time from 'parish ministry' to Christian students up to the mid-1960s, via 'enabling the Christian community' to act within the institution (1960s), to a pastoral responsibility to the institution as a whole (1970s).[158] Today, chaplains are more likely to be seen as humanistic professionals providing a pastoral ambulance service and institutional religious expertise to the institution as it seeks to ensure that a wider range of religious needs are accommodated and met.[159] She suggests that universities, like other public institutions, need to recognize the growing presence and significance of religious diversity and re-create themselves as holistic, but inclusive, communities. If that is to happen, some role akin to chaplaincy would seem indispensable.

There are many chaplaincies in other professional and industrial settings beyond the university. Some of these are simply aspects of the mission of churches and religious associations in which they seek to minister to certain sectors of the public. They have no formal connection with the organizations to which their target groups belong. Others operate with varying degrees of collaboration and support. For example, chaplains have been appointed to the police since the mid-nineteenth century, but police chaplaincy has been small, sporadic, and low profile. However, numbers have grown since the 1980s, and by 1988 there were 20 formally appointed chaplains.[160] Although some are paid, many are voluntary and part-time. There is now a National Association of Chaplains to the Police.

Other chaplaincies do have formal recognition, but are voluntary arrangements between churches and industries. For example, the Oil Chaplaincy

---

[156] Ibid, 71–3, 76.

[157] This model was identified as 'ideal' in a report of the National Consultation of Polytechnic Chaplains in 1985. Ibid, 30–3.   [158] Ibid, 29.

[159] Ibid, 69–71.

[160] Richard Armitage, 'Police Chaplaincy—Servant to the Service' (Home Office, Sept 1996).

was established in the late 1980s, receiving particular impetus following the Chinook helicopter accident. It provides pastoral services to the oil and gas industry through a programme of offshore visits, a counselling service, material support, and special services in a designated chapel in the Kirk of St Nicholas, Aberdeen. The chaplaincy is located in the headquarters of one of the oil companies and is funded by Oil and Gas UK, a trade association. It is Christian/interdenominational, but assists and advises anyone who seeks their services.[161]

The inclusion of chapels and prayer-rooms in airports is a widespread and, it would seem, growing phenomenon. There is an International Association of Civil Aviation Chaplaincies. Once again, these chaplaincies are essentially honorary, being funded by those religious associations with an interest in providing this type of service. In respect of the facilities provided they are dependent on the cooperation of airport authorities.

V. Chaplaincies and Human Rights

Legal and administrative provision for chaplaincy services now takes place against a general background of human rights. The right to religious liberty protects certain rights in respect of chaplaincies. The majority of directly relevant European human rights case-law is concerned with prisons, in which questions of religious access and exercise may be bound up with broader questions about the overall compatibility of the prison regime with rights not to be subject to degrading or inhuman treatment or punishment (article 3), or rights to respect for privacy and correspondence (article 8). Indeed, in some of the earlier cases heard by the Commission, there was a tendency to consider questions of access to ministers of religion as an aspect of article 8, not article 9, a tendency which may simply reflect the relatively late development of article 9 case-law.[162]

A series of applications involving prisoners' religious rights consistently failed before the Commission. These include the lack of access of a British prisoner in a German prison to a Church of England priest,[163] the desire of a Buddhist to publish articles in a religious magazine,[164] the diet and access to a minister of an orthodox Jew,[165] denial of registration, contact with outsiders and access to literature in respect of a Wicca pagan,[166] the refusal of a Sikh to wear prison clothes and clean his cell,[167] the lack of a suitable chapel for a prisoner in a secure unit,[168] and the refusal of a vegan to work in the prison print shop.[169]

---

[161] Information from <http://www.oilchaplaincy.com/>, accessed on 9 September 2009.
[162] See eg *Fell v United Kingdom* (1981) 23 DR 102.
[163] *X v Federal Republic of Germany* (1966) 23 Collections 1.
[164] *X v United Kingdom* (1974) 1 DR 41.
[165] *X v United Kingdom* (1976) 5 DR 8; *S v United Kingdom*, no 13669/88 (1990).
[166] *X v United Kingdom* (1977) 11 DR 55.   [167] *X v United Kingdom* (1982) 28 DR 5.
[168] *Chester v United Kingdom*, no 14747/89 (1990).
[169] *W v United Kingdom*, no 18187/91 (1993).

Although these applications all failed, they did so for different reasons, and in each case the Commission accepted the principle that prisoners enjoy article 9 rights to freedom of thought, conscience, and religion. Prison authorities have an obligation to make reasonable provision for the exercise of these rights. As regards the threshold question of what counts as a religion, there has been no question about any of the world faiths, and veganism was also accepted as coming within the scope of article 9.[170] The refusal to enter 'Wicca' as the religious affiliation of a prisoner was found not to amount to a breach, since the religion was 'not identifiable', although this application failed on other grounds as well. In the light of other cases (Druidism, for example[171]) and with more adequate evidence of the beliefs and practices of Wiccans, it is quite possible that a similar application could succeed at this point.

The Commission was more restrictive as regards the question of what counted as a protected religious practice. Engaging in collective worship, access to a minister, matters of diet and dress, and the refusal to engage in repugnant activity, such as cleaning for a high-caste Sikh and touching print dyes tested on animals for a vegan, have all been accepted as potentially relevant religious manifestations. Of course, in any given case the applicant may fail to show that the matter in question was in fact a matter of religious conscience for him personally. By contrast, contact with co-religionists outside the prison and engaging in external correspondence or publishing have been found not to be 'necessary' elements of religious practice.[172] This suggests that already at this stage the Commission applied a practicability test on the basis of certain plausible assumptions about what can and cannot be accommodated in the prison context. Strictly speaking, this is a matter of limitation, not manifestation.

The Commission was arguably the least demanding when it came to justifying restrictions. Thus the failure to supply a Church of England priest in a German prison was met with the response that 'there was no evidence that a Protestant pastor or facilities for worship in the Protestant religion are not available'.[173] It should be observed that there was no evidence that such religious provision would have been acceptable to the prisoner in question. Again, it was sufficient for the authorities to have done what they reasonably could to find a Buddhist minister and to have allowed an extra letter on the weeks one could not attend.[174] The fact that the Jewish Visitation Committee and Chief Rabbi had approved a certain prison regime was a sufficient answer to the ultra-orthodox Jew who objected.[175] Even if a prisoner could not attend chapel for reasons of security, the existence of special services in his segregation unit along with ministerial visits was a relevant and reasonable substitute.[176] And even if one could show that one

---

[170] Ibid.   [171] *Chappell v United Kingdom* (1987) 53 DR 241.
[172] *X v United Kingdom* (1974) 1 DR 41; *X v United Kingdom* (1977) 11 DR 55.
[173] *X v Federal Republic of Germany* (1966) 23 Collections 1.
[174] *X v United Kingdom* (1974) 1 DR 41.   [175] *X v United Kingdom* (1976) 5 DR 8.
[176] *Chester v United Kingdom*, no 14747/89 (1990).

had an objection of religious conscience to wearing prison clothes, doing routine acts of cleaning, or participating in the work programme, the limitation of rights involved could be justified as proportionate restrictions in pursuit of legitimate public interests of security, order, and health.[177]

Religious exercise is thus only clearly guaranteed in certain central instances such as access to a religious minister, participation in religious services, and provision of an acceptable and reasonable diet. Presumably access to basic literature (Bibles and Korans etc) and artefacts for personal devotion would also be covered, once again subject to proportionate limits in the interests of prison security.

The Court has now also considered the significance of religious belief and practice in restricted institutional contexts. The basic approach adopted in a subsequent series of cases can be found in the judgment in *Kalaç v Turkey*.[178] The applicant had been compulsorily retired as a judge advocate of the armed forces on account of 'breaches of discipline and scandalous conduct' revealing that he had adopted unlawful Islamic fundamentalist opinions. The Court found no breach of his article 9 rights:

It recalls that while religious freedom is primarily a matter of individual conscience, it also implies, *inter alia*, freedom to manifest one's religion not only in community with others, in public and within the circle of those whose faith one shares, but also alone and in private [...]. Article 9 lists a number of forms which manifestation of one's religion or belief may take, namely worship, teaching, practice and observance. Nevertheless, Article 9 does not protect every act motivated or inspired by a religion or belief. Moreover, in exercising his freedom to manifest his religion, an individual may need to take his specific situation into account.[179]

The Court noted that the applicant was able to fulfil the normal obligations of a Muslim such as prayer five times a day, keeping the fast of Ramadan, and attendance at Friday mosque. The Court further noted that it was not his opinions and beliefs as such which led to his dismissal, but his conduct and attitude. Compulsory retirement therefore did not interfere with his article 9 right.

In a recent series of cases, the Court has continued to uphold the dismissal of Islamic fundamentalist personnel from the Turkish armed forces.[180] The Court has stressed that while the military do enjoy article 9 rights, States are free to adopt disciplinary regulations forbidding certain forms of conduct, 'in particular an attitude inimical to an established order reflecting the requirements of military service'. These cases stress the fact that the individuals concerned could fulfil their 'normal' religious duties and that the dismissals must be based on conduct, not the mere belief or opinion of the individual concerned. These cases should be

---

[177] *X v United Kingdom* (1982) 28 DR 5; *W v United Kingdom*, no 18187/91 (1993).
[178] *Kalaç v Turkey* (1999) 27 EHRR 552.
[179] Ibid, para 27. The same principle can be found in *Larissis v Greece* (1999) 27 EHRR 329.
[180] See eg *Aksoy v Turkey*, no 45376/99 (2002); *Dal and Özen v Turkey*, no 45378/99 (2002); *Gündoğdu v Turkey*, no 47503/99 (2002).

read against the background of a general concern on the part of the Court that certain forms of Islam are incompatible with the Convention, and a consequent sympathy with Turkish secularism.[181]

The Court has now also ruled that the failure to provide a certain level of religious service in prisons amounts to a violation of article 9. The applicant in *Poltoratskiy v Ukraine* was a prisoner on death row.[182] The Court found violations of articles 3, 8, and 9 in respect of the conditions under which he was held. In respect of article 9 the Court held that very limited access to an orthodox priest[183] along with the applicant's inability to attend the weekly service available to other prisoners amounted to a limitation of his right. The question of necessity was not considered, since the limitation was not in accordance with law.

Closely related to *Poltoratskiy* is the decision in *JL v Finland*,[184] which contains a somewhat fuller discussion. JL had been convicted of serious criminal offences and compulsorily detained in a psychiatric hospital. Among several complaints about his treatment and the provision of care were some based on his faith as a Jehovah's Witness. In general terms the Court found that he had not been prevented from manifesting his belief up to the extent necessarily limited by his specific situation. On the facts, the Court found no evidence that his beliefs had not been respected in his diet, as alleged. It also found that he had been allowed for a time to attend meetings outside the institution and apart from that to receive regular visits. In any case there could be no absolute right to manifest religious beliefs outside the institution. He had no right to daily visits, or to proselytize by preaching and distributing literature, on account of the need to maintain order and protect non-believers in the institution. The Court may have overstated the position as regards proselytism. It seems to have assumed that because the restrictions on proselytism were general, applying to all hospital inmates, they could not amount to a violation of his right. This cannot be correct. The right to proselytize is undoubtedly included within article 9 and restrictions must be justified as for any other form of manifestation.[185] That includes, but is not exhausted by, uniform application of a restriction.

The fact that religious manifestation takes place in a restricted institutional context does not mean that limitations can be justified without reference to the usual tests of necessity and proportionality. The Convention organs have consistently rejected any notion that human rights are abandoned on entering certain institutions. However, in the place of this discredited doctrine, they have erected a substitute almost as problematic. One of the motifs running through several of the cases involving religious practice in restricted institutional contexts is the argument that applicants have voluntarily accepted a restriction of their rights.

---

[181] *Refah Partisi v Turkey* (2003) 37 EHRR 1.

[182] *Poltoratskiy v Ukraine* (2004) 39 EHRR 43.

[183] There was some difficulty establishing what requests had been made and whether or not they had been met.   [184] *JL v Finland*, no 32526/96 (2000).

[185] *Larissis v Greece* (1999) 27 EHRR 329.

This has been used as a complete answer in employment cases involving restrictions on religious practice,[186] and was also relied on substantially in the case of armed forces in *Kalaç v Turkey*. It is problematic in at least two respects. First, it is difficult to identify the precise level of sufficient voluntariness. Perhaps the only example of a complete lack of consent to a restriction arises in the case of military conscription combined with inadequate facilities for religious exercise. Even here one could decide to pay the penalty of conscientious objection. Imprisonment is voluntary, in that one could have resolved not to commit the criminal act which led to it; hospitalization is voluntary in the sense that one could refuse to attend for treatment. In reality, voluntariness is a spectrum from choices that are genuinely free to those that are highly constrained.

The effect of relying on voluntariness to justify restrictions is actually to close off choices for religious believers. If a certain industry requires Saturday labour, that industry will be closed off to practising Jews and Adventists. The argument from voluntariness can really only be safely relied on where there is a range of accessible options including those less burdensome to the religious believer. The proper question is thus not whether a burden on religious practice has been voluntarily accepted, but whether it is a burden appropriately imposed on the religious believers affected, or whether others—and the State in particular—have a responsibility to alleviate that burden. The existence of alternatives is relevant in answering this question, but not determining. Considerations of equal citizenship would suggest that at least in the centrally public spheres of the armed forces, prisons, and public service, the State has a responsibility so to structure the institutions concerned that burdens on religious believers are minimized. This responsibility could be extended to other broader public contexts such as healthcare and education.[187]

It follows that a number of classic distinctions break down in these institutional contexts. The obligation of States to provide prisoners with access to ministers of religion of their own persuasion could plausibly be viewed as either a negative or a positive obligation. The prison regime generally prevents outsiders from free communication with inmates; the State is under a negative obligation not to restrict such free communication in the case of ministers and believers. But this construction is strained. Having established a restrictive prison regime, the State is under an obligation to *facilitate* visits by ministers of religion. This point is even clearer in the case of special diets. The authorities must provide

---

[186] *Stedman v United Kingdom* (1997) 23 EHRR CD168; *Konttinen v Finland*, no 24949/94 (1996); *Kosteski v Macedonia* (2007) 45 EHRR 31.

[187] There is an important practical tension here between the State's duty to 'respect and protect' rights under art 1 ECHR and the restrictive assertion by UK courts of a public–private divide (*YL v Birmingham City Council* [2008] 1 AC 95). While the armed forces and prisons are clearly bound by human rights as public bodies, the extent to which hospitals and universities are bound is less clear. It may be that equality-based arguments stand a greater chance of success of raising the same substantive issues.

kosher and *halal* food, or at least an equivalently nutritious alternative to the normal, but unacceptable, diet; it would not be adequate for them simply to refrain from preventing prisoners from acquiring such food. A normative and practical structuring needs to take place requiring a series of positive legislative and executive acts.

It also follows that in institutionally restricted contexts the focus need not be exclusively on the individual applicant. This is sometimes seen in judgments of the European Court in which it is held to be an answer to a complaint that the applicant had not actually requested some facility. It is of course relevant that an individual should have been denied the facility, but this relevance is primarily procedural: the applicant is not a victim unless he has himself suffered in some way. The central question is whether the regime itself is an appropriate one for facilitating the sorts of religious practice that are to be permitted. An association may be as affected in its right to sustain its collective religious identity because it is shut out of an institution, or because the institution refuses to pass on information about the religious affiliation of individuals.

Furthermore, the public–private distinction breaks down in that chaplaincies require collaboration and coordination between public institutions and religious bodies.[188] The possibility of an ideological mismatch has already been noted, particularly in the context of recent reforms in the NHS, but a legal mismatch is also possible. As regards the Church of England, for example, this potential is addressed formally: according to Extra-parochial Ministry Measure 1967, the bishop of any diocese in which a 'university, college, school, hospital or public or charitable institution' is situated may license a clergyman to perform offices and services on the premises.[189] These may then be performed without the consent or control of the minister of the parish in which they are located.[190] This extends to the marriage of housebound and detained persons[191] and the conduct of funeral services at cemeteries and crematoria for deceased persons resident on the premises.[192] Provision is made for the registration of baptism and burials in adjoining or other appropriate parishes.[193] The licence may be revoked at any time.[194] The Clergy Discipline Measure 2003 provides that disciplinary proceedings against chaplains of prisons, hospitals, universities, schools, and other extra-parochial institutions may only be instituted by an authorized person, and in the case of a chaplain of one of the armed forces with the consent of the Archbishop of Canterbury.[195] The Clergy Discipline Rules set out the procedures to be followed, including the circumstances under which the employer (or in the case of

---

[188] An analogy may be drawn with collaboration in planning matters: see *Johannische Kirche and Peters v Germany*, no 41754/98 (2001).

[189] Extra-parochial Ministry Measure 1967, s 2(1).   [190] Ibid, s 2(2).

[191] Ibid, s 2(1A) as amended by Church of England (Legal Aid and Miscellaneous Provisions) Measure 1988, s 5.   [192] Church of England (Miscellaneous Provisions) Measure 1992, s 2.

[193] Parochial Registers and Records Measure 1978.   [194] Ibid, s 2(4).

[195] Clergy Discipline Measure 2003, s 42.

armed forces chaplains, the Secretary of State) are notified of a suspension.[196] More generally, and apart from internal law, religious associations need to be careful when disciplining their ministers who hold contracts as chaplains with other institutions, since they may commit the tort of interference with contract.[197] By the same token, institutions need to be confident that the person they appoint as chaplain really does have the appropriate legitimacy within the relevant religious community.

We can therefore conclude that the general human right of individuals to manifest their religion in worship, teaching, practice, and observance extends to those who are in restricted institutional contexts, and includes a right of access to suitable religious personnel and services. And just as there is a general human right of religious associations to carry on their associational life,[198] so also this includes a right to be present within restricted institutional contexts to maintain that associational life. This requires not merely bare toleration by the appropriate authorities but acts of positive structuring and collaboration which facilitate religious observance. Of course, limitations are inevitable, but they must be proportionate to the legitimate purposes of the institution in question. It must be possible for the religious life of individuals and associations to be sustained.

The question is how far the duty extends. At the very least, contact must be facilitated between individuals and ministers of religion. This must embrace the provision of basic information about chaplaincy services, along with time and space for meetings. Since collective prayer and worship is an important part of many religions, space should also be provided for such a purpose. However, one can question whether the obligation to facilitate extends to the purchase of sacred objects and literature or the payment of salaries. It may be good practice to do this, and if it is done at all, it must be done in a non-discriminatory fashion.[199] It may be that the only way to satisfy requirements of security and discipline in the context of the armed forces or prisons is to employ chaplains, with the degree of possible vetting and control that implies, but in principle there seems to be no reason why the State should pay for religious activity which normally carries on in public or private at the cost of believers.

VI. Conclusion

In many cases, the strict letter of the existing law represents a position which, with hindsight, we can already see as a consensus of the second half of the twentieth century. This consensus secured the dominance of the Church of England, with substantial openness to the larger Christian denominations and a tolerance

---

[196] Clergy Discipline Rules 2005/2022, rls 93 and 94.
[197] See *Conference of the Methodist Church of New Zealand v Gray* [1996] 2 NZLR 554.
[198] See ch 2 above.   [199] Art 14 ECHR applies here in the ambit of art 9.

of minority non-Christian faiths. The chaplains of the Church of England have, broadly speaking, a fourfold function: (1) to minister to members of that church; (2) to provide pastoral services to anyone else in need and prepared to receive their ministrations; (3) to facilitate the satisfaction of the religious needs of others; (4) to be the central bearers of religious identity and presence in their contexts. In practice, and fairly quickly, Church of England chaplains have teamed with other Christian ministers to provide inter-faith Christian chaplaincies. Although recognition and provision for non-Christian faiths is increasing, the personnel and structures necessary for multi-faith provision on a basis of strict neutrality are only now emerging and still embryonic.

This gradual development from tolerant establishment to pluralism has been reflected in the use of the term 'chaplain' which often only applies as a matter of law to the Church of England clergy. Application to other Christian ministers is now normal, and in some cases, but much more recently, ministers of other faiths have also been called 'chaplain'. Gilliat-Ray observes a process of 'approximation' taking place in which representatives of non-Christian religions begin to shape their ministry along lines suggested by the dominant tradition.[200] One suspects that in practice the term often goes with appointment on a full- or part-time salaried basis, as opposed to hourly-rate contractual arrangements entered into with 'visiting ministers'. This appointment carries with it the expanding role-assumption noted in the previous paragraph. Given that the term need have no necessary Christian connotations, broader use would seem entirely sensible.

Although it is arguable that there is a collective human right to provide and receive chaplaincy services, the implications of that right have not yet been fully articulated by the European Court. In practice, the actual level of accommodation and facilitation in domestic law goes beyond what is legally required. At the same time, the symbolic effect of human rights legislation has been to regularize, if not always strengthen, provision. In fact, the perceived need to offer chaplaincy services on a more neutral basis has enhanced the degree of involvement by the State. Yet chaplaincy services continue to face pressing practical questions of adequacy and neutrality, and are always vulnerable to the pressures of economic rationality. Humane public institutions will resist those pressures and continue to ensure adequate and fair access to chaplaincy services. This cannot be achieved without ongoing collaboration between the institution in question and organized religions.

---

[200] Gilliat-Ray, *op cit* n 151, 79–84.

8

Faith Schools

A case could be made that almost all schools in England and Wales are faith schools, even if in many cases 'faith' persists in a highly attenuated form. But the term is now generally used to identify those schools in which a faith-based ethos and institutional connections with churches and religious associations are formal and pronounced. Since the late 1990s, Government policy has changed significantly. Schools with a faith-based ethos no longer represent a tolerated historic residue, but have been welcomed as part of a new multicultural agenda. This openness has combined with equalities legislation to require a greater degree of legal clarity about the nature and limits of the religious dimensions of education.

There is nothing new about the association of religion with schools. The history of formal education in the British Isles is entwined with that of the Christian church, and past religious tensions and compromises still determine the structure of current arrangements. Education has long been the most contested area in the relationship between the State and organized religions, and this has resulted in considerable complexity.[1] It is not possible to make sense of current arrangements without some understanding of the history of this contestation. Furthermore, from the perspective of international human rights, education benefits from specific protections, particularly in its religious dimensions. This chapter therefore spends rather more time than others on the historical background and modern human rights context before looking at the ways in which English law regulates a religiously plural education system.[2]

I. Religion and Schools before 1902

At common law, all schools were subject to ecclesiastical oversight.[3] Whereas Augustine founded a school at Canterbury in 597, Governmental involvement in education only stems from the early decades of the nineteenth century. By that

---

[1] Neville Harris, *Education, Law and Diversity* (Oxford: Hart Publishing, 2007), is a full discussion of several of the issues raised in this chapter from the perspective of wider forms of diversity than the religious.

[2] Brief introduction in Philip Petchey, 'Legal Issues for Faith Schools in England and Wales' (2008) 10 Ecc LJ 174.

[3] *Cox's Case* (1700) 1 P Wms 29, 24 ER 281. But perhaps not elementary schools. The position of non-conformist school teachers was thus unclear until the Nonconformist Relief Act 1779,

time there was a widespread consensus among the ruling classes as to the desirability of universal education. Although derived in part from Enlightenment thought, which was often anti-religious, in practice the larger influence in this country was that of evangelical Christianity, both within the established church and on the part of dissent. Whatever else it might aspire to, education was first of all to be instruction in the Christian faith. Two key expressions of this were the growth of parish charity schools, often brought about by the work of the Society for the Promotion of Christian Knowledge (founded 1699), and the Sunday School movement, associated first with the work of Robert Raikes in Gloucester, but then promoted more widely through the Society for the Establishment and Support of Sunday Schools in the Different Counties of England (founded 1785). This used the one day that children were spared domestic, agricultural, and industrial labour to teach reading and Scripture. Sunday and parish schools were funded through voluntary subscription and small fees, and often represented the combined local efforts of Anglicans and non-conformists. By contrast, the endowed grammar schools, like the Universities of Oxford and Cambridge which they had originally supplied, were firmly within the grip of the established church. Schoolmasters still needed a bishop's licence,[4] and non-conformists were excluded. The grammar schools were also prevented by the strict application of the terms of their trust deeds from applying their endowments to subjects other than the classical languages. Since the universities were largely moribund, the torch of higher learning was carried in the eighteenth century to a disproportionate extent by dissenting academies, which had been formed to train ministers of religion and cater for the rising numbers of non-conformist middle classes.

In 1807 a Parochial Schools Bill designed to ensure the existence of a school in every parish funded by local rates failed on account of disagreement about the nature of the religious instruction to be provided. In 1808 the British and Foreign School Society was founded. It advocated non-denominational education and drew support from both Anglicans and non-conformists. But in 1811 the National Society for Promoting the Education of the Poor in the Principles of the Established Church throughout England and Wales was formed in response. The National Society was able to draw on considerably greater financial resources. Both societies adopted the monitorial system devised independently by Andrew Bell (Anglican) and Joseph Lancaster (Quaker) whereby older children taught

---

19 G III, c 44, s 2, rendered them free from all penalties. Section 3 ensured that relief did not apply to colleges or schools of royal foundation or endowed colleges or schools unless founded after 1688 for the immediate use and benefit of Protestant dissenters. For general background to this and the following section see John Lawson and Harold Silver, *A Social History of Education in England* (London: Methuen & Co, 1973); H C Barnard, *A History of English Education from 1760*, 2nd edn (London: University of London Press, 1961); James Murphy, *Church, State and Schools in Britain, 1800–1970* (London: Routledge & Kegan Paul, 1971).

[4] *R v Archbishop of York* (1795) 6 TR 490, 101 ER 664.

younger children, with a schoolteacher responsible only for the most senior. It was cheap, and within its didactic limits, effective. Thus were the lines drawn up between the advocates of non-denominational (Christian) instruction and denominational instruction using the catechisms of specific churches. Another model, the 'Irish system' of educating Protestants and Catholics together, except for religious instruction to be given by their respective ministers in designated school hours, was briefly attempted by the Liberals in Liverpool. However, in 1841, the Conservatives took control with a pledge to end it. When Catholics were refused exemption in 1842 from reading the Authorized Version of the Bible, they left for their own schools, and thereafter Catholic opinion was firmly in favour of separate denominational education. Separate religious instruction within combined schools rarely commended itself to British public opinion.

The view that education was the task of the church, not that of Government, was associated above all with the Congregationalist 'voluntaryists' Edward Miall and Edward Baines, whose principles led them to refuse both State oversight and State aid. But they were also supported after 1834 by the growing influence of the Anglo-Catholic Tractarian movement on the Church of England, which gave that church a reinvigorated sense of its distinctive social mission. In 1820 another Parish Schools Bill ran aground on the religious question, and in 1833 the first State funding for education was provided instead by way of central grants to the National and British Societies matching voluntary subscriptions for new schools. Given their support base, about 80 per cent of funding went to the National Society. In 1847, the Catholic Poor School Committee was formed to receive grants in the same way as the National and British Societies, and soon after, Jewish schools also received their first grants. The growing system of impartially aided religious schools was the genius and pride of Sir James Kay-Shuttleworth, secretary to the Education Committee of Privy Council from its inception in 1839.

The inclusion of a conscience clause to enable non-Anglican pupils to attend National schools was hotly debated within the National Society in the 1840s and 50s. The problem was particularly pressing in single-school areas, but required a tolerably clear division between secular and religious education to be put into practice. It was this division between the secular and the religious in education which provoked controversy. However, the Government was able to insist on the inclusion of a conscience clause as a condition of all grants from 1860 onwards.

The same period saw a reform movement throughout the grammar schools associated above all with Thomas Arnold, headmaster of Rugby School from 1828. Ironically, while the Grammar Schools Act 1840 freed up school endowments to be used more widely, Arnold was reinventing the classics as part of a liberal education. Although deeply committed to the alliance of faith and education, his own brand of liberal evangelicalism ensured that religious divisions remained muted in this context. However, major structural reform was still necessary, and this was provided by the Clarendon Commission (1861–4) and the Taunton

Commission (1864–8). The former, which considered nine major public schools, resulted in the Public Schools Act 1868.[5] This left them closely associated with the Church of England. But the latter inquiry, which considered the remaining 942 endowed and proprietory schools, made recommendations resulting in a greater degree of openness.[6] Schemes in respect of these schools were to ensure that in all cases there was a right for pupils to be exempted from religious worship and instruction on their parents or guardian giving notice in writing.[7] In the case of schools maintained out of cathedral or collegiate church endowments, or where the express terms of the endowment required pupils to be taught according to the doctrines of a particular denomination, no scheme was to be made without the consent of the governors.[8] But in all other cases, religious opinions or practice were no longer to be a bar to membership of the governing body,[9] and there was to be no requirement that a master be in holy orders.[10]

By the 1860s it was clear that even with substantial grants-in-aid, and in spite of considerable achievements, the voluntary system was not going to provide universal education. The approach was, in any case, seriously flawed. Government funds would only flow to areas of sufficient local interest and prosperity to found a school, so the poorest areas were not provided for. W E Forster's Elementary Education Act 1870 supplemented existing voluntary schools by allowing for the creation of rate-funded public elementary schools run by local boards. Thereafter, Parliamentary grants were only to be made to board schools. Provision for religious worship and instruction lay in the discretion of boards, but if provided at all 'no religious catechism or religious formulary which is distinctive of any particular denomination' could be taught.[11] In practice, nearly all boards did require non-denominational religious education. What was included in the Act was extensive protection for the dissenting pupil and his or her parents. The 'Cowper-Temple clause' gave parents the right to withdraw pupils from any religious observance or instruction.[12] Parents also had the right to withdraw a pupil on any day exclusively given to their own religious observance, and attendance, or non-attendance, at any place of worship could not be made a condition of admission, as it had been at many national schools. The Act required worship and instruction to be given at the start or end of the day to give effective protection to a right to withdraw.[13] Religious instruction was not subject to inspection.[14] In 1880, boards were required to make school attendance compulsory for all children between the ages of five and ten years.

---

[5] The schools were Eton, Winchester, Westminster, Charterhouse, Harrow, Rugby, Shrewsbury, Merchant Taylors', and St Paul's. The latter two were not covered by the subsequent legislation.

[6] This development was closely associated with the opening up of the universities of Oxford, Cambridge, and Durham. See Ch 7 above.   [7] Endowed Schools Act 1869, s 15.

[8] Ibid, s 19.   [9] Ibid, s 17.   [10] Ibid, s 18.

[11] Elementary Education Act 1870, s 14(2); Murphy, *op cit* n 3, 67–70.

[12] Elementary Education Act 1870, ss 7(1), 74(2), and 76.   [13] Ibid, s 7(2).

[14] Ibid, s 7(3).

In the three decades following the Act, the numbers of both voluntary and board schools rose significantly. The advent of board schools and the short deadline for final Government grant applications stimulated the church-based societies to a burst of frenetic action. However, funding became an increasing problem for voluntary schools as the century came to a close, reliant as they were on subscriptions and fees. At the same time, the State could not do without them. By 1900 two-thirds of schools were still voluntary schools, educating a little over half of all children. There were other problems as well: litigation had confirmed that school boards had no power to fund secondary education,[15] and the central Education Committee was increasingly unable to cope with the demands now placed upon it.

Thus on the eve of the twentieth century, fundamental questions about the relationship between State and organized religions in education remained unresolved: is the relationship one of competition or collaboration? How broad should religious education be, and who should deliver it? At the same time, the law had already come to prefer and reject certain possible answers. State-provided education was to reflect a religious consensus, which at the time implied a non-denominational Christianity. In both the context of State schools and that of schools associated with the historic Anglican establishment, individual religious liberty was to be protected though a right of conscientious objection. This right implied a widespread assumption that one could separate religious and non-religious dimensions of education. For those who rejected that assumption, or who wished religious education to be more closely tied to the teachings of a particular church, State-provided education was not to supplant denominationally-specific private education. The model of compulsory State education with time set aside for denominationally-specific religious education provided by the churches never caught on.

II. Faith-Based Education in the Twentieth Century

Balfour's Education Act of 1902 brought voluntary schools within the State-maintained sector for recurrent funding purposes, and established the main components of the current education system.[16] School boards were abolished, and local education authorities (LEAs) formed at Local Government level. The Act drew a basic distinction between schools provided by the LEA, and 'aided' schools, which were maintained but not provided, by the LEA. In the case of aided schools, two-thirds of the managers were to be foundation managers.[17] There was no control by the LEA over religious instruction, which was to be in accordance with the trust deed and under the control of the managers or any ecclesiastical authority to which the deed referred.[18] If the trust deed were silent, the newly

---

[15] *R v Cockerton* [1901] 1 QB 322.   [16] Murphy, *op cit* n 3, ch 6.
[17] Education Act 1902, s 6(2).   [18] Ibid, s 7(6).

formed Board of Education would determine the basis for religious instruction having regard to the ownership of the property and the historic basis on which education had been provided. As regards 'higher' education (ie above elementary level), LEAs were not to interfere in the arrangements of aided schools, but in the case of provided schools there was to be no pupil selection on religious criteria, and no catechism or formulary distinctive of any particular religious denomination was to be taught.[19] Parents could withdraw their children or could request (and pay for) specific religious instruction if they wished.[20]

The 1902 Act met with considerable initial hostility.[21] Since the substantial majority of voluntary schools had their origins in the Church of England's National Society, it was viewed in many quarters as a deliberate attempt by the Conservative party to shore up the establishment. However, Liberal attempts in the first decade of the twentieth century to undo the Act foundered, and it came increasingly to be seen as a 'settlement' not to be disturbed. In the economic depression following the First World War, another attempt was made to bring voluntary schools completely within the State system, replacing their provision with denominationally-specific religious instruction for the relevant groups within each school. Again this foundered on hostility from many quarters, principally non-conformists and teachers hostile to any denominational instruction and Roman Catholics strongly committed to it in a whole-school environment. The movement towards universal secondary education from the 1920s onwards placed the churches in considerable difficulties, not wishing to see themselves overtaken by better organized and funded State provision, yet largely unable to meet the demand for new schools themselves.

R A Butler's Education Act of 1944 was crafted against the background of Nazi aggression and expressed a renewed national commitment to the creation of Christian citizens. Denominational boundaries were to be transcended in an effort to ensure that the next generation were united in their resistance to alien ideologies. Religious education was defined as consisting of collective worship and religious instruction, and both were made compulsory in all schools, with the customary parental opt-out.[22] The school day was to begin with a single act of worship unless the premises made that impractical. In a new system of State-sponsored ecumenism, religious education in the county schools was to be in accordance with a syllabus agreed with representatives of the Church of England and other local churches, and not distinctive of any particular denomination, thereafter known as Standing Advisory Councils on Religious Education.[23]

In an attempt to meet the impoverished state of the church schools, a further distinction was created by the 1944 Act between voluntary aided and voluntary controlled schools.[24] The former had more independence in line with the 1902 Act: two-thirds of their managers/governors were foundation

---

[19] Ibid, s 4(1).   [20] Ibid, s 4(2).   [21] Murphy, *op cit* n 3, ch 7.
[22] Education Act 1944, s 25.   [23] Ibid, s 29 and sched 5.   [24] Ibid, s 15.

managers/governors, all staff could be appointed or dismissed with reference to their adherence to the faith of the school, and religious education was to be in accordance with the tenets of the religion. The price of this independence was an obligation to meet the costs of maintaining the premises of the school, with some exceptions and subject to a Central Government grant. In the case of voluntary controlled schools, only one-third of the managers/governors represented the foundation, the LEA paid for all the costs, and only 'reserved' teachers—up to one fifth—could be required to conform to the faith of the foundation.[25] Preference was given to teaching according to the agreed syllabus, although parents could request denominationally-specific education. In practice, Church of England schools were split fairly evenly between voluntary controlled and voluntary aided status, while the Roman Catholic Church made the Herculean effort to raise sufficient funds to secure the independence of voluntary aided status. Funding remained a challenge for the churches: the Central Government contribution to maintenance costs was originally set at 50 per cent, then raised progressively over the years to its current level of 90 per cent.[26]

The Act also set out a basic regulatory framework for all independent schools including a register, minimum standards for premises, accommodation, the quality of instruction and suitability of persons, an inspection regime, and a tribunal.[27]

The Education Reform Act 1988 was passed in the wake of Governmental concern both that the Christian ethos of schools was being eroded and the needs of religious minorities not being met.[28] It represented the first steps towards formalizing a more pluralist approach to the religious dimensions of education, which would be taken up and enhanced in New Labour's education legislation. The Act made explicit what was assumed in Butler's Act: that collective worship should be wholly or mainly of a broadly Christian character without being distinctive of any Christian denomination.[29] The precise balance was to be sensitive to the family background of the pupils.[30] At the same time it clarified the fact that the composition of Standing Advisory Councils was to include representatives of Christian and other religious denominations.[31] It also gave them the power to dispense with the Christian worship requirement.[32]

Although in theory new faith schools could be established within the maintained sector, in practice it was hard to do so. Quite apart from the initiative

[25] Ibid, s 27(2).

[26] Education Act 1944, s 102 (50%); Education Act 1959, s 1(1) (75%); Education Act 1967, s 1(1) (80%); Education Act 1975, s 3 (85%); School Standards and Framework Act 1998, sched 3, para 5(3)(a), as substituted by the Regulatory Reform (Voluntary Aided Schools Liability and Funding) (England) Order 2002, SI 2002/906, art 7(c).   [27] See, further, 260–1 below.

[28] Discussions in A Bradney, 'The Dewsbury Affair and the Education Reform Act 1988' (1989) 1 Education and the Law 51; Sebastian Poulter, 'The religious education provisions of the Education Reform Act 1988' (1990) 2 Education and the Law 1; J D C Harte, 'The Religious Dimensions of the Education Reform Act 1988' (1989) 1(5) Ecc LJ 32.

[29] Education Reform Act 1988, ss 7(1) and (2).   [30] Ibid, s 7(5).

[31] Ibid, s 11(4)(a). The reference to 'religious denomination' in Education Act 1944, sched 5, left the matter unclear.   [32] ERA 1988, s 7(6). ERA, n 29.

required on the part of parents and religious groups, the law required widespread consultation and the final decision was in the discretion of the Secretary of State.[33] Local education authorities were unlikely to look favourably on a proposal which would inevitably draw pupils away from other schools and, while catering for one faith community, would restrict choice for others. Although a number of applications were submitted on behalf of existing Muslim independent schools to receive State funding, none was successful.

The election of the Labour Government in 1997 brought about a noticeable change of attitude to towards non-Christian schools. In January 1998, the Education Secretary approved the applications of two Muslim primary schools for grant-maintained status. At the same time, the Government secured the passage of the School Standards and Framework Act 1998, which clarified the legal basis for faith schools within the maintained sector. This forms the foundation of the current law and is considered further below. Since that time, the numbers of faith schools, while still small as a proportion of all schools, have grown steadily, in spite of considerable controversy.

One of the effects of the 1998 legislation was to create a new categorization of schools in terms of 'religious designation'.[34] This now marks the basic distinction between faith schools and schools which have no specific religious character. In January 2007 there were 17,361 State-maintained primary schools in England; 11,106 had no religious designation.[35] Of the remaining 6,255 (36 per cent), the breakdown was 4,441 Church of England, 1,696 Roman Catholic, 84 other Christian (including 26 Methodist), 28 Jewish, 4 Muslim, and 2 other religion (Sikh and Hindu).[36] There were 3,399 secondary schools; 2,796 had no religious designation. Of the remaining 603 (18 per cent), the breakdown was 343 Roman Catholic, 205 Church of England, 41 other Christian, 9 Jewish, 3 Muslim, and 2 other religion (including Sikh).

In practice, there is a certain correlation between school type and religious designation.[37] Community schools form the largest group and are not permitted to have a religious designation. Nor may the very small numbers of City Technology Colleges. Academies, which are 'independent' but directly funded by Central Government subject to the terms of an individually negotiated agreement, may have a religious designation, and around half of them do. Foundation schools (formerly grant-maintained schools) may have a religious designation, but in practice tend not to. Of those that do, virtually all are Church of England. The significant

[33] The basic framework was established by Education Act 1944, ss 13–14. For the pre-1998 arrangements, see Education Act 1996, ss 41–58.

[34] School Standards and Framework Act 1998, s 69(3).

[35] Data drawn from DCSF/National Statistics, *Schools and Pupils in England*, SFR 30/2007 (Sept 2007), table 8a.

[36] The first Hindu primary school was opened in September 2008, and in January 2010 formally opened its purpose-built premises centred on a temple: *BBC News*, 29 January 2010.

[37] See the Designation of Schools Having a Religious Character (England) Order 1999, SI 1999/2432, and subsequent orders.

difference within the category of schools with a religious designation is between voluntary controlled and voluntary aided schools. Voluntary controlled schools are much closer in ethos to community schools, whereas voluntary aided schools have more independence and a more pronounced faith-based ethos. A little over half of Church of England schools are voluntary controlled, as are the single instances of Congregationalist, United Reformed, and Quaker schools. The vast majority of Methodist schools are also voluntary controlled, with two exceptions. There are at least 30 joint Church of England/Methodist schools, about half of which are voluntary controlled and half voluntary aided. By contrast, Roman Catholic, Jewish, Muslim, Hindu, and Sikh schools are all voluntary aided, as are the single instances of a Seventh Day Adventist school and a Greek Orthodox school. Voluntary aided schools tend to be slightly smaller than average.[38] Pupils attending a faith school tend to travel further to attend, on average by 1–2 miles, and this effect is marked among religious minorities.[39] Faith schools have slightly below average rates of social deprivation, as measured by entitlement to free school meals, with the notable exception of Muslim schools, which have substantially higher rates.[40]

As far as Wales is concerned, there are among maintained faith schools only Church in Wales and Roman Catholic schools.[41] As regards the former, 169 are primary schools and three are voluntary aided secondary schools. The primary schools are split 2:3 aided:controlled. The Roman Catholic schools are all voluntary aided, with 75 primary schools, 14 secondary schools, and one joint. There is also one joint Catholic/Anglican High School.

The overlap of interest between the State and organized religions in the area of education has thus resulted in a situation of considerable complexity. The law has never been subject to radical reform, but has added new layers of categorization and regulation onto existing provisions. Before considering the current law in more detail, the relevant human rights dimension needs to be taken into account.

III. The Human Rights Dimension

International human rights instruments contain various ambitious provisions bearing on education.[42] There is a universal right to education.[43] All education is to be directed to the full development of the human personality and the sense of

---

[38] Voluntary aided primary schools constitute 21.5 per cent of all schools in England and teach 19.1 per cent of all pupils; voluntary aided secondary schools constitute 16.3 per cent of all schools and teach 15.2 per cent of the pupils: *Schools and Pupils in England, op cit* n 35, tables 8(a) and 8(b).

[39] DCSF/National Statistics, *The Composition of Schools in England* (June 2008), table 7.4. Whereas 50.5 per cent of pupils at 'non-religious' schools are attending their nearest school, this drops to just under 40 per cent for Church of England and other Christian schools, 18.6 per cent Roman Catholic schools, 11.4 per cent Muslim, 6.8 per cent other religious, and 6.4 per cent Jewish schools: ibid, table 7.9.   [40] Ibid, tables 3.3–3.4.

[41] Designation of Schools Having a Religious Character (Wales) Order 2007, SI 2007/972.

[42] Carolyn Evans, 'Religious education in public schools: an international human rights perspective' (2008) 8 HRL Rev 449 is a useful recent overview.

[43] Universal Declaration of Human Rights (1948), art 26(1); International Covenant on Economic, Social and Cultural Rights (1966), art 13(1).

its dignity and to the strengthening of respect for human rights and fundamental freedoms.[44] Education must enable all persons to participate effectively in a free society; promote understanding, tolerance, and friendship among all nations and all racial, ethnic, or religious groups; and further the activities of the United Nations for the maintenance of peace.[45] The State is under a series of obligations to secure the effective enjoyment of the right to education, including the provision of free and compulsory elementary education and fair access to higher levels.[46]

As regards faith schools, the Universal Declaration simply protects the prior right of parents to choose the kind of education that shall be given to their children.[47] Article 13 of the International Covenant on Economic, Social and Cultural Rights contains a much fuller statement: parents and guardians have the right to choose schools, other than those established by public authorities, which conform to minimum educational standards laid down or approved by the State.[48] They also have the right to ensure the religious and moral education of their children in conformity with their own convictions.[49] There is a guarantee that individuals and bodies may establish private educational institutions subject to the substantive principles set out above, and minimum requirements set by States.[50] The UN Convention on the Rights of the Child highlights the fact that the child also enjoys rights, including a right to freedom of thought, conscience, and religion, and requires States to respect the rights and duties of the parents and guardians to provide direction to the child in the exercise of his or her right in a manner consistent with the evolving capacities of the child.[51] It also includes in the substantive content of education the development of respect for the child's parents, and the child's own cultural identity, language, and values.[52]

Article 18(4) International Covenant on Civil and Political Rights, which protects the right of parents and guardians to ensure the religious and moral education of their children in conformity with their own convictions, has been described as a 'modest' right.[53] It extends only to religious and moral education and imposes no positive duty on States to provide any specific form of teaching in State schools. However, it does protect the right to establish private religious schools as well as religious instruction out of school hours.[54] In *Hartikainen v Finland*,[55] the Human Rights Committee approved the provision of Christian religious instruction in State schools, with an alternative subject in history of religion and ethics for those who wished. Such alternative courses of instruction were acceptable 'if given in a neutral and objective way . . . respect[ing]

---

[44] UDHR, art 26(2); ICESCR, art 13(1).   [45] Ibid.
[46] UDHR, art 26(1); ICESCR, art 13(2).   [47] UDHR, art 26(3).
[48] ICESCR, art 13(3).   [49] Ibid.   [50] Art 13(4).   [51] UNCRC, art 14(2).
[52] Art 29(1)(c). Full discussion from this perspective in Sylvie Langlaude, *The Right of the Child to Religious Freedom in International Law* (Leiden: Martinus Nijhoff, 2007).
[53] Manfred Nowak, *CCPR Commentary* (Kehl: N P Engel, 1993), 331.   [54] *Loc cit.*
[55] No 40/1978.

the convictions of parents and guardians who do not believe in any religion'.[56] General Comment no. 22 states that instruction in a particular religion or belief is inconsistent with article 18(4) unless provision is made for non-discriminatory exemptions or alternatives that would accommodate the wishes of parents and guardians. States may make religious instruction dependent on the approval of church authorities, but only in respect of that church's religion.[57] In *Leirvåg v Norway*,[58] the Human Rights Committee applied these principles to a religious education and ethics curriculum which allowed for only partial exemption from 'those parts of the teaching at the individual school that [parents and pupils], on the basis of their own religion or philosophy of life, perceive as being the practice of another religion or adherence to another philosophy of life'. The Committee concluded that this was not even theoretically compliant with international law, because it imposed a considerable burden on teachers and parents of establishing which bits of the curriculum amounted to religious practice. In any case, on the facts, children with exemptions were being required to participate, for example by reciting Christian texts at Christmas celebrations. The system of partial exemptions was practically inoperable.

The non-discrimination provisions of article 26 ICCPR may also impose constraints on State action in this field. In *Waldman v Canada*,[59] the Human Rights Committee found a violation in Ontario's refusal to fund Jewish schools within the State system, while allowing for Roman Catholic schools. The only possible justification lay in the historic vulnerability of an unpopular minority, which no longer applied. Ontario had either to make all State schools secular, or open up funding for all religious denominations.

The 1981 Declaration on the Elimination of all Forms of Intolerance and of Discrimination based on Religion or Belief contains a stronger statement of the same principle: children not only have a right to access education in the matter of religion or belief in accordance with the wishes of their parents or guardians, but they are also not to be compelled to receive teaching on religion or belief against the wishes of their parents or guardians.[60] While the phrase 'have access to' still protects the State from necessarily having to provide religious education according to parental wishes, the second clause is a general right to exemption, even if the topic is taught 'neutrally and objectively'. It is not entirely clear that the binding human rights instruments reach quite that far, although a case will be made below that they do.

The European Convention and the case-law of its organs provides the richest source of relevant human rights doctrine. Article 2, First Protocol, states:

No person shall be denied the right to education. In the exercise of any functions which it assumes in relation to education and to teaching, the State shall respect the right of

---

[56] Ibid, para 10.4.   [57] General Comment no 22, para 6.   [58] C/82/D/1155/2003.
[59] No 694/96.   [60] Art 5(2).

parents to ensure such education and teaching in conformity with their own religious and philosophical convictions.[61]

In general, the second sentence is to be treated in the area of education as *lex specialis* to other potentially relevant articles such as 8, 9, and 10.[62] It is to be interpreted in the light of those articles,[63] and cases pleaded as a breach of parental rights to freedom of thought, conscience, and religion have been considered by the court of its own motion under this article instead.[64] At the same time, the article does not refer to the child's independent rights. Article 9 can be pleaded to defend the child's right to freedom of thought, conscience, and religion,[65] and has been used to evade Sweden's reservation to article 2 First Protocol requiring pupils to choose between different forms of denominational religious education.[66] The United Kingdom also entered a general reservation in respect of this article, accepting it 'only so far as it is compatible with the provision of efficient instruction and training and the avoidance of unreasonable public expenditure'. This reservation may not be valid,[67] but in any case the court has so far interpreted the article in such a way as to avoid onerous obligations on States.

The Court's basic approach to article 2 First Protocol, was set out in the early case of *Kjeldsen, Busk Madsen and Pedersen v Denmark*.[68] Parents objected to the implementation of compulsory sex education in Danish State schools on the grounds that it encouraged sexual activity they considered immoral. The European Court rejected their argument. The right contained in the second sentence is not limited to protecting private education; rather it aims at securing pluralism across the education system.[69] It covers all elements of education, not just the curriculum, extending, as the Court later held, to modes of school discipline.[70] The two sentences of the article are connected, in that parents have the prior duty to ensure that children receive an education, and the right to determine what that education shall be. State provision is only legitimate if it respects this prior parental responsibility.[71] But the reality is that the right to education requires considerable State action if it is to be enjoyed in practice.[72] States are thus responsible for the entire educational system, including both public and private schools, and they have considerable discretion in how they fulfil their responsibility.[73] It is not possible for the curriculum to avoid having some philosophical or religious dimension. The State's obligation is to ensure that information or

---

[61] See, generally, Pieter van Dijk *et al*, *Theory and Practice of the European Convention on Human Rights*, 4th edn (Oxford: Intersentia, 2006) ch 18 (Ben Vermeulen).

[62] *Folgerø v Norway* (2008) 46 EHRR 47, para 54.

[63] *Kjeldsen v Denmark* (1979–80) 1 EHRR 711, para 52

[64] eg *Çiftçi v Turkey*, no 71860/01 (2004).

[65] *Saniewski v Poland*, no 40319/98 (2001). See also *Sahin v Turkey* (2007) 44 EHRR 5.

[66] *Angelini v Sweden*, no 10491/83 (1986).

[67] See *Belilos v Switzerland* (1988) 10 EHRR 466. The point has never been resolved.

[68] *Kjeldsen, Busk Madsen and Pedersen v Denmark* (1979–80) 1 EHRR 711.

[69] Ibid, para 50.   [70] Ibid, para 51; *Campbell and Cosans v UK* (1982) 4 EHRR 293.

[71] *Kjeldsen*, para 52.   [72] Ibid, para 50.   [73] Ibid.

knowledge is conveyed in an 'objective, critical and pluralistic manner'.[74] The sex education programme was based on general moral considerations legitimately in the public interest. It did not encourage precocious sexual behaviour or prevent parents from advising their children as they saw fit.[75] The Court has since repeatedly stressed that 'respect' requires positive State action to ensure education in conformity with parental wishes. But while 'respect' is stronger than 'acknowledge' or 'take account of',[76] parents cannot use their convictions to evade compulsory education[77] nor require the State to deliver education according to their preferred model.[78]

The judgment in *Kjeldsen* has sometimes been read down simply to require that States refrain from 'indoctrination'.[79] But this does not reflect the judgment adequately. The requirement imposed on States is that topics be handled in an 'objective, critical and pluralistic' way. 'Indoctrination' is explained by the Court as the most extreme departure from this standard and is absolutely prohibited. Furthermore, the existence of substantially subsidized private schools, in which sex education was delivered more in keeping with the parents' views, and even the possibility of home schooling, were relevant factors in determining that the education system as a whole showed sufficient respect for those views.[80] The difference between the majority and Judge Verdross's dissenting opinion was that the latter considered that since the curriculum went beyond the merely biological, the education system would only show sufficient respect as a whole if it also allowed parents with children at State schools an individual exemption. In *Campbell and Cosans*, the next major case on article 2 First Protocol, the court effectively took Verdross's approach. It accepted that while the State could not be expected to maintain a system in which corporal punishment was both used and not used, it had to offer an individual exemption to parents who objected to it.

Thus the correct way to read *Kjeldsen* is this: just as the State has responsibility for the entire education system, so it can appeal to diversity within the system to satisfy its obligation to respect parental religious and philosophical views. Both private schooling and individual exemptions are means to this end of 'respect', and may—depending on the circumstances and the nature of State provision—be adequate, or even necessary.[81] Article 2 First Protocol will be breached when the State fails to make reasonable provision for parental convictions in the context of the entire education system. This still leaves open the question of whether there is a *right* to private schooling or a *right* to an exemption. Can a State avoid granting

---

[74] Ibid, para 53.   [75] Ibid, para 54.

[76] *Campbell and Cosans v UK* (1982) 4 EHRR 293, para 31.

[77] *Family H v UK*, no 10233/81 (1984).

[78] eg in respect of LEA-funded grammar schools: *X and Y v UK*, no 7527/76 (1977); *W and DM v UK*, no 10288/82 (1984), and in respect of special needs provision: *Northcott v UK*, no 13884/88 (1989); *J and BL v UK*, no 14136/88 (1989).   [79] See eg *Graeme v UK*, no 13887/88 (1990).

[80] *Kjeldsen, Busk Madsen and Pedersen v Denmark* (1979–80) 1 EHRR 711, para 54.

[81] See eg *Cederberg-Lappalainen v Sweden*, no 11356/85 (1987): making participation in a peace demonstration voluntary shows sufficient respect.

these rights so long as its own educational provision satisfies certain criteria of 'respect'?

As regards private schools, the matter has been settled along the lines of other international instruments. There is a free-standing right, regardless of State provision, to establish and run private schools, including faith-based schools, subject to State oversight and conformity to minimum standards.[82] The State is still responsible for the acts of private schools in breach of pupils' and parents' human rights, because allowing for private education is one way in which the State fulfils its basic obligation to educate.[83] However, it should not be concluded that private schools are bound to identical human rights standards as State-maintained schools. Although the point has never been tested, pupils' and parents' religious convictions are respected by the choice of a private education of the nature on offer. Thus where a State-maintained faith school might be required to offer an exemption from religious education, an equivalent private school would not be. To hold otherwise would be to undermine the very pluralism that private education is supposed to secure. This point receives indirect support from the recent tendency of the court to downplay the significance of the private education alternative when considering the neutrality of State provision.[84] State-maintained schools must respect all views; private schools may cater for a particular set of views.

There is still some uncertainty whether a school may vindicate its rights on its own behalf, or whether parents must bring a collective action. While it is now clear that a corporate person may enjoy rights under articles 9, 11, and 14, the wording of article 2 First Protocol, implies that it is a right only enjoyed by parents. Given the close relationship between the articles, a rigid distinction has not always been maintained, nor should it be.[85] The other source of difficulty lies in the uncertain boundary between public and private education. Organs of the State cannot claim to be victims of human rights violations. However, it is suggested that where school governing bodies have substantial autonomy from central and local Government, they should be treated as potential victims. The reasoning in respect of State churches should apply *mutatis mutandis*.[86] In England and Wales this problem might conceivably arise in respect of voluntary aided schools and academies in dispute with central or local Government.

There is no obligation on the State to fund any specific form of educational provision.[87] However, private schools have a right based on article 14 in the context

---

[82] *Ingrid Jordebo v Sweden*, no 11533/85 (1987); *Verein Gemeinsam Lernen v Austria* (1995) 20 EHRR CD 78. [83] *Costello-Roberts v UK* (1995) 19 EHRR 112, para 27.

[84] *Folgero v Norway* (2008) 46 EHRR 47, para 101.

[85] In *Ingrid Jordebo v Sweden*, the Commission denied that the Foundation could be a victim of a breach of First Protocol, art 2; but in *Verein Gemeinsam Lernen v Austria*, the association was able to mount a claim to non-discriminatory access to resources based on art 14 in the context of First Protocol, art 2. [86] See Ch 2 above.

[87] *40 Mothers v Sweden*, no 6853/74 (1977); *X v UK*, no 7782/77 (1978); *X and Y v UK*, no 9461/81 (1982).

of article 2 First Protocol to non-discriminatory conditions of existence, including equal access to State funding for schools of their type.[88] This has potential for challenging not only the basis on which faith schools are admitted into the State-maintained sector, but also the distinction between public and private schools. As standards for independent schools become more onerous and approximate to those applicable within the maintained sector, one can question both whether the right to establish private schools is genuinely guaranteed, and whether the differential funding regimes are justified. At the same time, as has already been pointed out, considerable leeway is given to States in this regard.[89]

The court has so far refused to recognize a right to home schooling.[90] States may thus take the view that education in a school context is indispensible at every level. However, the home schooling cases have so far not involved substantial analysis of whether the existing State and private provision taken as a whole shows sufficient respect for parental convictions in question.

As regards exemptions, the matter is less clear. The difficulty with the *Kjeldsen* approach is that it is open to a court to make an independent judgment about the neutrality of the educational provision in question, and simply find dissenting parents in the wrong.[91] This was the approach taken by the majority of the Court in *Valsamis v Greece*.[92] Jehovah's Witnesses had objected to compulsory participation in a National Day parade on the grounds that it was contrary to their pacifist convictions. While the Court expressed surprise that participation was compulsory on a national holiday, they simply disagreed with the parents' perception. Such commemorations of national events served both pacifist objectives and the public interest. The presence of military representatives at some of the parades which take place in Greece on the day in question did not in itself alter the nature of the parades.[93] It was sufficient that the pupil had been exempted from attendance at mass and religious instruction. By contrast, the minority took the position that the evaluation of the parents that the march was militaristic should be accepted unless it was obviously unfounded and unreasonable, which in their view it was not.

Folgerø v Norway arose from the same facts as the *Leirvåg* case before the Human Rights Committee and challenged the new Norwegian religion and ethics curriculum.[94] A narrow majority of the Court found a violation of article 2 First Protocol. The majority found that the quantitative imbalance in the time devoted to Christianity was acceptable given that 86 per cent of the population are members of the State church. However, they also found a qualitative

[88] *Verein Gemeinsam Lernen v Austria* (1995) 20 EHRR CD 78.
[89] *W and KL v Sweden*, no 10476/83 (1985); *Verein Gemeinsam Lernen v Austria* (1995) 20 EHRR CD 78.
[90] *Leuffen v Federal Republic of Germany*, no 19844/92 (1992); *BN and SN v Sweden*, no 17678/91 (1993); *Konrad v Germany* (2007) 44 EHRR SE8.
[91] See eg *Jimenez Alonso v Spain*, no 51188/99 (2000).
[92] *Valsamis v Greece* (1997) 24 EHRR 294.   [93] Ibid, para 31.
[94] *Folgerø v Norway* (2008) 46 EHRR 47.

imbalance preferring Christianity. This needed to be made acceptable by an exemption regime. However, inadequate information was given to parents about what would take place in each class to make the partial exemption regime workable, parents had to give reasons justifying their objections, which was inappropriate, and in practice children were not exempted from participating in acts of worship. The suggested distinction between 'observation' and 'participation' was too complicated and ineffective. Finally, the existence of heavily subsidized private schools could not exempt the State from its obligation to secure pluralism in State schools open to everyone. The minority disagreed on almost every point: there was no qualitative difference in the handling of other religions, and the exemption regime was reasonable and within the State's margin of appreciation. The minority tied their defence to the establishment clause of the Norwegian constitution, which also required parents who were members of the State church to bring up their children in accordance with its teaching: if that was legitimate, so was this curriculum.

Hasan and Eylem Zengin v Turkey is the latest decision on religious education.[95] The applicants were Alevi Muslims, who objected to their inability to gain exemption from a curriculum which they argued was dominated by Sunni Islam of the Hanafi school. The Court found that given the social composition of Turkey, the dominance of Islam in the curriculum was legitimate, but the virtual absence of reference to Alevism was disproportionate in the light of its social presence. In addition, the curriculum had indeed overstepped the boundary between 'transmitting information' and 'providing instruction' in Islam. The exemption system was not appropriate, both because it required parents to declare their faith and because it was limited to Jews and Christians. The Court noted that the vast majority of European States made religious education voluntary, either by making the subject optional, or by offering an exemption. It also noted two Recommendations of the Parliamentary Assembly of the Council of Europe calling for the promotion of education about religions, coupled with respect for the right of each person to believe that their faith is true.[96]

In December 2007, the OSCE Office for Democratic Institutions and Human Rights published the Toledo Guiding Principles on Teaching about Religions and Beliefs in Public Schools. These were prepared by the ODIHR Advisory Council of Experts on Freedom of Religion or Belief and also aim to encourage teaching about religions and beliefs in order to foster mutual respect and tolerance. The Guidelines draw a clear distinction between awareness and acceptance, between study and practice, and suggest various strategies concerning curriculum design, methodology, and teacher training including principles of multi-perspectivity, sensitivity, and inclusiveness. The importance of national, regional, and local

---

[95] *Hasan and Eylem Zengin v Turkey* (2008) 46 EHRR 44.
[96] Recommendation 1396 (1999) on Religion and Democracy; Recommendation 1720 (2005) on Religion and Education.

advisory bodies embracing a wide range of stake-holders is stressed as a valuable means of achieving consensus and resolving conflicts. The most interesting aspect of the Guidelines for present purposes is the view taken on exemptions for conscientious objectors.

The authors note that international human rights standards require opt-out provisions from religious instruction, but do not require exemptions if the education is 'neutral and objective'. However, they point out that opt-out provisions may still be a useful device for parents to raise issues of local malfeasance. In addition, some parents may take the view that teaching about religions and beliefs is indoctrination in relativism or secularism. Conscientious objection to this 'is precisely what the right to freedom of religion or belief (and the parallel right of parents to raise their children in accordance with those beliefs) is intended to protect'.[97] Neutrality is difficult to determine in advance and in the abstract. Exemptions—in any context in which teaching about religions or beliefs arises—make it more likely that the resulting courses actually meet international standards. Of course, opt-out regimes have to be sensitively structured so as not to result in discrimination or stigmatization. But the way in which schools respond to conscientious objectors 'send[s] a signal that may build or undermine the culture of tolerance and mutual respect in the school environment'.[98]

It should be noted that there are two separate arguments at work here. The first is that, at least in some areas of educational provision, it is very hard to satisfy tests that education be 'objective, critical and pluralist' or 'objective and neutral'. It is plausible that while there may be more or less objective ways of delivering subjects, at least in the area of religious education there is no truly neutral standpoint. For example, a phenomenological approach to the study of religions can easily imply that all religions are human constructs meeting universal psychological needs and are thus—in their distinctive metaphysical claims—all false. The other argument for exemptions is process-based: that an exemption creates a pressure-valve to test the acceptability of provision to parents. Rather than assuming that 'neutrality' is a fixed quality of a certain educational approach, provision is only genuinely neutral when parents do not in practice object to it. There is much to be said for such scepticism.

The overall effect of the European human rights case-law is unclear. In terms of the reasoning adopted by Convention organs it is rather demanding. Across the whole educational provision, principles of religious liberty and non-discrimination on grounds of religion must be observed. This has the potential to undermine historic preferences and imbalances. At their strongest, these principles conflict, since, for example, exemptions can never be perfectly non-discriminatory. It would be easy to set off on an endless search for an elusive neutrality. On the other hand, violations have only actually been found in respect

<hr/>

[97] OSCE/ODIHR, *Toledo Guiding Principles*, 71.   [98] Ibid, 74.

of compulsory involvement in faith-specific religious instruction, and liability to corporal punishment. This is a very minimal core of protection.

Even if the decisions of the European Court do not actually reach very far, international human rights law is arguably pointing in the direction of a general parental right to exempt children from any school activity on grounds of religion or belief. Of course, there must be a plausibility threshold. It is accepted that the objection must meet a certain level of 'cogency, seriousness, cohesion and importance'.[99] But courts—and anyone for that matter—should be cautious before concluding that a person's perception of forced breach of their own commitments, or unwilling complicity in another religion or belief, is simply wrong.

IV. Religious Pluralism in the Maintained Sector

We are now in a position to look more closely at the way in which the law regulates religion in education. This section considers the law applicable to the State-maintained sector; the following one considers the independent sector.[100]

1. School type and ethos

As has already been pointed out, under the School Standards and Framework Act 1998 and subsequent legislation, the principal difference is now between schools without a religious character and schools which have had a religious character designated by Order of the Secretary of State.[101] Each maintained school with a designated religious character must set out a description of the religious ethos of the school in its instrument of government.[102] However the old distinction between voluntary controlled and voluntary aided lives on, and the Equality Act 2006 uses a slightly different criterion to trigger the exceptions it contains for faith schools.

As well as requiring a formal statement of the school's ethos, designation affects staffing, admissions criteria, the form of religious education and collective worship, inspection processes, and the disposition of assets. It is not constitutive; it is simply a formal recognition of a matter of fact. Thus designation is based on a number of possible criteria.[103] The Secretary of State is required to designate

---

[99] *Campbell and Cosans v UK* (1982) 4 EHRR 293, para 36. See eg *Stevens v UK*, no 11674/85 (1986): objection to school uniform not *per se* protected.

[100] For these purposes, academies are treated as State-maintained rather than independent. Strictly speaking they are supposed to be both.

[101] School Standards and Framework Act 1998, s 69(3).

[102] Originally in School Standards and Framework Act 1998, sched 12. See now Education Act 2002, s 20(1); School Governance (Constitution) (England) Regulations 2003, SI 2003/348, reg 29(1)(j); School Governance (Constitution) (England) Regulations 2007, SI 2003/957, reg 30(1)(i); Government of Maintained Schools (Wales) Regulations 2005, SI 2005/2914, reg 33(1)(i).

[103] Religious Character of Schools (Designation Procedure) Regulations 1998, SI 1998/2535.

a school as having a religious character if it is a foundation or voluntary school
with at least one foundation governor appointed to represent the interests of one
or more religions or religious denominations, or if the land is held on trust to
revert to the benefit of a religion or religious denomination should it cease to be
a school, or if it is held on trust for the provision of education or the conduct of
an educational institution in accordance with the tenets of one or more religions
or religious denominations.[104] The Secretary of State may also designate a school
as having a religious character if he considers it appropriate having regard to the
practice of religious education prior to its first becoming a voluntary school, and
having regard to representations of relevant religious bodies.[105]

The designation procedure envisaged an initial stage up to 1 September 1999
whereby the Secretary of State would prepare as complete a list as possible, consulting first with a scheduled list of religious bodies, and then with the full governing body and any trustees of each school.[106] The scheduled list of consultees
consisted of the Church of England General Synod Board of Education, the
Board of Mission of the Church in Wales, the Catholic Education Service, the
Methodist Church, the Free Church Federal Council, the Seventh-Day Adventist
Church, the Board of Deputies of British Jews, and the Association of Muslim
Schools.

Thereafter, the procedure for new schools applies the same test with the addition that the application for designation in respect of schools associated with the
Church of England, Church in Wales, and Roman Catholic Church must have
been approved by the relevant diocesan authority.[107] There is also a power to
change designations should they prove incorrect, once again with a consultation
requirement.[108]

Employment equality legislation results in different regimes for teachers at
maintained and independent faith schools. These are considered further below.
However, in the context of the Equality Act 2006, the exceptions are harmonized.[109] In general terms it is unlawful for a body responsible for a school to
discriminate on grounds of religion or belief in the terms on which it offers to
admit a person as a pupil, by refusing to accept an application for admission, or
in the way in which it affords a pupil access to any benefit, facility, or service,
by refusing a pupil access to a benefit, facility, or service, by excluding a pupil
from the establishment, or by subjecting him or her to any other detriment.[110] In
the specific context of curriculum content and acts of worship or other religious
observance, all schools are excepted from the obligations in respect of access to
benefits, facilities, or services or the imposition of detriments.[111] However, this
does not extend to acts in respect of admission and exclusion. The practical effect

---

[104] Ibid, regs 5(1), 9(6).   [105] Ibid, reg 5(2).   [106] Ibid, reg 6.
[107] Ibid, reg 9(2).   [108] Ibid, reg 10.
[109] The position is continued under the Equality Act 2010, ss 84–89 and sched 11.
[110] Equality Act 2006, s 49(1).   [111] Ibid, s 50(2).

of this section is to preserve the religious aspects of non-faith schools, in other words, to prevent potential claims arising from religious education and worship. Once a maintained school has a designated religious character, only exclusion or 'other detriment' can give rise to a claim of unlawful discrimination.[112] Thus admissions decisions and access to benefits, facilities, and services can be made faith-sensitive. There is also a general exception for faith schools providing services other than to students of the institution.[113]

2. Staffing

The law reflects a long-standing underlying principle of religious non-discrimination in the employment of teachers at State-maintained schools.[114] No teacher is to be advantaged or disadvantaged by reference to religious beliefs or attendance, or by his or her refusal to give religious education.[115] The Employment Equality (Religion or Belief) Regulations 2003 now apply that principle much more generally, but preserve the specific regimes for teachers set out in the School Standards and Framework Act 1998.[116]

In respect of staffing, the difference between voluntary aided and voluntary controlled schools is still significant as a sub-division within the category of schools having a designated religious character. In the case of voluntary aided schools, preference may be given, in connection with the appointment, remuneration, or promotion of teachers at the school, to persons whose religious opinions are in accordance with the tenets of the religion or religious denomination specified in relation to the school, or who attend religious worship in accordance with those tenets, or who give, or are willing to give, religious education at the school in accordance with those tenets.[117] Furthermore, regard may be had, in connection with the termination of the employment or engagement of any teacher at the school, to any conduct incompatible with the precepts, or with the upholding of the tenets, of the religion or religious denomination so specified.[118]

Voluntary controlled and foundation schools with a religious character occupy a middle ground. Where the school has more than two teachers, up to a fifth of the total number of teachers (rounded up to the next multiple of five) may be 'reserved' for the delivery of appropriate religious education.[119] Reserved teachers are subject to the same rules as all teachers in voluntary aided schools.[120] Reserved teachers may only be appointed with the consent of the foundation

---

[112] Ibid, s 50(1)(a).   [113] Ibid, s 59.
[114] See Education Act 1944, s 30. The Education Act 1902, s 7, was rather more coy, permitting but not requiring non-discrimination.
[115] School Standards and Framework Act 1998, s 59.
[116] Employment Equality (Religion or Belief) Regulations 2003, SI 2003/1660, reg 39(1)(a). See Equality Act 2010, sched 22 para 3.
[117] School Standards and Framework Act 1998, s 60(5)(a).   [118] Ibid, s 60(5)(b).
[119] Ibid, s 58(2) and (3).   [120] Ibid, s 60(3).

governors, who can also require their dismissal if they fail to give appropriate religious education efficiently and suitably.[121] In the case of a head teacher who is not a reserved teacher, regard may be had to that person's ability and fitness to preserve and develop the religious character of the school.[122] Apart from that, the normal non-discrimination principles apply.

One small difference in this context between England and Wales was introduced by the Education and Inspections Act 2006. The appointment of non-teaching staff in England is now subject only to the general provisions of the Employment Equality Regulations, whereas in Wales the older general prohibition, which makes no allowance for a genuine occupational requirement, remains in force.[123]

At one level, the statutory regime resolves questions about the relevance of a school's religious ethos to staffing issues. However, the matter may not be as straightforward as it seems. The attempt to dismiss a Catholic religious education teacher for having an affair was argued (and won) as a sex discrimination case.[124] A challenge to the terms of appointment of a Christian headmaster in a Church of England school nearly succeeded on grounds of indirect race discrimination.[125] There are no relevant exceptions here, and given the Supreme Court's views on how to resolve boundary cases in the *JFS* case discussed below, aspects of a faith school's ethos which touch on questions of race, gender, or sexuality may be far from secure.

3. Admissions

Faith schools have always sought to use their admissions policies to prefer adherents and secure their ethos over time. This remains controversial, especially when the school has, or is perceived to have, higher educational or disciplinary standards and is popular among parents for reasons other than religious ones. When parents were given the right to express a preference for a particular school under the Education Act 1980, schools were allowed to refuse admission on religious criteria even if they were undersubscribed.[126] This right was strengthened under the Education Reform Act 1988 in order to 'preserve their character'.[127] Different local authorities adopted different approaches to balancing the need to provide places on a fair basis for all children with the exercise of parental preference. For example, in Lancashire, which has a substantial minority of Roman Catholic voluntary aided secondary schools (around 20 per cent), the local authority with the support of diocesan authorities gave an advantage to non-Catholic applicants to non-Catholic schools, to encourage indirectly the take-up of places at Catholic

---

[121] Ibid, s 58(5) and (6).   [122] Ibid, s 60(4).   [123] Ibid, s 60(6).
[124] *O'Neill v Governors of St Thomas More RC VA School* [1997] ICR 33.
[125] *Board of Governors of St Matthias CE School v Crizzle* [1993] ICR 401.
[126] This was the practical effect of Education Act 1980, s 6(3)(b).
[127] Education Reform Act 1988, s 30(3).

secondary schools by pupils who had attended Catholic primary schools. In spite of contravening Government advice, this survived legal challenge as a reasonable response to the problem of Catholic parents preferring a non-Catholic secondary education.[128] Of course, it had the effect of preserving the influence of Catholic secondary schools within the maintained sector.

In principle, any reasonable religious criteria may be used to determine admissions to a faith school.[129] Until recently, the courts have been unwilling to interfere except on general public law grounds. Thus the criteria must be sufficiently clear, the order of priority among applicants must be followed, or reasons for departure from them given.[130] An attempt by the Schools Adjudicator to prevent the London Oratory School, which is substantially oversubscribed, from using interviews to determine levels of genuine commitment among applicants, was also successfully challenged.[131] The use of interviews has since been prohibited, except for boarding schools and in remaining cases where selection by academic ability is permitted.[132] More recently, the courts have become more sensitive to the human rights dimensions of religiously-motivated parental choice. Parents have to be allowed to indicate that their preference for a single-sex education is religiously motivated.[133] However, religious identity is not in itself a Special Educational Need.[134]

The Government has now substantially centralized and regulated admissions policy. The status of the Code of Practice for School Admissions has changed. It is no longer adequate for admissions authorities to 'have regard to' it; they must act in accordance with it.[135] The Secretary of State is empowered to 'impose requirements' on local authorities and governing bodies.[136] Faith schools may only adopt religious criteria for admissions if they are oversubscribed.[137] In determining admissions policy, admissions authorities have a formal duty to give notice to such body or person representing the religion or religious denomination of the relevant foundation or voluntary school with a religious character as may be prescribed.[138] The prescribed bodies or persons are the appropriate

---

[128] *R v Lancashire County Council, ex parte Foster* [1995] ELR 33.

[129] *R v Governors of Bishop Challoner Roman Catholic School, ex parte Choudhury* [1992] 2 AC 182.

[130] Lack of clear criteria: *R v Governors of La Sainte Union Convent School, ex parte T* [1996] ELR 98; lack of reasons: *McKeown v Governors of Cardinal Heenan High School* [1998] ELR 578.

[131] *London Oratory School v Schools Adjudicator* [2005] ELR 162.

[132] School Standards and Framework Act 1998, ss 88A and 88R (inserted originally by the Education and Inspections Act 2006, s 44).

[133] *R (K) v Newham London Borough Council* [2002] EWHC 405.

[134] *G v London Borough of Barnet* [1998] ELR 480.

[135] School Standards and Framework Act 1998, s 84(3) as amended by the Education and Inspections Act 2006, s 40(4).

[136] Ibid, s 84(2) as amended by the Education and Inspections Act 2006, s 40(3).

[137] DCSF, *School Admissions Code* (2009), para 2.47.

[138] School Standards and Framework Act 1998, s 88F(3)(c) (England). In Wales, the earlier obligation to 'consult with' has been preserved: s 89(2)(e).

diocesan authority in the Church of England, the appropriate rabbinnic authority, the Methodist Connexional Education Secretary, the Association of Muslim
Schools UK, the Religious Society of Friends, the diocesan bishop or equivalent in the Roman Catholic Church, the British Union Conference of Seventh
Day Adventists, and the Network of Sikh Organisations UK. In the case of rabbinnic authorities, a schedule lists a range of authorities for the 38 maintained
Jewish schools, about half of which refer to the Chief Rabbi.[139] Objections may
be raised by these bodies to the Schools Adjudicator in England or the Welsh
Ministers.[140]

In 2006, the Government briefly considered requiring faith schools to admit
25 per cent of pupils from other religious backgrounds.[141] This was quickly abandoned, and the Government has proceeded instead by strengthening the role of
central religious authorities and reaching agreement with them. The Admissions
Code connects the admissions policies of faith schools to religious authorities in
several ways.[142] In determining criteria, admissions authorities for faith schools
should only use the methods and definitions agreed by their faith provider group
or religious authority. They must make clear how membership or practice is to be
demonstrated in line with guidance issued by the faith provider group or religious
authority. In the case of new voluntary aided or foundation schools, governing
bodies must obtain the consent of the relevant representative body before proposing or determining admissions arrangements which give priority for a proportion
of pupils from other religious backgrounds.

Designated religious schools are allowed to discriminate on religious grounds
in their admissions criteria. However, the admissions policies of orthodox Jewish
schools have recently been declared unlawful by the Supreme Court on grounds
of race discrimination, for which there is no exception. In *R(E) v Governing Body
of JFS*, the claimants had been rejected on the grounds that they were not Jewish
by matrilineal descent or conversion according to the principles of the Chief
Rabbi. At first instance, Munby J characterized this rule as being based primarily
on religious law which happened to refer to a criterion of descent.[143] Sedley LJ
for the Court of Appeal rejected this.[144] To be Jewish is to be of a certain ethnic
group, and therefore to treat someone less favourably because he is or is not (or
is or is not perceived to be) Jewish is to discriminate directly on racial grounds.
'Eligibility must depend on faith, however defined, and not on ethnicity.'[145] The
Supreme Court was divided, with a bare majority finding direct discrimination

---

[139] Education (Determination of Admissions Arrangements) 1999, SI 1999/126, reg 5ZA
as amended by SI 2007/3009. This has been replaced in England for 2010–11 by the School
Admissions (Admission Arrangements) (England) Regulations 2008, SI 2008/3089 with no substantial change in this respect.
[140] School Standards and Framework Act 1998, ss 88H(2) and 90(1) respectively.
[141] *BBC News Report*, 23 October 2006.
[142] DCSF, *School Admissions Code* (2009), paras 2.48–2.52.
[143] *R(E) v Governing Body of JFS* [2008] ELR 445.
[144] *R(E) v Governing Body of JFS* [2009] EWCA Civ 626.   [145] Ibid, para 33.

on grounds of ethnicity, a larger majority finding indirect discrimination in the alternative, and two Justices dissenting vigorously.[146] At root, the problem is that 'ethnicity' contains a religious component,[147] but the exception for admissions policies only applies to purely religious criteria. The law prohibiting religious discrimination, together with its exceptions, has been grafted onto existing law prohibiting race discrimination without careful thought being given to the interface between the two concepts.

From a technical point of view, the disagreement between the Justices of the Supreme Court on the question of direct discrimination turns on the meaning of 'grounds'. The majority characterized the use of a criterion of descent as a ground, and dismissed the fact that this derives from religious law as mere motivation. The adoption of a dual test of Jewish identity, one part of which is ethnic (descent), the other religious (maternal conversion) still draws a distinction on racial grounds. The minority considered that the religious context should not be ignored. Descent was only relevant until one had traced ancestry back to a mother who was halakhically Jewish. Whether an ancestor in the maternal line is halakhically Jewish is a religious question. Lord Phillips pointed out that a lawful test of religious practice could be formulated which would be likely to satisfy tests of matrilineal descent.[148] Lady Hale hinted that reform might be necessary to the law on direct discrimination.[149] But the underlying point is that the law as interpreted by the majority requires a non-Jewish definition of who is Jewish.[150] Only the adoption of a concept of religion which fits dominant (ie broadly Christian) understandings will satisfy the law.

4. Religious education and worship

Under the Education Act 1944, religious education consisted of instruction and worship. In 1988, 'instruction' was renamed 'education' for obvious pedagogical reasons, and then the 1996 consolidating legislation quietly separated out 'worship' into its own category.

Each maintained school must have a basic curriculum, which must include provision for religious education.[151] The religious education to be provided varies according to the school.[152] Community schools, foundation, and voluntary schools without a designated religious character must provide religious education according to the agreed syllabus for the school or the relevant pupils. In

---

[146] *R(E) v Governing Body of JFS* [2010] 2 WLR 153.
[147] *Mandla v Dowell Lee* [1983] 2 AC 548, per Lord Fraser at 562. It is Lord Fraser's interpretation of ethnicity which has dominated subsequent judgments. Helen Beynon and Nigel Love, '*Mandla* and the meaning of "racial group"' (1984) 100 LQR 120, are critical of this as an unwarranted expansion. The debate should be placed in the context of wider legal problems around the construction of 'Jewishness'. See Davina Cooper and Did Herman, 'Jews and other uncertainties: race, faith and English law' (1999) 19 Legal Studies 339.   [148] [2010] 2 WLR 153, 170.
[149] Ibid, 175–6.   [150] Lord Brown at 248.
[151] School Standards and Framework Act 1998, s 69(1).   [152] Ibid, s 69(2) and sched 19.

foundation and voluntary controlled schools with a religious character, religious education should be in accordance with the agreed syllabus, unless parents request provision in accordance with the trust deed or the tenets of the specified religion or religious denomination, in which case the foundation governors are to ensure that up to two periods a week of such education is provided. In the case of a voluntary aided school, religious education is under the control of the governing body and in accordance with the trust deed or the tenets of the specified religion or denomination. Parents may request alternative provision according to the agreed syllabus.

Agreed syllabuses are still drawn up according to the model established by the 1944 Act as amended by the Education Reform Act 1988.[153] They are agreed by a standing advisory council with representatives of the main religious denominations, the Church of England (in England), teachers, and the local authority. They are required to reflect the fact that the religious traditions in Great Britain are in the main Christian whilst taking account of the teaching and practices of the other principal religions represented in Great Britain. They are not to teach according to any catechism or formulary distinctive of any particular religion (but may include the study of such). Conferences must be reconvened at least every five years to reconsider the agreed syllabus, which may either be recommended again or replaced. If the conference is unanimous, and the substantive test set out above is satisfied, the local authority may adopt it. If they fail to reach agreement, or the recommended syllabus does not reflect the substantive test, or the local authority fail to act, the Secretary of State has the power to intervene and establish an agreed syllabus in a similarly constituted process. The non-statutory guidance on religious education has recently been updated to take account of the increasing diversity and perceived importance of religion in the United Kingdom as well as equalities and human rights legislation. It emphasizes its role in personal development and well-being as well as community cohesion.[154] Inevitably this growing degree of centralization reduces the scope for the syllabus to reflect local agendas and needs.

There is also a duty on schools to ensure that each pupil takes part in a daily act of collective worship.[155] Responsibility for the arrangements rests in a community school or foundation school without religious character with the head teacher in consultation with the governing body, and in the case of schools with a religious character with the governing body in consultation with the head teacher. Once again, the old model still applies: in 'non-faith' schools, the worship must be wholly or mainly of a broadly Christian character having regard to the family background of the pupils, their ages, and aptitudes. Standing Advisory Councils on Religious Education have the power to dispense with this requirement. In

---

[153] Ibid, s 69(2) and sched 19; Education Act 1996, s 375 and sched 31.
[154] DCSF, *Religious education in English schools: Non-statutory guidance*, 2009.
[155] School Standards and Framework Act 1998, s 70 and sched 20.

voluntary schools or schools with a religious character, collective worship must be in accordance with the trust deed, or failing that with the tenets and practices of the relevant religion.

Parents have the right to withdraw their child wholly or in part from religious education or worship.[156] The Education and Inspections Act 2006 extended that right to sixth-form pupils.[157] If parents wish their child to receive an alternative religious education, and it is not convenient to provide that at another school, there is a right to withdraw the pupil at the start or end of the school day to receive such education.[158] In the case of schools without a designated religious character, the local authority must also provide reasonable facilities for such education to take place on the school premises, but they must not bear the cost of such education.[159]

5. Other aspects of school life[160]

In 2007, the Muslim Council of Britain published *Towards Greater Understanding: meeting the needs of Muslim pupils in state schools*. It sets out what a school would need to do if it were to take social inclusion for Muslims seriously: provision for modest dress, including sportswear that covers completely; permission for beards and religious amulets; halal meals; provision for prayers including private washing facilities; special exemptions for Ramadan such as refraining from sport; sex education that respects Islamic morals; celebration of Islamic festivals; segregated sports; no communal showering; no dance; no use of religious images in art or worship; teaching of Arabic; no raffles; no alcohol; and much more. The document exposes the extent to which the current law of education is locked into a post-Christian paradigm, in which 'religion' only affects specifically religious instruction and collective worship. This still reflects the late-nineteenth century solution of dividing secular from religious and giving rights of conscience in respect of the latter. The right of conscientious withdrawal was in time extended to sex education,[161] but has not yet been applied to other subjects, such as biology or sport.

The courts have begun to consider the impact of religious freedom and non-discrimination as an individual right on school practices such as uniform requirements, with mixed results. In the leading case of *Begum*, the applicant failed to persuade the House of Lords that her rights were infringed when her school refused to allow her to wear a fuller form of Islamic dress than was permitted under the school uniform rules.[162] A majority held that she had no right to attend

---

[156] Ibid, s 71.   [157] Ibid, s 71(1B).   [158] Ibid, s 71(3) and (4).

[159] Ibid, s 71(5) and (6); sched 19, para 2(3).

[160] For a full discussion of several of the issues raised in this section, see Neville Harris, *Education, Law and Diversity* (Oxford: Hart Publishing, 2007), ch 7.

[161] Education Act 1993, s 241(3).

[162] *R (Begum) v Denbigh High School Governors* [2007] 1 AC 100; see also *R (X) v Governors and Teachers of Y School* [2008] 1 All ER 249.

a specific school, and that she could have attended a school which permitted the jilbab without undue inconvenience. Her rights had not even been limited. A minority accepted that her right to manifest her religion had been limited but accepted that it was justified to preserve the school's policy of rejecting the more radical form of Islam the jilbab was supposed to represent. Likewise in the 'silver ring' case a girl lost her challenge to a school jewellery rule when she failed to establish that she was required by her religion (Christianity) to wear a chastity ring.[163] However, in another case, a judge accepted that it was unjustified discrimination on both racial and religious grounds for a school to ban the Sikh bangle.[164] Clearly there is potential for further litigation as schools and courts grapple with the extent to which individual pupils and their parents can opt out of certain aspects of school life. The strength of the relevant religious convictions and the availability of alternatives will be key.

As regards the collective aspects of religious schooling, there has been as yet no case successfully challenging the range of different schools provided by public authorities or the terms under which faith schools are admitted within the maintained sector. The courts are likely to be unwilling to overturn major resource-sensitive decisions of education authorities.[165] Thus the cost of school transport has been a problem where parents have not been able to access a faith school of their choice in their home town. While the courts have steadily refused to see the provision of transport as required by religious rights,[166] legislation has recently extended the scope of local authority obligations to provide transport up to 15 miles.[167]

V. Religious Pluralism in the Independent Sector

Parents may comply with their statutory duty to ensure efficient and suitable full-time education for their children of compulsory school age by sending them to an independent school or by otherwise ensuring their education.[168] Some parents with strong religious convictions, and sufficient financial means, choose this option. Broadly speaking, an independent school is an educational institution for five or more children of compulsory school age not maintained by a local education authority.[169] About 7 per cent of children in England and Wales are educated in independent schools,[170] but this figure rises to about 15–16 per cent

---

[163] *R (Playfoot) v Millais School Governing Body* [2007] 3 FCR 754.

[164] *R (Watkins-Singh) v Aberdare Girls' High School Governors* [2008] 3 FCR 203.

[165] See *R (McDougal) v Liverpool City Council* [2009] EWHC 1821 unsuccessfully challenging a decision to close a non-faith school.   [166] *R(T) v Leeds City Council* [2002] ELR 91.

[167] Education and Inspections Act 2006, sched 8.   [168] Education Act 1996, s 7.

[169] Education Act 1996, s 463, as amended by the Education Act 2002, s 172 (which extended the definition to include any statemented or looked-after pupil).

[170] DCSF/National Statistics, *The Composition of Schools in England* (June 2008), table 2.1.

in the case of sixth-form education. The vast majority of independent schools are charities, or are run by charities, and in the case of long-established schools, they may well have a religious foundation or ethos. One of the main motives for establishing new independent schools is a desire to provide an education with a religious dimension not present in maintained schools. As we have seen, there is a human right to establish such schools, subject to State oversight to ensure compliance with minimum standards.

The Education Act 1944 established a basic framework for the State regulation of independent schools.[171] The key components of this framework were compulsory registration and inspection; the possibility of disqualification if the school premises, accommodation, instruction, the proprietor, or any teacher were unsuitable; notices of complaint with set periods to remedy the defect identified; appeals to an Independent Schools Tribunal; and criminal penalties to enforce the obligations. There was no further statutory specification of the standards a school had to achieve in order to provide 'efficient and suitable instruction'. This emerged instead in the practice of HM Inspectors and the decisions of the Independent Schools Tribunal. In the one case to reach the High Court in recent years, Woolf J (as he then was) interpreted the basic legal requirement in broad and tolerant terms. Education would be suitable if it

primarily equips a child for life within the community of which he is a member rather than the way of life in the country as a whole, as long as it does not foreclose the child's option in later years to adopt some other form of life if he wishes to do so.[172]

State regulation should be 'sensitive to the traditions of the minority sect' with interference not going beyond what is necessary.[173]

This regime survived, with minor modifications, until the Education Act 2002, which sets out in Part X a new framework for the regulation of independent schools. Both this framework and the employment equality agenda have served to emphasize questions of religious ethos and character. Every independent school is required to register with the Secretary of State. The information required on registration includes the religious ethos of the school, if any.[174] The Act authorizes the specification by regulation of standards for independent schools in respect of the quality of education; the spiritual, moral, social, and cultural development of pupils; the welfare, health, and safety of pupils; the suitability of proprietors and staff, premises, and accommodation; the provision of information; and the

---

[171] Education Act 1944, Part III.

[172] *R v Secretary of State for Education and Science, ex parte Talmud Torah Machzikei Hadass School Trust*, The Times, 12 April 1985.

[173] Discussion of the tensions between orthodox Jewish schools and liberal expectations in Anthony Bradney, *Law and Faith in a Sceptical Age* (Abingdon: Routledge-Cavendish, 2009), 131–40.

[174] Education Act 2002, s 160(1); Education (Provision of Information by Independent Schools (England) Regulations 2003, SI 2003/1934, sched 1, para 3(12).

manner in which complaints are handled.[175] The standards receive detailed specification in the Education (Independent School Standards) (England) Regulations
2003 and the Education (Independent School Standards) (Wales) Regulations
2003.[176] The information made available to pupils and parents must include
a statement of the school's ethos and aims, including any religious ethos.[177]
Educational quality is to be secured by a written policy on the curriculum which
provides, among many other things, for personal, social, and health education
reflecting the school's aims and ethos.[178]

There is no obligation to provide religious education, but in respect of the spiritual, moral, social, and cultural development of pupils, the school must promote
principles which—

(a) enable pupils to develop their self-knowledge, self-esteem and self-confidence;

(b) enable pupils to distinguish right from wrong and to respect the law;

(c) encourage pupils to accept responsibility for their behaviour, show initiative,
and understand how they can contribute to community life;

(d) provide pupils with a broad general knowledge of public institutions and
services (in England); and

(e) assist pupils to acquire an appreciation of and respect for their own and other
cultures in a way that promotes tolerance and harmony between different
cultural traditions.[179]

The Secretary of State has the power to require or arrange for inspection and to
issue orders identifying failures to meet standards and requiring action plans to be
drawn up to remedy the defects.[180] Ultimately, a school can be removed from the
register if it fails to meet standards or parts of the operation can be closed down.
There is an appeal to a tribunal. Appeals have been heard since September 2003
by the Care Standards Tribunal. Inspection services are carried out by approved
providers which currently include Ofsted, the Independent Schools Inspectorate
(which inspects the large number of schools affiliated to the Independent Schools
Council), and the School Inspection Service, which inspects schools affiliated
to the Focus Learning Trust.[181] This Trust is an association of Christian schools
within the Brethren denomination. The DCSF have also approved the Bridge
Schools Inspectorate to inspect schools affiliated to the Christian Schools Trust and
the Association of Muslim Schools. Presumably these arrangements create a further 'buffer' between Government and individual faith schools by allowing for an
inspectorate which is sensitive to the tensions between secular and religious requirements. Ofsted has a role in monitoring the quality of the other inspectorates.

---

[175] Education Act 2002, s 157.   [176] SI 2003/1910 and SI 2003/3234, as amended.
[177] Ibid, sched 1, para 6(d).   [178] Ibid, sched 1, para 1(2)(f).
[179] Ibid, sched 1, para 2.   [180] Education Act 2002, ss 162A–166.
[181] Education Act 2002, s 162A(1)(b). Formal agreements available at <http://www.dcsf.gov.
uk/reg-independent-schools/>, accessed 14 September 2009.

Equalities legislation has required the religious character of independent faith schools to become more formal. In respect of the appointment of staff, it is in principle unlawful to discriminate on grounds of religion or belief.[182] Since it would presumably be easy to show that the school has an ethos based on religion or belief, the test for an exception is the slightly weaker one of a 'genuine occupational requirement' (GOR) that the person be of a particular religion or belief as opposed to a 'genuine and determining occupational requirement'.[183] In either case, a faith school might struggle to demonstrate the proportionality of a faith test where the teacher is not directly involved in teaching the faith in question. One might be able to show a GOR for all staff, if, for example, it were a requirement of the job that all staff actively participate in acts of collective worship. But in the absence of such a rigorous and cohesive staffing policy forms of weaker preference would be unlawful.

However, provision is made for an exception to the employment equality legislation in respect of teachers at independent schools which have a religious character.[184] The designation procedure created by the School Standards and Framework Act 1998 for the provision of religious education and worship in maintained schools has been adapted to enable independent schools to have one or more designated religion(s) or religious denomination(s).[185]

The process for acquiring a designated religious character is set out in the Religious Character of Schools (Designation Procedure) (Independent Schools) (England) Regulations 2003 and the Independent Schools (Religious Character of Schools) (Designation Procedure) (Wales) Regulations 2003.[186] The school's proprietor may make an application to the Secretary of State for an order stating the religion or religious denomination of the school, including the grounds for the application and any supporting evidence, along with representations from any relevant religious body. The Regulations state that the Secretary of State may consult any religious body he considers appropriate. However, consultation with any body other than one to which it appears the school is connected would presumably be irrelevant and unlawful. The Secretary of State is required to designate if one of a number of conditions is fulfilled: the school is conducted or education is provided in accordance with the tenets of the religion; school property is held on trust for such purposes; at least one governor is appointed to represent the interests of a religion or religious denomination; or the governing instrument makes provision for education to be in accordance with a religion.[187] A school may also be designated even if none of these conditions applies if it is appropriate to do so.

---

[182] Employment Equality (Religion or Belief) Regulations 2003, SI 2003/1660, reg 3.
[183] Ibid, reg 7(3).   [184] Ibid, reg 39(1)(a).
[185] School Standards and Framework Act 1998, ss 124A and 124B, as inserted by the Independent Schools (Employment of Teachers in Schools with a Religious Character) Regulations 2003, SI 2003/2037.   [186] SI 2003/2314 and 2003/3233 respectively, as amended.
[187] Reg 5.

The terms used in the Regulations have a much broader reference than merely to religious education and worship. They embrace a whole range of aspects of the ethos and curriculum of the school. The same breadth is apparent in the consequences of designation for the employment of teachers. Preference may be given in connection with the appointment, promotion, or remuneration of teachers to those whose religious opinions are in accordance with the tenets of the religion or denomination specified, or to those who attend religious worship in accordance with those tenets, or to those who give, or who are willing to give, religious education in accordance with those tenets.[188] Furthermore, regard may be had in connection with the termination of employment or engagement of a teacher to conduct incompatible with the religion.[189]

A review of the orders listing independent schools with a designated religious character shows that to date over 600 schools have applied for designation.[190] Around 90 per cent of these are Christian, with substantial numbers designated simply as 'Christian', Anglican or Church of England, or Roman Catholic. In addition, there are small numbers of Methodist, Quaker, Evangelical Christian, Evangelical Anglican, United Reformed Church, Seventh Day Adventist, Baptist, Moravian, and Christian Science among others. Among the non-Christian religions, the majority are Muslim, with small number of Jewish, Hindu, and Buddhist schools. Sixteen schools in Wales have been designated, all 'Christian' except for one 'inter-denominational' (and presumably also Christian) and two Roman Catholic.[191]

It may not always be easy to determine whether a particular educational approach is 'religious' for the purposes of this legislation. Rudolf Steiner schools are a case in point. There are 35 Steiner schools in the UK, part of a worldwide movement of around 1,000 schools.[192] Although primarily an educational philosophy, Rudolf Steiner based his theories of child development on his anthroposophy, or 'spiritual science'. This is largely presupposed, rather than actively taught, but it is reflected in the religious education offered at Steiner schools, which focuses on spiritual sensitivity and striving.[193] Ultimately rooted in Christianity, it sees Christianity along with other religions as a phase through which humankind passes as our spiritual capacity evolves. Clearly, none of the Steiner schools have applied for a designated religious character; on the other hand a school which refused to appoint a teacher who objected on grounds of religious conscience to teaching anthroposophical views of human spirituality

---

[188] School Standards and Framework Act 1998, s 124A(2).   [189] Ibid, s 124A(3).

[190] There are now large numbers of Designation of Schools Having a Religious Character (Independent Schools) (England) Orders. See, most recently, SI 2009/510.

[191] Designation of Schools Having a Religious Character (Independent Schools) (Wales) Order 2009, SI 2009/1218.

[192] See website of the Steiner Waldorf Schools Fellowship, <http://www.steinerwaldorf.org.uk/>, accessed 15 October 2007.

[193] P Woods, M Ashley, and G Woods, *Steiner Schools in England*, DfES Research Report RR645, University of the West of England, 2005.

would seem to have discriminated on grounds of religion. It is not obvious that the influence of anthroposophy on Steiner schools is any less muted than the influence of Christianity on many traditional independent schools.

As indicated above, the pressure for formalizing the ethos of independent faith schools came first of all from the requirements of employment equality. However, this has been further strengthened by the Equality Act 2006. Once again, in general, it is unlawful for the proprietor of an independent school to discriminate on grounds of religion or belief. Along with other faith schools in the maintained sector, schools listed in the register of independent schools for England or for Wales and recorded as having a religious ethos are excepted from non-discrimination obligations in respect of admissions and access to benefits etc but not in respect of exclusions or detriments.[194] It should be noted that the judgment of the Supreme Court in the *JFS* case applies with equal relevance to the independent sector.[195] The exceptions do not extend to discrimination on grounds of race or ethnicity.

The regime established by the Equality Act 2006 sits awkwardly with that of the employment equality legislation and the regime for maintained schools. It is odd that the designation procedure was not adopted here also as a single point for the characterization of the school's ethos. It is also odd that the ultimate sanction of exclusion is not covered. Given that a teacher may be dismissed for failing to observe the religiously-determined conditions of his or her employment, it is strange that a school may not exclude pupils if they fail to observe the religiously-determined conditions of their education. From a human rights perspective, it may be more appropriate to draw a distinction here between State-maintained and independent schools. The Government is free to take the view that in schools funded by the public purse, a pupil once admitted should be accommodated. It is less clear that they have the right to impose that view on all schools. Of course, one could always fall back on the justification of indirect discrimination. If a pupil persistently fails to attend religious worship in an independent school which has made this a uniform condition of attendance, a court might still find this a proportionate way of preserving the ethos of the school and hence not in need of the exception in the first place.

These exceptions only apply in respect of non-discrimination on grounds of religion or belief. In principle, other forms of discrimination remain unlawful, and this may give rise to problems at the interface between religion and race, and religion and sexual ethics, as noted above.

In an early case under the Human Rights Act 1998, parents and teachers of a small independent Christian school sought to challenge the ban on corporal punishment in schools, which had finally been extended to independent schools by a backbench amendment to section 548 of the Education Act 1996.[196] The

---

[194] Equality Act 2006, s 50(1)(b).   [195] *R (E) v Governing Body of JFS* [2010] 2 WLR 153.
[196] *R (Williamson) v Secretary of State for Education and Employment* [2005] 2 AC 246.

House of Lords held that the restriction of parental religious rights was justified. However, the matter would have been better considered as an aspect of the diversity of educational provision and respect for parental convictions. It is hard to see why the boundary between lawful and unlawful chastisement (wherever one sets that) should be different for independent schools and the home environment. The argument that school punishment is 'institutional violence'[197] whereas parental punishment is not is, on the facts, rather implausible. In broader perspective, the *Williamson* case is one small part of the growing State regulation of the independent sector.

VI. Conclusion

The existence of faith schools has been controversial for as long as the State has funded education.[198] This controversy has been productive of considerable complexity within the education system as a whole as it engages not only with a diversity of beliefs, but with a range of views around the possibility of religious consensus and the degree to which 'religion' can be separated out from the rest of school life.

International human rights law makes clear that parents have a human right to establish faith schools themselves and a right of non-discriminatory access to such schools if they are provided within the State system. The schools themselves have rights as religious associations to defend their autonomy against disproportionate State intervention. The current Government has remained committed to such schools, defending them as offering valuable forms of partnership with civil society and the potential for higher degrees of social inclusion.[199] More cynically perhaps, faith schools are popular and are thought—whether for reasons associated with their faith or otherwise—to produce higher standards of attainment among their pupils.[200]

Within limits, faith schools represent a clear example of the law's commitment to religious autonomy and neutrality outside the narrow boundaries of worship and ritual. Religious communities are free to organize themselves in a way which enables parents to satisfy their obligations to secure suitable education for their children. That provision may be independent of State funding or within the State sector. However, the terms on which faith schools exist are deeply embedded in

---

[197] Ibid, per Lady Hale at para 86.

[198] Recent review of current arguments in John Flint, 'Faith-based schools: institutionalising parallel lives?' in Adam Dinham, Robert Furbey, and Vivien Lowndes, *Faith in the Public Realm: controversies, policies and practices* (Bristol: The Policy Press, 2009).

[199] DCSF, *Faith in the System: The role of schools with a religious character in England* (2007).

[200] This is a common perception. Demonstrating causation in this context is actually extremely difficult: see Stephen Gibbons and Olmo Silva, *Faith Primary Schools: better schools or better pupils*, DCSF research paper (2006).

the cultural and religious history of the United Kingdom. A principal feature of this is a clear distinction between 'religious' and 'secular' education. The commitment to protect individual conscience in respect of the former has continued, even though it has long left the pattern of nineteenth-century denominational instruction. Sensitivity here may now be excessive and hampering efforts to improve religious literacy. On the other hand, a belief in the neutrality of secular education also lives on, which greater religious diversity calls into question.

Although Government policy since 1997 has shifted noticeably in the direction of greater openness to religious minorities, the law has also been used to narrow down the significance that religion is allowed to have. From the perspectives of minority faiths, the law shapes the significance of religion in education in a more or less distorting fashion. This inevitably results in litigation and political pressure as the boundaries and contours of that shaping process are contested and renegotiated. Underlying these specific disputes are disagreements about the proper balance between education as a vehicle of cultural as well as political integration and as a means to sustain diverse faith and worldview groupings.[201]

---

[201] See also Neville Harris's conclusions in *op cit* n 1, 455–62.

9

Faith-Based Welfare

In historical perspective, the provision of community and welfare services in this country has been closely connected with religious belief and practice. Until recently, the relationship between organized religions and the State in this area of activity has been relatively uncontentious, at least in comparison with the provision of education. Provision has been separate and more or less complementary. However, shifts in the approach of Government to public service delivery have brought faith-based providers within the scope of 'third sector' regulation and started to subject them to alien values. The fundamental question is whether the new imposition of a uniform and non-religious ethos in all public welfare service delivery is legitimate.

With hindsight, it is possible to identify two significant moments of secularization in welfare provision. It may be that recent changes in public policy are evidence that the law is on the brink of a third such moment. For all their attempted inclusiveness, new forms of Government regulation may in fact prove exclusionary. This is brought to a point most graphically in the recent treatment of Roman Catholic agencies contracting to supply fostering and adoption services to local authorities. In order to understand the current potential for secularization and the role of law in that potential, it is helpful briefly to outline the first two.

The law relating to welfare and other public services covers a wide field of enquiry. Specific forms of welfare, such as housing law, or childcare outside the family, are subject to substantial and discrete bodies of regulation, which cannot be addressed here. Attention will be focused only on the question of the extent to which the law generally makes it possible or difficult for religious organizations to carry out social welfare services in a way that is integrated with their religious beliefs and practices.

I. Before the Welfare State

The dissolution of the monasteries by Henry VIII in the early 1530s removed at a stroke the central medieval institutions for the relief of the poor, the orphaned, the sick, and the aged. The giving of alms as a meritorious spiritual duty was also called into question by reformed Christian doctrine. Thus political insecurity and theological change combined to create a temporary hiatus in charitable giving and poor relief. The overall volume of giving dropped, and the proportion of that giving devoted to church purposes went into freefall.[1] New Tudor legislation to relieve the poor imposed an obligation on the parish, with funds to be raised by local rates and administered by local overseers.[2] A further source of welfare was secured by the creation of the Charity Commissioners in 1597.[3] This amounted to a public guarantee that endowments for local charitable purposes would be secured in perpetuity and prompted a wave of foundations, with charitable giving rising rapidly from 1600 onwards. These gifts had a strong emphasis on the relief of the poor and aged, on social rehabilitation such as prison relief, employment opportunities through the provision of loans, stock and apprenticeship schemes, the relief of the sick and the support of hospitals, marriage settlements, municipal works, and educational provision through scholarships and fellowships in schools and colleges and gifts to libraries.

As W K Jordan pointed out, this burst of charitable activity in the early years of the seventeenth century was a secularizing moment.[4] The absence of religious purposes from the preambles to the Elizabethan legislation has already been noted.[5] The purposes for which legacies were left had substantially shifted to the betterment of conditions in this life. Furthermore, the institutions which were created to advance those purposes were separate from the church and the now-disbanded religious orders. They were not secular in the sense of being atheistic, since they were regularly provided with chapels and chaplains. As often as not, their trustees were clergy, and Christian religion permeated all of their activities. Nor was the Poor Law secular in this sense either: two of the overseers were the churchwardens. But a point of structural differentiation had been reached which enabled a distinction to be drawn between religion and welfare.[6]

The potential for a growing divergence between the two is exemplified in some of the great eighteenth-century charitable foundations.[7] In 1739 Thomas Coram established the Foundling Hospital in London to care for and educate abandoned babies. This was nominally an Anglican foundation, but the governing body consisted of the great and the good without religious distinction. It had no clergy represented, apart from the Archbishops and the Bishop of London *ex officio*. Indeed, one of Coram's closest supporters was the Jewish banker Sampson Gideon.[8] Samuel Johnson caused a stir when he complained that the children

---

[1] See figures in the Appendix to W K Jordan, *Philanthropy in England 1480–1660* (London: George Allen & Unwin, 1959).

[2] Especially 14 Eliz, c 5 (1572); 39 Eliz C 3 (1597); see Jordan, *op cit* n 1, 91–108.

[3] 39 Eliz, c 10 (1597); 43 Eliz, c 4 (1601).   [4] *Op cit* n 1.   [5] Ch 5 above.

[6] On secularization as structural differentiation, see José Casanova, *Public Religions in the Modern World* (Chicago: University of Chicago Press, 1994), 20–5, 212.

[7] David Owen, *English Philanthropy 1660–1960* (Cambridge, Mass: Harvard University Press, 1964).

[8] For this reason the diversion *cy-près* of the estate in *Costa v De Pas* (1753) Amb 228, 27 ER 150, from a Jewish testator to the Foundling Hospital was not quite so outrageous as it seems at first sight.

were ignorant of the creed and the commandments.[9] Hospitals in the narrow modern sense of institutions for the care of the acute sick also show the imprint of mid-eighteenth century deism and 'rational religion'. Only two medieval hospitals had survived (St Thomas's and St Bartholomew's). Others were founded in a relatively short space of time during the first half of the eighteenth century, then through the voluntary hospital movement of the nineteenth century, with Poor Law hospitals only being established after 1867. Again, these were regularly provided with chaplains, but—and in distinction to many continental counterparts—they were not in any way religious foundations.

However, if 1600 was a secularizing moment, it was still compatible with a substantial revitalizing of religious expression. The Evangelical revival of the late eighteenth century, which had its most notable impact in the campaign to abolish slavery, also unleashed a torrent of voluntary activity.[10] This was rendered necessary not only by the social problems of rapidly expanding urbanization in the wake of the Industrial Revolution, but also by the harshness of the Poor Law, which was reformed in 1834 to create strong disincentives to claiming relief. Victorian philanthropy was no doubt motivated in part by reasons of social control, but it was also undeniably an expression of a desire to achieve a thoroughgoing social transformation, both spiritual and material. Kathleen Heasman estimated that three-quarters of all Victorian philanthropic institutions in the second half of the nineteenth century were run by Evangelical Christians.[11] The Earl of Shaftesbury, a figurehead for many of these institutions, exhausted himself and his estate in his support for hundreds of charitable endeavours, as well as in parliamentary agitation for asylum reform, public health, factory reform, and ragged schools. The origins of two great enduring social welfare institutions— the Salvation Army and Dr Barnado's—both lie in missions to the East End of London in 1865 and 1870 respectively.

The cause of voluntary effort was not limited to the evangelical social conscience. Starting with the influential foundation of Toynbee Hall in 1884, the University settlement movement sought to bring educated young men to live in poorer urban areas and had a pronounced High Anglican ethos. The Jewish Board of Guardians (from 1859) and allied bodies were highly effective in meeting the needs of the Jewish community, remarkably so as waves of immigration swelled their numbers towards the end of the century. Nor was religious effort limited to charity. Quakers such as Joseph Rowntree and George Cadbury successfully combined business acumen with social concern in the construction of model workers' villages.

---

[9] See R K McClure, 'Johnson's criticism of the Foundling Hospital and its consequences', *Review of English Studies* (New Series), vol XXVII, no 105 (1976).

[10] General accounts in Owen, *op cit* n 7; Maurice Bruce, *The Coming of the Welfare State*, 4th edn (London: B T Batsford, 1968); Geoffrey Finlayson, *Citizen, State and Social Welfare in Britain 1830–1990* (Oxford: Clarendon Press, 1994).

[11] K Heasman, *Evangelicals in Action* (London: Geoffrey Bles, 1962), 14.

The emphasis of Victorian social legislation was on improving the general conditions of society through the provision of public goods such as water, sanitation, paving, and lighting. People were encouraged towards self-help and mutual aid by the stick of grudging State provision in cases of extreme destitution and the carrot of charity for the deserving, but unlucky. This ethos received canonical expression in 1869 in the Goschen Minute of the Poor Law Commissioners, which called for a strict application of the principles of the 1834 Poor Law reform. In the same year the Charity Organization Society was founded to coordinate better the provision of charitable relief and to secure its more rational allocation. To do this it pioneered the use of case-workers to assess individual needs and recommend remedies.

A series of late nineteenth-century publications exposed the extent to which voluntary action was not adequately addressing social deprivation and brought about a gradual abandonment of these Victorian assumptions. *The Bitter Cry of Outcast London* (1883) by a Congregationalist clergyman was deliberately sensationalist, as was General William Booth's *In Darkest England* (1890). But their essential message was backed up by the monumental study of poverty in London by Charles Booth (1889–1903) and on a smaller scale by that of Seebohm Rowntree on conditions in York (1903). The change in public temper resulted not only in a Royal Commission on the Poor Law (1905–9) but also paved the way for the Liberal introductions of unemployment insurance, old age pensions, and national health insurance in 1908–11.

The Poor Law Commission was divided in its recommendations and produced two reports. That of the majority wished to maintain and reform the current model whereby a single Government agency provided relief for the 'less deserving' poor, leaving voluntary bodies to meet the needs of the 'more deserving'. The minority, dominated by Beatrice Webb, sought the introduction of a more thoroughgoing reform to ensure a national minimum of civilized life to all people through discrete public agencies for employment, health, education, and welfare. Voluntary bodies could provide a supplementary service beyond that guaranteed minimum.

The period between the First and Second World Wars saw the emergence of greater degrees of cooperation between the voluntary sector and the State.[12] The National Council of Social Services was founded in 1919 to coordinate action, and in its time distributed substantial sums of Government grant money to a wide range of voluntary social service agencies, including church societies. After the Local Government Act 1929 transferred most of the Poor Law functions to the larger local authorities there was considerable growth of State provision. This occurred most notably in the formation of public hospitals, which became the majority provider within a decade. In her review of charitable income to 1934, Constance Braithwaite estimated that charities were receiving between £35 and

---

[12] Henry A Mess (ed), *Voluntary Social Services since 1918* (London: Kegan Paul, 1948).

£50 million as opposed to a public social services income of £435 million.[13] But this masked considerable variation: charity might now be of little importance in general financial relief and in education, but it was still significant in hospitals, housing, welfare of disabled people, and institutions for children. In the case of the last example, religious organizations were of central importance.[14] But voluntary hospitals were rapidly becoming financially unsustainable, and local authorities were also increasingly providing services for disabled people. Although the Blind Persons Act 1920 had imposed a duty for the first time on local authorities to make arrangement for promoting the welfare of blind persons, this was done initially by funding voluntary agencies. Then in 1935 London County Council, for example, took the decision to operate the services themselves for reasons of efficiency, thus reducing their annual grants by 70 per cent.

In this way distinctive regimes of law and regulation emerged for different fields of welfare, some strongly dominated by the State, others largely a matter of voluntary, and often religiously-influenced, provision, still others subject to various forms of collaboration.[15] Views might differ on who was best placed to meet social need, or the relative roles of State and private provision, but in general terms, resources were too slender to turn the provision of welfare services into a competition between rivals.

II. Faith-Based Charity in the Welfare State

The culmination of the Welfare State after the Second World War was a second potentially secularizing moment. At the time of its creation, it was unknown whether the Welfare State would completely supplant voluntary endeavour. If Beveridge still saw a place for it, Richard Crossman, for example, hoped that the legislation of 1948 would sound the death-knell to 'churchly bourgeois attitudes'.[16] In the 1950s it seemed as if the State might indeed triumph. In many cases voluntary agencies were grateful to be relieved of historic financial obligations to the poor. Stagnating income levels, uncertainty about their role, and some hostility from statutory authorities combined to ensure that they tended to 'mark time'.[17]

[13] Constance Braithwaite, *The Voluntary Citizen* (London: Methuen, 1938).

[14] In 1944 the six members of the Associated Council of Children's Homes were responsible for 35,182 children. The six members were Dr Barnado's, the Church of England Waifs and Strays, the National Children's Home (Methodist), the Catholic Child Welfare Council, the Jewish Board of Guardians, and the Shaftesbury Homes. See Violet Creech-Jones, 'The Work of Voluntary Social Services among Children before School-Leaving Age' in Henry A Mess, *Voluntary Social Services since 1918* (London: Kegan Paul, 1948).

[15] For a detailed account of the development of regulation in housing law, see Morag McDermont, *Governing, Independence and Expertise: the business of housing associations* (Oxford: Hart Publishing, 2010).

[16] The experience of ministerial office later caused him to change his mind about the voluntary sector. Finlayson, *op cit* n 10, 249–50.

[17] Wolfenden Committee, *The Future of Voluntary Organisations* (London: Croom Helm, 1978), 20.

However, a number of factors resulted in their revival from the 1960s. The provision of personal social services (mainly the support and protection of children, physically and mentally disabled people, and the elderly) was from the start relatively poorly funded and locally disorganized until the recommendations of the Seebohm Committee resulted in integrated social services departments within local authorities from 1971. Education aside, those components of the Welfare State which were relatively well developed and funded—full employment and unemployment support, and universal healthcare—were not areas in which a faith-based ethos was particularly apparent. On the contrary, it was precisely in the personal social services, and to a lesser extent in the provision of social housing, that faith-based charities were most likely to be operating. Although the State was now the major provider, it could never completely dispense with the assistance of voluntary bodies.[18]

Furthermore, charities began to redirect their activities in ways complementary to existing State provision, for example in the direction of advocacy on behalf of minority groups, advice and counselling, specialist services, and in areas of concern not covered by the State such as international relief and the environment.[19] This change of direction was assisted by a growing political concern to achieve higher levels of civic participation and increased flexibility resulting from the reform of charity law. Finally, and in spite of a brief window of substantially increased resource from 1971–6, the economic downturn of the late 70s combined with the ageing population and rising expectations ensured that demand for such services always outstripped supply.

Thus when the Wolfenden Committee came to consider the place of the voluntary sector in the Welfare State it could conclude that it was an essential component in a model of 'welfare pluralism', which by the 70s could command cross-party support.[20] This model was characterized by a partnership between four sectors: informal care and support from family and friends, State support, commercial provision, and voluntary effort. It found formal expression in the establishment of the Voluntary Service Unit in the Home Office in 1973 as well as in a wide range of grants and agency agreements. At the same time, the Wolfenden Committee noted that the revival of voluntary effort had been accompanied by a process of secularization. While few voluntary organizations had died, among the ones that had, those concerned with moral welfare and having an explicit religious allegiance were more numerous.[21] The evidence the Committee heard showed that although the motivation of individuals within large bodies such as the Church of England Children's Society and Dr Barnado's might remain Christian and be valued as such, the expression of that faith had

---

[18] Rodney Lowe, *The Welfare State in Britain*, 3rd edn (London: Palgrave Macmillan 2005), ch 10.

[19] Maria Brenton, *The Voluntary Sector in British Social Services* (Harlow: Longman, 1985), ch 3; see eg Child Poverty Action Group (1965) and the emergence of Shelter (1966), the latter recounted in McDermont, *op cit* n 15, ch 7.

[20] Wolfenden Committee, *op cit* n 17. See also the wide-ranging discussion in Brenton, *op cit* n 19.

[21] Wolfenden Committee, *op cit* n 17, 185.

become more 'secular and materialist' and less inspired by the 'desire to rescue or evangelise'.[22] In short, the object of spiritual transformation which was so prominent in Victorian philanthropy, and which had lingered on into the first half of the twentieth century had been dropped, or at least transmuted into more generic spiritual values not specific to the religion in question.[23]

Internal secularization has been accompanied by a certain degree of pressure exerted by local authorities. Even if the evidence is only anecdotal, there is clearly a widespread sense that it is inappropriate to use public money to aid a community project that has an evangelistic or proselytizing dimension. There is also a growing insistence that organizations delivering public services or receiving grants comply with equal opportunity policies designed for public bodies.[24] This has led on occasion to the withdrawal of funding or pressure to conform to secular norms.[25]

The Conservative administrations from 1979–97 were committed to reducing State expenditure and promoting voluntary support. This redirected resources, but ironically had little practical impact on actual spending levels.[26] Indeed, the clarification that central Government would fund through social security the cost of private residential accommodation for the elderly with limited resources resulted in a cost increase of more than 100 times between 1979 and 1985, stimulating in the process a new market in nursing homes, both profit- and non-profit-making. When the NHS and Community Care Act 1990 was finally implemented in 1993 it required a minimum of 85 per cent of local authority expenditure on personal social services to be 'contracted out'. Thus internal and external markets were fostered, which created new opportunities—and a new discipline—for voluntary organizations. Indeed, in some areas the relationship between State and voluntary effort was reversed, with the latter becoming once again the principal provider, albeit under greater degrees of State oversight.[27] Paradoxically, the State became institutionally smaller, but ideologically more pervasive.

---

[22] Finlayson, *op cit* n 10, 330–2.

[23] This is made an explicit virtue in the case of the Mildmay Mission Hospital, which after losing its independence on the formation of the NHS, regained it in 1985 after being closed three years earlier: see text at <http://www.mildmay.org/history.aspx>, accessed 2 October 2009.

[24] See Robert Whelan, *The Corrosion of Charity* (Institute of Economic Affairs, 1996), 68–72, for an account of pressures on the Mayflower Centre, Canning Town. Another anecdote recalls the withdrawal of funding from a youth club because hymns were sung.

[25] This is just one facet of a wider concern about the impact of agency agreements on voluntary bodies. See Jane Lewis, 'What does Contracting do to Voluntary Agencies?' in David Billis and Margaret Harris (eds), *Voluntary Agencies: Challenges of Organisation and Management* (London: Macmillan, 1996).

[26] Figures in Maria Evandrou *et al*, *The State of Welfare: the economics of social spending*, 2nd edn (Oxford: Oxford University Press, 1998), ch 6.

[27] Marilyn Taylor, 'Voluntary Action and the State' in David Gladstone (ed), *British Social Welfare: past, present and future* (London: UCL Press, 1996); Lowe, *op cit* n 18, chs 12–13.

The 'third way' of New Labour seeks a partnership between Government and civil society in addressing a wide range of social need.[28] From the beginning of its time in office it has been open to cooperation with faith communities, and in that sense, the current policy environment is more congenial to faith-based community and welfare providers than at any time in the past century. The language has shifted 'from contract to compact' as the Government seeks 'shared values' in public service delivery on the basis of 'mutual respect'.[29] The extension of Gift Aid taxation relief to all charitable donations in 2000 and the creation of an Office of the Third Sector within the Cabinet Office in May 2006 are tangible expressions of this. This spirit of partnership has not been restricted to 'secular' organizations. Recent Government publications stress the importance of the 'faith sector' as a part of civil society. In 2008 *Face to Face and Side by Side: a framework for partnership in our multi faith society* was published.[30] Much of this is focused on promoting social cohesion and dialogue, and is considered at greater length in the next chapter. However, one of its four 'building blocks' is 'structures and processes which support dialogue and social action'.[31] And one of the practical steps to be taken by Government in this area includes 'working with faith communities, the Local Government Association and Charity Commission to produce a standardised version of a charter for excellence in public service delivery by faith communities'.[32] The intention was to prevent organizations from using public funding to proselytize or engage in other activities considered inappropriate for the State, but it would seem now to have been quietly dropped.[33]

A number of recent studies highlight the size and diversity of faith-based provision. An NCVO study in 2007 estimated the resources of faith-based charities at £4.6 billion, but spread very unevenly.[34] In many rural areas, the church continues to be a major focus of community life.[35] As public services are cut back for reasons of economy, in some cases churches have filled the gap. It is sometimes argued that they could do even more. In more diverse urban contexts, the studies highlight the enormous contribution made to civil society by faith-based organizations, but also the difficulties many faith-based organizations have both in preserving their distinctiveness in an homogenizing policy environment, and

---

[28] Anthony Giddens, *The Third Way: the renewal of social democracy* (Cambridge: Polity Press, 1998).

[29] Developments in the discourse are well summarized in Emma Carmel and Jenny Harlock, 'Instituting the "third sector" as a governable terrain: partnership, procurement and performance in the UK' (2008) 36(2) Policy and Politics 155.

[30] DCLG, *Face to Face and Side by Side: a framework for partnership in our multi faith society* (July 2008).　　　　　　　　　　　　　　　　　　　　　　　　　　[31] Ibid, 9.

[32] Ibid, 11.

[33] In the absence of an official announcement, the matter was transmitted through the British Humanist Association: *BHA News*, 27 July 2009.

[34] Véronique Jochum, Belinda Pratten, and Karl Wilding (eds), *Faith and Voluntary Action: an overview of current evidence and debates* (London: NCVO, 2007), 16.

[35] Jemma Grieve, Véronique Jochum, Belinda Pratten, and Claire Steel, *Faith in the Community: the contribution of faith-based organisations to rural voluntary action* (London: NCVO, 2007).

in addressing perceptions of distinctiveness that are not actually real.[36] Faith-based organizations are still particularly active in child welfare, personal care, informal clubs and community action, and overseas aid.[37] Yet public authorities are often suspicious, or at least cautious, before collaborating with them. It is easy to ground such suspicion in new legal obligations regulating the religious aspects of public life, and it is to the role of law in creating a difficult environment for faith-based welfare organizations that we now turn.

III. 'Equality and Diversity' as a Third Secularizing Moment?

It is possible that recent legislation to secure equality and diversity may prove to be a third secularizing moment in the development of welfare services. While it is clear that the State in its most central manifestations should not discriminate on grounds of religion or belief, it is equally clear that a religious body such as a church may be religiously distinctive, setting faith-specific tests for membership, office-holding, and standards of behaviour. What is not clear is the boundary between these two extremes. As the last chapter has shown, in the area of over-lap represented by education, the law has clearly recognized that religions have a large stake in the domain covered by the State, but this is much less clear in other areas of welfare. Applying norms of non-discrimination to a faith-based welfare provider may (on one approach) be required by a commitment to equality but may (on another) be destructive of the very diversity equality-norms are supposed to protect.

1. Private welfare

Faith-based welfare provision may be purely private, in the sense that it is funded by voluntary contributions in money or kind and operates independently of any public service. A youth club or care home may well take this form. The common law has long reflected the presumption that eleemosynary institutions (that is, those for the relief of the aged, impotent, and poor) are not specific to any religion. The law draws a threefold distinction between such objects and educational and religious objects.[38] In the case of eleemosynary institutions, the presumption of religious neutrality is very strong indeed. There are to be no religious restrictions on trustees or beneficiaries unless the founder has expressly declared there to

---

[36] Jochum *et al*, *op cit* n 34, 49–51, 56.

[37] Four of the 13 members of the Disasters Emergency Committee, which coordinates responses to major international aid requirements have a religious basis (Christian Aid, Tearfund, CAFOD, and Islamic Relief). Total income (2008) of £238m, about 20 per cent of DEC members' income, although some of them (eg Help the Aged and Save the Children) have a much wider remit. Source: *CaritasData*.

[38] *AG v Calvert* (1857) 23 Beav 248, 53 ER 97; *AG v Clifton* (1863) 32 Beav 596, 55 ER 234.

be such restrictions in the deeds.[39] In the case of religious trusts, by contrast, evidence may be heard to determine the founder's religion even if the deed is silent; trustees and beneficiaries are restricted accordingly.[40] Educational charities fall between the two. Where the school has a religious foundation, trustees must be appointed from within the relevant religion, but it is to be presumed that all may benefit from the education offered, even if religious education is to be provided in accordance with the tenets of the religion.[41] The Endowed Schools Act 1869 and subsequent legislation started the process of widening access to other religions more generally by restricting the evidence that could be brought to show that a school was truly denominational.[42]

Likewise, the law assumes that eleemosynary charities are institutions independent of any church body with which they might have informal connections. This is reflected in basic legal assumptions such as the duties of trustees not to fetter their discretion, but to act as fiduciaries in the best interests of the institution for which they are responsible, as well as in the separate legal personality or quasi-personality of unincorporated associations. Although it is possible to create links between a charity and a church or religious body, not least by careful specification of the objects and in the persons of the trustees, such as a bishop *ex officio*, tensions can still arise between the way in which a religion conceives of its internal relationships of authority and the way in which the law constructs those relationships. Thus where the trustees or governors of a Roman Catholic charity disagree with the church hierarchy on some matter of policy, it is the trustees whose view prevails in English law, even if the bishop has ultimate authority in canon law.[43]

When local Government was split away from church responsibility towards the end of the nineteenth century, local ecclesiastical charities were given a distinctive definition in legislation to distinguish them from the new secular rural parish councils.[44] Although the process of separating church and local Government is virtually complete, 'ecclesiastical charities' are still subject to special legal provision, being immune from local authority review and powers to approve schemes of consolidation otherwise available in respect of parochial charities.[45] Ecclesiastical charities, for these purposes, are defined very broadly to include endowments held for any spiritual purpose which is a legal purpose; for the benefit of any spiritual person or ecclesiastical officer as such; for use, if a building, as a church, chapel, mission room, or Sunday school, or otherwise by any particular church or denomination; for the maintenance, repair, or

---

[39] *AG v St. John's Hospital, Bath* (1876) 2 Ch D 554.   [40] See Ch 3 above.
[41] *Re Stafford Charities* (1857) 25 Beav 28, 53 ER 546; *Re Burnham National Schools* (1875) LR 17 Eq 241.   [42] See *Re St Leonards Parochial Schools* (1884) 10 App Cas 304.
[43] *R v Westminster Roman Catholic Diocese Trustee, ex parte Andrews* [1990] COD 25; discussion in Judith Hill, 'Roman Catholic religious orders as charities' (1997) 5 CL & PR 1. See also Helen Costigane, 'Catholic Adoption Agencies and "Gay Adopters"' [2008] Law & Justice 98.
[44] Local Government Act 1894, s 75(2).   [45] Charities Act 1993, ss 77, 79.

improvement of any such building as aforesaid, or for the maintenance of divine service therein; or otherwise for the benefit of any particular church or denomination, or of any members thereof as such.[46] Once again, one sees the assumption at work that church and some educational charities are likely to be religious in orientation, other public purposes are not.

Although the exceptions are not as widely drafted as they are for faith schools, recent equalities legislation has by and large left open the possibility for non-profit-making faith-based welfare organizations to exist and operate. The Equality Act 2006 creates an exception for organizations, the purpose of which is to 'enable persons of a religion or belief to receive any benefit, or engage in any activity, within the framework of that religion or belief'.[47] Restrictions on membership, participation in activities, access to goods, facilities and services, or the use of premises, may be justified by reason of or on grounds of the purpose of the organization or to avoid causing offence on grounds of the religion or belief to which the organization relates to persons of that religion or belief.[48] This exception does not apply if the sole or main purpose of the organization is commercial.[49] There is a similar exception for benefits restricted to persons of a religion or belief under the terms of a charitable instrument.[50] Government caution about interfering even with tenuously religious charities is exemplified by section 60 of the Act. This states that it is not unlawful for a charity to require members, or persons wishing to become members, to make a statement which asserts or implies membership or acceptance of a religion or belief, so long as this requirement was imposed before 18 May 2005 and has been continuously applied since. The parliamentary debates make clear that the Government had in mind organizations such as the Scouts, which have a residual faith ethos and which require members in the broad sense to refer to God in their pledge.[51]

One suspects that the problem of faith-restricted benefits may be limited to cases such as care homes for the elderly of a particular religious denomination and grants for widows and orphans of former ministers of religion. Many faith-based welfare organizations will be prepared to distribute their benefits without distinction, but wish to preserve a religious ethos or context for that work. In practice, it is therefore the Employment Equality Regulations which are more likely to present difficulties. As has already been shown, as well as a general exception for genuine and determining occupational requirements, the Regulations include a marginally broader exception for employers with an ethos based on religion or belief.[52] If, having regard to the ethos and the nature or context of the employment it is proportionate to apply a genuine (but not necessarily determining)

---

[46] Charities Act 1993, s 96(1). This is a rare legislative use of 'ecclesiastical' to refer (if only potentially) to non-Anglican charities.   [47] Equality Act 2006, s 57(1)(d).
    [48] s 57(3) and (5).   [49] s 57(2).   [50] s 58(1).
    [51] Hansard HC 6 Dec 2005, cols 219–224. The section thus does not prevent new incorporated faith-based charities from requiring their guarantors ('members' in the company law sense) from complying with a religious test.   [52] See Ch 4 above.

requirement relating to religion or belief, the employer may do so. This would seem to leave considerable discretion on the part of employers to design job specifications in ways which make it clear that the ethos is to have some expression in the work of the individual.

Private welfare is subject to the relevant general law of employment, charity, and company law as well as any specific regulatory regime for activities of that nature. In the case of voluntary social housing, the framework of charity law proved unacceptably restrictive and was replaced by special legal provision in the Housing Act 1974.[53] The gradually increasing body of law to secure health and safety and protection of the vulnerable undoubtedly creates costs and disincentives which are hard for voluntary bodies to comply with, and one can debate the appropriate balance between promoting socially advantageous activities of this nature and securing the well-being of participants. But these forms of regulation are not typically faith-specific and have hitherto not generally raised problems of a conflict between legal and religious requirements.

2. Publicly-funded welfare

Matters become more complex as faith-based welfare providers start to receive public funding. This can cover a spectrum of forms, from small one-off grants for a community project, through to open-ended contracts for substantial sums of money to provide public services. At the most extreme, major providers can become semi-autonomous branches of the Welfare State. As they come into closer proximity to the State, so questions about their distinctive religious ethos become more pressing. Two questions arise:

(1) To what extent are Governmental commissioning bodies under legal obligations not to have regard to the distinctive faith ethos of the faith-based provider, or not to create pressures on them to change in this respect?

(2) To what extent are faith-based providers under obligations to start looking more like a secular Governmental service provider, complying with norms of religious neutrality?

The starting-point is that Governmental contracting power is remarkably unfettered. It has been likened to a prerogative power, implying a high degree of discretion and low levels of political or legal accountability.[54] This leaves lots of room for local policy and even prejudice. During the 1970s and 80s some local authorities used this discretion to enforce anti-apartheid policies in their contracts. These were ultimately struck down by the courts on general public law grounds of fairness,[55] and a general statutory prohibition was enacted preventing the use

---

[53] McDermont, *op cit* n 15, ch 3.
[54] T Daintith, 'Regulation by Contract' (1979) 32 CLP 41.
[55] *Wheeler v Leicester City Council* [1985] AC 1054; *R v Lewisham Borough Council, ex parte Shell* [1988] 1 All ER 938.

of non-commercial criteria in contracting decisions.[56] This prohibition has now been loosened,[57] and although some courts have still been willing on occasion to interfere on general public law grounds with contracting decisions,[58] the general position would appear to be that the public law context is not to give the service-provider a procedural or substantive advantage. Thus in the *Supportways* case, a company whose contract to supply housing-related services to vulnerable people had been terminated on the basis of what it considered to be a flawed assessment of cost-effectiveness failed in its attempt to get the decision judicially reviewed.[59] In the context of public services, contract is both a tool of regulation and subject to regimes of audit and accountability.[60] However, in respect of the specifically religious dimensions of public service provision, 'freedom of contract' has until recently been the governing paradigm.

Onto this foundation of contractual freedom has now been grafted both the Human Rights Act 1998 and new public sector duties to respect and promote equality. As to the former, it is clear that a 'core' public authority is bound to respect Convention rights in all its activities—including the use of its contracting power.[61] As to the latter, in general terms public authorities may not discriminate on grounds of religion or belief.[62] This is subject to a series of exceptions in relation to legislation and judicial functions, and in faith-sensitive aspects of immigration and education.[63] It also does not apply to the power to do any act to promote the economic, social, or environmental well-being of an area.[64] This latter exception permits, for example, the positive favouring of minority religious community groups. But outside these areas, obligations to avoid direct and indirect discrimination on grounds of religion or belief apply. By contrast, the public sector duty positively to promote equality applies as yet only in respect of disability, race, and sex discrimination, although there are plans to extend it to other grounds, including religion or belief, as well.[65]

As far as the faith-based provider is concerned, the Human Rights Act 1998 left the question of direct effect somewhat obscure. Section 6 applies Convention rights to persons exercising functions of a public nature in respect of acts which are not private.[66] However, the courts have so far taken a narrow approach to its extent in the context of private rights. A parochial church council of the Church of England is not a 'core' public body and is not exercising a public function in

---

[56] Local Government Act 1988, s 7.

[57] Local Government Best Value (Exclusion of Non-commercial Considerations) Order 2001, SI 2001/909.   [58] eg *R v Legal Aid Board, ex parte Donn & Co* [1996] 3 All ER 1.

[59] *Hampshire County Council v Supportways Community Services Ltd* [2006] EWCA Civ 1035.

[60] See Carol Harlow and Richard Rawlings, *Law and Administration* 3rd edn (Cambridge: Cambridge University Press, 2009), esp ch 8.   [61] Human Rights Act 1998, s 6(1).

[62] Equality Act 2006, s 52(1).   [63] s 52(3) and (4).

[64] Local Government Act 2000, s 2.   [65] See 282–4 below.

[66] Human Rights Act 1998, s 6(3)(b) and (5).

enforcing a liability for chancel repairs.[67] Care homes providing services under contract with a public authority are not bound.[68] This judicial unwillingness to extend human rights obligations to private bodies acting under public contract is controversial, but is perhaps understandable in the light of the European Convention's binary distinction between public and private. State entities cannot be 'victims'. Since an established church can undoubtedly be a victim of a breach of its rights by the State, it must fall on the private side of the line. Where then is a faith-based welfare provider to be located? The Convention only awkwardly accommodates the 'both-and' implicit in religiously plural provision.[69]

Statute immediately reversed the recent decision concerning care homes. A person who provides accommodation together with nursing or personal care in a care home under arrangements made under statute is to be taken as exercising functions of a public nature.[70] More generally, though, the position stands, which is that faith-based welfare organizations are not constrained in their ethos and activities by virtue of their receipt of public funds, except to the extent that they are constrained by the terms of any contract they enter into with a public funding body.[71] However, the terms of that contract are themselves potentially subject to review on grounds of a breach of human rights or obligations of non-discrimination.

As yet, this leaves the question of substance unanswered. Do Convention rights or equality obligations make any difference? It is at least arguable that religious bodies have a Convention right to engage in charitable and humanitarian work.[72] Although no right to State funding flows from this, a right not to be discriminated against by the State within the ambit of this right certainly does. In this sense, human rights obligations and equality obligations coalesce. While it is clear that the prejudiced refusal to consider a faith-based provider for a public contract would be unlawful as directly discriminatory, it is much less clear that general rules impacting adversely on such bodies will in practice be challengeable. This turns on whether the constraints inherent in the terms of the contract are legitimate and proportionate.

At this point, a more careful consideration of proportionality would stand faith-based providers in good stead. A lot turns on the specification of the aim which might legitimate problematic contractual terms. If the aim is to ensure

---

[67] *Aston Cantlow and Wilmcote with Billesley Parochial Church Council v Wallbank* [2004] 1 AC 546.

[68] *R (Heather) v Leonard Cheshire Foundation* [2002] 2 All ER 936; *YL v Birmingham City Council* [2008] 1 AC 95.

[69] This is most obvious in relation to education. Since education is a public function, the State is liable for acts of private schools (*Costello-Roberts v UK* (1995) 19 EHRR 112), but private schools may be victims of a breach of rights by the State (*Verein Gemeinsam Lernen v Austria* (1995) 20 EHRR CD 78). See 247 above.   [70] Health and Social Care Act 2008, s 145.

[71] The Government resisted the opportunity to apply more onerous equality obligations to faith-based welfare providers acting under public contract during the course of the passage of the Equality Bill. See Hansard HC 6 Dec 2005, cols 218–219.

[72] There is no case on the point, but see discussion at 66 above.

that certain people receive certain benefits, then the first question should be whether the use of a faith-based provider creates obstacles for individuals seeking to access the service. It may have no impact at all. If it does create obstacles to access, the question should really be about the position of that provider in the 'market'—whether it dominates or even has a monopoly. For if there is equally accessible alternative provision, it is not necessary to exclude the faith-based provider from meeting part of the need. The question is essentially a pragmatic one: how best may people in need receive the benefits of the welfare service in question.

However, there are signs that some judges are willing to 'ideologize' the aim or object of the public authority's policy.[73] If the aim is re-characterized as one of ensuring that all publicly-funded welfare service provision is carried out in an ethos of religious neutrality or inclusivity, then of course contracting with distinctively faith-based providers becomes problematic. The very difficulty which gives rise to the *prima facie* breach of equality rights (the onerous policy or norm) also shows that the State must win. This brings us close to the fundamental question of this chapter, which is whether the imposition of ideological uniformity in the sphere of public welfare services is actually a legitimate and proportionate State aim. Clearly it would not be in the case of education; whether it would be so in welfare provision more broadly is less clear.

3. Emerging constraints on faith-based provision

Faith-based providers are under increasing constraints from two other related perspectives. The first is associated with the uncertainty surrounding the meaning and application of any new public sector equality duty; the second comes from the boundaries between religion or belief and other protected characteristics.

The public sector equality duty currently applies only in respect of sex, race, and disability discrimination.[74] The legislation uses slightly different terminology and different approaches to the definition of the public sector. The Equality Act 2010 harmonizes this legislation and extends it to all protected characteristics. Public authorities must have due regard to the need to eliminate discrimination, harassment, victimization and other prohibited conduct; advance equality of opportunity between those who share a relevant protected characteristic and those who do not; and foster good relations between the same two groups.[75] Having due regard includes removing or minimizing disadvantages,

---

[73] See, by analogy, *R (Williamson) v Secretary of State for Education and Employment* [2005] 2 AC 246 per Lady Hale; *R (Begum) v Denbigh High School Governors* [2007] 1 AC 100 per Lady Hale; *Islington LBC v Ladele* [2009] ICR 387 per Elias J.

[74] Sex Discrimination Act 1975, ss 76A–76C; Race Relations Act 1976, s 71(1); Disability Discrimination Act 1995, ss 49A–49D.

[75] Equality Act 2010, s 149(1).

meeting special needs, encouraging participation where rates are low, tackling prejudice, and promoting understanding.[76]

The public sector equality duty applies to public authorities and bodies exercising public functions.[77] The definition of the latter is connected to that in the Human Rights Act 1998, and thus does not itself extend to contracted bodies for as long as the courts maintain their current restrictive interpretation. The position of the Government is not entirely clear, in that although the decision of the House of Lords in *YL* has been publicly regretted,[78] and was reversed in that specific context, it has also been made clear that the decision not to require contracted bodies to comply with public sector equality duties more generally is deliberate.[79]

However, if this point is not entirely clear, there is considerable obscurity about what a public sector equality duty in respect of religion or belief actually means in practice.[80] In its response to the consultation exercise, the Government sought to allay widespread concerns. It suggested that the duty to advance equality of opportunity would not mean, for example, 'that the authority would have to provide a traditional festive meal to cater for every religious festival; it could just provide a traditional Christmas dinner on 25 December'.[81] But it also recognized the 'risk of unintended consequences' and was prepared to consider dropping the requirement to advance equality of opportunity in respect of religion or belief.[82]

The matter can be put quite starkly by considering whether a publicly funded faith school is in potential breach of the new duty by maintaining its distinctive religious ethos in accordance with the provisions of the School Standards and Framework Act 1998. Clearly there is little difficulty with the requirements to eliminate unlawful discrimination or to foster good relations, but superficially it is hard to see how preferential admissions criteria 'remove or minimise disadvantages' relating to religion or belief. One would have to argue that the very distinctiveness of the school is what advances equality. The difficulty is that in the final analysis, faith-specific school provision is not primarily, or only, about equality in the public sector sense. It is rather a recognition of parental freedom of religion, belief, and conscience in the semi-public sphere of education. 'Diversity' in this sense is rooted not only in equality rights but also in liberty rights.

The same arguments apply by analogy to faith-based welfare. 'Welfare pluralism' respects the distinctive religious motivation and expression of welfare services, particularly the personal welfare services. This is not merely a pragmatic response to diversity, but a recognition that the religious dimensions of welfare

---

[76] ss 149(3)–(5).   [77] s 149(2).

[78] See Joint Committee of Human Rights, 23rd Report (17 June 2008), Appendices 6–8.

[79] See n 57 above; Hansard HC 13 Jan 2009, col 572W.

[80] See also Anthony Lester and Paola Uccellari, 'Extending the equality duty to religion, conscience and belief: Proceed with caution' [2008] EHRLR 567.

[81] HM Government, *The Equality Bill—Government response to the consultation*, Cm 7454 (July 2008), para 2.60.   [82] Ibid.

can be very significant in promoting involvement and shaping delivery. In terms of strict law, the current Equality Bill makes little difference to the position of faith-based welfare providers. However, indirectly, the new public sector equality duty may further strengthen simplistic understandings of the 'culture of equality' as a homogeneous ethic applicable to all human relations.[83] Informal pressures created by the unthinking application of non-discrimination norms in the processes of grant-application and public service contracting can easily go beyond the requirements of the law and assume that norms of non-discrimination are identical for both Government and faith-based providers. It is easy to assume that if a public authority should not be distinctive on religious grounds, neither should the public service-provider. The law does not require this, and indeed, as has been shown, a case can be made that at present, a Governmental body behaving like this would itself be discriminating unlawfully.

The second source of constraint comes from legal requirements which from the perspective of the faith-based organization are faith-specific, but which from the perspective of the law are categorized differently. The difficulties of the Roman Catholic adoption agencies are a case in point. In brief, these agencies wished to continue a policy of refusing to consider same-sex couples as potential adoptive parents. This is ultimately rooted in an ethical position which maintains the inappropriateness of sexual relationships outside marriage. In many ways their difficulties parallel that of the JFS and other orthodox Jewish schools in respect of race discrimination in their admissions arrangements,[84] and the Church of Scotland in respect of alleged sex discrimination in clergy discipline.[85] In each case, the exceptions made for religion or belief discrimination do not apply. The plight of the Roman Catholic adoption agencies provides a case-study of the developments this chapter has been outlining.

IV. Roman Catholic Adoption Agencies under the New Secularism

While the prohibition of unlawful discrimination on grounds of religion or belief is contained in primary legislation, the equivalent body of rules in respect of sexual orientation was created under delegated powers.[86] The regulations contain a range of exceptions, including those for organizations relating to religion or belief (regulation 14), for adoption and fostering agencies (regulation 15), and for certain charities (regulation 18). During the passage of the regulations, a number

---

[83] See Government Equalities Office, *Framework for a Fairer Future—The Equality Bill*, Cm 7431 (June 2008), 5.   [84] See Ch 8 above.

[85] See Ch 4 above.

[86] Equality Act 2006, s 81(1), and Equality Act (Sexual Orientation) Regulations 2007, SI 2007/1263.

of Catholic adoption agencies realized that they might soon be acting unlawfully if they restricted their services to married couples or those in similarly stable heterosexual relationships. However, lobbying only produced a time-limited reprieve until 31 December 2008.[87] At least, that is what the Government intended to achieve, but the terms in which it did so make the matter far from clear.

Two of the agencies sought to change their charitable objects to bring themselves within the terms of the exception for charities instead. This was refused by the Charity Commission, and they appealed to the Charity Tribunal.[88] After an adverse preliminary ruling, the charity which continued proceedings was unable to propose objects acceptable both to itself and the Tribunal.[89] In the course of its rulings, the Tribunal inevitably formed a view of the relationship between the various exceptions. It is this relationship which is problematic.

Regulation 14 applies to an organization the purpose of which is to practise, advance, or teach the practice or principles of a religion or belief, or to enable persons of a religion or belief to receive any benefit or to engage in any activity within the framework of that religion or belief.[90] It is not unlawful to restrict membership, participation, or the provision of goods, facilities or services, or to restrict the use or disposal of premises on grounds of sexual orientation so long as the restriction is necessary to comply with the doctrine of the organization or to avoid conflict with the strongly held religious convictions of a significant number of the religion's followers.[91] There are additional exceptions for ministers of religion.[92] The exception does not apply to commercial organizations, to schools and education authorities, to the provision of goods, facilities or services to the public or a section of the public, or to the exercise of public functions on behalf of a public authority under the terms of a contract for provision of that kind.[93]

The contrast with section 57 Equality Act 2006, which contains the equivalent exceptions for religion or belief discrimination is marked. That section does not remove educational establishments, public supply, and public functions from its scope, and restrictions only have to be in place 'by reason of or on grounds of' the purpose of the organization or 'to avoid causing offence' on grounds of religion or belief.[94] Thus while there is clear scope for *religious* pluralism in education and welfare services, there is no scope for *sexual-ethical* pluralism. Or rather, what it means to be religious is partly defined by excluding sexual ethics from its scope. Catholic adoption agencies can be Catholic in some sense of the word, but they cannot act on the basis of a Catholic sexual ethic.

Regulation 18 provides that it is not unlawful for a person to provide benefits only to persons of a particular sexual orientation if he acts in pursuance of a charitable

[87] Reg 15(2).
[88] *Father Hudson's Society and Catholic Care (Diocese of Leeds) v Charity Commission for England and Wales*, preliminary ruling 13 March 2009.
[89] *Catholic Care (Diocese of Leeds) v Charity Commission for England and Wales*, 1 June 2009.
[90] Reg 14(1).   [91] Regs 14(3) and (5).   [92] Regs 14(4) and (6).
[93] Regs 14(2) and (8).   [94] Equality Act 2006, s 57(5).

instrument, and the restriction is imposed by reason of or on the grounds of the provisions of the charitable instrument.[95] Counsel for the Equality and Human Rights Commission, which intervened in the proceedings before the Charity Tribunal, argued for a very narrow 'special needs' interpretation of this regulation: the provision was only designed to render lawful charities for the promotion of minority orientations. This is supported by the Explanatory Note to the legislation. The Charity Commission argued for a slightly wider position: 'benefits' should be read by reference to the public benefit by virtue of which an organization is charitable. Since the object of the Catholic societies in question was to benefit children, not potential adoptive parents, distinguishing between parents on grounds of orientation was not within the regulation. The Charity Tribunal rejected both of these positions and accepted that the regulation covered 'benefits' in a wider sense: where an organization conferred benefits to achieve its ultimate charitable objects.[96]

Everything thus turns on the relationship between the different regulations. The Charity Tribunal took the view that regulation 18 only applies to a discrete area of pure charitable activity not otherwise prohibited by the regulations. It concluded in these words:

> ...regulation 18 does not permit a charity to act in a manner which is prohibited by the other regulations. However, if a charity limits itself to operating within the sphere of pure charitable activity permitted by regulation 18, the Tribunal takes the view that this could, subject to the expediency test in regulation 18(2) form the basis of a justified interference with the enjoyment of Convention rights in view of the benefit to society provided by such a charity.[97]

This is a very narrow reading indeed. When one recalls that the provision of goods, facilities, or services caught by the regulations includes those provided at no charge, the category of 'pure charitable activity' in which 'discrimination' is allowed looks rather small. Presumably what the Tribunal had in mind was activity such as making a discretionary grant, official teaching, and public awareness. Quite apart from adoption and fostering, charities offering any *service* which presumes a certain view of legitimate sexual relations and family structures are not protected, even if their charitable instruments make the underlying ethic explicit. One thinks of family housing, care for the elderly, or marriage counselling services, for example. Thus, in the case of the latter, the charity could teach that sex outside marriage is wrong, but it could not refuse counselling services to the unmarried.[98] Negotiating that boundary in practice might be difficult.

In this light, the reference to Convention rights is completely misconceived. If a charity promotes a traditional Christian sexual ethic in public, it is exercising its Convention rights of freedom of religion and speech. If B disagrees, is offended, or even turned away, there are no relevant Convention rights. There is no Convention right to receive a pure charitable service. The question is whether

---

[95] Reg 18(1).   [96] Preliminary Ruling, paras 46–53.   [97] Ibid, para 65.
[98] Even if not directly discriminatory on grounds of orientation, this would presumably be indirectly discriminatory, although the point is not unarguable.

the restrictions on charities by the State implicit in the Tribunal's reading of regulation 18 are justified, not the charities' restrictions on potential beneficiaries.[99]

On appeal by Catholic Care to the High Court, Briggs J rejected both constructions of regulation 18.[100] By definition a charity did not have beneficiaries as such; rather, its purposes might be pursued by conferring direct benefits on a range of people.[101] The question of public benefit should be addressed by weighing the positive advantages conferred by the charity against the disadvantage caused by discrimination.[102] Furthermore, the scope of regulation 18 should not be restricted to some new and 'elusive' category of purely charitable activity. Rather, the judge found the limits in (a) its restriction to charities; (b) the oversight of the Charity Commission; and (c) the requirements of non-discrimination in article 14 ECHR.[103] The case for a change of objects on the part of Catholic Care to ensure that it could continue to provide adoption services in line with its ethic was thus remitted to the Charity Commission. It was at least arguable that the benefits it conferred in respect of 'hard to place' children outweighed its restriction to married couples, and it was for the Commission to make that assessment.

The clarity brought by the judgment is welcome. However, it still depends on a very uncertain boundary in respect of Convention rights. The reference to article 14 requires a distinction to be drawn between acts in fulfilment of charitable purposes which engage Convention rights and those which do not. Only in the case of the former will there be a substantive human rights limit on the objects a charity may pursue. In general terms, Convention rights do not confer positive rights to receive public services, although where services are offered in the ambit of a right, they must be offered on a non-discriminatory basis. It is hard to state the extent of this 'ambit' test with precision, and thus hard to state when the refusal by a charity to confer benefits on a certain class of people will amount to a *prima facie* infringement of Convention rights. Furthermore, as is so often the case, the judgment fails to address the problem of horizontal effect, or the extent to which private welfare providers ought to be bound to the same standards as public bodies.[104] One suspects that the Charity Commission will continue simply to treat charities as if they were straightforwardly public bodies.

V. Conclusion

From the perspective of faith-based welfare, the Welfare State under New Labour has deliberately been refashioned according to a policy of collaboration rather than coordination. Unsurprisingly, this new overlap between the State and

---

[99] This point was recognized in respect of the harassment provisions of the equivalent Northern Irish regulations in *Christian Institute v Office of the First Minister* [2007] NIQB 66.

[100] *Catholic Care (Diocese of Leeds) v Charity Commission* [2010] EWHC 520 (Ch).

[101] *Op cit*, para 87.   [102] *Op cit*, paras 68, 97.   [103] *Op cit*, para 96.

[104] This is a particular weakness of cases decided under HRA 1998, s 3(1). See *Ghaidan v Godin-Mendoza* [2004] 2 AC 557.

organized religions is showing signs of the same tensions which have historically only been associated with the field of education. Whereas some measure of plural provision survived the earlier occupation of the welfare field by the State, the tendency of recent years has been to adopt a more individualistic conception of provision. Equality means equality between individuals as they come into contact with statutory or voluntary bodies, in their capacity as governors, workers, or beneficiaries. It is increasingly considered inappropriate for a voluntary welfare body to distinguish on any of the protected grounds of non-discrimination. Allowing the religious ethos to have an impact in these areas is only tolerated if the organization is self-funded, or in the purely 'private' sector.

However, there is a more pluralistic conception of equality, which sees the value of the voluntary sector precisely in its diversity of ethos and provision. Equality on this account does not require the imposition of a single secular ethos on all organizations which occupy the domain of the State's activity, but even-handed partnership with religiously-distinctive bodies. This not only allows for greater integration between motivation and activity on the part of these organizations, it also contributes to State legitimacy. The provision of welfare by the State is inevitable in the light of the failure of the great nineteenth-century experiment in voluntary effort. But the continued existence of voluntary bodies in the context of a dominant State is a tangible expression of individual preference and personal commitment which the State could be harnessing rather than suppressing.

There is thus a mismatch between the Government's avowed policy of welfare pluralism and partnership with faith-based organizations and the rather grudging exceptions found in non-discrimination law. Coupled with a dominant individualistic understanding, the law has the potential for excluding organizations which have anything more than very broad and tenuous links with their religious heritage. Religious diversity in welfare services is allowed to flavour the provision, but not to depart too far from the dominant secular ethos. In respect of religious dimensions of welfare provision, as more generally, new modes of governance by the State are having the effect of imposing alien values.[105] While there are many similarities between faith-based and non-faith-based voluntary providers, it may be preferable not to include faith-based organizations in the emerging 'third sector' if this is necessary to preserve their distinctiveness.[106]

---

[105] See Carmel and Harlock, *op cit* n 29.
[106] Rachel Chapman, 'Faith and the voluntary sector in urban governance: distinctive yet similar?' in Adam Dinham, Robert Furbey, and Vivien Lowndes, *Faith in the Public Realm: controversies, policies and practices* (Bristol: The Policy Press, 2009), at 219.

10

Access to Public Discourse

Furthest removed from the internal life of an organized religion in worship, teaching, and ritual is its participation in public consultation and discourse. The law has a role in shaping this participation. There is an obvious sense in which the maintenance of a place of public worship, the provision of chaplaincies in public institutions, and the operation of schools all result in certain forms of participation. They secure a presence in the community and make the actions of religious bodies a matter of public interest. However, this chapter is interested in formal and semi-formal rights of access to major public contexts of debate and decision-taking. Three quite different contexts are considered: formal representation in the House of Lords, engagement with central and local Government for consultation purposes, and access to broadcasting media. The principal feature of these three contexts is the extent to which religion is not only treated as a private matter of personal conviction and practice, but also as having a legitimate and formal public presence and role. The question is whether the shape that the law gives to this public religious participation presupposes a certain conception of the structure, purpose, and value of religions.

I. Representation in the House of Lords

The archbishops of Canterbury and York, the bishops of London, Durham, and Winchester, and the 21 most senior diocesan bishops by date of appointment, have seats as cross-benchers in the House of Lords.[1] They do not sit as peers, but as Lords of Parliament, and they are not strictly representative of the Church of England, receiving instead a personal writ of summons. The Bishops of Sodor and Man, and Gibraltar in Europe, are not eligible to sit.[2] By convention the

---

[1] The basic position is well described in Francis Brown, 'Influencing the House of Lords: the Role of the Lords Spiritual' (1994) 42 Political Studies 105; Anna Harlow, Frank Cranmer, and Norman Doe, 'Bishops in the House of Lords: a Critical Analysis' [2008] PL 490; R M Morris (ed), *Church and State in 21st Century Britain: The future of church establishment* (Basingstoke: Palgrave Macmillan, 2009), ch 13.

[2] On the position of the Bishop of Sodor and Man, see Augur Pearce, 'The Offshore Establishment: Church and Nation on the Isle of Man' (2003) 7 Ecc LJ 62. The bishop sits in the

bishops start each day's business with prayers, and Lambeth Palace maintains a 'duty bishop' rota to ensure the presence of at least one bishop to this end. Some attempt is also made to ensure that a bishop speaks in any matter in which the church has a particular interest.

Until the mid-nineteenth century, all diocesan bishops sat as Lords Spiritual and had a substantial impact on the deliberations and decisions of the House. Internal church reorganization required the creation of new dioceses, but met with growing political objections to the attendant increase in the influence of the established church. The current rule was the solution finally adopted in the Ecclesiastical Commissioners Act 1847, which created the new diocese of Manchester without an automatic right to sit.[3] Subsequent legislation creating new bishoprics contained the same rule.[4] Bishops of the Church of Ireland and the Church in Wales lost the right to sit in the House of Lords on disestablishment,[5] so that the 26 bishops are now selected from the total of 43 diocesan bishops eligible to sit. Senior members of other denominations and faiths are on occasion given life peerages,[6] as indeed are retired archbishops by convention and a few bishops whose individual contribution has been significant.[7] However, such peerages are given on a purely personal basis and not to ensure representation of other faith groups in the House of Lords.

A 1908 Select Committee recommended reducing the number of bishops to 10: the two archbishops with eight other bishops selected as the Church of England might determine.[8] The Committee also stated:

The Committee would gladly see within the House representatives of the other great Churches of England, Scotland, and Ireland; but they have not been able to formulate any definite recommendations with that object.[9]

Although formal religious representation in a legislative chamber is now unique among democratic nations,[10] this position of a reduction in numbers, together with an inchoate desire to widen representation to other religious denominations, has remained the 'middle ground' ever since. The Bryce Commission (1918) wanted to retain some bishops among the appointed members of a predominantly

---

Upper Branch of Tynwald instead. Given that the See of Gibraltar was created by letters patent in 1842, it must have been treated from the start as a colonial bishopric without the right to sit.

[3] Ecclesiastical Commissioners Act 1847, s 2.

[4] Bishopric of Truro Act 1876, s 5; Bishopric of St Albans Act 1875, s 7; Bishoprics Act 1878, s 5, the terms of which were then often referred to in subsequent legislation creating new sees. See also Bishopric of Leicester Measure 1925, s 8.

[5] See, respectively, Irish Church Act 1869, s 13; Welsh Church Act 1914, s 2(2).

[6] eg Lord Jacobovits, former Chief Rabbi; most recently Lord Sacks of Aldgate, currently Chief Rabbi; Lord Soper, former President of the Methodist Conference.

[7] eg Lord Harries of Pentregarth, Bishop of Oxford 1987–2006.

[8] House of Lords Select Committee on the House of Lords, Report (1908), paras 20–21, reproduced in part at (1953) 7 Parliamentary Affairs, 140, 142.   [9] Ibid.

[10] Earlier examples can be found in (eg) France before 1789 and in Ireland: Meg Russell, *Reforming the House of Lords: lessons from overseas* (Oxford: Oxford University Press, 2000), 61, 68.

elected House.[11] This was also the position of the cross-party Statement of 1948.[12] The 1968 White Paper likewise recommended that they remain in place, with relaxations of attendance qualifications for the senior bishops, and with a reduction over time to 16.[13]

Inevitably, over the course of the last century, the role of the bishops has changed considerably. Until about 1920, the bishops were still a significant partisan (Conservative) presence, after which the expectation of party-neutrality, or rather party-diversity, grew steadily.[14] Writing in 1953, the then Archbishop of York identified three functions of the bishops: 'a witness that England still claims to be a Christian nation', assisting the passage of church legislation and bringing a Christian conscience to bear on the problems of the day.[15] Around the same time, Bromhead found that bishops tended only to speak on issues in which they felt the church had a particular interest: typically questions of moral or social welfare and education.[16] Since the mid-century, contributions relating to matters of regional interest, and arising from personal expertise have increased.[17] Apart from the bishops, there are few members who can claim any sort of regional mandate in the upper house. However, there is evidence of a certain mismatch between the bishops' own perception of their contributions and their actual performance. A recent study finds that although they think they are likely to contribute on matters to do with education, the environment, ethics, and health, the top four are actually foreign policy, mental and physical health, offender management and prisons, and immigration and asylum.[18] At the same time it seems that many bishops now feel that their role is to represent a religious or ethical voice more generally,[19] sometimes to the frustration of lay Christian peers who wish their contribution to be more distinctive.[20]

Assessments of the contribution of the bishops varies. Given their diocesan duties, attendance is difficult and low, so their impact in terms of voting patterns is negligible. It could, of course, be more significant, were they all to attend. Their contributions tend to the general rather than the technical, so it is easy to dismiss them as 'visitors rather than contributors' or 'really more spectators than participants'.[21] However Drewry and Brock concluded that their impact

---

[11] Viscount Bryce, *Report of a Conference on the Second Chamber*, Cd 9038 (1918), para 26, reproduced in part at (1953) 7 Parliamentary Affairs, 151, 157.

[12] Cross-party Statement, Cmd 7380 (1948), para 5(6).

[13] Cabinet Office, *House of Lords Reform*, Cmnd 3799 (1968).

[14] See Gavin Drewry and Jenny Brock, 'Prelates in Parliament' (1971) 24 Parliamentary Affairs 222, 223–4.

[15] Archbishop of York, 'The Lords Spiritual' (1953) 7 Parliamentary Affairs 96, 100.

[16] P A Bromhead, *The House of Lords and Contemporary Politics 1911–1957* (London: Routledge & Paul, 1958), 55–6.

[17] Drewy and Brock, *op cit* n 14 at 238–42. Brown, *op cit* n 1 at 116, found 60.5 per cent contributions to do with church matters, 21 per cent diocesan area representation, and 18.5 per cent from personal expertise or experience. [18] Harlow, Cranmer and Doe, *op cit* n 1, 508.

[19] Ibid, 503. [20] Brown, *op cit* n 1, 108. [21] Quotations cited at ibid, 106.

is out of all proportion to their numbers.[22] As regards the scrutiny of legislation, Francis Brown identified four conditions for their effectiveness: there must be a general recognition that the church has a special and proper interest in the matter in hand, the bishops themselves must not be divided, the bill must not be a Government one, and other groups, such as Roman Catholic lay peers, must join in their support.[23] He concluded that the greatest contribution of the bishops during the period of his study was arguably to deny legitimacy to some of the Conservative Government's reforms.[24]

The Labour Government won the general election in 1997 with a mandate for constitutional reform, including reform of the composition of the House of Lords.[25] The first stage of reform, which removed all but 92 of the hereditary peers, left the position of the Lords Spiritual intact. A Royal Commission was then established in 1999 under the chairmanship of Lord Wakeham, and it included among its members the Bishop of Oxford.[26] In outline, the Commission proposed a chamber of around 550 members, with a substantial minority of regional elected members, an Independent Appointments Commission to appoint the rest, with a duty to ensure that a fifth of the membership were independent cross-benchers. Their report stressed the importance of the religious dimension in a plural society, and set out as a basic minimum the obligation of any Appointments Commission to ensure the presence of a wide range of philosophical, moral, and spiritual viewpoints.[27]

More controversially, a substantial majority of the Commission were also prepared to broaden the formal religious representation to include other Christian denominations and other faith communities.[28] The proposal was to reduce the Church of England representation to 16, allocating five places to other Christian denominations in England, and five to Christian denominations in Scotland, Wales, and Northern Ireland.[29] The logic behind this was that 21:5 matched the population distribution between England and the three other countries, and that 16:5 matched the proportion of Church of England and other baptized members of the English Christian denominations. Appointment would be in the hands of the Appointments Commission, but in close consultation with ecumenical structures such as Churches Together in England.[30] The Royal Commission recognized the difficulties the reduction to 16 would create for the Church of England if the current rule of seniority were to be maintained: bishops would on average

---

[22] *Op cit* n 14, 246.   [23] *Op cit* n 1, 114.   [24] Ibid, 119.

[25] A general account of the difficulties can be found in Gavin Phillipson, ' "The greatest quango of them all", "a rival Chamber" or "a hybrid nonsense"? Solving the Second Chamber Paradox' [2004] PL 352. A full and up-to-date chronology can be found in Chris Clarke and Matthew Purvis, *House of Lords Reform since 1997: a Chronology*, House of Lords Library Note 2009/007.

[26] Royal Commission on the Reform of the House of Lords, *A House for the Future*, Cm 4534 (Jan 2000).   [27] Ibid, paras 15.4–15.6; Recommendation 107.

[28] Ibid, paras 15.7–15.9; Recommendation 108.

[29] Ibid, paras 15.18–15.19; Recommendations 110 and 111.

[30] Ibid, paras 15.20–15.23; Recommendations 112 and 113.

wait for 10 years and sit for three or four. In response they expressed the hope that the church would find a way of ensuring that eligible bishops could sit for 15-year terms in the same way as other members.[31]

As regards non-Christian faiths, the Royal Commission proposed that there should be at least five members specifically appointed to represent these communities.[32] Once again, appointment would ultimately be in the hands of the Appointments Commission in consultation with inter-faith organizations. The basis for this number appears to be that fact that about 5–6 per cent of the population affirm a non-Christian faith. Presumably the percentage was applied to the number of independent members to produce the figure.

Charlotte Smith has commented on the fact that the Royal Commission failed to engage with the literature and theory of religious establishment.[33] She cites Thomas Arnold and William Gladstone in defence of the view that the church is the unique repository of moral knowledge, the voice of national conscience speaking to the power of State. By contrast, and perhaps not surprisingly, the Commission assumed that the Upper House should be representative of all the religious beliefs of the nation, facilitative of a dialogue between faiths and spiritualities, and symbolic of a general political accountability to a higher power.

But even within its own pluralist assumptions, the perceived need to secure proportionality of representation is an insurmountable obstacle to formal representation. The logic of proportionality should be that the entire House should reflect the religious composition of the United Kingdom as a whole, as indeed it should reflect other identities. This would not require any formal representation. On the other hand, if one is going to set aside about 30 seats for formal representatives, it would be hard to justify more than one or two for non-Christian faiths. And once one accepts that spiritual and moral insight can come from agnostics and atheists, one ought to secure proportionate quotas for these as well. Yet if the identification of representatives from faith communities organized as networks of small voluntary associations is hard enough, finding official spokespersons for agnostics and atheists is practically impossible, the efforts of the British Humanist Association notwithstanding. The very notion of formal religious representation is already a departure from proportionality.

In November 2001, the Government published a White Paper in response to the Royal Commission report.[34] This accepted the reduction in the number of bishops to 16, but took the view that the practical obstacles in the way of formal representation for other religions and denominations were too great.

---

[31] Ibid, paras 15.27–15.28; Recommendation 115.

[32] Ibid, paras 15.15–15.17; Recommendation 109.

[33] Charlotte Smith, 'The Place of Representatives of Religion in the Reformed Second Chamber' [2003] PL 674.

[34] Department for Constitutional Affairs, *The House of Lords—Completing the Reform*, Cm 5291 (Nov 2001).

Nevertheless, the Appointments Commission could be expected to give proper recognition to non-Church of England faith communities.[35] This effectively sidestepped the question of quotas, which had so exercised the Royal Commission. The Select Committee on Public Administration responded to the Government White Paper with its own, more radical, proposals.[36] They considered that the tradition of *ex officio* religious membership was an anachronism and should be abolished. In the context of a much smaller chamber, 60 per cent elected, 20 per cent appointed by political parties, and 20 per cent independent members appointed by a statutory appointments commission, formal representation could no longer be justified. Of course, senior members of religious bodies could be appointed by the Appointments Commission and would be free to stand for election.[37]

The Government responded by proposing that the Houses of Parliament should establish a Joint Committee to identify the options. This they did, but the resulting votes demonstrated the complete lack of consensus on the fundamental question of composition. In both Joint Committee Reports the question of religious representation was deferred.[38] In September 2003, the Government published a consultation paper proposing a fully-appointed second chamber.[39] The paper distanced itself from the earlier suggestion that the number of bishops should be reduced from 26 to 16, noting that this was in the context of a much more fundamental reform and a smaller Upper House.[40] The 'separate issue' of increasing representation for other faiths and denominations was noted and it was suggested that this was a matter for consideration by the proposed statutory Independent Appointments Commission. Responses to the consultation on this matter strongly supported the suggestion that the composition of the House of Lords should better reflect UK society, including its religious composition, but the difficulties of securing official representation from faith communities was again noticed.[41] On 18 March 2004 the Government announced that the recommendations in the consultation paper were being taken no further. An attempt in 2005 by senior politicians from across the parties to 'break the deadlock' recognized that wider questions about Church and State were raised by the problem, and once again settled on the figure of 16 for the sake of consensus.[42] The latest Government White Paper accepts that if an appointed

---

[35] Ibid, paras 83–5.
[36] Select Committee on Public Administration, *The Second Chamber: Continuing the Reform*, Fifth Report, 2001–2, HC 494-I (Feb 2002).   [37] Ibid, paras 154–9.
[38] Joint Committee on House of Lords Reform, *First Report*, HL17, HC171 (Dec 2002); id, *Second Report*, HL97, HC668 (April 2003).
[39] Department for Constitutional Affairs, *Constitutional Reform: Next Steps for the House of Lords*, CP 14/03 (Sept 2003).   [40] Ibid, para 19.
[41] See *Summary of Responses to the Consultation* at <http://www.dca.gov.uk/consult/holref/holresp.htm>.
[42] Kenneth Clarke *et al*, *Reforming the House of Lords: Breaking the Deadlock* (London: The Constitution Unit, 2005).

element remains, so should a proportionate number of bishops.[43] Rather disingenuously, it claims that:

After careful consideration, the Government proposes to endorse the recommendations of the Wakeham Commission that providing reserved places for other churches and faith communities other than the Church of England in a reformed second chamber would be problematic. Any appointments to represent other churches and faith groups should be made through the Appointments Commission in the usual way. The Government would welcome views on whether the Appointments Commission should be given a specific remit to provide for representation of other churches and faith groups in making its appointments.[44]

The Wakeham Commission expressly recommended that a set number of seats should go to other Christian denominations and non-Christian religions, while leaving an ultimate discretion in the hands of the Appointments Commission as to how that should be achieved. For the present, however, it seems that, *faute de mieux*, 26 Church of England bishops and no other formal faith representatives remain in the House of Lords.

Throughout the unresolved controversy about the composition of the House of Lords, it is worth highlighting two main assumptions. The first is that the religious voice is not to be excluded from public life. This is clearly articulated by virtually all, regardless of their views on formal representation.[45] The second is all the stronger for being unspoken and unchallenged: formal religious representatives do not, or should not, have party political affiliations, but are independent. Indeed, one cannot but observe the remarkable nature of the Anglican model: it is that senior religious ministers have a politically-relevant ethical role that transcends party division. Perhaps the biggest weakness of the Royal Commission in this area was its failure to consider the ecclesiastical, theological, and political preconditions for religious leaders to fulfil such a role. From a global perspective it is by no means guaranteed.

However, formal religious representation requires a stronger justification than the mere representation of diverse religious voices. It needs to be accepted that organized religions represent locations of authority in civil society which in some way stand over against Government and must be reconciled with Government. Just as Parliament legislates for the Church of England, so now the law reaches into the internal life of religions to a greater extent than before. As a result, institutional representation becomes more important, not less so. At the same time, organized religions can offer an alternative legitimacy that is capable of challenging and limiting Government. The critical stance towards Government adopted

---

[43] Ministry of Justice, *An Elected Second Chamber: Further reform of the House of Lords* Cm 7438 (July 2008), para 6.8.   [44] Ibid.

[45] Elizabeth Wicks, 'Religion, Law and Medicine: Legislating on Birth and Death in a Christian State' [2009] Med LR 410 has recently added her voice to those calling for the removal of bishops, but it is clear that her concern is *disproportionate* influence, not the exclusion of the religious dimension.

by the bishops during the Thatcher years has not lessened thereafter. In this they bring not just a personal opinion to bear, but one rooted in a part of organized civil society. In this area, as in others, the composition of Parliament stands to some extent as a proxy for unarticulated constitutional principles.

This is not to assert that wider formal representation is straightforward. If, for example, the Chief Rabbi were to be included, it should be not because he is the 'best representative' of British Jews, but because he is a leader of a substantial religious community whose distinctive insight and interest it is important to secure, and whose institutional position it is important to respect and protect. It may also be that some substantial religious communities are quite capable of identifying a person other than a religious leader to fill an *ex officio* place.[46] The efforts of the Royal Commission could perhaps have been better directed at identifying specific positions or processes by which the full range of organized religious opinion could be brought to bear in a reformed House.

II. New Consultation Processes

1. Outline of developments

Government departments have long maintained contacts with representatives of churches and other religious bodies in respect of matters where there is an obvious overlap of interest. Much more recently, Government has systematically attempted to promote and enhance processes of consultation with faith communities.[47] The origins of this recent and rapid development lie in the recognition that religious organizations are central in any successful programme of urban regeneration. Over the last decade the expectations and structures for consultation have become much more general. These new processes have taken place almost entirely in the absence of any statutory framework, although they have been facilitated by the new general local authority power contained in the Local Government Act 2000 to support economic, social, or environmental well-being.[48] The main exception to this rule is that the Greater London Authority is under a statutory obligation to consult with bodies which represent the interests of different religious groups in Greater London, if that is considered appropriate in the particular case.[49] This formal obligation to consult with religious representatives has now been extended to matters of local development and regional planning.[50]

---

[46] See Rachel Lampard, *The House of Lords: Completing the Reform—A response on behalf of the Methodist Church*, paras 6.3–6.4. The Methodist Church is very close in size to the Jewish population.

[47] The Better Regulation Executive lists 'faith/belief-based groups' among those that may 'warrant particular attention or specific approaches' under the general Government Code of Practice on Consultation.   [48] Local Government Act 2000, s 2(1).

[49] Greater London Authority Act 1999, s 32.

[50] Town and Country Planning (Regional Development) (England) Regulations 2004, SI 2004/2203; Town and Country Planning (Local Development Plan) (Wales) Regulations 2005,

The key body in this area was, until 2006, the Inner Cities Religious Council (ICRC). This had been established in 1992 as a new initiative to involve faith networks in seeking to address the social problems of inner cities.[51] It represented a recognition that organized religions had access to resources and solutions which Government could support and use in seeking to promote neighbourhood renewal and social inclusion. Containing representatives of five major faiths (Christian, Hindu, Jewish, Muslim, and Sikh), it was located in the Department of the Environment and chaired by a Government minister. It had some success in persuading Government departments to develop policies in faith-sensitive ways and enter into partnerships with faith-based organizations to deliver public services. Its role was strengthened after the change of Government in 1997 with an increasing number of policy documents emphasizing the role of religious organizations in areas of social deprivation, the importance of consulting with faith communities, and in particular the value of forums and workshops in redressing the weaknesses of more familiar forms of public consultation.[52] Neighbourhood renewal programmes also stressed the need for pragmatism in funding faith-based organizations and the need when making funding decisions to distinguish programmes of social inclusion (acceptable) from the direct promotion of religion (unacceptable).[53]

The Urban White Paper of November 2000 contained a high-level statement of the Government's commitment to consultation:

The Government is committed to the involvement of faith communities and supports the Inner Cities Religious Council in DETR. This multi-faith Council acts as a forum for consultation across government departments with a particular focus on regeneration and the drive for inclusion.[54]

The Prime Minister indicated his personal support for these developments in a speech in March 2001, and this was repeated in the 2001 Labour Party election manifesto:

We welcome the contribution of churches and other faith-based organisations as partners of local and central government in community renewal. We will use a successor to the Lambeth Group to look at government's interface with faith communities.[55]

As that quotation indicates, the planning process for the millennium had encouraged the Government to build on its experience of inter-faith dialogue. The Lambeth group was an *ad hoc* body established to plan the celebrations around

---

SI 2005/2839; Town and Country Planning (General Development Procedure) (Amendment) (England) Order 2006, SI 2006/1062.

[51] For an account of its origins and first decade, see Jenny Taylor, 'There's Life in Establishment—but not as we know it' (2004) 5 Political Theology 329.

[52] See DETR, *Involving Communities in Urban and Rural Regeneration: a Guide for Practitioners*, 2nd edn (September 1997); DETR, *Local Strategic Partnership Guidance* (March 2001), para 1.24.

[53] See Policy Action Team 9: *Community Self Help* (Sept 1999) Recommendation 25; *Compact: Black and Minority Ethnic Voluntary and Community Organisations* (Feb 2001), para 6.8.

[54] ODPM, *Our Towns and Cities: The Future—Delivering an Urban Renaissance* (Nov 2000), para 3.47.   [55] Labour Party, *Election Manifesto* (2001), 34.

the millennium and containing representatives of the same five faiths as the ICRC as well as Government departments, the Royal Households, and others. As well as being responsible for the Millennium Dome's 'Faith Zone' it produced guidelines on multi-faith events and produced the 'Shared Act of Reflection and Commitment' which took place in the House of Lords on 3 January 2000.

The experience of planning the Millennium was repeated two years later with a range of multi-faith events as part of the Golden Jubilee. Also, in 2002, the ICRC collaborated with the Local Government Association, the Active Communities Unit of the Home Office, and the InterFaith Network UK to produce *Faith and Community*, guidance for local Governments on relationships with local faith organizations.[56] Later in 2002, the Home Office agreed to take forward the manifesto commitment by establishing a wide-ranging review of existing consultation arrangements. This was announced in June 2003, and produced in due course a major report, *Working Together*.[57] In the same year, the religious issues section of the Home Office Race Equality Unit, which had been supporting the review, was re-formed as a separate Faith Communities Unit.

In the course of 2005, the Faith Communities Unit was renamed the 'Cohesion and Faiths Unit', and then in Spring 2006, the entire Race, Faith and Cohesion Directorate of which it was part was moved to the new Department for Communities and Local Government. This department now has responsibility for what are called with increasing uniformity 'faith communities'. At the same time, the Inner Cities Religious Council and the *Working Together* steering group were merged to form a new Faith Communities Consultative Council. This is also now located in the Department for Communities and Local Government. Most recently, in July 2008, that department produced another substantial review of Government engagement with religious bodies: *Face to Face and Side by Side*.[58] The last few years have also seen a growing number of local inter-faith and multi-faith bodies with consultative functions, as well as the establishment of regional bodies.

2. Three reports: three agendas?

It is instructive to contrast the three major Government reports touching on the relationship with faith communities. The Local Government Association publication, *Faith and Community*, arose from a joint project with the ICRC, the Department of Transport, Local Government and the Regions, the Active

---

[56] Local Government Association, *Faith and Community* (2002).
[57] Home Office Faith Communities Unit, *Working Together: Co-operation between Government and Faith Communities* (Feb 2004).
[58] DCLG, *Face to Face and Side by Side: A framework for partnership in our multi faith society* (July 2008).

Community Unit of the Home Office, and the UK Inter Faith Network.[59] It grounded its case for local authority engagement not in formal legal obligations, but in the post-Local Government Act 2000 role of local authorities as community leaders. Faith groups are an important part of the voluntary and community sector, not only advancing faith and worship, but engaged in community development, the representation of community interests, and the provision of services both to members and the wider public. They can offer networks, leadership, buildings, and volunteers. Funding is available through programmes such as *New Deal for Communities*, and the report instanced several faith-based community projects. However, the report also noted the inappropriateness of funding worship and the promotion of religion as such, as well as controversy about funding internal capacity-building within religious groups.[60]

In terms of structures for consultation, the report noted the difficulties minority faith communities can have in engaging with traditional consultation processes and the limited value of Standing Advisory Councils on Religious Education (SACREs) in advising on matters outside their distinctive educational remit. Instead, it stressed the value of including faith representatives in developing Local Compacts with the voluntary and community sector.[61] Its strongest support was reserved for the development of inter-faith initiatives, especially local councils of faiths.[62] The ICRC was expressly held up as a model for local and regional equivalents. While noting the dangers that can arise when local authorities seek to co-opt religious groups and stressing the need for patience and understanding, it encouraged the promotion of these councils. It identified five specific areas in which such bodies can make a contribution: working with local hospitals and hospices to meet patient needs, advising on facilities for burials and cremations, advising the police on community relations, contributing to planning and regeneration consultations in respect of places of worship and community groups, and working with SACREs.[63] But it also noted the intrinsic value of good relations between different religions at a local level. The report encouraged local authorities to establish a 'civic umbrella' promoting such an inter-faith structure where one does not yet exist, in the expectation that in due course it would become independently supported by local religious organizations.[64]

At around the same time, a pilot project commissioned by the Office of the Deputy Prime Minister on behalf of the ICRC found several obstacles to the involvement of faith communities in the *New Deal for Communities* (NDC) funding programme.[65] *Faith and Community* tied this initiative to the recognition

---

[59] See also the related publication of the Inter Faith Network in association with the Local Government Association, the Home Office, and the ICRC, *Partnership for the common good: inter-faith structures and local government*, 2003.   [60] Ibid, paras 5.1–5.2.

[61] Ibid, para 4.9.   [62] Ibid, para 7.9.   [63] Ibid, para 7.10.

[64] Ibid, paras 7.11–7.16.

[65] ODPM/Angoy Consultancy, *Pilot Project on Faith Community Involvement in the New Deal for Communities* (Feb 2005).

that there was a low level of involvement in NDC projects other than by the Christian churches.[66] The pilot project found that in three areas considered (Wolverhampton, Tower Hamlets, and Bradford), only in Bradford was there an effective working relationship. The project found that faith communities had access to resources—not least buildings, ideas, and enthusiasm—but that time would be needed to build relationships of trust between the communities and Local Government, if engagement was to produce benefits. Faith communities needed to see their ideas and projects validated and supported. Local faith community networks and a designated community engagement officer were obvious proposals to assist in this.

The *Working Together* Review, which can be considered together with the subsequent Progress Report on its implementation (August 2005), sought to map systematically the range of different consultation processes across Government departments, with a particular focus on Central Government. It suggested that there were five main categories of process: (1) standing arrangements such as committees of representatives, regular bilateral or multilateral meetings, or panels of faith advisers; (2) chaplaincies, which as well as providing religious ministry to individuals also give advice and guidance on policy and service delivery; (3) one-off time-limited groups to consider specific policy issues; (4) other *ad hoc* arrangements; and (5) relationships with local groups often based on departmental funding provision.[67]

Within the first category of standing arrangements, the Review noted the Central Religious Advisory Committee within the Department of Culture, Media and Sport, and the National Association of Standing Advisory Councils for Religious Education within the Department for Education and Skills, as well as regular meetings with bodies providing faith schools. The Department for International Development works closely with churches and faith groups and hosts regular meetings with representatives from Christian Aid, CAFOD, and Islamic Relief. There is a Muslim women's group within the Women and Equality Unit of the Department of Trade and Industry, and a Religious Freedom Panel within the Human Rights Policy Department of the Foreign and Commonwealth Office. At the time of the report, the Home Office contained the Community Cohesion Faith Practitioners' Group and the Office of the Deputy Prime Minister contained the Inner Cities Religious Council. Chaplaincies also provide a form of standing consultation arrangement, relevant particularly to the Department of Health, the Ministry of Defence, and HM Prison Service. The relevant bodies are, respectively, the Multi-faith Group on Healthcare Chaplaincy, the Religious Advisory Panel and multi-faith working group of chaplains, and the Chaplaincy Council and Prison Service Faith Advisers panel.[68] Although the Review noted that the Inner Cities Religious Council had to some extent functioned as a more

---

[66] *Faith and Community*, para 4.6.   [67] *Working Together*, para 6.2.7.
[68] Examples cited in *Working Together*, appendix 1 and *Progress Report*, section 3.

general consultation body beyond its core remit of urban regeneration and social inclusion, it concluded in the light of the diversity of formal arrangements that the case for a new central consultative body was not proven.[69]

As the reports pointed out, these formal, or relatively formal, processes of standing consultation are accompanied by a substantial number of examples of *ad hoc* engagement around specific issues. Examples can be found across all Government departments: the review of the BBC Charter (DCMS), a national framework for religious education (DES), a new policy on organ donations (DoH), a review of cremation (DEFRA), transport needs of ethnic minorities (DoT), and new language requirements for ministers of religion (HO/FCO). Many departments engage in regular consultation. In the light of this evidence, it is not surprising that the Review focused its attention on enhancing consultation processes generally. Its recommendations were addressed both to departments and to faith communities and sought to address a number of obstacles to effective consultation. It stressed the need to respect diversity between and within religions and to ensure that all views are included.[70] 'Faith literacy' within Government needed to be strengthened.[71] It pointed out the lack of capacity within some religious organizations to respond effectively, and the need for Departments to be willing to support consultation processes, if necessary by small grants.[72] It also emphasized the need to take sufficient time over consultations for constituencies to be contacted and to allow religious bodies to make their own positive suggestions.[73] On the part of faith communities, the reports make some fairly obvious points about the need to take the initiative in contacting Departments, to develop structures which meet the need to be consulted, to present a clear and common position, and to keep to deadlines.[74]

Perhaps the most notable feature of the *Working Together* Review was its respect for religious diversity. This is apparent not only in its regular plea that Government departments should not assume that all religions have the same concerns or are internally homogeneous, but also in its insistence that in principle the Church of England is not privileged as a consultee, either in comparison with other religions, or in comparison with other Christian churches such as the Roman Catholic Church, the Free Churches, or the Black Majority Churches.[75] Consultation should take place with all those affected, bearing in mind relative levels of adherence among the population as a whole.

However, this very clear multicultural agenda had two equally clear limits. The first was in the regular insistence that women, children, and older people should be represented in consultation processes.[76] If faith communities failed to show that they had included the perspectives of these people they were threatened with being ignored. The Report even went as far as suggesting a participation

---

[69] *Working Together*, paras 6.3.24–6.3.26.   [70] eg ibid, paras 2.2.15, 2.2.29.
[71] Ibid, paras 2.2.26–2.2.28.   [72] Ibid, paras 2.2.1–2.2.3.
[73] Ibid, paras 2.2.9–2.2.11.   [74] Ibid, ch 3.   [75] Ibid, para 2.2.38.
[76] Ibid, paras 2.2.31–2.2.34.

rate for women (30 per cent).[77] Secondly, the discussion of the representation of faith communities at national services and celebrations was unashamedly 'establishment'.[78] The Report emphasized the need to be sensitive both to views as to appropriate participation by one's own faith or others, and views as to the appropriateness of Government involvement. This set limits to what can be done. It divided events into three categories. First are national 'acts of worship' which are hosted by Christian churches and attended by other faith representatives. The Report was clear that there are limits on the involvement of other faiths (both from their point of view and those of the Christian churches hosting the event), that a national service based on another faith is unprecedented and unlikely, and that a multi-faith act of worship is 'strongly discouraged'. At this point, Christianity was recognized to be historically and culturally dominant. In England, the Church of England takes the lead. Secondly, there are faith-based celebrations organized by Government which are not acts of worship. The Millennium event is the only example of this and the Report candidly admitted that 'it may well remain unique for some time to come'. Finally, there are celebrations which are not faith-based but which have faith community representation. These were essentially unproblematic, although consultation was necessary to ensure an appropriate list of invitations.

The Government Report, *Face to Face and Side by Side: a framework for partnership in our multi faith society* is more wide-ranging than *Working Together* and has a notably different emphasis. It grew out of the 2007 Report of the Independent Commission on Integration and Cohesion. That report asserted that more constructive relationships were needed between people of different religions and beliefs. As a result, *Face to Face* calls for stronger dialogue and more practical cooperation.[79] The aims of the new framework it established are to encourage inter-faith dialogue which builds understanding and celebrates common values, to increase the level of collaborative social action involving different faith communities and wider civil society, to maintain and encourage the further development of good relations between faith communities and between faith communities and wider civil society, and to overcome barriers which may be faced by young people and women in participating in dialogue and social action.[80] It seeks to do this through a wide range of initiatives arranged into four 'building blocks': developing the confidence and skills to bridge and link, developing shared spaces for interaction and social action, developing structures and processes which support dialogue and social action, and providing opportunities for learning.[81]

The building blocks themselves contain a wide range of examples, ideas and initiatives. Within the first two blocks, many of these are directed towards providing advice and support to local authorities in bringing people from different religions together and in improving the quality of the physical infrastructure

---

[77] Ibid, para 3.2.14.   [78] Ibid, ch 4.   [79] *Face to Face*, 'Foreword', 5.
[80] Ibid, 21.   [81] Ibid, 23.

within which this can happen. There is strong encouragement for local authorities to implement principles of representation that include faith representatives, appoint an official with a faith communities brief, and support a local inter-faith group. Money was set aside for community building refurbishment and to support grassroots initiatives to create shared spaces. Faith communities are encouraged to open up, and local authorities to champion the sharing of space. The third building block is the most pertinent to this chapter. It sets out existing national, regional, and local structures for consultation and commits to strengthening the links between local authority 'faith leads' at regional level, investing in regional faith forums, and working with local authorities to update the 2002 *Faith and Community* guidance.[82] Finally, the fourth building block contains a range of ideas at every educational level to improve the understanding of religions among both young people and public officials. A new Faiths in Action Fund (2009–11) was announced to support activities and initiatives within any of the four blocks.[83] In accordance with its own ethos, the Report promoted a parallel report produced by the Church Urban Fund in partnership with the DCLG and the National Association of Councils for Voluntary Service giving examples and advice on successful partnership working.[84]

3. Current arrangements

The reformed Faith Communities Consultative Council has as its overarching aim, 'giving faith communities a strong role and clear voice in improving cohesion, regeneration and renewal in local communities'.[85] Its four objectives are 'to strengthen Government consultation with faith communities' by monitoring and promoting best practice in consultative processes and identifying gaps, duplication, problems, and solutions; 'to bring the voices of faith communities to Government' by providing advice to inform policy and guidance to improve faith literacy; 'to make a difference to communities' by identifying challenges and sharing best practice and resources; and 'to understand the context' by identifying and debating emerging issues. It is chaired by the Parliamentary Under-Secretary of State for Communities and Local Government. As well as Government standing representatives and those attending for specific items, it has representatives from a range of organizations which are themselves representative of the following nine faiths: Baha'i, Buddhist, Christian, Hindu, Jain, Jewish, Muslim, Sikh, and Zoroastrian, as well as a number of inter-faith bodies. There is multiple representation in the case of Christianity (Church of England, Roman Catholic Church, Methodist Church, the Free Churches Group, Churches Together in Britain

---

[82] Ibid, 74, 79, 89.   [83] Ibid, 112.
[84] Rosie Edwards, *Believing in Local Action* (Church Urban Fund, 2008).
[85] See <http://www.communities.gov.uk/communities/racecohesionfaith/faith/faithcommunities/faithcommunitiesconsultative/aimsobjectives/>, accessed 5 November 2009.

and Ireland, and the Evangelical Alliance), Hinduism (Hindu Council UK and
the Hindu Forum of Britain), Judaism (Board of Deputies and the Office of the
Chief Rabbi), Islam (Muslim Council of Britain and the British Muslim Forum),
and Sikhism (Network of Sikh Organisations and the British Sikh Consultative
Forum).[86] The Council has considered topics such as the funding of faith-based
organizations, pandemic influenza, Sunday trading, new forums for consultation, immigration services, programmes to reduce reoffending, supporting vulnerable adults, and local public partnerships.

There are now 10 regional multi-faith forums in England and Wales which typically have as their role the provision of information, training, consultation, and
input into regional Governmental structures.[87] All of these have been established
since the turn of the millennium. Some are supported by the Church of England
(North-East and North-West England) and some appear more independent.
The Faiths Forum for London and the South-East England Faith Forum are a
result of recent Government initiatives, and the equivalent bodies for the West
Midlands and Wales are also closely associated with Government consultation.
The Inter Faith Network's Directory also lists 212 local inter-faith or multi-faith
bodies in England and Wales. Of these, about 60 per cent list 'advice and assistance to public bodies' and slightly fewer 'acting as a consultation forum for local
government'. Other activities include the provision of training, participation in
Local Strategic Partnerships, and community regeneration projects. Of the type
of multi-faith group that has this public role, just under 30 per cent are serviced
by local Government. This support is spread throughout the country, but is particularly noticeable in the case of 11 London boroughs. To view that from the
opposite perspective, in 2007–8, 39 per cent of local authorities had provided
funding of one form or another to their local inter-faith body.[88]

There has been an exponential rise in new consultation processes between public and religious bodies over the last decade. It is a mark of the pace of change that
the 2002 Faith and Community Guidance, which in its time was far-reaching,
could be considered in need of updating within six years. Perhaps equally striking is the attempt, albeit brief, to refer to Christian theological justification for
inter-faith collaboration in a major Government publication.[89] The effect of this
change has been a substantial reversal of the implicit assumption that religion
and government are, for practical purposes, separate enterprises. This reversal
has come about through a number of causes, of which three stand out. First, we
can note the acceptance by Government that the problems of urban deprivation
can only be tackled by collaboration with religious organizations and the use
of their resources. This point has then been broadened out into a more general

---

[86] See Minutes of Inaugural Meeting (27 April 2006), Annex A.
[87] Information drawn from Inter Faith Network for the UK, *Inter Faith Organisations in the
UK: A Directory*, 2009.   [88] *Face to Face*, 89.
[89] Ibid, 70. The reference is to three Church of England publications: 'The Way of Dialogue'
(1988), 'The Mystery of Salvation' (1996) and 'Generous Love' (2008).

willingness to collaborate in public service delivery, as noted in the previous chapter. Secondly, there is the increasing public recognition of religious diversity, most notably through the 2001 National Census. This has highlighted the existing unremarked connections between Government departments and religious bodies and created a series of parallel questions around inclusion, fairness, and responsiveness to different religions. The relationship between Government and religious bodies thus has become a common theme. Finally, the urban riots of 2001 triggered a concern about the religious dimensions of civil unrest and desire to see greater levels of inter-faith cohesion. This agenda has been given additional impetus after the London bombings of July 2005 and is dominant in the latest Government publications.

These three causes see religions as respectively a positive social force, an unavoidable social reality, and potentially socially disruptive. In emphasizing the latter—however diplomatically—the Government inevitably prioritizes certain sorts of religion, namely those that downplay their distinctiveness and are prepared to focus on this-worldly social and moral improvement.[90]

III. Religious Broadcasting

1. Outline of developments

The development of religious broadcasting is dominated by its origins in the public service ethos of the BBC in the context of—and to some extent in spite of—increasing technological capacity. A year after the formation of the British Broadcasting Company in 1922, the 'Sunday Committee' was established to advise on the selection of religious broadcasters.[91] On receipt of the Royal Charter in 1927, this Committee became the Central Religious Advisory Committee (CRAC) and it remained in existence until 2007. Originally, it contained representatives only of the main Christian denominations in the UK. There was of course no question of the ownership of broadcasting facilities by churches or religious bodies, nor was any advertising of any nature permitted.

The introduction of independent television under the Television Act 1954 saw the adoption of a model which was to survive through subsequent legislation for almost 40 years. Under that Act, as well as the general obligation to ensure a proper balance in relation to subject-matter,[92] there was a specific prohibition of 'any religious service or any propaganda relating to matters of a religious nature' unless previous approval had been granted by the Independent Television

---

[90] These implications noted, and deplored, from a Christian theological perspective by Luke Bretherton, 'A New Establishment? Theological politics and the emerging shape of Church-State relations' (2006) 7 Political Theology 371.

[91] Background in Ian Leigh, 'Regulating Religious Broadcasting' (1992) 2 Ecc LJ 287.

[92] Television Act 1954, s 3(1)(b).

Authority (ITA).[93] The Act contained a statutory obligation to establish a Committee 'representative of the main streams of religious thought in the United Kingdom...to give advice as to the exercise of their functions [in respect of previous approval]...and on any other matters of a religious nature'.[94] In practice, the existing CRAC was used to fulfil this function, although meeting separately for the BBC and the ITA. This Committee thus became significant across all the broadcast media in its vetting of religious programmes. The Television Act 1964 added the power to draw up codes in respect of standards and practice of broadcasting.[95] As was the case for political advertising, advertising by religious bodies, or directed to religious ends, was prohibited.[96] There was, by contrast, no provision for churches to engage in religious equivalents to party political broadcasts.

By the mid-1970s the assumption that 'religious' meant Christian had given way to a more inclusive approach, and the CRAC membership was widened to include representatives of other faiths.[97] CRAC also adjusted its formal statement of the aims of religious broadcasting to become less declaratory and missionary in orientation.[98] Under the Sound Broadcasting Act 1972, the ITA took on responsibility for the provision of independent local radio as well, being renamed the Independent Broadcasting Authority. However, in practice the ban on advertising and the system of previous approval ensured that no contract was awarded to a religious radio station. The only development of note was the possibility of gaining a cable television licence under the Cable and Broadcasting Act 1984. Although this Act required that undue prominence should not be given to the views and opinions of particular persons or bodies on religious matters and that editorial comment should be excluded,[99] this did not prevent all ownership by religious bodies. From 1986 one Christian broadcaster started broadcasting cable television services for two hours every Sunday.[100]

The Broadcasting Act 1990 brought about a substantial shift of approach. Instead of providing independent broadcasting services, the newly formed Independent Television Commission and Radio Authority became licensing and regulatory bodies. The Act also brought with it a certain degree of liberalization. Although it included an obligation in respect of Channels 3 and 5 to ensure that

[93] Television Act 1954, s 3(4); Television Act 1964, s 3(5)(a); Independent Broadcasting Authority Act 1973, s 4(5)(a); Broadcasting Act 1981, s 4(5)(a).

[94] Television Act 1954, s 8(2)(a); Television Act 1964, s 9(2)(a); Independent Broadcasting Authority Act 1973, s 10(2)(a); Broadcasting Act 1981, s 16(2)(a).

[95] Television Act 1964, s 4(1)(a).

[96] Television Act 1954, sched 2, rl 8; Television Act 1964, sched 2, rl 6; Independent Broadcasting Authority Act 1973, sched 2, rl 6; Broadcasting Act 1981, sched 2, rl 6.

[97] Leigh, *op cit* n 91, 290.

[98] Rachel Viney, 'Religious broadcasting on UK television: Policy, public perception and programmes' (1999) 36 Cultural Trends 1.

[99] Cable and Broadcasting Act 1984, s 11(3)(a) and (b) respectively.

[100] VisionChannel (Swindon area): Leigh, *op cit* n 91, 293–4.

a sufficient amount of time was given to religious programmes,[101] the CRAC lost its statutory basis, and the system of previous approval was abandoned. At the same time, the complete prohibition on advertising was lifted, and some licensing of broadcast media by religious bodies was permitted: non-domestic satellite services, licensable programme services, and local radio.[102] The most significant substantive test for the acceptability of religious broadcasting was contained in section 6, requiring 'due responsibility' to be exercised and the avoidance of 'any improper exploitation of those watching' or 'any abusive treatment of these belonging to a particular religion or religious denomination'.

In spite of this liberalization, the Codes of Guidance and the practice of the regulatory bodies continued to be dominated by the former public service ethos. In an extensive analysis of the processes around the legal changes, Andrew and Juliet Quicke identified a 'hidden agenda' on the part of the regulators determined to prevent any form of US-style evangelism or proselytization.[103] In 1999, the Christian Channel was fined £20,000 for breaching four of the ITC Code rules in respect of a programme-length advertisement for the US evangelist Morris Cerullo.[104] Indeed, it was arguable that the Code of Practice on religious broadcasting was *ultra vires* since it was much more restrictive than the new legislation from which it now derived its authority.[105] In 1993, when the new licences came into operation, ITV reduced its religious broadcast time by 62 per cent and withdrew from the 'closed period' on Sunday evenings.[106] This period had originally been a time of no broadcasting on Sunday evenings out of deference to the churches, which was subsequently replaced by a convention that this period should be reserved for religious broadcasts.

2. Current arrangements for public service broadcasting

The advent of digital technology makes possible a far wider range of provision and strengthens still further the move away from a monopolistically-derived public service ethos to a regulated market in which consumer choice is paramount. The Communications Act 2003 was intended to meet the demands of the latter without abandoning the former.[107] At the same time, it coincided with an increased public awareness of the significance of world religions and some willingness on the part of broadcasters to move beyond the conventional diet dominated by acts of Christian worship. The current law is still found in the Broadcasting

---

[101] Broadcasting Act 1990, ss 16(2)(e), 25 and 29(1).
[102] Broadcasting Act 1990, sched 2, pt 2.
[103] Andrew Quicke and Juliet Quicke, *Hidden Agendas: the Politics of Religious Broadcasting in Britain 1987–1991* (Virginia Beach: Dominion Kings Grant Publications, 1992).
[104] Viney, *op cit* n 98, 11.   [105] This is the conclusion of Leigh, *op cit* n 91, 303–4.
[106] Viney, *op cit* n 98, 16.
[107] Department for Culture, Media and Sport, Communications White Paper—a new future for communications (Dec 2000).

Acts 1990 and 1996, but as substantially amended and supplemented by the Communications Act 2003. This latter Act established a single regulator, the Office of Communications (OFCOM), and transferred to it licensing and regulatory functions in respect of independent television and radio. The BBC Charter has also recently been reviewed, with arrangements for the next decade coming into force on 1 January 2007. OFCOM also has limited regulatory responsibilities for the BBC.

OFCOM has a statutory duty to report on the fulfilment across all services of the public service remit.[108] Among many other things, the services taken together must include a suitable quantity and range of programmes dealing with religions and other beliefs.[109] Programmes that deal with religions and other beliefs should include those that provide news and other information about different religions and other beliefs; programmes about the history of different religions and other beliefs; and programmes showing acts of worship and other ceremonies and practices, including some in their entirety.[110] Rather more briefly, the BBC Trust is under obligation in its Agreement with the Secretary of State to ensure that it reflects and strengthens cultural identities at local, regional, and national level and that it promotes awareness of different cultures and alternative viewpoints, and in doing so reflects different religious and other beliefs.[111]

Overall responsibility for regulating the content of broadcasting is delegated to the OFCOM Content Board whose general function is to protect audiences, and to ensure both creative diversity and the fulfilment of public service obligations.[112] At an early stage the Content Board approved the continuation of the relationship with the Central Religious Advisory Committee, whose members continued to be appointed jointly by the BBC Governors and the Board.[113] They were drawn from across the five main religious traditions represented in the UK, but acted as individuals not as delegates. During 2004–6 concerns surfaced about the way members of the Committee were appointed.[114] Reports emerged that it had been sidelined in discussions about contemporary major religious broadcasting controversies, such as the decision by ITV to cut religious broadcasting, and screening of *Jerry Springer: the Opera* as well as the Christmas 2004 edition of *The Vicar of Dibley*.[115]

The House of Lords Select Committee on BBC Charter Review supported positively a wide definition of broadcasting about religion and other beliefs.[116] It wanted to see more high-quality, innovative, and thought-provoking programmes as well as better-informed current affairs reporting. The Committee

---

[108] Communications Act 2003, s 264.   [109] s 264(6)(f).   [110] s 264(6)(g).

[111] Department for Culture, Media and Sport, *An Agreement Between Her Majesty's Secretary of State for Culture, Media and Sport and the British Broadcasting Corporation*, Cm 6872 (July 2006), para 9.   [112] Communications Act 2003, s 13.

[113] Minutes of the 6th meeting of the Ofcom Content Board, 11 Nov 2003, para 21.

[114] Minutes of the 13th meeting of the Ofcom Content Board, 6 April 2004, para 35.

[115] See Maggie Brown, 'Defender of the faith', *The Guardian*, 28 March 2005.

[116] *Second Report of the Select Committee on BBC Charter Review* HL128-I (March 2006), ch 8.

thought there should be an obligation to provide viewers and listeners with a better understanding of different religious and other belief systems. However, when it came to the CRAC, the Select Committee was rather negative:

We were surprised at the differing perceptions of CRAC's role that we observed between the BBC, CRAC's members and Ofcom. Indeed, it is not at all clear what the role of CRAC is or whether it adds value to the broadcasting of religion. We therefore recommend that the position of CRAC be reviewed and clarified by the BBC in consultation with Ofcom.[117]

During 2007, the new BBC Trust engaged in a public consultation exercise around audience engagement in which the CRAC made a spirited defence of its role.[118] It did this in terms of the rising significance of religion, the importance of expertise, and the need for social cohesion. As a multi-faith group of experts who were not representative of the faith communities with which they were familiar, and not an interest group as such, they could be the 'critical friend' the BBC needed. The BBC Trust acknowledged that it needed to find ways of the listening to interest groups including those defined by religion,[119] but at the end of 2007, the CRAC was disbanded. In April 2009, a successor body was announced— the Standing Conference on Religion and Belief—under the same chair (Bishop Graham James), but including for the first time a humanist. This has sparked a public debate about the nature of humanism and whether it should be treated as a religion in its own right, with proportionate access to programmes such as *Thought for the Day*.[120] It remains to be seen whether the new body gains the legitimacy its predecessor was clearly losing.

3. Negative constraints on programmes and advertising

The Communications Act 2003 has resulted in a revision and consolidation of the codes of practice in respect of religious broadcasting. Section 4 of the OFCOM Broadcasting Code 2008 is based on three statutory principles of a proper degree of responsibility with respect to the content of religious programmes,[121] no improper exploitation of the susceptibilities of the audience,[122] and no abusive treatment of the religious views or beliefs of those belonging to any religion or religious denomination.[123] This is expressly placed in the context of articles 9, 10, and 14 of the European Convention. Thereafter, the Code is brief, expanding on these principles in only four respects. Where a religion or religious denomination is the subject of a religious programme, then the identity of the religion or

---

[117] Ibid, para 171.
[118] See <http://www.bbc.co.uk/bbctrust/our_work/other/our_promise_audiences.shtml>, accessed 11 November 2009; *Audience Council and CRAC Responses*, part 2.
[119] BBC Trust, *Our Promise to You: how the Trust will engage with audiences* (Nov 2007), para 3.5.   [120] See eg HL Deb, 4 Nov 2009, cols GC95–108.
[121] Communications Act 2003, s 319(2)(e).   [122] Ibid, s 319(6)(a).
[123] Ibid, s 319(6)(b).

denomination must be clear to the audience.[124] Religious programmes must not seek to promote religious views or belief by stealth, and programmes on television services must not seek recruits, ie directly appeal to the audience to join a religion or religious denomination.[125] However, religious programmes on radio may seek recruits, as may those on specialist religious television services. Finally, claims that a living person or group has special powers or abilities must be treated with due objectivity and not broadcast when a significant number of children may be watching or listening.[126]

OFCOM also has obligations to set standards, publish codes, and secure observance of those codes in respect of advertising as well as regular programming.[127] The general statutory requirements are that persons under the age of 18 must be protected; advertising must not be misleading, harmful, or offensive; relevant international obligations must be complied with; and there should be no undue discrimination between advertisers. Unsuitable sponsorship should be avoided and subliminal techniques are unacceptable. Political advertising is prohibited. In respect of religious advertising, the same principles apply as for religious programmes: a proper degree of responsibility must be exercised, which means in particular that there should be no improper exploitation of any susceptibilities of the audience nor any abusive treatment of the religious views and beliefs of those belonging to a particular religion or religious denomination.

OFCOM has contracted out most of its advertising standards code functions in respect of broadcast advertising to the Broadcast Committee of Advertising Practice (BCAP).[128] It has contracted out its powers to secure observance of the codes by handling and resolving complaints to the Advertising Standards Authority (Broadcast) (ASAB).[129] BCAP have adopted the former ITC and Radio Authority Codes, both of which contain specific sections in respect of religious advertising.

The Radio Code and the TV Code are similar in substance, although the TV Code is rather fuller and slightly more restrictive. The TV Code uses the language of 'doctrinal' to refer to advertising by, or on behalf of, any organization or individual whose objectives are or appear to be wholly or mainly concerned with religion, faith, or other philosophies or beliefs.[130] The Radio Code effectively uses the same broad definition. The name and faith of the group concerned must be clearly identified.[131] The principal structural difference is that the TV Code contains an explicit statement of what is allowed:

(a) publicizing events such as services, meetings or festivals;

---

[124] OFCOM Broadcasting Code 2008, rule 4.3.   [125] Ibid, rules 4.4, 4.5.
[126] Ibid, rule 4.7.   [127] Communications Act 2003, ss 319, 324, and 325.
[128] Contracting Out (Functions Relating to Broadcast Advertising) and Specification of Relevant Functions Order 2004, SI 2004/1975.
[129] Communications Act 2003, s 325(1)(b)   [130] Ibid, para 10.1(a).
[131] TV Code, para 10.16; Radio Code, para 3.3.

(b) describing an organization's or individual's activities or publicizing their name or contact details;

(c) offering publications or merchandise.[132]

The Codes contain several prohibitions. Advertising is not acceptable from any body which practises or advocates illegal behaviour, whose rites or other forms of collective observance are not normally directly accessible to the public,[133] and in the case of TV advertising, which have been shown to apply unreasonable pressure on people wishing to join or leave, and which do not give written assurances that no representative will call on any respondent without prior arrangement. Doctrine may not be expounded as fact, or true, but must be presented as a matter of belief.[134] Viewers and listeners may not be exhorted to change their beliefs or behaviour, or threatened with any consequences should they fail to do so.[135] Various categories of vulnerable person must be protected, and in the case of children the only acceptable products for advertisement are age-appropriate publications and merchandise without any recruitment or fund-raising link.[136]

In some cases the TV Code is more restrictive. The Radio Code states that advertising must not make claims for the efficacy of faith healing, miracle working, or counselling, and that references to the benefits of religion for personal well-being should be restrained in manner and capable of substantiation.[137] Astrological and psychic services may be advertised, so long as no claim of efficacy is made.[138] By contrast, the TV Code states that testimonials and references to individual experiences and personal benefits are unacceptable, as is any offer of counselling.[139] Treatments of the occult, psychic practices, and exorcism are prohibited.[140] Both Codes subject religious charity advertising to the standard provisions for charitable appeals, but whereas the Radio Code simply requires that appeals may not state or imply that gifts are in exchange for prayers or other spiritual benefits,[141] the TV Code is quite restrictive: the charities must reliably demonstrate that the funds will be used exclusively for the benefit of disadvantaged third parties, and the benefit must not be associated with any other objective such as proselytizing.[142]

No TV or radio licensee is obliged to carry religious advertising, but must set its policy in a non-discriminatory way.[143] The TV Code recognizes that controls on advertising on specialized religious channels can be relaxed, in particular that expositions of doctrine and of the benefits of a religion are permissible. Services and ceremonies may be shown, and children may be targeted, so long as there

---

[132] TV Code, para 10.5   [133] TV Code, para 10.2; Radio Code, para 3.2.

[134] TV Code, para 10.8; Radio Code, para 3.6(a).

[135] TV Code, paras 10.8, 10.14; Radio Code, paras 3.4, 3.6(b).

[136] TV Code, para 10.15; Radio Code, para 3.8(a).   [137] Radio Code, para 3.7.

[138] Ibid, para 3.12.   [139] Ibid, paras 10.10, 10.11.

[140] TV Code, para 10.3. There are minor exceptions for tarot-based prediction services.

[141] Radio Code, para 3.9.   [142] TV Code, para 10.7.

[143] Ibid, Introductory Note 6; Radio Code, para 3.1.

is no recruitment or fund-raising. A specialized religious channel is a television licensable content service (ie cable TV) which has been granted a licence following a determination under Schedule 14, Part 4 of the Communications Act 2003.

4. Religious bodies as broadcasters

Religious bodies are disqualified from holding Channel 3 and 5 licences, a national sound broadcasting licence, a public teletext licence, an additional television service licence, and television or radio multiplex licences.[144] In respect of other licences, the applicant must not only be a fit and proper person in a position to secure compliance with licence conditions,[145] but OFCOM must make a prior determination that it is appropriate for the applicant to hold the licence of the description applied for.[146] The determination must remain in force for the duration of the licence. OFCOM are obliged to publish guidance as to the principles they will apply in making determinations. The guidance clarifies the types of licence a religious organization may hold.[147] These include restricted television and radio service licences,[148] local analogue radio services, local or national digital services, and content services.[149] The only significant substantive test is contained in paragraph 4:

OFCOM will consider the appropriateness of religious bodies to hold Broadcasting Act licences provided they do not:

(a) practise or advocate illegal behaviour;
(b) practise or advocate behaviour which is injurious to the health or morals of participants or others;
(c) practise or advocate behaviour which infringes the rights and freedoms of participants or others;
(d) pose a threat to public safety;
(e) pose a threat to national security or territorial integrity; or
(f) threaten the authority and impartiality of the judiciary.

Of course, it does not follow that a religious body satisfying these and the other general requirements will necessarily receive a licence.

5. European standards

OFCOM documentation now makes frequent reference to obligations under the Human Rights Act 1998. In regulating access to broadcast media, and the

---

[144] Broadcasting Act 1990, sched 2, pt 2, as amended.
[145] Communications Act 2003, ss 3(3) and 3(7) respectively.   [146] Ibid, sched 14, pt 4.
[147] OFCOM Guidance for religious bodies applying for a Broadcasting Act licence.
[148] ie for a particular establishment, location or event: Broadcasting Act 1990, s 42A.
[149] OFCOM Guidance, para 2.

content of religious broadcasting and advertising, OFCOM and the ASA exercise public functions and are subject to judicial review on traditional and human rights grounds. Article 10 European Convention states expressly that States are not prevented from requiring the licensing of broadcasting, television, or cinema enterprises, but such licensing must still be in proportionate pursuit of a legitimate public interest. Both the European Court of Human Rights and the European Court of Justice have accepted that technological advances are such that a public service monopoly is no longer justifiable.[150]

The European Court has repeatedly stated that the significance of article 10 in the context of audiovisual broadcasting is that it imposes a positive obligation on States to ensure objectivity and pluralism within the sector. States must secure access to impartial and accurate information as well as a range of opinion and comment.[151] Thus violations of the Convention have been found in cases in which an animal welfare organization was prevented from advertising, a political party from broadcasting its views, and a private religious radio station from gaining a licence.[152]

However, the Court has hitherto shown considerable deference to national authorities in their regulation of religious broadcasting. In *Murphy v Ireland*, the applicant was a minister attached to the Irish Faith Centre, which wished to advertise a video showing the evidence for the resurrection during Easter week.[153] The Independent Radio and Television Commission stopped the broadcast on the basis of legislation prohibiting the broadcast of any advertisement directed towards a religious end. The Court upheld the restriction on the grounds that, having regard to the national margin of appreciation, a complete ban on religious advertising was necessary. It accepted the Government's arguments that religious advertising could be offensive, and that a more limited restriction would be hard to apply fairly and objectively. It also accepted the argument that a limited freedom would benefit dominant religions with more adherents and resources at their disposal.

The judgment in *Murphy* is problematic on at least two counts. First, having recited the *Handyside* mantra of 'pluralism, tolerance and broad-mindedness' and concluded that article 10 does not 'protect a person from exposure to a religious view simply because it is not his own', the Court was not prepared to dissent from the view of the Irish High Court that the mere fact of religious advertising could be offensive and justify a restriction. Secondly, the Court allowed concerns about neutrality to override arguments about liberty. It is, of course, an

---

[150] *Informationsverein Lentia v Austria* (1994) 17 EHRR 93, para 39; *Vereniging Veronica Omroep Organisatie v Commissariaat voor de Media* C-148/91 [1993] ECR I-487. For further discussion of European Union and human rights dimensions of broadcasting regulation generally, see Rachael Craufurd Smith, *Broadcasting Law and Fundamental Rights* (Oxford: Clarendon Press, 1997).

[151] See, most recently, *Manole v Moldova*, no 13936/02 (2009), paras 95–102.

[152] See, respectively, *Vgt Verein gegen Tierfabriken v Switzerland* (2002) 34 EHRR 4; *TV Vest AS v Norway* (2009) 48 EHRR 51; *Glas Nadezhda EOOD v Bulgaria* (2009) 48 EHRR 35. The latter violation was on procedural grounds.   [153] *Murphy v Ireland* (2004) 38 EHRR 13.

almost inevitable consequence of liberty that certain products will succeed. The mere fact that religious advertising might lead to a 'free market' in religion hardly seems persuasive as a ground for restricting it. Andrew Geddis rightly notes a significant discrepancy in the way that the Court treats political as opposed to religious speech, suggesting that this is rooted in two questionable assumptions: that religious expression is less socially valuable and that State regulation of religion is less likely to be biased.[154]

The British ban on the licensing of a religious body to operate a national analogue radio station likewise survived scrutiny in *United Christian Broadcasters Ltd v UK*.[155] The applicants argued that to prevent them from even being considered was a disproportionate restriction on their freedom of expression in conjunction with freedom of religion and non-discrimination. However, the Court declared the application inadmissible on the grounds that the Government's decision was justified by its legitimate preference for greater local radio provision and the need to prevent the domination of one viewpoint in the light of spectrum scarcity.

IV. Conclusion

The last decade has seen a remarkable growth in public sector religious consultation bodies. This has been fuelled by a growing recognition of the relevance and diversity of religious belief and practice both in the UK and internationally. Just as civil servants come to accept that certain public policy questions have hitherto unremarked religious dimensions, so also new experiments in public service religious broadcasting show that it is increasingly difficult to separate out 'the religious broadcast' from a range of topics which have a religious dimension. This makes defining the remit of a faith-based consultation body quite tricky: CRAC no longer had an obvious 'slice' of programming in which it had a special interest. In that sense the problem here is a microcosm of the problem of the place of religion in public life more generally. If the rise of public sector consultation bodies has been about understanding and inclusion it also marks an opening up of settled boundaries between religion and public life.

The debate over the composition of the House of Lords shows that it is extremely difficult to construct formal multi-faith bodies on strict principles of proportionate representation. The depth and nature of religious conviction is too diverse—in what sense are Christians a majority or minority of the population, for example? The internal structures of religions do not necessarily produce persons able and willing to represent their faith in the way which the Government or public body would like. Yet in terms of helping a secular generation emerge

---

[154] Andrew Geddis, 'You can't say "God" on the Radio: Freedom of Expression, Religious Advertising and the Broadcast Media after Murphy v Ireland' [2004] EHRLR 180.
[155] *United Christian Broadcasters Ltd v UK*, no 44802/98 (2000).

from its religious illiteracy such bodies would seem to be indispensible. At least they make possible a systematic questioning of comfortable assumptions about what religion is and does and a point of contact towards greater understanding. Ultimately they may be the means of an ongoing renegotiation of hitherto settled boundaries between religions and the State. If they are to do this, a certain messiness around composition and remit has to be tolerated.

11

In Search of Principle

It is time to take a step back from the detailed exposition of legal doctrine set out in preceding chapters to consider the question of constitutional principle. A systematic attempt to understand the way in which English law regulates organized religions has been at the foundation of this entire study. We are now in a position to sketch a general statement.

It is not obvious that a general statement can take the form of constitutional principle. English law suffers from a characteristic absence of suitably authoritative materials. There is no constitutional text which sets out the fundamental values of the law, however briefly. Nor have common-law judges been prone to articulate these values, although that is to some extent a matter of judicial fashion, and their willingness to do so may once again be changing. The search is made particularly difficult on account of the absence of a tradition of textbook writing in this field. That is one of the consequences of establishment which this book seeks to redress. For it has largely been the systematic articulation of legal doctrine in textbooks which has provided English lawyers with their frameworks of principle.

One plausible response is to make a virtue of necessity and seek to evade the question of principle altogether. Perhaps the current law should be understood, not in normative terms, but as a contingent point in a process of gradual evolution which had as its starting point a single established church, and which has been subject to processes of secularization for at least 400 years. The current law is a fleeting moment in a movement from past practices and understandings to an uncertain future. With hindsight, it is possible to discern periods of relative stability and periods of rapid change. After the 'long eighteenth century' of Protestant toleration, the main components of the current law were set in place during a period of rapid change from 1830–1870. Change slowed notably from 1870 to 1920, and much of the twentieth-century law of organized religions has been a series of footnotes. As previous chapters have shown, a noticeable shift of emphasis has once again taken place in the law since the turn of the millennium. Only time will tell how significant a shift this is. It is easy enough to see such an historical account in broad terms as a journey from establishment to secularism, and recent changes as merely the next stage. If not universal, processes of secularization are at least widespread among 'western' liberal democracies. English law has its commonalities with other legal systems and its peculiarities, and there is little more to be said beyond tracing the legal dimensions of the story to date.

Nevertheless, in spite of its normative modesty, this response is inadequate. Unless they are to be wholly locked away in the isolated exaltation of the ivory tower, systematic treatments of the law cannot evade responsibility for playing a part in shaping its unfolding narrative, even when they masquerade as purely descriptive collections of legal miscellanea. The point has just been made that the articulation of legal doctrine in textbooks has been the English lawyers' typical substitute for constitutional principle. Even a reconstruction which sees the law on a journey from establishment to secularism cannot avoid having an agenda. Understood in this way, establishment and secularism provide paradigms for the relationship between law and religion, one descriptively historic and prescriptively undesirable, the other the *telos* of our constitutional development, both predicted and desired. There is a close relationship between such an account of the law and the secularization thesis of sociology. This too was no merely descriptive theory of modernization, but a matter for complacent self-congratulation on the part of an increasingly agnostic intellectual élite. Even if inevitable, one must ask whether such a development is good.

The closest the British constitution has ever come to a statement of constitutional principle in the law of organized religions can be found in the Church of Scotland Act 1921.[1] This short Act ended two centuries of dispute and schism within Scottish Presbyterianism about the extent to which the civil magistrate—we might say secular Government—may interfere in the life of the church. The Act enabled a reunion of the main Presbyterian Churches to take place by declaring to be lawful certain articles drafted by the Church of Scotland itself.[2] These articles set out its constitution in matters spiritual. Matters spiritual include matters as mundane as the disposition of church property and the terms on which its ministers are appointed. Article 4 states that the church 'has the right and power subject to no civil authority to legislate and [...] adjudicate finally in all matters of doctrine, worship, government and discipline'. The Act states that this does not affect the jurisdiction of the civil courts in civil matters.[3] Nor is it to prejudice the recognition of any other church protected in its spiritual functions.[4]

The Church of Scotland Act reflects the principles of autonomy and neutrality. Religious liberty is not only individual but requires self-government by the

---

[1] Strictly speaking, one should add, 'and the Church of Scotland (Property and Endowments) Act 1925'. Historical background in Lord Rodger of Earlsferry, *The Courts, the Church and the Constitution: Aspects of the Disruption of 1843* (Edinburgh: Edinburgh University Press, 2008); overview in R M Morris (ed), *Church and State in 21st Century Britain: The Future of Church Establishment* (Basingstoke: Palgrave Macmillan, 2009), ch 6. Of course, this does not imply that the whole of the Scottish law of Church and State is summed up in this short Act. For a general account, see Stair Memorial Encyclopaedia, *The Laws of Scotland*, vol 3 'Churches and Other Religious Bodies' (Edinburgh: Butterworths, 1994).   [2] Church of Scotland Act 1921, s 1.
[3] Ibid, s 3.   [4] Ibid, s 2.

church within a sphere defined as internal to the religion ('spiritual matters'). Religious equality requires this sphere of autonomy to be available to all. In this sense, the State ought to be neutral between religions. Both liberty and equality point to a certain conception of secularism: that there is a sphere of civil matters, which the State may regulate in a way which is not religiously distinctive, for the benefit of all. Church and State are separate. But this model of Church–State relations in turn requires the State and Church mutually to recognize each other's sovereignties. Thus the legislation reflects a 'concordat' which can properly be called constitutional.[5] It settles the question of the legal status of the church, which as a result is 'established' by law.[6] However, it is an establishment which was intended to be paradigmatic, not exclusive.

The English law of organized religions has never reflected the principles of autonomy and neutrality as clearly or succinctly as this. However, by the 1920s there was little doubt that this was the appropriate direction of travel. Twentieth-century legal developments were almost always further steps in this direction. The European Convention values of autonomy and neutrality reflect this model, and it is arguable that the limited discussion of concepts such as secularism and establishment by the European Court are also to be seen in this light. The idealized model set out in the Church of Scotland Act 1921 enables us to see the significance of recent legal developments: a different concept of secularism is at work, which is undermining the autonomy of organized religions and the neutrality of the State. It also reminds us that 'establishment' is not necessarily inimical to the securing of those same values.

I. The Inadequacy of Individual Rights

As values, autonomy and neutrality have a collective orientation. Indeed, it is possible to see them as the collective equivalents of individual religious liberty and equality. As Chapter 2 has shown, the European Court, along with other international human rights institutions, has developed these values on the foundation of individual rights. Their implications are being articulated with ever greater precision. However, international human rights instruments take individual rights as their starting point, and these rights are now reflected most clearly in the Human Rights Act 1998 and a growing body of equalities legislation, most notably the Employment Equality (Religion or Belief) Regulations 2003 and the Equality Acts 2006 and 2010. Since it is more natural to look for constitutional principle in individual rights, it is important to understand why these are inadequate and why they have to be developed in their collective dimension.

---

[5] Vernon Bogdanor, *The Monarchy and the Constitution* (Oxford: Clarendon Press, 1995), 237, uses the term 'treaty'. A concordat is a treaty between Church and State.
[6] Colin Munro, 'Does Scotland have an Established Church?' (1997) 4 Ecc LJ 639.

In the European context, individual rights to religious liberty and equality have developed broadly parallel structures. In the case of liberty, the right to have a religion is absolute. By contrast, the right to manifest that religion 'in public or private, individually or in community with others, in worship, teaching, practice or observance', may be limited by reference to the necessary pursuit of a legitimate public interest or the protection of the rights and freedoms of others. This requires a balancing exercise to be undertaken in accordance with the doctrine of proportionality. In the case of equality, direct discrimination prevents others from making the religion or belief of an individual a ground for the denial of some protected benefit such as employment, or the provision of goods or services. Indirect discrimination requires the application of burdensome general rules or policies to be justified by reference to the proportionate pursuit of a legitimate public interest. In each case there is a core of absolute (or near absolute) prohibition and a penumbra of *prima facie* prohibition.

It should now be obvious that the individual rights construction is only capable of explaining part of the law of organized religions. Questions of the ownership and control of religious property, the jurisdiction of religious tribunals and their relationship to courts of law, the appointment of ministers of religion or participation in formal consultation processes with Government cannot be recast as a matter of individual legal right. Even if one is prepared to look past legal or factual corporate personality to see these matters as the expression of an aggregate of individual rights, their practical dimension (property, finance, administration etc) can be too easily contrasted with an ethereal understanding of 'spirituality' to deny that religious freedom and equality are at stake. Individual religious believers benefit from these arrangements, but—as individuals—they do not have rights to them.

In other contexts, individual rights only tell half the story: the right of an individual religious believer to get married in accordance with the rites of their religion, to access chaplaincy services in prison, to attend a school with a religious ethos of which they approve, or receive welfare services in a faith-based context parallels the interest of the religious community in celebrating marriages with civil effect, in maintaining contact with co-religionists, in providing education or welfare services in what they take to be a more holistic context. Individual enjoyment requires the prior positive structuring by the law of the interface between public institutions and religious bodies.

The only cases in which a purely individual rights construction seems possible are those in which the religious believer wishes to continue some personal religious act, such as maintaining a distinctive diet, dress, or prayer, in a restricted public or semi-public context. There may be other believers in similar situations, but the problem is not necessarily collective. Even here, individualization has a tendency to distort. There are, of course, cases of genuinely individual conscience, but when, for example, a Sikh wishes to wear a ceremonial knife or a bangle in public, this is not primarily an act of individual religious commitment, but an expression of identification—of the individual with his or her community, and of the members of the community in public. Until the late nineteenth century, the growth of toleration of cases of conscience was expressly about creating spaces for minority groups, such as Quakers, Moravians, and Brethren, identified in law as groups not as individuals. It is not surprising that the laws which have accommodated the expression of Sikh identity in public have fluctuated between requiring the individual to be wearing the object as a Sikh or 'for religious reasons', which is potentially broader and a more individualistic test.[7]

The problem with individual rights to religious liberty and equality is not simply that they fail to qualify descriptively for the current law. They are also inherently weak. The weakness derives from the fact that they require balancing between the individual and the public or collective interest. Cases turning simply on the question of whether the litigant has been prevented from having a religious belief or has been subject to direct discrimination are rare. The normal case involves a decision or rule which burdens a religious individual by making it harder for them to practise their religion in a context covered by the right. Although in a few cases under the legislation just mentioned, courts have denied that the burden even brings the individual within the scope of the right, they have generally been quite quick to accept that the decision or rule subject to litigation has fallen *prima facie* within the protection of a religious liberty or equality right, in other words that the decision or rule needs justification.[8] They have then engaged in a balancing exercise in accordance with the doctrine of proportionality to determine whether or not the right of the individual is to prevail over the public or collective interest with which it conflicts. This balancing exercise is characteristic of the majority of both religious liberty and religious equality cases.

People are rarely prepared to litigate to defend a religious practice without being sincerely committed to it. One might add that they are rarely able to do so without some form of collective backing. However, courts are understandably unwilling to enter into questions of religious truth or orthodoxy, so an individual religious believer can only be asked to cross a very low plausibility threshold when they show that they actually have the belief in question as part of a broader metaphysical worldview. The question of accommodation thus resolves into one of convenience to the public or collective interest. Given that general rules are more or less burdensome on individuals anyway, and are formulated to maximize the public interest in spite of this cost to the individual, the decision is structurally weighted against the individual. It is not surprising that the religious cases litigated so far under the human rights and equality legislation have almost always resulted in failure for the individual.[9]

---

[7] See 31 above.

[8] The most obvious example in which a majority of the House of Lords denied that enjoyment of a right was even limited is *R (Begum) v Denbigh High School Governors* [2007] 1 AC 100.

[9] *R (Williamson) v Secretary of State for Education and Employment* [2005] 2 AC 246; *Copsey v WBB Devon Clays Ltd* [2005] ICR 1789; *R (R) v Leeds City Council* [2006] ELR 25; *R (Begum) v*

Courts often remind themselves that it does not matter whether the litigant is part of a recognized religious community asserting a right on behalf of many others, or an individual with idiosyncratic views; each deserves respect.[10] In saying this, there is a back-handed recognition that the size of the community tends to have an influence. In practice also, attempts to distinguish between religious acts which are obligatory and religious acts which are a matter of individual preference and decision reflect a covert reference to communities of belief.[11] Since courts cannot enter into theological debate, 'obligatory' in this context can only be determined by reference to one's membership of a community agreed on the obligatory nature of the act in question. In this light, an insistence that there is no difference between an individual and the representative of a substantial religious minority takes on a more restrictive significance. It risks treating the representative believer as an unconventional individual, with all the weakness in position which this implies, even if he or she is part of a minority group.

Individual rights to religious liberty and equality are not only weak, they even have a paradoxical tendency to undermine the freedom to be part of a religious community. Civil and political rights were conceived as rights against the State, yet were cast in universal terms. One of the intriguing features of human rights jurisprudence of the late twentieth century—whether international or domestic—has been the failure to think through the substantive implications of assuming that rights against the State can double up as rights against everyone.[12] The effect has been to create a presumption that non-State actors should respect these rights as well. In the case of religious liberty rights, the law has been consistent in seeing the right of the religious individual against his or her community as satisfied by the right of exit. However, one can find evidence of a growing assumption that everyone who wishes should be able to join any religious body, or that membership tests are suspect.[13] The implication is that it is up to the individual to decide if he or she qualifies for membership, not the body of which he or she is to be a member. Such an assumption represents an individualizing of religious liberty *against* the religious community. In the case of equality rights,

---

Denbigh High School Governors [2007] 1 AC 100; *R (Playfoot) v Millais School Governing Body* [2007] HRLR 34; *R (Swami Suryananda) v Welsh Ministers* [2007] EWCA Civ 893; *Ghai v Newcastle City Council* [2009] EWHC 978 (Admin); *McClintock v Department of Constitutional Affairs* [2008] IRLR 29; *Eweida v British Airways plc* [2009] ICR 303; *Ladele v Islington LBC* [2009] ICR 387, [2009] EWCA Civ 1357; *Azmi v Kirklees MBC* [2007] ICR 1154; *R (Watkins-Singh) v Aberdare Girls' High School Governors* [2008] ELR 561 is the exception.

[10] *R (Williamson) v Secretary of State for Education and Employment* [2005] 2 AC 246, 258.

[11] This distinction is reinforced by the structure of non-discrimination law. See *Eweida v British Airways plc* [2009] ICR 303. It is the obvious explanation for the different outcomes in *Playfoot* and *Watkins-Singh* (n 9 above).

[12] This is the central problem of 'horizontal effect'. See Julian Rivers, 'Translator's Introduction' in Robert Alexy, *A Theory of Constitutional Rights*, trans Julian Rivers (Oxford: Oxford University Press, 2002), xxxvi–xliv; See *Ghaidan v Godin-Mendoza* [2004] 2 AC 557 for a signal failure to spot the relevance of the property rights of the landlord on the other side of the relationship.

[13] See the comments of the Charity Commission at 165 above.

the law has had to create 'exceptions' for religious groups, which may be more or less adequate in preserving the group's right to maintain its identity. Again, the assumption is that the preservation of religious identity on the part of civil society groups needs justification *against* the individual who does not share that identity. The logic of many human rights cases has been to force the parties into a grid of State-versus-individual which is potentially destructive of the identity of non-State collectivities.[14]

In short, individual rights to religious liberty and equality, important though they undoubtedly are, do not represent an adequate grounding of principle for the law of organized religions. They fail to capture central parts of the subject-matter, they distort the underlying social reality, they are inherently weak, and they risk capture by a statist agenda that subjects all of civil society to its own ethos. As candidates for constitutional principle underlying the law of organized religions, they are descriptively inadequate and prescriptively unappealing.

II. Establishment by Law

The most obvious candidate for constitutional principle is the idea of establishment. Indeed, one might suppose that the law can be characterized as structured around a tolerant establishment, or in other words, by one paradigm of Church–State relations coupled with greater or lesser degrees of accommodation for other denominations and religions.

1. Establishment in the historic sense

In a very loose sense, a religion is established in a State when it is recognized as the official State religion or ideology. The fact that this definition is not at all helpful is exposed the moment one starts to consider the institutional expression of official State recognition. 'Islamic' States do not manifest their religious commitment in the law in the same way that 'Christian' ones do. Moreover, the scare quotes are necessary, because within each religion there is a range of opinion as to what the relationship with Government should be. Nor are these ranges parallel in the sense that each of a limited number of possible positions on the relationship between religion and the State can be found in each religion. Different religions are expressed in different institutional forms which result in different debates about the State–religion relationship.

---

[14] In *Wallbank v Aston Cantlow and Wilmcote with Billesley Parochial Church Council* [2002] Ch 51 CA, [2004] 1 AC 546 HL, the Court of Appeal thought the Church of England was the 'State' and the lay rectors the 'individual'. The House of Lords thought that the Church of England was on the individual side as a potential victim of human rights violations by the State. Neither construction is adequate.

It is therefore better to see establishment as a term only applying within Christian political thought and involving the recognition of a single State church. Moreover, if it is to be given any fixed or precise meaning, it has to be related to the historical context in which it arose. The two principal components of this context were the splitting of Latin Christendom in the sixteenth century as a result of the Protestant Reformation and the parallel rise of monarchical absolutism and the sovereign nation-state. Both Church and 'State' (ie royal government) pre-existed this turn of events for many centuries as complex and dynamic legal entities. Establishment meant the assertion of new forms of centralized Governmental control over the church and an elevation of the church to a bearer of national identity in an ideologically splintered international context.[15]

Although this development was pan-European, its expression varied from State to State. There was no single conception of a State church. Even before the Reformation, the jurisdictional boundaries between church courts and royal courts varied from country to country. Lutheranism diverged from Roman Catholicism in its ecclesiology, producing a range of different models for Governmental control over church property, for example. If one wishes to be completely precise, one has to consider the meaning of establishment in each separate emerging nation-state. To say that the Church of England is established by law is to point to its legal settling, securing, and control by the Crown with the aid of Parliament. In its oppressive form—which we might conveniently date from Henry VIII's assumption of papal powers in 1535 to the Toleration Act 1689—it was the only church. Membership and subordination to its ministry were as inescapable as political subjection. Vigorous internal debate might, and did, take place as to its doctrine, worship, discipline, and government, but there was no recognized alternative for dissenters. Legal history before 1535 is an account of conflict and collaboration between Church and State, not least in the violent suppression of heresy after 1401, but it is not obvious that we can call the mediaeval church 'established'. It was simply one jurisdiction among many, for it takes a 'State' to establish a church.[16] Legal history after 1689 is an account of the ways in which Church and State slowly part company. The story briefly sketched in Chapter 1 of this book has parallels in continental Europe, but they are only inexact.

Moreover, it would be hard to say what it might mean to return to an established church, even as a thought-experiment. The growth of the modern State has been intertwined with the continual rearticulation of the social role of the Christian church. For example, the social welfare function of the State is at one level as old as the Elizabethan Poor Law, although it was in organizational terms largely a local activity of the church. Having been through the history of

---

[15] The classic defence of the 'Elizabethan settlement' is that of Richard Hooker, *Of the Laws of Ecclesiastical Polity (1593–7)* (London: Dent, 1907).

[16] See the magisterial account in Harold J Berman, *Law and Revolution: The Formation of the Western Legal Tradition* (Cambridge, Mass: Harvard University Press, 1983).

independent religious voluntary effort, State coordination and assistance, centralized control and funding, and on into new forms of attempted plural collaboration, an 'establishment' of Christianity in the social welfare system could only mean yet new forms of provision and regulation.

Thus in one sense of the word, establishment was an unrepeatable historical moment in the development of the Christian church and the modern State, the legal incidents of which can be identified with precision in any one legal system, and with broad comparability across Latin Christendom. The impact of that historical moment can be seen not only in the legal residue of establishment as it still affects the Church of England, but also in the legal position of other organized religions as they were partially included in the incidents of establishment, and even in our understanding of the modern concept and functions of the State. In this sense, the established Church of England is an ever-receding memory.

2. Establishment in the comparative sense

If establishment in the historic sense is the characteristic of the monopolistic Christian church of a single political community, the Church of England was disestablished in 1689. Of course, the church continued to occupy a legal position very different from those of other tolerated religions. Establishment could then be defined in comparative terms as the ways in which the law governing the Church of England differed from the law governing other tolerated and oppressed religions. The process of expanding toleration has played out in different European countries in different ways. Only in England have bishops survived in the legislature. Thus in the comparative sense as well, establishment has no fixed content. It is a matter of contingent historical residue reflecting centuries of debate and re-adjustment. But for those interested in a programme of religious equality, or the justification of Anglican difference, it is still a useful definition.[17]

The main legal features of the Church of England which make it established in this sense of the term can be summarized as follows: the monarch is supreme Governor of the church and must be in communion with it.[18] She is styled *Fidei Defensor* and takes an oath on her coronation to uphold the church as established by law. Clergy must recognize her supremacy in the church. She makes senior appointments on the advice of her ministers, some of whom also have their own powers of appointment. Some churches (royal peculiars) are under her own direct jurisdiction, not that of the bishop in whose diocese they are located. The most senior bishops sit in the House of Lords. Parliament is still the legislature for

---

[17] This is the definition adopted by O Chadwick, *Church and State: Report of the Archbishop's Commission* (London: Church Information Office, 1970), 2. It also underlies R M Morris (ed), *Church and State in 21st Century Britain: the Future of Church Establishment* (Basingstoke: Palgrave Macmillan, 2009).

[18] Recent account of the monarchical aspects of establishment in Ian Leigh, 'By law established? The Crown, constitutional reform and the Church of England' [2004] PL 266.

the church, although the church has received a measure of autonomy—not by granting it independence in spiritual matters, but by giving it privileged access to the legislative process. The property and finances of the church are overseen by committees with Government representation. The church itself takes the form of a vast network of persons, both individual and corporate, and property, held together by one branch of the law of the land. This law is upheld by courts with coercive jurisdiction such as the ability to compel witnesses. Their judgments are overseen by the High Court as a matter of public law, rather than by way of private right. The content of that law is largely paralleled by other religious bodies, although there are special legal powers such as those to award special marriage licences, regulate notaries public, order exhumations, and award Lambeth degrees. There are also unique obligations such as those to parishioners in respect of baptism, marriage, and burial. Clergy of the Church of England have a guaranteed place on Standing Advisory Councils for Religious Education and are *primus inter pares* in arranging chaplaincy services within public institutions.

Although the Church in Wales was disestablished in 1920, it has been noted that general duties on clergy to marry and bury parishioners remain.[19] This is indicative of a continuing social position but is not in itself a mark of establishment in the comparative sense, since any religious body could take these obligations on itself. However, the Church in Wales does retain jurisdiction over useable pre-1662 burial grounds which must be available to all. Furthermore, the Church in Wales retains distinctive obligations in respect of prison chaplaincies. There is thus a minor residual 'establishment' even here.

As a term to assist in understanding the law of organized religions more generally the comparative concept of establishment is problematic. This is most clearly exposed in relation to the Church of Scotland, which can simultaneously be called established, since it enjoys a privileged position in relation to other churches and religions by virtue of legislation, but is at the same time the least established of all churches and religions by virtue of its independence from Government and the civil law. It is no accident that the language of 'establishment' is controversial in this context. The language comes naturally to lawyers, since one suspects that for all the professions of openness to other denominations, the twentieth-century position was only won on account of the Church of Scotland's earlier dominance. But how should one categorize the distinctive treatment of religious bodies which have never enjoyed an historic monopoly? If special provision is now made for the Salvation Army or the Dai al-Mutlak, are they thereby established?[20] If new arrangements were made for Jewish or Muslim tribunals would that be an example of a new establishment?

---

[19] T G Watkin, 'The vestiges of establishment: the ecclesiastical and canon law of the Church in Wales' (1990) 2 Ecc LJ 110; Norman Doe, *The Law of the Church in Wales* (Cardiff: University of Wales Press, 2002). Background to Welsh disestablishment in Morris (ed), *op cit* n 1, ch 8.

[20] See 87 above.

Establishment as a comparative term also fails to know how to categorize modes of preference and privilege which are mediated through continuing social factors. A programme of State funding for historic buildings, such as exists in France, or to some extent in the United Kingdom, will inevitably benefit disproportionately those religions with an historic presence.[21] Where the terms of the funding allow for the continued occupation and use of the buildings for their historic purposes, it is hard not to see this as a form of distinctive treatment. But is it establishment? *Laïque* France would like to believe not. By the same token it is not obvious that the endowments of the Church of England, or the involvement of lay patrons in appointments, are features of establishment relatively speaking. They are simply the social consequence of historic dominance. 'Disestablishment' may be—and was—accompanied by a measure of disendowment, but the two are not necessarily connected.

3. Plural establishment

Establishment in the comparative sense does not distinguish between two fundamentally opposed strategies to the removal of distinctive legal provision, the 'levelling down' involved in reducing the established church to the position of other religious bodies, and the 'levelling up' involved in admitting other religious bodies to the privileges of the established church. Lord Mansfield thought that the Toleration Act 1689 had 'established' dissenting societies, because their existence was now legally protected.[22] That was a form of levelling up, albeit minimal. This ambiguity emerges most notably in discussions about church taxation. Plural forms of taxation, where the taxpayer nominates the religious body to which the tax is to be transferred, are a form of disestablishment defined relatively. The German Basic Law proclaims that there shall be no State church, while retaining a plural tax regime.[23] Yet at the same time, James Madison inveighed against such a proposal in Virginia in 1785 as a failure to disestablish.[24] And there is no doubt that a plural church tax would fall foul of the no-establishment clause of the First Amendment today. However, one cannot condemn all forms of pluralization as 'plural establishment'. Characterizing new forms of consultation with religious bodies, or new public funding streams, as 're-establishment' does not

---

[21] On France, see Brigitte Basdevant-Gaudemet, 'State and Church in France', in Gerhard Robbers (ed), *State and Church in the European Union* (Baden-Baden: Nomos, 1996).

[22] In *Evans v Chamberlain of London*, noted in *AG v Pearson* (1817) 3 Mer 353, 420.

[23] Weimar Imperial Constitution 1919, arts 137(1), (5), and (6) incorporated by the Basic Law 1949, art 140. See Gerhard Robbers, 'Diversity of State-Religion Relations and European Union Unity' (2004) 7 Ecc LJ 304; Axel Freiherr von Campenhausen, 'Church Autonomy in Germany' in Gerhard Robbers (ed), *Church Autonomy* (Frankfurt a M: Peter Lang, 2001).

[24] Brief account in Martha C Nussbaum, *Liberty of Conscience: in defense of America's tradition of religious equality* (New York: Basic Books, 2008), 87–97.

make it inappropriate.[25] When municipal cemeteries allow distinct areas to be set aside for burial according to the rites of different religions, or when prisons secure chaplains for all faiths, they accommodate religious difference in ways which seem basically uncontroversial. Even to Americans.

It is true that most of the remaining incidents of Anglican establishment could only plausibly be levelled down. But as debates around the presence of bishops in the House of Lords show, serious thought can still be given to pluralization at least in that area. We should also be open to the possibility that the relationship between the internal law of an organized religion and the ordinary law is better expressed in the Anglican model of a system of law overseen by way of public law procedure, rather than through the private law analogy of contract and trust. In addition, Anglican ecclesiastical law is able to make the ownership of property (and thus to some extent the distribution of power) more diffuse while still upholding forms of connection which make it possible to talk of a single church. That may be valuable in the face of judicial attempts to squeeze organized religions into the mould of single entities.

In the English context, plural establishment has never had the connotation of a multiplicity of closed religio-political communities. If one takes 'establishment' in its historic sense of compulsory State religion, then it is logical enough to understand plural establishment in this way. But here one sees the influence of individual religious liberty at work. Religion became voluntary (1689) before establishment was pluralized (1830s onwards). Plural establishment may be undesirable, but not for reasons of compulsion.

It is easy to slip from the historic to the comparative and plural senses of establishment, and thence into a pejorative one, in which all possible forms of connection between religions and the State are rejected.[26] This assumes that levelling down is always the proper means to carry out a programme of disestablishment. Such a strategy adopted in 1689 would have resulted in all religions becoming unlawful. More to the point, among those who propound disestablishing in this way, surprisingly little thought is given to what one would be levelling down to. One of the main motivations for this book has been an attempt to state systematically what the law of organized religions is, so that one can answer that question more clearly. In reality, behind the pejorative sense of establishment, lies an assumption that religion and the State can and should be kept separate, or that the law of organized religions can be fully expressed in terms of secularism. This idea is also in need of clarification.

---

[25] Jenny Taylor, 'There's Life in Establishment—but not as we know it' (2004) 5 Political Theology 329; E R Norman, 'Notes on Church and State: a mapping exercise' in R M Morris (ed), *Church and State: some reflections on Church Establishment in England* (London: Constitution Unit, 2008), 9–13.

[26] Paul Avis, *Church, State and Establishment* (London: SPCK, 2001), ch 3, makes this point well.

III. Two Concepts of Legal Secularism

If in a rough sense, establishment is the connection between the State and a religion, so also in a rough sense secularism is the separation of State and religion. Christian political theology has always maintained a distinction between world and church, and between this age and the age to come, which has had a powerful impact on Western political thought.[27] The concept of the secular has been used in a wide variety of ways to identify the 'this-worldly' side of the divide. In one medieval sense of the word, the secular clergy were distinguished from regular clergy and referred to those clergy who were not subject to monastic rule. They were in the world, working in the present age. The secular could also refer to the domain of lay as opposed to clerical responsibility. After the Reformation, secularization referred to the transfer of functions, and particularly property, from the church to the emerging sovereign State. The appropriation of chantries by Edward VI to found colleges and hospitals is a central example. We can also see secularization happening in the formation of charitable trusts under lay control apart from the control of the church. In this sense, the Protestant rediscovery of the 'priesthood of all believers', and the re-formation of churches on a voluntary basis, also had a secularizing tendency.

In modern times, and as a term of sociological analysis, secularization refers to an aspect of modernization. As originally conceived, this was understood to contain interlocking components: individualization and privatization of faith, social and institutional differentiation as different bodies fulfilled what were once religious functions in non-religious ways, and the loss of faith consequent on technological and educational progress.[28] As a thesis of inexorable change, that thesis has had to be considerably modified in the face of overwhelming evidence to the contrary. Technologically advanced societies are not necessarily less religious. But at least processes of social and institutional differentiation are undeniable and, it would seem, irreversible.[29]

As a political agenda, secularism was originally a campaign for disestablishment, or the separation of Church and State.[30] This had no necessary connection

---

[27] Oliver O'Donovan, *The Desire of the Nations: Rediscovering the Roots of Political Theory* (Cambridge: Cambridge University Press, 1996) is a wide-ranging exploration of the evolution and impact of 'the Doctrine of the Two'.

[28] Introduction in Alan Aldridge, *Religion in the Contemporary World: A Sociological Introduction* (Cambridge: Polity Press, 2000), chs 4–5; Charles Taylor, *A Secular Age* (Cambridge, Mass: The Bellknap Press, 2007) is a monumental and wide-ranging study.

[29] See, above all, the work of Peter Berger and admission of his 'big mistake'. Appreciation in Linda Woodhead (ed), *Peter Berger and the Study of Religion* (London: Routledge, 2001). On structural differentiation, see José Casanova, *Public Religions in the Modern World* (London: University of Chicago Press, 1994).

[30] Useful collection of essays in Rajeev Bhargava (ed), *Secularism and its Critics* (Delhi: Oxford University Press, 1998).

with atheism or humanism, for it was entirely possible to find Christian co-belligerents in the anti-establishment cause. It is sometimes said, with more than a grain of truth, that in France the separation of Church and State was carried through to protect the State and in the United States it was carried through to protect the church. Yet as the nineteenth century drew to a close, secularism, rationalism, and atheism were often conflated. The view propounded in public debate by Charles Bradlaugh against George Holyoake in 1870 was that secularism leads to atheism.[31] Its programme assumed that political atheism would take a certain institutional form—both for the State and the societies by which secularism might be propounded. But different atheist States have expressed their ideology in quite different ways. The French revolutionary expression aped Roman Catholic Christianity—one thinks of 'temples of reason'—and the societies of late nineteenth-century English secularism aped liberal Protestantism. Communist States represent yet another expression of atheism as an official ideology.

It is therefore more helpful to distinguish secularism from various attempts to establish atheism as a State ideology. As a plausible alternative to establishment, secularism must be understood as an attempt to transcend the diversity of religious and non-religious systems of belief and practice, including atheism and agnosticism, by creating a public sphere which is not committed to any of them. This presupposes a conception of the proper extent of the State and a conception of how society apart from the State should be organized by law. The nineteenth-century 'voluntarists' sought to remove State funding for religious activity. This meant abolishing Government funding for churches and church schools, and leaving these to voluntary activity alone. It did not mean creating a system of State schools, because elementary education was intertwined in their minds with religion. The promotion of education by the State was to their minds as hostile to religion as the promotion of a particular church. As the century drew to a close there were growing numbers of secularists who thought that non-religious State education was a genuine possibility. This was, and remains, controversial. Even here, the solution adopted attempted to mark out a defined domain of 'religious education' which could kept separate, being neither compulsory nor subject to Government inspection.[32]

The separation model is very hard to implement consistently. The night watchman State of classic liberalism might be able to avoid any form of institutional overlap with organized religions, but the modern Welfare State certainly

---

[31] The Holyoake–Bradlaugh debate lives on. The National Secular Society (NSS) prefers a definition along the lines of the separation of Church and State; see <http://www.secularism.org.uk/whatissecularism.html>, accessed 21 January 2010. Yet while rejecting the conflation of secularism and atheism, the first 'general principle' of the NSS is that 'this life is the only one of which we have any knowledge and human effort should be directed wholly towards its improvement. It [sc. secularism] asserts that supernaturalism is based upon ignorance and assails it as the historic enemy of progress.' [32] See 237–8 above.

cannot.[33] Indeed, even in the minimal State there would presumably be prisons and armed forces, which would require chaplaincies as a matter of fundamental right. Chaplaincies in enclosed public institutions require collaboration between the State and religious authorities. The most rigorous attempts to expound a model of voluntary religious association within an egalitarian democracy must breach the wall of separation when it comes to education.[34] From a more technical point of view, the very core of the legal identity of religious groups in property and contract requires legal decisions to be made as to which interests will be enforceable before the secular courts and what standards will be applied.[35]

The basic problem is that the classification of something as 'religious' or a matter of 'public interest' is often hotly contested. Is ritual slaughter a religious practice which is none of the State's business, or is it an unacceptable breach of animal welfare which the State should prevent? Is the theory of evolution a religiously-netural scientific hypothesis which may compulsorily be taught to all children, or is it dependent on anti-religious metaphysical presuppositions? Is a church care home an unproblematic expression of religious mission or an alien presence in a rational system of care underwritten by the State? To adopt one answer or the other, while at the same time insisting that one is simply separating organized religion from the State, is to assert a legitimacy for the solution it does not actually possess. The separation model requires a high degree of consensus about the possibility of classifying acts as either religious or not. In reality, the classifications conflict and overlap.

From a legal point of view there is a further problem with the separation model. The model was never taken to mean that organized religions were exempt from the rule of law. Rather it presupposed the possibility of private legal ordering, based on an assumption that the use of private law did not implicate the State. But once courts conceive of themselves as State bodies, or if they insist that religious questions are non-justiciable, 'the separation of Church and State' comes to mean something quite different: the separation of law from religion. This renders the religious dimension invisible and irrelevant from the legal perspective.

It is very easy to slip from one form of separation to the other. The difference is merely between asserting that religious acts are legally irrelevant and that the religious dimensions of acts are legally irrelevant. For example, since this agreement is an arrangement for the appointment of a minister of religion, there is no intention to create civil contractual relations.[36] It is on the 'church' side of the Church–State divide. But one can also find examples, and increasingly so in recent years, in which the religious dimension makes no difference to the legal evaluation: of course this is a contract just like any other, it just happens to be to perform 'religious services'.[37]

[33] Robert Nozick, *Anarchy, State and Utopia* (Oxford: Basil Blackwell, 1974), 320–1.
[34] Brian Barry, *Culture and Equality* (Cambridge: Polity Press, 2001), ch 6.
[35] See Ch 3 above.   [36] *President of the Methodist Conference v Parfitt* [1984] QB 368.
[37] *New Testament Church of God v Stewart* [2008] ICR 282.

This slippage has the profound and paradoxical consequence that there is no particular reason to exclude religion from public life. If the religious dimension is insignificant, it no longer matters whether it is present or not. Thus 'secularism' can lead to the exclusion of religious expression from public contexts in an attempt to keep the public space free from religious contest. However, 'secularism' can equally well lead to an indifference towards religious expression as purely personal ornamentation. Some of the English puzzlement over continental European reactions to the headscarf may be explained by this difference. Sikh judges are allowed to wear turbans simply because we do not think their Sikhism makes any difference to how they do their job. Needless to say, if we thought it did make a difference, supporting arguments from individual religious liberty and equality would rapidly be outweighed by the public interest. But such indifference would be anathema to many of our liberal democratic neighbours: public officials should be beyond religious difference. For them, the presence of religion in public is still a threat.

The same ambiguity emerges in debates about the meaning of the First Amendment to the US Constitution. It is possible to construe the no-establishment and free exercise clauses so that they are fundamentally contradictory: the free exercise clause requires Government to relieve religious believers from the burdens of secular law and the no-establishment clause prevents Government from privileging religion by relieving believers from the burdens of secular law. This reading of the free exercise clause represents a view of secularism in which religion occurs in a shielded non-State sphere. This is why it mandates exemptions from general laws: the State has no business regulating religious acts. But the counterposed reading of the no-establishment clause represents a view of secularism expressed by Nelsonian blindness to the religious dimension.[38] In *Employment Division v Smith* the Supreme Court took a clear step in the latter direction, when it restricted the use of the free exercise clause to claim exemptions from burdensome general laws.[39] But the distinction can cut both ways: battle is also joined between those who think that the no-establishment clause prevents State support or funding of religious institutions, because the spheres should be separate, and those who think that the no-establishment clause requires the law to be completely neutral towards the category of the religious. On the latter basis it is possible to defend voucher schemes and support for non-theological subjects such as remedial mathematics and literacy schemes in schools, because the religious context is irrelevant.[40]

We thus need to distinguish secularism-as-separation from secularism-as-indifference. The effect of the former is to recognize distinct institutions of

---

[38] An approach defended vigorously by Marci A Hamilton, *God vs. The Gavel: Religion and the Rule of Law* (Cambridge: Cambridge University Press, 2005).

[39] *Employment Division v Smith* 494 US 872 (1990).

[40] Martha C Nussbaum, *Liberty of Conscience: in defense of America's tradition of religious equality* (New York: Basic Books, 2008), ch 7.

organized religions and the State, each with their own law. There is a 'private' sphere, in which religious belief and action may be expressed and organized as a matter of personal choice, and a 'public' sphere, in which religion is out of place. That is the secularism of the Church of Scotland Act 1921. Possible conflict is resolved through the identification of proper spheres of activity. By contrast, the effect of secularism-as-indifference is to create a single body of State law operating in an unlimited sphere of activity. Rowan Williams has recently referred to 'an unqualified secular legal monopoly'.[41] In such an environment, 'religious' considerations are no longer necessarily excluded, but they must always give way to the secular common good. They have no weight. As the law grants significance to an ever widening range of human action, religion is left to occupy the remaining extra-legal space of mere opinion and emotion. Legal subjects are still free to believe, but they are only free to believe. This development easily makes unholy alliance with the modern interest in 'spirituality' over organized forms of religion. Religion is not allowed to have a concrete expression which might compete with the standards of secular law. In that sense, religion in the secular State is entirely interstitial, playing its part in the gaps left by the law. The only question is the size of the gaps.

In the current legal and political context, slippage from secularism-as-separation to secularism-as-indifference is hard to resist.[42] Secularism-as-separation presupposes the existence of a private legal order which is 'natural', or part of the structure of civil society, which allows religious groups to form and operate lawfully and effectively, without rendering them subject to Government policy. This is its way of respecting the authority of non-State law, without subordinating it to the State. But the assumption that law can so neatly be divided into public and private is increasingly problematic. It also presupposes the construction of a legal category of 'religion' as an access point to distinctive forms of private legal regulation in order to transcend difference. But there is no religiously-neutral definition of religion.[43] As a legal category, it carries in itself the roots of its own destruction as its boundaries explode under the pressures of internal contradiction. In the interests of equality, every possible belief and practice has to be called 'religious'. There is no way one can keep the State separate from religion under such a broad definition. The legal effect of this disruption of the relatively settled boundary

---

[41] Rowan Williams, 'Civil and Religious Law in England: a Religious Perspective' (2008) 10 Ecc LJ 262. For an appreciative engagement, see Jonathan Chaplin, 'Legal monism and religious pluralism: Rowan Williams on religion, loyalty and law' (2008) 2 International Journal of Public Theology 418.

[42] Charles Taylor, 'Foreword. What is secularism?' in Geoffrey Brahm Levey and Tariq Modood, *Secularism, Religion and Multicultural Citizenship* (Cambridge: Cambridge University Press, 2009), makes the same point at xxi.

[43] Steven D Smith, *Foreordained Failure: The Quest for a Constitutional Principle of Religious Freedom* (Oxford: Oxford University Press, 1995) suggests that for this reason the quest is doomed to failure. Kent Greenawalt, 'Religion as a Concept in Constitutional Law' (1984) 72 Cal L Rev 753, proposes definition by analogy as the only plausible possibility; this is, of course, non-neutral.

between the religious and the non-religious has been noted particularly in the areas of education and broadcasting.[44] It is inevitable that religion is relativized as a result.

There is some evidence of this slippage, or at least ambiguity, in the use made of 'secularism' by the European Court of Human Rights. Most of the time it is content to see the principle of secularism as a legitimate aim in harmony with the rule of law, human rights, and democracy.[45] It is clearly understood as the exclusion of overt religious expression from public contexts such as education or the armed forces. However, in the *Refah Party* case, the court went further. Although disavowing any intention to consider the advantages and disadvantages of a plurality of legal systems in the abstract, it held that such a plural system would be incompatible with secularism and the Convention. It reiterated that freedom of religion and freedom to manifest religion were primarily a matter of individual conscience and that 'the sphere of individual conscience is quite different from the field of private law, which concerns the organisation and functioning of society as a whole'.[46] It is not clear whether this comment applies only to community law (ie coercive law) or to all forms of law.[47] Either way it appears to have a tendency to restrict the legal relevance of religious distinctions in any context, public or private.

We can now see that the developments in English law since the turn of the millennium have been desecularizing in the sense of secularism-as-separation, but secularizing in the sense of secularism-as-indifference. Examples can be found throughout this book: the loss of a special employment and general legal status for ministers of religion, new forms of regulation of organized religions by the Charity Commission, greater control and accountability of chaplains, a new legal framework for faith schools. There is thus a collective analogy to the development in individual religious rights noted earlier in this chapter: courts are very willing to recognize that a religious interest is at stake, and quite unwilling to allow it to outweigh considerations of the monistically-conceived public interest.

This development can be seen more subtly in the exceptions allowed to religious organizations in equalities legislation. If one is not simply going to blast a course through any religious objections, one could view the protection given from general non-discrimination norms either (a) as a legitimate ground of differentiation, or (b) as falling entirely outside of the scope of the relevant law. Both of these approaches would require the law to recognize the category of the religious, the former by accepting the validity of the religious perspective as a justifying ground for differentiation, the latter by creating a legally recognized domain of

---

[44] See 314–15 above.

[45] *Kalac v Turkey* (1999) 27 EHRR 552; *Dahlab v Switzerland*, no 42393/98 (2001); *Sahin v Turkey* (2007) 44 EHRR 5.

[46] *Refah Partisi v Turkey* (2003) 37 EHRR 1 (Grand Chamber), paras 127–8.

[47] The Chamber ((2002) 35 EHRR 3, para 70) referred to 'allegiance to a religious movement' as the relevant test, which might imply that even consensual plural laws are inappropriate.

liberty for religious bodies. On this approach, the Roman Catholic Church could continue to refuse to ordain women (a) because the institutional commitment to theological reasons for the refusal is seen by the law to be a valid reason, or (b) because the terms of appointment of priests are not a proper matter for State regulation. Instead, the law creates rather narrow exceptions expressed in terms which are unreasoned, or at best a matter of temporary political expedient. The implication is that if one could only get away with it politically, churches would be forced to ordain women. An exemption would surely be preferable to this sort of ideological bullying.[48]

In the same way, the exclusion of Catholic adoption agencies from public service contracting because of their refusal to consider unmarried and same-sex couples as potential parents was not grounded in any practical concern about ensuring that same-sex couples may adopt. It was driven by simple incompatibility between Catholic teaching and the new sexual ethic of the law. Here, a gap has just been closed. This is only the most obvious example of new tensions in the area of welfare provision, tensions which have historically been restricted to the field of education. One can expect a similar fate for the definition of religion for charitable purposes. It is almost inevitable that public benefit will become the sole and determining test for charitable status, and the religious or other dimension will carry no weight *as such*. In all these cases, the religious is coming within the scope of legal regulation (desecularization-as-separation), but the religious dimension has little or no weight (secularization-as-indifference).

IV. Autonomy

Establishment and secularism are, in different ways, inadequate to capture the law of organized religions. Indeed, the reason that English lawyers do not think in terms of a law of organized religions is precisely because the literature is dominated by these two alternatives. Textbooks have either started from Anglican ecclesiastical law, with occasional appendages referring to other Christian denominations or religions, or they have started from the premise of individual rights, in which religious rights may not even figure.[49] It is far more helpful to take our cue from the European Convention principles of autonomy and neutrality.

Autonomy is not merely the aggregate of several individual liberties, but is the power of a community for self-government under its own law.[50] The European Court of Human Rights refers to this principle when it states that 'the

---

[48] Rex Ahdar and Ian Leigh, *Religious Freedom in the Liberal State* (Oxford: Oxford University Press, 2005), 309–11.

[49] For the extremes, see *Halsbury's Laws of England*, 4th edn, vol 14 'Ecclesiastical Law' (London: Butterworths, 1975) and David Feldman, *Civil Liberties and Human Rights in England and Wales*, 2nd edn (Oxford: Oxford University Press, 2002).

[50] W Cole Durham, Jr, 'The Right to Autonomy in Religious Affairs: A Comparative View' in Gerhard Robbers (ed), *Church Autonomy: a Comparative Survey* (Frankfurt a M: Peter Lang, 2001).

autonomous existence of religious communities is indispensable for pluralism in a democratic society and is thus an issue at the very heart of the protection which Article 9 affords'.[51] It is not immediately obvious what it means for one system of law (State law) fully to respect the autonomy of another system (religious law) within its boundaries. It could mean that religious law is wholly other, entirely separate in its jurisdiction, sources, content, and sanctions—a parallel legal universe. This would make State law blind to its existence. Such blindness is actually disempowering. For example, religious law might recognize an obligation to use property for certain purposes, but State law see only the position according to its own norms, perhaps an unfettered power of disposal by the legal owner.

Thus autonomy requires not only the power of self-government under one's own law, it requires also the power to create legal effects in State law. Some degree of recognition of religious law and deference towards it by State courts is essential. For example, if the religious body appoints a minister, he or she needs to be appointed for the purposes of State law as well, at least to the minimal extent of providing a legal ground for the retention of property occupied or possessed by virtue of the office. The precise degree or type of recognition necessary to accord autonomy is a complex question.[52] There is also a question of extent, or the subject-matter over which religious law may range. Putting both of these dimensions together, a maximally autonomous system of religious law would presumably include the ability to determine over any area of life which of the entire range of possible consequences in State law follow from its precepts. It would, for example, not only be able to decide whether an agreement should be a binding contract for private law purposes, it would also be able to create criminal offences and punish for their commission. If it wished, it could itself become an entire system of religiously-grounded State or community law. Some expressions of some religions have tendencies in this direction.[53] For these, maximal autonomy is the right to create a complete legal/political community. Perhaps the closest example is the *millet*-system of the Ottoman empire, which accepted the existence of self-governing communities distinguished on a religious basis.[54] To a lesser extent the same approach characterized British India, with its acceptance of personal law in family and family property matters.[55]

---

[51] *Hasan and Chaush v Bulgaria*, no 30985/96 (2000), para 62.

[52] Perry Dane, 'The Varieties of Religious Autonomy' in Gerhard Robbers (ed), *Church Autonomy: a Comparative Survey* (Frankfurt a M: Peter Lang, 2001), 117, sets out a helpful typology of judicial techniques of respect for religious autonomy.

[53] H Patrick Glenn, *Legal Traditions of the World*, 2nd edn (Oxford: Oxford University Press, 2004) is the most accessible introduction to the major religious-legal traditions. Ihsan Yilmaz, *Muslim Laws, Politics and Society in Modern Nation States: Dynamic Legal Pluralisms in England, Turkey and Pakistan* (Aldershot: Ashgate, 2005) provides an instructive recent study of attempts to achieve greater degrees of control by Muslim communities over State law.

[54] Brief outline in Will Kymlicka, *Multicultural Citizenship* (Oxford: Clarendon Press, 1995), 156–8.

[55] See Asaf A A Fyzee, *Outlines of Muhammadan Law*, 4th edn (New Delhi: Oxford University Press, 1974).

Religious autonomy as a value within the liberal democratic tradition cannot be understood as maximal in this sense. One fundamental limit can be found in the value of individual religious liberty. Subjection to a religious community must remain voluntary from the perspective of the State law. There is in this sense a basic difference between subjection to State law and subjection to religious law, characterized in earlier English cases as the difference between coercive and consensual jurisdiction. The need to protect the right of exit renders unacceptable legal orders in which one can only choose between a limited range of religiously-determined community laws. Living outside of any organized religion must be possible. From the perspective of the State law, religious communities may only exist in organized form as associations.

Autonomy on this understanding derives its value from the fact that religions exist in an ideologically plural context dominated by the modern State. As well as arguments from individual autonomy, authenticity, self-expression, and conscience, all of which can be expressed collectively as well as individually, the existence of organizations which rival the State provides in addition a social location of legitimacy and coordination that has a real chance of resisting excessive State power.[56] This familiar argument for associational democracy, or mediating institutions, is particularly cogent in the case of religious associations.[57] Organized religions are not like any other civil society associations. In the minds of adherents, religious law can have a legitimacy superior to that of the State. By virtue of their other-worldly representation and this-worldly presence they fulfil an indispensable constitutional function in the preservation of civil liberty.[58]

If religious associations are to have a role in the preservation of civil liberty, they must to some degree compete with the institutions of the State. They cannot be purely spiritual communities, in the ethereal sense of the word, but must be expressed in the material goods common to all humankind. They must lay a claim to the proper ordering of those goods which presents itself as superior to the claims of the State. They can only do this being somewhat threatening to the authority of the State. On the other hand, if such associations are not to supplant the State, they must be bounded in their claims, bounded as to the persons for whom they claim to speak, and bounded as to the dimensions of human

---

[56] Michael Walzer, *Spheres of Justice* (Oxford: Basil Blackwell, 1983); Paul Hirst, *Associative Democracy* (Cambridge: Polity Press, 1994).

[57] See, classically, J N Figgis, *Churches in the Modern State*, 2nd edn (London: Longmans, Green & Co, 1914). Jurisprudential background in the work of Gierke and Rommen introduced in Jonathan Chaplin, 'Towards a Social Pluralist Theory of Institutional Rights (2005) 3 Ave Maria Law L Rev 147. Among modern statements, see Veit Bader, *Secularism or Democracy? Associational Governance of Religious Diversity* (Amsterdam: Amsterdam University Press, 2007). For a range of views, see also Nancy L Rosenblum (ed), *Obligations of Citizenship and Demands of Faith: Religious Accommodation in Pluralist Democracies* (Princeton, NJ: Princeton University Press, 2000).

[58] For an argument for (a particular) conception of liberal constitutionalism from within the Christian political tradition, see Julian Rivers, 'Liberal Constitutionalism and Christian Political Thought', in Paul Beaumont (ed), *Christian Perspectives on the Limits of Law* (Carlisle: Paternoster, 2002).

existence they seek to address. It is not surprising that writers have used terms such as 'multiple sovereignties',[59] 'two autonomies',[60] or 'twin toleration'.[61]

The law cannot live with a perpetual tension between the rival claims of civil society and the State, but must reflect a resolution in terms of boundaries. Broadly, one would expect to find areas of exclusive religious self-government, areas of exclusive State Government, and areas of overlap in which jointly acceptable regulation is negotiated by mutual agreement. It is this that makes the language of treaty or concordat between Church and State appropriate. From the perspective of the organized religion, one can think in terms of a core of absolute autonomy, with degrees of autonomy reducing as one moves towards the periphery of religiously-relevant regulation.[62] One would broadly expect a shift from a substantively defined domain of self-government in the core to procedural rights of negotiation and accommodation in areas of State interest.

As we have seen, international human rights institutions have started to elaborate the sphere within which religious bodies should enjoy autonomy. This includes rights to legal and religious entity status; a right to adopt an acceptable internal structure; a right to select, train, appoint, and dismiss leaders; rights to establish places of worship and meeting, raise funds, and uphold religious community life; rights of pastoral access to restricted institutions, and to establish educational, charitable and humanitarian institutions; a right to a public presence and State protection from attack.[63] Within these general categories, it is possible to discern a core and a periphery, possibly even concentric circles. Within the core, autonomy is guaranteed and must be respected by the State; within the periphery, the matter raises questions of legitimate State regulation. States are given discretion as to how they regulate the matter, and are sometime simply subject to a principle of fairness. The obvious example is that of education: religious groups are guaranteed a right to educate young people in a religion outside school hours with parental consent (core) and to provide private education of similar standard as an alternative to that provided at public expense (inner periphery).[64] This is peripheral in the sense that there is a right to provide suitable private education but the State also has an interest in oversight. Closer forms of collaboration between religions and the State, such as financial aid to religious schools through taxation, are subject to State discretion, in which the State is only obliged to act even-handedly (outer periphery). Finally, no religion may dominate the religious education offered in State-run schools.[65]

---

[59] Dane, *op cit* n 52, 122.   [60] Bader's preferred term, derived from a paper by Silvio Ferrari.
[61] A Stepan, 'Religion, Democracy and the "Twin Tolerations"' (2000) in 11 Journal of Democracy 37.
[62] This basic structural model is defended in a seminal article by Douglas Laycock, 'Towards a General Theory of the Religion Clauses: The Case of Church Labor Relations and the Right to Church Autonomy' (1981) 81 Columbia L Rev 1373. For a good summary of models and rationales in the US context, see Kathleen A Brady, 'Religious Group Autonomy: Further reflections about what is at stake' (2006–7) 22 J Law and Religion 153.   [63] See 55–69 above.
[64] ICESCR 1966, art 13(3); *Verein Gemeinsam Lernen v Austria* (1995) 20 EHRR CD 78.
[65] *Hasan and Eylem Zengin v Turkey* (2008) 46 EHRR 44.

The review of English law in preceding chapters suggests that it shows a commitment to religious autonomy over a long period of time. This has been most apparent as the State has grown in its competences. Obvious instances include the exceptional position of ministers of religion in the face of a growing body of employment legislation and internal accountability within religious denominations in the face of growing powers of the Charity Commission. Less obvious ones include the islands of religious regulation carved out as planning law (ecclesiastical exemption) and health and safety law (ritual slaughter) have expanded. It can also be seen in ongoing attempts in the twentieth century to secure to the Church of England the autonomy enjoyed by other churches.[66]

English law also follows the distinction between a core of religious activity in which autonomy is guaranteed and a periphery in which it must be negotiated. The distinction between core and periphery is broadly that between private and public law. At the core of the law of organized religions lies the rediscovery during the nineteenth century of the autonomy of churches in matters of doctrine, worship, discipline, and government. As noted above, this achieved its ultimate expression in the Church of Scotland Act 1921. The membership of a religious association, ownership of property, appointment of officers, religious teaching and the conduct of worship, and the determination of disputes in these areas are matters which are subject to the internal law of the body, but which have civil effect according to that law. They are subject to the private law-making power which religious individuals and groups share with everyone else. The move from trust-based to contract-based models of association ensures a degree of control by the religion over whether internal arrangements have any State legal consequences at all. By contrast, the extent of protection of ritual acts by the criminal law, joint regulation of acts having both religious and secular significance (eg circumcision and ritual slaughter), and presence in public institutions through chaplaincies, education, social welfare, and public consultation are all matters in which the terms of collaboration have had to be agreed with the State. There are elements of autonomy in this collaboration, but there is also a settlement or agreement of the terms which has required a degree of mutual compromise.

It is a matter of concern that one of the characteristics of legal developments in the last decade has been an erosion of autonomy in both the core and the periphery. Earlier chapters have shown how courts have become less willing to track the internal doctrine and government of religious bodies in resolving disputes over property after schism. The extension of elements of employment law to religious

---

[66] See eg Church of England (Worship and Doctrine) Measure 1974. On 3 July 2007, the Prime Minister issued a 'Constitutional Reform Statement' indicating his intention to relinquish prerogative powers over the appointment of bishops. *The Governance of Britain*, CM 7170 (July 2007), paras 57–66. David McLean concludes that the Church of England is 'not in reality subject...to State control': 'The changing legal framework of establishment' (2004) 7 Ecc LJ 292, 303.

office-holders and the widening of the definitions of employment have rendered the terms of appointment subject to norms of State law; recent reforms to charities law risk imposing a secular test of public benefit on religions and subject the finances of religious organizations to greater Governmental scrutiny. In respect of the periphery, the terms of collaboration in chaplaincies, education, welfare, and consultation have become more tightly defined and are designed more obviously to meet Governmental objectives.[67] Paradoxically, this development has taken place against the background of a provision within the Human Rights Act 1998 which was designed to reassure organized religions that their autonomy would be respected. The Act states that

if a court's determination of any question arising under this Act might affect the exercise by a religious organisation (itself or its members collectively) of the Convention right to freedom of thought, conscience and religion, it must have particular regard to the importance of that right.[68]

There is no evidence that this has had any affect at all on the post-HRA case-law. On the contrary, it has coincided with a reversal of approach.

In respect of autonomy, international human rights law and English law have thus been developing in opposite directions over the last decade. While the former has been engaged in a greater and more robust articulation of the rights of religious groups, the latter has seen a number of new modifications and limitations. Given the structure of European Convention rights, the ability to justify limitations of rights by reference to legitimate State interests, the relatively loose application of the doctrine of proportionality, and the availability of the margin of appreciation, it is unlikely that English law will be found in breach of the Convention. But cases such as those involving the appointment of church workers,[69] Roman Catholic adoption agencies,[70] and orthodox Jewish admission arrangements,[71] together with the continued revision of equalities legislation, show that the possibility of future incompatibility should not be ruled out. Regardless of the question of potential incompatibility, this represents a remarkable change in the direction of travel that English law had been following for well over 150 years.

---

[67] See *R (E) v Governing Body of JFS* [2010] 2 WLR 153, per Lord Mance JSC at 186 for a brief and entirely unconvincing dismissal of an argument from autonomy.

[68] Human Rights Act 1998, s 13(1). Discussion of background in Julian Rivers, 'From Toleration to Pluralism: Religious Liberty and Religious Establishment under the United Kingdom's Human Rights Act' in Rex J Ahdar (ed), *Law and Religion* (Aldershot: Ashgate, 2000); Peter Cumper, 'Religious Organisations and the Human Rights Act' in Peter W Edge and Graham Harvey (eds), *Law and Religion in Contemporary Society: Communities, individualism and the State* (Aldershot: Ashgate, 2000). [69] See 116–18 above.

[70] See 284–7 above.

[71] See 254–7 above.

V. Neutrality

The case-law of the European Court of Human Rights on organized religions refers regularly to the State's 'duty of neutrality and impartiality'.[72] The Court has given a particular meaning to that value: it means that the State must not attempt to assess the legitimacy of different religious viewpoints, nor must it take sides in disputes within or between religions. It also tends towards—or is at least compatible with—the exclusion of religious expression in public contexts.[73] The value of neutrality is closely associated in the Court's mind with the preservation of public order in a tolerant and pluralistic society, that is, with the legitimacy of the State.

As with autonomy, it is worth identifying what maximal neutrality might mean in order to see that a specific conception of neutrality is at work here, one which draws on other values in the liberal democratic tradition. Presumably, the law of a State would be maximally neutral between religions if each religion were equally able to access that form of legal regulation which best reflects its own understanding of the proper role of State law. Maximal autonomy and maximal neutrality are thus identical, albeit viewed from perspectives of liberty and equality respectively. The problem is that different religions differ (both between each other and within each other) as to the question of the proper role of State law. If adherents of one religion take the view that family law matters should be resolved by community courts according to religious law as part of a State-sanctioned system, and adherents of another religion think that the ethical underpinning of family law is not specific to any religion, but should be dealt with by State courts in the interests of society as a whole, a State which opts for one or the other solution is not maximally neutral. Indeed, it is not easy to see how a State can be maximally neutral, because it cannot adopt both strategies simultaneously. The closest it could get is to offer parties a choice of both forms of dispute resolution. But then the law must still settle the question of who is to decide if the choice is disputed, and neither the possibility of choice in such matters nor any particular allocation of decision-taking power is neutral. As with autonomy, one has to conclude that maximal neutrality can only be guaranteed in the context of a religiously homogeneous community, at which point the concept collapses. In any case, it is not our context.

Not only is religious homogeneity not our context, but also a particular conception of neutrality is operative which reflects the value of individual equality. The idea of equality within the liberal democratic tradition is rooted in a belief in moral sameness: people are at root the same.[74] There are no natural differences,

---

[72] See, most recently, *Holy Synod of the Bulgarian Orthodox Church (Metropolitan Inokentiy) v Bulgaria*, nos 412/03 and 35677/04 (2009), para 119, and cases listed at 53, n 92 above.

[73] *Leyla Sahin v Turkey* (2007) 44 EHRR 5 (Grand Chamber), para 113.

[74] The 'original position' in John Rawls, *A Theory of Justice* (Oxford: Oxford University Press, 1973) well expresses this conception of equality. Jeremy Waldron, *God, Locke and Equality:*

and in particular religious differences are not natural. Distinctions in treatment require justification in the way that identical treatment does not. This is the idea of equality found in human rights treaties: each person should enjoy equal rights, that is, the same set of liberties and opportunities. In fact, it is already implicit in the idea of human rights, which is the set of rights all people have simply as human beings. It also lies behind the moral disapprobation implicit in 'discrimination', which derives its force from the injustice of differential treatment, when sameness of treatment is morally required.[75] The commitment to individual equality leads to a preference for the State as the point at which religious difference is transcended.

This can be seen most clearly the moment one relates neutrality to the different spheres of regulation identified above. At a basic intuitive level, the law is neutral when the same law applies to all. In the core of autonomous ordering, this requires equal access to private law powers in such matters as the formation of legal persons, acquisition of property, the rights and duties of membership, and the employment of workers. In the sphere of public law, it means the adoption of laws which do not rely on religious tests or criteria. In the area of overlap, such as chaplaincies, education, and welfare it means access on equal (non-religious) terms by different religious groups to the same opportunities.

One might think that from the perspective of neutrality, the delineation of the different spheres is indifferent. It is not obvious that the State is more or less neutral between religions by (a) undertaking welfare functions itself in a non-religious context; (b) leaving social welfare up to private/religious effort; or (c) entering into collaborative arrangements with religious service providers on terms of equal access. However, from the perspective of the conception of neutrality moulded by a commitment to individual equality as well, there is a clear order of preference: (a) State welfare, then (b) private religious provision, then (c) collaboration.

In some contexts, this conception of neutrality leads to the suppression of difference. The State, or the public sphere more generally, is taken as the place in which religious difference may be avoided or subdued. The State is neutral not only when it has no overt connection to a religion as State ideology, but when it prevents religion from coming to expression in the State context. It is for this reason that the French Republic bans the Muslim veil and other ostensible signs of religious commitment in public schools: equality requires the suppression of difference and the expression of human sameness. The same logic is at work in

Christian Foundations in Locke's Political Thought (Cambridge: Cambridge University Press, 2002) subversively explores the theological underpinnings of such a conception.

[75] The disapprobation would be inexplicable for Aristotle, *Nichomachean Ethics*, trans David Ross (Oxford: Oxford University Press, 1925), V 3. It still is inexplicable for those who adopt similar conceptions. See eg Peter Westen, 'The Empty Idea of Equality' (1981–2) 95 Harv L Rev 537.

theories of public reason that require the subordination of religious discourse to secular discourse in democratic polities.[76]

The development of the law displays not only a growing commitment to neutrality, it gives some evidence of the preferential ordering of strategies to achieve neutrality referred to above. In first place was the creation of State institutions that transcend religious difference. The obvious examples here were the creation of new organs of secular public administration in the second half of the nineteenth century and the transfer of functions from the established church to those bodies. The same process happened again with the creation of the Welfare State in the second half of the twentieth century. Where this could not or should not be achieved, religious difference was the result of a private ordering of life under a law that was open to all religions. Even the distinction between the religious and the non-religious broke down at times. The law of trusts, contract, and legal persons was used as a vehicle for the creation of churches and other religious bodies, as it could be for non-religious groups, although the specific interest in religious autonomy set limits to that assimilation. Where privilege was conferred on religion (charitable status, registration as a place of worship) the tests were increasingly broad. Finally, where the non-religious State was impossible and privatization undesirable, State–religion collaboration was accepted. Education represents the main example.

At one level, the English law of organized religions has become increasingly neutral. A wide range of religious groups are free to form and organize themselves under the private law, and the law itself, both public and private, is phrased in non-religious terms. Considerable steps have been taken in the last decade to ensure that neutrality in the area of State–religion overlap is expanded beyond its historic limitation to Christian and Jewish denominations to a wide range of other religions. This is particularly apparent in chaplaincies, schools, and new forms of public consultation. A further level of neutrality is apparent: English law has historically been open to new forms of State–religion cooperation required by religious minorities: Jewish ritual slaughter and exemptions from Sunday trading legislation are obvious examples, as is the accommodation of Sikh dress.

At the same time, the historic presence of Christianity, which includes the legacy of religious establishment, has set clear limits to the neutrality of English law. Some of these are obvious. There is no symbolic neutrality in a State whose monarch is *ex officio* the supreme governor of a Christian church.[77] Establishment has also conferred a dominant position in State–religion relations, particularly

---

[76] See eg Robert Audi, *Religious Commitment and Secular Reason* (Cambridge: Cambridge University Press, 2000).

[77] The judgment of the European Court of Human Rights in *Lautsi v Italy*, no 30814/06 (3 Nov 2009), which finds the presence of crucifixes in State schools incompatible with Convention rights, may indicate a new level of opposition to symbolic establishment. The judgment has been referred to the Grand Chamber.

noticeable in the areas such as chaplaincies, religious education syllabuses, and Government consultation processes. However, Christianity has also had an influence on the delineation of the spheres of competence. What counts as religious education or religious broadcasting, or the nature of chaplaincy work, have been influenced by Christian conceptions. It is hard to be neutral at such a structural level. Indeed, there is evidence that minority religions to some extent have appropriated these structures and adopted new understandings of their social identity and role.[78] In spite of increasing levels of religious diversity, this book could *almost* have been called 'the law of church and state'.

The law of organized religions has been relatively settled in the period 1920–2000, to the point that litigation became rare and hardly ever reached the higher courts. The reason would seem to be the high degree of 'overlapping consensus' about the proper sphere of religious group autonomy and the possibility of transcending religious difference in secular law.[79] With hindsight it is possible to trace the dominance of Christian conceptions both of the sphere of religion ('Church') and the possibility of natural law ('State') at work here. Since the turn of the millennium, greater recognition has been given to the reality of increasing religious diversity, while at the same time State regulation has grown inexorably. This poses considerable challenges. Religious diversity makes it harder to transcend religious difference in the public sphere. Matters that appeared neutral become exposed as only impartial between versions of Christianity. It also calls into question the relatively settled domain of the religious/private. At the same time, areas of law traditionally considered private are becoming more and more subject to State regulation, and the obvious solution of religiously pluralized law runs directly counter to conceptions of neutrality which seek to transcend religious difference in the secular State.

What is curious about the legal developments of the last decade, is that they combine a certain commitment to greater State neutrality with new forms of closure towards alternative expressions of religiosity. Cases which evidence a loss of autonomy can also be seen as a forced remoulding of religions by the law into a paradigm of late twentieth-century liberal Protestantism. To be Jewish may not refer to matrilineal descent; to be Muslim may not extend to certain forms of dress; to be Roman Catholic may not affect judgments of sexual and family ethics. To be a religious school is to allow religion to influence school life in carefully managed ways precisely to stop it having too much influence. These developments are even affecting religious communities with a long-standing presence in this country. The new political commitment to greater State neutrality in respect of religious minorities is only superficial, masking an underlying current which flows in the opposite direction.

[78] See 233 above.

[79] The reference is to Rawls' central idea of political liberalism. See John Rawls, *Political Liberalism* (New York: Columbia University Press, 1993). For a brief summary, see id, 'The idea of an overlapping consensus' (1987) 7 OJLS 1.

VI. Between Establishment and Secularism

It is easy to dismiss establishment as an egregious breach of the principles of autonomy and neutrality. If the State has identified one church as peculiarly representative of its national identity, how can that church be free, and in what sense is the State neutral between religions? Yet this is too simple an analysis. There is no necessary incompatibility between State recognition and self-government. Indeed, in a legal context in which the norm for other religions and non-religious bodies is a certain degree of accountability to Government, establishment in the sense of special legal regulation may be necessary to secure greater levels of autonomy. The Church of Scotland Act 1921 stands as a reminder that a church may be established and free. And in some respects the Church of England enjoys a degree of self-government not available to other religious bodies.[80] Furthermore, although it is true that 'establishment' is only occasionally used to characterize plural arrangements which attempt a degree of neutrality, the established position of the Church of England has been combined with an expectation that its rights and privileges should, where possible, be available more widely. Part, at least, of the legitimacy of its position has been derived from its willingness to argue for widening access for others.

By the same token, it is too easy to assume that secularism necessarily secures autonomy and neutrality. Secularism-as-separation is one model of bounded autonomy within the sphere of 'church'. It also secures State neutrality expressed in terms of equal access to the sphere of church for all religions, and the transcending of religious difference within the State. But this depends on a substantial degree of consensus around the separability of the spheres and the possibility of transcending, as opposed to merely suppressing, religious difference in public. Increasing religious diversity challenges that consensus. By contrast, secularism-as-indifference might, or might not, secure autonomy and neutrality. Its effect is completely dependent on a one-sided perspective on what the State should regulate. On this version of secularism, religion is merely interstitial. But in the context of growing State regulation and a temptation to force a further interiorization of religion, it is likely to be unaccommodating to claims of self-government by organized religions. It thus also appears distinctly non-neutral.

The English law of organized religions is located between establishment and secularism. The established position of the Church of England has acted as a constitutional paradigm securing certain forms of connection (plural establishment) in a context in which separation is assumed, and ensuring the ongoing public significance of religion in a context in which it increasingly appears

---

[80] For example, it was given the power to initiate primary legislation affecting its affairs by the Church Assembly (Powers) Act 1919.

irrelevant.[81] This dynamic tension has been the substitute for any statement of constitutional principle.

The dynamic is exemplified well by that remarkable survival from earlier ages, the presence of bishops in the House of Lords. It is very difficult to remove them without raising questions about the nature of the Crown's relationship to the church, so they have to stay. But background commitments to neutrality make this an unsatisfactory state of affairs, which is reflected in attempts by the bishops to speak for religious perspectives more broadly, a willingness on the part of Government to grant life peerages to senior members of other denominations and religions, and a continual exploration of ways of broadening representation. Most recently, as Chapter 10 has also shown, there have been new forms of consultation and official presence in local, regional, and central Government. In part, at least, these have been brokered by the Church of England. A similar case can be made in respect of chaplaincies and schools, in which the Church of England has both attempted to use its dominance to secure a religious dimension generally, and also provided the model on which that dimension can be provided with greater diversity.

It is hard to believe that the Church of England would have been so accommodating if it were not operating against a background of secularism, of both varieties. This has forced it to justify its formal position of constitutional privilege. But then again, it is equally hard to believe that British secularism would be so accommodating to religions were it not for the constitutionally secure position of the Church of England. The two have played off against each other and have produced forms of legal regulation which are largely in accordance with principles of autonomy and neutrality.

It is important to note that the tension between establishment and secularism has resulted not only in forms of legal pluralism structured around the analogy of the established church. Other religions are not restricted to the legal forms desired by Anglicans. We have seen that the law also reflects elements of accommodation and overlap with minority religious practices, which reflects active State engagement with representatives of religions.[82] Yet, the dominance of the Anglican model is undeniable. At that structural level—the definition of religion and the place it is allowed to occupy within the law—there is no neutrality.

From an abstract perspective, the English law of organized religions is hardly ideal. In a recent and wide-ranging work, Veit Bader has cogently argued that the values of religious autonomy and State neutrality lead to a rejection of secularism in favour of a model of 'associative democracy'.[83] This seeks to pre-

---

[81] Rather than 'putting off an attempt to answer [the] question' of the relationship between religion and the State (Anthony Bradney, *Law and Faith in a Sceptical Age* (Abingdon: Routledge-Cavendish, 2009), 74) it has produced an answer.   [82] See 296–305 above.

[83] Veit Bader, *Secularism or Democracy? Associational Governance of Religious Diversity* (Amsterdam: Amsterdam University Press, 2007).

serve the voluntary nature of religious groups, as well as basic individual rights, but combines these with a greater degree of flexibility in State–religion relations. It would suggest a need both to remove the symbolic preference inherent in establishment, and to secure a more even-handed willingness continually to explore new forms of cooperation in law between the State and organized religions other than Christianity.[84] From this perspective, new forms of public consultation and dialogue are a key development,[85] and defences of establishment on the Anglican model can only seem pragmatic and temporary.[86]

Temporary they may indeed prove to be, but it is an open question what will replace them. There are three possible scenarios. It is of course possible that the status quo broadly remains in place: senior representatives of the Church of England may continue to attempt to use its position to defend the legal position of organized religions and to raise questions about new forms of interaction between religion and the State. The fate of the Archbishop of Canterbury's suggestions on the place of religious courts shows how difficult this has become.[87] In an age in which 'religion' almost exclusively meant 'church' such a role was at least plausible. Other religions can no longer be ignored like this.[88] But, arguably, there is no significant or widespread desire radically to change the legal place of religion. Even the calls for 'disestablishment' are muted.[89]

More likely, then, is a continued drift in the law towards secularism-as-indifference. This may, or may not, have a further impact on the autonomy of organized religions and the neutrality of the State. The point of this tendency lies precisely in its studied thoughtlessness. If there is a reason for legislating to

---

[84] This openness leads Bader to reject a constitutional grounding for the forms of pluralism: ibid, at 203. Yet surely the willingness to engage in dialogue requires constitutional grounding?

[85] Bikhu Parekh, *Rethinking Multiculturalism: Cultural Diversity and Political Theory* (Basingstoke: Macmillan Press Ltd, 2000), stresses the dialogical nature of multiculturalism. Tariq Modood, *Multiculturalism: a civic idea* (Cambridge: Polity Press, 2007), ch 4, also calls for greater inclusion of Muslims through organized religion.

[86] For such defences, see Jonathan Sacks, *The Persistence of Faith: Religion, Morality and Society in a Secular Age* (London: Weidenfeld, 1991), 61, and many of the essays in Tariq Modood (ed), *Church, State and Religious Minorities* (London: Policy Studies Institute, 1997).

[87] Rowan Williams, *op cit* n 41. Cautious responses by Samia Bano, 'In Pursuit of Religious and Legal Diversity: A response to the Archbishop of Canterbury and the "Sharia Debate" in Britain' (2008) 10 Ecc LJ 283; Adam Tucker, 'The Archbishop's Unsatisfactory Legal Pluralism' [2008] PL 463; and (indirectly) Lord Philips of Worth Matravers, 'Equality before the Law', a speech given at the East London Muslim Centre on 3 July 2008, reproduced in various places including (2008) 161 Law and Justice 75.

[88] Charlotte Smith, 'A very English affair: establishment and human rights in an organic constitution', in Peter Cane, Carolyn Evans, and Zoë Robinson (eds), *Law and Religion in Theoretical and Historical Context* (Cambridge: Cambridge University Press, 2008), 183: 'the time is now more than ripe for a fundamental reassessment and remodelling of the relationship between the church and state'.

[89] But see I McLean and B Linsey, *The Church of England and the State: Reforming Establishment for a Multi-faith Britain* (London: New Politics Network, 2004); R M Morris (ed), *Church and State in 21st Century Britain: the Future of Church Establishment* (Basingstoke: Palgrave Macmillan, 2009).

achieve some desirable social aim, the potential impact on organized religious belief and practice is not a reason for refraining. All the signs of the last decade are that it risks becoming worryingly oppressive. At its worst, it may yet prove to be a Trojan horse for State-sponsored atheism. For there is little sign that lawyers and judges will become bolder in applying Convention principles of autonomy and neutrality to resist such a tendency. 'Disestablishment' in this environment is only likely to exacerbate the trend.

One further possibility is more intriguing. It is that more general pressures for a major constitutional resettlement are productive of substantial change. Should this occur, it is unlikely that the established position of the Church of England will survive. At that point, it will be vital to ensure that the new constitution is not secular, in the sense of ignoring the question of the legal position of organized religions, leaving their position as merely interstitial. There is already a distinctive legal framework for organized religions in England and Wales; at various points throughout this book it has become apparent that there may be advantages in clarifying and extending that framework. If a new constitutional settlement is to reflect the principles of autonomy and neutrality, it must also continue to reflect a balance of forms of separation and connection between the State and organized religions. In that sense, it must continue to lie between establishment and secularism.

Bibliography

Ahdar, Rex and Leigh, Ian, *Religious Freedom in the Liberal State* (Oxford: Oxford University Press, 2005).

Aldridge, Alan, *Religion in the Contemporary World: A Sociological Introduction* (Cambridge: Polity Press, 2000).

Aristotle, *Nichomachean Ethics*, trans. David Ross (Oxford: Oxford University Press 1925).

Armitage, Richard, 'Police Chaplaincy—Servant to the Service' (Home Office, Sept 1996).

Atiyah, P S, 'Public Benefit and Charities' (1958) 21 MLR 138.

Audi, Robert, *Religious Commitment and Secular Reason* (Cambridge: Cambridge University Press, 2000).

Avis, Paul, *Church, State and Establishment* (London: SPCK, 2001).

Bader, Veit, *Secularism or Democracy? Associational Governance of Religious Diversity* (Amsterdam: Amsterdam University Press, 2007).

Baker, J H, 'The English Law of Sanctuary' (1990) 2 Ecc LJ 8.

Baker, J H, *Monuments of Endlesse Labours* (London: The Hambledon Press, 1998).

Bamforth, Nicholas, Malik, Maleiha, and O'Cinneide, Colm, *Discrimination Law: Theory and Context* (London: Sweet & Maxwell, 2008).

Bano, Samia, 'In Pursuit of Religious and Legal Diversity: A response to the Archbishop of Canterbury and the "Sharia Debate" in Britain' (2008) 10 Ecc LJ 283.

Barber, Paul, 'Outrageous behaviour' (1996) 4 Ecc LJ 584.

Barker, Christine R, 'Religion and Charity Law' [1999] Jur Rev 303.

Barnard, H C, *A History of English Education from 1760*, 2nd edn (London: University of London Press, 1961).

Barry, Brian, *Culture and Equality* (Cambridge: Polity Press, 2001).

Basdevant-Gaudemet, Brigitte, 'State and Church in France', in Gerhard Robbers (ed), *State and Church in the European Union* (Baden-Baden: Nomos, 1996).

BBC Trust, *Our Promise to You: How the Trust will engage with audiences* (Nov 2007).

Beckford, James A, 'Rational Choice Theory and Prison Chaplaincy: The chaplain's dilemma' (1999) 50 *British Journal of Sociology* 671.

Beckford, James A, and Gilliat, Sophie, *Religion in Prisons: Equal rites in a multi-faith society* (Cambridge: Cambridge University Press, 1998).

Berman, Harold J, *Law and Revolution: The Formation of the Western Legal Tradition* (Cambridge, Mass: Harvard University Press, 1983).

Beynon, Helen, and Love, Nigel, '*Mandla* and the meaning of "racial group"' (1984) 100 LQR 120.

Bhargava, Rajeev (ed), *Secularism and its Critics* (Delhi: Oxford University Press, 1998).

Blair, John, *The Church in Anglo-Saxon Society* (Oxford: Oxford University Press, 2005).

Blair, P H, *An Introduction to Anglo-Saxon England*, 2nd edn (Cambridge: Cambridge University Press, 1977).

Blakeney, Michael, 'Sequestered Piety and Charity—a comparative analysis' (1981) 2 J Leg Hist 207.

Blanco, Migual Rodriguez, 'Religion and the law of charities' (2005) 8 Ecc LJ 246.

Bloor, R H, 'Clocks, Bells and Cockerels' (1995) 3 Ecc LJ 393.

Bogdanor, Vernon, *The Monarchy and the Constitution* (Oxford: Clarendon Press, 1995).

Bonner, Gerald, 'Religion in Anglo-Saxon England', in Sheridan Gilley and W J Sheils (eds), *A History of Religion in Britain* (Oxford: Blackwell, 1994).

Botsford, Polly, 'Sharia Unveiled' (2008) 105 LSG 16.

Bradney, A, 'The Dewsbury Affair and the Education Reform Act 1988' (1989) 1 Education and the Law 51.

Bradney, Anthony, 'How not to marry people: formalities of the marriage ceremony' [1989] Fam Law 408.

Bradney, A, *Religions, Rights and Laws* (Leicester: Leicester University Press, 1993).

Bradney, Anthony, *Law and Faith in a Sceptical Age* (Abingdon: Routledge-Cavendish, 2009).

Brady, Kathleen A, 'Religious Group Autonomy: Further reflections about what is at stake' (2006–7) 22 J Law and Religion 153.

Braithwaite, Constance, *The Voluntary Citizen* (Methuen, 1938).

Braithwaite, Constance, *Conscientious Objection to Compulsions under the Law* (York: William Sessions Ltd, 1995).

Brenton, Maria, *The Voluntary Sector in British Social Services* (Harlow: Longman, 1985).

Bretherton, Luke, 'A New Establishment? Theological politics and the emerging shape of Church–State relations' (2006) 7 Political Theology 371.

Brodin, Emma, 'The employment status of ministers of religion' (1996) 25 ILJ 211.

Bromhead, P A, *The House of Lords and Contemporary Politics 1911–1957* (London: Routledge & Paul, 1958).

Bromley, Kathryn, and Bromley, E Blake, 'John Pemsel goes to the Supreme Court of Canada in 2001' [1999] CL & PR 115.

Brown, Francis, 'Influencing the House of Lords: the Role of the Lords Spiritual' (1994) 42 Political Studies 105.

Brown, Maggie, 'Defender of the faith', *The Guardian*, 28 March 2005.

Brown, Roger L, 'The Disestablishment of the Church in Wales' (1999) 5 Ecc LJ 252.

Bruce, Maurice, *The Coming of the Welfare State*, 4th edn (London: B T Batsford, 1968).

Bryce, Viscount, *Report of a Conference on the Second Chamber* Second Chamber Conference (1918), *Report*, Cd 9038, in (1953) 7 Parliamentary Affairs 151.

Burnside, Jonathan *et al*, *My Brother's Keeper: Faith-based units in prisons* (Cullompton: Willan Publishing, 2005).

Bursell, Rupert D H, 'The seal of the confessional' (1990) 2 Ecc LJ 84.

Cabinet Office, *House of Lords Reform*, Cmnd 3799 (1968).

Cabinet Office Strategy Unit, *Private Action Public Benefit—A Review of Charities and the Wider Not-For-Profit Sector* (Sept 2002).

Carmel, Emma, and Harlock, Jenny, 'Instituting the "third sector" as a governable terrain: partnership, procurement and performance in the UK' (2008) 36(2) Policy and Politics 155.

Casanova, José, *Public Religions in the Modern World* (Chicago: University of Chicago Press, 1994).

Chadwick, O, *Church and State: Report of the Archbishop's Commission* (London: Church Information Office, 1970).

Chaplin, Jonathan, 'Towards a Social Pluralist Theory of Institutional Rights' (2005) 3 Ave Maria Law L Rev 147.

Chaplin, Jonathan, 'Legal monism and religious pluralism: Rowan Williams on religion, loyalty and law' (2008) 2 International Journal of Public Theology 418.

Chapman, Rachel, 'Faith and the voluntary sector in urban governance: distinctive yet similar?' in Adam Dinham, Robert Furbey, and Vivien Lowndes, *Faith in the Public Realm: controversies, policies and practices* (Bristol: The Policy Press, 2009).

Charity Commission, *Draft Supplementary Guidance*, 'Public Benefit and the Advancement of Religion' (Feb 2008).

Charity Commission, *Supplementary Guidance*, 'The Advancement of Religion for the Public Benefit' (Dec 2008).

Clarke, Chris, and Purvis, Matthew, *House of Lords Reform since 1997: A Chronology*, House of Lords Library Note 2009/007.

Clarke, Kenneth *et al*, *Reforming the House of Lords: Breaking the Deadlock* (London: The Constitution Unit, 2005).

Coen, Mark, 'Religious ethos and employment equality: a comparative Irish perspective' (2008) 28 Legal Studies 452.

Coffey, John, *Persecution and Toleration in Protestant England* (Harlow: Pearson, 2000).

Collins, Lawrence (ed), *Dicey, Morris and Collins on the Conflict of Laws*, 14th edn (London: Sweet & Maxwell, 2006).

Commission for the Compact, *Compact: Black and Minority Ethnic Voluntary and Community Organisations* (Feb 2001).

Committee on Higher Education, *Report of the Committee on Higher Education* (the 'Robbins Report'), Cmnd 2154 (1963).

Cooper, Davina, and Herman, Didi, 'Jews and other uncertainties: race, faith and English law' (1999) 19 Legal Studies 339.

Costigane, Helen, 'Catholic Adoption Agencies and "Gay Adopters"' [2008] Law & Justice 98.

Cranmer, Frank, 'Christian Doctrine and Judicial Review: the Free Church Case revisited' in (2002) 6 Ecc LJ 318.

Cranmer, Frank, 'Regulation with the Religious Society of Friends' (2003) 7 Ecc LJ 176.

Cranmer, Frank, 'Parliamentary Report' (2008) 10 Ecc LJ 352.

Cranmer, Frank and Peterson, Scot, 'Employment: sex discrimination and the churches: the Percy case' (2006) 8 Ecc LJ 392.

Crawford, James, *The Creation of States in International Law*, 2nd edn (Oxford: Clarendon Press, 2006).

Creech-Jones, Violet, 'The Work of Voluntary Social Services among Children before School-Leaving Age', in Henry A Mess, *Voluntary Social Services since 1918* (London: Kegan Paul, 1948).

Cross, Stuart R, 'New Legal Forms for Charities in the United Kingdom' [2008] JBL 662.

Cross-party Statement, Cmd 7380 (1948).

Cumper, Peter, 'Religious Organisations and the Human Rights Act' in Peter W Edge and Graham Harvey (eds), *Law and Religion in Contemporary Society: Communities, individualism and the State* (Aldershot: Ashgate, 2000).

Daintith, T, 'Regulation by Contract' (1979) 32 CLP 41.

Dal Pont, G E, 'Charity Law and Religion', in Peter Radan, Denise Meyerson, and Rosalind F Croucher, *Law and Religion: God, the State and the Common Law* (London: Routledge, 2005).

Dane, Perry, 'The Varieties of Religious Autonomy' in Gerhard Robbers (ed), *Church Autonomy: a Comparative Survey* (Frankfurt a M: Peter Lang, 2001).

Deakin, Simon, and Morris, Gillian, *Labour Law*, 4th edn (Oxford: Hart Publishing, 2005).

Department for Children, Schools and Families/National Statistics, *Schools and Pupils in England*, SFR 30/2007 (Sept 2007).

Department for Children, Schools and Families/National Statistics, *The Composition of Schools in England* (June 2008).

Department of Communities and Local Government, *Face to Face and Side by Side: A framework for partnership in our multi faith society* (July 2008).

Department for Constitutional Affairs, *Constitutional Reform: Next Steps for the House of Lords*, CP 14/03 (Sept 2003).

Department for Constitutional Affairs, *The House of Lords—Completing the Reform*, Cm 5291 (Nov 2001).

Department for Culture, Media and Sport/Welsh Office, *Follow Up to the Review of the Ecclesiastical Exemption (The Newman Report)* (Jan 1999).

Department for Culture, Media and Sport, *Communications White Paper—a new future for communications* (Dec 2000).

Department for Culture, Media and Sport, *The Ecclesiastical Exemption: the Way Forward* (July 2005).

Department for Culture, Media and Sport, *An Agreement Between Her Majesty's Secretary of State for Culture, Media and Sport and the British Broadcasting Corporation*, Cm 6872 (July 2006).

Department for Culture, Media and Sport/Welsh Assembly Government, *Heritage Protection for the 21st Century*, Cm 7057 (March 2007).

Department of the Environment, Transport and the Regions, *Involving Communities in Urban and Rural Regeneration: A Guide for Practitioners*, 2nd edn (Sept 1997).

Department of the Environment, Transport and the Regions, *Local Strategic Partnership Guidance* (March 2001).

Dickinson, J C, *The Later Middle Ages* (London: A & C Black, 1979).

Dickson, Brice, 'The United Nations and freedom of religion' (1995) 44 ICLQ 327.

Doe, Norman, *The Legal Framework of the Church of England* (Oxford: Clarendon Press, 1996).

Doe, Norman, *The Law of the Church in Wales* (Cardiff: University of Wales Press, 2002).

Drewry, Gavin, and Brock, Jenny, 'Prelates in Parliament' (1971) 24 Parliamentary Affairs 222.

Duddington, John, 'God, Caesar and the Employment Rights of Ministers of Religion' [2007] Law and Justice 129.

Duffy, Eamon, *The Stripping of the Altars: traditional religion in England c. 1400–c. 1580*, 2nd edn (London: Yale UP, 2005).

Durham, W Cole, Jr, 'The Right to Autonomy in Religious Affairs: A Comparative View' in Gerhard Robbers (ed), *Church Autonomy: a Comparative Survey* (Frankfurt a M: Peter Lang, 2001).

Durham, Cole, *Freedom of Religion or Belief: Laws Affecting the Structuring of Religious Communities* (Warsaw: OSCE/ODIHR, 1999).

Edge, Peter W, 'Charitable Status for the Advancement of Religion: an abolitionist's view' (1995/6) 3 CL & PR 29.

Edge, Peter W, *Legal Responses to Religious Difference* (The Hague: Kluwer Law International, 2002).

Edge, Peter W, 'The construction of sacred places in English law' [2002] J Env L 161.

Edge, Peter W, *Religion and Law: An Introduction* (Aldershot: Ashgate, 2006).

Edge, Peter W, and Loughrey, Joan, 'Religious charities and the juridification of the Charity Commission' (2001) 21 Legal Studies 36.

Edwards, Rosie, *Believing in Local Action* (Church Urban Fund, 2008).

Elliott, D W, 'An evidential privilege for priest–penitent communications' (1995) 3 Ecc LJ 272.

Elton, G R, *England under the Tudors*, 3rd edn (London: Routledge, 1991).

English, Penny, 'Disputing Stonehenge: Law and Access to a National Symbol' (2002) 1 Entertainment Law 1.

Esau, A, '"Islands of Exclusivity": Religious Organizations and Employment Discrimination' (1993) 33 UB Col LR 719.

Evandrou, Maria *et al*, *The State of Welfare: the economics of social spending*, 2nd edn (Oxford: Oxford University Press, 1998).

Evans, Carolyn, *Freedom of Religion under the European Convention on Human Rights* (Oxford: Oxford University Press, 2001).

Evans, Carolyn, 'The Special Rapporteur on Freedom of Religion or Belief', in Nazila Ghanea (ed), *The Challenge of Religious Discrimination at the Dawn of the New Millennium* (Leiden/Boston: Martinus Nijhoff, 2003).

Evans, Carolyn, 'Religious education in public schools: an international human rights perspective' (2008) 8 HRL Rev 449.

Evans, Malcolm D, *Religious Liberty and International Law in Europe* (Cambridge: Cambridge University Press, 1997).

Evans, Malcolm D, 'Believing in Communities, European Style', in Nazila Ghanea (ed), *The Challenge of Religious Discrimination at the Dawn of the New Millennium* (Leiden: Martinus Nijhoff, 2003).

Evans, Malcolm D, 'Freedom of religion and the European Convention on Human Rights: approaches, trends and tensions', in Peter Cane, Carolyn Evans, and Zoë Robinson (eds), *Law and Religion in Theoretical and Historical Context* (Cambridge: Cambridge University Press, 2008).

Fairclough, Alexandra, 'Whose voice prevails? Faculties, hearings and heritage' [2002] JPL 1444.

Feldman, David, *Civil Liberties and Human Rights in England and Wales*, 2nd edn (Oxford: Oxford University Press, 2002).

Figgis, J N, *Churches in the Modern State*, 2nd edn (London: Longmans, Green & Co, 1914).

Finlayson, Geoffrey, *Citizen, State and Social Welfare in Britain 1830–1990* (Oxford: Clarendon Press, 1994).

Fisher, Simon, 'Clergy confidentiality and privileges: themes and prospects', in Peter Radan, Denise Meyerson, and Rosalind F Croucher, *Law and Religion: God, the State and the Common Law* (London: Routledge, 2005).

Flint, John, 'Faith-based schools: institutionalising parallel lives?', in Adam Dinham, Robert Furbey, and Vivien Lowndes, *Faith in the Public Realm: Controversies, policies and practices* (Bristol: The Policy Press, 2009).

Fredman, Sandra, *Discrimination Law* (Oxford: Oxford University Press, 2002).

Freiherr von Campenhausen, Axel, 'Church Autonomy in Germany' in Gerhard Robbers (ed), *Church Autonomy* (Frankfurt a M: Peter Lang, 2001).

Fyzee, Asaf A A, *Outlines of Muhammadan Law*, 4th edn (New Dehli: Oxford University Press, 1974).

Geddis, Andrew, 'You can't say "God" on the Radio: Freedom of Expression, Religious Advertising and the Broadcast Media after Murphy v Ireland' [2004] EHRLR 180.

George, Charles, 'Shared use of church buildings, or is nothing sacred?' (2002) 6 Ecc LJ 306.

Gerstenblith, Patty, 'Civil Court Resolution of Property Disputes among Religious Organizations', in James A Serritella *et al* (eds), *Religious Organizations in the United States* (Durham: Carolina Academic Press, 2006).

Ghanea, Nazila, 'The 1981 UN Declaration...Some Observations' in Nazila Ghanea (ed), *The Challenge of Religious Discrimination at the Dawn of the New Millennium* (Leiden: Martinus Nijhoff, 2003).

Gibbons, Julian, 'Discretionary Life Panels' (1994) 144 NLJ 524.

Gibbons, Stephen, and Silva, Olma, *Faith Primary Schools: Better schools or better pupils*, DCSF research paper (2006).

Gibson, Urban, and Lord, Karen S, 'Advancements in Standard Setting: Religious Liberty and OSCE Commitments', in Tore Lindholm *et al* (eds), *Facilitating Freedom of Religion or Belief: A Deskbook* (Leiden: Martinus Nijhoff, 2004).

Giddens, Anthony, *The Third Way: The renewal of social democracy* (Cambridge: Polity Press, 1998).

Gilbert, Howard, 'Time to reconsider the lawfulness of ritual male circumcision' [2007] EHRLR 279.

Gilliat-Ray, Sophie, *Religion in Higher Education: The politics of the multi-faith campus* (Aldershot: Ashgate, 2000).

Glenn, H Patrick, *Legal Traditions of the World*, 2nd edn (Oxford: Oxford University Press, 2004).

Godfrey, Gerald, 'The Judges and the Jews' (2003) 7 Ecc LJ 50.

Gordon, Keith, *Tolley's Guide to the Tax Treatment of Specialist Occupations* (Haywards Heath: Tottel Publishing Ltd, 2008).

Government Equalities Office, *Framework for a Fairer Future—The Equality Bill* Cm 7431 (June 2008).

Greenawalt, Kent, 'Religion as a Concept in Constitutional Law' (1984) 72 Cal L Rev 753.

Grieve, Jemma, Jochum, Véronique, Pratten, Belinda, and Steel, Claire, *Faith in the community: the contribution of faith-based organisations to rural voluntary action* (London: NCVO, 2007).

Gunn, T Jeremy, 'Adjudicating Rights of Conscience under the European Convention on Human Rights', in Johan D van der Vyver and John Witte, Jr (eds), *Religious Human Rights in Global Perspective: Legal perspectives* (The Hague: Kluwer Law International, 1996).

Guy, John, *Tudor England* (Oxford: Oxford University Press, 1988).

Halsbury's Laws of England, 3rd edn, vol 4, 'Charities' (London: Butterworths, 1953).

Halsbury's Laws of England, 4th edn, vol 10, 'Cremation and Burial' (London: Butterworths, 2002).

Halsbury's Laws of England, 4th edn, vol 14, 'Ecclesiastical Law' (London: Butterworths, 1975)

Halsbury's Laws of England, 4th edn, vol 35, 'Personal Property' (London: Butterworths, 1994).

Hamilton, Carolyn, *Family, Law and Religion*, (London: Sweet & Maxwell, 1995).

Hamilton, Marci A, *God vs. The Gavel: Religion and the Rule of Law* (Cambridge: Cambridge University Press, 2005).

Hansen, H Reese, 'Religious Organizations and the Law of Trusts', in James A Serritella *et al* (eds), *Religious Organizations in the United States* (Durham: Carolina Academic Press, 2006).

Harding, Matthew, 'Trusts for Religious Purposes and the Question of Public Benefit' (2008) 71 MLR 159.

Harlow, Anna, Cranmer, Frank, and Doe, Norman, 'Bishops in the House of Lords: a Critical Analysis' [2008] PL 490.

Harlow, Carol, and Rawlings, Richard, *Law and Administration*, 3rd edn (Cambridge: Cambridge University Press, 2009).

Harris, Neville, *Education, Law and Diversity* (Oxford: Hart Publishing, 2007).

Harris, Sarah, Schultz, Jenny, and Castan, Melissa, *The International Covenant on Civil and Political Rights*, 2nd edn (Oxford: Oxford University Press, 2004).

Harte, J D C, 'The Religious Dimensions of the Education Reform Act 1988' (1989) 1(5) Ecc LJ 32.

Heasman, K, *Evangelicals in Action* (London: Geoffrey Bles, 1962).

Hedley, Stephen, 'Keeping Contract in its Place' (1965) 5 OJLS 391.

Helmholz, R H, *The ius commune in England: Four Studies* (Oxford: Oxford University Press, 2001).

Helmholz, R H, *The Oxford History of the Laws of England*, vol 1: The Canon Law and Ecclesiastical Jurisdiction from 597 to the 1640s (Oxford: Oxford University Press, 2004).

Henig, Martin, 'Religion in Roman Britain' in Sheridan Gilley and W J Sheils (eds), *A History of Religion in Britain* (Oxford: Blackwell, 1994).

Henriques, H S Q, *The Jews and the English Law* (London: J Jacobs, 1908).

Hill, Christopher, 'Episcopal lineage: a theological reflection on Blake v Associated Newspapers Ltd' (2004) 7 Ecc LJ 334.

Hill, Judith, 'Roman Catholic religious orders as charities' (1997) 5 CL & PR 1.

Hill, Mark, 'Judicial Review of Ecclesiastical Courts', in Norman Doe, Mark Hill, and Robert Ombres, *English Canon Law* (Cardiff: University of Wales Press, 1998).

Hinnells, John R, *Zoroastrians in Britain* (Oxford: Clarendon Press, 1996).

Hirst, Paul, *Associative Democracy* (Cambridge: Polity Press, 1994).

HM Government, *The Governance of Britain*, CM 7170 (July 2007).

HM Government, *The Equality Bill—Government response to the consultation*, Cm 7454 (July 2008).

HM Prison Service, *Directory and Guide on Religious Practice in HM Prison Service*, 1988.

Holt, J C, *Magna Carta* (Cambridge: Cambridge University Press, 1965).

Home Office, Policy Action Team 9: *Community Self Help* (Sept 1999).

Home Office, *Charities and Not-for-Profits: A modern legal framework* (July 2003).

Home Office Faith Communities Unit, *Working Together: Co-operation between Government and Faith Communities* (Feb 2004).

Home, R K, 'Planning decision statistics and the Use Classes debate' [1987] JPL 167.

Hooker, Richard, *Of the Laws of Ecclesiastical Polity (1593–7)* (London: Dent, 1907).

House of Lords Select Committee on the House of Lords, 1908 Report, in (1953) 7 Parliamentary Affairs 140.

House of Lords Select Committee on Religious Offences in England and Wales, HL 95-I (April 2003).

House of Lords Select Committee on BBC Charter Review, *Second Report of the Select Committee on BBC Charter Review*, HL 128-I (March 2006).

Hudson, Anne, *The Premature Reformation* (Oxford: Clarendon Press, 1988).

Hylson-Smith, K, *The Churches in England from Elizabeth I to Elizabeth II*, vol II (London: SCM Press, 1997).

Inter Faith Network, *Partnership for the common good: interfaith structures and local government*, 2003.

Inter Faith Network for the UK, *Inter Faith Organisations in the UK: A Directory*, 2009.

Iwobi, Andrew, 'Out with the old, in with the new: religion, charitable status and the Charities Act 2006' (2009) 29 Legal Studies 619.

Jochum, Véronique, Pratten, Belinda, and Wilding, Karl (eds), *Faith and voluntary action: an overview of current evidence and debates* (London: NCVO, 2007).

Joint Committee on House of Lords Reform, *First Report*, HL17, HC171 (Dec 2002).

Joint Committee on House of Lords Reform, *Second Report*, HL97, HC668 (April 2003).

Jones, Gareth, *History of the Law of Charity, 1532–1827* (Cambridge: Cambridge University Press, 1969).

Jones, T Hughie, 'Outrageous behaviour—a postscript' (1997) 4 Ecc LJ 664.

Jordan, W K, *Philanthropy in England 1480–1660* (London: Allen & Unwin, 1959).

Junor, Gordon, 'Church heritage—law and religion' [2008] SLT 167.

Jupp, Peter C, *From Dust to Ashes: Cremation and the British way of life* (Basingstoke: Palgrave Macmillan, 2005).

Katz, David S, *The Jews in the History of England* (Oxford: Oxford University Press, 1994).

Kauper, Paul G, and Ellis, Stephen C, 'Religious Corporations and the Law' (1972–3) 71 Mich L Rev 1499.

Khaliq, Urfan, 'The Accommodation and Regulation of Islam and Muslim Practices in English Law' (2002) 6 Ecc LJ 332.

Krishnaswami, Arcot, 'Study of Discrimination in the matter of Religious Rights and Practices' UN Doc. E/CN.4/Sub.2/200/Rev.1 (1960), reproduced at (1978–9) 11 NYUJ Int'l L & Pol 227.

Kunz, Josef L, 'The Status of the Holy See in International Law' (1952) 46 AJIL 308.

Kymlicka, Will, *Multicultural Citizenship* (Oxford: Clarendon Press, 1995).

Lampard, Rachel, *The House of Lords: Completing the Reform—A response on behalf of the Methodist Church*, available at <http://www.methodist.org.uk/index.cfm?fuseaction=opentogod.content&cmid=695>.

Langlaude, Sylvie, *The Right of the Child to Religious Freedom in International Law* (Leiden: Martinus Nijhoff, 2007).

Larsen, Timothy, *Friends of Religious Equality: Non-conformist Politics in Mid-Victorian England* (Woodbridge: The Boydell Press, 1999).

Last, Kathryn, 'The privileged position of the Church of England in the control of works to historic buildings: the provenance of the ecclesiastical exemption from listed building control' [2002] CLWR 205.

Law Commission, *Working Paper on Offences against Religion and Public Worship*, no 79 (1981).

Law Commission, *Report on Offences against Religion and Public Worship*, no. 145 (1985).

Law Commission, *Criminal Law: Consent in the Criminal Law*, Consultation Paper no 139 (1995).

Lawson, John, and Silver, Harold, *A Social History of Education in England* (London: Methuen & Co, 1973).

Laycock, Douglas, 'Towards a General Theory of the Religion Clauses: The Case of Church Labor Relations and the Right to Church Autonomy' (1981) 81 Columbia L Rev 1373.

Lee, Natalie (ed), *Revenue Law—Principles and Practice*, 26th edn (Haywards Heath: Tottel Publishing, 2008).

Leigh, Ian, 'Regulating Religious Broadcasting' (1992) 2 Ecc LJ 287.

Leigh, Ian, 'By law established? The Crown, constitutional reform and the Church of England' [2004] PL 266.

Lerner, Natan, 'Religious Human Rights under the United Nations', in Johann D van der Vyver and John Witte, Jr (eds), *Religious Human Rights in Global Perspective: Legal perspectives* (The Hague: Kluwer Law International, 1996).

Lester, Anthony, and Uccellari, Paola, 'Extending the equality duty to religion, conscience and belief: Proceed with caution' [2008] EHRLR 567.

Lewis, Jane, 'What does Contracting do to Voluntary Agencies?' in David Billis and Margaret Harris (eds), *Voluntary Agencies: Challenges of Organisation and Management* (London: Macmillan, 1996).

Local Government Association, *Faith and Community*, 2002.

Lowe, Rodney, *The Welfare State in Britain*, 3rd edn (London: Palgrave Macmillan 2005).

Luxton, Peter, *The Law of Charities* (Oxford: Oxford University Press, 2001).

Lynch, Andrew, 'The constitutional significance of the Church of England', in Peter Radan, Denise Meyerson, and Rosalind F Croucher, *Law and Religion: God, the State and the Common Law* (London: Routledge, 2005).

McClure, R K, 'Johnson's criticism of the Foundling Hospital and its consequences', Review of English Studies (New Series), vol XXVII, no 105 (1976).

McColgan, Aileen, 'Class wars? Religion and (in)equality in the workplace' [2009] ILJ 1.

McCoubrey, Hilaire, 'The Protection of Creed and Opinion in the Laws of Armed Conflict' (2000) 5 Journal of Conflict and Security Law 135.

MacCulloch, Diarmaid, *Tudor Church Militant: Edward VI and the Protestant Reformation* (London: Allen Lane, 1999).

McDermont, Morag, *Governing, Independence and Expertise: The business of housing associations* (Oxford: Hart Publishing, 2010).

Macdonald, Ian A, and Webber, Frances, (eds), *Immigration Law and Practice in the United Kingdom*, 6th edn (London: LexisNexis Butterworths, 2005).

McFarlane, K B, *Wycliffe and English Non-conformity* (Harmondsworth: Penguin, 1972).

McLean, David, 'The changing legal framework of establishment' (2004) 7 Ecc LJ 292.

McLean, I, and Linsey, B, *The Church of England and the State: Reforming Establishment for a Multi-faith Britain* (London: New Politics Network, 2004).

Maitland, F W, 'The deacon and the Jewess; or, apostasy at common law' (1886) 2 LQR 153.

Manning, Bernard, Lord, *The Protestant Dissenting Deputies* (Cambridge: Cambridge University Press, 1952).

Masson, J M, Bailey-Harris, R, and Probert, R J (eds), *Cretney's Principles of Family Law*, 8th edn (London: Sweet & Maxwell, 2008).

Matlary, Janne Haaland, 'Implementing Freedom of Religion or Belief: Experiences from the Norwegian Chairmanship' in Tore Lindholm *et al* (eds), *Facilitating Freedom of Religion or Belief: A Deskbook* (Leiden: Martinus Nijhoff, 2004).

Meah, Nafees, and Petchey, Philip, 'Liability of Churches and Religious Organizations for Sexual Abuse of Children by Ministers of Religion' (2005) 34 CLWR 39.

Mess, Henry A (ed), *Voluntary Social Services since 1918* (London: Kegan Paul, 1948).

Ministry of Justice, *An Elected Second Chamber: Further reform of the House of Lords* Cm 7438 (July 2008).

Modood, Tariq (ed), *Church, State and Religious Minorities* (London: Policy Studies Institute, 1997).

Modood, Tariq, *Multiculturalism: a civic idea* (Cambridge: Polity Press, 2007).

Morris, Rachel, and Clements, Luke, 'Fraudulent and incompetent mediums' (1996) 146 NLJ 1574

Morris, R M (ed), *Church and State in 21ˢᵗ Century Britain: The future of church establishment* (Basingstoke: Palgrave Macmillan, 2009).

Mullett, Michael, 'Radical Sects and Dissenting Churches, 1600–1750' in Sheridan Gilley and W J Sheils (eds), *A History of Religion in Britain* (Oxford: Blackwell, 1994).

Mundill, Robin R, *England's Jewish Solution* (Cambridge: Cambridge University Press, 1998).

Munro, Colin, 'Does Scotland have an Established Church? (1997) 4 Ecc LJ 639.

Murphy, James, *Church, State and Schools in Britain, 1800–1970* (London: Routledge & Kegan Paul, 1971).

Mynors, Charles, *Listed Buildings, Conservation Areas and Monuments*, 4th edn (London: Sweet & Maxwell, 2006).

Nathan, Lord, *The Charities Act 1960* (London: Butterworths, 1962).

National Health Service, *Appointment of chaplains*, HMC (48) 62 (1948).

National Health Service, *Meeting the religious and spiritual needs of patients and staff* (Nov 2003).

Newark, F H, 'Public Benefit and religious Trusts' (1946) 62 LQR 234.

Newman, John, *A Review of the Ecclesiastical Exemption from Listed Buildings Controls* (DCMS, September 1997).

Newth, John, 'NIC and Special Occupations—Part I' *Tolley's Practical NIC Newsletter*, 15 PNN 6.

Nielsen, Jørgen, *Muslims in Western Europe* (Edinburgh: Edinburgh University Press, 1992).

Nolte, Georg (ed), *European Military Law Systems* (Berlin: W de Gruyter, 2003).

Norman, E R, 'Notes on Church and State: A mapping exercise' in R M Morris (ed), *Church and State: some reflections on Church Establishment in England* (London: Constitution Unit, 2008).

Nowak, Manfred, *CCPR Commentary* (Kehl am Rhein: Engel, 1993).

Nozick, Robert, *Anarchy, State and Utopia* (Oxford: Basil Blackwell, 1974).

Nussbaum, Martha C, *Liberty of Conscience: In defense of America's tradition of religious equality* (New York: Basic Books, 2008).

O'Brien, Derek, 'Rastafarianism and the Law' (2001) 151 NLJ 509.

O'Donovan, Oliver, *The Desire of the Nations: Rediscovering the Roots of Political Theory* (Cambridge: Cambridge University Press, 1996).

Office of the Deputy Prime Minister/Angoy Consultancy, *Pilot Project on Faith Community Involvement in the New Deal for Communities* (Feb 2005).

Office of the Deputy Prime Minister, *Our Towns and Cities: The Future—Delivering an Urban Renaissance* (Nov 2000).

Office for National Statistics, *Civil Registration: Vital change*, Cm 5355 (Jan 2002).

Office for National Statistics, *Focus on Religion* (Oct 2004).

Office for National Statistics, *Marriage, divorce and adoption statistics*, 2005 (Series FM2, no 32).

O'Hara, James B, 'The Modern Corporation Sole' (1988–9) 93 Dick L Rev 23.

OSCE Ministry of Foreign Affairs, *Seminar on Freedom of Religion or Belief in the OSCE Region: Challenges to Law and Practice* (The Hague, 2001).

Outhwaite, R B, *Clandestine Marriage in England 1500–1850* (London: The Hambledon Press, 1995).

Outhwaite, R B, *The Rise and Fall of the English Ecclesiastical Courts, 1500–1860* (Cambridge: Cambridge University Press, 2006).

Owen, David, *English Philanthropy 1660–1960* (Cambridge, Mass: Harvard University Press, 1964).

Owen, Gale R, *Rites and Religions of the Anglo-Saxons* (Newton Abbot: David & Charles, 1981).

Parekh, Bikhu, *Rethinking Multiculturalism: Cultural Diversity and Political Theory* (Basingstoke: Macmillan Press Ltd, 2000).

Pearce, Augur, 'The Offshore Establishment: Church and Nation on the Isle of Man' (2003) 7 Ecc LJ 62.

Petchey, Philip, 'Ministers of Religion and Employment Rights: An examination of the issues' (2003) 7 Ecc LJ 157.

Petchey, Philip, 'Legal Issues for Faith Schools in England and Wales' (2008) 10 Ecc LJ 174.

Philips of Worth Matravers, Lord, 'Equality before the Law' (2008) 161 Law and Justice 75.

Phillipson, Gavin, ' "The greatest quango of them all", "a rival Chamber" or "a hybrid nonsense"? Solving the Second Chamber Paradox' [2004] PL 352.

Picarda, Hubert, *The Law and Practice relating to Charities*, 3rd edn (London: Butterworths, 1999).

Pillay, Anashri, 'South Africa: freedom of religion—religiously motivated use of cannabis' (2003) 1 IJCL 152.

Poulter, Sebastian, 'The religious education provisions of the Education Reform Act 1988' (1990) 2 Education and the Law 1.

Poulter, Sebastian, *Ethnicity, Law and Human Rights: The English Experience* (Oxford: Clarendon Press, 1998).

Quicke, Andrew, and Quicke, Juliet, *Hidden Agendas: The Politics of Religious Broadcasting in Britain 1987–1991* (Virginia Beach: Dominion Kings Grant Publications, 1992).

Rawls, John, *A Theory of Justice* (Oxford: Oxford University Press, 1973).

Rawls, John, 'The idea of an overlapping consensus' (1987) 7 OJLS 1.

Rawls, John, *Political Liberalism* (New York: Columbia University Press, 1993).

Rex, Richard, *The Lollards* (Basingstoke: Palgrave, 2002).

Rivers, Julian, 'From Toleration to Pluralism: Religious Liberty and Religoius Establishment under the United Kingdom's Human Rights Act', in Rex J Ahdar (ed), *Law and Religion* (Aldershot: Ashgate, 2000).

Rivers, Julian, 'Religious Liberty as a Collective Right', in Richard O'Dair and Andrew Lewis (eds), *Law and Religion* (Oxford: Oxford University Press, 2001).

Rivers, Julian, 'Translator's Introduction' in Robert Alexy, *A Theory of Constitutional Rights*, trans Julian Rivers (Oxford: Oxford University Press, 2002).

Rivers, Julian, 'Liberal Constitutionalism and Christian Political Thought', in Paul Beaumont (ed), *Christian Perspectives on the Limits of Law* (Carlisle: Paternoster, 2002)

Rivers, Julian, 'In Pursuit of Pluralism: The Ecclesiastical Policy of the European Union' (2004) 7 Ecc LJ 267.

Rivers, Julian, 'The Question of Freedom of Religion or Belief and Defamation' (2007) 2 Religion and Human Rights 113.

Rivers, Julian, 'Law, Religion and Gender Equality' (2007) 9 Ecc LJ 24.

Robbers, Gerhard, 'Diversity of State-Religion Relations and European Union Unity' (2004) 7 Ecc LJ 304.

Robbins, Keith, 'Religion and Community in Scotland and Wales since 1800' in Sheridan Gilley and W J Sheils (eds), *A History of Religion in Britain* (Oxford: Blackwell, 1994).

Robilliard, St John A, *Religion and the Law: Religious liberty in modern English law* (Manchester: Manchester University Press, 1984).

Rodes, Robert E, *Law and Modernization in the Church of England* (Notre Dame: University of Notre Dame Press, 1991).

Rodger of Earlsferry, Lord, *The Courts, the Church and the Constitution: Aspects of the Disruption of 1843* (Edinburgh: Edinburgh University Press, 2008).

Rosenblum, Nancy L (ed), *Obligations of Citizenship and Demands of Faith: Religious Accommodation in Pluralist Democracies* (Princeton, NJ: Princeton University Press, 2000).

Roth, Cecil, *A History of the Jews in England* (Oxford: Clarendon Press, 1941).

Rowe, Peter, *Defence: the Legal Implications* (London: Brassey's, 1987).

Rowe, Peter, *The Impact of Human Rights Law on Armed Forces* (Cambridge: Cambridge University Press, 2006).

Royal Commission on the Reform of the House of Lords, *A House for the Future*, Cm 4534 (Jan 2000).

Rubin, G R, 'United Kingdom Military Law: Autonomy, civilianisation, juridification' (2002) 65 MLR 36.

Rupp, Gordon, *Religion in England, 1688–1791* (Oxford: Clarendon Press, 1986).

Russell, Meg, *Reforming the House of Lords: Lessons from overseas* (Oxford: Oxford University Press, 2000).

Sacks, Jonathan, *The Persistence of Faith: Religion, Morality and Society in a Secular Age* (London: Weidenfeld, 1991).

Sandberg, Russell, and Doe, Norman, 'Religious Exemptions in Discrimination Law' (2007) 66 CLJ 302.

Scheinin, Martin, 'The Human Rights Committee and Freedom of Religion or Belief', in Tore Lindholm *et al* (eds), *Facilitating Freedom of Religion or Belief: A Deskbook* (Leiden: Martinus Nijhoff, 2004).

Schiltz, Patrick J, and Laycock, Douglas, 'Employment in Religious Organizations', in James A Serritella *et al* (eds), *Religious Organizations in the United States* (Durham: Carolina Academic Press, 2006).

Scotland, Nigel, *Sectarian Religion in Contemporary Britain* (Carlisle: Paternoster Press, 2000).

Select Committee on Public Administration, *The Second Chamber: Continuing the Reform*, Fifth Report, 2001–2, HC 494-I.

Short, K R M, 'The English Indemnity Acts, 1726–1867' (1973) 42 Church History 366.

Simpson, A W B, 'Innovation in 19th century contract law' (1975) 91 LQR 247.

Smale, David A (ed), *Davies' Law of Burial, Cremation and Exhumation,* 7th edn (London: Shaw & Sons, 2002).

Smith, Charlotte, 'The Place of Representatives of Religion in the Reformed Second Chamber' [2003] PL 674.

Smith, Charlotte, 'A very English affair: establishment and human rights in an organic constitution', in Peter Cane, Carolyn Evans, and Zoë Robinson (eds), *Law and Religion in Theoretical and Historical Context* (Cambridge: Cambridge University Press, 2008).

Smith, Rachel Craufurd, *Broadcasting Law and Fundamental Rights* (Oxford: Clarendon Press, 1997).

Smith, Steven D, *Foreordained Failure: The Quest for a Constitutional Principle of Religious Freedom* (Oxford: Oxford University Press, 1995).

Spring, Thomas, and Quint, Francesca, 'Religion, Charity Law and Human Rights' (1999) 5 CL & PR 153.

Stepan, A, 'Religion, Democracy and the "Twin Tolerations"' (2000) in 11 Journal of Democracy 37.

Sullivan, Donna J, 'Advancing the Freedom of Religion or Belief through the UN Declaration on the Elimination of Religious Intolerance and Discrimination' (1988) 82 AJIL 487.

Sullivan, Winnifred Fallers, *Prison Religion: Faith-based Reform and the Constitution* (Princeton; Princeton University Press, 2009).

Sutton, David St John *et al*, *Russell on Arbitration*, 23rd edn (London: Sweet & Maxwell, 2007).

Sutton, Teresa, 'Modern Sanctuary' (1996) 4 Ecc LJ 487.

Swift, Christopher, *Hospital Chaplaincy in the Twenty-first Century: The crisis of spiritual care on the NHS* (Farnham: Ashgate, 2009).

Tackaberry, John, and Marriott, Arthur *et al*, *Bernstein on Arbitration*, 4th edn (London: Sweet & Maxwell, 2003).

Taylor, Charles, *A Secular Age* (Cambridge, Mass: The Bellknap Press, 2007).

Taylor, Charles, 'Foreword. What is secularism?' in Geoffrey Brahm Levey and Tariq Modood, *Secularism, Religion and Multicultural Citizenship* (Cambridge: Cambridge University Press, 2009).

Taylor, Jenny, 'There's Life in Establishment—but not as we know it' (2004) 5 Political Theology 329.

Taylor, Marilyn, 'Voluntary Action and the State' in David Gladstone (ed), *British Social Welfare: Past, present and future* (London: UCL Press, 1996).

Taylor, Paul M, *Freedom of Religion* (Cambridge: Cambridge University Press, 2005).

Thomas, Charles, *Christianity in Roman Britain to AD 500* (London: Batsford, 1985).

Tiley, John, *Revenue Law*, 6th edn (Oxford: Hart Publishing, 2008).

Tucker, Adam, 'The Archbishop's unsatisfactory legal pluralism' [2008] PL 463.

Van Boven, Theo, 'The United Nations Commission on Human Rights and Freedom of Religion or Belief', in Tore Lindholm *et al* (eds), *Facilitating Freedom of Religion or Belief: A Deskbook* (Leiden: Martinus Nijhoff, 2004).

Van Dijk, Pieter *et al*, *Theory and Practice of the European Convention on Human Rights*, 4th edn (Oxford: Intersentia, 2006).

Vickers, Lucy, *Religious Freedom, Religious Discrimination and the Workplace* (Oxford: Hart Publishing, 2008).

Viney, Rachel, 'Religious broadcasting on UK television: Policy, public perception and programmes' (1999) 36 Cultural Trends 1.

Wade, H W R, and Forsyth, C, *Administrative Law*, 8th edn (Oxford: Oxford University Press, 2000).

Waldron, Jeremy, *God, Locke and Equality: Christian Foundations in Locke's Political Thought* (Cambridge: Cambridge University Press, 2002).

Walzer, Michael, *Spheres of Justice* (Oxford: Basil Blackwell, 1983).

Warburton, Jean (ed), *Tudor on Charities*, 9th edn (London: Sweet & Maxwell, 2003).

Watkin, T G, 'The vestiges of establishment: the ecclesiastical and canon law of the Church in Wales' (1990) 2 Ecc LJ 110.

Watkin, Thomas Glyn, 'A Happy Noise to Hear?' (1996) 4 Ecc LJ 545.

Watkin, Thomas Glyn, and Thomas, Sarah, 'Oh, Noisy Bells, be Dumb: Church Bells, Statutory Nuisance and Ecclesiastical Duties' [1995] JPL 1097.

Watts, Michael, *The Dissenters*, 2 vols (Oxford: Clarendon Press, 1978, 1995).

Webster, G, *The British Celts and their Gods* (London: Batsford, 1986).

Westen, Peter, 'The Empty Idea of Equality' (1981–2) 95 Harv L Rev 537.

Whelan, Robert, *The Corrosion of Charity* (Institute of Economic Affairs, 1996).

Wicks, Elizabeth, 'Religion, Law and Medicine: Legislating on Birth and Death in a Christian State' [2009] Med LR 410.

Williams, Rowan, 'Civil and Religious Law in England: a Religious Perspective' (2008) 10 Ecc LJ 262.

Wolfenden Committee, *The Future of Voluntary Organisations* (London: Croom Helm, 1978).

Woodhead, Linda (ed), *Peter Berger and the Study of Religion* (London: Routledge, 2001).

Woods, P, Ashley, M, and Woods, G, *Steiner Schools in England*, DfES Research Report RR645, (University of the West of England, 2005).

Woolf, Lord, 'Judicial Review: A Possible Programme for Reform' [1992] PL 211.

Yilmaz, Ihsan, *Muslim Laws, Politics and Society in Modern Nation States: Dynamic Legal Pluralisms in England, Turkey and Pakistan* (Aldershot: Ashgate, 2005).

York, The Rt Hon the Archbishop of, 'The Lords Spiritual' (1953) 7 Parliamentary Affairs 96.

Yu, Hong-lin, 'Section 46(1)(b) of the English Arbitration Act 1996: its past and future' [1999] Int ALR 43.

Index